S0-ACA-228

READINGS IN EUROPEAN HISTORY

READINGS IN

EUROPEAN

HISTORY

COMPILED AND EDITED BY

LEON BERNARD, Ph. D.
UNIVERSITY OF NOTRE DAME

AND

THEODORE B. HODGES, Ph. D.
UNIVERSITY OF NOTRE DAME

THE MACMILLAN COMPANY • NEW YORK

Printed in the United States of America

First Printing

Library of Congress catalog card number: 58-5465

FOREWORD

A perennial difficulty confronting the college teacher of European history has been the coordination of textbook and source readings. There is surely no shortage of source collections from which to choose, and in recent years the "problem" approach has enjoyed a considerable vogue. The problem method has the distinct advantage of giving unity to a body of diverse material, but in actual practice it presents several formidable obstacles. The problem itself is often an artificial creation, with the material forced together in a distorted or exaggerated fashion. In addition, problem units rarely fit easily into a syllabus based on textbook assignments.

Somewhat older than the problem approach is the more encyclopedic type of source book incorporating a multitude of original selections without much unity, either real or artificial. Such books include splendid material on certain topics but are woefully weak on others, with the result that the book is used sparingly and spottily by the teacher.

It is our purpose in this volume to provide readings organized in such a way as to supplement the college text effectively. Both the rigidity of the problem studies and the discursiveness of the older source books are avoided by presenting significant, short, and carefully edited selections on a wide range of topics from the fifth century Greeks to World War II. These readings are especially intended to serve as a supplement to the well-known *History of Europe,** by Carlton J.H. Hayes, Marshall W. Baldwin, and Charles W. Cole, but they can be easily adapted to any college text.

Each of the forty-one topics is deliberately restricted in length to permit full use of all component selections without disrupting textbook assignments. Each selection illumines a key idea, event, or personality treated in the accompanying chapter of the Hayes, Baldwin, and Cole text, thereby

* New York, The Macmillan Company, 1956.

giving the text a new richness and meaning for the student. For the most part, the writers drawn upon in this book either participated in or were contemporary to the events described. In selecting the material, we have sought a balance among intellectual, political, military, religious, social, and economic elements of European history. It is our belief that recent collections of source material have tended to become anthologies of the history of ideas and are overloaded with rather arid excerpts from the great thinkers. We have attempted to redress the balance and give the student a sense of the color and action that abound in European history. With some optimism, we hope that these selections will stimulate the student to pursue further reading and study.

L.L. Bernard
T.B. Hodges

South Bend, Indiana

CONTENTS

I. *THE HERITAGE OF ANCIENT TIMES*

1. THE GREEKS

2. *ROME: REPUBLIC AND EARLY EMPIRE*

3. *CHRISTIANITY*

IV. *THE LATE MIDDLE AGE*

15. *THE GROWTH OF NATIONAL MONARCHY IN ENGLAND AND FRANCE*

16. *WANING PRESTIGE AND INFLUENCE OF THE CHURCH*

17. *HUMANISM AND RENAISSANCE ART*

21. THE CATHOLIC REFORMATION

22. THE THIRTY YEARS' WAR

VI. *POWER POLITICS AND "ENLIGHTENMENT"*

23. *THE AGE OF LOUIS XIV*

24. *THE ENGLISH REVOLUTIONS OF THE SEVENTEENTH CENTURY*

25. *THE RISE OF RUSSIA AND PRUSSIA*

32. *THE REVOLUTIONS OF 1848*

VIII. *MATERIAL PROGRESS AND DEMOCRATIC POLITICS*

33. *THE INDUSTRIAL REVOLUTION*

34. *THE UNIFICATION OF ITALY AND GERMANY*

37. *SCIENCE, SOCIALISM, AND RELIGION IN THE LATE NINETEENTH CENTURY*

IX. *EUROPE IN THE TWENTIETH CENTURY*

38. *WORLD WAR I AND VERSAILLES*

39. *THE RISE OF TOTALITARIANISM*

40. TOTALITARIAN AGGRESSION

41. THE SECOND WORLD WAR

I

THE HERITAGE OF ANCIENT TIMES

1

THE GREEKS

The foundation of Western civilization is ancient Greece. The story of Western art, architecture, literature, science, and philosophy begins with the Greeks. Their contribution to our way of life is visible all about us to this day—most obviously in our architecture and vocabulary, but, in an equally real sense, in virtually every field of human endeavor. Perhaps most notable is the Greek discovery of the importance of the individual and of a type of government which enabled the individual to retain his personal freedom.

1. THE ATHENIANS DEFEAT THE PERSIANS AT MARATHON, 490 B.C.

Greek civilization came to full fruition in the fifth century B.C. However, before the Golden Age could be realized, the invasion of the Persians had to be beaten off. With little aid from her sister city-states. Athens defeated the army of Emperor Darius at Marathon. Thus, the first great threat to the West from an alien Eastern civilization was repulsed; there would be many more in the centuries to come. The following account was written by Herodotus (484–425 B.C.), often called the "Father of History."

The Athenian generals were divided in their opinions; and some advised not to risk a battle, because they were too few to engage such a host as that of the Medes [Persians]; while others were for fighting at once, and among these last was Miltiades. He, therefore, seeing that opinions were thus divided, and that the less worthy counsel appeared likely to prevail, resolved to go to the polemarch [commander of the army], and have a conference

The History of Herodotus, VI, 109–114, 120, adapted from the translation of George Rawlinson (New York: D. Appleton & Co., 1860), pp. 408–417.

with him. . . . The polemarch at this juncture was Callimachus of Aphidnae; to him therefore Miltiades went, and said:

"With you it rests, Callimachus, either to bring Athens to slavery, or, freedom. . . . We generals are ten in number, and our votes are divided; half of us wish to engage, half to avoid a combat. . . . You have only to add your vote to my side and your country will be free, and not free only, but the first state in Greece. Or, if you prefer to give your vote to them who would decline the combat, then the reverse will follow."

Miltiades by these words gained Callimachus; and the addition of the polemarch's vote caused the decision to be in favor of fighting. Hereupon all those generals who had been desirous of hazarding a battle, when their turn came to command the army, gave up their right to Miltiades. He however, though he accepted their offers, nevertheless waited, and would not fight, until his own day of command arrived in due course.

Then at length, when his own turn was come, the Athenian army was set in array, and this was the order of it. Callimachus the polemarch led the right wing, for it was at that time a rule with the Athenians to give the right wing to the polemarch. After this followed the tribes, according as they were numbered, in an unbroken line; while last of all came the Plataeans [a city-state allied with Athens], forming the left wing. And ever since that day it has been a custom with the Athenians, in the sacrifices and assemblies held each fifth year at Athens, for the Athenian herald to implore the blessing of the gods on the Plataeans conjointly with the Athenians. Now as they marshalled the host upon the field of Marathon, in order that the Athenian front might be of equal length with the Median, the ranks of the centre were diminished, and it became the weakest part of the line, while the wings were both made strong with a depth of many ranks.

So when the army was set in array, and the sacrifices were favourable, instantly the Athenians, so soon as they were let go, charged the barbarians at a run. Now the distance between the two armies was little short of a mile. The Persians, therefore, when they saw the Greeks coming on at speed, made ready to receive them, although it seemed to them that the Athenians were bereft of their senses, and bent upon their own destruction; for they saw a mere handful of men coming on at a run without either horsemen or archers. Such was the opinion of the barbarians; but the Athenians in close array fell upon them, and fought in a manner worthy of being recorded. They were the first of the Greeks, so far as I know, who introduced the custom of charging the enemy at a run, and they were likewise the first who dared to look upon the Median garb, and to face men clad in that fashion. Until this time the very name of the Medes had been a terror to the Greeks to hear.

The two armies fought together on the plain of Marathon for a length of time; and in the middle of the line, where the Persians themselves and the Sacae had their place, the barbarians were victorious, and broke and pursued the Greeks into the inner country; but on the two wings the Athenians and the Plataeans defeated the enemy. Having so done, they routed the barbarians, and joining the two wings in one, fell upon those who had broken their own centre, and fought and conquered them. These likewise fled, and now the Athenians hung upon the runaways and cut them down, chasing them all the way to the shore, on reaching which they laid hold of the ships and called aloud for fire.

It was in the struggle here that Callimachus the polemarch, after greatly distinguishing himself, lost his life; Stesilaus too, the son of Thrasilaus, one of the generals, was slain; and Cynaegirus, the son of Euphorion, having seized on a vessel of the enemy's by the ornament at the stern, had his hand cut off by the blow of an axe, and so perished; as likewise did many other Athenians of note and name.

Nevertheless the Athenians secured in this way seven of the vessels, while with the remainder the barbarians pushed off . . . doubled Cape Sunium, hoping to reach Athens before the return of the Athenians. . . .

. . . But the Athenians with all possible speed marched away to the defence of their city, and succeeded in reaching Athens before the appearance of the barbarians; . . . The barbarian fleet arrived, and lay to off Phalerum, which was at that time the haven of Athens; but after resting awhile upon their oars, they departed and sailed away to Asia.

After the full of the moon 2,000 Lacedaemonians came to Athens. So eager had they been to arrive in time, that they took but three days to reach Attica from Sparta. They came, however, too late for the battle; yet, as they had a longing to behold the Medes, they continued their march to Marathon and there viewed the slain. Then, after giving the Athenians all praise for their achievement, they departed and returned home.

2. PERICLES TELLS OF THE GREATNESS OF ATHENS

Between 431 and 404 B.C., Athens and Sparta fought a civil war for the mastery of Greece. At the end of the first year of the war, Pericles delivered his famous funeral oration commemorating the Athenian soldiers who had fallen in battle. It is a highly idealized speech, and the recorder, Thucydides, makes no claim that

Thucydides, *The History of the Peloponnesian War*, II, 36–41, translated by B. Jowett (London: Oxford University Press, 1900), pp. 127–131.

he is reporting the speech exactly as it was delivered. He is simply giving the "general purport of what was actually said." In any case, the speech stands as one of the greatest ever delivered.

Before I praise the dead, I should like to point out by what principles of action we rose to power, and under what institutions and through what manner of life our empire became great. For I conceive that such thoughts are not unsuited to the occasion, and that this numerous assembly of citizens and strangers may profitably listen to them.

Our form of government does not enter into rivalry with the institutions of others. We do not copy our neighbours, but are an example to them. It is true that we are called a democracy, for the administration is in the hands of the many and not of the few. But while the law secures equal justice to all alike in their private disputes, the claim of excellence is also recognized; and when a citizen is in any way distinguished, he is preferred to the public service, not as a matter of privilege, but as the reward of merit. Neither is poverty a bar, but a man may benefit his country whatever be the obscurity of his condition. There is no exclusiveness in our public life, and in our private intercourse we are not suspicious of one another, nor angry with our neighbour if he does what he likes; we do not put on sour looks at him which, though harmless, are not pleasant. While we are thus unconstrained in our private intercourse, a spirit of reverence pervades our public acts; we are prevented from doing wrong by respect for the authorities and for the laws, having an especial regard to those which are ordained for the protection of the injured as well as to those unwritten laws which bring upon the transgressor of them the reprobation of the general sentiment.

And we have not forgotten to provide for our weary spirits many relaxations from toil; we have regular games and sacrifices throughout the year; our homes are beautiful and elegant; and the delight which we daily feel in all these things helps to banish melancholy. Because of the greatness of our city the fruits of the whole earth flow in upon us; so that we enjoy the goods of other countries as freely as of our own.

Then, again, our military training is in many respects superior to that of our adversaries. Our city is thrown open to the world, and we never expel a foreigner or prevent him from seeing or learning anything of which the secret if revealed to an enemy might profit him. We rely not upon management or trickery, but upon our own hearts and hands. And in the matter of education, whereas they from early youth are always undergoing laborious exercises which are to make them brave, we live at ease, and yet are equally ready to face the perils which they face. And here is the proof. The Lacedaemonians [Spartans] come into Attica not by themselves, but with their whole confederacy following; we go alone into a neighbour's country; and although our opponents are fighting for their homes and we on a foreign soil, we have seldom any difficulty in overcoming them. Our enemies have never yet felt our united strength; the care of a navy divides our attention, and on land we are obliged to send our own citizens everywhere. But they, if they meet and defeat a part of our army, are as proud as if they had routed us all, and when defeated they pretend to have been vanquished by us all.

If then we prefer to meet danger with a light heart but without laborious training, and with a courage which is gained by habit and not enforced by law, are we not greatly the gainers? Since we do not anticipate the pain, although, when the hour comes, we can be as brave as those who never allow themselves to rest; and thus too our city is equally admirable in peace and in war. For we are lovers of the beautiful, yet simple in our tastes, and we cultivate the mind without loss of manliness. Wealth we employ, not for talk and ostentation, but when there is a real use for it. To avow poverty with us is no disgrace; the true disgrace is in doing nothing to avoid it. An Athenian citizen does not neglect the state because he takes care of his own household; and even those of us who are engaged in business have a very fair idea of politics. We alone regard a man who takes no interest in public affairs, not as a harmless, but as a useless character; and if few of us are originators, we are all sound judges of a policy. The great impediment to action is, in our opinion, not discussion, but the want of that knowledge which is gained by discussion preparatory to action. For we have a peculiar power of thinking before we act and of acting too, whereas other men are courageous from ignorance but hesitate upon reflection. And they are surely to be esteemed the bravest spirits who, having the clearest sense both of the pains and pleasures of life, do not on that account shrink from danger. In doing good, again, we are unlike others; we make our friends by conferring, not by receiving favours. Not he who confers a favour is the firmer friend, because he would fain by kindness keep alive the memory of an obligation; but the recipient is colder in his feelings, because he knows that in requiting another's generosity he will not be winning gratitude but only paying a debt. We alone do good to our neighbours not upon a calculation of interest, but in the confidence of freedom and in a frank and fearless spirit. To sum up: I say that Athens is the school of Hellas, and that the individual Athenian in his own person seems to have the power of adapting himself to the most varied forms of action with the utmost versatility and grace. This is no passing and idle word, but truth and fact; and the assertion is verified by the position to which these qualities have raised the state. For in the hour of trial Athens alone among her contemporaries is superior to the report of her. No enemy who comes against her is indignant at the reverses which he sustains at the hands of such a city; no subject complains that his masters are unworthy of him. And we shall assuredly not be without witnesses; there are mighty monuments of our power which will make us the wonder of this and of succeeding ages; we shall not need the praises of Homer or of any other panegyrist whose poetry may please for the moment, although his representation of the facts will not bear the light of day. For we have compelled every land and every sea to open a path for our valour, and have everywhere planted eternal memorials of our friendship and of our enmity. Such is the city for whose sake these men nobly fought and died; they could not bear the thought that she might be taken from them; and every one of us who survive should gladly toil on her behalf. . . .

3. A GREAT ATHENIAN PHILOSOPHER MEETS DEATH

Socrates was brought to trial on charges of disrespect to the gods and of corrupting the youth of Athens. In reality, he was a victim of the times. The Athenians, disastrously defeated in the Peloponnesian War, were in no mood to accept Socrates' constant challenging of conventional ideas and ways. He was condemned by an Athenian jury and drank hemlock in 399 B.C. He left no writings. Most of our knowledge of the man is based on what his disciple, Plato, says about him. An extract from one of Plato's dialogues, the* Phaedo, *follows.

. . . [Socrates] got up and went into a room to bathe, and Crito followed him, but he told us to wait. We waited, therefore, chatting amongst ourselves and reviewing the discussion that we had had, and then again speaking of the magnitude of our misfortune. It was as though we were losing a father, and we felt that when he had gone we should be living the rest of our lives as orphans. After he had had his bath . . . he talked with [his children and womenfolk] in Crito's presence and gave his instructions, and then asked the women and the children to go away, and came over to us. It was now almost sunset, for he had been a long time inside. He came and sat down, fresh from his bath, and did not say much after that. Then the servant of the Eleven came and stood by him and said, "Socrates, I shall not have to reproach you, as I do others, for being angry with me and cursing me when, on the instructions of the archons, I tell you to drink the poison. I have found you during this period the noblest and most kindly and best man who has ever come here; and now, I am sure, you are not angry with *me*, but with those who you know are responsible. So now—

Plato, *Phaedo*, 116A–118A, adapted from the translation of R.S. Bluck (London: Routledge & Kegan Paul Ltd., 1955), pp. 140–143. Used by permission of the publisher.

you know what I have come to tell you—good-bye, and try to bear the inevitable as easily as you can." He burst into tears, turned round, and went away.

And Socrates looked up at him and said, "Good-bye to you too. We will do as you say"; and to us he said, "What a fine fellow! He always used to come and visit me, and sometimes would chat with me, and was the best of men; and now, how good of him to weep for me! But now, Crito, let us do as he asks, and let the poison be brought, if it has been prepared. If not, let the pounding be done."

"I think, Socrates," said Crito, "that the sun is still on the mountains; it hasn't set yet. What's more, I know that others drink the poison very late after they have been told to, after a good dinner and a good deal of drinking, and after enjoying the society of their lovers. Don't be in a hurry; there is still time left."

"It is natural, Crito," said Socrates, "that those whom you mention should do this—they think they gain something by doing it; and it is natural, too, that I should not do this, for in my opinion the only thing I shall gain, if I drink a little later, will be to make myself a laughing-stock in my own eyes—clinging to life and being sparing with it when my cup has been drained to the dregs. Come now," he said, "do as I say, please."

At this Crito nodded to the boy who was standing near; and the boy went out and after some while returned with the man who was going to administer the poison, which he brought ready-pounded in a cup. Socrates, when he saw the fellow, said, "Well, my friend, you know all about these things, what do I have to do?"

"Simply drink it," he said, "and then walk about until a heaviness comes over your legs; then lie down. Then it will do the work itself." With this, he handed Socrates the cup. . . .

. . . he raised [it] to his lips, and showing not the least distaste, quite unperturbed, he drained the draught. Most of us had till then been more or less able to restrain our tears, but when we saw him drinking and then that he had drunk it, we could do so no longer. For my part, despite my efforts I found that the tears flooded down my cheeks; I wrapped my face in my cloak and wept for my misfortune—not for his, but for my own, to think what a friend I had lost. Crito had got up and gone away even before me, unable to restrain his tears. Apollodorus even before this had been weeping ceaselessly, and then he burst out crying aloud, and distressed us so much that he made everyone present break down, except Socrates himself.

"What are you doing, strange fellows?" he said. "That was my chief reason for sending the women away, so that they shouldn't make this mistake; I have heard that it is better to die in silence. Please remain quiet, and be brave."

At this we felt ashamed, and checked our weeping. Socrates walked about, and when he said his legs felt heavy, he lay down on his back—as the fellow told him to; and after a while, this man who had given the poison felt him, examining his feet and his legs, and then pinching his foot hard he asked if he felt it, and Socrates replied, "No." After that, the man did the same to his shins; and then, passing upwards in this way, he showed us that he was becoming numbed and rigid. And he himself continued to feel him, and said that when the coldness reached his heart, then he would be gone.

The region about the groin was now becoming more or less numb, and uncovering his head (for it had been covered up), he said—and these were the last words he uttered: "Crito, we owe a cock to Asclepius [1]; please pay it—do not neglect it."

"It shall be done," said Crito. "Is there anything else?"

Socrates gave no reply to this question, but after a little while he made a movement, and the man uncovered him, and his eyes had become fixed. Seeing this, Crito closed his lips and his eyes.

Such, Echecrates, was the end of our friend—the best man of his time, in our opinion, that we had ever come across, and in general the wisest, and the most just.

4. ALEXANDER THE GREAT HELLENIZES THE NEAR EAST

Alexander the Great became king of Macedonia in 336 B.C. In 323, at the age of thirty-two, he died in Babylon. His short reign is one of the most extraordinary in all history. By the time of his death he had come close to fulfilling his ambition to conquer the civilized world. His influence was lasting. To the Near East he brought Greek culture, which, blended with the older Oriental civilizations, produced the Hellenistic World.

. . . The statues that gave the best representation of Alexander's person, were those of Lysippus, (by whom alone he would suffer his image to be made,) those peculiarities which many of his successors afterwards and his friends used to affect to imitate, the inclination of his head a little on one side towards his left shoulder, and his melting eye, having been ex-

Plutarch, "Alexander," condensed from the translation of John Dryden in *Everybody's Plutarch*, edited by Raymond T. Bond, pp. 534–566.

[1] The god of healing. A cock was the customary offering in gratitude for a cure. Socrates regards death as release from all human ills.

pressed by this artist with great exactness. . . . He was fair and of a light color, passing into ruddiness in his face and upon his breast. Aristoxenus in his Memoirs tells us that a most agreeable odor exhaled from his skin, and that his breath and body all over was so fragrant as to perfume the clothes which he wore next him; . . . His temperance, as to the pleasures of the body, was apparent in him in his very childhood, as he was with much difficulty incited to them, and always used them with great moderation; though in other things he was extremely eager and vehement, and in his love of glory, and the pursuit of it, he showed a solidity of high spirit and magnanimity far above his age. . . . He seems in general to have looked with indifference, if not with dislike, upon the professed athletes. He often appointed prizes, for which not only tragedians and musicians, pipers and harpers, but rhapsodists also, strove to outvie one another; and delighted in all manner of hunting and cudgel-playing, but never gave any encouragement to contests either of boxing or of the pancratium.[1] . . .

. . . the Grecians . . . declared their resolution of joining with Alexander in the war against the Persians and proclaimed him their general. Many public ministers and philosophers came from all parts to visit him, and congratulated him on his election, but contrary to his expectation, Diogenes of Sinope, who then was living at Corinth, thought so little of him, that instead of coming to compliment him, he never so much as stirred out of the suburb called the Cranium, where Alexander found him lying along in the sun. When he saw so much company near him, he raised himself a little, and vouchsafed to look upon Alexander; and when he kindly asked him whether he wanted any thing, "Yes," said he, "I would have you stand from between me and the sun." Alexander was so struck at this answer, and surprised at the greatness of the man, who had taken so little notice of him, that as he went away, he told his followers who were laughing at the moroseness of the philosopher, that if he were not Alexander, he would choose to be Diogenes. . . .

Among the treasures and other booty that was taken from Darius, there was a very precious casket, which being brought to Alexander for a great rarity, he asked those about him what they thought fittest to be laid up in it; and when they had delivered their various opinions, he told them he should keep Homer's *Iliad* in it. . . . Homer was neither an idle, nor an unprofitable companion to him in his expedition. For when he was master of Egypt, designing to settle a colony of Grecians there, he resolved to build a large and populous city, and give it his own name. . . . He

[1] A form of athletics in which boxing and wrestling were combined. The bare hands were used and were curved but not clenched in the boxing.

chanced one night in his sleep to see a wonderful vision; a grey-headed old man, of a venerable aspect, appeared to stand by him, and pronounce these verses:

> An island lies, where loud the billows roar,
> Pharos they call it, on the Egyptian shore.

Alexander upon this immediately rose up and went to Pharos, which, at that time, was an island lying a little above the Canobic mouth of the river Nile, though it has now been joined to the main land by a mole. As soon as he saw the commodious situation of the place, it being a long neck of land, stretching like an isthmus between large lagoons and shallow waters on one side, and the sea on the other, the latter at the end of it making a spacious harbor, he said, Homer, besides his other excellences, was a very good architect, and ordered the plan of a city to be drawn out answerable to the place. To do which, for want of chalk, the soil being black, they laid out their lines with flour, taking in a pretty large compass of ground in a semicircular figure. . . . While he was pleasing himself with his design, on a sudden an infinite number of great birds of several kinds, rising like a black cloud out of the river and the lake, devoured every morsel of the flour that had been used in setting out the lines; at which omen even Alexander himself was troubled, till the augurs restored his confidence again by telling him, it was a sign the city he was about to build would not only abound in all things within itself, but also be the nurse and feeder of many nations. . . .

Some little time after the battle with Porus,[1] Bucephalas [Alexander's beloved war-horse] died, as most of the authorities state, under cure of his wounds, or as Onesicritus says, of fatigue and age, being thirty years old. Alexander was no less concerned at his death, than if he had lost an old companion or an intimate friend, and built a city, which he named Bucephalia, in memory of him, on the bank of the river Hydaspes. He also, we are told, built another city, and called it after the name of a favorite dog, Peritas, which he had brought up himself. . . .

. . . the combat with Porus took off the edge of the Macedonians' courage, and stayed their further progress into India. For having found it hard enough to defeat an enemy who brought but twenty thousand foot and two thousand horse into the field, they thought they had reason to oppose Alexander's design of leading them on to pass the Ganges too, which they were told was four miles broad and six hundred feet deep, and the banks on the further side covered with multitudes of enemies. For they were told that the kings of the Gandaritans and Praesians expected

[1] Porus was the ruler of a country in the Indus Valley who opposed Alexander's invasion of India.

them there with eighty thousand horse, two hundred thousand foot, eight thousand armed chariots, and six thousand fighting elephants. . . . Alexander at first was so grieved and enraged at his men's reluctancy, that he shut himself up in his tent, and threw himself upon the ground, declaring, if they would not pass the Ganges, he owed them no thanks for any thing they had hitherto done, and that to retreat now, was plainly to confess himself vanquished. But at last the reasonable persuasions of his friends and the cries and lamentations of his soldiers, who in a suppliant manner crowded about the entrance of his tent, prevailed with him to think of returning. Yet he could not refrain from leaving behind him various deceptive memorials of his expedition, to impose upon after-times, and to exaggerate his glory with posterity, such as arms larger than were really worn, and mangers for horses, with bits of bridles above the usual size, which he set up, and distributed in several places. He erected altars, also, to the gods, which the kings of the Praesians even in our time do honor to when they pass the river, and offer sacrifice upon them after the Grecian manner. . . .

2

ROME: REPUBLIC AND EARLY EMPIRE

While Alexander the Great was subduing the Near East, the obscure agrarian city-state of Rome was maintaining a steady pressure on its Italian neighbors. Soon after 275 B.C., Rome became head of a federation which included all Italy south of the Po River. In the south of the peninsula contact was made with Greek colonists, and a transplantation of Greek ideas and institutions began which in the course of time justifies the term Graeco-Roman civilization. In this merger Rome's primary contributions were in the realms of law, government, and the applied sciences, while those of Greece were intellectual and cultural.

1. HOW ROME BECAME A NAVAL POWER

The desire for ever more land, commercial advantage, and military power inevitably caused Rome to become involved in war with Carthage, the dominant power of the western Mediterranean. In the course of this war Rome was transformed from an agrarian city-state into a formidable commercial and naval power. Polybius' (c. 205–c. 125 B.C.) account of the beginnings of the Roman navy follows.

. . . so long as the Carthaginians were in undisturbed command of the sea, the balance of success could not incline decisively in [the favor of Rome]. . . .

It was because they saw that the war they had undertaken lingered to a weary length, that [the Romans] first thought of getting a fleet built, consisting of a hundred quinqueremes and twenty triremes [261 B.C.]. But one part of their undertaking caused them much difficulty. Their shipbuilders were entirely unacquainted with the construction of quinqueremes,

The Histories of Polybius, I, 20–22, translated by E.S. Shuckburgh (London and New York: Macmillan, 1889), pp. 22–24.

because no one in Italy had at that time employed vessels of that description. There could be no more signal proof of the courage, or rather the extraordinary audacity of the Roman enterprise. . . . It was [at this time] that, the Carthaginians having put to sea in the Strait to attack them, a decked vessel of theirs charged so furiously that it ran aground, and falling into the hands of the Romans served them as a model on which they constructed their whole fleet. And if this had not happened it is clear that they would have been completely hindered from carrying out their design by want of constructive knowledge.

Meanwhile, however, those who were charged with the shipbuilding were busied with the construction of the vessels; while others collected crews and were engaged in teaching them to row on dry land: which they contrived to do in the following manner. They made the men sit on rower's benches on dry land, in the same order as they would sit on the benches in actual vessels: in the midst of them they stationed the Celeustes, and trained them to get back and draw in their hands all together in time, and then to swing forward and throw them out again, and to begin and cease these movements at the word of the Celeustes. By the time these preparations were completed the ships were built. They therefore launched them, and, after a brief preliminary practice of real sea-roving, started on their coasting voyage along the shore of Italy, in accordance with the Consul's order. . . .

. . . Now their ships were badly fitted out and not easy to manage, and so some one suggested to them as likely to serve their turn in a fight the construction of what were afterwards called "crows." Their mechanism was this. A round pole was placed in the prow, about twenty-four feet high, and with a diameter of four palms. The pole itself had a pulley on the top, and a gangway made with cross planks nailed together, four feet wide and thirty-six feet long, was made to swing round it. Now the hole in the gangway was oval shaped, and went round the pole twelve feet from one end of the gangway, which had also a wooden railing running down each side of it to the height of a man's knee. At the extremity of this gangway was fastened an iron spike like a miller's pestle, sharpened at its lower end and fitted with a ring at its upper end. The whole thing looked like the machines for braising corn. To this ring the rope was fastened with which, when the ships collided, they hauled up the "crows," by means of the pulley at the top of the pole, and dropped them down upon the deck of the enemy's ship, sometimes over the prow, sometimes swinging them round when the ships collided broadsides. And as soon as the "crows" were fixed in the planks of the decks and grappled the ships together, if the ships were alongside of each other, the men leaped on board anywhere along the side, but if they were prow to prow, they used the "crow" itself for boarding, and advanced over it two abreast. The first two protected their front by holding up before them their shields, while those who came after them secured their sides by placing the rims of their shields upon the top of the railing. Such were the preparations which they made; and having completed them they watched an opportunity of engaging at sea.

2. *LIVY DESCRIBES HANNIBAL'S CROSSING OF THE ALPS*

The First Punic War (264–241 B.C.) made Rome the foremost power of the western Mediterranean. In an effort to compensate for her losses (Sicily, Sardinia, and Corsica), Carthage began to expand in Spain, thereby intruding on Roman interests and provoking a declaration of war by Rome in 218 B.C. A Roman army was dispatched to deal with Hannibal in Spain, but Hannibal, with characteristic daring, marched into southern France, crossed the Alps with 26,000 men and a few elephants, and ravaged Italy until recalled in 203 B.C.

On the ninth day [the Carthaginians] arrived at the summit of the Alps, having come for the most part over trackless wastes and by roundabout routes, owing either to the dishonesty of their guides, or—when they would not trust the guides—to their blindly entering some valley, guessing at the way. For two days they lay encamped on the summit. The soldiers, worn with toil and fighting, were permitted to rest; and a number of baggage animals which had fallen among the rocks made their way to the camp by following the tracks of the army. Exhausted and discouraged as the soldiers were by many hardships, a snow-storm . . . threw them into a great fear. The ground was everywhere covered deep with snow when at dawn they began to march, and as the column moved slowly on, dejection and despair were to be read in every countenance. Then Hannibal, who had gone on before the standards, made the army halt on a certain promontory which commanded an extensive prospect, and pointing out Italy to them, and just under the Alps the plains about the Po, he told them that they were now scaling the ramparts not only of Italy, but of Rome itself; the rest of the way would be level or downhill; and after one, or, at the most, two battles, they would have in their hands and in their power the citadel and capital of Italy.

The column now began to make some progress, and even the enemy [native Gauls] had ceased to annoy them, except to make a stealthy raid, as occasion offered. But the way was much more difficult than the ascent

Livy, *Annals*, XXI, 35–39 (Cambridge, Mass.: Harvard University Press, 1949), Vol. V, pp. 103–111. Reprinted by permission of the publishers and the Loeb Classical Library, translated by B.O. Foster.

had been, as indeed the slope of the Alps on the Italian side is in general more precipitous in proportion as it is shorter. For practically every road was steep, narrow, and treacherous, so that neither could they keep from slipping, nor could those who had been thrown a little off their balance retain their footing, but came down, one on top of the other, and the beasts on top of the men.

They then came to a much narrower cliff, and with rocks so perpendicular that it was difficult for an unencumbered soldier to manage the descent, though he felt his way and clung with his hands to the bushes and roots that projected here and there. The place had been precipitous before, and a recent landslip had carried it away to the depth of a good thousand feet. There the cavalry came to a halt, as though they had reached the end of the road, and as Hannibal was wondering what it could be that held the column back, word was brought to him that the cliff was impassable. Going then to inspect the place himself, he thought that there was nothing for it but to lead the army round, over trackless and untrodden steeps, however circuitous the detour might be. But that way proved to be insuperable; for above the old, untouched snow lay a fresh deposit of moderate depth, through which, as it was soft and not very deep, the men in front found it easy to advance; but when it had been trampled down by the feet of so many men and beasts, the rest had to make their way over the bare ice beneath and the slush of the melting snow. Then came a terrible struggle on the slippery surface, for it afforded them no foothold, while the downward slope made their feet the more quickly slide from under them; so that whether they tried to pull themselves up with their hands, or used their knees, these supports themselves would slip, and down they would come again! Neither were there any stems or roots about, by which a man could pull himself up with foot or hand—only smooth ice and thawing snow, on which they were continually rolling. But the baggage animals, as they went over the snow, would sometimes even cut into the lowest crust, and pitching forward and striking out with their hoofs, as they struggled to rise, would break clean through it, so that numbers of them were caught fast, as if entrapped, in the hard, deep-frozen snow.

At last, when men and beasts had been worn out to no avail, they encamped upon the ridge, after having, with the utmost difficulty, cleared enough ground even for this purpose, so much snow were they obliged to dig out and remove. The soldiers were then set to work to construct a road across the cliff—their only possible way. Since they had to cut through the rock, they felled some huge trees that grew near at hand, and lopping off their branches, made an enormous pile of logs. This they set on fire, as soon as the wind blew fresh enough to make it burn, and pouring vinegar over the glowing rocks, caused them to crumble. After thus heating the crag with fire, they opened a way in it with iron tools, and relieved the steepness of the slope with zigzags of an easy gradient, so that not only the baggage animals but even the elephants could be led down. Four days were consumed at the cliff, and the animals nearly perished of starvation; for the mountain tops are all practically bare, and such grass as does grow is buried under snow. Lower down one comes to valleys and sunny slopes and rivulets, and near them woods, and places that begin to be fitter for man's habitation. There the beasts were turned out to graze, and the men, exhausted with toiling at the road, were allowed to rest. Thence they descended in three days' time into the plain, through a region now that was less forbidding, as was the character of its inhabitants.

3. *THE RISE OF THE GENERALS: (1) MARIUS AND SULLA*

The years between 133 and 31 B.C. were marked by almost continuous civil war and revolution in the Roman Republic. The basic cause was the inability of the governing class to find remedies for the numerous ailments resulting from the enormous expansion of Rome. One of the disturbing trends of the time was the rise of autocratic generals such as Marius and Sulla. Each of these bitter rivals had his own solution for Rome's problems; neither hesitated to violate constitutional precedent. The following selection is from Plutarch, a Greek historian of the second century A.D.

. . . Matching the very common soldiers in labor and abstemiousness, [Marius] gained great popularity with them; as indeed any voluntary partaking with people in their labor is felt as an easing of that labor, as it seems to take away the constraint and necessity of it. It is the most obliging sight in the world to the Roman soldier to see a commander eat the same bread as himself, or lie upon an ordinary bed, or assist the work in the drawing a trench and raising a bulwark. For they do not so much admire those that confer honors and riches upon them, as those that partake of the same labor and danger with themselves; but love them better that will vouchsafe to join in their work, than those that encourage their idleness.

Marius thus employed, and thus winning the affections of the soldiers, before long filled both Africa and Rome with his fame, and some, too,

Plutarch, "Caius Marius," translated by John Dryden in *Everybody's Plutarch*, edited by Raymond T. Bond, pp. 377–378, 394–396.

wrote home from the army that the war with Africa would never be brought to a conclusion, unless they chose Caius Marius consul. . . .

. . . Marius . . . began his voyage, and in four days, with a favorable wind, passed the sea; he was welcomed with great joy by the [Roman] people, and being brought into the assembly by one of the tribunes, sued for the consulship. . .

He was elected triumphantly [107 B.C.], and at once proceeded to levy soldiers, contrary both to law and custom, enlisting slaves and poor people; whereas former commanders never accepted of such, but bestowed arms, like other favors, as a matter of distinction, on persons who had the proper qualification, a man's property being thus a sort of security for his good behavior. These were not the only occasions of ill-will against Marius; some haughty speeches, uttered with great arrogance and contempt, gave great offence to the nobility; as, for example, his saying that he had carried off the consulship as a spoil from the effeminacy of the wealthy and high-born citizens, and telling the people that he gloried in wounds he had himself received for them, as much as others did in the monuments of dead men and images of their ancestors. . . .

Marius was now in his fifth consulship, and he sued for his sixth [100 B.C.] in such a manner as never any man before him had done, even for his first; he courted the people's favor and ingratiated himself with the multitude by every sort of complaisance; not only derogating from the state and dignity of his office, but also belying his own character, by attempting to seem popular and obliging, for which nature had never designed him. His passion for distinction did, indeed, they say, make him exceedingly timorous in any political matters, or in confronting public assemblies; and that undaunted presence of mind he always showed in battle against the enemy, forsook him when he was to address the people; he was easily upset by the most ordinary commendation or dispraise. The need they had of him in time of war procured him power and dignity; but in civil affairs, when he despaired of getting the first place, he was forced to betake himself to the favor of the people, never caring to be a good man, so that he were but a great one. . . . He thus became very odious to all the nobility. . . .

[After his sixth consulship, Marius] built a house close by the forum, either, as he himself gave out, that he was not willing his clients should be tired with going far, or that he imagined distance was the reason why more did not come. This, however, was not so; the real reason was, that being inferior to others in agreeableness of conversation and the arts of political life, like a mere tool and implement of war, he was thrown aside in time of peace. Amongst all those whose brightness eclipsed his glory, he was most incensed against Sulla, who had owed his rise to the hatred which the nobility bore Marius; and had made his disagreement with him the one principle of his political life. When Bocchus, king of Numidia, who was styled the associate of the Romans, dedicated some figures of Victory in the capital, and with them a representation in gold, of himself delivering Jugurtha to Sulla, Marius upon this was almost distracted with rage and ambition, as though Sulla had arrogated this honor to himself, and endeavored forcibly to pull down these presents; Sulla, on the other side, as vigorously resisted him. . . .

4. THE RISE OF THE GENERALS: (2) JULIUS CAESAR

The popular (anti-senatorial) party found an able leader in another victorious general, Julius Caesar. Declared a public enemy by the Senate in January, 49 B.C., Caesar promptly crossed the Rubicon in northern Italy ("the die is cast") and marched on Rome with one legion. Most of the senatorial party, with its leader, Pompey, fled the city. Another member of this party, Cicero, met Caesar en route to the capital and described his interview in letters to his friend Atticus.

Cicero to Atticus, Formiae, March 25, 49 B.C.

. . . a letter reached me from Capua saying that Caesar would see me either here or at Alba on the 28th. . . . As Caesar wrote to me, he has stationed one legion each at Brundisium, Tarentum and Sipontum. He seems to me to be cutting off retreat by sea and yet himself to have Greece in view rather than Spain. But these are remote considerations. Now I am stirred by the thought of meeting him; for the meeting is close at hand, and I am alarmed at the first steps he will take, for he will want, I am sure, a decree of the Senate and a decree of the augurs (we shall be hurried off to Rome or harassed, if we are absent), so that the praetor may hold an election of consuls or name a dictator, both acts unconstitutional. . . .

. . . Now I long to go away and it never strikes me that there is any chance of return. Not only is there no outcry of any in town or country, but on the contrary all are afraid of Pompey as cruel in his anger. . . .

Formiae, March 27, 49 B.C.

. . . What a wretched age this is! I have no doubt Caesar will urge me to come to Rome. For he gave orders that notices should be posted

Cicero, *Letters to Atticus*, translated by E.O. Winstedt (New York: The Macmillan Company, 1921), Vol. II, pp. 255–269. Reprinted by permission of the publishers and the Loeb Classical Library, Cambridge, Mass.: Harvard University Press.

even at Formiae that he wanted a full house on the first. Must I refuse? But why do I anticipate? I will write you all about it at once. . . .

Arpinum, March 28, 49 B.C.

. . . I spoke so as to gain Caesar's respect rather than his gratitude; and I persisted in my resolve not to go to Rome. We were mistaken in thinking he would be easy to manage. I have never seen anyone less easy. He kept on saying that my decision was a slur on him, and that others would be less likely to come, if I did not come. I pointed out that my case was very unlike theirs. After much talk he said, "Well, come and discuss peace." "On my own terms?" I asked. "Need I dictate to you?" said he. "Well," said I, "I shall contend that the Senate cannot sanction your invasion of Spain or your going with an army into Greece, and," I added, "I shall lament Pompey's fate." He replied, "That is not what I want." "So I fancied," said I: "but I do not want to be in Rome, because either I must say that and much else, on which I cannot keep silent, if I am present, or else I cannot come." The upshot was that I was to think over the matter, as Caesar suggested, with a view to closing our interview. I could not refuse. So we parted. I am confident then he has no liking for me. But I like myself, as I have not for a long time.

For the rest, ye gods what a following! What "damned souls," in your phrase! . . . What an abandoned cause, and what desperate gangs! . . . I see no end to our evil days. . . .

Arpinum, March 31, 49 B.C.

Since Rome was out of bounds, I celebrated my son's coming of age at Arpinum in preference to any other place, and so doing delighted my fellow-townsmen. Though they were pleased, yet I must tell you they and all others I have met are sad and sorry. So dark and direful is the *coup d'oeil* of this vast calamity. Levies are being made; troops are being drafted into winter quarters. These measures are hardships in themselves even when taken by loyalists, when the war is just, when there is some consideration. You can imagine how bitter they are when taken quite tyrannically by desperadoes in wicked civil war. But you must remember that every scoundrel in Italy is of [Caesar's] party. I saw them all together at Formiae. I could hardly believe them to be human. I knew every one of them, but I had never seen the whole collection together.

5. *AUGUSTUS HARANGUES THE ROMAN BACHELORS*

The spectacular success of Roman imperialism resulted in a complete transformation of the old republican city-state. No less than the political, social, and economic structure of Rome, standards of personal morality were affected—for the worse, as Augustus and many other thinking contemporaries well perceived. The following selection illustrates his concern for this problem.

. . . [Augustus] assembled in one part of the Forum the unmarried men . . . and in another those who were married, including those who also had children. Then, perceiving that the latter were much fewer in number than the former, he was filled with grief and addressed them somewhat as follows:

"Though you are but few altogether, in comparison with the vast throng that inhabits this city, and are far less numerous than the others, who are unwilling to perform any of their duties, yet for this very reason I for my part praise you the more, and am heartily grateful to you because you have shown yourselves obedient and are helping to replenish the fatherland. . . .

". . . is there anything better than a wife who is chaste, domestic, a good house-keeper, a rearer of children; one to gladden you in health, to tend you in sickness; to be your partner in good fortune, to console you in misfortune; to restrain the mad passion of youth and to temper the unseasonable harshness of old age? And is it not a delight to acknowledge a child who shows the endowments of both parents, to nurture and educate it, at once the physical and the spiritual image of yourself, so that in its growth another self lives again? . . . for the State, for whose sake we ought to do many things that are even distasteful to us, how excellent and how necessary it is . . . that there should be a multitude of men, to till the earth in time of peace, to make voyages, practise arts, and follow handicrafts, and, in time of war, to protect what we already have. . . . Therefore, men,—for you alone may properly be called men,—and fathers,—for you are as worthy to hold this title as I myself,—I love you and praise you for this; and I not only bestow the prizes I have already offered but will distinguish you still further by other honours and offices, so that you may not only reap great benefits yourselves but may also leave them to your children undiminished. I will now go over to the other group, whose actions will bear no comparison with yours and whose reward, therefore, will be directly the opposite. . . ."

Dio's Roman History, LVI, translated by Ernest Cary (New York: G.P. Putnam's Sons, 1924), pp. 5–23. Reprinted by permission of the publishers and the Loeb Classical Library, Cambridge, Mass.: Harvard University Press.

After this speech he made presents to some of them at once and promised to make others; he then went over to the other crowd and spoke to them as follows:

"A strange experience has been mine, O—what shall I call you? Men? But you are not performing any of the offices of men. Citizens? But for all that you are doing, the city is perishing. Romans? But you are undertaking to blot out this name altogether. Well, at any rate, whatever you are and by whatever name you delight to be called, mine has been an astonishing experience; for though I am always doing everything to promote an increase of population among you and am now about to rebuke you, I grieve to see that there are a great many of you. I could rather have wished that those others to whom I have just spoken were as numerous as you prove to be, and that preferably you were ranged with them, or otherwise did not exist at all. For you, heedless alike of the providence of the gods and of the watchful care of your forefathers, are bent upon annihilating our entire race and making it in truth mortal, are bent upon destroying and bringing to an end the entire Roman nation. . . .

". . . How can the State be preserved, if we neither marry nor have children? For surely you are not expecting men to spring up from the ground to succeed to your goods and to the public interests, as the myths describe! And yet it is neither right nor creditable that our race should cease, and the name of Romans be blotted out with us, and the city be given over to foreigners—Greeks or even barbarians. Do we not free our slaves chiefly for the express purpose of making out of them as many citizens as possible? And do we not give our allies a share in the government in order that our numbers may increase? And do you, then, who are Romans from the beginning and claim as your ancestors the famous Marcii, the Fabii, the Quintii, the Valerii, and the Julii, do you desire that your families and names alike shall perish with you? . . . Have done with your madness, then, and stop at last to reflect, that with many dying all the time by disease and many in war it is impossible for the city to maintain itself, unless its population is continually renewed by those who are ever and anon being born. . . ."

Such were his words to the two groups at that time. Afterwards he increased the rewards to those who had children and in the case of the others made a distinction between the married men and the unmarried by imposing different penalties; furthermore, he granted a year's time to those who were remiss in either respect, in which to obey him and thus escape the penalties. . . .

6. TACITUS ASSESSES AUGUSTUS' REIGN

The greatest, but not the most impartial, Roman historian is Tacitus (died c. 117 A.D.). His* Annals *begin with the death of Augustus. In the selection below he gives his description of Augustus' funeral and a brief assessment of his reign. Tacitus' point of view is that of one who bemoans the death of the Republic and the decline of the old Roman virtues.

On the day of the funeral soldiers stood round as a guard, amid much ridicule from those who had either themselves witnessed or who had heard from their parents of the famous day when slavery was still something fresh, and freedom had been resought in vain, when the slaying of Caesar, the Dictator, seemed to some the vilest, to others, the most glorious of deeds. "Now," they said, "an aged sovereign, whose power had lasted long, who had provided his heirs with abundant means to coerce the State, requires forsooth the defence of soldiers that his burial may be undisturbed."

Then followed much talk about Augustus himself. . . . People extolled, too, the number of his consulships . . . the continuance for thirty-seven years of the tribunitian power, the title of Imperator twenty-one times earned, and his other honours which had been either frequently repeated or were wholly new. Sensible men, however, spoke variously of his life with praise and censure. Some said "that dutiful feeling towards a father, and the necessities of the State in which laws had then no place, drove him into civil war, which can neither be planned nor conducted on any right principles. . . . The only remedy for his distracted country was the rule of a single man. Yet the State had been organized under the name neither of a kingdom nor a dictatorship, but under that of a prince. The ocean and remote rivers were the boundaries of the empire; the legions, provinces, fleets, all things were linked together; there was law for the citizens; there was respect shown to the allies. The capital had been embellished on a grand scale; only in a few instances had he resorted to force, simply to secure general tranquillity."

It was said, on the other hand, "that filial duty and State necessity were merely assumed as a mask. It was really from a lust of sovereignty that he had excited the veterans by bribery, had, when a young man and a subject, raised an army, tampered with the Consul's legions, and feigned an attachment to the faction of Pompey. By a decree of the Senate he had usurped the high functions and authority of Praetor . . . wrested the

Tacitus, *Annals*, I, 8–10, *The Complete Works of Tacitus,* translated by A.J. Church and W.J. Brodribb (New York: The Modern Library, 1942), pp. 9–11. Used by permission of Macmillan & Company, Ltd., London.

consulate from a reluctant Senate, and turned against the State the arms with which he had been intrusted against Antony. Citizens were proscribed, lands divided, without so much as the approval of those who executed these deeds. . . . No doubt, there was peace after all this, but it was a peace stained with blood; . . .

". . . No honour was left for the gods, when Augustus chose to be himself worshipped with temples and statues, like those of the deities, and with flamens and priests. He had not even adopted Tiberius as his successor out of affection or any regard to the State, but, having thoroughly seen his arrogant and savage temper, he had sought glory for himself by a contrast of extreme wickedness."

3

CHRISTIANITY

In the reign of Augustus, about 4 B.C., was born a Man whose life and death would provide the principal unifying element of Western civilization. The time was opportune for His coming. The Mediterranean World was beginning the longest uninterrupted reign of peace in history. Communication had never been easier. Spiritually and intellectually, there existed a void which neither the official Roman religion nor the mystery cults imported from the East could fill. Christianity, with its rational foundation, its emphasis on the dignity and worth of human life, its promise of redemption and eternal happiness, gave life a new meaning for increasing numbers. By the end of the fourth century the entire Roman world was Christian.

1. A SECOND CENTURY SAINT DESCRIBES CHRISTIAN WORSHIP

St. Justin Martyr (c. 100–c. 165 A.D.) was of pagan, Graeco-Roman ancestry and a native of Samaria in Palestine. He received an excellent education in pagan culture but found no peace in the pagan philosophies of his day. By accident, he was introduced to Christianity and, in his words, was "set on fire" by the teachings of Christ and the heroic conduct of His followers in the face of persecution. His* First Apology, *one of the earliest Christian writings extant, was designed to explain Christianity to the hostile Roman people.

After baptizing the one who has believed and given his assent, we escort him to the place where are assembled those whom we call brethren, to offer up sincere prayers in common for ourselves, for the baptized person,

Saint Justin Martyr, *The First Apology,* 65–68, translated by T.B. Falls in *The Fathers of the Church* (New York: Christian Heritage, Inc., 1948), Vol. IV, pp. 104–107. Copyright 1948 by Ludwig Schopp. Used by permission of the Fathers of the Church, Inc.

and for all other persons wherever they may be, in order that, since we have found the truth, we may be deemed fit through our actions to be esteemed as good citizens and observers of the law, and thus attain eternal salvation. At the conclusion of the prayers we greet one another with a kiss. Then, bread and a chalice containing wine mixed with water are presented to the one presiding over the brethren. He takes them and offers praise and glory to the Father of all, through the name of the Son and of the Holy Spirit, and he recites lengthy prayers of thanksgiving to God in the name of those to whom He granted such favors. At the end of these prayers and thanksgiving, all present express their approval by saying "Amen." This Hebrew word, "Amen," means "So be it." And when he who presides has celebrated the Eucharist, they whom we call deacons permit each one present to partake of the Eucharistic bread, and wine and water; and they carry it also to the absentees.

We call this food the Eucharist, of which only he can partake who has acknowledged the truth of our teachings, who has been cleansed by baptism for the remission of his sins and for his regeneration, and who regulates his life upon the principles laid down by Christ. Not as ordinary bread or as ordinary drink do we partake of them, but just as, through the word of God, our Savior Jesus Christ became Incarnate and took upon Himself flesh and blood for our salvation, so, we have been taught, the food which has been made the Eucharist by the prayer of His word, and which nourishes our flesh and blood by assimilation, is both the flesh and blood of that Jesus who was made flesh. The Apostles in their memoirs, which are called Gospels, have handed down what Jesus ordered them to do; that He took bread and, after giving thanks, said: "Do this in remembrance of Me; this is My body." In like manner, He took also the chalice, gave thanks, and said: "This is My blood"; and to them only did He give it. The evil demons, in imitation of this, ordered the same thing to be performed in the Mithraic mysteries. [The worship of the Persian sun-god became very popular in Justin's lifetime.] For, as you know or may easily learn, bread and a cup of water, together with certain incantations, are used in their mystic initiation rites.

Henceforward, we constantly remind one another of these things. The rich among us come to the aid of the poor, and we always stay together. For all the favors we enjoy we bless the Creator of all, through His Son Jesus Christ and through the Holy Spirit. On the day which is called Sunday we have a common assembly of all who live in the cities or in the outlying districts, and the memoirs of the Apostles or the writings of the Prophets are read, as long as there is time. Then, when the reader has finished, the president of the assembly verbally admonishes and invites all to imitate such examples of virtue. Then we all stand up together and offer up our prayers, and, as we said before, after we finish our prayers, bread and wine and water are presented. He who presides likewise offers up prayers and thanksgivings, to the best of his ability, and the people express their approval by saying "Amen." The Eucharistic elements are distributed and consumed by those present, and to those who are absent they are sent through the deacons. The wealthy, if they wish, contribute whatever they desire, and the collection is placed in the custody of the president. [With it] he helps the orphans and widows, those who are needy because of sickness or any other reason, and the captives and strangers in our midst; in short, he takes care of all those in need. . . .

2. *A LAY INTELLECTUAL PRESENTS THE CHRISTIAN CASE*

Minucius Felix, like Justin, was the son of a well-to-do pagan colonist family. He was trained as a lawyer and moved to Rome. There, in the courts of law, he had ample opportunity to witness the steadfastness of the Christians in the face of persecution. Their example determined him to join their ranks. His* Octavius, *the earliest known work of Latin Christian literature, purports to be a colloquy between himself ("Marcus"), his Christian friend Octavius, and the pagan Caecilius.

. . . Caecilius neither paid attention nor laughed at the game. [The three friends were at the seashore watching boys skim flat rocks over the water.] Silent, uneasy, and distracted, he betrayed by the expression on his face that he was troubled by something. I said to him: "What is the matter, Caecilius? How is it I fail to see your usual liveliness and . . . cheerfulness . . . ?"

He rejoined: "For a long time I have been greatly annoyed, and actually cut to the quick, by the remarks of our friend Octavius. . . . I would [like] an exhaustive and comprehensive discussion with him. . . . Let us just sit down on those piles of rocks . . . so that we can both rest from our walk and debate with more concentration."

. . . The two opponents taking their place on either side flanked me as the middle of the three. This was done . . . so that I, as arbiter, sitting close to both, might give heed to them, and, being in the middle, might separate the two contestants.

Caecilius then began as follows: . . . "There will be no difficulty in showing that in human affairs everything is doubtful, uncertain and un-

Minucius Felix, *Octavius*, translated by R. Arbesmann, O.S.A., in *The Fathers of the Church* (New York: Christian Heritage, Inc., 1948), Vol. X, pp. 324–402, *passim.*

settled; that everything is a matter of probability rather than truth. . . . Since this is the case, everyone must feel a righteous indignation and be annoyed that certain persons—persons, in addition, innocent of learning, untouched by letters, unskilled even in manual arts—boldly utter categorical statements concerning the majesty of the universe; a problem over which countless schools of philosophy have pondered through so many centuries and are continuing to do so up to this day. And not without good reason. For, man, because of the limitation of his intellectual power, is so incapable of exploring things divine that neither is he privileged to know, nor does religious awe allow him to examine thoroughly, things which are suspended high above us in heaven or lie deeply submerged within the womb of the earth; . . .

". . . How much more reverent and better it is to accept the teaching of our forefathers as a guide to truth, to cherish the religious practices handed down to us, to adore the gods whom your parents taught you to fear rather than to know more familiarly! . . . Is it not deplorable that fellows (you will excuse me for the vehement and unrestrained expression of my thoughts) . . . fellows, I say, belonging to an incorrigible, outlawed, and desperate gang, riot against the gods? Fellows who gather together ignoramuses from the lowest dregs of society, and credulous women, an easy prey because of the instability of their sex, and thus organize an unholy mob of conspirators who become leagued together in nocturnal gatherings, by solemn fasts and atrocious repasts, not by any rite, but by an inexpiable crime—a furtive race which shuns the light, mute in the open but garrulous in the corners. They despise the temples as no better than sepulchres, abominate the gods, sneer at our sacred rites. Pitiable themselves, they pity (if this is possible at all) the priests; half-naked themselves, they spurn positions of honor and purple robes. What strange folly! What incredible insolence! . . .

". . . The stories told about the initiation of their novices . . . are as detestable as they are notorious. An infant covered with a dough crust to deceive the unsuspecting is placed beside the person to be initiated into their sacred rites. This infant is killed at the hands of the novice by wounds inflicted unintentionally and hidden from his eyes, since he has been urged on as if to harmless blows upon the surface of the dough. The infant's blood—oh, horrible—they sip up eagerly; its limbs they tear to pieces, trying to outdo each other; by this victim they are leagued together; by being privy to this crime they pledge themselves to mutual silence. These sacred rites are more shocking than any sacrilege.

"Many things I pass over purposely, for even those I mentioned are more than enough; that either all or most of them are true is evident from the mysterious conduct of this perverted religion. Why do they strive with so much effort to keep secret and conceal whatever the object of their worship is? Is it not because honorable deeds rejoice in publicity, while evil deeds keep in hiding? Why do they have no altars, no temples, none of the usual images of the gods? Why do they never speak in public, never assemble in open? Is it not because the very object of their worship and secretiveness is something shameful or liable to punishment?" . . .

Thus Caecilius came to an end and said with a triumphant smile (for the impetuous flow of his discourse had relieved the swelling of his indignation): "And, now, is there anything that Octavius ventures to answer to these things, Octavius, a man of the progeny of Plautus: the best of bakers, but the poorest of philosophers?" . . .[1]

Octavius then began: . . . "Our good brother has disclosed feelings of displeasure, annoyance, indignation, and grief that unlearned, poor, and ignorant people should discuss heavenly things. Yet, he should know that all human beings, without respect to age, sex, or rank, are born capable of and fit for reasoning and understanding; they do not acquire wisdom by good fortune, but receive it as an innate gift from nature. . . . Talents are not furnished by wealth or obtained through studies, but are begotten with the very fashioning of the mind. There is, then, no reason for indignation or grief if a common man makes inquiries into things divine and holds and pronounces his views on the subject, since it is not the authority in the discussing person, but the truth in his discussion, that matters. Further, the more unskilled the speech, the clearer is the reasoning, because it is not vitiated by a display of eloquence and graceful style, but sustained in its true character by the rule of right.

"I feel . . . convinced that people who hold this universe of consummate artistic beauty to be not the work of divine planning, but a conglomeration of some kind of fragments clinging together by chance, are themselves devoid of reason and perception—even of the very power of seeing. For, what is so manifest, so acknowledged, and so evident, when you lift your eyes to heaven and examine all the things which are below and around you, than that there exists some divine Being of unequaled mental power by whom all nature is inspired, moved, nourished, and governed? . . .

"Our ancestors were ready to believe in any product of imagination. . . . What about those old women's tales of human beings turned into birds and wild beasts, and of people transformed into trees and flowers? If such things had ever happened, they would still happen today; but, since

[1] Plautus, the great Latin comedy writer, worked for a miller as a youth. Millers belonged to the lowest class of Roman society.

they cannot happen today, they never happened at all. In a similar way, our ancestors were mistaken about their gods; uncritical, credulous, they formed their faith with naive simplicity. . . .

"Do not the very forms and appearances of your gods expose them to ridicule and contempt?—Vulcan, a lame and crippled god; Apollo, still beardless after all the years; Aesculapius, with a bushy beard, although he is the son of the ever-youthful Apollo; Neptune, with sea-green eyes; Minerva, cat-eyed; Juno, ox-eyed; Mercury, with winged feet; Pan, with hoofs; Saturn, with shackled feet. Yes, and Janus sports two faces as if he meant to walk backward, also; Diana is sometimes short-skirted like a huntress, while at Ephesus she is represented with many breasts and paps, and, as goddess of the crossroads, she is horrible to behold, with three heads and many hands. Why, your Jupiter himself is at one time shown beardless and at another is displayed with a beard. When he is called Hammon, he has horns; when the Capitoline, he wields thunderbolts; when Latiaris, he is drenched in blood; and as Feretrius, he wears a wreath. And, not to linger too long over multitudinous Jupiters, there are as many strange forms for him as there are names. . . .

"Accept it from us, as from people who remember with sorrow their own attitude, how unfair it is to pass judgment, as you do, without knowledge and examination of the facts. We, too, were once not different from you; still blind and ignorant, we thought the same as you, fancying that Christians worshipped monsters, devoured infants, and joined in incestuous banquets. We were unaware that it was by the demons that such stories were continually spread about, without ever being investigated or proved; that in all that time there was not one who played the traitor in order to gain not only pardon for his offense, but also reward for his denunciation; and that criminal action is so little involved that Christians, when accused, neither blushed nor were afraid, but regretted one thing only: not having been Christians sooner. . . .

". . . To your great mortification, we practice mutual love, because we do not know how to hate; and to your displeasure, we call ourselves brethren, as being human children of one divine Father, sharers in one faith, and joint heirs of the same hope. You, on the other hand, do not acknowledge each other, and a fit of bad temper leads you to mutual hatred; nor do you recognize each other as brothers unless for the purpose of fratricide."

Octavius had ended his speech. Stunned into silence, we kept our eyes intently fixed upon him for a while. . . . Caecilius burst out, saying: "I extend my heartiest congratulations to my friend Octavius and to myself, nor do I wait for a decision. As things turned out, we have both won. . . .

I acknowledge Providence, agree with you on the concept of God, and recognize the moral purity of the religion which has just become my own." . . .

After this we left, rejoicing and in good spirits—Caecilius, because he had found the faith; Octavius, because he had won a victory; and I, because of the faith of the one and the victory of the other.

3. THE DEATH OF A CHRISTIAN MARTYR: BLANDINA OF LYONS

The ensuing account of the martyrdom of Blandina and her co-religionists in Lyons is from a letter written by a Christian of that city who survived the persecution. The letter was sent to "the brethren in Asia and Phrygia [Asia Minor] who have the same faith and hope of redemption as we." The persecution described took place in the reign of Marcus Aurelius (161–180 A.D.) and was one of the most severe in the history of the Empire.

. . . The holy martyrs endured punishments beyond all description, as Satan strove to wring some blasphemy even from them. And all the wrath of the mob and of the governor and of the soldiers beyond all measure fell upon Sanctus, the deacon from Vienne, and against Maturus, very much of a novice but a noble contender, and on Attalus, a Pergamene [native of Pergamus in Asia Minor] by race, who had always been a pillar and a bulwark for the Christians there, and against Blandina. . . . Blandina was filled with so much strength that she was released and those who tortured her in relays in every manner from morning until evening became exhausted, even confessing of their own accord that they were beaten, since they had nothing further to do to her, and that they marveled at the fact that she was still alive, for her whole body was broken and opened, and that they testified that one form of torture was enough to drive out life, to say nothing of the different nature and number of the tortures. But the blessed woman, like a noble athlete, renewed her strength in the confession, and her comfort and rest and release from the pain of what was happening to her was in saying: "I am a Christian woman and nothing wicked happens among us."

Sanctus himself also nobly endured beyond all measure and human endurance all the ill-treatment of men. When the wicked hoped through persistence and the severity of the tortures that they would hear something from him which should not be said, he resisted them with such firmness

Eusebius, *Ecclesiastical History,* V, 1, translated by R.J. Deferrari in *The Fathers of the Church* (New York: Christian Heritage, Inc., 1955), Vol. XIX, pp. 276-285.

that he did not even tell his own name nor of what race or city he was, nor whether he was a slave or free, but to all their interrogations he answered in the Latin language: "I am a Christian." This he confessed for name and for city and for race and for everything in succession, and the heathen heard no other word from him. . . .

When the tyrant's torments had been brought to naught by Christ through the endurance of the blessed, the Devil invented other schemes: imprisonments in cells of darkness and in the most loathsome places, stretching the feet in the stocks, separated to the fifth hole, and other outrages. . . .

. . . Now, Maturus and Sanctus and Blandina and Attalus were led to the wild beasts, for a public and general exhibition of the inhumanity of the heathen. . . . Maturus and Sanctus again passed through every torture in the amphitheatre, as if they had suffered nothing at all before, but rather as if they had already overpowered their opponent in several bouts and were now holding the contest for the crown. They endured again the customary running of the gauntlet and the violence of the wild beasts and all such things as the maddened people, some here and others there, shouted for and commanded—above all the iron chair on which their bodies were roasted, covering them with reek. Not even there did the persecutors cease, but again they raved even more, seeking to overcome their endurance. But not even thus did they hear anything else from Sanctus than the sound of the confession which he had been accustomed to say from the beginning.

These, then, while their life lingered long through a great contest, at last were sacrificed, they themselves having been a spectacle for the world throughout that day in place of the usual variety of gladiatorial combats; but Blandina was hung on a stake and was offered as food for the wild beasts that were let in. Since she seemed to be hanging in the form of a cross, and by her firmly intoned prayer, she inspired the combatants with great zeal, as they looked on during the contest and with their outward eyes saw through their sister Him who was crucified for them, that He might persuade those who believe in Him that everyone who suffers for the glory of Christ always has fellowship with the living God. And when none of the wild beasts then touched her, she was taken down from the stake and again cast into the prison, being saved for another contest, that by conquering through more trials she might make the condemnation of the crooked Serpent irrevocable, and might encourage the brethren. Although small and weak and greatly despised, she had put on the great and invincible athlete Christ, and in many contests had overcome the Adversary and through the conflict had gained the crown of immortality. . . .

Finally . . . on the last day of the gladiatorial combats, Blandina was again brought in, together with Ponticus, a boy of about fifteen, and they had been brought in daily to witness the torture of the others, and attempts were made to force them to swear by the very idols, and because they remained steadfast and regarded them as nothing, the mob was roused to fury so that they had neither pity for the youth of the boy nor respect for the feminine sex, and they exposed them to all the horrors and led them in turn through every torture, repeatedly trying to force them to swear but being unable to do this. For Ponticus was encouraged by his sister, so that even the heathen saw that she was urging him on and encouraging him, and after he had nobly endured every torture he gave up the ghost. But the blessed Blandina, last of all, like a noble mother who has encouraged her children and sent them forth triumphant to the king, herself also enduring all the conflicts of the children, hastened to them, rejoicing and glad at her departure, as if called to a marriage feast and not being thrown to the beasts. And after the scourging, after the wild beasts, after the roasting seat, she finally was placed in a net and thrown to a bull. She was tossed about for some time by the animal, but was insensitive to what was happening to her because of her hope and hold upon what had been entrusted to her and her communion with Christ. And she also was sacrificed, and the heathen themselves confessed that never had a woman among them suffered so many and such horrible tortures.

4. A ROMAN GOVERNOR IS PERPLEXED BY THE CHRISTIANS

We should not think of the relations between Christians and the Roman Empire only in terms of such cruel and senseless persecutions as the foregoing. Christianity presented a real political problem with which many fair-minded Roman emperors and civil servants tried to cope without useless shedding of blood. Such moderation is evidenced in the exchange of letters between Pliny the Younger, governor of Bithynia, in Asia Minor, and the Emperor Trajan (98–117 A.D.).

Pliny to the Emperor Trajan

It is a rule, Sir, which I inviolably observe, to refer myself to you in all my doubts; for who is more capable of guiding my uncertainty or informing my ignorance? Having never been present at any trials of the Christians, I am unacquainted with the method and limits to be observed either in examining or punishing them. Whether any difference is to be

Pliny, *Letters*, X, 96–97 (Cambridge, Mass.: Harvard University Press, 1935), pp. 401–407. Reprinted by permission of the publishers and the Loeb Classical Library, translated by W. Melmouth.

made on account of age, or no distinction allowed between the youngest and the adult; whether repentance admits to a pardon, or if a man has been once a Christian it avails him nothing to recant; whether the mere profession of Christianity, albeit without crimes, or only the crimes associated therewith are punishable—in all these points I am greatly doubtful.

In the meanwhile, the method I have observed towards those who have been denounced to me as Christians is this: I interrogated them whether they were Christians; if they confessed it I repeated the question twice again, adding the threat of capital punishment; if they still persevered, I ordered them to be executed. . . .

Accusations spread (as is usually the case) from the mere fact of the matter being investigated. . . . A placard was put up, without any signature, accusing a large number of persons by name. Those who denied they were, or had ever been, Christians, who repeated after me an invocation to the gods, and offered adoration, with wine and frankincense, to your image, which I had ordered to be brought for that purpose, together with those of the gods, and who finally cursed Christ—none of which acts, it is said, those who are really Christians can be forced into performing—these I thought it proper to discharge. . . .

. . . The matter seemed to me well worth referring to you—especially considering the numbers endangered. Persons of all ranks and ages, and of both sexes are, and will be, involved in the prosecution. For this contagious superstition is not confined to the cities only, but has spread through the villages and rural districts; it seems possible, however, to check and cure it. . . .

The Emperor Trajan to Pliny

The method you have pursued, my dear Pliny, in sifting the cases of those denounced to you as Christians is extremely proper. It is not possible to lay down any general rule which can be applied as the fixed standard in all cases of this nature. No search should be made for these people; when they are denounced and found guilty they must be punished; with the restriction, however, that when the party denies himself to be a Christian, and shall give proof that he is not (that is, by adoring our gods) he shall be pardoned on the ground of repentance, even though he may have formerly incurred suspicion. Informations without the accuser's name subscribed must not be admitted in evidence against anyone, as it is introducing a very dangerous precedent, and by no means agreeable to the spirit of the age.

5. *THE CHRISTIANS ARE GRANTED TOLERATION—THE EDICT OF MILAN*

In 311 A.D., Emperor Galerius, in what the Christian historian Eusebius describes as a deathbed repentence for the wickedness of his life, granted conditional liberty to the Christians. Two years later, the joint emperors, Constantine and Licinius, issued the much more famous Edict of Milan granting toleration not only to the Christians but to all religions.

When under happy auspices I, Constantine Augustus, and I, Licinius Augustus, had come to Milan and held an inquiry about all matters such as pertain to the common advantage and good . . . we resolved to issue decrees by which esteem and reverence for the Deity might be procured, that is, that we might give all Christians freedom of choice to follow the ritual which they wished, so that whatever is of the nature of the divine and heavenly might be propitious to us and to all those living under our authority. Accordingly, with sound and most correct reasoning we decided upon this our plan: that authority is to be refused no one at all to follow and to choose the observance or the form of worship of the Christians, and that authority be given to each one to devote his mind to that form of worship which he himself considers to be adapted to himself, in order that the Deity may be able in all things to provide for us His accustomed care and goodness. . . .

And this, also, besides the rest, we resolve with respect to the Christians: that their places at which they were formerly accustomed to assemble . . . must be handed over to [them] immediately and without delay.

And since the same Christians had not only those places in which they used to assemble, but are known to have had others, also, which belonged not to individuals among them, but to the rightful claim of their whole body, that is, of the Christians, all these, in accordance with the law which we have just mentioned, you [the imperial governors] are to order to be restored without delay to the same Christians, that is, to their group and to each assembly, guarding clearly . . . that whoever restore the same places without compensation . . . may hope for indemnification from our own generosity.

In all these matters you should exercise the utmost care for the aforementioned group of Christians, so that our order may be carried out as quickly as possible, and that also in this forethought may be exercised through our beneficence for the common and public peace. For by this

Eusebius, *Ecclesiastical History*, V, 1, translated by R.J. Deferrari in *The Fathers of the Church* (New York: Christian Heritage, Inc., 1955), Vol. XXIX, pp. 269–272.

means, as has been mentioned before, the divine zeal in our behalf, which we have already experienced in many things, will remain steadfast forever. And that the scope of this our decree and generosity may be brought to the knowledge of all, it is fitting that these matters as decreed by us be declared everywhere, and brought to the knowledge of all by being published at your order, so that the decree of this our generosity may escape the notice of no one.

6. THE PERSECUTED BECOME THE PERSECUTORS

In the reign of Theodosius I (379–395 A.D.) not only was Christianity the official religion of the Empire, but all other religions were declared illegal.

It is our desire that all the various nations which are subject to our Clemency and Moderation, should continue in the profession of that religion which was delivered to the Romans by the divine Apostle Peter, as it hath been preserved by faithful tradition; and which is now professed by the Pontiff Damasus and by Peter, Bishop of Alexandria, a man of apostolic holiness. According to the apostolic teaching and the doctrine of the Gospel, let us believe the one deity of the Father, the Son and the Holy Spirit, in equal majesty and in a holy Trinity. We authorize the followers of this law to assume the title of Catholic Christians; but as for the others, since, in our judgement, they are foolish madmen, we decree that they shall be branded with the ignominious name of heretics, and shall not presume to give to their conventicles the name of churches. They will suffer in the first place the chastisement of the divine condemnation, and in the second the punishment which our authority, in accordance with the will of Heaven, shall decide to inflict.

The Theodosian Code, XVI, i, 2, as found in Henry Bettenson, ed., *Documents of the Christian Church* (London: Oxford University Press, 1943), p. 31. Used by permission of the publisher.

4

THE BARBARIAN INVASIONS

Since the early Republic the Germans had pressed upon the Roman frontier. Although many Germans had peacefully entered the Roman Empire, no forceful break-through took place until the end of the fourth century. In the following century Roman rule disintegrated in the western half of the Empire. In its place appeared a number of Germanic states, the precursors of modern England, France, Spain, and Italy. However, there was no clean break with classical civilization. In the fusion between the Germanic and the Catholic Graeco-Roman civilizations, the latter element was predominant. The end product was Europe.

1. TACITUS DESCRIBES THE GERMANS

Next to Caesar's* Gallic Wars, *the earliest account of the Germans that has survived is the* Germania *of the Roman historian Tacitus. It was written in 98 A.D. Because of its emphasis on the alleged purity of morals, love of liberty, and individualism of the Germans—qualities hardly characteristic of Tacitus's fellow Romans—the* Germania *has often been interpreted as an indirect condemnation of the early Empire.

. . . [The Germans] have fierce blue eyes, red hair, huge frames, fit only for a sudden exertion. They are less able to bear laborious work. Heat and thirst they cannot in the least endure; to cold and hunger their climate and their soil inure them. . . .

. . . Few use swords or long lances. They carry a spear . . . with a narrow and short head, but so sharp and easy to wield that the same weapon serves, according to circumstances, for close or distant conflict.

Tacitus, *Germania*, 4–21, *The Complete Works of Tacitus,* translated by A.J. Church and W.J. Brodribb (New York: The Modern Library, 1942), pp. 710–720. Used by permission of Macmillan & Company, Ltd., London.

As for the horse-soldier, he is satisfied with a shield and spear; the foot-soldiers also scatter showers of missiles, each man having several and hurling them to an immense distance. . . . On the whole, one would say that their chief strength is in their infantry, which fights along with the cavalry; admirably adapted to the action of the latter is the swiftness of certain foot-soldiers, who are picked from the entire youth of their country, and stationed in front of the line. . . . Their line of battle is drawn up in a wedge-like formation. To give ground, provided you return to the attack, is considered prudence rather than cowardice. The bodies of their slain they carry off even in indecisive engagements. To abandon your shield is the basest of crimes; nor may a man thus disgraced be present at the sacred rites, or enter their council; many, indeed, after escaping from battle, have ended their infamy with the halter.

. . . They carry with them into battle certain figures and images taken from their sacred groves. And what most stimulates their courage is, that their squadrons or battalions, instead of being formed by chance or by a fortuitous gathering, are composed of families and clans. Close by them, too, are those dearest to them, so that they hear the shrieks of women, the cries of infants. *They* are to every man the most sacred witnesses of his bravery—*they* are his most generous applauders. The soldier brings his wounds to mother and wife, who shrink not from counting or even demanding them and who administer both food and encouragement to the combatants.

About minor matters the chiefs deliberate, about the more important the whole tribe. Yet even when the final decision rests with the people, the affair is always thoroughly discussed by the chiefs. . . . The king or the chief, according to age, birth, distinction in war, or eloquence, is heard, more because he has influence to persuade than because he has power to command. If his sentiments displease [the multitude], they reject them with murmurs; if they are satisfied, they brandish their spears. The most complimentary form of assent is to express approbation with their weapons.

In their councils an accusation may be preferred or a capital crime prosecuted. Penalties are distinguished according to the offence. Traitors and deserters are hanged on trees; the coward, the unwarlike, the man stained with abominable vices, is plunged into the mire of the morass, with a hurdle put over him. This distinction in punishment means that crime, they think, ought, in being punished, to be exposed, while infamy ought to be buried out of sight. Lighter offences, too, have penalties proportioned to them; he who is convicted, is fined in a certain number of horses or of cattle. . . .

They transact no public or private business without being armed. It is not, however, usual for anyone to wear arms till the state has recognized his power to use them. Then in the presence of the council one of the chiefs, or the young man's father, or some kinsman, equips him with a shield and a spear. These arms are what the "toga" is with us, the first honour with which youth is invested. Up to this time he is regarded as a member of a household, afterwards as a member of the commonwealth. Very noble birth or great services rendered by the father secure for lads the rank of a chief; such lads attach themselves to men of mature strength and of long approved valour. It is no shame to be seen among a chief's followers. . . .

When they go into battle, it is a disgrace for the chief to be surpassed in valour, a disgrace for his followers not to equal the valour of the chief. And it is an infamy and a reproach for life to have survived the chief, and returned from the field. To defend, to protect him, to ascribe one's own brave deeds to his renown, is the height of loyalty. The chief fights for victory; his vassals fight for their chief. If their native state sinks into the sloth of prolonged peace and repose, many of its noble youths voluntarily seek those tribes which are waging some war, both because inaction is odious to their race, and because they win renown more readily in the midst of peril, and cannot maintain a numerous following except by violence and war. . . .

Whenever they are not fighting, they pass much of their time in the chase, and still more in idleness, giving themselves up to sleep and to feasting, the bravest and the most warlike doing nothing, and surrendering the management of the household, of the home, and of the land, to the women, the old men, and all the weakest members of the family. They themselves lie buried in sloth, a strange combination in their nature that the same men should be so fond of idleness, so averse to peace. . . .

It is well known that the nations of Germany have no cities, and that they do not even tolerate closely contiguous dwellings. They live scattered and apart, just as a spring, a meadow, or a wood has attracted them. Their villages they do not arrange in our fashion, with the buildings connected and joined together, but every person surrounds his dwelling with an open space, either as a precaution against the disasters of fire, or because they do not know how to build. No use is made by them of stone or tile; they employ timber for all purposes, rude masses without ornament or attractiveness. Some parts of their buildings they stain more carefully with a clay so clear and bright that it resembles painting, or a coloured design. They are wont also to dig out subterranean caves, and pile on them great heaps of dung, as a shelter from winter and as a receptacle for the year's produce, for by such places they mitigate the rigour of the cold. And should an enemy approach, he lays waste the open country, while what is hidden and buried is either not known to exist, or else escapes him from the very fact that it has to be searched for.

No nation indulges more profusely in entertainments and hospitality. To exclude any human being from their roof is thought impious; every German, according to his means, receives his guest with a well-furnished table. When his supplies are exhausted, he who was but now the host becomes the guide and companion to further hospitality, and without invitation they go to the next house. It matters not; they are entertained with like cordiality. No one distinguishes between an acquaintance and a stranger, as regards the rights of hospitality. It is usual to give the departing guest whatever he may ask for, and a present in return is asked with as little hesitation. They are greatly charmed with gifts, but they expect no return for what they give, nor feel any obligation for what they receive.

2. *THE HUNS FORCE THE VISIGOTHS ACROSS THE ROMAN FRONTIER*

Late in the second century A.D. the Germanic Goths settled on the northern shores of the Black Sea. Two centuries later, from across the steppes of Asia, the awesome Huns arrived in the same region. The East Goths (Ostrogoths) were crushed and subjugated. In desperation, the West Goths (Visigoths) asked permission to cross the Danube and enter the Roman Empire. Emperor Valens gave his consent, and in 376 the first German "nation" entered the Empire.

. . . The people of the Huns . . . exceed every degree of savagery. Since the cheeks of the children are deeply furrowed with the steel from their very birth, in order that the growth of hair, when it appears at the proper time, may be checked by the wrinkled scars, they grow old without beards and without any beauty, like eunuchs. They all have compact, strong limbs and thick necks, and are so monstrously ugly and misshapen, that one might take them for two-legged beasts or for the stumps, rough-hewn into images, that are used in putting sides to bridges. But although they have the form of men, however ugly, they are so hardy in their mode of life that they have no need of fire nor of savory food, but eat the roots of wild plants and the half-raw flesh of any kind of animal whatever, which they put between their thighs and the backs of their horses, and thus warm it a little. They are never protected by any buildings, but they

Ammianus Marcellinus, *Roman History*, XXXI, 2–4 (Cambridge, Mass.: Harvard University Press, 1939), Vol. III, pp. 381–387, 399–405. Reprinted by permission of the publishers and the Loeb Classical Library, translated by J.C. Rolfe.

avoid these like tombs, which are set apart from everyday use. For not even a hut thatched with reed can be found among them. But roaming at large amid the mountains and woods, they learn from the cradle to endure cold, hunger, and thirst. When away from their homes they never enter a house unless compelled by extreme necessity; for they think they are not safe when staying under a roof. They dress in linen cloth or in the skins of field-mice sewn together, and they wear the same clothing indoors and out. But when they have once put their necks into a faded tunic, it is not taken off or changed until by long wear and tear it has been reduced to rags and fallen from them bit by bit. They cover their heads with round caps and protect their hairy legs with goatskins; their shoes are formed upon no lasts, and so prevent their walking with free step. For this reason they are not at all adapted to battles on foot, but they are almost glued to their horses, which are hardy, it is true, but ugly, and sometimes they sit them woman-fashion and thus perform their ordinary tasks. From their horses by day or night every one of that nation buys and sells, eats and drinks, and bowed over the narrow neck of the animal relaxes into a sleep so deep as to be accompanied by many dreams. . . . They are subject to no royal restraint, but they are content with the disorderly government of their important men, and led by them they force their way through every obstacle. . . . They enter the battle drawn up in wedge-shaped masses, while their medley of voices makes a savage noise. And as they are lightly equipped for swift motion, and unexpected in action, they purposely divide suddenly into scattered bands and attack, rushing about in disorder here and there, dealing terrific slaughter; . . . And on this account you would not hesitate to call them the most terrible of all warriors, because they fight from a distance with missiles having sharp bone, instead of their usual points, joined to the shafts with wonderful skill; then they gallop over the intervening spaces and fight hand to hand with swords, regardless of their own lives; and while the enemy are guarding against wounds from the sabre-thrusts, they throw strips of cloth plaited into nooses over their opponents and so entangle them that they fetter their limbs and take from them the power of riding or walking. No one in their country ever plows a field or touches a plow-handle. They are all without fixed abode, without hearth, or law, or settled mode of life, and keep roaming from place to place, like fugitives, accompanied by the wagons in which they live; . . . In truces they are faithless and unreliable, strongly inclined to sway to the motion of every breeze of new hope that presents itself, and sacrificing every feeling to the mad impulse of the moment. Like unreasoning beasts, they are utterly ignorant of the difference between right and wrong; they are deceitful and ambiguous in speech, never bound by any reverence for religion or for superstition. . . .

When the report spread widely among the other Gothic peoples, that a race of men hitherto unknown had now arisen from a hidden nook of the earth, like a tempest of snows from the high mountains, and was seizing or destroying everything in its way, the greater part of the people . . . looked for a home removed from all knowledge of the savages; and after long deliberation what abode to choose they thought that Thrace offered them a convenient refuge. . . .

Therefore . . . they took possession of the banks of the Danube, and sending envoys to Valens, with humble entreaty begged to be received, promising that they would not only lead a peaceful life but would also furnish auxiliaries, if circumstances required. . . . The affair caused more joy than fear [among the Romans], and experienced flatterers immoderately praised the good fortune of the prince, which unexpectedly brought him so many young recruits from the ends of the earth, that by the union of his own and foreign forces he would have an invincible army; also that instead of the levy of soldiers which was contributed annually by each province, there would accrue to the treasuries a vast amount of gold. In this expectation various officials were sent with vehicles to transport the savage horde, and diligent care was taken that no future destroyer of the Roman state should be left behind, even if he were smitten with a fatal disease. Accordingly, having by the emperor's permission obtained the privilege of crossing the Danube and settling in parts of Thrace, they were ferried over for some nights and days, embarked by companies in boats, on rafts, and in hollowed treetrunks; and because the river is by far the most dangerous of all and was then swollen by frequent rains, some who, because of the great crowd, struggled against the force of the waves and tried to swim were drowned; and they were a good many.

With such stormy eagerness on the part of insistent men was the ruin of the Roman world brought in. . . .

3. *ST. JEROME VIEWS THE WRECKAGE OF THE ROMAN WORLD*

The traditional, but now discredited, view of the fifth century A.D. as an age of sudden cataclysmic change from light to darkness is reflected very well in the following selections from St. Jerome's writings. That it was a tragic age no one

can doubt, but it should be kept in mind that St. Jerome, writing from Bethlehem, was not an eyewitness to the events he describes. His testimony should be compared with that of the calmer witnesses in the ensuing selections.

Jerome to Heliodorus, 396 A.D.

. . . My soul shrinks from reciting the ruins of our times. For twenty years and more, the blood of Rome has been poured out daily between the city of Constantine and the Julian Alps. In Scythia, Thrace, Macedonia, Thessaly, Dardania, Dacia, Epirus, Dalmatia, and all the Pannonias, the Goth, Sarmatian, Quade, Alan, Hun, Vandal, and Marcoman lay waste, pillage, and drag away. How many matrons, how many virgins of God, how many of the free-born and noble have been used for the mirth of these beasts! Bishops have been seized, elders and other officials slain, churches overthrown, horses stabled at the altars of Christ, the mortal relics of the martyrs dug up. Everywhere are lamentations, everywhere groanings, and on every hand the image of death. The Roman world is tumbling in ruins. And yet our head is erect and unbent. In what state of mind and soul now do you suppose are the people of Corinth, of Athens, of Lacedaemon, of Arcadia, and of entire Greece, all of them in the control of barbarians? And indeed I have named only a few cities that once had no slight power. The East seemed immune from these misfortunes . . . when, look you, in the past year from the farthest cliffs of the Caucasus the wolves of the North came sweeping down on us, and in this short time have ranged over these big provinces. How many monasteries have been seized, how many rivers have had their waters changed to human blood! . . .

Jerome to Principia, 412 A.D.

. . . A terrifying rumor comes to me from the West that Rome has been besieged and her citizens' safety bought with gold; that, once despoiled, they were again beset, so that after losing their substance they might yield up life as well. My voice is stopped, and sobs cut off the words as I try to speak. Captive is the city which once took captive all the world; yea, it perished from famine ere touched by the sword, and few were found to be rendered captive. Maddening hunger drove to the use of meats unspeakable; they tore their own members, the one the other, mothers not sparing the sucking babe, and consuming again the fruits of their own bosoms. . . . The city of old, the queen of the world for many years, is fallen to ruin, and the lifeless bodies of men lie thickly scattered in its streets and homes, and everywhere is the spectre of death.

From The Preface to Ezechiel III

No doubt everything which is born is doomed to die, that which has matured must grow old, there is no work of man but decay attacks it or age ends by destroying it. But who would have believed that Rome, raised by so many victories above the universe, could one day crumble to pieces, and be at once the mother and the tomb of her people? That she who had reckoned the East, and Egypt, and Africa among her slaves, should herself become a slave in her turn? Who would have believed that obscure Bethlehem would see, begging at its gates, nobles lately loaded with wealth? The daughters of the queenly city now wander from shore to shore, to Africa, to Egypt, to the East; her ladies have become servants; the most illustrious personages ask bread at the gates of Bethlehem, and when we cannot give it to them all, we give them at least our tears. In vain I try to snatch myself from the sight of such sufferings by resuming my unfinished work; I am incapable of study. I feel that this is the time for translating the precepts of Scripture not into words but into deeds, and not for saying holy things but doing them.

4. *A ROMAN COUNTRY GENTLEMAN DESCRIBES LIFE AMONG THE BARBARIANS*

Apollinaris Sidonius (c. 430–c. 487 A.D.) was a native of Lyons. He belonged to the Gallo-Roman nobility, served briefly as prefect of Rome (467), then entered the Church, and was consecrated bishop of Clermont in 472. His letters are one of our best sources for evaluating relations between Romans and barbarians in the fifth century.

Sidonius to His Friend Donidius, c. 465 A.D.

. . . I have passed the most delightful time in the most beautiful country [southern France] in the company of Tonantius Ferreolus and Apollinaris, the most charming hosts in the world. Their estates march together; their houses are not far apart; and the extent of intervening ground is just too far for a walk and just too short to make the ride worth while. The hills above the houses are under vines and olives; . . . The view from one villa is over a wide flat country, that from the other over woodland; yet different though their situations are, the eye derives equal pleasure from both. But

The Letters of Sidonius, translated by O.M. Dalton in the *Oxford Translation Series* (Oxford: The Clarendon Press, 1915), Book II, p. 9, Book IV, p. 20. Used by permission of the publisher.

enough of sites; I have now to unfold the order of my entertainment. Sharp scouts were posted to look out for our return; and not only were the roads patrolled by men from each estate, but even winding short-cuts and sheep-tracks were under observation, to make it quite impossible for us to elude the friendly ambush. Into this of course we fell, no unwilling prisoners; and our captors instantly made us swear to dismiss every idea of continuing our journey until a whole week had elapsed. And so every morning began with a flattering rivalry between the two hosts, as to which of their kitchens should first smoke for the refreshment of their guest; . . . From the first moment we were hurried from one pleasure to another. Hardly had we entered the vestibule of either house when we saw two opposed pairs of partners in the ball-game repeating each other's movements as they turned in wheeling circles; in another place one heard the rattle of dice boxes and the shouts of the contending players; in yet another, were books in abundance ready to your hand; you might have imagined yourself among the shelves of some grammarian, or the tiers of the Athenaeum, or a bookseller's towering cases. They were so arranged that the devotional works were near the ladies' seats; where the master sat were those ennobled by the great style of Roman eloquence. . . . An envoy from the cook [arrived] to warn us that the moment of bodily refreshment is at hand. . . . The dinner was short, but abundant, served in the fashion affected in senatorial houses where inveterate usage prescribes numerous courses on very few dishes, though to afford variety, roast alternated with stew. Amusing and instructive anecdotes accompanied our potations; wit went with the one sort, and learning with the other. To be brief, we were entertained with decorum, refinement, and good cheer. After dinner, if we were at Vorocingus (the name of one estate) we walked over to our quarters and our own belongings. If at Prusianum, as the other is called . . . Tonantius and his brothers turned out of their beds for us because we could not be always dragging our gear about: they are surely the elect among the nobles of our own age. The siesta over, we took a short ride to sharpen our jaded appetites for supper. . . .

Sidonius to His Friend Domnicius, c. 470 A.D.

You take such pleasure in the sight of arms and those who wear them, that I can imagine your delight if you could have seen the young prince Sigismer on his way to the palace of his father-in-law in the guise of a bride-groom or suitor in all the pomp and bravery of the tribal fashion. His own steed with its caparisons, other steeds laden with flashing gems, paced before and after; but the conspicuous interest in the procession centred in the prince himself, as with a charming modesty he went afoot amid his bodyguard and footmen, in flame-red mantle, with much glint of ruddy gold, and gleam of snowy silken tunic, his fair hair, red cheeks and white skin according with the three hues of his equipment. But the chiefs and allies who bore him company were dread of aspect, even thus on peace intent. Their feet were laced in boots of bristly hide reaching to the heels; ankles and legs were exposed. They wore high tight tunics of varied color hardly descending to their bare knees, the sleeves covering only the upper arm. Green mantles they had with crimson borders; baldrics supported swords hung from their shoulders, and pressed on sides covered with cloaks of skin secured by brooches. No small part of their adornment consisted of their arms; in their hands they grasped barbed spears and missile axes; their left sides were guarded by shields, which flashed with tawny golden bosses and snowy silver borders, betraying at once their wealth and their good taste. Though the business in hand was wedlock, Mars was no whit less prominent in all this pomp than Venus. Why need I say more? Only your presence was wanting to the full enjoyment of so fine a spectacle. . . .

5. *A ROMAN CITIZEN CHOOSES TO LIVE AMONG THE BARBARIANS*

There can be little doubt that, quite apart from the menace of the barbarians, life in the declining Roman Empire was oppressive and generally unattractive for the majority of the inhabitants. For many, the coming of the barbarians meant simply the substitution of one tyranny for another. Such an attitude is revealed in the following selection, written by an envoy sent to Attila, king of the Huns, by the emperor at Constantinople.

. . . a man, whom from his Scythian dress I took for a barbarian, came up and addressed me in Greek, with the word "Hail!" I was surprised at a Scythian speaking Greek. For the subjects of the Huns, swept together from various lands, speak, besides their own barbarous tongues, either Hunnic or Gothic, or—as many as have commercial dealings with the western Romans —Latin; but none of them easily speak Greek, except captives from the Thracian or Illyrian sea-coast; and these last are easily known to any stranger by their torn garments and the squalor of their heads, as men who have met with a reverse. This man, on the contrary, resembled a well-to-do Scythian, being well dressed, and having his hair cut in a circle after Scythian fashion. Having returned his salutation, I asked him who he was and whence he had

J.B. Bury, *History of the Later Roman Empire* (London, Macmillan and Co., Ltd., 1923), Vol. 1, pp. 283–285. Used by permission of Dover Publications, New York 10, N. Y.

come into a foreign land and adopted Scythian life. When he asked me why I wanted to know, I told him that his Hellenic speech had prompted my curiosity. Then he smiled and said that he was born a Greek and had gone as a merchant to Viminacium, on the Danube, where he had stayed a long time, and married a very rich wife. But the city fell a prey to the barbarians, and he was stript of his prosperity, and on account of his riches was allotted to Onegesius in the division of the spoil, as it was the custom among the Scythians for the chiefs to reserve for themselves the rich prisoners. Having fought bravely against the Romans and the Acatiri, he had paid the spoils he won to his master, and so obtained freedom. He then married a barbarian wife and had children, and had the privilege of eating at the table of Onegesius.

He considered his new life among the Scythians better than his old life among the Romans, and the reasons he gave were as follows: "After war the Scythians live in inactivity, enjoying what they have got, and not at all, or very little, harassed. The Romans, on the other hand, are in the first place very liable to perish in war, as they have to rest their hopes of safety on others, and are not allowed, on account of their tyrants, to use arms. And those who use them are injured by the cowardice of their generals, who cannot support the conduct of war. But the condition of the subjects in time of peace is far more grievous than the evils of war, for the exaction of taxes is very severe, and unprincipled men inflict injuries on others, because the laws are practically not valid against all classes. A transgressor who belongs to the wealthy classes is not punished for his injustice, while a poor man, who does not understand business, undergoes the legal penalty, that is if he does not depart this life before the trial, so long is the course of lawsuits protracted, and so much money is expended on them. The climax of the misery is to have to pay in order to obtain justice. For no one will give a court to the injured man unless he pay a sum of money to the judge and the judge's clerks."

In reply to this attack on the Empire, I asked him to be good enough to listen with patience to the other side of the question. "The creators of the Roman republic," I said, "who were wise and good men, in order to prevent things from being done at haphazard, made one class of men guardians of the laws, and appointed another class to the profession of arms, who were to have no other object than to be always ready for battle, and to go forth to war without dread, as though to their ordinary exercise, having by practice exhausted all their fear beforehand. Others again were assigned to attend to the cultivation of the ground, to support both themselves and those who fight in their defence, by contributing the military corn-supply. . . . To those who protect the interests of the litigants a sum of money is paid by the latter, just as a payment is made by the farmers to the soldiers. Is it not fair to support him who assists and requite him for his kindness? The support of the horse benefits the horseman. . . . Those who spend money on a suit and lose it in the end cannot fairly put it down to anything but the injustice of their case. And as to the long time spent on lawsuits, that is due to concern for justice, that judges may not fail in passing correct judgments, by having to give sentence offhand; it is better that they should reflect, and conclude the case more tardily, than that by judging in a hurry they should both injure man and transgress against the Deity, the institutor of justice. . . . The Romans treat their servants better than the king of the Scythians treats his subjects. They deal with them as fathers or teachers, admonishing them to abstain from evil and follow the lines of conduct which they have esteemed honourable; they reprove them for their errors like their own children. They are not allowed, like the Scythians, to inflict death on them. They have numerous ways of conferring freedom; they can manumit not only during life, but also by their wills, and the testamentary wishes of a Roman in regard to his property are law."

My interlocutor shed tears, and confessed that the laws and constitution of the Romans were fair, but deplored that the governors, not possessing the spirit of former generations, were ruining the State.

5

THE AGE OF JUSTINIAN

The Roman Empire did not collapse with the Germanization of the western provinces. The traditions of Rome continued in the state which came to be known as the Byzantine Empire. The emperors were in direct succession to Augustus, and the inhabitants referred to themselves as Roman. But as political, economic, and religious contacts diminished between the western Mediterranean and Constantinople, the Byzantine Empire became less Roman and increasingly Greek and Oriental. This distinctive Byzantine amalgam produced a civilization which, from both the material and the cultural standpoints, outshone anything western Europe produced until the twelfth and thirteenth centuries.

1. PROCOPIUS TELLS THE "INSIDE" STORY OF JUSTINIAN AND THEODORA

One of the problems of the historian is to assess the credibility of sources. Assuming a writer was in a position to know the truth, the historian must decide whether, for one reason or another, the truth was actually colored or contradicted. A case in point is Procopius. He is acknowledged to be the most eminent historian of the age of Justinian. He was private secretary to Justinian's foremost general, Belisarius. He spent years at court. In most of his works he lauds Justinian and Theodora, but in a later work, the **Secret History,** ***he professes to tell the unvarnished truth for the benefit of future generations. Historians have never reached agreement on the overall reliability of this work. Some passages are so venomous and exaggerated as to make acceptance impossible. Other passages, like the one below, most historians consider at least credible.***

Procopius, *Secret History*, XIII, XV (Cambridge, Mass.: Harvard University Press, 1934), pp. 157–181, *passim.* Reprinted by permission of the publishers and the Loeb Classical Library, translated by H.B. Dewing.

[Justinian] never allowed himself to show anger or exasperation, and thus to reveal his feelings to those who had given offence, but with gentle mien and with lowered brows and in a restrained voice he would give orders for the death of thousands of innocent men, for the dismantling of cities, and for the confiscation of all monies to the Treasury. And one would infer from this characteristic that he had the spirit of a lamb. Yet if anyone sought to intercede through prayers and supplications for those who had given offence and thus to gain for them forgiveness, then, "enraged and showing his teeth," he would seem to be ready to burst, so that no one of those who were supposed to be intimate with him had any hope after that of getting the desired pardon.

And while he seemed to have a firm belief as regards Christ, yet even this was for the ruin of his subjects. For he permitted the priests with comparative freedom to outrage their neighbours, and if they plundered the property of the people whose lands adjoined theirs, he would congratulate them, thinking that thus he was showing reverence for the Deity. And in adjudicating such cases, he considered that he was acting in a pious manner if any man in the name of religion succeeded by his argument in seizing something that did not belong to him, and, having won the case, went his way. . . . For he was lighter than dust in his judgment. . . .

He was not given to sleep, as a general thing, and he never filled himself to repletion with either food or drink, but he usually touched the food with the tips of his fingers and went his way. For such matters seemed to him a kind of side-issue imposed upon him by Nature, for he often actually remained without food two days and nights, especially . . . before the festival called Easter. . . . And yet, if he had been willing to spend just this Easter-tide on good deeds, affairs would have advanced to a high pitch of prosperity. But as it was, by employing his natural strength for the ruin of the Romans, he succeeded in pulling down to the ground their whole political structure. For he made it his task to be constantly awake and to undergo hardships and to labour for no other purpose than to contrive constantly and every day more grievous calamities for his subjects. . . .

. . . As for Theodora, she had a mind fixed firmly and persistently upon cruelty. For she never did anything at any time as the result of persuasion or compulsion by another person, but she herself, applying a stubborn will, carried out her decisions with all her might, no one daring to intercede for the victim who had given offence. . . . To state the matter briefly, no one ever saw Theodora reconciled with one who had given offence, even after the person had died, but the son of the deceased received the Empress' enmity as an inheritance from him, just as he received anything else that had been his father's, and passed it on to the third generation. . . .

Her body she treated with more care than was necessary, yet less than she herself could have wished. For instance, she used to enter the bath very early and quit it very late, and after finishing her bathing, she would go thence to her breakfast. After partaking of breakfast she would rest. At luncheon, however, and dinner she partook of all manner of foods and drinks; and sleep for long stretches of time would constantly lay hold of her, both in the daytime up to nightfall and at night up to sunrise; and though she had to such an extent strayed into every path of incontinence for so long a portion of the day, she claimed the right to administer the whole Roman Empire. . . .

. . . The Empress . . . could not be approached even by one of the magistrates, except at the expense of much time and labour, but actually, they all had to wait constantly upon her convenience with a servile kind of assiduity, waiting in a small and stuffy ante-room for an endless time. For it was a risk beyond bearing for any one of the officials to be absent. And they stood there constantly upon the tips of their toes, each one straining to hold his head higher than the persons next to him, in order that the eunuchs when they came out might see him. And some of them were summoned at last, after many days, and going in to her presence in great fear they very quickly departed, having simply done obeisance and having touched the instep of each of her feet with the tips of their lips. [According to Procopius, one of the innovations of Justinian and Theodora was a new and humiliating kind of obeisance. Subjects, regardless of rank, had to prostrate themselves, holding their heads and feet stretched far out, and kiss one foot of Emperor and Empress before rising.] For there was no opportunity to speak or to make any request unless she bade them to do so. For the Government had sunk into a servile condition, having her as slave-instructor. . . .

In their thinking and in their habits of life the contrast between them was clear, yet they had in common their avarice, their lust for murder and their untruthfulness to all. . . .

2. *JUSTINIAN SUPPRESSES THE NIKA REVOLT, 532*

While Procopius' reliability in the **Secret History** ***is somewhat questionable, the same cannot be said of the following passage from his*** **History of the Wars.** ***It is one of the most colorful episodes in his writings. It deals with the revolt of the Blue and Green factions (temporarily allied) against Justinian.***

Procopius, *History of the Wars,* I, xxiv, translated by H.B. Dewing (New York: The Macmillan Company, 1914), pp. 219–230. Reprinted by permission of the publishers and the Loeb Classical Library, Cambridge, Mass.: Harvard University Press.

At this time [January 1, 532] an insurrection broke out unexpectedly in Byzantium among the populace, and, contrary to expectation, it proved to be a very serious affair, and ended in great harm to the people and to the senate, as the following account will show. In every city the population has been divided for a long time past into the Blue and the Green factions; but within comparatively recent times it has come about that, for the sake of these names and the seats which the rival factions occupy in watching the games, they spend their money and abandon their bodies to the most cruel tortures, and even do not think it unworthy to die a most shameful death. And they fight against their opponents knowing not for what end they imperil themselves, but knowing well that, even if they overcome their enemy in the fight, the conclusion of the matter for them will be to be carried off straightway to the prison, and finally, after suffering extreme torture, to be destroyed. So there grows up in them against their fellow men a hostility which has no cause, and at no time does it cease or disappear, for it gives place neither to the ties of marriage nor of relationship nor of friendship, and the case is the same even though those who differ with respect to these colours be brothers or any other kin. . . . I, for my part, am unable to call this anything except a disease of the soul. . . .

At this time the officers of the city administration in Byzantium were leading away to death some of the rioters. But the members of the two factions, conspiring together and declaring a truce with each other, seized the prisoners and then straightway entered the prison and released all those who were in confinement there. . . . Fire was applied to the city as if it had fallen under the hand of an enemy. . . . The emperor and his consort with a few members of the senate shut themselves up in the palace and remained quietly there. Now the watch-word which the populace passed around to one another was Nika [i.e., "Conquer"]. . . .

. . . On the fifth day of the insurrection in the late afternoon the Emperor Justinian gave orders to Hypatius and Pompeius, nephews of the late emperor, Anastasius, to go home as quickly as possible, either because he suspected that some plot was being matured by them against his own person, or, it may be, because destiny brought them to this. But they feared that the people would force them to the throne (as in fact fell out), and they said that they would be doing wrong if they should abandon their sovereign when he found himself in such danger. When the Emperor Justinian heard this, he inclined still more to his suspicion, and he bade them quit the palace instantly. . . .

On the following day at sunrise it became known to the people that both men had quit the palace where they had been staying. So the whole population ran to them, and they declared Hypatius emperor and prepared to lead him to the market place to assume the power. But the wife of Hypatius, Mary, a discreet woman, who had the greatest reputation for prudence, laid hold of her husband and would not let go, but cried out with loud lamentation and with entreaties to all her kinsmen that the people were leading him on the road to death. But since the throng overpowered her, she unwillingly released her husband, and he by no will of his own came to the Forum of Constantine, where they summoned him to the throne; . . .

The emperor and his court were deliberating as to whether it would be better for them if they remained or if they took to flight in the ships. And many opinions were expressed favouring either course. And the Empress Theodora also spoke to the following effect: ". . . My opinion then is that the present time, above all others, is inopportune for flight, even though it bring safety. . . . For one who has been an emperor it is unendurable to be a fugitive. May I never be separated from this purple, and may I not live that day on which those who meet me shall not address me as mistress. If, now, it is your wish to save yourself, O Emperor, there is no difficulty. For we have much money, and there is the sea, here the boats. However consider whether it will not come about after you have been saved that you would gladly exchange that safety for death. For as for myself, I approve a certain ancient saying that royalty is a good burial-shroud." When the queen had spoken thus, all were filled with boldness, and, turning their thoughts towards resistance, they began to consider how they might be able to defend themselves if any hostile force should come against them. . . . All the hopes of the emperor were centred upon Belisarius and Mundus, of whom the former, Belisarius, had recently returned from the Persian war bringing with him a following which was both powerful and imposing, and in particular he had a great number of spearmen and guards who had received their training in battles and the perils of warfare. . . .

When Hypatius reached the hippodrome, he went up immediately to where the emperor is accustomed to take his place and seated himself on the royal throne from which the emperor was always accustomed to view the equestrian and athletic contests. And from the palace Mundus went out through the gate which, from the circling descent, has been given the name of the Snail. . . . Belisarius, with difficulty and not without danger and great exertion, made his way over ground covered by ruins and half-burned buildings, and ascended to the stadium. . . . Concluding that he must go against the populace who had taken their stand in the hippodrome—a vast multitude crowding each other in great disorder—he drew his sword from its sheath and, commanding the others to do likewise, with a shout he advanced upon them at a run. But the populace, who were standing in a mass and not in order, at the sight of armoured soldiers who had a great reputation for bravery and experience in war, and seeing that they struck out with their swords unsparingly, beat a hasty retreat. . . . [Mundus] straightway made a sally into the hippodrome through the entrance which they call the Gate of Death. Then indeed from both sides the partisans of Hypatius were assailed with might and main and destroyed. . . . There perished among the populace on that day more than thirty thousand. . . . The soldiers killed both [Hypatius and Pompeius] on the following day and threw their bodies into the sea. . . . This was the end of the insurrection in Byzantium.

3. *CONSTANTINOPLE CELEBRATES THE RECONQUEST OF NORTH AFRICA*

A year after the suppression of the Nika Revolt, the hero of that occasion was sent at the head of an army to overthrow the Vandal Kingdom in northern Africa. Although Belisarius won an easy victory, his expedition marked only the first stage in a long and costly effort to reconquer the lost imperial provinces in the West. The triumph which was accorded Belisarius upon his return to Constantinople in 534 is described below by Procopius. Note especially the continuity in the old Roman traditions.

Belisarius, upon reaching Byzantium with Gelimer [last king of the Vandals, captured by Belisarius in 534] and the Vandals, was counted worthy to receive such honours, as in former times were assigned to those generals of the Romans who had won the greatest and most noteworthy victories. And a period of about six hundred years had now passed since anyone had attained these honours, except, indeed, Titus and Trajan, and such other emperors as had led armies against some barbarian nation and had been victorious. For he displayed the spoils and slaves from the war in the midst of the city and led a procession which the Romans call a "triumph," not, however, in the ancient manner, but going on foot from his own house to the hippodrome and then again from the barriers [the starting point for the racers at the open end of the Hippodrome] until he reached the place where the imperial throne is. And there was booty,—first of all, whatever articles are wont to be set apart for the royal service,—thrones of gold and carriages in which it is customary for a king's consort to ride, and much jewelry made of precious stones, and golden drinking cups, and all the other

Procopius, *History of the Wars*, IV, ix, translated by H.B. Dewing (New York: G.P. Putnam's Sons, 1916), pp. 279–283. Reprinted by permission of the publishers and the Loeb Classical Library, Cambridge, Mass.: Harvard University Press.

things which are useful for the royal table. And there was also silver weighing many thousands of talents and all the royal treasure amounting to an exceedingly great sum (for Gizeric [leader of the Vandals who had sacked Rome in 455] had despoiled the Palatium in Rome) . . . and among these were the treasures of the Jews, which Titus, the son of Vespasian, together with certain others, had brought to Rome after the capture of Jerusalem [70 A.D.]. And one of the Jews, seeing these things, approached one of those known to the emperor and said: "These treasures I think it inexpedient to carry into the palace in Byzantium. Indeed, it is not possible for them to be elsewhere than in the place where Solomon, the king of the Jews, formerly placed them. For it is because of these that Gizeric captured the palace of the Romans, and that now the Roman army has captured that of the Vandals." When this had been brought to the ears of the Emperor, he became afraid and quickly sent everything to the sanctuaries of the Christians in Jerusalem. And there were slaves in the triumph, among whom was Gelimer himself, wearing some sort of a purple garment upon his shoulders, and all his family, and as many of the Vandals as were very tall and fair of body. And when Gelimer reached the hippodrome and saw the emperor sitting upon a lofty seat and the people standing on either side and realized as he looked about in what an evil plight he was, he neither wept nor cried out, but ceased not saying over in the words of the Hebrew scripture: "Vanity of vanities, all is vanity." And when he came before the emperor's seat, they stripped off the purple garment, and compelled him to fall prone on the ground and do obeisance to the Emperor Justinian. This also Belisarius did, as being a suppliant of the emperor along with him. And the Emperor Justinian and the Empress Theodora presented the children of Ilderic [one-time king of the Vandals and friend of Justinian; overthrown by Gelimer] and his offspring and all those of the family of the Emperor Valentinian with sufficient sums of money, and to Gelimer they gave lands not to be despised in Galatia and permitted him to live there together with his family. However, Gelimer was by no means enrolled among the patricians, since he was unwilling to change from the faith of Arius.

A little later the triumph [in honor of his inauguration as consul] was celebrated by Belisarius in the ancient manner also. For he had the fortune to be advanced to the office of consul, and therefore was borne aloft by the captives, and as he was thus carried in his curule chair, he threw to the populace those very spoils of the Vandalic war. For the people carried off the silver plate and golden girdles and a vast amount of the Vandals' wealth of other sorts as a result of Belisarius' consulship, and it seemed that after a long interval of disuse an old custom was being revived. . . .

4. JUSTINIAN REGULATES CHURCH DISCIPLINE AND RITUAL

The concept of a free and independent Church was unacceptable to Justinian. He regarded himself as head of the Church and insisted on his right and duty not only to regulate the smallest details of discipline but also to dictate the theological opinions of the Church. Samples of his ecclesiastical legislation follow.

If, for the general welfare, We have taken measures to render the civil laws more effective, with whose execution, God, through His good will towards men, has entrusted Us, how much more reason is there not for Us to compel the observance of the sacred canons, and Divine Laws, which have been promulgated for the safety of Our souls? For those who observe the sacred canons become worthy of the assistance of Our Lord God, while those who disobey them render themselves liable to be punished by Him. Therefore, the most holy bishops who are charged with the enforcement of these laws are liable to severe penalties when they allow any breaches of them to remain unpunished. And, indeed, as the sacred canons have not been, up to this time, strictly observed, various complaints have been made to Us of clerks, monks, and certain bishops, on the ground that they do not live in accordance with the divine canons; and indeed there are even some among them who are either ignorant of, or do not perform the holy service of the mass, or of the ceremony of baptism.

Therefore We, conceding the authority of the sacred canons, do promulgate the present law, by which We decree that every time it may be necessary to consecrate a bishop in any city, the clergy and principal citizens of the said city shall assemble, and issue proclamations by which they nominate three persons, and then make oath on the Holy Gospels, in conformity with the Scriptures. This oath, inserted in the proclamations, shall be worded as follows: "That they did not select the three persons whom they have nominated in consideration of any gifts or promises made to them; nor through friendship, nor induced by any affection whatsoever, but for the reason that they knew that the candidates whom they have chosen are steadfast in the Catholic Faith, and of honorable life; that they have passed the age of thirty years, and have neither wives nor children; and that they have had neither concubines nor natural children, nor have any at present; and if any of them formerly had a wife, he had but one, and she was neither a widow, nor sepa-

Justinian, *Novella*, CXXXVII, translated by S.P. Scott in *The Civil Law* (Cincinnati, Ohio: 1932), Vol. XVII, pp. 152–156. Reprinted from *Corpus Juris Civilis*, with permission of the copyright owners, the Estate of Elizabeth W. Scott, Deceased, and The Jefferson Medical College of Philadelphia.

rated from her husband, and that his marriage with her was not prohibited, either by the sacred canons, or by secular laws; that neither of the three candidates is charged with the duties of any public office. . . .

As what is laid down in the canons relating to the episcopal synods, which should be held in every province, is not observed, this is the first thing that should be remedied. . . . We order that one synod shall assemble in each province in the month of June or September. . . . We desire that ecclesiastical questions having reference to the Faith, to canonical points, and such as relate to the administration of church property; . . . and . . . to all matters which have need of correction, shall be debated and examined in each synod, and We desire that abuses shall be disposed of in accordance with Our laws and the sacred canons.

. . . We order all bishops and priests to repeat the divine service and the prayer, when baptism is performed, not in an undertone, but in a loud voice which can be heard by the faithful people, in such a way that the minds of the listeners may be induced to manifest greater devotion, and a higher appreciation of the praises and blessings of God. . . . We notify all ecclesiastics that if they should violate any of these provisions, they must render an account of their conduct on the terrible Judgment Day of Our Lord and Saviour Jesus Christ; and that We, when informed of these matters, shall not disregard them, and leave them unpunished.

We also order that if the Governors of provinces should ascertain that any of the rules which We have promulgated are not observed, they shall first compel the metropolitans and other bishops to call the synods together, and do what We have just prescribed; and when the bishops do not immediately obey, the Governors must notify Us of the fact, in order to enable Us to promptly punish those who refuse to convoke the synods; and We hereby warn the Governors, as well as their courts, that if they do not see that what We have decreed is executed, they shall be put to death.

5. *JUSTINIAN CODIFIES THE LAWS OF ROME*

Incomparably the greatest achievement of Justinian is the* Corpus Juris Civilis. *The codification of Roman law, which Justinian ordered and supervised, has greatly infinenced modern law. The following selection is from Justinian's "confirmation of the Digest."

In the name of our Lord God Jesus Christ.

The Emperor Caesar Flavius Justinianus Alamannicus Gothicus Francicus Germanicus Anticus Alanicus Vandalicus Africanus pious happy re-

The Digest of Justinian, translated by C.H. Monro (Cambridge: University Press, 1904), Vol. I, XXV–XXXVI, *passim*. Used by permission of the publisher.

nowned conqueror and triumpher ever Augustus to the Senate and to all peoples.

So great in our behalf is the foresight of Divine Humanity that it ever deigns to support us with eternal acts of liberality. After the Parthian wars were hushed in eternal peace, after the nation of the Vandals was destroyed, and Carthage, nay rather all Libya, was again taken into the Roman Empire, then I contrived also that the ancient laws, already bowed down with age, should by my care reach new beauty and come within moderate bounds; a thing which before our command none ever expected or deemed to be at all possible for human endeavour. It was indeed a wondrous achievement when Roman jurisprudence from the time of the building of the city to that of our rule, which period well-nigh reaches to one thousand and four hundred years . . . [was brought] into one harmonious system, so that it should present no contradiction, no repetition and no approach to repetition, and that nowhere should two enactments appear dealing with one question. This was indeed proper for Heavenly Providence, but in no way possible to the weakness of man. We therefore have after our wont fixed our eyes on the aid of Immortality, and, calling on the Supreme Deity, we have desired that God should be made the originator and the guardian of the whole work, and we have entrusted the entire task to Tribonianus, a most distinguished man, Master of the Offices, ex-quaestor of our sacred palace and ex-consul, and we have laid on him the whole service of the enterprise described, so that with other illustrious and most learned colleagues he might fulfil our desire. Besides this, our Majesty, ever investigating and scrutinizing the composition of these men, whensoever anything was found doubtful or uncertain, in reliance on the heavenly Divinity, amended it and reduced it to suitable shape. . . . Now the Imperial statutes we have already placed, arranged in twelve books, in the Code which is illuminated with our name. After this, undertaking a very great work, we allowed the same exalted man both to collect together and to submit to certain modifications the very most important works of old times, thoroughly intermixed and broken up as they may almost be called. . . . It was intimated to us by the said exalted person that there were nearly two thousand books written by the old lawyers, and more than three million lines were left us by them, all of which it was requisite to read and carefully consider and out of them to select whatever might be best. This, by the grace of Heaven and the favour of the Supreme Trinity, was accomplished in accordance with our instructions such as we gave at the outset to the exalted man above mentioned, so that everything of great importance was collected into fifty books, and all ambiguities were settled, without any refractory passage being left. We gave these books the name of Digest or Pandects. . . . Everyone of the old lawyers who wrote on law has been mentioned in our Digest; all that we did was to provide that if, in the rules given by them, there appeared to be anything superfluous or imperfect or of small importance, it should be amplified or curtailed to the requisite extent and be reduced to the most correct form; . . .

We saw however that the burden of all this mass of knowledge is more than such men are equal to bearing as are insufficiently educated and are standing in the vestibules of law, though on their way towards the secrets thereof, and we therefore were of opinion that a further compendious summary should be prepared, so that, thereby tinctured and so to speak imbued with the first elements of the whole subject, they might proceed to the innermost recesses thereof and take in with eyes undazzled the exquisite beauty of the law. We therefore summoned Tribonianus, that eminent man who had been chosen for the direction of the whole work, also Theophilus and Dorotheus, illustrious persons and most eloquent professors, and commissioned them to collect one by one the books composed by old authors in which the first principles were to be found, and thereupon, whatever they found in them that was useful and most to the purpose and polished in every point of view and in accordance with the practice of the present age, all this they were to endeavour to grasp and to put it into four books, so as to lay the first foundations and principles of education in general, and thus enable young men, supported thereon, to be ready for weightier and more perfect rules of law. . . . The whole work, as accomplished by these men, was put before us and read through; whereupon we received it willingly and judged it to be not unworthy of our mind. . . .

Now therefore let all our judges in their respective jurisdictions take up this law, and both within their own provinces and in this royal city observe and apply it, more especially that distinguished man the Prefect of this revered city. It will be the duty of the three distinguished Pretorian Prefects, the Oriental, the Illyrian, and the Libyan, to make the same known by the exercise of their authority to all those who are subject to their jurisdiction.

Given on the seventeenth day before the Kalends of January in the third Consulship of our Lord Justinianus.

II

THE EARLY MIDDLE AGE

6

EXPANSION OF THE CATHOLIC CHRISTIAN CHURCH

When the Roman Empire in the West gave way to various Germanic kingdoms, one institution preserved its identity, the Roman Catholic Church. The Church acted as a bridge in the early Middle Ages between classical civilization and the barbarian peoples—German and Slavic. Primarily, of course, the Church's role was spiritual, but it fulfilled a great mission in other respects as well. The Church struggled to maintain a degree of unity in a society bordering on the anarchic. Only the Church had an effective organization commanding the obedience of large numbers of human beings. Finally, the Church preserved much of the classical heritage for the day when western Europe would once again show an interest in matters of the intellect.

1. ST. BENEDICT INSTITUTES "A SCHOOL FOR THE SERVICE OF GOD"

Benedict was born about 480 of a noble Roman family. Educated in Rome, he soon became disgusted with the viciousness of life there and decided to become a hermit. He lived in a cave for several years, but his sanctity attracted so many disciples that he found himself head of a rather large community which in time established itself on a hill called Monte Cassino. It was there, in 529, that he published the Rule which shaped much of medieval monastic life, selections from which follow.

The Rule of St. Benedict, translated by Justin McCann (London: Burns Oates & Washbourne Ltd., 1952), *passim*. Copyright by Burns Oates & Washbourne Ltd., London, and The Newman Press, Westminster, Maryland. Used by permission of the copyright holders.

Let [the abbot] not make any distinction of persons in the monastery. Let him not love one more than another, unless he find him better in good works and obedience. Let not a freeborn monk be put before one that was a slave, unless there be some other reasonable ground for it. But if the abbot, for just reason, think fit so to do, let him fix anyone's order as he will; otherwise let them keep their due places; because, whether slaves or freemen, we are all one in Christ and have to serve alike in the army of the same Lord. . . . In this regard only are we distinguished in his sight, if we be found better than others in good works and humility. Therefore let the abbot show an equal love to all, and let the same discipline be imposed on all in accordance with their deserts. . . .

As often as any important business has to be done in the monastery, let the abbot call together the whole community and himself set forth the matter. And, having heard the advice of the brethren, let him take counsel with himself and then do what he shall judge to be most expedient. . . .

In winter, that is from the first of November until Easter, prudence dictates that the brethren shall rise at the eighth hour of the night [about one o'clock in the morning], so that their sleep may extend for a moderate space beyond midnight, and they may rise with digestion completed. Those brethren, who need a better knowledge of them, should devote the time that remains after Matins to the study of the psalms and lessons. From Easter to the aforesaid first of November, let the hour of rising be so arranged that there be a very short interval after Matins, in which the brethren may go out for the necessities of nature, to be followed at once by Lauds, which should be said at dawn. . . .

The prophet saith: *Seven times a day have I given praise to thee.* We shall observe this sacred number of seven, if we fulfill the duties of our service in the Hours of Lauds, Prime, Terce, Sext, None, Vespers, and Compline; for it was of these Day Hours that he said: *Seven times a day have I given praise to thee.* But of the Night Office the same prophet saith: *At midnight I rose to give praise to thee.* At these times, therefore, let us render praise to our Creator *for the judgments of his justice*: that is, at Lauds, Prime, Terce, Sext, None, Vespers, and Compline; and let us rise in the night to praise him. . . .

The vice [of private property] especially ought to be utterly rooted out of the monastery. Let no one presume to give or receive anything without the abbot's leave, or to have anything as his own, anything whatever, whether book or tablets or pen or whatever it may be; for monks should not have even their bodies and wills at their own disposal. . . .

We believe it to be sufficient for the daily meal, whether that be at the sixth or the ninth hour, that every table should have two cooked dishes, on account of individual infirmities, so that he who perchance cannot eat of the one, may make his meal of the other. Therefore, let two cooked dishes suffice for all the brethren; and if any fruit or young vegetables are available, let a third be added. Let a good pound weight of bread suffice for the day, whether there be one meal only, or both dinner and supper. If they are to have supper, let a third part of the pound be reserved by the cellarer, to be given to them for their supper. But if their work chance to be heavier, the abbot shall have the choice and power, should it be expedient, to increase this allowance. Above all things, however, gluttony must be avoided, so that a monk never be surprised by a surfeit; . . .

Every man hath his proper gift from God, one after this manner, and another after that. It is therefore with some misgiving that we determine how much others should eat or drink. Nevertheless, keeping in view the needs of weaker brethren, we believe that a hemina of wine a day is sufficient for each. But those upon whom God bestows the gift of abstinence, should know that they shall have a special reward.

But if the circumstances of the place, or their work, or the heat of summer require more, let the superior be free to grant it. Yet let him always take care that neither surfeit nor drunkenness supervene. We do, indeed, read that wine is no drink for monks; but since nowadays monks cannot be persuaded of this, let us at least agree upon this, to drink temperately and not to satiety: for *wine maketh even the wise to fall away.* . . .

Idleness is the enemy of the soul. The brethren, therefore, must be occupied at stated hours in manual labour, and again at other hours in sacred reading. To this end we think that the times for each may be determined in the following manner. From Easter until September the 14th, the brethren shall start work in the morning and from the first hour until about the fourth do the tasks that have to be done. From the fourth hour until about the sixth let them apply themselves to reading. After the sixth hour, having left the table, let them rest on their beds in perfect silence; or if anyone wishes to read by himself, let him read so as not to disturb the others. Let None be said early, at the middle of the eighth hour; and let them again do what work has to be done until Vespers. But if the circumstances of the place or their poverty require them to gather the harvest themselves, let them not be discontented; for then are they truly monks when they live by the labour of their hands, like our fathers and the apostles. Yet let all things be done in moderation on account of the faint-hearted. . . .

Let all guests that come be received like Christ, for he will say: *I was a stranger and ye took me in.* And let fitting honour be shown to all, but especially to churchmen and pilgrims. As soon, therefore, as a guest is announced, let the superior or some brethren meet him with all charitable service. And first of all let them pray together, and then let them unite in the kiss of peace. This kiss of peace shall not be offered until after the prayers have been said, on account of the delusions of the devil. In the greeting of all guests, whether they be arriving or departing, let the greatest humility be shown. Let the head be bowed or the whole body prostrated on the ground, and so let Christ be worshipped in them, for indeed he is received in their persons.

When the guests have been received, let them be led to prayer, and afterwards let the superior, or a monk appointed by him, sit with them. Let the law of God be read before the guest for his edification, and then let all kindness be shown to him. . . .

Let [the monks] bear with the greatest patience one another's infirmities, whether of body or character. Let them vie in paying obedience one to another. Let none follow what seems good for himself, but rather what is good for another. Let them practise fraternal charity with a pure love. Let them fear God. Let them love their abbot with a sincere and humble affection. Let them prefer nothing whatever to Christ. And may he bring us all alike to life everlasting.

2. *CLOVIS AND THE FRANKS ACCEPT CHRISTIANITY*

The first Germanic kingdom to be converted to Catholic Christianity was that of the Franks. The baptism of King Clovis in 496 had momentous political as well as religious consequences. Powerful episcopal and papal support was assured Clovis in his wars with his Arian German neighbors. In addition, Clovis' Gallo-Roman subjects were naturally more amenable to the rule of a fellow-Catholic than to that of heathen. The way was thus paved for a relatively quick and painless fusion of German and Roman cultures in the Frankish Kingdom. The ensuing account is from the* History *of Bishop Gregory of Tours (d. 593).

Now the king of the Burgundians was Gundevech. . . . He had four sons; Gundobad, Godegisel, Chilperic and Godomar. Gundobad killed his brother Chilperic with the sword, and sank his wife in water with a stone tied to her neck. His two daughters he condemned to exile; the older of these, who became a nun, was called Chrona, and the younger Clotilda. And as Clovis often sent embassies to Burgundy, the maiden Clotilda was found by his envoys. And when they saw that she was of good bearing and wise, and learned that she was of the family of the king, they reported this to King Clovis, and he sent an embassy to Gundobad without delay asking her in marriage. And Gundobad was afraid to refuse, and surrendered her to the

Gregory of Tours, *History of the Franks*, II, 28–31, translated by E. Brehaut (New York: Columbia University Press, 1916), pp. 38–41.

men, and they took the girl and brought her swiftly to the king. The king was very glad when he saw her, and married her, having already by a concubine a son named Theodoric. . . .

The queen did not cease to urge [Clovis] to recognize the true God and cease worshiping idols. But he could not be influenced in any way to this belief, until at last a war arose with the Alamanni, in which he was driven by necessity to confess what before he had of his free will denied. It came about that as the two armies were fighting fiercely, there was much slaughter, and Clovis' army began to be in danger of destruction. He saw it and raised his eyes to heaven, and with remorse in his heart he burst into tears and cried: "Jesus Christ, whom Clotilda asserts to be the son of the living God, who art said to give aid to those in distress, and to bestow victory on those who hope in thee, I beseech the glory of thy aid, with the vow that if thou wilt grant me victory over these enemies, and I shall know that power which she says that people dedicated in thy name have had from thee, I will believe in thee and be baptized in thy name. For I have invoked my own gods, but, as I find, they have withdrawn from aiding me; and therefore I believe that they possess no power, since they do not help those who obey them. I now call upon thee, I desire to believe thee, only let me be rescued from my adversaries." And when he said this, the Alamanni turned their backs, and began to disperse in flight. . . .

Then the queen asked saint Remi, bishop of Rheims, to summon Clovis secretly, urging him to introduce the king to the word of salvation. And the bishop sent for him secretly and began to urge him to believe in the true God, maker of heaven and earth, and to cease worshiping idols, which could help neither themselves nor any one else. But the king said: "I gladly hear you, most holy father; but there remains one thing: the people who follow me cannot endure to abandon their gods; but I shall go and speak to them according to your words." He met with his followers, but before he could speak the power of God anticipated him, and all the people cried out together: "O pious king, we reject our mortal gods, and we are ready to follow the immortal God whom Remi preaches." This was reported to the bishop, who was greatly rejoiced, and bade them get ready the baptismal font. The squares were shaded with tapestried canopies, the churches adorned with white curtains, the baptistery set in order, the aroma of incense spread, candles of fragrant odor burned brightly, and the whole shrine of the baptistery was filled with a divine fragrance: . . . And so the king confessed all-powerful God in the Trinity, and was baptized in the name of the Father, Son and holy Spirit, and was anointed with the holy ointment with the sign of the cross of Christ. And of his army more than 3000 were baptized. . . .

3. *ST. AUGUSTINE BEGINS THE CONVERSION OF THE ENGLISH*

The second of the major Germanic peoples to accept Catholic Christianity were the Anglo-Saxons. Augustine, the leader of a group of forty Benedictine monks from Pope Gregory's own monastery in Rome, arrived in England in 596. He baptized Ethelbert, king of Kent, the next year. The following account is from the eighth century historian Bede.

. . . [Pope Gregory] being moved by Divine inspiration . . . sent the servant of God, Augustine, and with him several other monks, who feared the Lord, to preach the word of God to the English nation. They having, in obedience to the pope's commands, undertaken that work, were, on their journey, seized with a sudden fear, and began to think of returning home, rather than proceed to a barbarous, fierce, and unbelieving nation, to whose very language they were strangers; and this they unanimously agreed was the safest course. In short, they sent back Augustine, who had been appointed to be consecrated bishop in case they were received by the English, that he might, by humble entreaty, obtain of the holy Gregory, that they should not be compelled to undertake so dangerous, toilsome, and uncertain a journey. The pope, in reply, sent them a hortatory epistle, persuading them to proceed in the work of the Divine word, and rely on the assistance of the Almighty. . . .

Augustine . . . strengthened by the confirmation of the blessed Father Gregory, returned to the work of the word of God, with the servants of Christ, and arrived in Britain. The powerful Ethelbert was at that time king of Kent; . . . On the east of Kent is the large Isle of Thane. . . . In this island landed the servant of our Lord, Augustine, and his companions, being, as is reported, nearly forty men. They had, by order of the blessed Pope Gregory, taken interpreters of the nation of the Franks, and sending to Ethelbert, signified that they were come from Rome, and brought a joyful message, which most undoubtedly assured to all that took advantage of it everlasting joys in heaven, and a kingdom that would never end, with the living and true God. The king having heard this, ordered them to stay in that island where they had landed, and that they should be furnished with all necessaries, till he should consider what to do with them. For he had before heard of the Christian religion, having a Christian wife of the royal family of the Franks, called Bertha; whom he had received from her parents, upon

The Venerable Bede, *The Ecclesiastical History of the English Nation,* I, 23–26; II, 1. Everyman's Library Edition, pp. 33–37, 59, 64. Published by E.P. Dutton & Co., Inc. Reprinted by permission of E.P. Dutton & Co., Inc., New York, and J.M. Dent & Sons Ltd., Publishers, London.

condition that she should be permitted to practise her religion with the Bishop Luidhard, who was sent with her to preserve her faith. Some days after, the king came into the island, and sitting in the open air, ordered Augustine and his companions to be brought into his presence. For he had taken precaution that they should not come to him in any house, lest, according to an ancient superstition, if they practised any magical arts, they might impose upon him, and so get the better of him. But they came furnished with Divine, not with magic virtue, bearing a silver cross for their banner, and the image of our Lord and Saviour painted on a board; and singing the litany, they offered up their prayers to the Lord for the eternal salvation both of themselves and of those to whom they were come. When he had sat down, pursuant to the king's commands, and preached to him and his attendants there present, the word of life, the king answered thus:—"Your words and promises are very fair, but as they are new to us, and of uncertain import, I cannot approve of them so far as to forsake that which I have so long followed with the whole English nation. But because you are come from far into my kingdom, and, as I conceive, are desirous to impart to us those things which you believe to be true, and most beneficial, we will not molest you, but give you favourable entertainment, and take care to supply you with your necessary sustenance; nor do we forbid you to preach and gain as many as you can to your religion." Accordingly he permitted them to reside in the city of Canterbury, which was the metropolis of all his dominions, and, pursuant to his promise, besides allowing them sustenance, did not refuse them liberty to preach. . . .

As soon as they entered the dwelling-place assigned them, they began to imitate the course of life practised in the primitive church; applying themselves to frequent prayer, watching and fasting; preaching the word of life to as many as they could; despising all worldly things, as not belonging to them; receiving only their necessary food from those they taught; living themselves in all respects conformably to what they prescribed to others, and being always disposed to suffer any adversity, and even to die for that truth which they preached. In short, several believed and were baptized, admiring the simplicity of their innocent life, and the sweetness of their heavenly doctrine. . . .

When [the King], among the rest, induced by the unspotted life of these holy men, and their delightful promises, which, by many miracles, they proved to be most certain, believed and was baptized, greater numbers began daily to flock together to hear the word, and, forsaking their heathen rites, to associate themselves, by believing, to the unity of the church of Christ. Their conversion the king so far encouraged, as that he compelled none to embrace Christianity, but only showed more affection to the believers, as to his fellow-citizens in the heavenly kingdom. For he had learned from his instructors and leaders to salvation, that the service of Christ ought to be voluntary, not by compulsion. Nor was it long before he gave his teachers a settled residence in his metropolis of Canterbury, with such possessions of different kinds as were necessary for their subsistence. . . .

4. *IRISH MONASTICISM INVADES THE CONTINENT*

In their missionary endeavors, Benedictine monks often encountered rivals in the persons of Irish monks. The latter in their comparative isolation had developed religious practices and traditions of church government somewhat at variance with those of the Roman Church. One of these Irish missionary monks was St. Columban, who founded two of the most notable medieval monasteries, Luxeuil in what is now eastern France, and Bobbio in the Apennines.

Having collected a band of brethren, St. Columban . . . started out [from a monastery in Ireland] in the twentieth year of his life, and under the guidance of Christ went to the seashore with twelve companions. . . . They embarked, and began the dangerous journey across the channel and sailed quickly with a smooth sea and favorable wind to the coast of Brittany. . . . They decided to enter the land of Gaul. . . .

. . . At that time, either because of the numerous enemies from without, or on account of the carelessness of the bishops, the Christian faith had almost departed from that country. The creed alone remained. But the saving grace of penance and the longing to root out the lusts of the flesh were to be found only in a few. Everywhere that he went the noble man preached the Gospel. And it pleased the people, because his teaching was adorned by eloquence and enforced by examples of virtue.

. . . He found a place formerly strongly fortified . . . which had . . . been called Luxovium. . . . A great number of stone idols, which in the old heathen times had been worshiped with horrible rites, stood in the forest near at hand. Here then the excellent man began to build a monastery [Luxeuil]. At the news of this people streamed in from all directions in order to consecrate themselves to the practice of religion, so that the large number of monks scarcely had sufficient room. The children of the nobles from all directions strove to come thither; despising the spurned trappings of the world and the pomp of present wealth, they sought eternal rewards. Columban perceived that the people were rushing in from all directions to the remedy of penance, and that the walls of one monastery could with

Jonas, *The Life of St. Columban*, in *Translations and Reprints from the Original Sources of European History* (Philadelphia: University of Pennsylvania, n.d.), Series I, Vol. II, No. 7, *passim.*

difficulty hold so great a throng of converts. Although they were of one purpose and heart, yet one monastery was insufficient for the abode of so great a number. Accordingly he sought out another spot especially remarkable for its bountiful supply of water and founded a second convent to which he gave the name of *Fontaines.* In this he placed men whose piety could not be doubted. After he had settled the bands of monks in these places, he stayed alternately at the two convents, and full of the Holy Ghost, he established the rule which they were to follow. . . .

The fame of Columban had already penetrated into all parts of Gaul and Germany, and everyone was praising the venerable man. King Theuderich, too, came often to him and humbly begged his prayers. . . . As he very often visited Columban, the holy man began to reprove him because he sinned with concubines. . . . After this reproof from Columban, the king promised to abstain from such sinful conduct. But the old serpent came to his grandmother Brunhilda, who was a second Jezebel, and aroused her pride against the holy man, because she saw that Theuderich was obedient to him. For she feared that her power and honor would be lessened if, after the expulsion of the concubines, a queen should rule the court.

St. Columban happened one day to go to Brunhilda. . . . As she saw him enter the court, she led to him the illegitimate sons of Theuderich. When St. Columban saw her, he asked what she wanted of him. Brunhilda answered, "These are the king's sons; give them thy blessing." He replied, "Know that these boys will never bear the royal sceptre, for they were begotten in sin." Enraged, she told the boys to go. When after this Columban left the court, a loud cracking noise was heard, the whole house trembled and everyone shook with fear. But that did not avail to check the wrath of the wretched woman.

From that time she began to persecute the neighboring monasteries. She issued an order that none of the monks should be allowed to leave the lands of the monasteries, no one should receive them into other houses or give them any aid. . . .

. . . Brunhilda began again to incite the king against Columban in every way; urged all the nobles and others at court to do the same, and influenced the bishops to attack Columban's faith and to abolish his monastic rule. She succeeded so fully that the holy man was obliged to . . . leave the country. . . .

[After many years of labor among the Alamans, Columban went to northern Italy—to "a lonely spot in the Apennines."] . . . The place had many advantages, it was unusually fertile, the water was full of fishes; it had long been called *Bobbio,* from the brook that flowed by it. There was another river in the neighborhood, by which Hannibal had once passed a winter and suffered the loss of a very great number of men, horses and elephants. Thither Columban now went, and with all diligence restored to its old beauty the church which was already half in ruins.

. . . After a single year in his monastery of Bobbio, Columban, the man of God, ended his devout life on the eleventh day before the Kalends of December [November 1, 615]. . . . His remains are buried there, where they have proved their virtues, by the aid of Christ. . . .

5. ST. BONIFACE CARRIES CHRISTIANITY TO THE GERMANS BEYOND THE RHINE

The mission of St. Augustine was destined to yield rich dividends a century later in the career of the Anglo-Saxon Benedictine monk Boniface (680–755). Called the "Apostle of Germany," Boniface worked principally in the eastern part of the Frankish Kingdom—Bavaria, Thuringia, Hesse, and Friesland. Christianity was not unknown in most of this region, but it suffered from poor organization and a scandalous breakdown of clerical discipline. Boniface created a strong ecclesiastical system under the control of the Papacy.

Letter of Boniface to Pope Zacharias, 742

We have . . . to inform Your Paternity that by the grace of God we have appointed three bishops over those peoples in Germany who have been to a certain extent won over and converted and we have divided the province into three dioceses. The bishoprics of these three towns or cities where they were ordained we beg you to confirm and establish by your authority in writing. We have appointed one episcopal see in the fortress called Würzburg, another in the town of Buraburg, and a third in a place called Erfurt, which was formerly a city of heathen rustics. The choice of these three places we earnestly pray you to strengthen and confirm by your own charter and by authority of your apostolic office, so that, God willing, there may be in Germany three episcopal sees founded and established by apostolic order and under the authority and direction of St. Peter. And may neither the present nor any future generation presume to break up these dioceses or to defy the orders of the Apostolic See.

Be it known also to Your Paternity that Karlmann, duke of the Franks, summoned me to him and requested me to bring together a council in the part of the Frankish kingdom which is under his rule. He promised that he would do something toward reforming and reestablishing the ecclesiastical discipline, which for a long time, not less than sixty or seventy years, has

The Letters of Saint Boniface, XL, translated by E. Emerton (New York: Columbia University Press, 1940), pp. 79–82.

been despoiled and trampled upon. If, therefore, he is really willing, under divine inspiration, to carry out this purpose, I should have the advice and direction of your authority—that is, the authority of the Apostolic See. The Franks, according to their elders, have not held a council for more than eighty years, nor have they had an archbishop or established or restored anywhere the canon law of the Church. For the most part the episcopal sees in cities are in the hands of greedy laymen or are exploited by adulterous and vicious clergymen and publicans for secular uses. If, then, I am to undertake this business by your orders and at the instance of the aforesaid duke, I desire to have at once the command and the suggestions of the Apostolic See, together with the Church canons.

If I find among these men certain so-called deacons who have spent their lives since boyhood in debauchery, adultery, and every kind of filthiness, who entered the diaconate with this reputation, and who now, while they have four or five concubines . . . still read the Gospel and are not ashamed or afraid to call themselves deacons—nay rather, entering upon the priesthood, they continue in the same vices, add sin to sin, declare that they have a right to make intercession for the people in the priestly office and to celebrate Mass, and, still worse, with such reputations advancing from step to step to nomination and appointment as bishops—may I have the formal prescription of your authority as to your procedure in such cases so that they may be convicted by an apostolic judgment and dealt with as sinners? And certain bishops are to be found among them who, although they deny that they are fornicators or adulterers, are drunkards and shiftless men, given to hunting and to fighting in the army like soldiers and by their own hands shedding blood, whether of heathens or Christians. Since I am the recognized servant and legate of the Apostolic See, my word here and your word there ought to agree, in case I should send messengers, as I have done in the past, to learn the decision of your authority. . . .

Some of the ignorant common people, Alemanians, Bavarians, and Franks, hearing that many of the offenses prohibited by us are practiced by the city of Rome imagine that they are allowed by the priests there and reproach us for causing them to incur blame in their own lives. They say that on the first day of January year after year, in the city of Rome and in the neighborhood of St. Peter's church by day or night, they have seen bands of singers parading the streets in pagan fashion, shouting and chanting sacrilegious songs and loading tables with food day and night, while no one in his own house is willing to lend his neighbor fire or tools or any other convenience. They say also that they have seen there women with amulets and bracelets of heathen fashion on their arms and legs, offering them for sale to willing buyers. All these things, seen by evil-minded and ignorant people, are a cause of reproach to us and a hindrance to our preaching and teaching. . . .

Some bishops and priests of the Frankish nation who were adulterers and fornicators of the worst kind, whose children born during their episcopate or priesthood bear witness against them, now declare, on returning from the Apostolic See, that the Roman Pontiff has given them permission to carry on their episcopal service in the Church. Against this we maintain that we have never heard that the Apostolic See had ever given a decision contrary to canonical decrees.

All these things, beloved master, we make known to you that we may give an answer to these people upon your authority and that under guidance of your instruction the sheep of the Church may not be led astray and that the ravening wolves may be overcome and destroyed.

We are sending you some trifling gifts, not as being worthy of Your Paternity, but as a token of our affection and our devoted obedience, a warm rug and a little silver and gold.

7

THE RISE OF ISLAM

Even after the incursion of the Germanic tribes and the official demise of the Roman Empire in western Europe, a considerable degree of unity remained in the Mediterranean World. Most of the Germans acknowledged a vague sort of suzerainty to the emperor at Constantinople. Economic and cultural contacts between Rome, Constantinople, and the shores of North Africa continued. Virtually all the Mediterranean peoples were, or became, Christians. But with the advent of Mohammedanism in the seventh century more than half the perimeter of the Mediterranean was lost to Christendom. The Mediterranean became a Moslem sea. Long-range commerce declined almost to the vanishing point. The trend towards isolationism and agrarianism in western Europe was intensified.

1. A MODERN BIOGRAPHER EVALUATES THE PROPHET'S CHARACTER

It goes without saying that Mohammed is a highly controversial figure. To a Christian, he seems a somewhat hysterical and immoral charlatan. To his followers, Mohammed is a heroic and divinely inspired religious leader. A reasonably detached (but Western) view of the founder of one of the world's great religions can be found in Sir William Muir's standard biography, a selection from which follows.

A patriarchal simplicity pervaded Mohammed's life. His custom was to do everything for himself. If he gave an alms he would place it with his own hand in that of the petitioner. He aided his wives in their household duties; he mended his clothes; he tied up the goats; he even cobbled his sandals.

Sir William Muir, *The Life of Mahomet* (London: Smith, Elder and Co., 1877), pp. 524–534.

His ordinary dress was of plain white cotton stuff, made like his neighbours'; but on high and festive occasions he wore garments of fine linen, striped or dyed in red. He never reclined at meals. He ate with his fingers; and, when he had finished, he would lick them before he wiped his hands. The indulgences to which he was most addicted were women, scents, and food.

Mohammed, with his wives, lived . . . in a row of low and homely cottages built of unbaked bricks; the apartments were separated by walls of palm-branches rudely daubed with mud; curtains of leather, or of black hair-cloth, supplied the place of doors and windows. His abode was to all easy of access. . . . [Yet no familiarity was tolerated.] The Prophet must be addressed in subdued accents and in a reverential style. His word was absolute; his bidding law.

A remarkable feature was the urbanity and consideration with which Mohammed treated even the most insignificant of his followers. Modesty and kindliness, patience, self-denial, and generosity, pervaded his conduct, and riveted the affections of all around him. He disliked to say *No*; if unable to answer a petitioner in the affirmative, he preferred silence. "He was more bashful," says Ayesha, "than a veiled virgin; and if anything displeased him, it was rather from his face, than by his words, that we discovered it; he never smote any one but in the service of the Lord, not even a woman or a servant." He was not known ever to refuse an invitation to the house even of the meanest, nor to decline a proffered present however small. . . .

In the exercise at home of a power absolutely dictatorial, Mohammed was just and temperate. Nor was he wanting in moderation towards his enemies, when once they had cheerfully submitted to his claims. . . . [But] magnanimity or moderation are nowhere discernible as features in the conduct of Mohammed towards such of his enemies as failed to tender a timely allegiance. Over the bodies of the Coreish who fell at Bedr, he exulted with a savage satisfaction; and several prisoners—accused of no crime but that of scepticism or political opposition—were deliberately executed at his command. The Prince of Kheibar, after being subjected to inhuman torture for the purpose of discovering the treasures of his tribe, was, with his cousin, put to death on the pretext of having treacherously concealed them, and his wife led away captive to the conqueror's tent. Sentence of exile was enforced by Mohammed with rigorous severity on two whole Jewish tribes residing at Medina; and of a third, likewise his neighbours, the women and children were sold into captivity, while the men, amounting to six or eight hundred, were butchered in cold blood before his eyes.

In domestic life the conduct of Mohammed, with one grave exception, was exemplary. As a husband his fondness and devotion were entire, bordering at times upon jealousy. As a father he was loving and tender. In his youth he is said to have lived a virtuous life. At the age of twenty-five he married a widow forty years old, and during her lifetime for five-and-twenty years he was a faithful husband to her alone. Yet it is remarkable that during this period were composed most of those passages of the Koran in which the black-eyed Houris reserved for believers in Paradise, are depicted in such glowing colours. Shortly after the death of Khadîja, the Prophet married again; but it was not till the mature age of fifty-four that he made the dangerous trial of polygamy, by taking Ayesha, yet a child, as the rival of Sauda. . . . In his fifty-sixth year he married Haphsa; and the following year, in two succeeding months, Zeinab . . . and Omm Salma. . . . A few months after . . . a second Zeinab [by divine command joined his harem]. . . . In the same year he married a seventh wife, and also a concubine. And at last, when he was full threescore years of age, no fewer than three new wives, besides Mary the Coptic slave, were within the space of seven months added to his already well-filled harem. . . .

Proceeding now to consider the religious and prophetical character of Mohammed, the first point which strikes the biographer is his constant and vivid sense of a special and all-pervading Providence. This conviction moulded his thoughts and designs, from the minutest actions in private and social life to the grand conception that he was destined to be the Reformer of his people and of the world. He never entered a company "but he sat down and rose up with the mention of the Lord." When the first fruits of the season were brought to him, he would kiss them, place them upon his eyes, and say: "Lord, as thou hast shown us the first, show unto us likewise the last." In trouble and affliction, as well as in prosperity and joy, he ever saw and humbly acknowledged the hand of God. A fixed persuasion that every incident, small and great, was ordered by the divine will, led to the strong expressions of predestination which abound in the Koran. . . .

The growth in the mind of Mohammed of the conviction that he was appointed to be a prophet and a reformer, was intimately connected with his belief in a special Providence embracing the spiritual as well as the material world; and simultaneously with that conviction there arose an implicit confidence that the Almighty would crown his mission with success. The questionings and aspirations of his inner soul were regarded by him as proceeding directly from God; the light which gradually illuminated his mind with a knowledge of the divine unity and perfections, and of the duties and destiny of man,—light amidst gross darkness,—must have emanated from the same source; and He who in his own good pleasure had thus begun the work would surely carry it through to a successful ending. What was Mohammed himself but an instrument in the hand of the great Worker? It was this belief which strengthened him, alone and unsupported, to brave for many weary years the taunts and persecutions of a whole people. In estimating the signal moral courage thus displayed, it must not be overlooked that for what is ordinarily termed *physical* courage Mohammed was not remarkable. It may be doubted whether he ever engaged personally in active conflict on the battle-field; though he accompanied his forces, he never himself led them into action, or exposed his person to avoidable danger. And there were occasions on which . . . he showed symptoms of a faint heart. Yet even if this be admitted, it brings out in still higher relief the singular display of moral daring. . . . We search in vain through the pages of profane history for a parallel to the struggle in which for thirteen years the Prophet of Arabia, in the face of discouragement and threats, rejection and persecution, retained his faith unwavering, preached repentance, and denounced God's wrath against his godless fellow citizens. Surrounded by a little band of faithful men and women, he met insults, menace, and danger with a lofty and patient trust in the future. . . .

From the earliest period of his religious convictions, the idea of ONE great Being who guides with almighty power and wisdom the whole creation, while yet remaining infinitely above it, gained a thorough possession of his mind. Polytheism and idolatry, utterly at variance with this first principle of his faith, were indignantly condemned as levelling the Creator with the creature. . . .

. . . The Prophet himself was but the passive organ which received and transmitted a heavenly message. His revelations were not the fruit of a subjective process in which a soul burning with divine life and truth, seeks to impress the stamp of its own convictions on those around; the process, on the contrary, was one which Mohammed professed to be entirely external to himself, and independent of his own reasoning, affections, and will. . . . In the Meccan period of his life there certainly can be traced no personal ends or unworthy motives for his revelations. . . .

But the scene changes altogether at Medina. There the acquisition of temporal power, aggrandisement, and self-glorification mingled rapidly with the grand object of the Prophet's life; and they were sought after and attained by precisely the same instrumentality. Messages from heaven were freely brought down to justify political conduct, in precisely the same manner as to inculcate religious precept. Battles were fought, executions inflicted, and territories annexed, under pretext of the Almighty's sanction. Even grosser actions were not only excused but encouraged by the divine approval or command. A special license was produced, allowing Mohammed a double number of wives; the discreditable affair with Mary the Coptic slave was justified in a separate Sura; and the passion for the wife of his own adopted son and bosom friend, was the subject of an inspired message in which the Prophet's scruples were rebuked by God, a divorce permitted, and marriage with the object of his unhallowed desires enjoined! . . . . . . we trace from the period of Mohammed's arrival at Medina a marked and rapid deterioration in the system he inculcated. Intolerance quickly took the place of freedom; force, of persuasion. The spiritual weapons designed at first for higher objects were no sooner prostituted to the purposes of temporal authority, than temporal authority was employed to impart a fictitious weight and power to those spiritual weapons. The name of the Almighty, impiously borrowed, imparted a terrible strength to the sword of the State; and the sword of the State yielded a willing return by destroying "the enemies of God" and sacrificing them at the shrine of the new religion. "Slay the unbelievers wheresoever ye find them," was now the watchword of Islam. "Fight in the ways of God until opposition be crushed and the Religion becometh the Lord's alone!" The warm and earnest devotion breathed by the Prophet and his followers at Mecca, soon became at Medina dull and vapid; it degenerated into a fierce fanaticism, or evaporated in a lifeless round of cold and formal ceremonies. The Jewish faith . . . as well as the less familiar system of Christianity, were both, in spite of former protestations of faith and allegiance, cast aside without hesitation and without enquiry; . . .

2. *MOHAMMED TRANSMITS ALLAH'S MESSAGES*

When Mohammed was forty years old he fell into a trance. He heard a voice say, "Read!" Twice he protested he could not read, but each time the fearsome voice commanded that he do so. The speaker identified himself as the Angel Gabriel and told Mohammed that he was henceforth to be Allah's messenger. When Mohammed awoke the words remained "as if inscribed upon his heart." This was the first of many such revelations which eventually were collected in the sacred book of the Mohammedans, the Koran or "Reading." It is a very difficult book to read, lacking, as it does, any logical order. It is divided into chapters **(sûrahs),** ***each one representing one or more messages from Allah via Gabriel.*** **Sûrah II** ***dates for the most part to 623 and 624, shortly after the Prophet's flight from Mecca to Medina. More than any other*** **sûrah,** ***it summarizes the tenets of the new religion. Selections from this*** **sûrah** ***follow.***

In the name of Allah, the Beneficent, the Merciful.

1. I am Allah, the best Knower.

2. This book, there is no doubt in it, is a guide to those who guard (against evil),

The Holy Qur-án, translated by Maulvi Muhammad Ali (Lahore, Punjab, India: Ahmadiyya Anjuman I Ishaat-i-Islam, 1920), pp. 11–132, *passim*. Used by permission of the publisher.

3. Those who believe in the unseen and keep up prayer and spend out of what We have given them:

4. And who believe in that which has been revealed to *you* [Mohammed] and that which was revealed before *you* [to Christian and other prophets], and they are sure of the hereafter.

5. These are on a right course from their Lord, and these it is that shall be successful.

6. Surely those who disbelieve, it being alike to them whether *you* warn them or do not warn them, will not believe.

7. Allah has set a seal upon their hearts and upon their hearing, and there is a covering over their eyes, and there is a great chastisement for them.

8. And there are some people who say: We believe in Allah and the last day; and they are not at all believers.

9. They desire to deceive Allah and those who believe, and they deceive only themselves and they do not perceive.

10. There is a disease in their hearts, so Allah added to their disease, and they shall have a painful chastisement because they lied.

23. . . . if you are in doubt as to that which We have revealed to Our servant [Mohammed], then produce a chapter like it and call on your *helpers* besides Allah if you are truthful.

24. But if you do (it) not—and never shall you do (it)—then be on your guard against the fire of which men and stones are the fuel; it is prepared for the unbelievers.

87. And most certainly We gave Moses the book and We sent apostles after him one after another: and We gave Jesus, the son of Mary, clear arguments and strengthened him with the holy spirit. What! whenever then an apostle came to you with that which your souls did not desire, you were insolent so you called some liars and some you slay. [Much of *Sûrah II* is a diatribe against the Jews. Many Jews in the city of Yathrib, later Medina, had supported Mohammed's coming, thinking him to be their long-awaited Messiah. They soon came to think otherwise. Nevertheless, Mohammed continued to think of Allah as identical to the God of the Jews and the Christians.]

88. And they say: Our hearts are *covered.* Nay, Allah has cursed them on account of their unbelief; so little it is that they believe.

89. And when there came to them a Book from Allah verifying that which they have, and aforetime they used to pray for *victory* against those who disbelieved, but when there came to them that which they recognized, they disbelieved in it; so Allah's curse is on the unbelievers.

111. And they say: None shall enter the garden (of Paradise) except he who is a Jew or the Christians. These are their vain desires. Say: Bring your proof if you are truthful.

112. Yea! whoever submits himself entirely to Allah and he is the doer of good (to others), he has his reward from his Lord, and there is no fear for *him* nor shall *he* grieve.

113. And the Jews say, The Christians do not follow anything (good), and the Christians say, The Jews do not follow anything (good), while they recite the (same) Book. Even thus say those who have no knowledge, like to what they say; so Allah shall judge between them on the day of resurrection in what they differ. [The Jews and the Christians are blamed for denying all good in each other, notwithstanding they both believe in the Old Testament. The Koran asserts that there is partial truth in all religions.]

135. And they say: Be Jews or Christians, you will be on the right course. Say: Nay! (we follow) the religion of Abraham, the upright one, and he was not one of the polytheists.

136. Say: We believe in Allah and (in) that which has been revealed to us, and (in) that which was revealed to Abraham and Ishmael and Isaac and Jacob and the tribes, and (in) that which was given to Moses and Jesus, and (in) that which was given to the prophets from their Lord: we do not make any distinction between any of them, and to Him do we submit.

144. Indeed We see the turning of *your* face to heaven, so We shall surely turn *you* to a qiblah which *you shall* like; turn then *your* face towards the sacred mosque, and wherever you are, turn your faces towards it, and those who have been given the Book most surely know that it is the truth from their Lord; and Allah is not at all heedless of what they do. [The *qiblah* is the place towards which the face is turned at prayer. The first *qiblah* of the Moslems was Jerusalem, but after the falling-out with the Jews, Mohammed found this Hebraic orientation embarrassing and hoped for a new revelation and a new *qiblah.*]

173. He has only forbidden you what dies of itself, and blood, and flesh of swine, and that over which any other (name) than (that of) Allah has been invoked; but whoever is driven to necessity, not desiring, nor exceeding the limit, no sin shall be upon him; surely Allah is Forgiving, Merciful.

183. O you who believe! fasting is prescribed for you, as it was prescribed for those before you, so that you may guard (against evil),

184. For a certain number of days; but whoever among you is sick or on a journey, then (he shall fast) a (like) number of other days; and those

who are able to do it may effect a redemption by feeding a poor man; so whoever does good spontaneously it is better for him; and that you fast is better for you if you know.

185. The month of Ramadan is that in which the Koran was revealed, a guidance to men and clear proofs of the guidance and the distinction; therefore whoever of you is present in the month, he shall fast therein, and whoever is sick or upon a journey, then (he shall fast) a (like) number of days; Allah desires ease for you, and He does not desire for you difficulty, and (He desires) that you should complete the number and that you should exalt the greatness of Allah for His having guided you and that you may give thanks.

190. Fight in the way of Allah against those who fight against you, but begin not hostilities. Lo! Allah loves not aggressors. [This is probably the earliest revelation regarding the permission to fight.]

191. And kill them wherever you find them, and drive them out from whence they drove you out [Mecca], and persecution is severer than slaughter; and do not fight with them at the sacred mosque until they fight with you in it, but if they do fight you, then slay them; such is the recompense of the unbelievers.

192. But if they desist, then surely Allah is Forgiving, Merciful.

193. And fight with them until there is no persecution, and religion should be only for Allah; but if they desist, then there should be no hostility except against the oppressors.

196. And accomplish the pilgrimage and the visit for Allah, but if you are prevented, (send) whatever offering is easy to obtain, and do not shave your heads until the offering reaches its destination; but whoever among you is sick or has an ailment of the head, he (should effect) a compensation by fasting or alms or sacrificing; then when you are secure, whoever profits by combining the visit with the pilgrimage (should take) whatever offering is easy to obtain; but he who cannot find (any offering) should fast for three days during the pilgrimage and for seven days when you return; these (make) ten (days) complete; this is for him whose family is not present in the sacred mosque, and be careful (of your duty) to Allah, and know that Allah is severe in requiting (evil).

197. The pilgrimage is (performed in) the well-known months; so whoever determines the performance of the pilgrimage therein, there shall be then no foul speech nor abusing nor disputing in the pilgrimage; and whatever good you do, Allah knows it; and make provision, for surely the best provision is the guarding of oneself, and be careful (of your duty) to Me, O men of understanding.

211. Ask the Israelites how many a clear sign have We given them;

and whoever changes the favour of Allah after it has come to him, then surely Allah is severe in requiting (evil).

216. Fighting is enjoined on you, and it is an object of dislike to you; and it may be that you dislike a thing while it is good for you, and it may be that you love a thing while it is evil for you, and Allah knows, while you do not know.

219. They ask you about intoxicants and games of chance. Say: In both of them there is a great sin and means of profit for men, and their sin is greater than their profit. And they ask *you* as to what they should spend. Say: What you can spare. Thus does Allah make clear to you the communications, that you may ponder,

220. On this world and the hereafter. And they ask you concerning the orphans. Say: To set right for them (their affairs) is good, and if you become copartners with them, they are your brethren; and Allah knows the mischief-maker and the peace-maker; and if Allah had pleased, He would certainly have caused you to fall into a difficulty; surely Allah is Mighty, Wise.

221. And do not marry the idolatresses until they believe, and certainly a believing maid is better than an idolatress woman, even though she should please you; and do not give (believing women) in marriage to idolaters until they believe, and certainly a believing servant is better than an idolater, even though he should please you; these invite to the garden and to forgiveness by His will, and makes clear His communications to men, that they may be mindful.

229. Divorce may be (pronounced) twice; then keep (them) in good fellowship or let (them) go with kindness; and it is not lawful for you to take any part of what you have given them, unless both fear that they cannot keep within the limits of Allah; then if you fear that they cannot keep within the limits of Allah, there is no blame on them for what she gives up to become free thereby. These are the limits of Allah, so do not exceed them, and whoever exceeds the limits of Allah, these it is that are the unjust. [Islam permits a couple two divorces, with a prescribed waiting period of three months before marital relations can be resumed.]

230. So if he divorces her [the third time] she shall not be lawful to him afterwards until she marries another husband; then if he divorces her there is no blame on them both if they return to each other (by marriage), if they think that they can keep within the limits of Allah; and these are the limits of Allah which He makes clear for a people who know. [After the third divorce is pronounced, the husband cannot remarry the divorced wife until she has been married elsewhere to another man and then divorced from him.]

271. If you give alms openly, it is well, and if you hide it and give it

to the poor, it is better for you; and this will do away with some of your evil deeds; and Allah is aware of what you do.

278. O you who believe! be careful of (your duty to) Allah and relinquish what remains (due) from usury, if you are believers.

279. But if you do (it) not, then be apprised of war from Allah and His Apostle, and if you repent, then you shall have your capital; neither shall you make (the debtor) suffer loss, nor shall you be made to suffer loss.

280. And if (the debtor) is in straitness, then let there be postponement until (he is in) ease; and that you remit (it) as alms is better for you, if you knew.

281. And guard yourselves against a day in which you shall be returned to Allah; then every soul shall be paid back in full what it has earned, and they shall not be dealt with unjustly.

3. *WESTERN CHRISTENDOM REPULSES THE MOSLEMS: TOURS, 732*

In 711 a force of Arabs and North African Berbers crossed the Straits of Gibraltar (which derives its name from the leader of the expedition) and with a minimum of effort overthrew the decadent Visigothic Kingdom. In less than a decade the Moslems were across the Pyrenees conducting incessant raiding expeditions into southern France. In 732, under the command of Abderrahman, they were decisively defeated by Charles Martel and the Franks at Tours. The ensuing selection is from an Arabian chronicle.

. . . The Moslems smote their enemies, and passed the river Garonne, and laid waste the country, and took captives without number. And that army went through all places like a desolating storm. Prosperity made those warriors insatiable. At the passage of the river, Abderrahman overthrew the count, and the count retired into his stronghold, but the Moslems fought against it, and entered it by force, and slew the count; for everything gave way to their scimitars, which were the robbers of lives. All the nations of the Franks trembled at that terrible army, and they betook them to their king Caldus [Charles Martel], and told him of the havoc made by the Moslem horsemen, and how they rode at their will through all the land of Narbonne, Toulouse, and Bordeaux, and they told the king of the death of their count. Then the king bade them be of good cheer, and offered to aid them. . . . He mounted his horse, and he took with him a host that could not be numbered, and went against the Moslems. And he came upon them at the great

Quoted from an unidentified Arabian chronicle in the book *Fifteen Decisive Battles of the World* by Sir Edward Creasy. Everyman's Library Edition, pp. 168–169. Published by E.P. Dutton & Co., Inc. Reprinted by permission of E.P. Dutton & Co., Inc., New York, and J.M. Dent & Sons Ltd., Publishers, London.

city of Tours. And Abderrahman and other prudent cavaliers saw the disorder of the Moslem troops, who were loaded with spoil; but they did not venture to displease the soldiers by ordering them to abandon everything except their arms and war-horses. And Abderrahman trusted in the valour of his soldiers, and in the good fortune which had ever attended him. But such defect of discipline always is fatal to armies. So Abderrahman and his host attacked Tours to gain still more spoil, and they fought against it so fiercely that they stormed the city almost before the eyes of the army that came to save it; and the fury and the cruelty of the Moslems towards the inhabitants of the city were like the fury and cruelty of raging tigers. It was manifest that God's chastisement was sure to follow such excesses; and fortune thereupon turned her back upon the Moslems.

Near the river Owar [Loire], the two great hosts of the two languages and the two creeds were set in array against each other. The hearts of Abderrahman, his captains, and his men were filled with wrath and pride, and they were the first to begin to fight. The Moslem horsemen dashed fierce and frequent forward against the battalions of the Franks, who resisted manfully, and many fell dead on either side, until the going down of the sun. Night parted the two armies: but in the grey of the morning the Moslems returned to the battle. Their cavaliers had soon hewn their way into the center of the Christian host. But many of the Moslems were fearful for the safety of the spoil which they had stored in their tents, and a false cry arose in their ranks that some of the enemy were plundering the camp; whereupon several squadrons of the Moslem horsemen rode off to protect their tents. But it seemed as if they fled; and all the host was troubled. And while Abderrahman strove to check their tumult, and to lead them back to battle, the warriors of the Franks came around him, and he was pierced through with many spears, so that he died. Then all the host fled before the enemy, and many died in the flight. . . .

8

CHARLEMAGNE'S EMPIRE

If any period in European history merits the appellation "Dark Ages," it is the long stretch from the rise of Islam to the eleventh century. However, in the middle of this period, with Charlemagne, there was a momentary revival. For the first time since the disappearance of Roman authority, western Europe experienced large-scale government. There was a small but promising renaissance of classical learning. The religious climate, too, improved as the Papacy reoriented itself to the cooperative Carolingians. But the revival was only temporary. With the death of Charlemagne and new waves of hostile invaders, Europe plunged deeper than ever before into localism, agrarianism, and ignorance.

1. EINHARD WRITES OF THE PRIVATE LIFE AND CHARACTER OF CHARLEMAGNE

Easily our best source for the history of Charlemagne is Einhard's all-too-brief **Life of Charlemagne.** ***A brilliant product of the newly established monastic school of Fulda, Einhard went to Charlemagne's court to complete his education at the palace school. In short time he became the King's private secretary and intimate friend. His biography is the best work of its kind of the early Middle Ages.***

After his father's death, while sharing the kingdom with his brother, [Charlemagne] bore his unfriendliness and jealousy most patiently, and, to the wonder of all, could not be provoked to be angry with him. Later he married a daughter of Desiderius, King of the Lombards, at the instance of his mother, but he repudiated her at the end of a year for some reason unknown, and married Hildegard, a woman of high birth, of Suabian origin. He had

Einhard, *Life of Charlemagne,* translated by S.E. Turner (New York: Harper & Brothers, 1880), *passim.*

three sons by her—Charles, Pepin, and Lewis—and as many daughters. . . . He had three other daughters besides these—Theoderada, Hiltrud, and Ruodhaid—two by his third wife, Fastrada, a woman of East Frankish (that is to say, of German) origin, and the third by a concubine, whose name for the moment escapes me. At the death of Fastrada, he married Liutgard, an Alemannic woman, who bore him no children. After her death he had three concubines. . . .

. . . He was so careful of the training of his sons and daughters that he never took his meals without them when he was at home, and never made a journey without them; his sons would ride at his side, and his daughters follow him, while a number of his body-guard, detailed for their protection, brought up the rear. Strange to say, although they were very handsome women, and he loved them very dearly, he was never willing to marry any of them to a man of their own nation or to a foreigner, but kept them all at home until his death, saying that he could not dispense with their society. . . .

Charles was large and strong, and of lofty stature, though not disproportionately tall (his height is well known to have been seven times the length of his foot); the upper part of his head was round, his eyes very large and animated, nose a little long, hair fair, and face laughing and merry. Thus his appearance was always stately and dignified, whether he was standing or sitting; although his neck was thick and somewhat short, and his belly rather prominent; but the symmetry of the rest of his body concealed these defects. His gait was firm, his whole carriage manly, and his voice clear, but not so strong as his size led one to expect. His health was excellent, except during the four years preceding his death, when he was subject to frequent fevers; at the last he even limped a little with one foot. Even in those years he consulted rather his own inclinations than the advice of physicians, who were almost hateful to him, because they wanted him to give up roasts, to which he was accustomed, and to eat boiled meat instead. . . .

He used to wear the national, that is to say, the Frank, dress. . . . He despised foreign costumes, however handsome, and never allowed himself to be robed in them, except twice in Rome, when he donned the Roman tunic, chlamys, and shoes; the first time at the request of Pope Hadrian, the second to gratify Leo, Hadrian's successor. . . .

Charles was temperate in eating, and particularly so in drinking, for he abominated drunkenness in anybody, much more in himself and those of his household; . . . He very rarely gave entertainments, only on great feast-days, and then to large numbers of people. His meals ordinarily consisted of four courses, not counting the roast, which his huntsmen used to bring in on the spit; he was more fond of this than of any other dish. While at table, he listened to reading or music. The subjects of the readings were the stories and deeds of olden time: he was fond, too, of St. Augustine's books, and especially of the one entitled *The City of God*. . . .

. . . He most zealously cultivated the liberal arts, held those who taught them in great esteem, and conferred great honours upon them. He took lessons in grammar of the deacon Peter of Pisa, at that time an aged man. Another deacon, Albin of Britain, surnamed Alcuin, a man of Saxon extraction, who was the greatest scholar of the day, was his teacher in other branches of learning. The King spent much time and labour with him studying rhetoric, dialectics, and especially astronomy; he learned to reckon, and used to investigate the motions of the heavenly bodies most curiously, with an intelligent scrutiny. He also tried to write, and used to keep tablets and blanks in bed under his pillow, that at leisure hours he might accustom his hand to form the letters; however, as he did not begin his efforts in due season, but late in life, they met with ill success.

. . . He cherished the Church of St. Peter the Apostle at Rome above all other holy and sacred places, and heaped its treasury with a vast wealth of gold, silver, and precious stones. He sent great and countless gifts to the popes; and throughout his whole reign the wish that he had nearest at heart was to re-establish the ancient authority of the city of Rome under his care and by his influence, and to defend and protect the Church of St. Peter, and to beautify and enrich it out of his own store above all other churches. Although he held it in such veneration, he only repaired to Rome to pay his vows and make his supplications four times during the whole forty-seven years that he reigned.

When he made his last journey thither, he had also other ends in view. The Romans had inflicted many injuries upon the Pontiff Leo, tearing out his eyes and cutting out his tongue, so that he had been compelled to call upon the King for help. Charles accordingly went to Rome, to set in order the affairs of the Church, which were in great confusion, and passed the whole winter there. It was then that he received the titles of Emperor and Augustus, to which he at first had such an aversion that he declared that he would not have set foot in the Church the day that they were conferred, although it was a great feast-day, if he could have foreseen the design of the Pope. He bore very patiently with the jealousy which the Roman [i.e., Byzantine] emperors showed upon his assuming these titles, for they took this step very ill; and by dint of frequent embassies and letters, in which he addressed them as brothers, he made their haughtiness yield to his magnanimity, a quality in which he was unquestionably much their superior. . . .

Towards the close of his life, when he was broken by ill-health and old age, he summoned Lewis, King of Aquitania, his only surviving son by Hildegard, and gathered together all the chief men of the whole kingdom of the Franks in a solemn assembly. He appointed Lewis, with their unanimous consent, to rule with himself over the whole kingdom, and constituted him heir to the imperial name; then, placing the diadem upon his son's head, he bade him be proclaimed Emperor and Augustus. This step was hailed by all present with great favour, for it really seemed as if God had prompted him to it for the kingdom's good; it increased the King's dignity, and struck no little terror into foreign nations. After sending his son back to Aquitania, although weak from age he set out to hunt, as usual, near his palace at Aix-la-Chapelle, and passed the rest of the autumn in the chase, returning thither about the first of November. While wintering there, he was seized, in the month of January, with a high fever, and took to his bed. As soon as he was taken sick, he prescribed for himself abstinence from food, as he always used to do in case of fever, thinking that the disease could be driven off, or at least mitigated, by fasting. Besides the fever, he suffered from a pain in the side, which the Greeks call pleurisy; but he still persisted in fasting, and in keeping up his strength only by draughts taken at very long intervals. He died January twenty-eighth, the seventh day from the time that he took to his bed, at nine o'clock in the morning, after partaking of the holy communion, in the 72d year of his age and the 47th of his reign [814].

2. *CHARLEMAGNE ADMONISHES THE STEWARDS OF HIS ESTATES*

No document better reveals the agrarian character of Charlemagne's kingdom than his* Capitulare de Villis*—his instructions to the stewards on the proper management of the royal estates. Charlemagne's estates were not just a hobby. With the disappearance of city-life and commerce, the King's estates provided almost all his revenues, to say nothing of food for his table.

22. In each of our estates our stewards are to have as many cow-houses, piggeries, sheep-folds, stables for goats, as possible, and they ought never to be without these. And let them have in addition cows furnished by our serfs for performing their service, so that the cow-houses and plows shall be in no way weakened by the service on our demesne. And when they have to provide meat, let them have steers lame, but healthy, and cows and horses which are not mangy, or other beasts which are not diseased and, as we have said, our cow-houses and plows are not to be weakened for this.

34. They must provide with the greatest care, that whatever is pre-

Translations and Reprints from the Original Sources of European History (Philadelphia: University of Pennsylvania, 1902), Series II, Vol. III, No. 2, pp. 3–4.

pared or made with the hands, that is, lard, smoked meat, salt meat, partially salted meat, wine, vinegar, mulberry wine, cooked wine, *garns* [a kind of fermented liquor], mustard, cheese, butter, malt, beer, mead, honey, wax, flour, all should be prepared and made with the greatest cleanliness.

40. That each steward on each of our domains shall always have, for the sake of ornament, swans, peacocks, pheasants, ducks, pigeons, partridges, turtle-doves.

42. That in each of our estates, the chambers shall be provided with counterpanes, cushions, pillows, bed-clothes, coverings for the tables and benches; vessels of brass, lead, iron and wood; andirons, chains, pot-hooks, adzes, axes, augers, cutlasses and all other kinds of tools, so that it shall never be necessary to go elsewhere for them, or to borrow them. And the weapons, which are carried against the enemy, shall be well cared for, so as to keep them in good condition; and when they are brought back they shall be placed in the chamber.

43. For our women's work they are to give at the proper time, as has been ordered, the materials, that is the linen, wool, wood, vermillion, madder, wool-combs, teasels, soap, grease, vessels and the other objects which are necessary.

44. Of the food-products other than meat, two-thirds shall be sent each year for our own use, that is of the vegetables, fish, cheese, butter, honey, mustard, vinegar, millet, panic, dried and green herbs, radishes, and in addition of the wax, soap and other small products; and they are to tell us how much is left by a statement, as we have said above; and they shall not neglect this as in the past; because from those two-thirds, we wish to know how much remains.

45. That each steward shall have in his district good workmen, namely, blacksmiths, gold-smiths, silver-smiths, shoemakers, turners, carpenters, sword-makers, fishermen, foilers, soap-makers, men who know how to make beer, cider, berry, and all the other kinds of beverages, bakers to make pastry for our table, net-makers who know how to make nets for hunting, fishing and fowling, and the other who are too numerous to be designated.

3. *CHARLEMAGNE INSTRUCTS THE* MISSI DOMINICI

In an effort to check the decentralizing tendencies of his day, Charlemagne created the* missi. *These "messengers of the lord" traveled in pairs, inspecting all parts of Charlemagne's realm and reporting back their findings to the ruler. In 802, Charlemagne prepared a special capitulary to serve as a guide for the* missi. *Sections of this document follow.

Translations and Reprints from the Original Sources of European History (Philadelphia: University of Pennsylvania, 1900), Series I, Vol. VI, No. 5, pp. 16–27.

1. . . . The most serene and most Christian lord emperor Charles has chosen from his nobles the wisest and most prudent men, both archbishops and some of the other bishops also, and venerable abbots and pious laymen, and has sent them throughout his whole kingdom. . . . Where anything which is not right and just has been enacted in the law, he has ordered them to inquire into this most diligently and to inform him of it; he desires, God granting, to reform it. And let no one, through his cleverness or astuteness, dare to oppose or thwart the written law, as many are wont to do, or the judicial sentence passed upon him, or to do injury to the churches of God or the poor or the widows or the wards or any Christian. But all shall live entirely in accordance with God's precept, justly and under a just rule, and each one shall be admonished to live in harmony with his fellows in his business or profession; the canonical clergy ought to observe in every respect a canonical life without heeding base gain, nuns ought to keep diligent watch over their lives, laymen and the secular clergy ought rightly to observe their laws without malicious fraud, and all ought to live in mutual charity and perfect peace. . . .

2. . . . [The Emperor] commanded that every man in his whole kingdom, whether ecclesiastic or layman, and each one according to his vow and occupation, should now promise to him as emperor the fidelity which he had previously promised to him as king; and all of those who had not yet made that promise should do likewise, down to those who were twelve years old. . . .

10. That bishops and priests shall live according to the canons and shall teach others to do the same.

11. That bishops, abbots, abbesses, who are in charge of others, with the greatest veneration shall strive to surpass their subjects in this diligence and shall not oppress their subjects with a harsh rule or tyranny, but with sincere love shall carefully guard the flock committed to them with mercy and charity or by the examples of good works.

18. Monasteries for women shall be firmly ruled, and the women shall not be permitted to wander about at all, but they shall be guarded with all diligence, and they shall not presume to arouse litigations or strife among themselves, nor shall they dare to be disobedient or refractory in any way toward their rulers and abbesses. . . .

19. That no bishops, abbots, priests, deacons, or other members of the clergy shall presume to have dogs for hunting, or hawks, falcons and sparrow-hawks, but each shall observe fully the canons or rule of his order. If any one shall presume to do so, let him know that he shall lose his office. . . .

21. That priests and the remaining canonical clergy, whom they have as associates in their ministry, shall be wholly subject to their bishops, as

the canonical institution orders; let them consent to be taught the sacred discipline fully by their bishops, as they desire to have our favor or their own offices.

25. That counts and *centenarii* [rulers of subdivisions of counties] shall compel all to do justice in every respect, and shall have such assistants in their ministries as they can securely confide in, who will observe law and justice faithfully, who will oppress the poor in no manner, who will not dare under any pretext, on account of flattery or reward, to conceal thieves, robbers, murderers, adulterers, magicians, wizards or witches, and all sacrilegious men, but instead will give them up that they may be punished and chastised in accordance with the law, so that, God granting it, all of these evils may be removed from the Christian people.

28. Concerning embassies coming from the lord emperor. That the counts and *centenarii* shall provide most carefully, as they desire the grace of the lord emperor, for the *missi* who are sent out, so that they may go through their departments without any delay; and he commands to all everywhere that they ought to see to it that no delay is encountered anywhere. . . .

32. Murders, by which a multitude of the Christian people perishes, we command in every way to be shunned and to be forbidden; . . . In order that the greatest enmities may not arise among Christians, when by the persuasions of the devil murders happen, the criminal shall immediately hasten to make amends and with all celerity shall pay the fitting composition for the evil done to the relatives of the murdered man. And we forbid firmly, that the relatives of the murdered man shall dare in any way to continue their enmities on account of the evil done, or shall refuse to grant peace to him who asks it, but having given their pledges they shall receive the fitting composition and shall make a perpetual peace; moreover, the guilty one shall not delay to pay the composition. . . . But if any one shall have scorned to make the fitting composition, he shall be deprived of his property until we shall render our decision.

35. That all shall wholly venerate their bishops and priests with all honor in the service and will of God. That they shall not dare to pollute themselves and others by incestuous nuptials; that they shall not presume to be married before the bishops and priests together with the elders of the people have inquired diligently into the consanguinity of those marrying; and then they shall be married with a benediction. Let them shun drunkenness, avoid greed, commit no theft; let them wholly shun strifes and contentions and blasphemies, both at feasts and assemblies, but let them live in charity and concord. . . .

39. That in our forests no one shall dare to steal our game, which we

have already many times forbidden to be done; and now we again strictly forbid that any one shall do so in the future; . . . But if any count or *centenarius* . . . shall have stolen our game, he shall be brought to our presence without fail to render account. . . .

40. Lastly, therefore, we desire all our decrees to be known in our whole kingdom through our *missi* now sent out. . . . Where we believe there is anything unpunished, we shall so strive to correct it with all our zeal and will that with God's aid we may bring it to correction, both for our own eternal glory and that of all our faithful. Likewise we desire all the above to be fruitfully known by our counts or *centenarii*. . . .

4. *HOW CHARLEMAGNE RAISED HIS ARMY*

The enlargement of his realm by military conquest was Charlemagne's main preoccupation. An obvious requirement was a large and loyal army. But because of the economic breakdown of western Europe, no money was available to Charlemagne to raise and maintain an armed force. How he solved this problem (not that the solution was entirely original with Charlemagne) is described in the following selections. The first two are from his capitularies relating to the army; the last selection shows how a large landholder, in this case a cleric, was called upon to render military service.

[808] Ch. 1. Every free man who has four *mansi* [a *mansus* is about one hundred acres] of his own property, or as a benefice from any one, shall equip himself and go to the army, either with his lord, if the lord goes, or with his count. He who has three *mansi* of his own property shall be joined to a man who has one *mansus*, and shall aid him so that he may serve for both. He who has only two *mansi* of his own property shall be joined to another who likewise has two *mansi*, and one of them, with the aid of the other, shall go to the army. He who has only one *mansus* of his own shall be joined to one of three who have the same and shall aid him, and the latter shall go alone; the three who have aided him shall remain at home.

Ch. 4. From the men who have been enfeoffed by the counts the following are to be excepted and are not commanded to pay the ban: two who shall have been left behind with the wife of a count and two others who shall have been commanded to remain to guard his territory and to perform our service. . . .

* * *

[811] Ch. 3. If any man holding an office under us shall have been summoned to the host [i.e., army] and shall not have come to the appointed

Translations and Reprints from the Original Sources of European History (Philadelphia: University of Pennsylvania, 1900), Series I, Vol. VI, No. 5, pp. 8–12.

muster, he shall abstain from flesh and wine for as many days as he shall have been proved to be late in coming to the appointed muster.

Ch. 4. If any one, without the license or permission of the prince, shall have returned from the army (the Franks call this *herisliz*), we wish the ancient law to be preserved, that is, he shall be punished by a capital sentence.

Ch. 5. If any one of those who hold a royal benefice shall have abandoned his peer proceeding in the army against the common enemies, and shall have been unwilling to go or stay with him, he shall lose his office and benefice.

Ch. 6. That in the host no one shall ask his peer or any other man to drink. And if any drunken person shall have been found in the army, he shall be so excommunicated that in drinking he shall use nothing but water until he acknowledges that he has acted wrongly. . . .

Ch. 8. It has been enacted that the preparation for serving in the army shall be defined and continued in accordance with the ancient custom, namely, victuals for a three months' march and arms and clothing for a half-year. But, nevertheless, it has been decided that this shall be observed in the following manner, so that those who march from the Rhine to the Loire shall compute the beginning of their provision from the Loire; those, indeed, who make their journey from the Loire to the Rhine shall compute their victuals for the three months from the Rhine; those, moreover, who dwell across the Rhine and proceed through Saxony shall know that the Elbe is their boundary; and those who remain across the Loire and ought to go to Spain shall know that the Pyrenees Mountains are their boundary.

Ch. 9. If it shall have been learned that any free man has not been, during the present year, in the army with his lord, he shall be compelled to pay the full *heribannum* [fine for failure to render military service]. And if his lord or count shall have permitted him to remain at home, the former shall pay the same fine on his account; and as many *heribanni* shall be demanded as he has allowed men to remain at home. . . .

* * *

Letter of Charlemagne to Abbot Fulrad, c. 808

In the name of the Father, Son and Holy Ghost. Charles, most serene, august, crowned by God, great pacific Emperor, and also, by God's mercy, King of the Franks and Lombards, to Abbot Fulrad.

Be it known to you that we have decided to hold our general assembly this year in the eastern part of Saxony, on the river Bode, at the place which is called Stassfurt. Therefore, we have commanded you to come to the aforesaid place, with all your men well armed and prepared, on the fifteenth day before the Kalends of July, that is, seven days before the festival of St. John the Baptist. Come, accordingly, so equipped with your men to the aforesaid place that thence you may be able to go well prepared in any direction whither our summons shall direct; that is, with arms and gear also, and other equipment for war in food and clothing. So that each horseman shall have a shield, lance, sword, dagger, bow and quivers with arrows; and in your carts utensils of various kinds, that is, axes, planes, augers, boards, spades, iron shovels, and other utensils which are necessary in an army. In the carts also supplies of food for three months, dating from the time of the assembly, arms and clothing for a half-year. And we command this in general, that you cause it to be observed that you proceed peacefully to the aforesaid place, through whatever part of our realm your journey shall take you, that is, that you presume to take nothing except fodder, wood and water; and let the men of each one of your vassals march along with the carts and horsemen, and let the leader always be with them until they reach the aforesaid place, so that the absence of a lord may not give an opportunity to his men of doing evil.

5. *EUROPEAN CIVILIZATION TOUCHES BOTTOM*

After the brief and limited revival under Charlemagne's leadership, western European civilization continued its downward trend, intensified by new invasions. No history worthy of the name was written in this melancholy period, but a number of monastic annals have survived which throw dramatic light on conditions in Europe. One of these annals is that of the monastery of Xanten, located near the mouth of the Rhine River and thus in constant danger from Norse marauders.

[845] Twice in the canton of Worms there was an earthquake; the first in the night following Palm Sunday, the second in the holy night of Christ's Resurrection. In the same year the heathen broke in upon the Christians at many points, but more than twelve thousand of them were killed by the Frisians. Another party of invaders devastated Gaul; of these more than six hundred men perished. Yet owing to his indolence Charles [the Bald] agreed to give them many thousand pounds of gold and silver if they would leave Gaul, and this they did. Nevertheless the cloisters of most of the saints were destroyed and many of the Christians were led away captive.

J.H. Robinson, *Readings in European History* (New York: Ginn and Company, 1904), Vol. I, pp. 158–161. Copyright 1904 by James Harvey Robinson. Used by permission of the publisher.

[846] According to their custom the Northmen plundered Eastern and Western Frisia and burned the town of Dordrecht, with two other villages, before the eyes of Lothaire, who was then in the castle of Nimwegen, but could not punish the crime. The Northmen, with their boats filled with immense booty, including both men and goods, returned to their own country.

At this same time, as no one can mention or hear without great sadness, the mother of all churches, the basilica of the apostle Peter, was taken and plundered by the Moors, or Saracens, who had already occupied the region of Beneventum. The Saracens, moreover, slaughtered all the Christians whom they found outside the walls of Rome, either within or without this church. They also carried men and women away prisoners. They tore down, among many others, the altar of the blessed Peter, and their crimes from day to day bring sorrow to Christians. Pope Sergius departed life this year.

[847] After the death of Sergius no mention of the apostolic see has come in any way to our ears. . . .

[848] On the fourth of February, towards evening, it lightened and there was thunder heard. The heathen, as was their custom, inflicted injury on the Christians. . . .

[849] While King Louis was ill his army of Bavaria took its way against the Bohemians. Many of these were killed and the remainder withdrew, much humiliated, into their own country. The heathen from the North wrought havoc in Christendom as usual and grew greater in strength; but it is revolting to say more of this matter.

[850] On January 1st of that season, in the octave of the Lord, towards evening, a great deal of thunder was heard and a mighty flash of lightning seen; and an overflow of water afflicted the human race during this winter. In the following summer an all too great heat of the sun burned the earth. Leo, pope of the apostolic see, an extraordinary man, built a fortification round the church of St. Peter the apostle. The Moors, however, devastated here and there the coast towns in Italy. . . .

[852] The steel of the heathen glistened; excessive heat; a famine followed. There was not fodder enough for the animals. . . .

[853] A great famine in Saxony so that many were forced to live on horse meat.

III

THE HIGH MIDDLE AGE

9

THE CRUSADES

An outstanding feature of western European life in the High Middle Age was the expansion of feudal society out of the lands which had comprised Charlemagne's empire. While the boundaries of Christendom were advanced south into Spain and Portugal, north into the Baltic lands, Scandinavia, and Scotland, and east into the Slavic lands of east-central Europe, the most dramatic aspect of European expansion consisted of a series of religiously inspired military expeditions to the Holy Land, known as the Crusades. Although the First Crusade proved to be unexpectedly successful, later expeditions accomplished little, and eventually the Christian States of the Levant were retaken by the Moslems. In the late thirteenth century Christian missionaries and traders found their way across the vast Asian landmass to the rich court of the Mongols in North China.

1. POPE URBAN CALLS FOR A CRUSADE, 1095

In the last half of the eleventh century the Seljuk Turks swept out of central Asia, conquered Persia, adopted the Islamic religion, and overwhelmed the Byzantine army at Manzikert (1071). Not only was the Byzantine Empire, the eastern bastion of Christendom, endangered, but pilgrimages to Jerusalem were disrupted. To meet the Turkish threat, Pope Urban II convened a council at Clermont in central France, where on November 25, 1095, he delivered the following oration, calling for a Crusade. It was one of the most dramatic and successful appeals of all time.

Oh, race of Franks, race from across the mountains, race beloved and chosen by God—as is clear from many of your works,—set apart from all other nations by the situation of your country, as well as by your catholic faith and the honor which you render to the holy church. To you our dis-

The version of Robert the Monk, in *Translations and Reprints from the Original Sources of European History* (Philadelphia: University of Pennsylvania, 1894), Series I, Vol. I, No. 2, pp. 5-8.

course is addressed and for you our exhortations are intended. We wish you to know what a grievous cause has led us to your country, and that it is the imminent peril threatening you and all the faithful, which has brought us hither.

From the confines of Jerusalem and from the city of Constantinople a horrible tale has gone forth and very frequently has been brought to our ears. Namely, that a race from the kingdom of the Persians, an accursed race, a race wholly alienated from God, a generation forsooth which has not directed its heart and has not entrusted its spirit to God, has violently invaded the lands of those Christians and has depopulated them by pillage and fire. They have led away a part of the captives into their own country, and a part they have destroyed by cruel tortures. They have either destroyed the churches of God or appropriated them for the rites of their own religion. They destroy altars, after having defiled them with their uncleanness. They circumcise the Christians, and the blood of the circumcision they either spread upon the altars or pour into the baptismal vases.

When they wish to torture anyone by a base death, they perforate his navel and dragging forth the extremity of the intestines, bind it to a stake; then by blows they compel the victim to run around the stake, until the viscera gush forth and the victim falls prostrate on the ground. Others they bind to a post and pierce with arrows. Others they compel to extend their necks and then, attacking them with naked swords, attempt to cut through the neck with a single blow. What shall I say of the abominable rape of the women? To speak of it is worse than to be silent. The kingdom of the Greeks is now dismembered by them and deprived of territory so vast in extent that it could not be traversed in two month's time.

On whom therefore is the labor of avenging these wrongs and recovering this territory incumbent, if not upon you? You, upon whom above all other nations God has conferred remarkable glory in arms, great courage, bodily activity, and strength to humble the heads of those who resist you. Let the deeds of your ancestors encourage you and incite your minds to manly achievements; the glory and greatness of king Charlemagne, and of his son Louis, and of your other monarchs, who have destroyed the kingdoms of the Turks and have extended the sway of the holy church over the lands of the pagans. Let the holy sepulchre of our Lord and Saviour, which is possessed by the unclean nations, especially incite you, and the holy places which are now treated with ignominy and irreverently poluted with the filth of the unclean. Oh, most valiant soldiers and descendents of invincible ancestors, be not degenerate, but recall the valor of your progenitors.

But if you are hindered by love of children, parents or wife, remember what the Lord says in the Gospel, "He that loveth father or mother more than me, is not worthy of me." "Everyone that hath forsaken houses, or brethren, or sisters, or father, or mother, or wife, or children, or lands for my name's sake shall receive an hundred-fold and shall inherit everlasting life." Let none of your possessions retain you, no solicitude for your family affairs. For this land which you inhabit, shut in on all sides by the seas and surrounded by the mountain peaks, is too narrow for your large population; nor does it abound in wealth; and it furnishes scarcely food enough for its cultivators. Hence it is that you murder and devour one another, that you wage war, and that very many among you perish in intestine strife.

Let therefore hatred depart from among you, let your quarrels end, let wars cease, and let all dissentions and controversies slumber. Enter upon the road to the Holy Sepulchre; wrest that land from the wicked race, and subject it to yourselves. That land which as the Scripture says "floweth with milk and honey," was given by God into the power of the children of Israel. Jerusalem is the center of the earth; the land is fruitful above all others, like another paradise of delights. This the Redeemer of mankind has made illustrious by His advent, has beautified by His residence, has consecrated by His passion, has redeemed by His death, has glorified by His burial.

This royal city, however, situated at the center of the earth, is now held captive by the enemies of Christ, and is subjected by those who do not know God, to the worship of the heathens. . . . Accordingly undertake this journey for the remission of your sins, with the assurance of the imperishable glory of the kingdom of heaven.

When Pope Urban had said these and very many similar things in his urbane discourse, he so influenced to one purpose the desires of all who were present, that all cried out, "It is the will of God! It is the will of God!" When the venerable Roman pontiff heard that, with eyes uplifted to heaven he gave thanks to God and, with his hand commanding silence, said:

Most beloved brethren, to-day is manifest in you what the Lord says in the Gospel, "Where two or three are gathered together in my name there am I in the midst of them." For unless God had been present in your spirits, all of you would not have uttered the same cry. For, although the cry issued from numerous mouths, yet the origin of the cry was one. Therefore I say to you that God, who implanted this in your breasts, has drawn it forth from you. Let that then be your war-cry in combats, because it is given to you by God. When an armed attack is made upon the enemy, let this one cry be raised by all the soldiers of God: It is the will of god! It is the will of God!

And we do not command or advise that the old or feeble, or those incapable of bearing arms, undertake this journey. Nor ought women to set out at all, without their husbands or brothers or legal guardians. For such are more of a hindrance than aid, more of a burden than advantage. Let the rich aid the needy; and according to their wealth, let them take with them experienced soldiers. The priests and clerks of each order are not to go without consent of their bishop; for this journey would profit them nothing if they went without permission. Also, it is not fitting that laymen should enter upon the pilgrimage without the blessing of their priests.

Whoever, therefore, shall determine upon this holy pilgrimage and shall make his vow to God to that effect and shall offer himself to Him for sacrifice, as a living victim, holy and acceptable to God, shall wear the sign of the cross of the Lord on his forehead or on his breast. When, truly, in fulfillment of his vow he wishes to enter upon his journey, let him place the cross on his back between his shoulders. Such, indeed, by this two-fold action will fulfill the precept of the Lord, as He commanded in the Gospel, "He that taketh not his cross and followeth after me, is not worthy of me."

2. THE CRUSADERS CAPTURE JERUSALEM, 1099

The final battle of the First Crusade was the ferocious Christian assault on the Moslem-held fortified city of Jerusalem. Its capture on July 15, 1099, brought to a successful conclusion the three-year campaign of the Crusaders. Fulk of Chartres, the author of this account, participated in the storming of the city and in the bloody massacre which followed.

On the seventh of June the Franks besieged Jerusalem. The city is located in a mountainous region, which is lacking in rivers, woods, and springs, except the Fountain of Siloam, where there is plenty of water, but it empties forth only at certain intervals. This fountain empties into the valley, at the foot of Mount Zion, and flows into the course of the brook of Kedron, which, during the winter, flows through the valley of Jehosaphat. There are many cisterns, which furnish abundant water within the city. When filled by the winter rains and well cared for, they offer both men and beasts an unfailing supply at all times. Moreover, the city is laid out most beautifully, and cannot be criticized for too great length or as being disproportionately narrow. On the west is the tower of David, which is flanked on both sides by the broad wall of the city. The lower half of the wall is solid masonry, of square stones and mortar, sealed with molten lead. So strong is this wall that, if fifteen or twenty men should be well supplied with provisions, they would never be taken by any army. . . .

Fulk of Chartres, *Gesta Francorum Jerusalem Expugnantium* ("The Deeds of the Franks Who Attacked Jerusalem"), in Frederick Duncalf and August C. Krey, eds., *Parallel Source Problems in Medieval History* (New York: Harper & Brothers, 1912), pp. 109–115.

When the Franks saw how difficult it would be to take the city, the leaders ordered scaling ladders to be made, hoping that by a brave assault it might be possible to surmount the walls by means of ladders and thus take the city, God helping. So the ladders were made, and on the day following the seventh, in the early morning, the leaders ordered the attack, and, with the trumpets sounding, a splendid assault was made on the city from all sides. The attack lasted till the sixth hour, but it was discovered that the city could not be entered by the use of ladders, which were few in number, and sadly we ceased the attack.

Then a council was held, and it was ordered that siege machines should be constructed by the artisans, so that by moving them close to the wall we might accomplish our purpose, with the aid of God. This was done. . . .

. . . When the tower had been put together and had been covered with hides, it was moved nearer to the wall. Then knights, few in number, but brave, at the sound of the trumpet, took their places in the tower and began to shoot stones and arrows. The Saracens defended themselves vigorously, and, with slings, very skilfully hurled back burning firebrands, which had been dipped in oil and fresh fat. Many on both sides, fighting in this manner, often found themselves in the presence of death.

. . . On the following day the work again began at the sound of the trumpet, and to such purpose that the rams, by continual pounding, made a hole through one part of the wall. The Saracens suspended two beams before the opening, supporting them by ropes, so that by piling stones behind them they would make an obstacle to the rams. However, what they did for their own protection became, through the providence of God, the cause of their own destruction. For, when the tower was moved nearer to the wall, the ropes that supported the beams were cut; from these same beams the Franks constructed a bridge, which they cleverly extended from the tower to the wall. About this time one of the towers in the stone wall began to burn, for the men who worked our machines had been hurling firebrands upon it until the wooden beams within it caught fire. The flames and smoke soon became so bad that none of the defenders of this part of the wall were able to remain near this place. At the noon hour on Friday, with trumpets sounding, amid great commotion and shouting "God help us," the Franks entered the city. When the pagans saw one standard planted on the wall, they were completely demoralized, and all their former boldness vanished, and they turned to flee through the narrow streets of the city. Those who were already in rapid flight began to flee more rapidly.

Count Raymond and his men, who were attacking the wall on the other side, did not yet know of all this, until they saw the Saracens leap from the wall in front of them. Forthwith, they joyfully rushed into the city to pursue and kill the nefarious enemies, as their comrades were already doing. Some Saracens, Arabs, and Ethiopians took refuge in the tower of David, others fled to the temples of the Lord and of Solomon. A great fight took place in the court and porch of the temples, where they were unable to escape from our gladiators. Many fled to the roof of the temple of Solomon, and were shot with arrows, so that they fell to the ground dead. In this temple almost ten thousand were killed. Indeed, if you had been there you would have seen our feet colored to our ankles with the blood of the slain. But what more shall I relate? None of them were left alive; neither women nor children were spared.

This may seem strange to you. Our squires and poorer footmen discovered a trick of the Saracens, for they learned that they could find byzants [1] in the stomachs and intestines of the dead Saracens, who had swallowed them. Thus, after several days they burned a great heap of dead bodies, that they might more easily get the precious metal from the ashes. Moreover, Tancred broke into the temple of the Lord and most wrongfully stole much gold and silver, also precious stones, but later, repenting of his action, after everything had been accounted for, he restored all to its former place of sanctity. . . .

The carnage over, the crusaders entered the houses and took whatever they found in them. However, this was all done in such a sensible manner that whoever entered a house first received no injury from any one else, whether he was rich or poor. Even though the house was a palace, whatever he found there was his property. Thus many poor men became rich.

Afterward, all, clergy and laymen, went to the Sepulcher of the Lord and His glorious temple, singing the ninth chant. With fitting humility, they repeated prayers and made their offering at the holy places that they had long desired to visit. . . .

It was the eleven hundredth year of our Lord, if you subtract one, when the people of Gaul took the city. It was the 15th day of July when the Franks in their might captured the city. It was the eleven hundredth year minus one after the birth of our Lord, the 15th day of July in the two hundred and eighty-fifth year after the death of Charles the Great and the twelfth year after the death of William I of England.

3. *CHRISTIAN POWER IN THE HOLY LAND DECLINES*

Capturing the Holy Land was hard enough; preserving Christian rule there was even more difficult. There were never enough knights to form an adequate gar-

Letter from Aymeric, patriarch of Antioch, to Louis VII of France, 1164, in *Translations and Reprints from the Original Sources of European History* (Philadelphia: University of Pennsylvania, 1894), Series I, Vol. I, No. 4, pp. 14–17.

[1] Gold coins of the Byzantine Empire.

rison, and the Christian settlements were widely scattered and easily isolated. The fall of the County of Edessa to the Moslems in 1144 marked the beginning of the end. The Second Crusade failed completely. This left Christians in the Levant in a desperately weak position. Aymeric of Antioch, in this appeal to King Louis VII of France, depicts the plight of the badly outnumbered Christian knights in the face of a resurgent Moslem unity under Nureddin (Nourrddin).

Aymeric, by the grace of God, patriarch of the holy Apostolic See of Antioch, to Louis, illustrious king of the French,—greeting and Apostolic benediction.

It would be fitting that we should always write joyful tidings to his royal majesty and should increase the splendor of his heart by the splendor and delight of our words. But the reverse has ever been our lot. The causes for tears, forsooth, are constant, the grief and the groaning are continuous, and we are unable to speak except of what concerns us. For the proverb says: "Where the grief is, there is also the tongue and hand." The deaths of the Christians are frequent and the captures which we see daily. Moreover, the wasting away of the church in the East afflicts with ineradicable grief us who, tortured internally even to our destruction, are dying while living in anguish of soul, and, leading a life more bitter than death, as a culmination of our miseries, are wholly unable to die. Nor is there anyone who turns his heart towards us and out of pity directs his hand to aid us. But not to protract our words, the few Christians who are here cry out to you, together with us, and implore your clemency, which with God's assistance is sufficient to liberate us and the church of God in the East.

And now we will tell you of all the events which have happened to us. In the Lent which has just passed, a certain one (Nourrddin) of the men who are about us, who is held as chief among the Saracens, and who oppresses our Christian population far more than all who have gone before, and the leader of his army . . . having gotten possession of Damascus, the latter entered Egypt with a great force of Turks, in order to conquer the country. . . .

Therefore, the great devastator of the Christian people, who rules near us, collected together from all sides the kings and races of the infidels and offered a peace and truce to our prince and very frequently urged it. His reason was that he wished to traverse our land with greater freedom in order to devastate the kingdom of Jerusalem and to be able to bear aid to his vassal fighting in Egypt. But our prince was unwilling to make peace with him until the return of our lord king.

When the former saw that he was not able to accomplish what he had proposed, full of wrath, he turned his weapons against us and laid siege to a certain fortress of ours, called Harrenc, twelve miles distant from our city. But those who were besieged—7000 in number including warriors, men and women—cried loudly to us, ceasing neither day nor night, to have pity on them, and fixed a day beyond which it would be impossible for them to hold out. Our prince having collected all his forces, set out from Antioch on the day of St. Lawrence and proceeded as far as the fortress in entire safety. For the Turks in their cunning gave up the siege and withdrew a short distance from the fortress to some narrow passes in their own country.

On the next day our men followed the enemy to that place and while they were marching without sufficient circumspection, battle was engaged and they fled. The conflict was so disastrous that hardly anyone of ours of any rank escaped, except a few whom the strength of their horses or some lucky chance rescued from the tumult. . . . Of the people, some were killed, others captured; very few escaped; men, horses and weapons were almost entirely destroyed.

After the slaughter of the Christians the Turks returned to the abovementioned fortress, captured it, and by compact conducted the feeble multitude of women, children and wounded as far as Antioch. Afterwards they advanced to the City, devasted the whole country as far as the sea with fire and sword and exercised their tyranny according to their lusts on everything which met their eyes.

God is witness that the remnant which is left us is in no way sufficient to guard the walls night and day, and owing to the scarcity of men, we are obliged to entrust their safety and defense to some whom we suspect. Neglecting the church services, the clergy and presbyters guard the gates. We ourselves are looking after the defense of the walls and, as far as possible, are repairing, with great and unremitting labor, the many portions which have been broken down by earthquakes. And all this in vain, unless God shall look upon us with a more kindly countenance. For we do not hope to hold out longer, inasmuch as the valor of the men of the present day has been exhausted and is of no avail. But we do, in order that whatever can be done may not be left undone by us.

Above all, the only anchor which is left in this extremity for our hope is in you. Because we have heard from everybody of your greatness, because we have understood that you, more than all the other kings of the West, always have the East in mind. From that we are given to understand that your joy will not be full until you accomplish at some time what we are unable through our misdeeds to accomplish. And it is our hope that by your hand the Lord will visit His people and will have compassion on us.

May the sighings and groanings of the Christians enter the ear of the most high and incomparable prince; may the tortures and griefs of the captives strike his heart! And, not to make our letter too long, lest we should waste away in this vain hope and be for a long time consumed by the shadow of death, may his royal majesty deign to write to us and tell us his pleasure. Whatever we undergo by his command will not be difficult for us. May our Lord Jesus Christ increase in the heart of the king the desire which we desire, and may He in whose hand are the hearts of kings enkindle that heart! Amen.

4. A FRANCISCAN MISSIONARY REPORTS FROM CHINA, 1305

John of Monte Corvino (1247–1328), a Franciscan priest, became the first archbishop of Cambalec (present-day Peiping) in 1307. John, a missionary of great ability and boundless energy, crossed central Asia during a rare interval of peace when that region was controlled by the Mongol Khans. In the early fourteenth century Christians could travel freely and with relative safety through the vast Mongol domains. However, the break-up of the Mongol empire in 1368 brought a long period of turbulence to central Asia, and permanently severed communications between the popes and Christian missionaries in the Far East.

I, Friar John of Monte Corvino, of the order of Minor Friars, departed from Tauris, a city of the Persians, in the year of the Lord 1291, and proceeded to India. And I remained in the country of India, wherein stands the church of St. Thomas the Apostle, for thirteen months, and in that region baptized in different places about one hundred persons. The companion of my journey was Friar Nicholas of Pistoia, of the order of Preachers, who died there, and was buried in the church aforesaid.

I proceeded on my further journey and made my way to Cathay, the realm of the Emperor of the Tartars who is called the Grand Cham. To him I presented the letter of our lord the Pope, and invited him to adopt the Catholic Faith of our Lord Jesus Christ, but he had grown too old in idolatry. However he bestows many kindnesses upon the Christians, and these two years past I am abiding with him. . . .

In this mission I abode alone and without any associate for eleven years; but it is now going on for two years since I was joined by Friar Arnold, a German of the province of Cologne.

I have built a church in the city of Cambaliech, in which the king has his chief residence. This I completed six years ago; and I have built a bell-tower to it, and put three bells in it. I have baptized there, as well as I can estimate, up to this time some 6000 persons; and if those charges against

Letter of John Monte Corvino, in *Cathay and the Way Thither,* translated and edited by Sir Henry Yule, second edition revised by Henri Cordier (London: Hakluyt Society, 1914), Vol. III, Second Series, Vol. 37, pp. 45–51, *passim.* Used by permission of the Hakluyt Society.

me of which I have spoken had not been made, I should have baptized more than 30,000. And I am often still engaged in baptizing.

Also I have gradually bought one hundred and fifty boys, the children of pagan parents, and of ages varying from seven to eleven, who had never learned any religion. These boys I have baptized, and I have taught them Greek and Latin after our manner. Also I have written out Psalters for them, with thirty Hymnaries and two Breviaries. By help of these, eleven of the boys already know our service, and form a choir and take their weekly turn of duty as they do in convents, whether I am there or not. Many of the boys are also employed in writing out Psalters and other things suitable. His Majesty the Emperor moreover delights much to hear them chaunting. I have the bells rung at all the canonical hours, and with my congregation of babes and sucklings I perform divine service, and the chaunting we do by ear because I have no service book with the notes. . . .

Indeed if I had had but two or three comrades to aid me 'tis possible that the Emperor Cham would have been baptized by this time! I ask then for such brethren to come, if any are willing to come, such I mean as will make it their great business to lead exemplary lives. . . .

As for the road hither I may tell you that the way through the land of the Goths, subject to the Emperor of the Northern Tartars, is the shortest and safest; and by it the friars might come, along with the letter-carriers, in five or six months. The other route again is very long and very dangerous, involving two sea-voyages; . . . But, on the other hand, the first-mentioned route has not been open for a considerable time, on account of wars that have been going on.

It is twelve years since I have had any news of the Papal court, or of our Order, or of the state of affairs generally in the west. . . .

I have myself grown old and grey, more with toil and trouble than with years; for I am not more than fifty-eight. I have got a competent knowledge of the language and character which is most generally used by the Tartars. And I have already translated into that language and character the New Testament and the Psalter, and have caused them to be written out in the fairest penmanship they have; and so by writing, reading, and preaching, I bear open and public testimony to the Law of Christ. . . .

As far as I ever saw or heard tell, I do not believe that any king or prince in the world can be compared to his majesty the Cham in respect of the extent of his dominions, the vastness of their population, or the amount of his wealth. Here I stop.

Dated at the city of Cambalec in the kingdom of Cathay, in the year of the Lord 1305, and on the 8th day of January.

10

ECONOMIC REVIVAL

The political expansion of Christian Europe in the twelfth and thirteenth centuries was accompanied by a remarkable economic revival. External maritime commerce developed markedly, partly because of the Crusades to the East. The rise in Mediterranean trade was matched by that of the North and Baltic Sea areas, which came under the domination of the Hanseatic League. As overland trade gradually increased, a number of fairs arose, providing marketing facilities at favorable commercial locations. New towns, outside the feudal structure of society, either fought for or were granted rights as self-governing "communes." Within the towns industry and trade were closely regulated by the guilds. At the same time agricultural life was considerably influenced by the population growth, the eastward expansion, and the decline of serfdom in western Europe.

1. GODRIC, THE BEACHCOMBER, BECOMES A MERCHANT

While historians still disagree about the origins of medieval towns, it is certain that the essential element of town-life was the community of merchants. These merchants had originally been itinerant peddlers, and some, like Godric, acquired great wealth by a combination of luck, hard work, and intelligence. Godric's career had an unusual ending, for he renounced his business life, gave all his possessions to the poor, and became a monk.

. . . how are we to explain the formation of a class of free merchants and artisans in the midst of an exclusively rural society, where serfdom was the normal condition of the people? Scarcity of information prevents us from replying with that precision which the importance of the problem demands, but it is at least possible to indicate the chief factors. First, it is

Henri Pirenne, *Economic and Social History of Medieval Europe,* translated by I.E. Clegg, pp. 46–48. Copyright 1936 by Harcourt, Brace and Company, Inc. Reprinted by permission of Harcourt, Brace and Company, Inc., New York, and Routledge & Kegan Paul Ltd., London.

incontestable that commerce and industry were originally recruited from among landless men, who lived, so to speak, on the margin of a society where land alone was the basis of existence. Now these men were very numerous. Apart altogether from those, who in times of famine or war left their native soil to seek a livelihood elsewhere and returned no more, we have to remember all the individuals whom the manorial organisation itself was unable to support. The peasants' holdings were of such a size as to secure the regular payment of the dues assessed upon them. Thus the younger sons of a man over-burdened with children were often forced to leave their father in order to enable him to make his payments to the lord. Thenceforth they swelled the crowd of vagabonds who roamed through the country, going from abbey to abbey taking their share of alms reserved for the poor, hiring themselves out to the peasants at harvest time or at the vintage, and enlisting as mercenaries in the feudal troops in times of war.

These men were quick to profit by the new means of livelihood offered them by the arrival of ships and merchants along the coasts and in the river estuaries. Many of the more adventurous certainly hired themselves to the Venetian and Scandinavian boats as sailors; others joined the merchant caravans which took their way more and more frequently to the "ports". With luck, the best among them could not fail to seize the many opportunities of making a fortune, which commercial life offered to the vagabonds and adventurers who threw themselves into it with energy and intelligence. Strong probability would suffice to support such a reconstruction of the facts, even if we did not possess, in the story of St. Godric of Finchale, a valuable example of the way in which the *nouveaux riches* were then formed. Godric was born towards the end of the eleventh century in Lincolnshire of poor peasant stock and, forced, no doubt, to leave his parents' holding, he must have had to use all his wits to get a living. Like many other unfortunates in every age he became a beachcomber, on the look-out for wreckage thrown up by the waves. Shipwrecks were numerous and one fine day a lucky chance furnished him with a windfall which enabled him to get together a pedlar's pack. He had amassed a little store of money, when he met with and joined a band of merchants. Their business prospered and he soon made enough profit to enable him to form a partnership with others, in common with whom he loaded a ship and engaged in coastal trade along the shores of England, Scotland, Flanders and Denmark. The partnership prospered. Its operations consisted in taking abroad goods which were known to be scarce there and bringing back a return cargo, which was then exported to places where the demand was greatest and where, in consequence, the largest profits could be realised.

The story of Godric was certainly that of many others. In an age when local famines were continual, one had only to buy a very small quantity of grain cheaply in regions where it was abundant, to realize fabulous profits, which could then be increased by the same methods. Thus speculation, which is the starting-point in this kind of business, largely contributed to the foundation of the first commercial fortunes. The savings of a little pedlar, a sailor, a boatman, or a docker, furnished him with quite enough capital, if only he knew how to use it. . . .

2. *THE COMMUNE OF LAON REVOLTS AGAINST ITS BISHOP*

In 1115 the town of Laon in northern France revolted against its bishop and the nobility. The townsmen, who had endured for years the extortion of the nobles and the tyranny of the bishop, suddenly rose in a violent and bloody orgy of revenge. The events at Laon were recorded by the abbot of a nearby monastery.

Now after some time when he [Bishop of Laon] had set out for England to extract money from the English king, whom he had served, and who had formerly been his friend, the Archdeacons Walter and Guy, with the nobles of the city, devised the following plan: Of old time such ill-fate had settled upon that city that neither God nor any lord was feared therein, but according to each man's power and lust the state involved in rapine and murder. For to begin with the source of the plague, whenever it happened that the king came there, he who ought to have exacted respect for himself with royal severity, was himself first shamefully fined on his own property. When his horses were led to the water morning or evening, his grooms were beaten and the horses carried off. It was known that the very clergy were held in such contempt, that neither their persons nor their goods were spared, as it is written, "Like as the people, so the priest." But what shall I say about the baser people? No one of the countrymen came into the city, no one except under the safest conduct approached it, who was not thrown into prison and held to ransom, or was not, as opportunity served, drawn without cause into a lawsuit.

As an example let me adduce one practice, which occurring amongst barbarians or Scythians, men having no code of laws, would be regarded as most iniquitous. When on the Saturday the country populace from different parts came there to buy and sell, the townfolk carried round as for sale, beans, barley or any kind of corn in cup and platter or other kind of measure in the marketplace, and when they had offered them for sale to the countrymen seeking such things, the latter having settled the price

The Autobiography of Guibert, Abbot of Nogent-sous-Coucy, translated by C.C. Swinton Bland (London: George Routledge & Sons, Ltd., 1925), pp. 152–155, 157–159, 161–164. Used by permission of Routledge & Kegan Paul Ltd., London.

promised to buy. "Follow me," said the seller, "to my house that you may there see the rest of the corn which I am selling you, and when you have seen it, may take it away." He followed, but when he came to the bin, the honest seller, having raised and held up the lid, would say, "Bend your head and shoulders over the bin, that you may see that the bulk does not differ from the sample which I shewed you in the market-place." And when the buyer getting up on the pediment of the bin leaned his belly over it, the worthy seller standing behind lifted up his feet and pushed the unwary man into the bin, and having put the lid down on him as he fell, kept him in safe prison until he ransomed himself. Such and like things were done in the city. No one was safe going out at night. There remained for him nothing but plunder, capture or murder.

The clergy with the archdeacons considering this, and the nobles catching at pretexts for exacting money from the people, offer them through agents the choice of making composition by paying a sum to cover them. Now Commune is a new and a bad name of an arrangement for all the poorest classes to pay their usual due of servitude to their lords once only in the year, and to make good any breach of the laws they have committed by the payment fixed by law, and to be entirely free from all other exactions usually imposed on serfs. The people seizing on this opportunity for freeing themselves gathered huge sums of money to fill the gaping mouths of so many greedy men. And they, pleased with the shower poured upon them, took oaths binding themselves in the matter.

A pledge of mutual aid had been thus exchanged by the clergy and nobles with the people, when the Bishop returned with much wealth from England and being moved to anger against those responsible for this innovation, for a long time kept away from the city. . . .

Saying therefore that he was moved with relentless wrath against those who had taken that oath and the principals in the transaction, in the end his loud-sounding words were suddenly quieted by the offer of a great heap of silver and gold. Therefore he swore that he would maintain the rights of the Commune according to the terms duly drawn up at Noyon and Saint-Quintin. The King too was induced by a bribe from the people to confirm the same by oath. O my God, who could say how many disputes arose when the gifts of the people were accepted, how many after oath had been sworn to reverse what they had agreed to, whilst they sought to bring back the serfs who had been freed from the oppression of their yoke, to their former state. At least there was implacable hate by the Bishop and nobles against the citizens. . . . Whenever one of the people entered a court of law, where he was dependent not on the justice of God, but on his ability to please his judges, if I may say so, he was drained of his substance to the last penny. . . .

Having therefore summoned the nobles and certain of the clergy on the last day of Lent in the holy days of the Passion of our Lord . . . [the Bishop] determined to urge the annulment of the Commune, to which he had sworn, and had by bribes induced the King to swear, and the day before the Passover, that is to say, on the day of the Lord's Supper, he summoned the King to this pious duty and instructed the King and all his people to break their oaths. . . .

The compact of the Commune being broken, such rage, such amazement seized the citizens that all the officials abandoned their duties and the stalls of the craftsmen and cobblers were closed and nothing was exposed for sale by the innkeepers and hucksters, who expected to have nothing left when the lords began plundering. For at once the property of all was calculated by the Bishop and nobles, and whatever any man was known to have given to arrange the Commune, so much was demanded of him to procure its annulment. . . . All the efforts of the prelate and the nobles in these days were reserved for fleecing their inferiors. But those inferiors were no longer moved by mere anger, but goaded into a murderous lust for the death of the Bishop and his accomplices and bound themselves by oath to effect their purpose. Now they say that four hundred took the oath. . . .

The next day, that is, the fifth in Easter week, after midday, as . . . [the Bishop] was engaged in business with Archdeacon Walter about the getting of money, behold there arose a disorderly noise throughout the city, men shouting 'Commune!' and again through the middle of the chapel of the Blessed Mary through that door by which the murderers of Gerard had come and gone, there citizens now entered the Bishop's court with swords, battle-axes, bows and hatchets, and carrying clubs and spears, a very great company. As soon as this sudden attack was discovered, the nobles rallied from all sides to the Bishop, having sworn to give him aid against such an onset, if it should occur. In this rally Guinimon, the chatelain, an aged nobleman of handsome presence and guiltless character, armed only with shield and spear, ran out through the church and as he entered the Bishop's hall, was the first to fall, struck on the back of the head with a battle-axe by a certain Rainbert, who was his fellow-citizen. . . .

Next the outrageous mob attacking the Bishop and howling before the walls of his palace, he with some who were succouring him fought them off by hurling of stones and shooting of arrows. For he now, as at all times, shewed great spirit as a fighter; but because he had wrongly and in vain taken up another sword, by the sword he perished. Therefore being unable to stand against the reckless assaults of the people, he put on the clothes of one of his servants and flying to the vaults of the church hid himself in a cask, shut up in which with the head fastened on by a faithful follower he thought himself safely hidden. And as they ran hither and thither demanding where, not the Bishop, but the hangdog, was, they seized one of his pages, but through his faithfulness could not get what they wanted. Laying hands on another, they learn from the traitor's nod where to look for him. Entering the vaults, therefore, and searching everywhere, at last they found him. . . .

. . . And as he piteously implored them, ready to take oath that he would henceforth cease to be their Bishop, that he would give them unlimited riches, that he would leave the country, and as they with hardened hearts jeered at him, one named Bernard . . . lifting his battle-axe brutally dashed out the brains of that sacred, though sinner's, head, and he slipping between the hands of those who held him, was dead before he reached the ground stricken by another thwart blow under the eye-sockets and across the middle of the nose. . . .

3. *THE GARMENT CUTTERS OF STENDAL REVISE THEIR GUILD LAWS*

Industry in the Early Middle Age had been the work of serfs on the manor, providing for local needs. With the growth of towns, however, free craftsmen became numerous and sought mutual advantages by forming craft guilds. The following selection is from guild regulations of Stendal, drawn up in 1231.

. . . John and Otto, by the grace of God, margraves of Brandenburg. . . . We make known . . . that we . . . desiring to provide properly for our city of Stendal, have changed, and do change, for the better, the laws of the gild brethren, and of those who are called cloth-cutters, so that they might have the same laws in this craft as their gild brethren the garment-cutters in Magdeburg have been accustomed to observe in the past.

These are the laws:

1. No one shall presume to cut cloth, except he be of our craft; those who break this rule will amend to the gild with three talents.

2. Thrice a year there ought to be a meeting of the brethren, and whoever does not come to it will amend according to justice.

3. Whoever wishes to enter the fraternity whose father was a brother and cut cloth will come with his friends to the meeting of the brethren, and if he conduct himself honestly, he will be able to join the gild at the first request on payment of five solidi, and he will give six denarii to the master. And if he be dishonest and should not conduct himself well, he should be put off until the second or third meeting. But any of our citizens who wish to enter the gild, if he be an honest man, and worthy, will give

Roy C. Cave and Herbert H. Coulson, *A Source Book for Medieval Economic History* (Milwaukee, Wis.: The Bruce Publishing Company, 1936), pp. 246–247.

a talent to the brethren on entry into the gild, and will present a solidus to the master. But if a guest who is an honest man should decide to join our fraternity, he will give thirty solidi to the gild on his entry, and eighteen denarii to the master.

4. But in the time of the fairs, that is of the annual fair, any guest, even if he be not of the craft, will be able to cut cloth during the whole fair.

5. If any of our burgesses holding office wish to enter the crafts he will abjure his office, and, on entrance to the gild, will present one mark of gold freely to the brethren, and to the master eighteen denarii.

6. If any brother has been accustomed to prepare cloth in his house and is wont to cut or sell it at the wish of others, he will either cease or have no part in his fraternity.

7. Whatever two parts of the brethren have decreed to do the third part ought to consent to do; but if that third be unwilling, each will amend with three solidi, and will pay them at the next meeting.

8. Every year a master and four other good men who shall preside over the affairs of the gild will be faithfully chosen.

9. Moreover whoever goes contrary to these decrees and is unwilling to obey the master and brethren according to justice, his contumacy ought to be referred to the judgment of his superior. . . .

4. LÜBECK AND HAMBURG SEEK MUTUAL PROTECTION

In the thirteenth century the port cities of the Baltic and North Sea areas drew together to combat common problems of piracy, excessive customs, and discrimination. The treaty of Lübeck and Hamburg in 1241, presented below, led to a league of German towns, the Hanseatic League.

The advocate and common council of Lübeck. . . . We have made an agreement with our beloved friends the citizens of Hamburg.

1. That if by chance robbers or other evil men rise against our citizens or theirs, from that place where the river which is called the Trave flows into the sea to Hamburg, and thence along the Elbe to the sea, and if they assail our citizens or theirs, whatever costs or expenses are incurred for extirpating those robbers we ought to share with them, and they with us.

2. If by chance any criminal should outrageously kill, wound, beat, or, God forbid, in any way ill-treat outside the city any burgess of Hamburg or Lübeck whom he has accused, whatever expense is incurred in taking him and punishing him, we shall share with them and they with us,

Roy C. Cave and Herbert H. Coulson, *A Source Book for Medieval Economic History* (Milwaukee, Wis.: The Bruce Publishing Company, 1936), pp. 232–233.

this condition being added, that whatever happens to their citizens near their city, and to our citizens near our city, they with their citizens, and we with ours, shall punish at the expense of the city.

3. Further, if any burgesses of theirs near our city of Lübeck, or our burgesses near the city of Hamburg, should be ill-treated, we shall surrender the doer or doers of the deed for punishment, and they will surrender such people to us at the expense of the commune likewise.

5. THE MERCHANTS FIND INCONVENIENCES AT THE WESTMINSTER FAIR

To the merchants who traded with distant lands the medieval fair was a vital institution serving as both bank and market. In addition, kings and nobles usually found it profitable to encourage fairs in their domains.

. . . The king then declared it as his pleasure, and ordered it to be proclaimed by herald throughout the whole city of London, and elsewhere, that he instituted a new fair to be held at Westminster, to continue for a fortnight entire. He also strictly interdicted, under penalty of heavy forfeiture and loss, all fairs which usually lasted for such a length of time in England; for instance, that of Ely and other places, and all traffic usually carried on at London, both in and out of doors, in order that by these means the Westminster fair might be more attended by people, and better supplied with merchandise. . . . But all the merchants, in exposing their goods for sale there, were exposed to great inconveniences, as they had no shelter except canvas tents; for owing to the changeable gusts of wind assailing them, as is usual at that time of the year, they were cold and wet, and also suffered from hunger and thirst; their feet were soiled by the mud, and their goods rotted by the showers of rain. . . .

Roy C. Cave and Herbert H. Coulson, *A Source Book for Medieval Economic History* (Milwaukee, Wis.: The Bruce Publishing Company, 1936), p. 125. Copyright 1936 by The Bruce Publishing Company. Used by permission.

6. ST. THOMAS AQUINAS EXPLAINS USURY AND THE JUST PRICE

St. Thomas Aquinas (1225–1274) was a Dominican theologian, whose most important work, the* Summa Theologica, *based on Aristotelian rationalism, summarizes theological knowledge. His views on usury and a just price reflect accurately

St. Thomas Aquinas, *Summa Theologica,* Part II, Second Number, QQ LXXVII–LXXVIII, translated by the Fathers of the English Dominican Province (London: Benziger Brothers, Inc., 1918), pp. 327–328, 330–331, 336–337. Used by permission of Benziger Brothers, Inc., New York, Publishers and Copyright Owners, and Burns Oates & Washbourne Ltd., London.

canon law decrees of the Church. At that time any interest on loans was considered usury.

. . . A tradesman is one whose business consists in the exchange of things. . . . exchange of things is twofold; one, natural as it were, and necessary, whereby one commodity is exchanged for another, or money taken in exchange for a commodity, in order to satisfy the needs of life. Suchlike trading, properly speaking, does not belong to tradesmen, but rather to housekeepers or civil servants who have to provide the household or the state with the necessaries of life. The other kind of exchange is either that of money for money, or of any commodity for money, not on account of the necessities of life, but for profit, and this kind of exchange, properly speaking, regards tradesmen. . . . The former kind of exchange is commendable because it supplies a natural need: but the latter is justly deserving of blame, because, considered in itself, it satisfies the greed for gain, which knows no limit and tends to infinity. Hence trading, considered in itself, has a certain debasement attaching thereto, in so far as, by its very nature, it does not imply a virtuous or necessary end. Nevertheless gain which is the end of trading, though not implying, by its nature, anything virtuous or necessary, does not, in itself, connote anything sinful or contrary to virtue: . . .

Not everyone that sells at a higher price than he bought is a tradesman, but only he who buys that he may sell at a profit. If, on the contrary, he buys not for sale but for possession, and afterwards, for some reason wishes to sell, it is not a trade transaction even if he sell at a profit. For he may lawfully do this, either because he has bettered the thing, or because the value of the thing has changed with the change of place or time, or on account of the danger he incurs in transferring the thing from one place to another, or again in having it carried by another. In this sense neither buying nor selling is unjust. . . .

To take usury for money lent is unjust in itself, because this is to sell what does not exist, and this evidently leads to inequality which is contrary to justice.

In order to make this evident, we must observe that there are certain things the use of which consists in their consumption: thus we consume wine when we use it for drink, and we consume wheat when we use it for food. Wherefore in suchlike things the use of the thing must not be reckoned apart from the thing itself, and whoever is granted the use of the thing, is granted the thing itself; and for this reason, to lend things of this kind is to transfer the ownership. Accordingly if a man wanted to sell wine separately from the use of the wine, he would be selling the same thing twice, or he would be selling what does not exist, wherefore he would evidently commit a sin of injustice. In like manner he commits an injustice who lends wine or wheat, and asks for double payment, viz. one, the return of the thing in equal measure, the other, the price of the use, which is called usury.

On the other hand there are things the use of which does not consist in their consumption: thus to use a house is to dwell in it, not to destroy it. Wherefore in such things both may be granted: for instance, one man may hand over to another the ownership of his house while reserving to himself the use of it for a time, or vice versa, he may grant the use of the house, while retaining the ownership. For this reason a man may lawfully make a charge for the use of his house, and, besides this, revendicate the house from the person to whom he has granted its use, as happens in renting and letting a house.

Now money . . . was invented chiefly for the purpose of exchange: and consequently the proper and principal use of money is its consumption or alienation whereby it is sunk in exchange. Hence it is by its very nature unlawful to take payment for the use of money lent, which payment is known as usury: and just as a man is bound to restore other ill-gotten goods, so is he bound to restore the money which he has taken in usury. . . .

. . . he that entrusts his money to a merchant or craftsman so as to form a kind of society, does not transfer the ownership of his money to them for it remains his, so that at his risk the merchant speculates with it, or the craftsman uses it for his craft, and consequently he may lawfully demand as something belonging to him, part of the profits derived from his money.

7. A SARACEN ARRANGES A SEA LOAN AT MARSEILLES

By the thirteenth century the Mediterranean ports of Christian Europe were conducting a thriving business with Moslem lands, as this selection indicates. As this is a sea loan, the borrower, al-Hakim, agrees to repay the loan only if the ship carrying the goods for which he borrowed the money arrives safely in port.

MARSEILLES, APRIL 2, 1227. . . . Be it known to all that I, al-Hakim, Saracen of Alexandria, acknowledge and recognize that I have had and have received, by virute of a purchase from you, Bernard Manduel, 2 quintals of Socotran aloes and 1 quintal 80 pounds of cassia bark, and 2 *cen-*

Robert S. Lopez and Irving W. Raymond, *Medieval Trade in the Mediterranean World* (New York: Columbia University Press, 1955), pp. 170–171.

tenaria of coral, for all of which I owe you 135 bezants . . . waiving, with my full knowledge, the exception that the goods have not been delivered to me. And these 135 bezants . . . I promise by stipulation to pay fully and to deliver peacefully to you, said Bernard, or to your accredited messenger, in Ceuta within a space of twenty days after the ship 'The Falcon' arrives there. And for these I pledge to you as security all the aforesaid goods which I bought from you, and these goods are to go and remain at your risk for the said value of 135 bezants and any surplus value (to be) at my (risk). (This is to be) so done that if I do not pay you the said 135 bezants by the established time limit, you are then to be permitted on your own authority to sell all said security or to pledge (it) as security, and to do what you want with it, until you have been fully paid of the aforesaid 135 bezants . . . just as has been stated above. And I (also) promise in good faith, under pledge of all my goods, to restore to you the whole of what (may) be lacking. And I waive in regard to all this the period of grace of twenty days and four months and any other delay and any legal (rights). This was done in a certain house of the late Anselme, in which Januaire, notary, lives. . . . I, Januaire, public notary of Marseilles, by commission of both parties, wrote this.

8. *THE VENETIAN SENATE CONDEMNS A COTTON MONOPOLY*

Medieval town governments often encouraged cartels and monopolies, if the purpose lay in securing an advantage for the townsmen against foreigners. In the selection below, however, the cotton cartel was condemned on the grounds that the members were seeking only their own profit against the interests of their fellow-Venetians.

VENICE, APRIL 28, [1358]. On April 28 (motion was) passed (in the Senate as follows):

Whereas our (fellow citizens) frequenting Cyprus have of late engaged in the formation of rings and conspiracies . . . in the business of transporting cotton to Venice, entering upon mutual obligations and pacts to prevent the transport of more than a certain amount (of cotton);

And (whereas) this is against the interest of the Commune, which loses its customs duties upon what would be imported and used to be imported beyond the said amount; and it is also against the welfare of the city because cotton needed in the West is transported to Ancona and elsewhere

Robert S. Lopez and Irving W. Raymond, *Medieval Trade in the Mediterranean World* (New York: Columbia University Press, 1955), pp. 129–130.

while it ought to be transported to Venice, and (thus the conspirators) are building up foreign countries while ruining ours; and it is also against the good of the community and of individual persons because such profits as used to be distributed among the whole community is turned over to three or four (persons);

And (whereas) it is useful in view of all above considerations to provide a remedy to this (situation):

Let a motion be put to vote that three wisemen shall be elected within the assembly of the Senate, who shall make an inquiry in regard to these rings (of dealers) in cotton as well as to (others dealing) in powdered sugar, salt, and other merchandise, and also in regard to those in shipping and to all conspiracies that may be formed in Venice, in Cyprus, and in any other place. And they shall draft provisions and give us their advice in writing. We shall meet here with this (advice at hand), and we shall act as shall seem proper, and any one (of us) shall be entitled to put a motion to vote. And (the wisemen) may be chosen from any post, but each is to accept only one office.

And the first vote is to be for the said proposal and (its individual) articles, and the second for the election (of the wisemen).

And (the wisemen) are to have as a deadline (for the completion of the inquiry) the end of the coming month of May.

9. *A SERF GAINS HIS FREEDOM*

In the thirteenth and fourteenth centuries serfdom declined greatly in western Europe, as individual serfs either purchased their freedom, or were freely granted it, or ran away from the manor.

Be it manifest to all by these presents that we, brother Robert, Abbot of Stoneleigh, and the convent of the same place, have granted for us and our successors that Geoffrey son of the late William Austyn of Wottonhull be free of his body with all his brood and his chattels hereafter for ever; so that neither we nor our successors shall be able to demand or claim anything in him or his brood or his chattels, but by these presents we are wholly excluded. In witness whereof we have put our seal to these presents. Given at Stonle on Monday next after the feast of the Purification of the Blessed Virgin Mary in the eighth year of the reign of King Edward the third after the conquest.

A.E. Bland, P.A. Brown, and R.H. Tawney, eds., *English Economic History: Select Documents* (London: G. Bell & Sons, Ltd., 1925), pp. 97–98. Used by permission of the publisher.

11

CONSOLIDATION OF FEUDAL MONARCHY IN WESTERN EUROPE

Although the forms of feudalism still dominated government in the High Middle Age, considerable progress was achieved in the centralizing of royal power in England and France. The Norman-French kings of England in the twelfth century extended royal justice, often at the expense of ecclesiastical jurisdiction. In the next century English kings lost ground to the feudal barons, as seen in Magna Carta and the Provisions of Oxford. Edward I stabilized government at the end of the thirteenth century by calling representatives from four classes to meet as a parliament. On the other hand, French kings after the ninth century faced an immense task of re-establishing royal authority in the great fiefs of France. Philip II (Augustus), king from 1180 to 1223, was notably successful in extending royal control. His successors, Louis IX and Philip IV, were equally able rulers, one a saint, the other decidedly unsaintly.

1. THOMAS A. BECKET IS MURDERED IN CANTERBURY CATHEDRAL

Under Henry II, a vigorous proponent of strong monarchy, royal justice was considerably expanded in England, sometimes in conflict with ecclesiastical jurisdiction. In the controversy of royal* vs. *canon law, Henry encountered bitter opposition from the Archbishop of Canterbury, Thomas à Becket, formerly his loyal chancellor. An idle remark by the irritated king was interpreted by his followers as an invitation to assassinate Becket, the execution of whom is described below.

Edward Grim, *Materials for the History of Archbishop Becket*, translated by W.H. Hutton (London: 1889), Rolls Series, Vol. II, p. 430, as found in Charles W. Colby, *Selections from the Sources of English History* (New York: Longmans, Green and Co., 1905), pp. 56–59.

When the monks had entered the church, already the four knights followed behind with rapid strides. With them was a certain subdeacon, armed with malice like their own, Hugh, fitly surnamed for his wickedness, Mauclerc, who showed no reverence for God or the saints, as the result showed. When the holy archbishop entered the church, the monks stopped vespers which they had begun and ran to him, glorifying God that they saw their father, whom they had heard was dead, alive and safe. They hastened, by bolting the doors of the church, to protect their shepherd from the slaughter. But the champion, turning to them, ordered the church doors to be thrown open, saying, "It is not meet to make a fortress of the house of prayer, the church of Christ: though it be not shut up it is able to protect its own; and we shall triumph over the enemy rather in suffering than in fighting, for we came to suffer, not to resist." And straightway they entered the house of peace and reconciliation with swords sacrilegiously drawn, causing horror to the beholders by their very looks and the clanging of their arms.

All who were present were in tumult and fright, for those who had been singing vespers now ran hither to the dreadful sight.

Inspired by fury the knights called out, "Where is Thomas Becket, traitor to the king and realm?" As he answered not they cried out the more furiously, "Where is the archbishop?" At this, intrepid and fearless, as is written, "The just, like a bold lion, shall be without fear," he descended from the stair where he had been dragged by the monks in fear of the knights, and in a clear voice answered, "I am here, no traitor to the king, but a priest. Why do ye seek me?" And whereas he had already said that he feared them not, he added, "So I am ready to suffer in His name, Who redeemed me by His Blood: be it far from me to flee from your swords, or to depart from justice." Having thus said, he turned to the right, under a pillar, having on one side the altar of the blessed Mother of God and ever Virgin Mary, on the other that of St. Benedict the Confessor: by whose example and prayers, having crucified the world with its lusts, he bore all that the murderer could do with such constancy of soul as if he had been no longer in the flesh. The murderers followed him; "Absolve," they cried, "and restore to communion those whom you have excommunicated, and restore their powers to those whom you have suspended." He answered: "There has been no satisfaction, and I will not absolve them." "Then you shall die," they cried, "and receive what you deserve." "I am ready," he replied, "to die for my Lord, that in my blood the Church may obtain liberty and peace. But in the name of Almighty God, I forbid you to hurt my people whether clerk or lay." Thus piously and thoughtfully, did the noble martyr provide that no one near him should be hurt or the innocent be brought to death, whereby his glory should be dimmed as he hastened to Christ. Thus did it become the martyr-knight to follow in the footsteps of his Captain and Saviour Who when the wicked sought Him said: "If ye seek Me, let these go their way." Then they laid sacrilegious hands on him, pulling and dragging him that they might kill him outside the Church, or carry him away a prisoner, as they afterwards confessed. But when he could not be forced away from the pillar, one of them pressed on him and clung to him more closely. Him he pushed off calling him "pander," and saying, "Touch me not, Reginald; you owe me fealty and subjection, you and your accomplices act like madmen." The knight, fired with terrible rage at this severe repulse, waved his sword over the sacred head. "No faith," he cried, "nor subjection do I owe you against my fealty to my lord the king." Then the unconquered martyr seeing the hour at hand which should put an end to this miserable life and give him straightway the crown of immortality promised by the Lord, inclined his neck as one who prays, and joining his hands he lifted them up, and commended his cause and that of the Church to God, to S. Mary, and to the blessed martyr Denys. Scarce had he said the words than the wicked knight fearing lest he should be rescued by the people and escape alive, leapt upon him suddenly and wounded this lamb who was sacrificed to God, on the head, cutting off the top of the crown which the sacred unction of the chrism had dedicated to God; and by the same blow he wounded the arm of him who tells this. For he, when the others, both monks and clerks, fled, stuck close to the sainted archbishop and held him in his arms till the one he interposed was almost severed. Behold the simplicity of the dove, the wisdom of the serpent, in the martyr who opposed his body to those who struck that he might preserve his head, that is his soul and the Church, unharmed, nor would he use any forethought against those who destroyed the body whereby he might escape. O worthy shepherd, who gave himself so boldly to the wolves that his flock might not be torn. Because he had rejected the world, the world in wishing to crush him unknowingly exalted him. Then he received a second blow on the head but still stood firm. At the third blow he fell on his knees and elbows, offering himself a living victim, and saying in a low voice, "For the name of Jesus and the protection of the Church I am ready to embrace death." Then the third knight inflicted a terrible wound as he lay, by which the sword was broken against the pavement, and the crown which was large was separated from the head; so that the blood white with brain and the brain red with blood, dyed the surface of the virgin mother Church with the life and death of the confessor and martyr in the colours of the lily and the rose. The fourth knight prevented any from interfering so that the others might freely perpetrate the murder. As to the fifth, no knight but that clerk who had entered with the knights, that a fifth blow might not be wanting to the martyr who was in other things like to Christ, he put his foot on the neck of the holy priest and precious martyr, and, horrible to say, scattered the brains and blood over the pavement, calling out to the others: "Let us away, knights; he will rise no more."

2. *KING JOHN MEETS THE BARONS AT RUNNYMEDE*

Royal power, which had expanded under Henry II, declined notably in the reign of his son John (1199–1216). Following the loss of most of his possessions in France, John faced a revolt of his feudal barons in England. The rebellious barons in June, 1215, forced John to sign the Great Charter (Magna Carta), which defined the relationship of lord and vassal. Though originally a feudal document, Magna Carta was later interpreted as a guarantee of the rights of all Englishmen, and a landmark on the road to limited monarchy.

King John, when he saw that he was deserted by almost all, so that out of his regal superabundance of followers he scarcely retained seven knights, was much alarmed lest the barons would attack his castles and reduce them without difficulty, as they would find no obstacle to their so doing; and he deceitfully pretended to make peace for a time with the aforesaid barons, and sent William Marshal earl of Pembroke, with other trustworthy messengers, to them, and told them that, for the sake of peace, and for the exaltation and honour of the kingdom, he would willingly grant them the laws and liberties they required; he also sent word to the barons by these same messengers, to appoint a fitting day and place to meet and carry all these matters into effect. The king's messengers then came in all haste to London, and without deceit reported to the barons all that had been deceitfully imposed on them; they in their great joy appointed the fifteenth of June for the king to meet them, at a field lying between Staines and Windsor. Accordingly, at the time and place pre-agreed on, the king and nobles came to the appointed conference, and when each party had stationed themselves apart from the other, they began a long discussion about terms of peace and the aforesaid liberties. . . . At length, after various points on both sides had been discussed, king John, seeing that he was inferior in strength to the barons, without raising any difficulty, granted the underwritten laws and liberties, and confirmed them by his charter. . . .

Roger of Wendover, *Flowers of History,* translated by J.A. Giles (London: Henry G. Born, 1849), Vol. II, pp. 308–309.

3. *MAGNA CARTA SETS A LIMIT TO ROYAL POWER*

John, by the grace of God, King of England, Lord of Ireland, Duke of Normandy and Aquitaine, Count of Anjou, to the archbishops, bishops, abbots, earls, barons, justiciars, foresters, sheriffs, reeves, servants, and all bailiffs and his faithful people greeting. Know that by the suggestion of God and for the good of our soul and those of all our predecessors and of our heirs, to the honor of God and the exaltation of holy church, and the improvement of our kingdom, by the advice of our venerable fathers . . . and of the noblemen . . . and others of our faithful.

1. In the first place we have granted to God, and by this our present charter confirmed, for us and our heirs forever, that the English church shall be free, and shall hold its rights entire and its liberties uninjured; and we will that it be thus observed; which is shown by this, that the freedom of elections, which is considered to be most important and especially necessary to the English church, we, of our pure and spontaneous will, granted, and by our charter confirmed, before the contest between us and our barons had arisen; and obtained a confirmation of it by the lord Pope Innocent III.; which we will observe and which we will shall be observed in good faith by our heirs forever. We have granted moreover to all free men of our kingdom for us and our heirs forever all the liberties written below, to be had and holden for themselves and their heirs from us and our heirs. . . .

9. Neither we nor our bailiffs will seize any land or rent for any debt, so long as the chattels of the debtor are sufficient for the payment of the debt; nor shall the pledges of a debtor be distrained so long as the principal debtor himself has enough for the payment of the debt; and if the principal debtor fails in the payment of the debt, not having the wherewithal to pay it, the pledges shall be responsible for the debt; and if they wish, they shall have the lands and the rents of the debtor until they shall have been satisfied for the debt which they have before paid for him, unless the principal debtor shall have shown himself to be quit in that respect towards those pledges. . . .

13. And the city of London shall have all its ancient liberties and free customs, as well by land as by water. Moreover, we will and grant that all other cities and boroughs and villages and ports should have all their liberties and free customs. . . .

28. No constable or other bailiff of ours shall take anyone's grain or other chattels, without immediately paying for them in money, unless he is able to obtain a postponement at the good-will of the seller. . . .

Translations and Reprints from the Original Sources of European History (Philadelphia: University of Pennsylvania, 1894), Series I, Vol. I, No. 6, pp. 7, 9, 11–12, 15, 17.

35. There shall be one measure of wine throughout our whole kingdom, and one measure of ale, and one measure of grain, that is the London quarter, and one width of dyed cloth and of russets and of halbergets, that is two ells within the selvages; of weights, moreover it shall be as of measures.

36. Nothing shall henceforth be given or taken for a writ of inquisition concerning life or limbs, but it shall be given freely and not denied. . . .

38. No bailiff for the future shall place any one to his law on his simple affirmation, without credible witnesses brought for this purpose.

39. No free man shall be taken or imprisoned or dispossessed, or outlawed, or banished, or in any way destroyed, nor will we go upon him, nor send upon him, except by the legal judgment of his peers or by the law of the land.

40. To no one will we sell, to no one will we deny, or delay right or justice. . . .

60. Moreover, all those customs and franchises mentioned above which we have conceded in our kingdom, and which are to be fulfilled, as far as pertains to us, in respect to our men; all men of our kingdom, as well clergy as laymen, shall observe as far as pertains to them, in respect to their men. . . .

63. . . . Witness the above named and many others. Given by our hand in the meadow which is called Runnymede, between Windsor and Staines, on the fifteenth day of June, in the seventeenth year of our reign.

4. EDWARD I SUMMONS THE "MODEL PARLIAMENT"

Edward I (1272–1307), in carrying out a vigorous foreign policy and an ambitious legislative program, found it advantageous to expand his Great Council or Parliament to include representatives of the urban and rural middle classes. The "Model Parliament" of 1295 was not the first meeting of such representative groups, but most later Parliaments were composed of the same elements as that of 1295: great nobles, high clergy, knights of the shire, and burgesses.

The King to the venerable father in Christ, Robert, by the same grace Archbishop of Canterbury, primate of all England, greeting. As a most just law, established by the careful providence of sacred princes, exhorts and decrees that what affects all, should be approved by all, so also, very evidently should common danger be met by means provided in common. You know sufficiently well, and it is now, as we believe, known through all regions of the world, how the King of France fraudulently and craftily de-

Elizabeth Kimball Kendall, ed., *Source-Book of English History* (New York: The Macmillan Company, 1900), pp. 89–91.

prived us of our land of Gascony, by withholding it unjustly from us. Now, however, not satisfied with the aforesaid fraud and injustice, having gathered together for the conquest of our kingdom a very great fleet, and a very large force of warriors, with which he has made a hostile attack on our kingdom and the inhabitants of the kingdom, he now proposes to stamp out the English language altogether from the earth if his power should be equal to the detestable task of the proposed iniquity, which God forbid. Because, therefore, darts seen beforehand do less injury, and your interest especially, as that of other fellow citizens of the same realm, is concerned in this affair, we command you, strictly enjoining you in the fidelity and love in which you are bound to us, that on the Lord's day next after the feast of St. Martin, in the approaching winter, you be present in person at Westminster; citing beforehand the dean and chapter of your church, the archdeacons and all the clergy of your diocese, causing the same dean and archdeacons in their own persons, and the said chapter by one suitable proctor, and the said clergy by two, to be present along with you, having full and sufficient power of themselves from the chapter and clergy, for considering, ordaining and providing along with us and with the rest of the prelates and principal men and other inhabitants of our kingdom how the dangers and threatened evils of this kind are to be met. Witness, the King at Wengham, the thirtieth day of September. (Like summons were sent to the Archbishop of York, to eighteen bishops, and with the omission of the last paragraph, to seventy abbots and other great churchmen.)

The King to his beloved and faithful kinsman, Edmund, Earl of Cornwall, greeting. Because we wish to have a conference and meeting with you and with the rest of the principal men of our kingdom, to provide remedies for the dangers which in these days threaten our whole kingdom; we command you, strictly enjoining you by the fidelity and love in which you are bound to us, that on the Lord's day next after the feast of St. Martin, in the approaching winter, you be present in person at Westminster, for considering, ordaining and doing with us, and with the prelates, and the rest of the magnates and other inhabitants of our kingdom, as may be necessary to meet dangers of this kind. Witness, the King at Canterbury, on the first day of October. (Like summons were sent to seven earls and forty-one barons.)

The King to the sheriff of Northamptonshire. Since we purpose to have a conference and meeting, with the earls, barons, and other principal men of our kingdom to provide remedies for the dangers which in these days threaten the same kingdom; and on that account, have commanded them to be with us, on the Lord's day next after the feast of St. Martin, in the approaching winter, at Westminster, to consider, ordain, and do, as may be necessary for the avoidance of these dangers; we strictly require you to cause two knights from the aforesaid county, two citizens from each city in the same county, and two burgesses from each borough, of the more discreet and capable, to be elected without delay, and to cause them to come to us, at the aforesaid time and place.

Moreover, the said knights are to have full and sufficient power, for themselves and for the commonalty of the aforesaid county, and the said citizens and burgesses for themselves and for the commonalty of the aforesaid cities and boroughs separately, then and there to do what shall be ordained by the common advice in the premises; so that the aforesaid business shall not remain unfinished in any way for defect of this power. And you shall have there the names of the knights, citizens and burgesses, and this writ.

Witness, the King at Canterbury, on the third day of October. (A like summons was sent to the sheriff of each county.)

5. LOUIS IX COMBINES PIETY WITH A ZEAL FOR JUSTICE

Louis IX (St. Louis), king of France from 1226 to 1270, followed the political tradition set by his grandfather, Philip Augustus. With great energy and remarkable wisdom, he crushed feudal warfare, improved the administration and the collection of taxes, and extended royal justice on the basis of the newly rediscovered Roman law. France, under Louis IX, enjoyed unprecedented peace, prosperity, and cultural progress. Jean de Joinville, author of the following account, was an advisor and close friend of St. Louis.

This holy man, King St. Louis, loved and feared God during his life above all things, and, as is very apparent, was in consequence favoured in all his works. As I have before said that our God died for his people, so in like manner did St. Louis several times risk his life and incur the greatest dangers for the people of his realm, as shall be touched on hereafter.

The good king, being once dangerously ill at Fontainebleau, said to my Lord Louis, his eldest son, "Fair son, I beseech thee to make thyself beloved by the people of thy kingdom; for, in truth, I should like better that a Scotsman, fresh from Scotland, or from any other distant and unknown country, should govern the subjects of my realm well and loyally, than that thou shouldst rule them wickedly and reproachfully."

The holy king loved truth so much, that even to the Saracens and infidels, although they were his enemies, he would never lie, nor break his

Jean de Joinville, Memoires of St. Louis IX, translated by Colonel Johnes in *Chronicles of the Crusades* (London: G. Bell & Sons, Ltd., 1882), pp. 351–353, 355, 363–364.

word in any thing he had promised them, as shall be noticed hereafter. With regard to his food, he was extremely temperate; for I never in my whole life heard him express a wish for any delicacies in eating or drinking, like too many rich men; but he sat and took patiently whatever was set before him.

In his conversation he was remarkably chaste; for I never heard him, at any time, utter an indecent word, nor make use of the devil's name, which, however, is now very commonly uttered by every one, by which I firmly believe is so far from being agreeable to God, that it is highly displeasing to him. . . .

My good lord the king asked me at another time, if I should wish to be honoured in this world, and afterwards to gain paradise; to which I answered, that I should wish it were so. "Then," replied he, "be careful never knowingly to do or say any thing disgraceful, that should it become public, you may not have to blush, and be ashamed to say I have done this, or I have said that." In like manner he told me never to give the lie, or contradict rudely whatever might be said in my presence, unless it should be sinful or disgraceful to suffer it, for oftentimes contradiction causes coarse replies and harsh words, that bring on quarrels, which create bloodshed, and are the means of the deaths of thousands.

He also said, that every one should dress and equip himself according to his rank in life, and his fortune, in order that the prudent and elders of this world may not reproach him, by saying such a one has done too much, and that the youth may not remark, that such a one has done too little, and dishonours his station in society. On this subject, I remember once the good lord king, father to the king now on the throne, speaking of the pomp of dress, and the embroidered coats of arms that are now daily common in the armies. I said to the present king, that when I was in the Holy Land with his father, and in his army, I never saw one single embroidered coat or ornamented saddle in the possession of the king his father, or of any other lord. He answered, that he had done wrong in embroidering his arms; and that he had some coats that had cost him eight hundred Parisian livres. I replied, that he would have acted better if he had given them in charity, and had his dress made of good sendal, lined and strengthened with his arms, like as the king, his father, had done. . . .

He loved every one who, with uprightness of heart, feared and loved God; insomuch that from the great reputation he had heard of my brother Sir Giles de Bruyn, who was not a Frenchman, for his fear and love of God, as was the truth, he appointed him constable of France.

In like manner, from the favourable report which he had heard of Master Robert de Sorbon being a courageous and discreet man, he made him one of his personal attendants, and permitted him to partake of his table. One time, as we were sitting near each other, and eating and drinking at the king's table, we conversed together in a low voice, which the good king observing, reprimanded us by saying, "You act wrong thus to whisper together; speak out, that your companions may not suspect you are talking of them to their disadvantage, and railing at them. When eating in company, if you have any things to say that are pleasant and agreeable, say them aloud, that every one may hear them: if not, be silent." . . .

Many times have I seen this holy saint, after having heard mass in the summer, go and amuse himself in the wood of Vincennes; when, seating himself at the foot of an oak, he would make us seat ourselves round about him, and every one who wished to speak with him came thither without ceremony, and without hindrance from any usher or others. He then demanded aloud if there were any who had complaints to make; and when there were some, he said, "My friends, be silent, and your cause shall be despatched one after another." Then, oftentimes, he called to him the lord Peter de Fontaines, and the lord Geoffrey de Villette, and said to them, "Despatch these causes;" and whenever he heard any thing that could be amended in the speeches of those who pleaded for others, he most graciously corrected them himself. I have likewise seen this good king ofttimes come to the garden of Paris, dressed in a coat of camlet, a surcoat of tyretaine, without sleeves, and a mantle of black sendal, and have carpets spread for us to sit round him, and hear and discuss the complaints of his people with the same diligence as in the wood of Vincennes.

6. CLARICOS LAICOS *FORBIDS ROYAL TAXATION OF THE CLERGY*

Boniface VIII, pope from 1294 to 1303, attempted unsuccessfully to assert papal political supremacy in the face of rising national monarchy in western Europe. In the bull **Clericos Laicos** ***(1296) he tried to prevent Philip IV of France from illegally taxing the clergy. Philip was a formidable opponent, and the dispute was a bitter one, reaching a climax in 1302–1303. Philip responded to*** **Clericos Laicos** ***by cutting off the flow of money from France to Rome. Boniface thereupon issued two further bulls, strongly condemning Philip's action. Philip countered by summoning representatives from the three estates (nobles, clergy, and townsmen) to support his stand. This brief meeting in 1302 was France's first Estates General.***

Bishop Boniface, servant of the servants of God, in perpetual memory of this matter. Antiquity shows us that the laity has always been exceeding

"The Bull *Clericos Laicos* of Pope Boniface VIII, 1296," from Rymer's *Foedora* (1727), Vol. II, pp. 706–707, as found in *Translations and Reprints from the Original Sources of European History* (Philadelphia: University of Pennsylvania, 1896), Series I, Vol. III, No. 6, pp. 22–23.

hostile to the clergy; and this the experience of the present time clearly demonstrates, since, not content with their limitations, the laity strive for forbidden things and give free reign to the pursuit of illicit gain.

They do not prudently observe that all control over the clergy, as well as over all ecclesiastical persons and their possessions, is denied them, but impose heavy burdens upon the prelates of the churches, upon the churches themselves, and upon ecclesiastical persons both regular and secular, exacting talliages and other contributions from them. From such persons they require and extort the payment of a half, a tenth, a twentieth or some other quota of their property or income, and strive in many other ways to subject the churchmen to slavery and bring them under their control.

And (with grief do we declare it) certain prelates of the churches and ecclesiastical persons, fearing where they ought not to fear, and seeking a temporary peace, dreading to offend a temporal more than the eternal majesty, do, without having received the permission or sanction of the Apostolic See, acquiesce in such abuses, not so much from recklessness, as want of foresight. We, therefore, desiring to check these iniquitous practices, by the council of our brothers, do, of our apostolic authority, decree that whatever prelates and ecclesiastical persons, whether monastic or secular, whatever their order, condition or status, shall pay, or promise or agree to pay to laymen, any contributions or talliages, tenths, twentieths or hundredths of their own, or their churches' revenues or possessions, or shall pay any sum, portion or part of their revenues or goods, or of their estimated or actual value, in the form of an aid, loan, subvention, subsidy or gift, or upon any other pretense or fiction whatsoever, without authority from this same Apostolic See,—likewise emperors, kings and princes, dukes, counts, barons, podestà, captains, officers, rectors, whatever their title, of cities, castles or other places wherever situated, or any other persons, whatever their rank, condition or status, who shall impose, exact or receive such payments, or who shall presume to lay hands upon, seize or occupy the possessions of churches, or of ecclesiastical persons deposited in the sacred edifices, or who shall order such to be seized or occupied, or shall receive such things as shall be seized or occupied,—likewise all who shall consciously lend aid, council or support in such undertakings, either publicly or privately,—shall, by the very act, incur the sentence of excommunication; corporations, moreover, which shall show themselves guilty in these matters, we place under the interdict.

We strictly command all prelates and ecclesiastical persons above mentioned, in virtue of their obedience, and under penalty of deposition, that they shall not hereafter acquiesce in any such demands without the express permission of the aforesaid Chair. Nor shall they pay anything under pretext of any obligation, promise or declaration made in the past, or which may be made before this notice, prohibition or order shall be brought to their attention. Nor shall the above mentioned laymen in any way receive any such payments. And if the former pay, or the latter receive anything, they shall incur, by the act itself, the sentence of excommunication. . . .

7. *PHILIP IV CALLS THE FIRST ESTATES GENERAL*

Philip, by the grace of God King of the French, to the seneschal of Beaucaire, or his lieutenant, greeting. We wish to deliberate with the prelates, barons and other our loyal subjects on many serious matters closely touching ourselves, our estate and liberty, and that of our kingdom, as well as of the churches, ecclesiastics, nobles and secular persons, and all the inhabitants of the said kingdom. We bid you on our behalf to order and command the consuls and communities of the cities of Nîmes, Uzès, le Puy, Mende and Viviers, and the towns of Montpellier and Beaucaire . . . to be present at Paris on the coming Sunday before Palm Sunday, in the persons of two or three of the more prominent and learned of their several communities. These last are to have full and express powers from the said consuls and communities, without making any excuse about the need for reporting back (to their principals), to hear, receive, do and consent to everything that shall be ordained by us in this matter. . . .

G. Picot, *Documents relatifs aux États Généraux . . . sous Philippe le Bel* (Paris: 1901), p. 1, as found in R.C.D. Laffan, ed., *Select Documents of European History, 800–1492* (New York: Henry Holt and Company, Inc., 1929), pp. 160–161. Used by permission of Methuen & Co., Ltd., London.

12

THE CHURCH IN THE HIGH MIDDLE AGE

In the latter half of the eleventh century the Church freed itself from the danger of submersion in the feudal order, as Pope Gregory VII resolutely attacked the central issue of lay investiture. Gregory was drawn into a dramatic struggle with Emperor Henry IV, and in his *Dictatus* laid the foundations for later papal claims to political supremacy. Innocent III, presiding over the "Papal Monarchy" in the early thirteenth century, met with vigor the threat of the Albigensian heresy, encouraged the new mendicant orders, and convoked the greatest Church gathering of the Middle Ages, the Fourth Lateran Council. The political power of the Papacy declined during the late thirteenth century, and Pope Boniface VIII in his conflict with Philip IV of France found the spiritual weapons of Innocent III no longer effective.

1. THE BISHOP OF COLOGNE PROCLAIMS A TRUCE OF GOD

In the hope of limiting feudal violence, a number of bishops of France and Germany in the eleventh century issued Truce of God decrees. Most of these decrees provided severe ecclesiastical penalties for violators of the Truce.

Inasmuch as in our own times the church, through its members, has been extraordinarily afflicted by tribulations and difficulties, so that tranquillity and peace were wholly despaired of, we have endeavored by God's help to aid it, suffering so many burdens and perils. And by the advice of our faith-

"The Truce of God for the Diocese of Cologne, April 20, 1083," in *Translations and Reprints from the Original Sources of European History* (Philadelphia: University of Pennsylvania, 1894), Series I, Vol. I, No. 2, pp. 9–10.

ful subjects we have at length provided this remedy, so that we might to some extent re-establish, on certain days at least, the peace which, because of our sins, we could not make enduring. Accordingly we have enacted and set forth the following: . . .

Namely, that from the first day of the Advent of our Lord through Epiphany, and from the beginning of Septuagesima to the eighth day after Pentecost and through that whole day, and throughout the year on every Sunday, Friday and Saturday, and on the fast days of the four seasons, and on the eve and the day of all the apostles, and on all days canonically set apart—or which shall in the future be set apart—for fasts or feasts, this decree of peace shall be observed; so that both those who travel and those who remain at home may enjoy security and the most entire peace, so that no one may commit murder, arson, robbery or assault, no one may injure another with a sword, club or any kind of weapon, and so that no one irritated by any wrong . . . may presume to carry arms, shield, sword or lance, or moreover any kind of armor. . . . If it shall happen that any castle is besieged during the days which are included within the peace the besiegers shall cease from attack unless they are set upon by the besieged and compelled to beat the latter back.

And in order that this statute of peace should not be violated by anyone rashly or with impunity, a penalty was fixed by the common consent of all: if a free man or noble violates it, *i.e.*, commits homicide or wounds anyone or is at fault in any manner whatever, he shall be expelled from our territory, without any indulgence on account of the payment of money or the intercession of friends, and his heirs shall take all his property; if he holds a fief, the lord to whom it belongs shall receive it again. . . .

2. *HENRY REJECTS GREGORY'S CONDEMNATION OF LAY INVESTITURE*

Gregory VII, the former monk Hildebrand, had been trained in the Cluny movement. As pope (1073–1085) he found it his duty directly to attack the crucial issue, lay investiture of bishops and abbots. Emperor Henry IV, whose government was largely composed of bishop-vassals loyal to himself, chose to ignore Gregory's decree. The first selection below, a famous letter from Henry to Gregory, written in either January or March, 1076, shows the violence of Henry's reaction; the second selection is Gregory's formal excommunication of Henry; the third is an excerpt from Gregory's letter to the German princes, describing the dramatic scene at Canossa in January, 1077; the final document, the **Dictatus Papae,** ***is Gregory's statement of papal authority.***

Doeberl, ed., *Monumenta Germaniae Historica Selecta,* Vol. III, pp. 24 *seqq.*, as found in J.H. Robinson, *Readings in European History* (New York: Ginn and Company, 1904), Vol. I, pp. 279–281.

Henry, King not by usurpation but by holy ordination of God, to Hildebrand, now no Pope but false monk:

Such greeting as this hast thou merited through thy disturbances, for there is no rank in the Church but thou hast brought upon it, not honor but disgrace, not a blessing but a curse. To mention a few notable cases out of the many, thou hast not only dared to assail the rulers of the holy Church, the anointed of the Lord,—archbishops, bishops, and priests,—but thou hast trodden them under foot like slaves ignorant of what their master is doing. By so crushing them thou hast won the favor of the common herd; thou hast regarded them all as knowing nothing,—thyself alone as knowing all things. Yet this knowledge thou hast exerted, not for their advantage but for their destruction; so that with reason we believe St. Gregory, whose name thou hast usurped, prophesied of thee when he said, "The pride of the magistrate commonly waxes great if the number of those subject to him be great, and he thinks that he can do more than they all."

We, forsooth, have endured all this in our anxiety to save the honor of the apostolic see, but thou hast mistaken our humility for fear, and hast, accordingly, ventured to attack the royal power conferred upon us by God, and threatened to divest us of it. As if we had received our kingdom from thee! As if the kingdom and the empire were in thy hands, not in God's! For our Lord Jesus Christ did call us to the kingdom, although he has not called thee to the priesthood: that thou hast attained by the following steps.

By craft abhorrent to the profession of monk, thou hast acquired wealth; by wealth, influence; by influence, arms; by arms, a throne of peace. And from the throne of peace thou hast destroyed peace; thou hast turned subjects against their governors, for thou, who wert not called of God, hast taught that our bishops, truly so called, should be despised. Thou hast put laymen above their priests, allowing them to depose or condemn those whom they themselves had received as teachers from the hand of God through the laying on of bishops' hands.

Thou hast further assailed me also, who, although unworthy of anointing, have nevertheless been anointed to the kingdom, and who, according to the traditions of the holy fathers, am subject to the judgment of God alone, to be deposed upon no charge save that of deviation from the faith,—which God avert! For the holy fathers by their wisdom committed the judgment and deposition of even Julian the Apostate not to themselves but to God alone. Likewise the true pope, Peter, himself exclaims: "Fear God. Honor the king." But thou, who dost not fear God, art dishonoring me, his appointed one. Wherefore, St. Paul, since he spared not an angel of heaven if he should preach other than the gospel, has not excepted thee, who dost teach other doctrine upon earth. For he says, "If any one, whether I, or an angel from heaven, shall preach the gospel other than that which has been preached to you, he shall be damned."

Thou, therefore, damned by this curse and by the judgment of all our bishops and ourselves, come down and relinquish the apostolic chair which thou hast usurped. Let another assume the seat of St. Peter, who will not practice violence under the cloak of religion, but will teach St. Peter's wholesome doctrine. I, Henry, king by the grace of God, together with all our bishops, say unto thee: "Come down, come down, to be damned throughout all eternity!"

3. *GREGORY EXCOMMUNICATES HENRY*

O St. Peter, chief of the apostles, incline to us, I beg, thy holy ears, and hear me thy servant whom thou hast nourished from infancy, and whom, until this day, thou hast freed from the hand of the wicked, who have hated and do hate me for my faithfulness to thee. Thou, and my mistress the mother of God, and thy brother St. Paul are witnesses for me among all the saints that thy holy Roman church drew me to its helm against my will; that I had no thought of ascending thy chair through force, and that I would rather have ended my life as a pilgrim than, by secular means, to have seized thy throne for the sake of earthly glory. And therefore I believe it to be through thy grace and not through my own deeds that it has pleased and does please thee that the Christian people, who have been especially committed to thee, should obey me. And especially to me, as thy representative and by thy favour, has the power been granted by God of binding and loosing in Heaven and on earth. On the strength of this belief therefore, for the honour and security of thy church, in the name of Almighty God, Father, Son and Holy Ghost, I withdraw, through thy power and authority, from Henry the king, son of Henry the emperor, who has risen against thy church with unheard of insolence, the rule over the whole kingdom of the Germans and over Italy. And I absolve all Christians from the bonds of the oath which they have made or shall make to him; and I forbid any one to serve him as king. For it is fitting that he who strives to lessen the honour of thy church should himself lose the honour which belongs to him. And since he has scorned to obey as a Christian, and has not returned to God whom he had deserted—holding intercourse with the excommunicated; practising manifold iniquities; spurning my commands

Ernest F. Henderson, trans. and ed., *Select Historical Documents of the Middle Ages* (London: G. Bell & Sons, Ltd., 1892), pp. 376–377.

which, as thou dost bear witness, I issued to him for his own salvation; separating himself from thy church and striving to rend it—I bind him in thy stead with the chain of the anathema. And, leaning on thee, I so bind him that the people may know and have proof that thou art Peter, and above thy rock the Son of the living God hath built His church, and the gates of Hell shall not prevail against it.

4. *HENRY SEEKS ABSOLUTION AT CANOSSA*

Bishop Gregory, servant of the servants of God, to all the Archbishops, Bishops, Dukes, Counts, and other princes of the realm of the Germans, defenders of the Christian faith, greeting and apostolic benediction:

Inasmuch as for the love of justice ye have assumed common cause and danger with us in the stress of this Christian warfare, we have bethought us to relate to you, beloved, in sincere affection, how the king, humbled to penance, has obtained the pardon of absolution, and how the whole matter has progressed since his entry into Italy up to the present day.

As had been arranged with the legates whom you dispatched to us, we came into Lombardy about twenty days before the date on which one of the nobles was to meet us at the pass, and awaited his coming before we crossed over to the other side of the Alps.

When the time fixed upon had quite passed, we were told, as we could well believe, that at that season, on account of the numerous obstacles, an escort could not be sent to meet us. We were then involved in no little anxiety as to what we would best do, since we had no means of crossing over to you.

Meanwhile, however, we learned positively that the king was approaching. Indeed, before he entered Italy he had sent us suppliant messages, offering to render satisfaction, in all respects, to God, St. Peter, and ourselves. He also renewed his promise that he would be perfectly obedient in the matter of amending his life if only he might win from us the favor of absolution and of the apostolic benediction.

When, after many delays and after much consultation, we had, through all the envoys who passed between us, severely reprimanded him for his offenses, he at length came of his own accord, accompanied by a few followers, with no hostility or arrogance in his bearing, to the town of Canossa, where we were tarrying. And there, laying aside all the trappings of royalty,

Register of Gregory VII, Lib. IV, No. 12, as found in J.H. Robinson, *Readings in European History* (New York: Ginn and Company, 1904), Vol. I, pp. 282–283.

he stood in wretchedness, barefooted and clad in woolen, for three days before the gate of the castle, and implored with profuse weeping the aid and consolation of the apostolic mercy, until he had moved all who saw or heard of it to such pity and depth of compassion that they interceded for him with many prayers and tears and wondered at the unaccustomed hardness of our heart; some even protested that we were displaying not the seriousness of the apostolic displeasure but the cruelty of tyrannical ferocity.

At last, overcome by his persistent remorse and by the earnest entreaties of those with us, we loosed the chain of anathema and received him into the favor of our fellowship and into the lap of the holy mother Church, accepting the pledges given below. We also obtained a confirmation of the transaction from the abbot of Cluny, from our daughters Matilda and the countess Adelaide, and from such princes, ecclesiastical and lay, as seemed to us proper.

5. *GREGORY INDICATES THE SCOPE OF PAPAL AUTHORITY*

The Roman church was founded by God alone.

The Roman bishop alone is properly called universal.

He alone may depose bishops and reinstate them.

His legate, though of inferior grade, takes precedence, in a council, of all bishops and may render a decision of deposition against them.

He alone may use the insignia of empire.

The pope is the only person whose feet are kissed by all princes.

His title is unique in the world.

He may depose emperors.

No council may be regarded as a general one without his consent.

No book or chapter may be regarded as canonical without his authority.

A decree of his may be annulled by no one; he alone may annul the decrees of all.

He may be judged by no one.

No one shall dare to condemn one who appeals to the papal see.

The Roman church has never erred, nor ever, by the witness of Scripture, shall err to all eternity.

He may not be considered Catholic who does not agree with the Roman church.

The pope may absolve the subjects of the unjust from their allegiance.

Register of Gregory VII, Lib. II, No. 55a, as found in J.H. Robinson, *Readings in European History* (New York: Ginn and Company, 1904), Vol. I, pp. 274–275.

6. ST. FRANCIS PREACHES TO THE BIRDS

The following selection is from* The Little Flowers of St. Francis, *a collection of stories about St. Francis of Assisi and his followers, based upon memories and oral tradition. These stories reveal St. Francis' tremendous love of God and man and nature, which has made him the most appealing figure of the Middle Ages.

St. Francis, humble servant of God, a short time after his conversion, having gathered together many companions and received them into the Order, fell into great perplexity and doubt touching what it behoved him to do—whether to be wholly intent on prayer or sometimes to preach. And greatly he desired to know the will of God touching these things. But since the holy humility wherewith he was filled suffered him not to lean overmuch on his own judgment, nor on his own prayers, he bethought him to seek the divine will through the prayers of others. Wherefore he called Friar Masseo to him and spake to him thus, "Go to Sister Clare and bid her from me that she and some of the most spiritual of her companions pray devoutly unto God, that He may be pleased to reveal to me which is the more excellent way: whether to give myself up to preaching or wholly to prayer; then go to Friar Silvester and bid him do the like." Now he had been in the world and was that same Friar Silvester that beheld a cross of gold issue from the mouth of St. Francis, the length whereof was high as heaven, and the breadth whereof reached to the uttermost parts of the earth. And this Friar Silvester was a man of such great devotion and holiness that whatsoever he asked of God he obtained, and the same was granted to him; and ofttimes he spake with God, wherefore great was the devotion of St. Francis to him. Friar Masseo went forth and gave his message first to St. Clare, as St. Francis had commanded, and then to Friar Silvester, who no sooner had heard the command than he straightway betook himself to prayer, and when he had received the divine answer, he returned to Friar Masseo and spake these words, "Thus saith the Lord God, 'Go to Friar Francis and say unto him that God hath not called him to this state for himself alone, but that he may bring forth fruit of souls and that many through him may be saved.'" Friar Masseo, having received this answer, returned to Sister Clare to learn what answer she had obtained of God; and she answered that she and her companions had received the selfsame response from God that Friar Silvester had. And Friar Masseo returned with this answer to St. Francis, who greeted him with greatest charity, washing his feet and setting meat before him. And St. Francis called Friar Masseo, after he had eaten, into the wood, and

The Little Flowers of St. Francis of Assisi, translated by T. Okey (Mt. Vernon, N.Y.: The Peter Pauper Press, 1944), pp. 46–50. Used by permission of the publisher.

there knelt down before him, drew back his cowl, and making a cross with his arms, asked of him, "What doth my Lord Jesus Christ command?" Friar Masseo answers, "Thus to Friar Silvester and thus to Sister Clare and her sisterhood hath Christ answered and revealed His will: that thou go forth to preach throughout the world, for He hath not chosen thee for thyself alone, but also for the salvation of others." Then St. Francis, when he had heard these words and learned thereby the will of Christ, rose up and said with great fervour, "Let us then go forth in God's name." And with him he took Friar Masseo and Friar Agnolo, holy men both, and setting forth with great fervour of spirit and taking heed neither of road nor path, they came to a city called Saburniano. And St. Francis began to preach, first commanding the swallows to keep silence until his sermon were ended; and the swallows obeying him, he preached with such zeal that all the men and women of that city desired in their devotion to follow after him and forsake the city. But St. Francis suffered them not, saying, "Be not in haste to depart, for I will ordain what ye shall do for the salvation of your souls." And then he bethought him of the third Order which he stablished for the universal salvation of all people. And so, leaving them much comforted and well disposed to penitence, he departed thence and came to a place between Cannara and Bevagna. And journeying on in that same fervour of spirit, he lifted up his eyes and beheld some trees by the wayside whereon were an infinite multitude of birds; so that he marvelled and said to his companions, "Tarry here for me by the way and I will go and preach to my little sisters the birds." And he entered into the field and began to preach to the birds that were on the ground; and anon those that were on the trees flew down to hear him, and all stood still the while St. Francis made an end of his sermon; and even then they departed not until he had given them his blessing. And according as Friar Masseo and Friar James of Massa thereafter related, St. Francis went among them, touching them with the hem of his garment, and not one stirred. And the substance of the sermon St. Francis preached was this, "My little sisters the birds, much are ye beholden to God your Creator, and alway and in every place ye ought to praise Him for that He hath given you a double and a triple vesture; He hath given you freedom to go into every place, and also did preserve the seed of you in the ark of Noe, in order that your kind might not perish from the earth. Again, ye are beholden to Him for the element of air which He hath appointed for you; moreover, ye sow not, neither do ye reap, and God feedeth you and giveth you the rivers and the fountains for your drink; He giveth you the mountains and the valleys for your refuge, and the tall trees wherein to build your nests, and forasmuch as ye can neither spin nor sew God clotheth you, you and your children: wherefore your Creator loveth you much, since He hath dealt so bounteously with you; and therefore beware, little sisters mine, of the sin of ingratitude, but ever strive to praise God." While St. Francis was uttering these words, all those birds began to open their beaks, and stretch their necks, and spread their wings, and reverently to bow their heads to the ground, showing by their gestures and songs that the holy father's words gave them greatest joy: and St. Francis was glad and rejoiced with them, and marvelled much at so great a multitude of birds and at their manifold loveliness, and at their attention and familiarity; for which things he devoutly praised the Creator in them. Finally, his sermon ended, St. Francis made the sign of holy cross over them and gave them leave to depart; and all those birds soared up into the air in one flock with wondrous songs, and then divided themselves into four parts after the form of the cross St. Francis had made over them; and one part flew towards the east; another towards the west; the third towards the south, and the fourth towards the north. And each flock sped forth singing wondrously, betokening thereby that even as St. Francis, standard-bearer of the cross of Christ, had preached to them and had made the sign of the cross over them, according to which they had divided themselves, singing, among the four quarters of the world, so the preaching of Christ's cross, renewed by St. Francis, was, through him and his friars, to be borne throughout the whole world; the which friars possessing nothing of their own in this world, after the manner of birds, committed their lives wholly to the providence of God.

7. AN INQUISITOR DESCRIBES THE ALBIGENSIAN HERETICS

The Albigensians, or* Cathari, *were relapsed Christians of southern France, who adhered to an oriental Gnostic cult. Pope Innocent III took vigorous action against the heresy by sending preachers (followers of St. Dominic) into the affected area, by proclaiming the Albigensian Crusade, and by establishing a new institution, the Papal Inquisition. Bernard Gui, author of this selection, was a just and efficient inquisitor of the thirteenth century.

It would take too long to describe in detail the manner in which these same Manichean heretics preach, and teach their followers, but it must be briefly considered here.

In the first place they usually say of themselves that they are good Christians, who do not swear, or lie, or speak evil of others; that they do

Bernard Gui, *Practica Inquisitionis Heretice Pravitatis,* Part V, Ch. I, Sec. 4, in *Translations and Reprints from the Original Sources of European History* (Philadelphia: University of Pennsylvania, 1896), Series I, Vol. III, No. 6, pp. 7–8.

not kill any man or animal nor any thing having the breath of life, and that they hold the faith of the Lord Jesus Christ and His Gospel, as Christ and His Apostles taught. They assert that they occupy the place of the apostles, and that on account of the above mentioned things those of the Roman Church, namely, the prelates, clerks and monks, persecute them, especially the Inquisitors of Heresy, and call them heretics, although they are good men and good Christians, and that they are persecuted just as Christ and his apostles were by the Pharisees.

They moreover talk to the laity of the evil lives of clerks and prelates of the Roman Church, pointing out, and setting forth their pride, cupidity, avarice and uncleanness of life and such other evils as they know. They invoke with their own interpretation, and according to their abilities, the authority of the Gospels and the Epistles against the condition of the prelates, churchmen and monks, whom they call Pharisees and false prophets, who say, but do not.

Then they attack and vituperate, one after the other, all the sacraments of the church, especially the sacrament of the Eucharist, saying that it cannot contain the body of Christ, for had this been as great as the largest mountain, Christians would have consumed it entirely before this. They assert that the host comes from straw, that it passes through the tails of horses, to wit, when the flour is cleaned by a sieve (of horse hair). That moreover it passes through the body and comes to a vile end which, they say, could not happen if God were in it. Of baptism, they assert that water is material and corruptible, and is therefore the creation of the Evil Power and cannot sanctify the soul, but that the churchmen sell this water out of avarice, just as they sell earth for the burial of the dead, and oil to the sick when they anoint them, and as they sell the confession of sins as made to the priests. Hence, they claim that confession made to the priests of the Roman Church is useless, and that since the priests may be sinners, they can not loose nor bind, and being unclean themselves, cannot make another clean. They assert, moreover, that the Cross of Christ should not be adored or venerated, because, as they urge, no one would venerate or adore the gallows upon which a father, relative or friend had been hung. They urge farther that they who adore the cross ought for similar reasons to worship all thorns and lances because, as Christ's body was on the cross during the passion, so was the crown of thorns on his head, and the soldier's lance in his side. They proclaim many other scandalous things in regard to the sacraments. They, moreover, read from the Gospels and the Epistles in the vulgar tongue, applying and expounding them in their favor and against the condition of the Roman Church in a manner which it would take too long to describe in detail, but all that relates to this subject may be read more fully in the books they have written and infected, and may be learned from the confessions of such of their followers as have been converted.

8. THE FOURTH LATERAN COUNCIL BRINGS A VARIETY OF REFORMS

The Fourth Lateran Council of 1215 was called by Pope Innocent III to complete a program of reform begun by the Cluny-inspired pontiffs of the eleventh century. At the council of 1215 a number of difficult theological issues were clarified, and exact definitions of dogma were pronounced.

3. . . . Convicted heretics shall be handed over for due punishment to their secular superiors, or the latter's bailiffs. If they are clerks, they shall first be degraded. The goods of the laymen thus convicted shall be confiscated: those of the clergy shall be applied to the churches from which they drew their stipends.

. . . If a temporal lord neglects to fulfill the demand of the Church that he shall purge his land of this contamination of heresy, he shall be excommunicated by the metropolitan and other bishops of the province. If he fails to make amends within a year, it shall be reported to the supreme pontiff, who shall pronounce his vassals absolved from fealty to him and offer his land to catholics. The latter shall exterminate the heretics, possess the land without dispute and keep it in the true faith; saving the rights of the overlord, provided that he himself is under no disqualification. . . .

Catholics, who assume the cross and devote themselves to the extermination of heretics, shall enjoy the same indulgence and privilege as those who go to the Holy Land. . . .

Further we add that every archbishop and bishop, in person or by his archdeacon or suitable and trustworthy persons, shall visit each of his parishes, in which there are said to be heretics, twice or at least once a year. And he shall compel three or more men of good reputation, or even, if necessary, the whole neighbourhood, to swear that, if any of them knows of any heretics or of any who frequent secret ceremonies or who practise manners and customs different from those common amongst Christians, he will report them to the bishop. The bishop shall call the accused into his presence; and, unless they clear themselves of the accusation, or if they relapse into their former mischief, they shall receive canonical punishment. . . .

C.J. Hefele, *Histoire des Conciles,* edited and translated by H. Leclerq, V, 1330 *et seq.*, as found in R.C.D. Laffan, ed., *Select Documents of European History, 800–1492* (New York: Henry Holt and Company, Inc., 1929), pp. 104–106. Used by permission of Methuen & Co., Ltd., London.

6\. . . . Metropolitans shall hold provincial councils with their suffragan bishops every year. Thereat earnestly and in the fear of God they shall consider methods of correcting abuses and reforming evils, especially amongst the clergy. . . . And, that this may be more thoroughly carried out, they shall appoint in every diocese suitable, discreet and trustworthy persons who shall quietly take note during the year of whatever requires correction and shall make a faithful report to the metropolitan, the bishops and others at the next council; . . . and what [the bishops] decide, they shall enforce, publishing their decisions in their episcopal synods, which shall be held annually in all dioceses. . . .

18\. No cleric shall draw up or pronounce a sentence entailing the shedding of blood; nor execute any such punishment; nor be present at it. . . . Nor shall any cleric pronounce any form of benediction or consecration over an ordeal by boiling or cold water or molten iron. Prohibitions already promulgated against single combats or duels retain their force. . . .

21\. Every Christian of either sex, after reaching years of discretion, shall faithfully confess all his sins, at least once a year, privately to his own priest; he shall fulfill the penance imposed on him to the best of his ability; and reverently receive the sacrament of the Eucharist at least at Easter. . . . The priest shall take care not to betray the confidence of the sinner by word, by sign, or in any other way. . . . We declare that whoever shall reveal a sin confessed at the penitential tribunal, shall not only be deposed from his priestly office, but shall be imprisoned in a severe monastery to do perpetual penance. . . .

13

INTELLECTUAL LIFE IN THE HIGH MIDDLE AGE

The "Renaissance" of the twelfth century was essentially a revival of classical studies, or humanism, stimulated in part by the rediscovery of many of Aristotle's works, as translated from the Arabic. In the thirteenth century, humanism yielded the center of the intellectual stage to philosophy and theology. As the universities arose, that of Paris became an outstanding seat of learning for theological studies, while Salerno and Montpellier specialized in medicine, and the University of Bologna boasted an outstanding medical school and a renowned faculty of canon and civil law.

1. A PAPAL LEGATE LAYS DOWN RULES FOR THE UNIVERSITY OF PARIS

The status of the University of Paris was not at the beginning clearly established. A student riot in 1200 led to a serious dispute of university against city, during which the masters threatened to move to another town unless their rights were clearly defined. King Philip Augustus intervened by confirming in a charter the exemption of the university from all municipal jurisdiction. When the university next challenged the local ecclesiastical authority, the following regulations were laid down in 1215 by a legate of Pope Innocent III.

Robert . . . legate of the apostolic see, to all the masters and scholars of Paris eternal greeting in the Lord. Let all know that, since we have had a special mandate from the pope to take effective measures to reform the state of the Parisian scholars for the better, wishing with the counsel of

Chartularium Universitatis Parisiensis, I, 78–79, as found in Lynn Thorndike, *University Records and Life in the Middle Ages* (New York: Columbia University Press, 1944), pp. 27–30. Copyright 1944 by Columbia University Press. Used by permission.

good men to provide for the tranquillity of the scholars in the future, we have decreed and ordained in this wise:

No one shall lecture in the arts at Paris before he is twenty-one years of age, and he shall have heard lectures for at least six years before he begins to lecture, and he shall promise to lecture for at least two years. . . . He shall not be stained by any infamy, and when he is ready to lecture, he shall be examined according to the form which is contained in the writing of the lord bishop of Paris, where is contained the peace confirmed between the chancellor and scholars by judges delegated by the pope. . . . And they shall lecture on the books of Aristotle on dialectic old and new in the schools. . . . They shall also lecture on both Priscians [books of grammar] ordinarily, or at least on one. They shall not lecture on feast days except on philosophers and rhetoric and the quadrivium [arithmetic, geometry, music, and astronomy]. . . . They shall not lecture on the books of Aristotle on metaphysics and natural philosophy or on summaries of them. . . .

In the . . . meetings of the masters and in the responsions or oppositions of the boys and youths there shall be no drinking. They may summon some friends or associates, but only a few. Donations of clothing or other things as has been customary, or more, we urge should be made, especially to the poor. None of the masters lecturing in arts shall have a cope except one round, black and reaching to the ankles, at least while it is new. Use of the pallium is permitted. No one shall wear with the round cope shoes that are ornamented or with elongated pointed toes. . . . If any master in arts or theology dies, all the masters shall keep vigils, each shall read or cause to be read the Psalter, each shall attend the church where is celebrated the watch until midnight or the greater part of the night, unless reasonable cause prevent. On the day when the master is buried, no one shall lecture or dispute. . . .

Each master shall have jurisdiction over his scholar. No one shall occupy a classroom or house without asking the consent of the tenant, provided one has a chance to ask it. No one shall receive the licentiate from the chancellor or another for money given or promise made or other condition agreed upon. Also, the masters and scholars can make both between themselves and with other persons obligations and constitutions supported by faith or penalty or oath in these cases: namely, the murder or mutilation of a scholar or atrocious injury done a scholar, if justice should not be forthcoming, arranging the prices of lodgings, costume, burial, lectures and disputations, so, however, that the university be not thereby dissolved or destroyed.

As to the status of the theologians, we decree that no one shall lecture at Paris before his thirty-fifth year and unless he has studied for eight years at least, and has heard the books faithfully and in classrooms, and has attended lectures in theology for five years before he gives lectures himself publicly. And none of these shall lecture before the third hour on days when masters lecture. No one shall be admitted at Paris to formal lectures or to preachings unless he shall be of approved life and science. No one shall be a scholar at Paris who has no definite master.

Moreover, that these decrees may be observed inviolate, we by virtue of our legatine authority have bound by the knot of excommunication all who shall contumaciously presume to go against these our statutes, unless within fifteen days after the offense they have taken care to emend their presumption before the university of masters and scholars or other persons constituted by the university. Done in the year of Grace 1215, the month of August.

2. *A FATHER SENDS ADVICE TO HIS SONS AT THE UNIVERSITY OF TOULOUSE*

The following letter was written in 1315 by a physician of Valencia, Spain, to his two sons at the University of Toulouse, and gives a valuable insight into the personal habits and daily lives of students.

Beware of eating too much and too often especially during the night. Avoid eating raw onions in the evening except rarely, because they dull the intellect and senses generally.

Avoid all very lacteal foods such as milk and fresh cheese except very rarely. Beware of eating milk and fish, or milk and wine, at the same meal, for milk and fish or milk and wine produce leprosy.

Don't have fresh pork too often. Salt pork is all right.

Don't eat many nuts except rarely and following fish. I say the same of meat and fruit, for they are bad and difficult to digest.

Thy drink be twice or thrice or four times during a meal. Between meals drink little, for it would be better once in a while to drink too much at table than to drink away from table. Don't take wine without water, and, if it is too cold, warm it in winter. For 'tis bad to grow used to strong wine without admixture of water.

Remember about the well water of Toulouse. Wherefore boil it, and the same with water of the Garonne, because such waters are bad.

Also, after you have risen from table wash out your mouth with wine. . . .

British Museum, Ms. Sloane 3124, Fols. 74r–77r, as found in Lynn Thorndike, *University Records and Life in the Middle Ages* (New York: Columbia University Press, 1944), pp. 156–160.

Sufficient and natural sleep is to sleep for a fourth part of a natural day or a trifle more or less. To do otherwise is to pervert nature. Too much is a sin, wherefore shun it, unless the case is urgent and necessary.

Avoid sleeping on your back except rarely, for it has many disadvantages, but sleep on your side or stomach, and first on the right side, and then on the left.

Don't sleep in winter with cold feet, but first warm them at the fire or by walking about or some other method. And in summer don't sleep with bed slippers on your feet, because they generate vapors which are very bad for the brain and memory.

Don't go straight to bed on a full stomach but an hour after the meal. Also, unless some urgent necessity prevents, walk about for a bit after a meal, at least around the square, so that the food may settle in the stomach and not evaporate in the mouth of the stomach, since the vapors will rise to the head and fill it with rheum and steal away and cut short memory. . . .

Choose lodgings removed from all foul smells as of ditches or latrines and the like, since in breathing we are continually drawing in air which, if it is infected, infects us more and more forcibly than tainted food and drink do.

Likewise in winter keep your room closed from all noxious wind and have straw on the pavement lest you suffer from cold.

Furthermore, if you can have coals or chopped wood in a clay receptacle of good clay, or if you have a chimneyplace and fire in your room, it is well.

Also, be well clad and well shod, and outdoors wear pattens to keep your feet warm. . . .

And when you see other students wearing their caps, do you do likewise, and, if need be, put on one of fur. . . .

Moreover, at the time of the great rains it is well to wear outdoors over your cap a bonnet or helmet of undressed skin, that is, a covering to keep the head from getting wet. . . .

Also, look after your stockings and don't permit your feet to become dirty.

Also, wash the head, if you are accustomed to wash it, at least once a fortnight with hot lye and in a place sheltered from draughts on the eve of a feast day towards nightfall. Then dry your hair with a brisk massage; afterwards do it up; then put on a bonnet or cap.

Also comb your hair daily, if you will morning and evening before eating or at least afterwards, if you cannot do otherwise.

Also look out that a draught does not strike you from window or crack while you study or sleep, or indeed at any time, for it strikes men without their noticing.

Also, in summer, in order not to have fleas or to have no more of them, sweep your room daily with a broom and not sprinkle it with water, for they are generated from damp dust. But you may spray it occasionally with strong vinegar which comforts heart and brain.

If you will, walk daily somewhere morning and evening. And if the weather is cold, if you can run, run on empty stomach, or at least walk rapidly, that the natural heat may be revived. For a fire is soon extinguished unless the sticks are moved about or the bellows used. However, it is not advisable to run on a full stomach but to saunter slowly in order to settle the food in the stomach.

If you cannot go outside your lodgings, either because the weather does not permit or it is raining, climb the stairs rapidly three or four times, and have in your room a big heavy stick like a sword and wield it now with one hand, now with the other, as if in a scrimmage, until you are almost winded. This is splendid exercise to warm one up and expel noxious vapors through the pores and consume other superfluities. Jumping is a similar exercise. Singing, too, exercises the chest. And if you will do this, you will have healthy limbs, a sound intellect and memory, and you will avoid rheum. The same way with playing ball. All these were invented not for sport but for exercise. Moreover, too much labor is to be avoided as a continual practice.

Accidents of the soul have the greatest influence, such as anger, sadness, and love of women, fear, excessive anxiety: concerning all which I say nothing more than that you avoid all passions of the soul harmful to you and enjoy yourself happily with friends and good companions, and cultivate honesty and patience which bring the more delights to the soul, and especially if you love God with your whole heart. . . .

Thus it ends. Thanks to God. Amen, Amen.

3. *THE HAZING OF FRESHMEN IS FORBIDDEN*

As this decree of the year 1340 of the University of Paris indicates, freshmen in the medieval universities were often picked on by upper-classmen, a practice which did not die with the Middle Ages.

This is the ordinance made by the deputies of the university as to the punishment of those hazing Freshmen. First, that no one, of whatever faculty he be, shall take any money from a Freshman because of his class or anything else, except from roommates with whom he lives or as a volun-

Chartularium Universitatis Parisiensis, II, 496, as found in Lynn Thorndike, *University Records and Life in the Middle Ages* (New York: Columbia University Press, 1944), pp. 192–193.

tary gift, under penalty of deprivation of any honor now held or to be held from the university, which deprivation from now as from then the said university brings upon any offending thus.

* * *

Fourth, the said university bids the said Freshmen, under penalty of deprivation of any honor from the said university, that if anyone does any wrong to them by word or deed on account of their class, they shall straightway secretly reveal this to the proctors and deans of the faculties who in general congregation shall be required to reveal the names of the offenders by their oaths.

4. *FERNANDO OF CORDOVA, BOY WONDER, COMES TO TOWN*

Although the following three selections concern intellectual events of a later period, it is fitting to include them here, since university life changed remarkably little between the thirteenth and fifteenth centuries.

In the year 1445 there came to the Collège de Navarre a certain youth of twenty summers who was past master of all good arts, as the most skilled masters of the university testified with one accord. He sang beautifully to the flute: he surpassed all in numbers, voice, modes and symphony. He was a painter and laid colors on images best of all. In military matters he was most expert: he swung a sword with both hands so well and mightily that none dared fight with him. . . .

Of this adolescent John Trithemius writes thus in his Sponheim Chronicle: "But as we write this, we recall Ferrandus of Cordova, who in the year 1445, a young gilded knight of twenty, doctor of arts, medicine and sacred theology, came from Spain to France with eight horses and stupefied the entire university of Paris by his marvelous science. For he was most learned in every faculty of the scriptures, most honorable in life and conversation, not proud and arrogant like him (of whom we were just speaking) but very humble and full of reverence. He knew the whole Bible by heart, also Nicholas of Lyra, the writings of St. Thomas Aquinas, Alexander of Hales, John the Scot, Bonaventura and many others in theology. Likewise the *Decretum* and all the books of both laws, and in medicine Avicenna, Galen, Hippocrates, and Aristotle and Albertus and all the books

Launoy, *Regii Navarrae Gymnasii Parisiensis Historia,* I, 157–158, as found in Lynn Thorndike, *University Records and Life in the Middle Ages* (New York: Columbia University Press, 1944), pp. 341–343.

of philosophy and metaphysics and commentaries he remembered to the nail, as the saying is. Finally, he read, wrote and understood perfectly Hebrew, Greek, Latin, Arabic and Chaldean. . . . There was a diversity of opinion concerning him among the doctors of Paris, some accusing him of being a magician and full of the demon, others thinking the contrary. Nor were those lacking who deemed him antichrist because of his incredible knowledge of scriptures, in which he seemed to excel all mortals."

5. *THE CITY OF FERRARA TAKES ACTION AGAINST IGNORANT TEACHERS, 1443*

There exists at this time in this city a seminary of evil learning and ignorance. Our citizens desire to instruct their sons and their adolescents in good letters, and they are sunk in I know not what pit from which they can never extricate themselves. That is, certain barbarous teachers—who, far from knowing, never even saw, any good literature—have invaded our city, opened schools, and professed grammar. Citizens ignorant of these men's ignorance entrust their sons to them to be educated. They want them to learn and to graduate learned, but they learn those things which later they must unlearn. Lest this calamity and pest progress further, they decree that no one take scholars to train, nor hold a school, unless first he shall have demonstrated that he is acquainted with good literature or had been approved by the board of the Twelve Wise as suited to open a school. If anyone shall dare to do different, let him be ejected from the city as a pestiferous beast.

"Decree by Joannes de Gualengis and the Board of Wise Men, July 11, 1443," from Borsetti, *Historia Almi Ferrarieae Gymnasii,* as found in Lynn Thorndike, *University Records and Life in the Middle Ages* (New York: Columbia University Press, 1944), p. 337.

6. *SURGEONS PRACTICE DISSECTION AT BOLOGNA, 1405*

Medieval medical schools carried the level of medical knowledge beyond that of the Hellenistic Age, as significant advances were made in sanitation and in surgery. By the early fourteenth century, dissection of human corpses was a regular practice in Italian universities.

Since the performance of dissection regards and pertains to the industry and advantage of scholars, and quarrels and rumors have often been customary in finding or searching for bodies from which or of which dissection should

Carlo Malagola, *Statuti dell'universita e dei Collegii dello studio Bolognese,* 1888, Rubric 96, as found in Lynn Thorndike, *University Records and Life in the Middle Ages* (New York: Columbia University Press, 1944), p. 283.

be made, they decreed and ordained that any doctor or scholar or anyone else shall not dare or presume to acquire for himself any dead body for such purpose of dissection, unless he has first obtained permission from the rector then in office. . . . Also, that not more than twenty persons may attend the dissection of a male; and not over thirty, the dissection of the corpse of a woman. And that no one may attend a dissection unless he has been a student of medicine for two whole years and is in his third year, even if he has attended classes at a forbidden time. . . .

7. *THE WANDERING STUDENT BURSTS INTO SONG*

The twelfth century student was often a wanderer, begging for alms in his summer "vacation," or traveling from one university to another to hear the lectures of renowned scholars. The Latin lyric poems of the wandering students are known as "goliardic" poetry. A famous goliardic poem,* Gaudeamus Igitur, *is here presented in translation.

GAUDEMAUS IGITUR
No. 60

Let us live then and be glad
While young life's before us!
After youthful pastime had,
After old age hard and sad,
Earth will slumber o'er us.

Where are they who in this world,
Ere we kept, were keeping?
Go ye to the gods above;
Go to hell; inquire thereof:
They are not; they're sleeping.

Brief is life, and brevity
Briefly shall be ended:
Death comes like a whirlwind strong,
Bears us with his blast along;
None shall be defended.

Live this university,
Men that learning nourish;

"Gaudeamus Igitur," in J.A. Symonds, *Wine, Women and Song* (Portland, Me.: T.B. Mosher, 1899), pp. 170–171.

Live each member of the same,
Long live all that bear its name;
Let them ever flourish!

Live the commonwealth also,
And the men that guide it!
Live our town in strength and health,
Founders, patrons, by whose wealth
We are here provided!

Live all girls! A health to you,
Melting maids and beauteous!
Live the wives and women too,
Gentle, loving, tender, true,
Good, industrious, duteous!

Perish cares that pule and pine!
Perish envious blamers!
Die the Devil, thine and mine!
Die the starch-necked Philistine!
Scoffers and defamers!

8. PETER ABELARD RECALLS HIS STUDENT DAYS

Peter Abelard (1079–1142), the outstanding intellectual of his century, came from a noble family of Brittany. A talented and precocious youth, Abelard quickly abandoned a projected military career and took up the wandering life of the scholar. As the first selection reveals, he made life miserable for his teachers. Abelard's fame rested on his brilliant lectures and his new system of dialectic, which was explained in his treatise,* Sic et Non *("Yes and No"). The second selection below is taken from the introduction to* Sic et Non, *in which Abelard listed 158 theological propositions, together with authoritative views for and against.

Consequently (he says) I traversed the various provinces, engaging in disputation and visiting all those places where I heard that the art of logic flourished. I came finally to Paris, where this art was wont to be most cultivated, to William of Champeaux, my preceptor, who at that time was quite justly famous in his profession. I remained with him for a time and was at first favorably received; later he came to dislike me heartily, when I at-

P. Abaelardus, *Opera,* edited by V. Cousin (Paris: 1849–1859), Vol. I, as found in J.H. Robinson, *Readings in European History* (New York: Ginn and Company, 1904), Vol. I, pp. 447–449.

tempted to oppose certain of his opinions. I began frequently to argue against him, and sometimes appeared to get the better of him in debate. Moreover those among my fellow-students who stood highest were especially indignant with me, since I was reckoned of slight consequence owing to my youth and the brief period I had been studying. Here my calamities had their beginning and they still continue.

(In spite of his youthfulness Abelard ventured to begin teaching for himself near Paris, and attracted many students. But he speedily broke down in health and went back to Brittany for several years. Later he returned to Paris, and forced poor William of Champeaux to change the formulation of his doctrine in a single point. The master being thus discredited, the students now flocked to listen to the new teacher. Before long, however, Abelard decided to turn to theology. He accordingly went to Laon, to study under Master Anselm, then famous in that subject.)

I accordingly betook myself to this old man, but found that he owed his name rather to mere tradition than to any special ability. If one applied to him, uncertain as to some question, one left him still more uncertain. He was marvelous in the eyes of those who merely listened, but contemptible to those who asked questions. He enjoyed an astonishing facility in words but was despicable in his understanding and fatuous in his reasoning. . . . When I discovered that he was like a tree full of leaves but without fruit, I did not spend many days lying idle in his shade. I went more and more infrequently to his lectures. Some of the most prominent among his students took this ill, since I seemed to despise their great master.

(One day Abelard's fellow-students, who regarded him as very ill prepared for the study of theology, asked him jokingly what he thought of the reading of the Scriptures. Abelard replied that he believed that any one who could read ought to be able to understand the writings of the saints without a long course under a master.) Those who heard laughed and asked if I would presume to interpret the Scriptures myself. I said that if they wished to try me I was ready. They then exclaimed, amid renewed laughter, that they gladly assented.

(They agreed upon a very obscure passage in Ezekiel. Abelard insisted upon the students coming on the morrow, although they advised him to take more time to think over the passage.) I said indignantly that it was not my custom to reach my goal by long practice but by my wits. I added that they should either let me off altogether or come to my lecture when I wished them to come.

At my first lecture few were present, since it seemed absurd to them all that I, hitherto almost wholly inexperienced in the Scriptures, should undertake the task so suddenly. However, all who came were so pleased that, one and all, they praised my words and urged me to proceed with my comments according to my interpretation. As the affair became known, those who had not been present at the first lecture began to come in great numbers to the second and third. All were, moreover, eager to make notes from the very beginning, upon the explanation which I had given the first day.

(Not unnaturally Anselm was very much irritated and made the audacious and self-complacent lecturer a great deal of trouble later.)

9. *ABELARD INTRODUCES THE* SIC ET NON *METHOD*

There are many seeming contradictions and even obscurities in the innumerable writings of the church fathers. Our respect for their authority should not stand in the way of an effort on our part to come at the truth. The obscurity and contradictions in ancient writings may be explained upon many grounds, and may be discussed without impugning the good faith and insight of the fathers. A writer may use different terms to mean the same thing, in order to avoid a monotonous repetition of the same word. Common, vague words may be employed in order that the common people may understand; and sometimes a writer sacrifices perfect accuracy in the interest of a clear general statement. Poetical, figurative language is often obscure and vague.

Not infrequently apocryphal works are attributed to the saints. Then, even the best authors often introduce the erroneous views of others and leave the reader to distinguish between the true and the false. Sometimes, as Augustine confesses in his own case, the fathers ventured to rely upon the opinions of others.

Doubtless the fathers might err; even Peter, the prince of the apostles, fell into error; what wonder that the saints do not always show themselves inspired? The fathers did not themselves believe that they, or their companions, were always right. Augustine found himself mistaken in some cases and did not hesitate to retract his errors. He warns his admirers not to look upon his letters as they would upon the Scriptures, but to accept only those things which, upon examination, they find to be true.

All writings belonging to this class are to be read with full freedom to criticise, and with no obligation to accept unquestioningly; otherwise the way would be blocked to all discussion, and posterity be deprived of the excellent intellectual exercise of debating difficult questions of language

Petrus Abelardus, *Sic et Non*, edited by Henke and Lindenkohl (Marburg: 1851), as found in J.H. Robinson, *Readings in European History* (New York: Ginn and Company, 1904), Vol. I, pp. 450–451.

and presentation. But an explicit exception must be made in the case of the Old and New Testaments. In the Scriptures, when anything strikes us as absurd, we may not say that the writer erred, but that the scribe made a blunder in copying the manuscripts, or that there is an error in interpretation, or that the passage is not understood. The fathers make a very careful distinction between the Scriptures and later works. They advocate a discriminating, not to say suspicious, use of the writings of their own contemporaries.

In view of these considerations, I have ventured to bring together various dicta of the holy fathers, as they came to mind, and to formulate certain questions which were suggested by the seeming contradictions in the statements. These questions ought to serve to excite tender readers to a zealous inquiry into truth and so sharpen their wits. The master key of knowledge is, indeed, a persistent and frequent questioning. Aristotle, the most clear-sighted of all the philosophers, was desirous above all things else to arouse this questioning spirit, for in his *Categories* he exhorts a student as follows: "It may well be difficult to reach a positive conclusion in these matters unless they be frequently discussed. It is by no means fruitless to be doubtful on particular points." By doubting we come to examine, and by examining we reach the truth.

10. ROGER BACON PRAISES A FELLOW SCIENTIST

It was once thought that Roger Bacon in the thirteenth century was the only man of his age to appreciate experimental science. However, historians have since discovered that a number of other scientists shared Bacon's views, and that Bacon, himself, devoted considerable attention to alchemy, astrology, and magic. In spite of this, Bacon did have a real feeling for the importance of experimental science, as this selection reveals.

One man I know, and one only, who can be praised for his achievements in experimental science.[1] Of discourses and battles of words he takes no heed: he pursues the works of wisdom and in them finds satisfaction. What others strive to see dimly and blindly, like bats blinking at the sun in the twilight, he gazes at in the full light of day, because he is a master of experiment. Through experiment he gains knowledge of natural things, medical, chemical, indeed of everything in the heavens and on earth.

He is ashamed that things should be known to laymen, old women,

Roger Bacon, *Opus Tertium* c. cxiii, *Opera Quaedam Hactenus Inedita*, edited by Brewer, in the Rolls Series, 1859, pp. 46 *seq.*, as found in J.H. Robinson, *Readings in European History* (New York: Ginn and Company, 1904), Vol. I, pp. 460–461.

[1] Of Peter of Maricourt, to whom Bacon refers, very little is known.

soldiers, plowmen, of which he is ignorant. Therefore he has looked closely into the doings of those who melt metals and who work in gold and silver and other metals and in minerals of all sorts; he knows everything relating to the art of war, the making of weapons, and the chase; he has looked carefully into agriculture, mensuration, and farming works; he has even taken note of remedies, lot casting, and charms used by old women and by wizards and magicians, and of the devices and deceptions of conjurers, so that nothing which deserves investigation should escape him, and in order that he might be able to expose the impostures of the magicians.

If philosophy is to be carried to its perfection and is to be handled with certainty and advantage, his aid is indispensable. As for reward, he neither receives it nor looks for it. If he frequented the courts of kings and princes he would easily find those who would bestow upon him both honor and wealth. Or if he would show the results of his researches in Paris the whole world would follow him. But since either of these courses would hinder him from pursuing the great experiments in which he takes delight, he puts honor and wealth aside, knowing well that his knowledge would secure him wealth whenever he chose. For the last three years he has been working at the invention of a mirror which should produce combustion at a fixed distance, and he will, with God's aid, soon reach his end.

14

LITERATURE AND ART OF THE HIGH MIDDLE AGE

Although Latin remained the language of the medieval university and of scholarly writing, the vernacular languages were increasingly used in popular literature. *Chansons de geste,* epic poems, usually in French, were originally sung in the castles and were designed to appeal to an audience of feudal nobles. Other literary forms, such as the lyric poems of the troubadours, and the legends and romances, were more universal in their appeal. The great masterpiece of the High Middle Age is Dante's long narrative poem *The Divine Comedy.* These notable achievements in literature were matched by the emergence of spectacular new art forms, particularly the development of Romanesque and Gothic cathedral architecture.

1. ROLAND IS SLAIN IN BATTLE AGAINST THE SARACENS

The eleventh century poem* The Song of Roland *was the earliest and the greatest of the* chansons de geste. *The historical Roland, Charlemagne's prefect of Brittany, was killed in 778, when the rear guard of Charlemagne's army was ambushed by Basques in the Pyrenees. In the poem Roland appears as Charlemagne's nephew and is the perfect vassal, loyal and courageous. His friend Count Olivier is equally brave, but somewhat more prudent, and Archbishop Turpin is a blood-stained warrior. It was entirely a man's world, for the dying Roland has no thought for his fiancée, remembering only his feudal lord and his native land.

The Song of Roland, translated by John O'Hagan, in *Epic and Saga, The Harvard Classics,* edited by Charles W. Eliot (New York: P.F. Collier & Son Corp., 1910), Vol. XLIX, pp. 125–126, 136–137, 147, 162–163, 184.

LXVIII

Through Roncesvalles the march began;
Ogier, the baron, led the van;
For them was neither doubt nor fear,
Since Roland rested to guard the rear,
With twenty thousand in full array:
Theirs the battle—be God their stay.
Gan knows all; in his felon heart
Scarce hath he courage to play his part.

LXIX

High were the peaks, and the valleys deep,
The mountains wondrous dark and steep;
Sadly the Franks through the passes wound,
Full fifteen leagues did their tread resound.
To their own great land they are drawing nigh,
And they look on the fields of Gascony.
They think of their homes and their manors there,
Their gentle spouses and damsels fair.
Is none but for pity the tear lets fall;
But the anguish of Karl is beyond them all.
His sister's son at the gates of Spain
Smites on his heart, and he weeps amain.

XC

Roland is daring and Olivier wise,
Both of marvellous high emprise;
On their chargers mounted, and girt in mail,
To the death in battle they will not quail.
Brave are the counts, and their words are high,
And the Pagans are fiercely riding nigh.
"See, Roland, see them, how close they are,
The Saracen foemen, and Karl how far!
Thou didst disdain on thy horn to blow.
Were the king but here we were spared this woe.
Look up through Aspra's dread defile,
Where standeth our doomed rear-guard the while;
They will do their last brave feat this day,
No more to mingle in mortal fray."

"Hush!" said Roland, "the craven tale—
Foul fall who carries a heart so pale;
Foot to foot shall we hold the place,
And rain our buffets and blows apace."

XCII

Archbishop Turpin, above the rest,
Spurred his steed to a jutting crest.
His sermon thus to the Franks he spake:—
"Lords, we are here for our monarch's sake;
Hold we for him, though our death should come;
Fight for the succor of Christendom.
The battle approaches—ye know it well,
For ye see the ranks of the infidel.
Cry *mea culpa*, and lowly kneel;
I will assoil you, your souls to heal.
In death ye are holy martyrs crowned."
The Franks alighted, and knelt on ground;
In God's high name the host he blessed,
And for penance gave them—to smite their best.

CXVI

Wild and fierce is the battle still:
Roland and Olivier fight their fill;
The Archbishop dealeth a thousand blows
Nor knoweth one of the peers repose;
The Franks are fighting commingled all,
And the foe in hundreds and thousands fall;
Choice have they none but to flee or die,
Leaving their lives despighteously.
Yet the Franks are reft of their chivalry,
Who will see nor parent nor kindred fond,
Nor Karl who waits them the pass beyond.

CLII

Archbishop Turpin their strife hath heard,
His steed with the spurs of gold he spurred,
And thus rebuked them, riding near:
"Sir Roland, and thou, Sir Olivier,
Contend not, in God's great name, I crave.
Not now availeth the horn to save;

And yet behoves you to wind its call,—
Karl will come to avenge our fall,
Nor hence the foemen in joyance wend.
The Franks will all from their steeds descend;
When they find us slain and martyred here,
They will raise our bodies on mule and bier,
And, while in pity aloud they weep,
Lay us in hallowed earth to sleep;
Nor wolf nor boar on our limbs shall feed."
Said Roland, "Yea, 't is a goodly rede."

CLIV

With deadly travail, in stress and pain,
Count Roland sounded the mighty strain.
Forth from his mouth the bright blood sprang,
And his temples burst for the very pang.
On and onward was borne the blast,
Till Karl hath heard as the gorge he passed,
And Naimes and all his men of war.
"It is Roland's horn," said the Emperor,
"And, save in battle, he had not blown."

CXCVI

Roland feeleth his hour at hand;
On a knoll he lies towards the Spanish land.
With one hand beats he upon his breast:
"In thy sight, O God, be my sins confessed.
From my hour of birth, both the great and small,
Down to this day, I repent of all."
As his glove he raises to God on high,
Angels of heaven descend him nigh.

2. *AUCASSIN SEARCHES FOR NICOLETTE*

A precious gem of medieval literature is the story of Aucassin and Nicolette, by an unknown French author of the thirteenth century. The story, composed in a unique half-prose, half-verse style, should be read in its entirety to be fully appreciated. The plot is quite simple: Aucassin, the only son of a feudal lord, falls in love with Nicolette, a Saracen slave girl. Aucassin's father will not allow them to marry and succeeds in separating them. Each undergoes a series of wild adventures, until at last they are reunited.

Aucassin and Nicolette, translated by Andrew Lang (New York: Thomas Y. Crowell Company, n.d.), pp. 15–17, 18–19, 22–26. Used by permission of the publisher.

'T IS OF AUCASSIN AND NICOLETTE

Who would list to the good lay
Gladness of the captive grey?
'T is how two young lovers met,
Aucassin and Nicolette,
Of the pains the lover bore
And the sorrows he outwore,
For the goodness and the grace,
Of his love, so fair of face.

Sweet the song, the story sweet,
There is no man hearkens it,
No man living 'neath the sun,
So outwearied, so foredone,
Sick and woful, worn and sad,
But is healed, but is glad
'T is so sweet.

So say they, speak they, tell they the Tale:

How the Count Bougars de Valence made war on Count Garin de Biaucaire, war so great, and so marvellous, and so mortal that never a day dawned, but alway he was there, by the gates and walls, and barriers of the town with a hundred knights, and ten thousand men at arms, horsemen and footmen: so burned he the Count's land, and spoiled his country, and slew his men. Now the Count Garin de Biaucaire was old and frail, and his good days were gone over. No heir had he, neither son nor daughter, save one young man only; such an one as I shall tell you. Aucassin was the name . . . fair was he, goodly, and great, and featly fashioned of his body, and limbs. His hair was yellow, in little curls, his eyes blue and laughing, his face beautiful and shapely, his nose high and well set, and so richly seen was he in all things good, that in him was none evil at all. But so suddenly overtaken was he of Love, who is a great master, that he would not, of his will, be dubbed knight, nor take arms, nor follow tourneys, nor do whatsoever him beseemed. Therefore his father and mother said to him; "Son, go take thine arms, mount thy horse, and hold thy land, and help thy men, for if they see thee among them more stoutly will they keep in battle their lives, and lands, and thine, and mine."

"Father," said Aucassin, "I marvel that you will be speaking. Never may God give me aught of my desire if I be made knight, or mount my horse, or face stour and battle wherein knights smite and are smitten again, unless thou give me Nicolette, my true love, that I love so well."

"Son," said the father, "this may not be. Let Nicolette go, a slave girl she is, out of a strange land, and the captain of this town bought her of the Saracens, and carried her hither, and hath reared her and let christen the maid, and took her for his daughter in God, and one day will find a young man for her, to win her bread honourably. Herein hast thou naught to make or mend, but if a wife thou wilt have, I will give thee the daughter of a King, or a Count. There is no man so rich in France, but if thou desire his daughter, thou shalt have her."

"Faith! my father," said Aucassin, "tell me where is the place so high in all the world, that Nicolette, my sweet lady and love, would not grace it well? If she were Empress of Constantinople or of Germany, or Queen of France or England, it were little enough for her; so gentle is she and courteous, and debonaire, and compact of all good qualities."

* * *

When the Count Garin de Biaucaire knew that he would not avail to withdraw Aucassin his son from the love of Nicolette, he went to the Captain of the city, who was his man, and spake to him, saying:

"Sir Count; away with Nicolette thy daughter in God; cursed be the land whence she was brought into this country, for by reason of her do I lose Aucassin, that will neither be dubbed knight, nor do ought of the things that fall to him to be done. . . ."

. . . Now the Captain was a right rich man: so had he a rich palace with a garden in face of it; in an upper chamber thereof he let place Nicolette, with one old woman to keep her company, and in that chamber put bread and meat and wine and such things as were needful. Then he let seal the door, that none might come in or go forth, save that there was one window, over against the garden, and strait enough, where through came to them a little air.

* * *

While Aucassin was in the chamber sorrowing for Nicolette his love, even then the Count Bougars de Valence, that had his war to wage, forgat it no whit, but had called up his horsemen and his footmen, so made he for the castle to storm it. And the cry of battle arose, and the din, and knights and men at arms busked them, and ran to walls and gates to hold the keep. And the towns-folk mounted to the battlements, and cast down bolts, and pikes. Then while the assult was great, and even at its height, the Count Garin de Biaucaire came into the chamber where Aucassin was making lament. . . .

"Ha! son," quoth he, "how caitiff art thou, and cowardly, that canst see men assail thy goodliest castle and strongest. Know thou that if thou lose it, thou losest all. Son, go to, take arms, and mount thy horse, and defend thy land, and help thy men, and fare into the stour. . . ."

"Father," said Aucassin, "what is this thou sayest now? God grant me never aught of my desire, if I be dubbed knight, or mount steed, or go into the stour where knights do smite and are smitten, if thou givest me not Nicolette, my sweet lady, whom I love so well."

"Son," quoth his father, "this may never be: rather would I be quite disinherited and lose all that is mine, than that thou shouldst have her to thy wife. . . ."

"Father, go to now, I will make with thee fair covenant."

"What covenant, fair son?"

"I will take up arms, and go into the stour, on this covenant, that, if God bring me back sound and safe, thou wilt let me see Nicolette my sweet lady, even so long that I may have of her two words or three, and one kiss."

"That will I grant," said his father.

At this was Aucassin glad. . . .

Aucassin was armed and mounted as ye have heard tell. . . . Now believe ye not that his mind was on kine, nor cattle of the booty, nor thought he how he might strike a knight, nor be stricken again: nor no such thing. Nay, no memory had Aucassin of aught of these; rather he so dreamed of Nicolette, his sweet lady, that he dropped his reins, forgetting all there was to do, and his horse that had felt the spur, bore him into the press and hurled among the foe, and they laid hands on him all about, and took him captive, and seized away his spear and shield, and straightway they led him off a prisoner, and were even now discoursing of what death he should die.

And when Aucassin heard them,

"Ha! God," said he, "sweet Saviour. Be these my deadly enemies that have taken me, and will soon cut off my head? And once my head is off, no more shall I speak with Nicolette, my sweet lady that I love so well. Natheless have I here a good sword, and sit a good horse unwearied. If now I keep not my head for her sake, God help her never, if she love me more!"

. . . And he laid hand to sword, and fell a-smiting to right and left, and smote through helm and *nasal*, and arm and clenched hand, making a murder about him, like a wild boar when hounds fall on him in the forest, even till he struck down ten knights, and seven he hurt, and straightway he hurled out of the press, and rode back again at full speed, sword in hand. The Count Bougars de Valence heard say that they were about hanging Aucassin, his enemy, so he came into that place, and Aucassin was ware of him, and gat his sword into his hand, and lashed at his helm with such a stroke that he drave it down on his head, and he being stunned, fell grovelling. And Aucassin laid hands on him, and caught him by the *nasal* of his helmet, and gave him to his father.

"Father," quoth Aucassin, "lo here is your mortal foe, who hath so warred on you with all malengin. Full twenty years did this war endure, and might not be ended by man."

"Fair son," said his father, "thy feats of youth shouldst thou do, and not seek after folly."

"Father," saith Aucassin, "sermon me no sermons, but fulfil my covenant."

"Ha! what covenant, fair son?"

"What, father, hast thou forgotten it? . . . Didst thou not covenant with me when I took up arms, and went into the stour, that if God brought me back safe and sound, thou wouldst let me see Nicolette, my sweet lady, even so long that I may have of her two words or three, and one kiss? . . ."

"I!" quoth the father, "God forsake me when I keep this covenant! Nay, if she were here, I would let burn her in the fire, and thyself shouldst be sore adread."

"Is this thy last word?" quoth Aucassin.

"So help me God," quoth his father, "yea!"

"Certes," quoth Aucassin, "this is a sorry thing meseems when a man of thine age lies!"

3. DANTE MEETS VIRGIL, HIS GUIDE THROUGH THE INFERNO

Dante Alighieri (1265–1321), the greatest of Italian poets, wrote extensively in Latin and in the Tuscan dialect of Italian.* The Divine Comedy, *his great work, opens with the scene presented below, in which Dante is lost in a forest on the night before Good Friday, in the year 1300. Symbolic wild beasts block his way until the spirit of Virgil appears, to usher him through the nine circles of Hell, thence to Purgatory and finally to Paradise.

CANTO I

In the middle of the journey of our life, I found myself in a dark wood; for the straight way was lost. Ah! how hard a thing it is to tell what a wild, and rough, and stubborn wood this was, which in my thought renews the fear: so bitter is it, that scarcely more is death. But to treat of the good that I there found, I will relate the other things that I discerned.

Dante's Divine Comedy: The Inferno, translated by John A. Carlyle, Seventh Edition (London: G. Bell & Sons, Ltd., 1894), pp. 2–4, 7–9, 11–12.

I cannot rightly tell how I entered it, so full of sleep was I about the moment that I left the true way. But after I had reached the foot of a Hill there, where that valley ended, which had pierced my heart with fear, I looked up and saw its shoulders already clothed with the rays of the Planet that leads men straight on every road. Then the fear was somewhat calmed, which had continued in the lake of my heart the night that I passed so piteously. And as he, who with panting breath has escaped from the deep sea to the shore, turns to the dangerous water and gazes; so my mind, which still was fleeing, turned back to see the pass that no one ever left alive.

After I had rested my wearied body, I took the way again along the desert strand, so that the firm foot always was the lower. . . .

Whilst I was rushing downwards, there appeared before my eyes one who seemed hoarse from long silence. When I saw him in the great desert, I cried: "Have pity on me, whate'er thou be, whether shade or veritable man!"

He answered me: "Not man, a man I once was; and my parents were Lombards, and both of Mantua by country. I was born *sub Julio,* though it was late; and lived at Rome under the good Augustus, in the time of the false and lying gods. A Poet I was; and sang of that just son of Anchises, who came from Troy after proud Ilium was burnt. But thou, why returnest thou to such disquiet? why ascendest not the delectable mountain, which is the beginning and the cause of all gladness?"

"Art thou then that Virgil, and that fountain which pours abroad so rich a stream of speech?" I answered him, with bashful front. "O glory, and light of other poets! May the long zeal avail me, and the great love, that made me search thy volume. Thou art my master and my author. Thou alone art he from whom I took the good style that hath done me honour. . . .

". . . Wherefore I think and discern *this* for thy best, that thou follow me. And I will be thy guide, and lead thee hence through an eternal place, where thou shalt hear the hopeless shrieks, shalt see the ancient spirits in pain; so that each calls for second death. And thou shalt see those who are contented in the fire; for they hope to come, whensoever it be, amongst the blessed. Then to these, if thou desirest to ascend, there shall be a Spirit worthier than I to guide thee. With her will I leave thee at my parting. For that Emperor who reigns above, because I was rebellious to his law, wills not that I come into his city. In all parts he rules; and there he dwells. There is his city, and his high seat. O happy whom he chooses for it!"

And I to him: "Poet, I beseech thee by that God whom thou knewest not: in order that I may escape this ill and worse, lead me where thou now hast said, so that I may see the Gate of St. Peter, and those whom thou makest so sad."

Then he moved; and I kept on behind him.

4. FRANCESCA DA RIMINI TELLS HER TRAGIC STORY TO DANTE

On entering Hell, Dante and Virgil reach the outer circle, or Limbo, where dwell spirits of renowned pagans and unbaptized persons. In the second circle, guarded by the judge, Minos, are found the souls of those whose sins were of carnal love. Francesca da Rimini, whom Dante meets here, was married by proxy to the crippled Giovanni Malatesta, but at once fell in love with the proxy, Giovanni's younger brother, Paolo. The lovers were discovered and killed by the outraged husband.

CANTO V

Thus I descended from the first circle down into the second, which encompasses less space, and so much greater pain, that it stings to wailing. There Minos sits horrific, and grins: examines the crimes upon the entrance; judges, and sends according as he girds himself. I say, that when the ill-born spirit comes before him, it confesses all; and that sin-discerner sees what place in hell is for it, and with his tail makes as many circles round himself as the degrees he will have it to descend.

Always before him stands a crowd of them. They go each in its turn to judgment: they tell, and hear; and then are whirled down. . . .

Now begin the doleful notes to reach me; now am I come where much lamenting strikes me. I came into a place void of all light, which bellows like the sea in tempest, when it is combated by warring winds. The hellish storm, which never rests, leads the spirits with its sweep; whirling, and smiting it vexes them. When they arrive before the ruin, there the shrieks, the moanings, and the lamentation; there they blaspheme the divine power.

I learnt that to such torment were doomed the carnal sinners, who subject reason to lust. And as their wings bear along the starlings, at the cold season, in large and crowded troop; so that blast, the evil spirits. Hither, thither, down, up, it leads them. No hope ever comforts them, not of rest but *even* of less pain. And as the cranes go chanting their lays, making a long streak of themselves in the air; so I saw the shadows come, uttering wails, borne by that strife *of winds*. . . .

I began: "Poet, willingly would I speak with those two that go together, and seem so light upon the wind."

Dante's Divine Comedy: The Inferno, translated by John A. Carlyle, Seventh Edition (London: G. Bell & Sons, Ltd., 1894), pp. 48–51, 53–58.

And he to me: "Thou shalt see when they are nearer to us: and do thou then entreat them by that love, which leads them; and they will come."

Soon as the wind bends them to us, I raise my voice: "O wearied souls! come to speak with us, if none denies it."

As doves called by desire, with open and steady wings fly through the air to their loved nest, borne by their will; so those spirits issued from the band where Dido is, coming to us through the malignant air. Such was the force of my affectuous cry.

"O living creature, gracious and benign! that goest through the black air, visiting us who stained the earth with blood. If the King of the Universe were our friend, we would pray him for thy peace; seeing that thou hast pity of our perverse misfortune. Of that which it pleases thee to hear and to speak, we will hear and speak with you, whilst the wind, as now, is silent.

"The town, where I was born, sits on the shore, where Po descends to rest with his attendant *streams.* Love, which is quickly caught in gentle heart, took him with the fair body of which I was bereft; and the manner still afflicts me. Love, which to no loved one permits excuse for loving, took me so strongly with delight in him, that, as thou seest, even now it leaves me not. Love led us to one death. Caïna waits for him who quenched our life." These words from them were offered to us.

After I had heard those wounded souls, I bowed my face, and held it low until the Poet said to me: "What art thou thinking of?"

When I answered, I began: "Ah me! what sweet thoughts, what longing led them to the woeful pass!"

Then I turned again to them; and I spoke, and began: "Francesca, thy torments make me weep with grief and pity. But tell me: in the time of the sweet sighs, by what and how love granted you to know the dubious desires?"

And she to me: "*There is* no greater pain than to recall a happy time in wretchedness; and this thy teacher knows. But if thou hast such desire to learn the first root of our love, I will do like one who weeps and tells.

"One day, for pastime, we read of Lancelot, how love constrained him. We were alone, and without all suspicion. Several times that reading urged our eyes to meet, and changed the colour of our faces. But one moment alone it was that overcame us. When we read how the fond smile was kissed by such a lover, he, who shall never be divided from me, kissed my mouth all trembling. . . . That day we read in it no farther."

Whilst the one spirit thus spake, the other wept so, that I fainted with pity, as if I had been dying; and fell, as a dead body falls.

5. EUROPE IS SEIZED BY A CHURCH-BUILDING CRAZE

Raul Glaber, a monk at Cluny, was one of the first writers to note the remarkable upsurge of interest in church building after the year 1000.

Therefore, after the above-mentioned year of the millennium which is now about three years past, there occurred, throughout the world, especially in Italy and Gaul, a rebuilding of church basilicas. Notwithstanding the greater number were already well established and not in the least in need, nevertheless each Christian people strove against the others to erect nobler ones. It was as if the whole earth, having cast off the old by shaking itself, were clothing itself everywhere in the white robe of the church. Then, at last, all the faithful altered completely most of the episcopal seats for the better, and likewise, the monasteries of the various saints as well as the lesser places of prayer in the towns. . . .

V. Mortet, *Recueil de textes relatifs à l'histoire de l'architecture* . . . (Paris: 1911), Vol. I, p. 4, translated by Charles P. Parkhurst, Jr., as found in Elizabeth Gilmore Holt, ed., *Literary Sources of Art History* (Princeton, N.J.: Princeton University Press, 1947), p. 3.

6. ABBOT SUGER REBUILDS THE CHURCH OF ST. DENIS

Suger (1081–1151) emerged from obscure origins to become the chief minister of Kings Louis VI and Louis VII. In 1122, Suger was named abbot of St. Denis, the great monastery and church near Paris where most of the kings of France are buried.

XXIV. OF THE CHURCH'S DECORATION. Having assigned the increase of the revenue in this manner, we turned our hand to the memorable construction of buildings, so that by this thanks might be given to Almighty God by us as well as by our successors; and that by good example their ardor might be aroused to the continuation and, if necessary, to the completion of this (work). For neither any want nor any hindrance by any power will have to be feared if, for the love of the Holy Martyrs, one takes safely care of oneself by one's own resources. The first work on this church which we began under the inspiration of God (was this): because of the age of the old walls and their impending ruin in some places, we summoned the best

Abbot Suger, on the Abbey-Church of St. Denis and Its Art Treasures, edited, translated, and annotated by Edwin Panofsky (Princeton: 1946), as found in Elizabeth Gilmore Holt, ed., *Literary Sources of Art History* (Princeton, N.J.: Princeton University Press, 1947), pp. 20–21.

painters I could find from different regions, and reverently caused these (walls) to be repaired and becomingly painted with gold and precious colors. I completed this all the more gladly because I had wished to do it, if ever I should have an opportunity, even while I was a pupil in school.

XXV. OF THE FIRST ADDITION TO THE CHURCH. However, even while this was being completed at great expense, I found myself, under the inspiration of the Divine Will and because of that inadequacy which we often saw and felt on feast days, namely the Feast of the blessed Denis, the Fair, and very many others (for the narrowness of the place forced the women to run toward the altar upon the heads of the men as upon pavement with much anguish and noisy confusion), encouraged by the counsel of wise men and by the prayers of many monks (lest it displease God and the Holy Martyrs) to enlarge and amplify the noble church consecrated by the Divine Hand; and I set out at once to begin this very thing. In our chapter as well as in church I implored Divine mercy that He Who is the One, *the beginning and the end, Alpha and Omega,* might join a good end to a good beginning by a safe middle; that He might not repel from the building of the temple a *bloody man* who desired this very thing, with his whole heart, more than to obtain the treasures of Constantinople. Thus we began work at the former entrance with the doors. We tore down a certain addition asserted to have been made by Charlemagne on a very honorable occasion (for his father, the Emperor Pepin, had commanded that he be buried, for the sins of his father Charles Martel, outside at the entrance with the doors, face downward and not recumbent); and we set our hand to this part. As is evident we exerted ourselves incessantly with the enlargement of the body of the church as well as with the trebling of the entrance and the doors, and with the erection of high and noble towers.

IV

THE LATE MIDDLE AGE

15

THE GROWTH OF NATIONAL MONARCHY IN FRANCE AND ENGLAND

In the fourteenth and fifteenth centuries, government in England and France underwent gradual transition from feudal to national monarchy. The rising class of bourgeoisie often allied itself with the kings to check the ambitions of a still powerful military nobility. Most Englishmen and Frenchmen experienced a greater consciousness of nationality, which was considerably stimulated by the events of the Hundred Years' War (1340–1453). English victories in the early phases of this struggle at Crécy and Poitiers and the triumph of Henry V at Agincourt (1415) were eventually offset by the dramatic emergence of Joan of Arc, the champion of French nationalism. By 1500, France had recovered from the devastation of the war and was moving politically in the direction of absolutism. England's Parliament gained considerable power during the war with France, but was eclipsed by the Tudor kings at the end of the fifteenth century.

1. THE FRENCH CROWN PASSES TO THE VALOIS HOUSE, 1328

Although the origins of the Hundred Years' War are exceedingly complex, the basic political conflict centered on the issue of succession to the throne of France. In 1328 the line of male descendants of Hugh Capet came to an end, leaving Edward III of England as nearest male heir to the throne of France.

Besides this daughter (Isabella of France, wife of Edward II of England) of whom I have spoken above, King Philip the Fair (Philip IV) had three

Jean le Bel of Liége, *Chronicle,* as found in R.C.D. Laffan, ed., *Select Documents of European History, 800–1492* (New York: Henry Holt and Company, Inc., 1929), pp. 161–162. Used by permission of Methuen & Co., Ltd., London.

sons. And these three sons were very handsome. Of them, the eldest was called Louis, who in his father's lifetime became king of Navarre and was called the quarrelsome king; the second was called Philip the Fair; the third Charles. And, after the death of their father, they were all three kings of France in lawful succession, one after the other. . . .

Accordingly, after the death of King Charles, the twelve peers and the barons of France did not give the kingdom to the sister, who was queen of England, because they wished to say and maintain (as they still do) that the kingdom of France is so noble that it ought on no account to go to a woman; nor, consequently, to her eldest son, the king of England; for, as they declared, the son of a woman can have no right of succession through his mother, where his mother herself has none. For these reasons the twelve peers and the barons of France by common consent gave the kingdom of France to my lord Philip, son of my lord Charles of Valois, the brother of the aforesaid King Philip the Fair. Thus they set aside the queen of England and her son, who was heir male and son of the sister of the late king, Charles. Thus the kingdom passed away from the true line, as it seemed to many people; and hence great wars arose and great destruction of people and lands in the kingdom of France, as you may hear hereafter. . . .

2. *ENGLISH FORCES WIN A SWEEPING VICTORY AT CRÉCY, 1346*

The battle of Crécy in 1346, the first major land engagement of the Hundred Years' War, marked the triumph of a new weapon, the long-bow, over feudal military equipment. The source for this selection is Jean Froissart's* Chronicles, *one of the great literary and historical works of the Late Middle Age.

(Having reached a point near Crécy) the king of England was well informed how the French king followed after him to fight. Then he said to his company: "Let us take here some plot of ground, for we will go no farther till we have seen our enemies. I have good cause here to abide them, for I am on the right heritage of the queen, my mother, the which land was given her at her marriage; I will challenge it of mine adversary, Philip of Valois." And because he had not the eighth part in number of men that the French king had, therefore he commanded his marshals to

The Chronicles of Froissart, translated by John Bourchier, Lord Berners, edited by G.C. Macaulay, *The Globe Edition* (London: Macmillan and Co., Ltd., 1899), pp. 102–107, as found in J.H. Robinson, *Readings in European History* (New York: Ginn and Company, 1904), Vol. I, pp. 466–470. Copyright 1904 by James Harvey Robinson. Used by permission of the publisher.

choose a plot of ground somewhat for his advantage; and so they did, and thither the king and his host went. . . .

That night the king made a supper to all his chief lords of his host, and made them good cheer; and when they were all departed to take their rest, then the king entered into his oratory and kneeled down before the altar, praying God devoutly that if he fought the next day he might achieve the expedition to his honor. Then about midnight he laid him down to rest, and in the morning he rose betimes and heard mass, and the prince his son with him; and the most part of his company were confessed and received the communion; and after the mass was said, he commanded every man to be armed and to draw to the field, to the same place before appointed. . . .

Then (after arranging his army in three divisions,) the king lept on a palfrey, with a white rod in his hand, one of his marshals on the one hand and the other on the other hand. He rode from rank to rank, desiring every man to take heed that day to his right and honor. He spake it so sweetly and with so good countenance and merry cheer that all such as were discomfited took courage in the seeing and hearing of him. And when he had thus visited all his battles (i.e., divisions) it was then nine of the day. Then he caused every man to eat and drink a little, and so they did at their leisure. And afterward they ordered again their battles. Then every man lay down on the earth, his helmet and his bow by him, to be the more fresher when their enemies should come.

This Saturday the French king rose betimes and heard mass in Abbeville, in his lodging in the abbey of St. Peter, and he departed after the sun rising. (He dispatched four knights to view the English, who let them alone and permitted them to return to the king as they had come. The knights advised the king that the French should defer the attack until the morrow.) Then the king commanded that it should be so done. Then his two marshals rode, one before, another behind, saying to every banner, "Tarry and abide here in the name of God and St. Denis." They that were foremost tarried, but they that were behind would not tarry, but rode forth, and said how they would in no wise abide till they were as far forward as the foremost. And when they that were before saw them come on behind, then they rode forward again, so that the king nor his marshals could not rule them.

So they rode without order or good array till they came in sight of their enemies; and as soon as the foremost saw them, they reculed them aback without good array, whereof they behind had marvel and were abashed, and thought that the foremost company had been fighting. Then they might have had leisure and room to have gone forward if they had listed, but some went forth while some abode still.

The commons, of whom all the ways between Abbeville and Crécy were full, when they saw that they were near to their enemies, took their swords and cried, "Down with them! Let us slay them all." There were no man, though he were present, that could imagine or show the truth of the evil order that was among the French party,—and yet they were a marvelous great number. What I write in this book I learned especially of the Englishmen, who beheld their dealing; and also certain knights of Sir John of Hainault's, who was always about King Philip, showed me what they knew.

The Englishmen, who were in three battles lying on the ground to rest them, as soon as they saw the Frenchmen approach, they rose upon their feet, fair and easily without any haste, and arranged their battles. The first was the prince's battle, and the archers there stood in manner of a harrow and the men-at-arms in the bottom of the battle. The earl of Northampton and the earl of Arundel with the second battle were on the wing in good order, ready to comfort the prince's battle, if need were.

The lords and knights of France came not to the engagement together in good order, for some came before and some came after, in such evil order that one of them did trouble another. When the French king saw the Englishmen his blood changed and he said to his marshals, "Make the Genoese go on before and begin the battle in the name of God and St. Denis." There were of the Genoese crossbows about fifteen thousand, but they were so weary of going afoot that day a six leagues armed with their crossbows that they said to their constables, "We be not well ordered to fight this day, for we be not in the case to do any great deed of arms; we have more need of rest." . . .

Also the same season there fell a great rain, and a flash of lightning with a terrible thunder, and before the rain there came flying over both battles a great number of crows for fear of the tempest coming. Then anon the air began to wax clear, and the sun to shine fair and bright, the which was right in the Frenchmen's eyen and on the Englishmen's backs.

When the Genoese were assembled together and began to approach they uttered a great cry to abash the Englishmen, but these stood still and stirred not for all that. Then the Genoese a second time made a fell cry and stept forward a little, but the Englishmen removed not one foot. Thirdly they shouted again and went forth until they came within shot. Then they shot fiercely with their crossbows. Then the English archers stepped forth one pace and let fly their arrows so wholly and so thick that it seemed snow. When the Genoese felt the arrows piercing through their heads, arms, and breasts, many of them cast down their crossbows and did cut their strings and returned discomfited.

When the French king saw them fly away he said, "Slay these rascals, for they shall let and trouble us without reason." Then ye should have seen the men-at-arms dash in among them and they killed a great number of them; and ever still the Englishmen shot where they saw the thickest press. The sharp arrows ran into the men-at-arms and into their horses, and many fell, horses and men, among the Genoese, and when they were down they could not rise again; the press was so thick that one overthrew another. And also among the Englishmen there were certain rascals that went afoot with great knives, and they went in among the men-at-arms and slew and murdered many as they lay on the ground, both earls, barons, knights, and squires; whereof the king of England was after displeased, for he had rather that they had been taken prisoners. . . .

(The division led by the king's son, the Black Prince, being hard pressed,) they sent a messenger to the king, who was on a little windmill hill. Then the knight said to the king, "Sir, the earl of Warwick and the earl of Oxford, Sir Raynold Cobham, and others, such as be about the prince your son, are fiercely fought withal and are sorely handled; wherefore they desire you that you and your battle will come and aid them; for if the Frenchmen increase, as they doubt they will, your son and they will have much ado." Then the king said, "Is my son dead, or hurt, or on the earth felled?" "No, sir," quoth the knight, "but he is hardly matched, wherefore he hath need of your aid." "Well," said the king, "return to him and to them that sent you hither, and say to them that they send no more to me for any adventure that falleth, as long as my son is alive; and also say to them that they suffer him this day to win his spurs; for if God be pleased, I will that this expedition be his, and the honor thereof, and to them that be about him."

3. *FRANCE ENDURES THE DISASTROUS YEAR OF 1356*

In the early stages of the Hundred Years' War, brutality and destruction appeared as normal characteristics of this unfortunate conflict. The following selection is taken from a contemporary chronicle of Jean de Venette, a Carmelite friar.

In the same year, 1356, the luxury and dissoluteness of many of the nobles and the knights became still more deeply rooted. I have described above

The Chronicle of Jean de Venette, translated by Jean Birdsall, edited by Richard A. Newhall (New York: Columbia University Press, 1953), pp. 62–67.

the far too brief and scanty garments which they had already adopted. Now they began to disfigure themselves in a still more extravagant way. They wore pearls on their hoods or on their gilded and silver girdles and elaborately adorned themselves from head to foot with gems and precious stones. So assiduously did all men, from the least to the greatest, cover themselves with these luxuries that pearls and other precious stones were sold for high prices and could hardly be found at all in Paris. I myself remember seeing two small pearls which had been bought long before for 8 denarii and which sold at this time for 10 librae. Men also began to wear the plumes of birds fastened on their hats. By night they devoted themselves immoderately to the pleasures of the flesh or to games of dice; by day, to ball or tennis. Wherefore the common people had reason to lament, and did lament greatly, that the taxes levied on them for the war were uselessly spent on such sports and converted to such uses. It was at this time that the nobles in derision called peasants and simple folk Jacques Bonhomme. That year men sent to the wars who bore arms in rustic fashion of peasants were given the name Jacques Bonhomme by those who mocked and despised them, and thus lost the name of peasant. Both French and English called peasants this for a long time afterward. But, woe is me! many who then derided peasants with this name were later made mortal sport of by them. For many nobles, as shall be told, perished miserably at the hands of peasants and many peasants in turn were cruelly slain by the nobles and their villages burned in revenge. Let us leave these matters for the present and turn to still more remarkable and terrible events.

In the same year, 1356, the prince of Wales, eldest son of Edward, king of England, was sent by his father to France with a great multitude of men-at-arms, English and Gascon and German mercenaries. While his father remained in England he rose along through the kingdom, burning and destroying until he came to the borders of Poitou. John, king of France, heard of his approach and, after defeating and ejecting enemies who had established themselves in the castle of Breteuil and the castle of Verneuil in the neighborhood of Chartres, he straightway assembled a very large and mighty army. With Charles, duke of Normandy, his eldest son, two other sons, and Philip, his youngest, he soon drew near to Poitou against the English prince and his army. In the French army were the duke of Bourbon, a great noble, the duke of Athens, constable of France, and many marshals, barons, counts, knights, and nobles. There were also two prelates in arms, William of Melun, archbishop of Sens, and the bishop of Châlons, and a very large number of foot soldiers. There came there also two cardinals sent by the Church to arrange a peace. When both armies had come within about two leagues of Poitiers the cardinals went back and forth between the lines, solicitously interposing their good offices. But impeded by that enemy of human kind, Belial, and some of his sons, they failed to bring peace to the discordant parties. On the contrary, pride reigned, confidence in the might and multitude of armed men persisted, and as a result a pitched battle was agreed upon. King John came to battle in high spirits. He desired to fight on foot with his men, and this he did. After he had sent away his horses, he entered the conflict and attacked the enemy boldly and bravely. He slew several and wounded many mortally. Had all the nobles and knights borne themselves as bravely as the king they would have triumphed gloriously over all their enemies. But many, became pusillanimous and sluggish, were loath to attack their adversaries. The English, emboldened by this, made a spirited attack on King John. Though he defended himself manfully and slew many, he could not withstand so overwhelming an attack. Many of the French nobility were killed, for example the duke of Bourbon and all his men, and the duke of Athens, the constable, with his, and, by the will of God and the opposition of Fortune who makes the outcome of wars uncertain, King John with his youngest son Philip was taken by the English and made prisoner. When his eldest son Charles, duke of Normandy, saw this, he and his men abandoned the battle and retreated, and his brothers the duke of Anjou and the count of Poitou did likewise. All who could escape fled from the battle. The English pursued the fugitives, slew many, and took and plundered many knights and foot soldiers. Some unable to flee surrendered themselves indiscriminately to varlets and servants without offering any defense; others who did not know how to yield to the fury and the swords of their foes were slain.

In this way, then, the king was captured and held a prisoner, some of the people slain, others put to flight and scattered, and others captured and held for ransom, including many knights and barons and the archbishop of Sens. The bishop of Châlons was killed. King John, his younger son Philip, and many other prisoners were taken by the English and the Gascons, who had come to the aid of the English, by the direct route to Bordeaux. The king, though a prisoner, was treated with great honor by the prince of Wales and the English. As soon as they came to Bordeaux they drew up a treaty of peace, which, however, was never put into effect; for the king of England was unwilling to approve the treaty and commanded that John be taken a prisoner to England. And this was done very soon. He was taken overseas to the city of London in England. . . .

The three estates were still the rulers of the state when the regent returned, but they did not retain that office much longer. For the nobles utterly refused to settle certain matters as the other two estates, the clergy and the burgesses, wished. Thus discord arose and all three estates abandoned the task they had begun. From that time on all went ill with the kingdom, and the state was undone. Thieves and robbers rose up everywhere in the land. The nobles despised and hated all others and took no thought for the mutual usefulness and profit of lord and men. They subjected and despoiled the peasants and the men of the villages. In no wise did they defend their country from its enemies. Rather did they trample it underfoot, robbing and pillaging the peasants' goods. The regent, it appeared clearly, gave no thought to their plight. At that time the country and whole land of France began to put on confusion and mourning like a garment, because it had no defender or guardian. For this land, which before all the kingdoms and parts of the world had been secure in glory and honor and the blessings of peace and renown, and opulent in the affluence of every good thing, came more and more to be held by the other nations in derision and opprobrium, woe is me! Highways and roads were almost everywhere uncertain and dangerous on account of freebooters and robbers. What more can I say? Thenceforward infinite harm, misfortune, and danger befell the French people for lack of good government and adequate defense.

In the same year, 1356, the citizens of Paris, fearing the enemy and putting little trust in the nobility, placed iron chains across the streets and crossways of Paris. They dug a ditch round the walls on the west and round the suburbs on the east where no walls had been before, and they built new walls with gates and bastilles like the others, in addition to digging a ditch. They fortified the towers with ballista, garrots, cannons, machines, and other instruments of war. They destroyed all the houses which adjoined the wall either within or without. At that time many handsome and splendid dwellings both within and without the walls were condemned to complete demolition and ruin so that ditches might take their way over the ground on which these dwellings and manors stood. I myself saw the destruction of houses and the construction of ditches and walls, diligently pursued the next year and thereafter. . . .

4. *JOAN OF ARC TESTIFIES AT HER TRIAL*

The revival of French national feeling in the final stages of the Hundred Years' War owed much to the inspiring example of Joan of Arc (Jeanne d'Arc). The following selection is taken from a translation of the record of the Inquisition trial at Rouen in 1431, in which Joan was charged with heresy and witchcraft. She had been captured by Burgundians, sold to the English, and turned over to the local ecclesiastical court.

The Trial of Jeanne d'Arc, translated by W.P. Barrett (London: George Routledge & Sons, Ltd., 1931), pp. 49–51, 54–55, 70, 101, 113, 279, 281–282, 303, 306, 313–329, *passim.* Used by permission of Routledge & Kegan Paul Ltd.

Whilst we were saying these things this woman was brought in by our usher. Since she was appearing in judgment before us we began to explain how this Jeanne had been taken and apprehended within the boundaries and limits of our diocese of Beauvais; how many of her actions, not in our diocese alone but in many other regions also, had injured the orthodox faith, and how common report of them had spread through all the realms of christendom. . . .

. . . according to our office, we lawfully required the said Jeanne to take proper oath, with her hands on the holy gospels, to speak the truth in answer to such questions put to her, as beforesaid.

The said Jeanne replied in this manner: "I do not know what you wish to examine me on. Perhaps you might ask such things that I would not tell." Whereupon we said: "Will you swear to speak the truth upon those things which are asked you concerning the faith, which you know?" She replied that concerning her father and her mother and what she had done since she had taken the road to France, she would gladly swear; but concerning the revelations from God, these she had never told or revealed to anyone, save only to Charles whom she called King; nor would she reveal them to save her head; for she had them in visions or in her secret counsel; and within a week she would know certainly whether she might reveal them. . . .

When she had thus taken the oath the said Jeanne was questioned by us about her name and her surname. To which she replied that in her own country she was called Jeannette, and after she came to France, she was called Jeanne. . . . Consequently she was questioned about the district from which she came. She replied she was born in the village of Domrémy. . . .

Asked about the name of her father and mother, she replied that her father's name was Jacques d'Arc, and her mother's Isabelle. . . .

Asked if in her youth she had learned any craft, she said yes, to sew and spin: and in sewing and spinning she feared no woman in Rouen. . . .

. . . Afterwards she declared that at the age of thirteen she had a voice from God to help her and guide her. And the first time she was much afraid. And this voice came towards noon, in summer, in her father's garden: and the said Jeanne had (not) fasted on the preceding day. . . .

Asked what instruction this voice gave her for the salvation of her soul: she said it taught her to be good and to go to church often; and it told her that she must come to France. . . . and the voice told her again that she should raise the siege of the city of Orleans. . . .

Asked whether, when she saw the voice coming to her, there was a light, she answered that there was a great deal of light on all sides, as was most fitting. She added to the examiner that not all the light came to him alone! . . .

Asked whether she thought she had committed a sin when she left her father and mother, she answered that since God commanded, it was right to do so. She added that since God commanded, if she had had a hundred parents, or had been the king's daughter, she would have gone nevertheless. . . .

And first why she jumped from the tower at Beaurevoir. She answered that she had heard that the people of Compiègne, all of them to the age of seven years, were to be put to fire and to the sword, and she would rather die than live after such a destruction of good people. That was one reason why she jumped: the other was that she knew she had been sold to the English, and she would have died rather than fall into the hands of her enemies the English.

Asked whether the leap was made at the counsel of her voices, she answered that St. Catherine told her almost every day not to jump, and God would help her, and the people of Compiègne too. And Jeanne told St. Catherine that since God was going to help the people of Compiègne, she wanted to be there. And St. Catherine said: "You must be resigned and not falter; you will not be delivered until you have seen the King of the English." Jeanne answered: "Truly I do not want to see him, and I would rather die than fall into the hands of the English." . . .

And Jeanne was required and admonished to speak the truth on many different points contained in her trial which she had denied or to which she had given false replies, whereas we possessed certain information, proofs, and vehement presumptions upon them. Many of the points were read and explained to her, and she was told that if she did not confess them truthfully she would be put to the torture, the instruments of which were shown to her all ready in the tower. There were also present by our instruction men ready to put her to the torture in order to restore her to the way and knowledge of truth, and by this means to procure the salvation of her body and soul which by her lying inventions she exposed to such grave perils.

To which the said Jeanne answered in this manner: "Truly if you were to tear me limb from limb and separate my soul from my body, I would not tell you anything more: and if I did say anything, I should afterwards declare that you had compelled me to say it by force." . . .

. . . in view of her disposition and will and of the circumstances, we concluded that it was neither necessary nor expedient to submit her to the torture, and that we should proceed further in the matter. . . .

. . . the clergy declare you to be a traitor, perfidious, cruel, desiring human bloodshed, seditious, an instigator of tyranny, a blasphemer of God's commandments and revelations. . . .

. . . the clergy affirm that if you had the revelations and saw the apparitions of which you boast in such a manner as you say, then you are an idolatress, an invoker of demons, an apostate from the faith, a maker of rash statements, a swearer of an unlawful oath.

* * *

Jeanne's Abjuration

. . . I, *Jeanne*, commonly called *The Maid*, a miserable sinner, recognizing the snares of error in which I was held, and being by God's grace returned to Our Holy Mother Church, in order to show that my return is made not feignedly but with a good heart and will, I confess that I have most grievously sinned in falsely pretending to have had revelations and apparitions from God, His angels, St. Catherine and St. Margaret; . . . In making superstitious divinations, in blaspheming God and His Saints; in breaking the divine law, Holy Scripture, and the canon laws; in wearing a dissolute, ill-shaped and immodest dress against the decency of nature, and hair cropped round like a man's, against all the modesty of womankind; also in bearing arms most presumptuously; in cruelly desiring the shedding of human blood; . . .

Sentence After the Abjuration

. . . inasmuch as you have rashly sinned against God and the Holy Church, we finally and definitely condemn you for salutary penance to perpetual imprisonment, with the bread of sorrow and water of affliction. . . .

On Monday following, the day after Holy Trinity Sunday, we the said judges repaired to Jeanne's prison to observe her state and disposition. . . .

. . . She said that what she had declared and recanted on Thursday was done only for fear of the fire.

Asked if she believed her voices to be St. Catherine and St. Margaret, she answered yes, and they came from God. . . .

Afterwards . . . we the said judges repaired to the Old Market of Rouen, near the church of St. Sauveur. . . . The said Jeanne was led before us in view of a great multitude of people assembled in this place; she was placed upon a scaffold or platform. . . .

. . . we proceeded to the final sentence in these terms:

. . . we declare that you are fallen again into your former errors and under the sentence of excommunication which you originally incurred we decree that you are a relapsed heretic; and by this sentence which we deliver in writing and pronounce from this tribunal, we denounce you as a rotten member, which, so that you shall not infect the other members of Christ, must be cast out of the unity of the Church, cut off from her body, and given over to the secular power. . . .

5. *ENGLAND'S PARLIAMENT ASSUMES GREATER POWERS*

The English Parliament was gradually transformed in the fourteenth and fifteenth centuries from a feudal advisory body into a judicial and legislative branch of government. Early in the Hundred Years' War the hard-pressed Edward III reluctantly recognized Parliament's right to control the purse. The following account is drawn from a fourteenth century description of the working of Parliament.

The king is the head, beginning and end of parliament; and thus he has no peer in his grade, and the first grade consists of the king alone. The second grade consists of the archbishops, bishops, abbots, priors, who hold by barony. The third grade consists of the representatives of the clergy. The fourth, of earls, barons, and other magnates and chiefs, whose holding is of the value of a county and barony—as has been explained in the clause concerning laymen. The fifth is of knights of the shires. The sixth, of citizens and burgesses. And thus parliament consists of six grades. . . .

. . . the two principal clerks of parliament elected by the king and his council, and the other secondary clerks . . . are bound to be present on the first day. The chancellor of England, the treasurer, the chamberlain, and the barons of the exchequer, the justices, all the clerks and knights of the king, together with those who serve the king with regard to the pleas, and who are of the king's council: are bound to be present on the second day. . . .

The king is in every way bound to be personally present in parliament, unless he be detained by bodily sickness; and then he can keep his room, provided it do not lie beyond the manor, or at least the town, where the parliament is held. . . .

The king does not usually ask aid from his kingdom unless for imminent war, or for knighting his sons, or for marrying his daughters; and then such aids ought to be sought in full parliament; . . . if the commonality—the clergy and laity—have been summoned to parliament, as they have a right to be, and are not willing to come for certain causes; as if they were to maintain that the lord king did not rule them as he ought to, and were

"The Manner of Holding Parliament," in Ernest F. Henderson, trans. and ed., *Select Historical Documents of the Middle Ages* (London: G. Bell & Sons, Ltd., 1892), pp. 158–165.

to signify in what especial respect he did not do so; then it would not be a parliament at all, even though the archbishops, bishops, counts and barons and all their peers, were present with the king. And so it is necessary that all things which are to be affirmed or cancelled, granted or denied, or done by the parliament, should be granted by the commonality of the parliament, which consists of the three grades or divisions of parliament: viz. of the representatives of the clergy, the knights of the shires, the citizens and burgesses, who represent the whole commonality of England; and not by the magnates. . . .

Parliament ought not to be dismissed so long as any petition remains undiscussed. . . .

. . . Parliament shall be held in whatever place of the kingdom it pleases the king.

16

WANING PRESTIGE AND INFLUENCE OF THE CHURCH

The Church in the Late Middle Age experienced a series of misfortunes. From 1309 to 1377 popes lived at Avignon in southern France, in luxurious surroundings. The collection of papal revenues caused numerous complaints from all parts of Christian Europe. While many clergymen were honest, devout, and hardworking like Chaucer's parson, others like the pardoner were thoroughly corrupt. Among the laity deep devotion was revealed by the popularity of the *Imitation of Christ*, and crude superstition was evidenced by the witchcraft hysteria. In the early fifteenth century the serious problems of the Great Schism, the need for reform, and the heresies of Huss and Wycliffe led to the calling of a general Church council at Constance in 1415.

1. PETRARCH DEPLORES THE PAPAL COURT AT AVIGNON

Much of the bitter criticism of the Avignon Papacy by subsequent historians stems from the well-publicized letters of condemnation by Petrarch, an Italian humanist, who lived for many years in and near Avignon. While luxury and venality in the papal court no doubt existed, Petrarch failed to appreciate such vital spiritual achievements as the great missionary work in Asia and Africa. The second selection below serves as a corrective to Petrarch's dismal denunciation.

. . . The sun, in its travels sees nothing more hideous than this place on the shores of the wild Rhone, which suggests the hellish streams of Cocytus and Acheron. Here reign the successors of the poor fishermen of Galilee;

Petrarch, *Untitled Letters*, in *Translations and Reprints from the Original Sources of European History* (Philadelphia: University of Pennsylvania, 1896), Series I, Vol. III, No. 6, pp. 26–27.

they have strangely forgotten their origin. I am astounded, as I recall their predecessors, to see these men loaded with gold and clad in purple, boasting of the spoils of princes and nations; to see luxurious palaces and heights crowned with fortifications, instead of a boat turned downwards for shelter. We no longer find the simple nets which were once used to gain a frugal sustenance from the Lake of Galilee, and with which, having labored all night and caught nothing, they took, at day break, a multitude of fishes, in the name of Jesus. One is stupified nowadays to hear the lying tongues, and to see worthless parchments, turned by a leaden seal, into nets which are used, in Christ's name, but by the arts of Belial, to catch hordes of unwary Christians. These fish, too, are dressed and laid on the burning coals of anxiety before they fill the insatiable maw of their captors. Instead of holy solitude we find a criminal host and crowds of the most infamous satellites: instead of soberness, licentious banquets; instead of pious pilgrimages, preternatural and foul sloth; instead of the bare feet of the apostles, the snowy coursers of brigands fly past us, the horses decked in gold and fed on gold, soon to be shod with gold, if the Lord does not check this slavish luxury. In short, we seem to be among the kings of the Persians or Parthians, before whom we must fall down and worship, and who can not be approached except presents be offered. O, ye unkempt and emaciated old men, is it for this you labored? Is it for this that you have sown the field of the Lord and watered it with your holy blood? . . .

2. *A MODERN CATHOLIC HISTORIAN DEPLORES PETRARCH'S VIEWS*

The dark points of the Avignon period have certainly been greatly exaggerated. The assertion that the Government of the Avignon Popes was wholly ruled by the "will and pleasure of the Kings of France," is, in this general sense, unjust. The Popes of those days were not all so weak as Clement V., who submitted the draft of the Bull, by which he called on the Princes of Europe to imprison the Templars, to the French King. Moreover, even this Pope, the least independent of the fourteenth century Pontiffs, for many years offered a passive resistance to the wishes of France, and a writer, who has thoroughly studied the period, emphatically asserts that only for a few years of the Pontificate of Clement V. was the idea so long associated with the "Babylonian Captivity" of the Popes fully realized. The extension of this epithet to the whole of the Avignon sojourn is an unfair exaggeration. The eager censors of the dependence into which the

Ludwig Pastor, *The History of the Popes from the Close of the Middle Ages*, translated and edited by F.I. Antrobus (London: Kegan Paul, Trench, Trubner, and Co., Ltd., 1891), Vol. I, pp. 64–68.

Avignon Popes sank, draw attention to the political action of the Holy See during this period so exclusively, that hardly any place is left for its labours in the cause of religion. A very partial picture is thus drawn, wherein the noble efforts of these much-abused Pontiffs for the conversion of heathen nations become almost imperceptible in the dim background. Their labours for the propagation of Christianity in India, China, Egypt, Nubia, Abyssinia, Barbary, and Morocco have been very imperfectly appreciated. The earliest of the Avignon Popes, Clement V. and John XXII., gave the greatest attention to Eastern affairs, and were the originators of a series of grand creations, from which the best results were to be expected. Their successors were chiefly occupied in the maintenance and preservation of the works established by the wisdom of their predecessors, yet in the time of Clement VI. an effort was made to extend the sphere of the Church even to the furthest limits of Eastern Asia. The unwearied assiduity of the Avignon Popes in taking advantage of every favourable event in the East, from the Crimea to China, to promote the spread of Christianity by sending out missions and founding Bishoprics, is all the more admirable because of the great difficulties with which the Papacy was at that time beset. . . .

Petrarch judges the French Popes with the greatest severity. In theory he condemns every one, worthy or unworthy, who lived at Avignon. No expression is too strong when he speaks of this city, which he compares to the Babylon of the Apocalypse. . . . It would be, however, a great mistake to consider his picture of the wickedness of Avignon and the corruption of the Church, painted with true Italian fervour, as strictly trustworthy and accurate. Petrarch here speaks as a poet and as a fiery, enthusiastic, Roman patriot. His judgments are often intemperate and unjust. His own life was not such as to give him the right to come forward as a preacher of morals. Passing over his other failings, we need here only allude to his excessive greed for benefices. This passion has much to do with his bitterness against Avignon and the Papal Court. We are led to suspect that there were many unsuccessful suits. Petrarch did nothing towards the amendment of this evil world; the work of reformation was in his own case begun very late. He was a dreamer, who contented himself with theories, and in practice eschewed all improvements which demanded any greater effort than that of declamation.

The unmitigated condemnation of the Avignon Popes must have been based in great measure on Petrarch's unjust representations, to which, in later times and without examination, an undue historical importance has been attached. He is often supposed to be a determined adversary of the Papacy; but this is a complete mistake. He never for a moment questioned its divine institution. . . .

But however much we may question Petrarch's right to find fault with the moral delinquencies of the Court at Avignon; however much we may, in many respects, modify the picture he paints of it, no impartial inquirer can deny that it was pervaded by a deplorable worldliness. For this melancholy fact we have testimony more trustworthy than the rhetorical descriptions of the Italian poet. Yet it must in justice be borne in mind that the influx of thousands of strangers into the little French provincial town, so suddenly raised to the position of capital of the world, had produced all the evils which appertain to densely populated places. Moreover, even if we are to believe all the angry assertions of contemporaries as to the corruption prevailing in Avignon, evidence is not wanting, on the other hand, of ardent yearnings for a life conformable to the precepts of the Gospel.

Side by side with the profligacy which was the characteristic of the age, and, therefore, prominent in its history, there were still to be found scattered in various places many homes of quiet and devout contemplation. Thence went forth an influence, winning noble souls to a higher ideal of existence, and gently, but perseveringly, striving by means of self-denial and persuasion, to allay the passionate feuds of parties and disentangle their intrigues. As this higher life only manifested itself here and there, history passes it by; it is dealt with in commonplace phrases, judged, or rather misjudged, by the measure of the later movements of the sixteenth century, as if they formed a canon for the historical investigation of all religious phenomena. At no time were there wanting good and earnest men, who were doing their utmost in their own circle to stem the tide of corruption, and exerting a salutary influence on their age and surroundings. . . .

3. *CHAUCER'S PARSON AND PARDONER REPRESENT THE BEST AND WORST OF MEDIEVAL CHURCHMEN*

The Prologue to Chaucer's* Canterbury Tales *comprises a magnificent panorama of medieval society. The company that assembled at the Tabard Inn at Southwark for the journey to the shrine of St. Thomas à Becket at Canterbury included individuals from every walk of life, each vividly portrayed by the poet.

A good man was there of religion,
And was a poor Parson of a town,
But rich he was of holy thought and work.
He was also a learned man, a cleric
That Christ's gospel truly would preach;
His parishioners devoutly would he teach,

Prologue to Chaucer's *Canterbury Tales,* rendered into modern English by Ruth C. Hodges, 1958.

Benign he was, and wonderfully diligent
And in adversity full patient,
And such he was proved often times.
Full loath was he to excommunicate to get his tithes
But rather would he give in case of doubt
Unto his poor parishioners about
Of his offering and also of his substance.
He could in little things have contentment.
Wide was his parish, and houses far asunder,
But he never forgot, in rain nor thunder,
In sickness nor in misfortune, to visit
The farest of his parishioners, high or low,
On foot, and in his hand a staff.
This noble example to his flock he gave,
That first he wrought, and afterward he taught,
Out of the gospel he these words caught,
And this figure of speech he added also thereto,
That if gold rusts, what should iron do?
For if a priest be evil, in whom can we trust,
No wonder does a wicked man rust;
And shame it is, if a priest takes heed,
An evil shepherd and a pure flock.
Well ought a priest an example give,
By his purity, how that his flock should live.
He put not his benefice for hire
And left his flock encumbered in the mire.
Nor ran to London unto St. Paul's
To seek for himself a chanterie for Souls,[1]
Or with a gild to be retained as chaplain;
But dwelt at home, and kept well his fold;
So that the wolf never made it come to harm.
He was a shepherd and not a mercenaire [2]
And though he was holy and virtuous,
He was to sinful men not scornful,
Nor was his speech severe nor disdainful,
But in his teaching he was discreet and benign.
To draw folk to heaven by fairness,
By good example, this was his business.

[1] "Chanterie"—provision for a priest to sing daily for the repose of a soul for a remuneration.

[2] "Mercenaire"—a priest who made a living entirely by saying Mass.

But if were any persons obstinate,
Whomever they were, of high or low estate,
Them would he rebuke sharply at the time.
A better priest I believe that nowhere none is.
He demanded no pomp and reverence,
Nor made himself an over-scrupulous conscience,
But Christ's teachings and those of His Twelve Apostles,
He taught, but first he followed them himself.

* * *

With him [the Summoner] there rode a gentle Pardoner
Of Rouncivale, his friend and compeer,
That straight was come from the court of Rome.
Full loud he sang, "Come hither, love, to me!"
The Summoner joined him with a stiff basic melody;
And never did a trumpet make half so great a sound.
This Pardoner had hair as yellow as wax,
But smooth it hung as does a hank of flax;
By small bunches hung the locks that he had,
And therewith his shoulders it overspread;
But there it lay, by wisps one by one.
But hood, for jollity, he wore none,
For it was tucked up in his pouch.
It seemed to him he rode all in the newest fashion
With loose hair; save his cap, he went all bareheaded.
Such glaring eyes had he as a hare.
A vernycle had he sewed on his cap.[3]
His wallet lay before him in his lap,
Brimful of pardons, come from Rome all hot.
A voice he had as small as has a goat.
No beard had he, nor never should have,
As smooth his face was as it were lately shaven.
I think he was a gelding or a mare.
But of his craft, from Berwyk to Ware,[4]
Never was there such another pardoner.
For in his bag he had a pillowcase
Which he said was Our Lady's Veil:
He said he had a piece of the sail

[3] "Vernycle"—a reproduction of the sacred handkerchief that bore the miraculous impression of Christ's face.

[4] "Berwyk to Ware"—meaning from the north of England to the south.

That St. Peter had, when that he went
Upon the sea, till Jesus Christ him caught.
He had a cross of latten full of stones,[5]
And in a glass he had pigs' bones.
And with these relics, when that he found
A poor parson dwelling in the country
Upon that day he got him more money
Than that the parson got in two months.
And thus, with feigned flattery and jokes
He made the parson and his people fools.
But truly to tell at last,
He was in the church a noble ecclesiastic.
Well could he read a lesson or a story,
But best of all he sang the offertory
For well he knew, when that song was sung,
He must preach, and well use his smooth tongue
To win silver, as he full well could
Therefore he sang so merrily and loud.

4. A WITCH CONFESSES HIS WORSHIP OF THE DEVIL

A distressing feature of the Late Middle Age was the witchcraft hysteria, which began in the fifteenth century and continued sporadically for the next two hundred years, affecting all parts of Christian Europe. The selection below describes witch-persecution at Bern, Switzerland, in 1437.

I will relate to you some examples, which I have gained in part from the teachers of our faculty, in part from the experience of a certain upright secular judge, worthy of all faith, who from the torture and confession of witches and from his experiences in public and private has learned many things of this sort—a man with whom I have often discussed this subject broadly and deeply—to wit, Peter, a citizen of Bern, in the diocese of Lausanne, who has burned many witches of both sexes, and has driven others out of the territory of the Bernese. I have moreover conferred with one Benedict, a monk of the Benedictine order, who, although now a very devout cleric in a reformed monastery at Vienna, was a decade ago, while still in the world, a necromancer, juggler, buffoon, and strolling player, well-known as an expert among the secular nobility. I have likewise heard

Johannes Nider, *Formicarius,* Augsburg Edition (c. 1476), Lib. V, Cap. 3, in *Translations and Reprints from the Original Sources of European History* (Philadelphia: University of Pennsylvania, 1896), Series I, Vol. III, No. 4, pp. 6–7.

[5] "Latten"—a mixed metal compounded chiefly of copper and zinc.

certain of the following things from the Inquisitor of Heretical Pravity at Autun, who was a devoted reformer of our order in the convention at Lyons, and has convicted many of witchcraft in the diocese of Autun.

[Relating then two or three anecdotes derived from these sources, the theologian closes his answer with this one:]

The same procedure was more clearly described by another young man, arrested and burned as a witch, although, as I believe, truly penitent, who had earlier, together with his wife, a witch invincible to persuasion, escaped the clutches of the aforesaid judge, Peter. The aforesaid youth, being again indicted at Bern, with his wife, and placed in a different prison from hers, declared: "If I can obtain absolution for my sins, I will freely lay bear all I know about witchcraft, for I see that I have death to expect." And when he had been assured by the scholars that, if he should truly repent, he would certainly be able to gain absolution for his sins, then he gladly offered himself to death, and disclosed the methods of the primeval infection.

The ceremony, he said, of my seduction was as follows: First, on a Sunday, before the holy water is consecrated, the future disciple with his masters must go into the church, and there in their presence must renounce Christ and his faith, baptism, and the church universal. Then he must do homage to the *magisterulus,* that is, to the little master (for so, and not otherwise, they call the Devil). Afterward he drinks from the aforesaid flask (filled with a liquid made from murdered infants); and, this done, he forthwith feels himself to conceive and hold within himself an image of our art and the chief rites of this sect. After this fashion was I seduced; and my wife also, whom I believe of so great pertinacity that she will endure the flames rather than confess the least whit of the truth; but, alas, we are both guilty. What the young man had said was found in all respects the truth. For, after confession, the young man was seen to die in great contrition. His wife, however, though convicted by the testimony of witnesses, would not confess the truth even under the torture or in death; but, when the fire was prepared for her by the executioner, uttered in most evil words a curse upon him, and so was burned.

5. *THE* IMITATION OF CHRIST *REFLECTS INTENSE CHRISTIAN PIETY*

The* Imitation of Christ, *one of the great devotional works of Christian literature, was written probably in the early fifteenth century, by either Gerard Groote or

Imitation of Christ, translated by William Benham, in *The Harvard Classics,* edited by Charles W. Eliot (New York: P.F. Collier & Son Corp., 1909), Vol. VII, pp. 213–215.

Thomas à Kempis (1379–1471). Groote was the founder, and Thomas a member, of the Brethren of the Common Life, an order devoted to preaching and teaching in the Netherlands.

He that followeth me shall not walk in darkness, saith the Lord. These are the words of Christ; and they teach us how far we must imitate His life and character, if we seek true illumination, and deliverance from all blindness of heart. Let it be our most earnest study, therefore, to dwell upon the life of Jesus Christ.

2. His teaching surpasseth all teaching of holy men, and such as have His Spirit find therein *the hidden manna.* But there are many who, though they frequently hear the Gospel, yet feel but little longing after it, because they have not the mind of Christ. He, therefore, that will fully and with true wisdom understand the words of Christ, let him strive to conform his whole life to that mind of Christ.

3. What doth it profit thee to enter into deep discussion concerning the Holy Trinity, if thou lack humility, and be thus displeasing to the Trinity? For verily it is not deep words that make a man holy and upright; it is a good life which maketh a man dear to God. I had rather feel contrition than be skilful in the definition thereof. If thou knewest the whole Bible, and the sayings of all the philosophers, what should all this profit thee without the love and grace of God? *Vanity of vanities, all is vanity,* save to love God, and Him only to serve. That is the highest wisdom, to cast the world behind us, and to reach forward to the heavenly kingdom.

4. It is vanity then to seek after, and to trust in, the riches that shall perish. It is vanity, too, to covet honours, and to lift up ourselves on high. It is vanity to follow the desires of the flesh and be led by them, for this shall bring misery at the last. It is vanity to desire a long life, and to have little care for a good life. It is vanity to take thought only for the life which now is, and not to look forward to the things which shall be hereafter. It is vanity to love that which quickly passeth away, and not to hasten where eternal joy abideth.

5. Be ofttimes mindful of the saying, *The eye is not satisfied with seeing, nor the ear with hearing.* Strive, therefore, to turn away thy heart from the love of the things that are seen, and to set it upon the things that are not seen. For they who follow after their own fleshly lusts, defile the conscience, and destroy the grace of God.

* * *

There is naturally in every man a desire to know, but what profiteth knowledge without the fear of God? Better of a surety is a lowly peasant who serveth God, than a proud philosopher who watcheth the stars and neglecteth the knowledge of himself. He who knoweth himself well is vile in his own sight; neither regardeth he the praises of men. If I knew all the things that are in the world, and were not in charity, what should it help me before God, who is to judge me according to my deeds?

2. Rest from inordinate desire of knowledge, for therein is found much distraction and deceit. Those who have knowledge desire to appear learned, and to be called wise. Many things there are to know which profiteth little or nothing to the soul. And foolish out of measure is he who attendeth upon other things rather than those which serve to his soul's health. Many words satisfy not the soul, but a good life refresheth the mind, and a pure conscience giveth great confidence towards God.

3. The greater and more complete thy knowledge, the more severely shalt thou be judged, unless thou hast lived holily. Therefore be not lifted up by any skill or knowledge that thou hast; but rather fear concerning the knowledge which is given to thee. If it seemeth to thee that thou knowest many things, and understandest them well, know also that there are many more things which thou knowest not. *Be not high-minded,* but rather confess thine ignorance. Why desirest thou to lift thyself above another, when there are found many more learned and more skilled in the Scripture than thou? If thou wilt know and learn anything with profit, love to be thyself unknown and to be counted for nothing.

4. That is the highest and most profitable lesson, when a man truly knoweth and judgeth lowly of himself. To account nothing of one's self, and to think always kindly and highly of others, this is great and perfect wisdom. Even shouldest thou see thy neighbour sin openly or grievously, yet thou oughtest not to reckon thyself better than he, for thou knowest not how long thou shalt keep thine integrity. All of us are weak and frail; hold thou no man more frail than thyself.

6. *POPE GREGORY XI CONDEMNS THE TEACHINGS OF JOHN WYCLIFFE*

John Wycliffe (1320–1384) was a priest and scholar at Oxford, who also held a county parish as a means of support. His close study of the Bible led him to the belief that it could be fully understood by any Christian, without the aid of priests or church. Wycliffe, like the Protestants of the sixteenth century, denied the efficacy of most of the sacraments of the Church. Although he was never tried for heresy, Wycliffe gave up his preaching and retired to the seclusion of his parish.

"Bull of Pope Gregory XI, against John Wycliffe," in Guy Carleton Lee, *Source-Book of English History* (New York: Henry Holt and Company, Inc., 1900), pp. 211–212.

Gregory, bishop, servant of the servants of God, to his beloved sons the chancellor and University of Oxford, in the diocese of Lincoln, grace and apostolic benediction.

We are compelled to wonder and grieve that you, who, in consideration of the favours and privileges conceded to your University of Oxford by the apostolic see, and on account of your familiarity with the Scriptures, in whose sea you navigate, by the gift of God, with auspicious oar, you, who ought to be, as it were, warriors and champions of the orthodox faith, without which there is no salvation of souls,—that you through a certain sloth and neglect allow tares to spring up amidst the pure wheat in the fields of your glorious university aforesaid; and what is still more pernicious, even continue to grow to maturity. And you are quite careless, as has been lately reported to us, as to the extirpation of these tares; with no little clouding of a bright name, danger to your souls, contempt of the Roman church, and injury to the faith above mentioned. And what pains us the more is that this increase of the tares aforesaid is known in Rome before the remedy of extirpation has been applied in England where they sprang up. By the insinuation of many, if they are indeed worthy of belief, deploring it deeply, it has come to our ears that John de Wycliffe, rector of the church of Lutterworth, in the diocese of Lincoln, Professor of the Sacred Scriptures, (would that he were not also Master of Errors,) has fallen into such a detestable madness that he does not hesitate to dogmatize and publicly preach, or rather vomit forth from the recesses of his breast certain propositions and conclusions which are erroneous and false. He has cast himself also into the depravity of preaching heretical dogmas which strive to subvert and weaken the state of the whole church and even secular polity, some of which doctrines, in changed terms, it is true, seem to express the perverse opinions and unlearned learning of Marsilio of Padua of cursed memory, and of John of Jandun, whose book is extant, rejected and cursed by our predecessor, Pope John XXII, of happy memory. This he has done in the kingdom of England, lately glorious in its power and in the abundance of its resources, but more glorious still in the glistening piety of its faith, and in the distinction of its sacred learning; producing also many men illustrious for their exact knowledge of the holy Scriptures, mature in the gravity of their character, conspicuous in devotion, defenders of the catholic church. He has polluted certain of the faithful of Christ by besprinkling them with these doctrines, and led them away from the right paths of the aforesaid faith to the brink of perdition.

Wherefore, since we are not willing, nay, indeed, ought not to be willing, that so deadly a pestilence should continue to exist with our connivance, a pestilence which, if it is not opposed in its beginnings, and torn out by the roots in its entirety, will be reached too late by medicines when it has infected very many with its contagion; we command your university with strict admonition, by the apostolic authority, in virtue of your sacred obedience, and under penalty of the deprivation of all the favours, indulgences, and privileges granted to you and your university by the said see, for the future not to permit to be asserted or proposed to any extent whatever, the opinions, conclusions, and propositions which are in variance with good morals and faith, even when those proposing strive to defend them under a certain fanciful wresting of words or of terms. Moreover, you are on our authority to arrest the said John, or cause him to be arrested and to send him under a trustworthy guard to our venerable brother, the Archbishop of Canterbury, and the Bishop of London, or to one of them.

Besides, if there should be, which God forbid, in your university, subject to your jurisdiction, opponents stained with these errors, and if they should obstinately persist in them, proceed vigorously and earnestly to a similar arrest and removal of them, and otherwise as shall seem good to you. Be vigilant to repair your negligence which you have hitherto shown in the premises, and so obtain our gratitude and favour, and that of the said see, besides the honour and reward of the divine recompense.

Given at Rome, at Santa Maria Maggiore, on the 31st of May, the sixth year of our pontificate.

17

HUMANISM AND RENAISSANCE ART

Italy in the fourteenth century was the scene of a very substantial increase of interest in classical literature by humanists such as Petrarch and Boccaccio. This was accompanied by an even more amazing series of changes in the fine arts. The pioneering efforts of Giotto encouraged succeeding generations of Italian artists, which included the versatile Michelangelo and the universal genius Leonardo da Vinci. This renaissance of literature and art reached northern Europe in the fifteenth century, but northern humanism remained essentially Christian, resisting the pagan aspects of the Italian writers. Erasmus, greatest of the northern humanists, vigorously attacked abuses in the Church, hoping thereby to effect a reform movement. The invention of movable type in the mid-fifteenth century served as a link between Italy and the North, making the new learning more accessible in the form of printed books.

1. PETRARCH ADDRESSES POSTERITY

Francesco Petrarch (1304–1374), the first of the Italian humanists, composed near the end of his career an autobiographical letter to posterity, in which he described his early literary life. Although an ordained priest, Petrarch devoted more attention to women and literature than to religion.

. . . On the windy banks of the river Rhone I spent my boyhood, guided by my parents, and then, guided by my own fancies, the whole of my youth. Yet there were long intervals spent elsewhere, for I first passed four years at the little town of Carpentras, somewhat to the east of Avignon: in these two places I learned as much of grammar, logic, and rhetoric as

James Harvey Robinson and Henry Winchester Rolfe, *Petrarch: The First Modern Scholar and Man of Letters,* Second Revised Edition (New York and London: G.P. Putnam's Sons, 1914), pp. 66–73. Used by permission of the publisher.

my age permitted, or rather, as much as it is customary to teach in school: how little that is, dear reader, thou knowest. I then set out for Montpellier to study law, and spent four years there, than three at Bologna. I heard the whole body of the civil law, and would, as many thought, have distinguished myself later, had I but continued my studies. I gave up the subject altogether, however, so soon as it was no longer necessary to consult the wishes of my parents. My reason was that, although the dignity of the law, which is doubtless very great, and especially the numerous references it contains to Roman antiquity, did not fail to delight me, I felt it to be habitually degraded by those who practise it. . . .

So at the age of two and twenty I returned home. . . .

. . . About this time, a youthful desire impelled me to visit France and Germany. While I invented certain reasons to satisfy my elders of the propriety of the journey, the real explanation was a great inclination and longing to see new sights. I first visited Paris, as I was anxious to discover what was true and what fabulous in the accounts I had heard of that city. On my return from this journey I went to Rome, which I had since my infancy ardently desired to visit. . . .

While leading a leisurely existence in this region, I received, remarkable as it may seem, upon one and the same day, letters both from the Senate at Rome and the Chancellor of the University of Paris, pressing me to appear in Rome and Paris, respectively, to receive the poet's crown of laurel. In my youthful elation I convinced myself that I was quite worthy of this honour; the recognition came from eminent judges, and I accepted their verdict rather than that of my own better judgment. . . .

So I decided, first to visit Naples, and that celebrated king and philosopher, Robert, who was not more distinguished as a ruler than as a man of culture. He was, indeed, the only monarch of our age who was the friend at once of learning and of virtue, and I trusted that he might correct such things as he found to criticise in my work. . . . After talking over a great many things, I showed him my *Africa,* which so delighted him that he asked that it might be dedicated to him in consideration of a handsome reward. This was a request that I could not well refuse, nor, indeed, would I have wished to refuse it, had it been in my power. . . . Having thus tested my poor attainments for three days, the King at last pronounced me worthy of the laurel. He offered to bestow that honour upon me at Naples, and urged me to consent to receive it there, but my veneration for Rome prevailed over the insistence of even so great a monarch as Robert. At length, seeing that I was inflexible in my purpose, he sent me on my way accompanied by royal messengers and letters to the Roman Senate, in which he gave enthusiastic expression to his flattering opinion of me. . . .

On arriving at Rome, I continued, in spite of my unworthiness, to rely upon the judgment of so eminent a critic, and, to the great delight of the Romans who were present, I who had been hitherto a simple student received the laurel crown. This occasion is described elsewhere in my letters, both in prose and verse. The laurel, however, in no way increased my wisdom, although it did arouse some jealousy—but this is too long a story to be told here.

2. *ERASMUS SATIRIZES INTELLECTUALS*

Desiderius Erasmus (1466–1536), the greatest humanist north of the Alps, skillfully employed satire in his best-known work,* Praise of Folly, *to expose the weaknesses and errors of his age. He was unsparing in his criticism of those groups he knew well, theologians, scientists, and writers. In the following selection the first person pronouns refer to "Folly," supposedly the narrator.

But I should be most foolish myself . . . if I should go on counting forms of folly and madness among the folk. Let me turn to those who maintain among mortals an appearance of wisdom and, as the saying is, seek for the golden bough. Among these the grammarians hold first place. Nothing could be more calamity-stricken, nothing more afflicted, than this generation of men, nothing so hated of God, if I were not at hand to mitigate the pains of their wretched profession by a certain sweet infusion of madness. For they are not only liable to the five curses which the Greek epigram calls attention to in Homer, but indeed to six hundred curses; as being hunger-starved and dirty in their schools—I said "their schools," but it were better said "their knowledge-factories" or "their mills" or even "their shambles"—among herds of boys. There they grow old with their labors, they are deafened by the noise, they sicken by reason of the stench and nastiness. Yet thanks to me, they see themselves as first among men; so greatly do they please themselves when they terrify the timorous band by a menacing look and tone; when they beat the little wretches with ferules, rods, or straps; and when . . . they storm fiercely in all directions, as whim may dictate. . . .

Of the same brand also are those who pursue fame by turning out books. All of them are highly indebted to me, but especially those who blacken paper with sheer triviality. For the ones who write learnedly for

Desiderius Erasmus, *The Praise of Folly,* translated from the Latin, with an Essay and Commentary, by Hoyt Hopewell Hudson (Princeton, N.J.: Princeton University Press, 1941), pp. 70–71, 73–74, 76–79.

the verdict of a few scholars . . . seem to me more pitiable than happy, since they continuously torture themselves: they add, they alter, they blot something out, they put it back in, they do their work over, they recast it, they show it to friends, they keep it for nine years; yet they never satisfy themselves. At such a price they buy an empty reward, namely, praise—and that the praise of a handful. They buy it with such an expense of long hours, so much loss of that sweetest of all things, sleep, so much sweat, so many vexations. Add also the loss of health, the wreck of their good looks, weakness of eyes or even blindness, poverty, malice, denial of pleasures, premature old age, and early death—and if there are other things like these, add them. The scholar considers himself compensated for such ills when he wins the approbation of one or two other weak-eyed scholars. But my author is crazy in a far happier way, since without any prolonged thought he quickly puts in writing whatever has come into his head or chanced to his pen, even his dreams; and all this with little waste of paper, knowing that if the trifles he has written are trivial enough the greater number of readers—that is, the fools and ignoramuses—will approve. Of what consequence is it to ignore the two or three scholars, even if they chance to read the work? Or what weight will the censure of a few learned men have, as against the great multitude of those who will shout acclaim?

But the wiser writers are those who put out the work of others as their own. By a few strokes of the pen they transfer to their own account the glory which was the fruit of much toil on another's part, drawing comfort from the thought that even if it should happen that they are publicly convinced of plagiarism, meanwhile they shall have enjoyed for a period the emoluments of authorship. . . .

Perhaps it were better to pass over the theologians in silence. . . . For they may attack me with six hundred arguments, in squadrons, and drive me to make a recantation; which if I refuse, they will straightway proclaim me an heretic. By this thunderbolt they are wont to terrify any toward whom they are ill-disposed. . . . They are protected by a wall of scholastic definitions, arguments, corollaries, implicit and explicit propositions; they have so many hideaways that they could not be caught even by the net of Vulcan; for they slip out on their distinctions, by which also they cut through all knots as easily as with a double-bitted axe from Tenedos; and they abound with newly-invented terms and prodigious vocables. . . .

. . . The methods our scholastics pursue only render more subtle these subtlest of subtleties; for you will escape from a labyrinth more quickly than from the tangles of Realists, Nominalists, Thomists, Albertists, Occamists, Scotists—I have not named all, but the chief ones only. But in all these sects there is so much learning and so much difficulty that I should think the apostles themselves must needs have the help of some other spirit if they were to try disputing on these topics with our new generation of theologues.

3. *POPE JULIUS II APPEARS AT THE GATE OF HEAVEN*

The dialogue* Julius II Exclusus *appeared in Paris in 1513 without an author's name. Erasmus denied having written it, but most of his contemporaries attributed it to him, and, although the authorship has never been thoroughly established, it is generally assumed to be his work.

JULIUS. What the devil is this? The gates not opened! Something is wrong with the lock.

SPIRIT. You have brought the wrong key perhaps. The key of your money-box will not open the door here. You should have brought both keys. This is the key of power, not of knowledge.

JULIUS. I never had any but this, and I don't see the use of another. Hey there, porter! I say, are you asleep or drunk?

PETER. Well that the gates are adamant, or this fellow would have broken in. He must be some giant, or conqueror. Heaven, what a stench! Who are you? What do you want here?

JULIUS. Open the gates, I say. Why is there no one to receive me?

PETER. Here is fine talk. Who are you, I say?

JULIUS. You know this key, I suppose, and the triple crown, and the pallium?

PETER. I see a key, but not the key which Christ gave to me a long time since. The crown? I don't recognize the crown. No heathen king ever wore such a thing, certainly none who expected to be let in here. The pallium is strange too. And see, there are marks on all three of that rogue and impostor Simon Magus, that I turned out of office.

JULIUS. Enough of this. I am Julius the Legurian, P.M., as you can see by the letters if you can read.

PETER. P.M.! What is that? Pestis Maxima? [Greatest Plague.]

JULIUS. Pontifex Maximus, you rascal.

"Julius II Exclusus," in J.A. Froude, *Life and Letters of Erasmus* (New York: Charles Scribner's Sons, 1895), pp. 149–151, 168.

PETER. If you are three times Maximus, if you are Mercury Trismegistus, you can't come in unless you are Optimus too.

JULIUS. Impertinence! You, who have been no more than Sanctus all these ages—and I Sanctissimus, Sanctissimus Dominus, Sanctitas, Holiness itself, with Bulls to show it.

PETER. Is there no difference between being Holy and being called Holy? Ask your flatterers who called you these fine names to give you admittance. Let me look at you a little closer. Hum! Signs of impiety in plenty, and none of the other thing. Who are these fellows behind you? Faugh! They smell of stews, drink-shops, and gunpowder. Have you brought goblins out of Tartarus to make war with heaven? Yourself, too, are not precisely like an apostle. Priest's cassock and bloody armour below it, eyes savage, mouth insolent, forehead brazen, body scarred with sins all over, breath loaded with wine, health broken with debauchery. Ay, threaten as you will, I will tell you what you are for all your bold looks. You are Julius the Emperor come back from hell. . . .

JULIUS. Will you make an end of your talking and open the gates? We will break them down else. You see these followers of mine.

PETER. I see a lot of precious rogues, but they won't break in here.

JULIUS. Make an end, I say, or I will fling a thunderbolt at you. I will excommunicate you. I have done as much to kings before this. Here are the Bulls ready.

PETER. Thunderbolts! Bulls! I beseech you, we had no thunderbolts or Bulls from Christ.

JULIUS. You shall feel them if you don't behave yourself. . . .

PETER. You must show your merits first; no admission without merits.

JULIUS. What do you mean by merits?

PETER. Have you taught true doctrine?

JULIUS. Not I. I have been too busy fighting. There are monks to look after doctrine, if that is of any consequence.

PETER. Have you gained souls to Christ by pious example?

JULIUS. I have sent a good many to Tartarus.

PETER. Have you worked any miracles?

JULIUS. Pshaw! miracles are out of date.

PETER. Have you been diligent in your prayers?

SPIRIT. You waste your breath. This is mockery.

PETER. These are the qualities which make a respectable pope. If he has others better, let him produce them. . . .

JULIUS. Then you won't open the gates?

PETER. Sooner to anyone than to such as you. We are not of your communion in this place. You have an army of sturdy rogues behind you, you have money, and you are a famous architect. Go build a paradise of your own, and fortify it, lest the devils break in on you.

4. GUTENBERG INVENTS MOVABLE TYPE

Credit for the invention of movable type is still a matter of historical dispute, although it has been assigned most frequently to Johan Gutenberg of Mainz. The following passage contains one of the few contemporary references to the invention of the printing press.

The eternal God has out of his unfathomable wisdom brought into existence the laudable art, by which men now print books, and multiply them so greatly that every man may for himself read or hear read the way of salvation. . . .

Item this most valuable art aforesaid is found first of all in Germany at Mainz on the Rhine. And it is a great honor for the German nation that such ingenious men are there to be found. And this came to pass about the year of our Lord 1440 and from thence forward until 1450 is written the art was investigated and what belongs to it. And in the year of our Lord which is written 1450, there was a Golden year and men began to print and the first book that they printed was the Bible in Latin, and it was printed in a large character, such as the character with which Missal Books are now printed.

Item although the art is found at Mainz as aforesaid in the manner as it is now generally used, yet the first prefiguration is found in Holland out of the Donatuses which were in that very (country) printed before that time. And from and out of them was taken the beginning of the aforesaid art. And it is found much more masterly and subtilely [*sic.*] than that same manner was and the longer (it was practiced) the more skillful it became. . . . The first inventor of printing was a burgher at Mainz, and he was born at Strassburg, and named Johan Gutenburg. Item from Mainz the aforesaid art came first of all to Cologne, then to Strassburg, and thereafter to Venice. The beginning and development of the aforesaid art was told me by word of mouth by the honorable man Master Ulrich Zell of Hanau, still, *Anno* 1490, a printer at Cologne by whome the aforesaid art came to Cologne.

"Chronicle of Cologne," 1499, from H.E. Hodgkin, *Rariora*, Vol. II, *The Dawn of Typography* (London: 1901), p. 231. Reprinted by permission of the publishers from Abbott Payson Usher, *A History of Mechanical Inventions*, Rev. Ed., p. 242. Cambridge, Mass.: Harvard University Press, Copyright, 1929, 1954, by The President and Fellows of Harvard College.

5. GIOTTO BRINGS NEW FORM AND MOVEMENT TO ART

Giotto di Bondone (c. 1266–c. 1336), one of the monumental figures in the history of art, revolutionized Italian painting by abandoning the static, conventional Byzantine art forms and stressing naturalism and movement.

The gratitude which the masters in painting owe to Nature—who is ever the truest model of him who, possessing the power to select the brightest parts from her best and loveliest features, employs himself unweariedly in the reproduction of these beauties—this gratitude, I say, is due, in my judgment, to the Florentine painter. Giotto, seeing that he alone—although born amidst incapable artists, and at a time when all good methods in art had long been entombed beneath the ruins of war—yet, by the favour of Heaven, he, I say, alone succeeded in resuscitating art, and restoring her to a path that may be called the true one. And it was in truth a great marvel, that from so rude and inapt an age, Giotto should have had strength to elicit so much, that the art of design, of which the men of those days had little, if any, knowledge, was, by his means, effectually recalled into life. The birth of this great man took place in the hamlet of Vespignano, fourteen miles from the city of Florence, in the year 1276. His father's name was Bondone, a simple husbandman, who reared the child, to whom he had given the name of Giotto, with such decency as his condition permitted. The boy was early remarked for extreme vivacity in all his childish proceedings, and for extraordinary promptitude of intelligence; so that he became endeared, not only to his father, but to all who knew him in the village and around it. When he was about ten years old, Bondone gave him a few sheep to watch, and with these he wandered about the vicinity—now here and now there. But, induced by Nature herself to the arts of design, he was perpetually drawing on the stones, the earth, or the sand, some natural object that came before him, or some fantasy that presented itself to his thoughts. It chanced one day that the affairs of Cimabue took him from Florence to Vespignano, when he perceived the young Giotto, who, while his sheep fed around him, was occupied in drawing one of them from the life, with a stone slightly pointed, upon a smooth clean piece of rock,—and that without any teaching whatever, but such as Nature herself had imparted. Halting in astonishment, Cimabue inquired of the boy if he would accompany him to his home, and the child replied he would go willingly, if his father were content to permit it. Cimabue therefore requesting the consent of Bondone, the latter granted it readily, and suffered the artist to conduct his son to Florence, where, in a short time, instructed

Giorgio Vasari, *Lives of the Most Eminent Painters, Sculptors, and Architects,* translated by Mrs. Jonathan Foster (London: Henry G. Bohn, 1855), Vol. I, pp. 93–95.

by Cimabue and aided by Nature, the boy not only equalled his master in his own manner, but became so good an imitator of Nature, that he totally banished the rude Greek manner,—restoring art to the better path adhered to in modern times, and introducing the custom of accurately drawing living persons from nature, which had not been used for more than two hundred years. . . .

6. LEONARDO DA VINCI PRESENTS HIS QUALIFICATIONS FOR EMPLOYMENT

Leonardo da Vinci (1452–1519), the universal genius of the Italian Renaissance, wandered for most of his life from one Italian city to another, offering to various patrons his remarkable talents. In the following letter, addressed to Ludovico Sforza **(Il Moro)*****, despot of Milan, Leonardo asked for a job and submitted his qualifications. The reader should observe the relative importance Leonardo attached to painting and sculpture.***

MOST ILLUSTRIOUS LORD,—Having now sufficiently considered the specimens of all those who proclaim themselves skilled contrivers of instruments of war, and that the invention and operation of the said instruments are nothing different to those in common use: I shall endeavor, without prejudice to anyone else, to explain myself to your Excellency, showing your Lordship my secrets, and then offering them to your best pleasure and approbation to work with effect at opportune moments on all those things which, in part, shall be briefly noted below.

I have a sort of extremely light and strong bridges, adapted to be most easily carried, and with them you may pursue, and at any time flee from the enemy; and others, secure and indestructible by fire and battle, easy and convenient to lift and place. Also method of burning and destroying those of the enemy.

I know how, when a place is besieged, to take water out of the trenches, and make endless variety of bridges, and covered ways and ladders, and other machines pertaining to such expeditions.

ITEM. If, by reason of the height of the banks, or the strength of the place and its position, it is impossible, when besieging a place, to avail oneself of the plan of bombardment, I have methods of destroying every rock or other fortress, even if it were founded on a rock, etc.

Again, I have kinds of mortars; most convenient and easy to carry;

"Letter of Leonardo da Vinci to Il Moro (Ludovico Sforza, despot of Milan), 1493," in J.P. and I.A. Richter, *The Literary Works of Leonardo da Vinci* (New York: Oxford University Press, Inc., 1939), Vol. II, pp. 325–327, No. 1341, as found in Elizabeth Gilmore Holt, ed., *Literary Sources of Art History* (Princeton, N.J.: Princeton University Press, 1947), pp. 169–170.

and with these I can fling small stones almost resembling a storm; and with the smoke of these cause great terror to the enemy, to his great detriment and confusion.

And if the fight should be at sea I have kinds of many machines most efficient for offence and defence; and vessels which will resist the attack of the largest guns and powder and fumes.

ITEM. I have means by secret and tortuous mines and ways, made without noise to reach a designated [spot], even if it were needed to pass under a trench or a river.

ITEM. I will make covered chariots, safe and unattackable, which, entering among the enemy, with their artillery, there is no body of men so great but they would break them. And behind these, infantry could follow quite unhurt and without any hindrance.

ITEM. In case of need I will make big guns, mortars, and light ordnance of fine and useful forms, out of the common type.

Where the operation of bombardment might fall, I would contrive catapults, mangonels, *trabocchi* and other machines of marvellous efficacy and not in common use. And in short, according to the variety of cases, I can contrive various and endless means of offence and defence.

In time of peace I believe I can give perfect satisfaction and to the equal of any other in architecture and the composition of buildings, public and private; and in guiding water from one place to another.

ITEM. I can carry out sculpture in marble, bronze, or clay, and also I can do in painting whatever may be done, as well as any other, be he whom he may.

Again, the bronze horse may be taken in hand, which is to be the immortal glory and eternal honour of the prince your father of happy memory, and of the illustrious house of Sforza.

And if any one of the above-named things seem to anyone to be impossible or not feasible, I am most ready to make the experiment in your park, or in whatever place may please your Excellency, to whom I commend myself with the utmost humility.

7. MACHIAVELLI DEPICTS POLITICAL REALISM IN THE LATE MIDDLE AGE

Niccolo Machiavelli (1469–1527), who rose no higher than a secretarial position in the government of Florence, presented in* The Prince *a masterfully realistic

Niccolo Machiavelli, *The Prince and the Discourses,* translated by Luigi Ricci and revised by E.R.P. Vincent (New York: The Modern Library, 1940), pp. 56, 60-65. From *The Prince and Other Discourses* by Machiavelli, published by the Oxford University Press in the World's Classics series. Used by permission of the Oxford University Press.

***and candid portrayal of Italian political behavior in the Late Middle Age. His model prince, Cesare Borgia, was an utterly immoral tyrant of the Papal States. Not without reason did Pope Paul IV in 1557 condemn* The Prince *and place it on the* Index.**

It now remains to be seen what are the methods and rules for a prince as regards his subjects and friends. . . . How we live is so far removed from how we ought to live, that he who abandons what is done for what ought to be done, will rather learn to bring about his own ruin than his preservation. A man who wishes to make a profession of goodness in everything must necessarily come to grief among so many who are not good. Therefore it is necessary for a prince, who wishes to maintain himself, to learn how not to be good, and to use this knowledge and not use it, according to the necessity of the case.

* * *

Proceeding to the other qualities before named, I say that every prince must desire to be considered merciful and not cruel. He must, however, take care not to misuse this mercifulness. Cesare Borgia was considered cruel, but his cruelty had brought order to the Romagna, united it, and reduced it to peace and fealty. . . . A prince, therefore, must not mind incurring the charge of cruelty for the purpose of keeping his subjects united and faithful; for, with a very few examples, he will be more merciful than those who, from excess of tenderness, allow disorders to arise, from whence spring bloodshed and rapine; for these as a rule injure the whole community, while the executions carried out by the prince injure only individuals. And of all princes, it is impossible for a new prince to escape the reputation of cruelty, new states being always full of dangers. . . .

From this arises the question whether it is better to be loved more than feared, or feared more than loved. The reply is, that one ought to be both feared and loved, but as it is difficult for the two to go together, it is much safer to be feared than loved, if one of the two has to be wanting. For it may be said of men in general that they are ungrateful, voluble, dissemblers, anxious to avoid danger, and covetous of gain; as long as you benefit them, they are entirely yours; they offer you their blood, their goods, their life, and their children, as I have before said, when the necessity is remote; but when it approaches, they revolt. And the prince who has relied solely on their words, without making other preparations, is ruined; for the friendship which is gained by purchase and not through grandeur and nobility of spirit is bought but not secured, and at a pinch is not to be expended in your service. And men have less scruple in offending one who makes himself loved than one who makes himself feared; for love is held by a chain of obligation which, men being selfish, is broken whenever it serves their purpose; but fear is maintained by a dread of punishment which never fails.

Still, a prince should make himself feared in such a way that if he does not gain love, he at any rate avoids hatred; for fear and the absence of hatred may well go together, and will be always attained by one who abstains from interfering with the property of his citizens and subjects or with their women. And when he is obliged to take the life of any one, let him do so when there is a proper justification and manifest reason for it; but above all he must abstain from taking the property of others, for men forget more easily the death of their father than the loss of their patrimony. Then also pretexts for seizing property are never wanting, and one who begins to live by rapine will always find some reason for taking the goods of others, whereas causes for taking life are rarer and more fleeting.

But when the prince is with his army and has a large number of soldiers under his control, then it is extremely necessary that he should not mind being thought cruel; for without this reputation he could not keep an army united or disposed to any duty. . . .

* * *

How laudable it is for a prince to keep good faith and live with integrity, and not with astuteness, every one knows. Still the experience of our times shows those princes to have done great things who have had little regard for good faith, and have been able by astuteness to confuse men's brains, and who have ultimately overcome those who have made loyalty their foundation.

You must know, then, that there are two methods of fighting, the one by law, the other by force: the first method is that of men, the second of beasts; but as the first method is often insufficient, one must have recourse to the second. It is therefore necessary for a prince to know well how to use both the beast and the man. . . .

A prince being thus obliged to know well how to act as a beast must imitate the fox and the lion, for the lion cannot protect himself from traps, and the fox cannot defend himself from wolves. One must therefore be a fox to recognize traps, and a lion to frighten wolves. Those that wish to be only lions do not understand this. Therefore, a prudent ruler ought not to keep faith when by so doing it would be against his interest, and when the reasons which made him bind himself no longer exist. If men were all good, this precept would not be a good one; but as they are bad, and would not observe their faith with you, so you are not bound to keep faith with them. Nor have legitimate grounds ever failed a prince who wished to show colourable excuse for the non-fulfilment of his promise. Of this one could furnish an infinite number of modern examples, and show how many times peace has been broken, and how many promises rendered worthless, by the faithlessness of princes, and those that have been best able to imitate the fox have succeeded best. But it is necessary to be able to disguise this character well, and to be a great feigner and dissembler; and men are so simple and so ready to obey present necessities, that one who deceives will always find those who allow themselves to be deceived.

I will only mention one modern instance. Alexander VI did nothing else but deceive men, he thought of nothing else, and found the occasion for it; no man was ever more able to give assurances, or affirmed things with stronger oaths, and no man observed them less; however, he always succeeded in his deceptions, as he well knew this aspect of things.

It is not, therefore, necessary for a prince to have all the above-named qualities, but it is very necessary to seem to have them. I would even be bold to say that to possess them and always to observe them is dangerous, but to appear to possess them is useful. Thus it is well to seem merciful, faithful, humane, sincere, religious, and also to be so; but you must have the mind so disposed that when it is needful to be otherwise you may be able to change to the opposite qualities. . . .

18

ECONOMIC DISLOCATION AND THE BEGINNINGS OF OVERSEAS EXPANSION

Generally speaking, the fourteenth century lacked the economic stability and growth of the High Middle Age. It was a period marked by the decay of at least two of the great institutions of earlier years: the manor and the guild. Territorial expansion, land reclamation, and population all leveled off. For the common folk of both town and country, life seemed much harder. In the following century, however, Europe came out of the doldrums. The new optimism and enthusiasm found spectacular expression in world-wide voyages of discovery. Western Europe began to "export" its civilization, a development which would terminate only in our own day.

1. THE "FOUL DEATH" STRIKES ENGLAND, 1349

The worst epidemic in the history of Europe struck in 1348–1350. The course of the pestilence, probably the bubonic plague, can be traced from the Black Sea region to Italy and then northward to all Europe. Perhaps as much as a third of the population perished. The following is a contemporary account.

Then the grievous plague penetrated the seacoasts from Southampton, and came to Bristol, and there almost the whole strength of the town died, struck as it were by sudden death; . . . There died at Leicester in the small parish of S. Leonard more than 380, in the parish of Holy Cross more than

Henry Knighton, *History of England,* as found in Elizabeth Kimball Kendall, ed., *Source-Book of English History* (New York: The Macmillan Company, 1900), pp. 102–106.

400; in the parish of S. Margaret of Leicester more than 700; and so in each parish a great number. Then the bishop of Lincoln sent through the whole bishopric, and gave general power to all and every priest, both regular and secular, to hear confessions, and absolve with full and entire episcopal authority except in matters of debt, in which case the dying man, if he could, should pay the debt while he lived, or others should certainly fulfil that duty from his property after his death. Likewise, the pope granted full remission of all sins to whoever was absolved in peril of death, and granted that this power should last till next Easter, and everyone could choose a confessor at his will. In the same year there was a great plague of sheep everywhere in the realm, so that in one place there died in one pasturage more than 5,000 sheep, and so rotted that neither beast nor bird would touch them. And there were small prices for everything on account of the fear of death. For there were very few who cared about riches or anything else. . . . Sheep and cattle went wandering over fields and through crops, and there was no one to go and drive or gather them, so that the number cannot be reckoned which perished in the ditches in every district, for lack of herdsmen; for there was such a lack of servants that no one knew what he ought to do. In the following autumn no one could get a reaper for less than 8d. with his food, a mower for less than 12d. with his food. Wherefore many crops perished in the fields for want of some one to gather them; but in the pestilence year, as is above said of other things, there was such abundance of all kinds of corn that no one troubled about it. The Scots, hearing of the cruel pestilence of the English, believed it had come to them from the avenging hand of God, and—as it was commonly reported in England—took for their oath when they wanted to swear, "By the foul death of England." But when the Scots, believing the English were under the shadow of the dread vengeance of God, came together in the forest of Selkirk, with purpose to invade the whole realm of England, the fell mortality came upon them, and the sudden and awful cruelty of death winnowed them, so that about 5,000 died in a short time. Then the rest, some feeble, some strong, determined to return home, but the English followed and overtook them and killed many of them.

Master Thomas of Bradwardine was consecrated by the pope archbishop of Canterbury, and when he returned to England he came to London, but within two days was dead. . . . At the same time priests were in such poverty everywhere that many churches were widowed and lacking the divine offices, masses, mattins, vespers, sacraments, and other rites. A man could scarcely get a chaplain under £10 or 10 marks to minister to a church. And when a man could get a chaplain for 5 or 4 marks or even for two marks with his food when there was an abundance of priests before the pestilence, there was scarcely anyone now who was willing to accept a vicarage for £20 or 20 marks; but within a short time a very great multitude of those whose wives had died in the pestilence flocked into orders, of whom many were illiterate and little more than laymen, except so far as they knew how to read although they could not understand.

Meanwhile the king sent proclamation into all the countries that reapers and other labourers should not take more than they had been accustomed to take, under the penalty appointed by statute. But the labourers were so lifted up and obstinate that they would not listen to the king's command, but if anyone wished to have them he had to give them what they wanted, and either lose his fruit and crops, or satisfy the lofty and covetous wishes of the workmen. And when it was known to the king that they had not observed his command, and had given greater wages to the labourers, he levied heavy fines upon abbots, priors, knights, greater and lesser, and other great folk and small folk of the realm. . . . And afterwards the king had many labourers arrested, and sent them to prison; many withdrew themselves and went into the forests and woods; and those who were taken were heavily fined. Their ringleaders were made to swear that they would not take daily wages beyond the ancient custom, and then were freed from prison. And in like manner was done with the other craftsmen in the boroughs and villages. . . . After the aforesaid pestilence, many buildings, great and small, fell into ruins in every city, borough, and village for lack of inhabitants, likewise many villages and hamlets became desolate, not a house being left in them, all having died who dwelt there; and it was probable that many such villages would never be inhabited. In the winter following there was such a want of servants in work of all kinds, that one would scarcely believe that in times past there had been such a lack. . . . And so all necessaries became so much dearer that what in times past had been worth a penny, was then worth 4d. or 5d.

Magnates and lesser lords of the realm who had tenants made abatements of the rent in order that the tenants should not go away on account of the want of servants and the general dearness, some half the rent, some more, some less, some for two years, some for three, some for one year, according as they could agree with them. Likewise, those who received of their tenants daywork throughout the year, as is the practice with villeins, had to give them more leisure, and remit such works, and either entirely to free them, or give them an easier tenure at a small rent, so that homes should not be everywhere irrecoverably ruined, and the land everywhere remain entirely uncultivated.

2. THE ENGLISH PEASANTS RISE IN FUTILE REVOLT, 1381

The fourteenth century was not a happy one for western European peasants. The old manorial relations, which in former times had provided the peasants with a measure of stability and security, seemed to be breaking down. To make matters worse, agricultural expansion virtually ceased, and peasants no longer enjoyed the opportunities offered by new lands. Peasants' wars broke out in many parts of Europe. A contemporary historian gives an account in the following selection of the revolt of 1381 in England.

In the year 1381, the second of the reign of King Richard Second, during the month of May, on Wednesday, the fourth day after the feast of Trinity, that impious band began to assemble from Kent, from Surrey, and from many other surrounding places. Apprentices also, leaving their masters, rushed to join these. And so they gathered on Blackheath, where, forgetting themselves in their multitude, and neither contented with their former cause nor appeased by smaller crimes, they unmercifully planned greater and worse evils and determined not to desist from their wicked undertaking until they should have entirely extirpated the nobles and great men of the kingdom. . . .

On the Friday following the feast of the Consecration they came over the bridge to London; here no one resisted them, although, as was said, the citizens of London knew of their advance a long time before; and so they directed their way to the Tower where the king was surrounded by a great throng of knights, esquires, and others. . . . The people had determined to kill the archbishop and [certain] others. . . . The king, however, desired to free the archbishop and his friends from the jaws of the wolves, so he sent to the people a command to assemble outside the city, at a place called Mile End, in order to speak with the king and to treat with him concerning their designs. The soldiers who were to go forward, consumed with folly, lost heart, and gave up, on the way, their boldness of purpose. Nor did they dare to advance, but, unfortunately, struck as they were by fear, like women, kept themselves within the Tower.

But the king advanced to the assigned place, while many of the wicked mob kept following him. . . . More, however, remained where they were. When the others had come to the king they complained that they had been seriously oppressed by many hardships and that their condition of servitude was unbearable, and that they neither could nor would endure it longer.

Henry Knighton, *History of England,* as found in Edward P. Cheyney, ed., *Readings in English History* (New York: Ginn and Company, 1908), pp. 261–265.

The king, for the sake of peace, and on account of the violence of the times, yielding to their petition, granted to them a charter with the great seal, to the effect that all men in the kingdom of England should be free and of free condition, and should remain both for themselves and their heirs free from all kinds of servitude and villeinage forever. This charter was rejected and decided to be null and void by the king and the great men of the kingdom in the parliament held at Westminster in the same year, after the feast of St. Michael.

[While the Conference at Mile End was going on, the part of the mob which had stayed in the city murdered the Archbishop of Canterbury and many royal officials.]

On the following day, which was Saturday, [the rebels] gathered in Smithfield, where there came to them in the morning the king, who although only a youth in years yet was in wisdom already well versed. Their leader, whose real name was Wat Tyler, approached him; already they were calling him by the other name of Jack Straw. He kept close to the king, addressing him for the rest. He carried in his hand an unsheathed weapon which they call a dagger, and, as if in childish play, kept tossing it from one hand to the other in order that he might seize the opportunity, if the king should refuse his requests, to strike the king suddenly (as was commonly believed); and from this thing the greatest fear arose among those about the king as to what might be the outcome.

They begged from the king that all the warrens, and as well waters as park and wood, should be common to all, so that a poor man as well as a rich should be able freely to hunt animals everywhere in the kingdom. . . . When the king hesitated about granting this concession Jack Straw came nearer, and, speaking threatening words, seized with his hand the bridle of the horse of the king very daringly. When John de Walworth, a citizen of London, saw this, thinking that death threatened the king, he seized a sword and pierced Jack Straw in the neck. . . . He sank back, slowly letting go with his hands and feet, and then died. A great cry and much mourning arose: "Our leader is slain." When this dead man had been meanly dragged along by the hands and feet into the church of St. Bartholomew, which was near by, many withdrew from the band, and, vanishing, betook themselves to flight, to the number it is believed of ten thousand. . . .

After these things had happened and quiet had been restored the time came when the king caused the offenders to be punished. So Lord Robert Tresillian, one of the judges, was sent by order of the king to inquire into the uprisings against the peace and to punish the guilty. Wherever he came he spared no one, but caused great slaughter. . . . For whoever was accused before him in this said cause, whether justly or as a matter of spite, he immediately passed upon him the sentence of death. He ordered some to be beheaded, others to be hanged, still others to be dragged through the city and hanged in four different parts thereof; others to be disemboweled, and the entrails to be burned before them while they were still alive, and afterwards to be decapitated, quartered, and hanged in four parts of the city according to the greatness of the crime and its desert. John Ball was captured at Coventry and led to St. Alban's, where, by order of the king, he was drawn and hanged, then quartered, and his quarters sent to four different places.

3. *THE JOURNEYMEN SADDLERS OF LONDON ATTEMPT TO ORGANIZE, 1396*

The manor was not the only medieval institution which was undergoing painful alteration in the fourteenth century. Guilds, too, were rapidly changing character. One tendency was towards monopolistic control by the masters, closing off the journeymen's opportunity for advancement. In self-protection, the latter began to form journeymen's guilds. These were looked upon by the masters as conspiratorial organizations. With the help of the town authorities they were suppressed wherever possible, as in the following example which occurred in 1396.

Whereas there had arisen no small dissension and strife between the masters of the trade of Saddlers of London, and the serving-men [journeymen] in that trade; because that the serving-men aforesaid against the consent, and without leave of their masters, were wont to array themselves all in a new and like suit once in the year, and often times held divers meetings, at Stratford and elsewhere [outside] the said city, as well as in divers places within the city; whereby many inconveniences and perils ensued to the trade aforesaid; and also, very many losses might happen thereto in future times, unless some quick and speedy remedy should by the rulers of the said city be found for the same; therefore the masters of the said trade on the 10th day of the month of July, in the 20th year, etc., made grievous complaint thereon to the excellent men, William More, Mayor, and the Aldermen of the City aforesaid, urgently entreating that, for the reasons before mentioned, they would deign to send for Gilbert Dustone, William Gylowe, John Clay, John Hiltone, William Berigge, and Nicholas Mason, the then governors of the serving-men aforesaid; to appear before them on the 12th day of July then next ensuing.

. . . [Said] Governors of the serving-men appeared, and, being interrogated as to the matters aforesaid, they said that time out of mind the

London Guildhall Records, as found in A.E. Bland, P.A. Brown, and R.H. Tawney, eds., *English Economic History: Select Documents* (London: G. Bell & Sons, Ltd., 1925), pp. 138–141. Used by permission of the publisher.

serving-men of the said trade had had a certain Fraternity among themselves, and had been wont to array themselves all in like suit once in the year, and, after meeting together at Stratford, on the Feast of the Assumption of the Blessed Virgin Mary to come from thence to the Church of St. Vedast, in London, there to hear Mass on the same day, in honour of the said glorious Virgin.

But the said masters of the trade asserted to the contrary of all this, and said that the fraternity, and the being so arrayed in like suit among the serving-men, dated from only thirteen years back, and even then had been discontinued of late years; and that under a certain feigned colour of sanctity, many of the serving-men in the trade had influenced the journeymen among them and had formed covins [conspiracies] thereon, with the object of raising their wages greatly in excess; to such an extent, namely, that whereas a master in the said trade could before have had a serving-man or journey-man for 40 shillings or 5 marks yearly, and his board, now such a man would not agree with his master for less than 10 or 12 marks or even 10 pounds, yearly; to the great deterioration of the trade.

[Various petitions and arguments having been presented by masters and journeymen, the Mayor and Aldermen] determined that the serving-men in the trade aforesaid should in future be under the governance and rule of the masters of such trade; the same as the serving-men in other trades in the same city are wont, and of right are bound to be; and that in future they should have no fraternity, meetings, or covins, or other unlawful things under a penalty, etc. And that the said masters must properly treat and govern their serving-men in the trade in such manner as the serving-men in like trades in the city have been wont to be properly treated and governed. And that if any serving-men should in future wish to make complaint to the Mayor and Aldermen, for the time being, as to any grievance unduly inflicted upon him by the masters aforesaid, such Mayor and Aldermen would give to him his due and speedy meed of justice as to the same.

4. COLUMBUS REPORTS TO FERDINAND AND ISABELLA ON HIS FIRST VOYAGE

Promptly upon his return from the New World, Columbus wrote a brief and somewhat colored report of his discoveries to his royal patrons. Since it was considered disrespectful for a commoner to address himself directly to the monarchs, the Admiral wrote to the Royal Treasurer Sanchez, who doubtless passed the letter on to Ferdinand and Isabella. It was quickly published in a Latin trans-

Old South Leaflets (Boston: Old South Meeting House, n.d.), Vol. II, No. 33.

lation and went through seventeen editions between 1493 and 1499. It is the first piece of Americana.

As I know that it will afford you pleasure that I have brought my undertaking to a successful result, I have determined to write you this letter to inform you of everything that has been done and discovered in this voyage of mine.

On the thirty-third day after leaving Cadiz [October 12, 1492] I came into the Indian Sea, where I discovered many islands inhabited by numerous people. I took possession of all of them for our most fortunate King by making public proclamation and unfurling his standard, no one making any resistance. To the first of them I have given the name of our blessed Saviour [San Salvador], trusting in whose aid I had reached this and all the rest; but the Indians call it Guanahani. . . . As soon as we reached the island which . . . was called Johana [Cuba], I sailed along its coast some considerable distance toward the west, and found it to be so large, without any apparent end, that I believed it was not an island, but a continent, a province of Cathay. . . . At last, finding that no discoveries rewarded our further progress . . . I concluded not to attempt any other adventures; so, turning back, I came again to a certain harbor, which I had remarked. . . . I continued along toward the east, as much as 322 miles, always hugging the shore, where was the very extremity of the island. From there I saw another island to the eastwards, distant fifty-four miles from this Johana, which I named Hispana [Haiti], and proceeded to it. . . .

In . . . Hispana, there are very lofty and beautiful mountains, great farms, groves and fields, most fertile both for cultivation and for pasturage, and well adapted for constructing buildings. The convenience of the harbors in this island, and the excellence of the rivers, in volume and salubrity, surpass human belief, unless one should see them. In it the trees, pasture-lands, and fruits differ much from those of Johana. Besides, this Hispana abounds in various kinds of spices, gold, and metals. The inhabitants of both sexes of this and of all the other islands I have seen, or of which I have any knowledge, always go as naked as they came into the world, except that some of the women cover parts of their bodies with leaves or branches, or a veil of cotton, which they prepare themselves for this purpose. They are all, as I said before, unprovided with any sort of iron, and they are destitute of arms, which are entirely unknown to them, and for which they are not adapted; not on account of any bodily deformity, for they are well made, but because they are timid and full of terror. . . . They are very guileless and honest, and very liberal of all they have. No one refuses the asker anything that he possesses; on the contrary, they themselves invite us to ask for it. They manifest the greatest affection toward all of us, exchanging valuable things for trifles, content with the very least thing or nothing at all. But I forbade giving them a very trifling thing and of no value, such as bits of plates, dishes, or glass, also nails and straps; although it seemed to them, if they could get such, that they had acquired the most beautiful jewels in the world. . . .

They do not practise idolatry; on the contrary, they believe that all strength, all power, in short, all blessings, are from Heaven, and that I have come down from there with these ships and sailors; and in this spirit was I received everywhere, after they had got over their fear. They are neither lazy nor awkward, but, on the contrary, are of an excellent and acute understanding. Those who have sailed these seas give excellent accounts of everything; but they have never seen men wearing clothes, or ships like ours.

In all these islands, as I understand, every man is satisfied with only one wife, except the princes or kings, who are permitted to have twenty. The women appear to work more than the men, but I could not well understand whether they have private property or not; for I saw that what every one had was shared with the others, especially meals, provisions, and such things. I found among them no monsters, as very many expected, but men of great deference and kind; nor are they black like the Ethiopians, but they have long, straight hair. They do not dwell where the rays of the sun have most power, although the sun's heat is very great there, as this region is twenty-six degrees distant from the equinoctial line. From the summits of the mountains there comes great cold, but the Indians mitigate it by being inured to the weather, and by the help of very hot food, which they consume frequently and in immoderate quantities.

I saw no monsters, neither did I hear accounts of any such except in an island called Charis [Dominica], the second as one crosses over from Spain to India, which is inhabited by a certain race regarded by their neighbors as very ferocious. They eat human flesh, and make use of several kinds of boats by which they cross over to all the Indian islands, and plunder and carry off whatever they can. But they differ in no respect from the others except in wearing their hair long after the fashion of women. They make use of bows and arrows made of reeds, having pointed shafts fastened to the thicker portion, as we have before described. For this reason they are considered to be ferocious, and the other Indians consequently are terribly afraid of them; but I consider them of no more account than the others. . . .

. . . Finally, to sum up in a few words the chief results and advantages of our departure and speedy return, I make this promise to our most invincible Sovereigns, that, if I am supported by some little assistance from them, I will give them as much gold as they have need of, and in addition spices, cottons, and mastic, which is found only in Chios, and as much aloes-wood, and as many heathen slaves as their Majesties may choose to demand; besides these, rhubarb and other kinds of drugs, which I think the men I left in the fort before alluded to have already discovered, or will do so; as I have myself delayed nowhere longer than the winds compelled me, except while I was providing for the construction of a fort in the city of Nativity, and for making all things safe.

Although these matters are very wonderful and unheard of, they would have been much more so if ships to a reasonable amount had been furnished me. But what has been accomplished is great and wonderful, and not at all proportionate to my deserts, but to the sacred Christian faith, and to the piety and religion of our Sovereigns. For what the mind of man could not compass, the spirit of God has granted to mortals. . . .

Therefore let King and Queen and Princes, and their most fortunate realms, and all other Christian provinces, return thanks to our Lord and Saviour Jesus Christ, who has bestowed so great a victory and reward upon us; let there be processions and solemn sacrifices prepared; let the churches be decked with festal boughs; let Christ rejoice upon earth as he rejoices in heaven, as he foresees that so many souls of so many people heretofore lost are to be saved; and let us be glad not only for the exaltation of our faith, but also for the increase of temporal prosperity, in which not only Spain, but all Christendom is about to share.

As these things have been accomplished, so have they been briefly narrated. Farewell.

5. HENRY VII ISSUES LETTERS PATENT TO CABOT FOR THE EXPLORATION OF NORTH AMERICA

Less than three years after Columbus' great voyage, another Italian, Giovanni Caboto, crossed the Atlantic and landed on Cape Breton Island. The official document he received from Henry VII of England authorizing his voyage is given below.

The Letters patents of King Henry the seventh granted unto John Cabot and his three sonnes, Lewis, Sebastian, and Sancius for the discoverie of new and unknowen lands.

Richard Hakluyt, *The Principal Navigations, Voyages, Traffiques and Discoveries of the English Nation* (New York: The Macmillan Company, 1904), Vol. VII, pp. 141–144.

Henry by the grace of God, king of England and France, and lord of Ireland, to all to whom these presents shall come, Greeting.

Be it knowen that we have given and granted, and by these presents do give and grant for us and our heires, to our welbeloved John Cabot citizen of Venice, to Lewis, Sebastian, and Santius, sonnes of the sayd John, and to the heires of them, and every of them, and their deputies, full and free authority, leave, and power to saile to all parts, countreys, and seas of the East, of the West, and of the North, under our banners and ensignes, with five ships of what burthen or quantity soever they be, and as many mariners or men as they will have with them in the sayd ships, upon their owne proper costs and charges, to seeke out, discover, and finde whatsoever isles, countreys, regions or provinces of the heathen and infidels whatsoever they be, and in what part of the world soever they be, which before this time have bene unknowen to all Christians: we have granted to them, and also to every of them, the heires of them, and every of them, and their deputies, and have given them licence to set up our banners and ensignes in every village, towne, castle, isle, or maine land of them newly found. And that the aforesayd John and his sonnes, or their heires and assignes may subdue, occupy and possesse all such townes, cities, castles and isles of them found, which they can subdue, occupy and possesse, as our vassals, and lieutenants, getting unto us the rule, title, and jurisdiction of the same villages, townes, castles, & firme land so found. Yet so that the aforesayd John, and his sonnes and heires, and their deputies, be holden and bounden of all the fruits, profits, gaines, and commodities growing of such navigation, for every their voyage, as often as they shall arrive at our port of Bristoll (at the which port they shall be bound and holden onely to arrive) all maner of necessary costs and charges by them made, being deducted, to pay unto us in wares or money the fifth part of the capitall gaine so gotten. We giving and granting unto them and to their heires and deputies, that they shall be free from all paying of customes of all and singular such merchandize as they shall bring with them from those places so newly found. And moreover, we have given and granted to them, their heires and deputies, that all the firme lands, isles, villages, townes, castles and places whatsoever they be that they shall chance to finde, may not of any other of our subjects be frequented or visited without the licence of the foresayd John and his sonnes, and their deputies, under paine of forfeiture aswell of their shippes as of all and singuler goods of all them that shall presume to saile to those places so found. Willing, and most straightly commanding all and singuler our subjects aswell on land as on sea, to give good assistance to the aforesayd John and his sonnes and deputies, and that as well in arming and furnishing their ships or vessels, as in provision of food, and in buying of victuals for their money, and all other things by them to be provided necessary for the sayd navigation, they do give them all their helpe and favour. In witnesse whereof we have caused to be made these our Letters patents. Witnesse our selfe at Westminster the fifth day of March, in the eleventh yeere of our reigne [1495].

V

EARLY MODERN TIMES

19

LUTHERANISM AND CALVINISM

The starting point of the Protestant Revolt was a spiritual crisis in the life of an obscure German monk which led him to repudiate Church doctrine on indulgences. But behind Martin Luther was a whole complex of currents going back into the Middle Ages which made the times propitious for a revolt against Rome. The development of national monarchies created many sources of friction between kings and popes. The growth of commerce and town-life helped produce a secular state of mind. Increased lay education and humanism often undermined the prestige of the Church. Most important of all, the discipline and spiritual health of the Church declined greatly in the century before Luther, and a purely secularized Papacy showed no inclination toward reform.

1. LUTHER LAYS DOWN SOME FUNDAMENTAL PRINCIPLES OF THE REFORMATION

The two selections below are from Luther's great reform tracts of 1520. They were provoked by the publication of the pope's bull of excommunication in June, 1520. In them are beautifully summarized the basic religious, political, and economic principles of the reform movement. The "Address to the German Nobility" shows Luther's utilization of German nationalism against Rome. The second pamphlet, "Of Christian Liberty," gives the theological basis of the revolt.

To his most Serene and Mighty Imperial Majesty and to the Christian Nobility of the German Nation.

Martin Luther, "Address to the German Nobility" and "Concerning Christian Liberty," in *The Harvard Classics*, edited by Charles W. Eliot (New York: P.F. Collier & Son Corp., 1910), Vol. XXXVI, pp. 276–352. Copyright 1910 by P.F. Collier & Son Corp. Used by permission.

The Romanists have, with great adroitness, drawn three walls round themselves, with which they have hitherto protected themselves, so that no one could reform them, whereby all Christendom has fallen terribly.

Firstly, if pressed by the temporal power, they have affirmed and maintained that the temporal power has no jurisdiction over them, but, on the contrary, that the spiritual power is above the temporal.

Secondly, if it were proposed to admonish them with the Scriptures, they objected that no one may interpret the Scriptures but the Pope.

Thirdly, if they are threatened with a council, they pretend that no one may call a council but the Pope.

Let us, in the first place, attack the first wall.

It has been devised that the Pope, bishops, priests, and monks are called the *spiritual estate,* princes, lords, artificers, and peasants are the *temporal estate*. This is an artful lie and hypocritical device, but let no one be made afraid by it, and that for this reason: that all Christians are truly of the spiritual estate, and there is no difference among them, save of office alone. . . . We are all consecrated as priests by baptism, as St. Peter says: "Ye are a royal priesthood, a holy nation;" . . . to put the matter even more plainly, if a little company of pious Christian laymen were taken prisoners and carried away to a desert, and had not among them a priest consecrated by a bishop, and were there to agree to elect one of them, born in wedlock or not, and were to order him to baptise, to celebrate the mass, to absolve, and to preach, this man would as truly be a priest, as if all the bishops and all the popes had consecrated him. . . .

The second wall is even more tottering and weak: that they alone pretend to be considered masters of the Scriptures; although they learn nothing of them all their life. . . . It is a wickedly devised fable—and they cannot quote a single letter to confirm it—that it is for the Pope alone to interpret the Scriptures or to confirm the interpretation of them. They have assumed the authority of their own selves. And though they say that this authority was given to St. Peter when the keys were given to him, it is plain enough that the keys were not given to St. Peter alone, but to the whole community. Besides, the keys were not ordained for doctrine or authority, but for sin, to bind or loose; and what they claim besides this from the keys is mere invention. But what Christ said to St. Peter: "I have prayed for thee that thy faith fail not" (St. Luke xxii. 32), cannot relate to the Pope, inasmuch as the greater part of the Popes have been without faith, as they are themselves forced to acknowledge; nor did Christ pray for Peter alone, but for all the Apostles and all Christians. . . .

The third wall falls of itself, as soon as the first two have fallen; for if the Pope acts contrary to the Scriptures, we are bound to stand by the

Scriptures, to punish and to constrain him. . . . When need requires, and the Pope is a cause of offence to Christendom, in these cases whoever can best do so, as a faithful member of the whole body, must do what he can to procure a true free council. This no one can do so well as the temporal authorities, especially since they are fellow-Christians, fellow-priests, sharing one spirit and one power in all things, and since they should exercise the office that they have received from God without hindrance. . . .

And now I hope the false, lying spectre will be laid with which the Romanists have long terrified and stupefied our consciences. . . .

Now though I am too lowly to submit articles that could serve for the reformation of these fearful evils, I will yet sing out my fool's song, and will show, as well as my wit will allow, what might and should be done by the temporal authorities or by a general council.

1. Princes, nobles, and cities should promptly forbid their subjects to pay the *annates* [a papal tax developed in the fourteenth century by which a newly elected bishop or abbot had to pay the Papacy the first year's income of his office] to Rome and should even abolish them altogether. . . .

2. [The nobility] should ordain, order, and decree that henceforth no benefice shall be drawn away to Rome. . . . And if a courtling came from Rome, he should receive the strict command to withdraw, or to leap into the Rhine, or whatever river be nearest, and to administer a cold bath to the Interdict, seal and letters and all. . . .

4. Let it be decreed that no temporal matter shall be submitted to Rome, but all shall be left to the jurisdiction of the temporal authorities. . . .

7. The Roman See must abolish the papal offices, and diminish that crowd of crawling vermin at Rome, so that the Pope's servants may be supported out of the Pope's own pocket, and that his court may cease to surpass all royal courts in its pomp and extravagance; . . .

9. The Pope should have no power over the Emperor, except to anoint and crown him at the altar, as a bishop crowns a king; . . .

11. The custom of kissing the Pope's feet must cease. It is an unchristian, or rather an anti-Christian, example that a poor sinful man should suffer his feet to be kissed by one who is a hundred times better than he. . . .

12. Pilgrimages to Rome must be abolished. . . . This I say, not because pilgrimages are bad in themselves, but because at the present time they lead to mischief; for at Rome a pilgrim sees no good examples, but only offence. They themselves have made a proverb, "The nearer to Rome, the farther from Christ". . . .

13. Now we come to the great crowd that promises much and per-

forms little. . . . Let no more mendicant monasteries be built! [The principal mendicant orders were the Franciscans, Dominicans, and Luther's own order, the Augustinians.] God help us! there are too many as it is. Would to God they were all abolished, or at least made over to two or three orders! It has never done good, it will never do good, to go wandering about over the country. . . . For their preaching and confession has led to nought but mere hatred and envy between priests and monks, to the great offence and hindrance of the people. . . . It does not look at all improbable that the Holy Roman See had its own reasons for encouraging all this crowd of monks: the Pope perhaps feared that priests and bishops, growing weary of his tyranny, might become too strong for him, and begin a reformation unendurable to his Holiness.

14. We see also how the priesthood is fallen, and how many a poor priest is encumbered with a woman and children and burdened in his conscience. . . . My advice is to restore liberty, and to leave every man free to marry or not to marry. . . .

16. It were also right to abolish annual festivals, processions, and masses for the dead, or at least to diminish their number; for we evidently see that they have become no better than a mockery, exciting the anger of God and having no object but money-getting gluttony, and carousals. . . .

17. One should also abolish certain punishments inflicted by the canon law, especially the interdict, which is doubtless the invention of the evil one. . . .

18. One should abolish all saints' days, keeping only Sunday. But if it were desired to keep the festivals of Our Lady and the greater saints, they should all be held on Sundays, or only in the morning with the mass; the rest of the day being a working day. My reason is this: with our present abuses of drinking, gambling, idling, and all manner of sin, we vex God more on holy days than on others. . . .

21. It is one of the most urgent necessities to abolish all begging in Christendom. No one should go about begging among Christians. . . .

24. It is high time to take up earnestly and truthfully the cause of the Bohemians. . . . First of all, we must honestly confess the truth, without attempting self-justification, and own one thing to the Bohemians, namely that John Huss and Jerome of Prague were burnt at Constance in violation of the papal, Christian and imperial oath and safe-conduct, and that thus God's commandment was broken and the Bohemians excited to great anger. . . .

25. The universities also require a good, sound reformation. . . . What are the universities, as at present ordered, but, as the book of Maccabees says, "schools of 'Greek fashion' and 'heathenish manners'" . . . full

of dissolute living, where very little is taught of the Holy Scriptures and of the Christian faith, and the blind heathen teacher, Aristotle, rules even further than Christ? Now, my advice would be that the books of Aristotle, the *Physics,* the *Metaphysics, Of the Soul, Ethics,* which have hitherto been considered the best, be altogether abolished. . . .

. . . I daresay I have sung a lofty strain, that I have proposed many things that will be thought impossible, and attacked many points too sharply. But what was I to do? . . . I have hitherto made many offers of peace to my adversaries; but, as I see, God has forced me through them to open my mouth wider and wider, and, because they do not keep quiet, to give them enough cause for speaking, barking, shouting, and writing. Well, then, I have another song still to sing concerning them and Rome; if they wish to hear it, I will sing it to them, and sing with all my might. Do you understand, my friend Rome, what I mean?

* * *

From "Of Christian Liberty," 1520

. . . Man is composed of a two-fold nature, a spiritual and a bodily. As regards the spiritual nature, which they name the soul, he is called the spiritual, inward, new man; as regards the bodily nature, which they name the flesh, he is called the fleshly, outward, old man. . . .

. . . One thing, and one alone, is necessary for life, justification, and Christian liberty; and that is the most holy word of God, the Gospel of Christ, as He says: "I am the resurrection and the life; he that believeth in me shall not die eternally" (John xi. 25); and also (John viii. 36) "If the Son shall make you free, ye shall be free indeed"; and (Matt. iv. 4) "Man shall not live by bread alone, but by every word that proceedeth out of the mouth of God."

Let us therefore hold it for certain and firmly established that the soul can do without everything, except the word of God, without which none at all of its wants are provided for. . . .

The first care of every Christian ought to be, to lay aside all reliance on works, and strengthen his faith alone more and more, and by it grow in the knowledge, not of works, but of Christ Jesus, who has suffered and risen again for him, as Peter teaches, when he makes no other work to be a Christian one. . . .

Now let us turn to the other part, to the outward man. Here we shall give an answer to all those who, taking offense at the word of faith and at what I have asserted, say: "If faith does everything, and by itself suffices for justification, why then are good works commanded? Are we then to take our ease and do no works, content with faith?" Not so, impious men, I reply; not so. . . .

Although, as I have said, inwardly, and according to the spirit, a man is amply enough justified by faith, having all that he requires to have, except that this very faith and abundance ought to increase from day to day, even till the future life; still he remains in this mortal life upon earth, in which it is necessary that he should rule his own body, and have intercourse with men. Here then works begin; here he must not take his ease; here he must give heed to exercise his body by fastings, watchings, labor, and other moderate discipline, so that it may be subdued to the spirit, and obey and conform itself to the inner man and faith, and not rebel against them nor hinder them, as is its nature to do if it is not kept under. . . .

These works, however, must not be done with any notion that by them a man can be justified before God—for faith, which alone is righteousness before God, will not bear with this false notion—but solely with this purpose, that the body may be brought into subjection, and be purified from its evil lusts, so that our eyes may be turned only to purging away those lusts. . . .

True then are these two sayings: Good works do not make a good man, but a good man does good works. Bad works do not make a bad man, but a bad man does bad works. . . .

2. *THE LOWER CLASSES IN GERMANY REBEL AND ARE DENOUNCED BY LUTHER*

Until the Peasants' War, Luther was hailed by the great majority of Germans as a national hero. His position changed radically, however, after his violent denunciation of the peasants and artisans in 1525. He thereby alienated the lower classes in Germany and became the leader of only a faction. The first selection below is from a diary of a citizen of Rothenburg in Bavaria; the second is from Luther's famous denunciation of the rebels.

From the Diary of Michael Eisenhart, 1525

On March 21, a Tuesday, thirty or forty peasants got together in a mob in Rothenburg, bought a kettledrum, and marched about the town, a part going to Pretheim and a part toward Orenbach. . . .

The working classes in the town now begin to revolt. . . .

MARCH 24. This evening between five and six o'clock some one knocked off the head of Christ's image on a crucifix and struck off the arms.

J.H. Robinson, *Readings in European History* (New York: Ginn and Company, 1904), Vol. II, pp. 101–108. Copyright 1904 by James Harvey Robinson. Used by permission of the publisher.

MARCH 26. Chrischainz, the baker, knocked the missal out of the priest's hand in the chapel of our Lady and drove away the priest from mass. . . .

On Tuesday eight hundred peasants came together. Those who would not join them willingly they forced to do so or took their property, as happened to a peasant at Wettring.

On this same day all the artisans were to lay all their complaints and demands before a committee. The taxes, wages, and methods of weighing were discussed. . . .

On Saturday the blind monk, Hans Rotfuchs, spoke contemptuously of the holy sacrament, calling it idolatry and heresy.

APRIL 19. The peasants take three casks of wine from the priest at Scheckenpach and drink it up.

On Wednesday (April 26) Lorenz Knobloch was hewn to pieces by the peasants at Ostheim, and then they pelted one another with the fragments. They said he was a traitor and that he wanted to mislead them. Divine retribution! He had said he would not die until he had killed three priests, but, thank God, not one fell into his hands.

In Rothenburg the citizens are summoned to decide whether, like the neighboring towns of Heilbronn, Dinkelsbühl, and Wimfen, they will aid the peasants. The majority decide to send them guns and pikes, powder and lead.

MAY 15. The bell summoned the community. In spite of the protests of the old Christians, they are forced to obey the majority, and Rothenburg that day fell away from the empire and joined the peasants. . . .

MAY 21. Certain Hohenlohe peasants burn their lord's castle.

On the next Monday Margrave Casimir proceeds with his forces to subdue and punish the peasants. . . .

On Monday after Whitsunday eight thousand peasants are slaughtered by the troops of the League [the Swabian League under Casimir] near Büttart and Sulzdorf. In all these battles the League lost not over one hundred and fifty men.

On June 6 messengers are sent from Rothenburg to Casimir to ask for pardon. Next day others are sent to the League, but they are told that they must surrender unconditionally.

On Thursday following, after the League had retaken the town of Würzburg, they beheaded sixty-two.

After the League had attacked Bamberg they beheaded twenty-one.

On Friday after Corpus Christi, mass was once more chanted in Rothenburg, as formerly.

On the eve of Peter and Paul's day Margrave Casimir rides into Rothenburg with four hundred horsemen, a thousand footmen, and two hundred wagons full of arms and equipments.

JUNE 30. The citizens of Rothenburg are summoned to the market place by a herald and surrounded by pikemen. They are accused of deserting the empire and joining the peasants, and are threatened with the vengeance they deserve.

The names of a number of citizens are read off, and they are beheaded on the spot. Their bodies are left on the market place all day. Some got away through the ring of soldiers: Lorenz Diem, the sexton, Joseph Schad, a tanner, Fritz Dalck, a butcher, and others, but were nevertheless executed.

JULY 1. Fifteen more are beheaded in the market place, including the blind monk. All the bodies are left on the market place all day, then buried. All of these died without confession or the last sacrament, and did not even ask for it.

* * *

From Luther, "Against the Murdering and Robbing Bands of the Peasants"

With threefold horrible sins against God and men have these peasants loaded themselves, for which they have deserved a manifold death of body and soul.

First, they have sworn to their true and gracious rulers to be submissive and obedient, in accord with God's command (Matt. xxii. 21), "Render therefore unto Caesar the things which are Caesar's," and (Rom. xiii. 1), "Let every soul be subject unto the higher powers." But since they have deliberately and sacrilegiously abandoned their obedience, and in addition have dared to oppose their lords, they have thereby forfeited body and soul, as perfidious, perjured, lying, disobedient wretches and scoundrels are wont to do. . . .

Second, they cause uproar and sacrilegiously rob and pillage monasteries and castles that do not belong to them, for which, like public highwaymen and murderers, they deserve the twofold death of body and soul. It is right and lawful to slay at the first opportunity a rebellious person, who is known as such, for he is already under God's and the emperor's ban. Every man is at once judge and executioner of a public rebel; just as, when a fire starts, he who can extinguish it first is the best fellow. Rebellion is not simply vile murder, but is like a great fire that kindles and devastates a country; it fills the land with murder and bloodshed, makes widows and orphans, and destroys everything, like the greatest calamity. Therefore, whosoever can, should smite, strangle, and stab, secretly or publicly, and should remember that there is nothing more poisonous, pernicious, and devilish than a rebellious man. Just as one must slay a mad dog, so, if you do not fight the rebels, they will fight you, and the whole country with you.

Third, they cloak their frightful and revolting sins with the gospel, call themselves Christian brethren, swear allegiance, and compel people to join them in such abominations. Thereby they become the greatest blasphemers and violators of God's holy name, and serve and honor the devil under the semblance of the gospel, so that they have ten times deserved death of body and soul, for never have I heard of uglier sins. . . . Lo, how mighty a prince is the devil, how he holds the world in his hands and can put it to confusion: who else could so soon capture so many thousands of peasants, lead them astray, blind and deceive them, stir them to revolt, and make them the willing executioners of his malice. . . .

3. *CALVIN ASSERTS THE DOCTRINE OF PREDESTINATION*

The most characteristic doctrine of the Calvinists is that of predestination. Calvin's uncompromising view of this doctrine is clearly expressed in his great theological treatise,* The Institutes of the Christian Religion *(1536).

The predestination by which God adopts some to the hope of life, and adjudges others to eternal death, no man who would be thought pious ventures simply to deny; but it is greatly cavilled at, especially by those who make prescience its cause. We, indeed, ascribe both prescience and predestination to God; but we say that it is absurd to make the latter subordinate to the former. When we attribute prescience to God, we mean that all things always were, and ever continue under his eye; that to his knowledge there is no past or future, but all things are present, and indeed so present, that it is not merely the idea of them that is before him, but that he truly sees and contemplates them as actually under his immediate inspection. This prescience extends to the whole circuit of the world, and to all creatures. By predestination we mean the eternal decree of God, by which he determined with himself whatever he wished to happen with regard to every man. All are not created on equal terms, but some are preordained to eternal life, others to eternal damnation; and, accordingly, as each has been created for one or other of these ends, we say that he has been predestinated to life or to death. This God has testified, not only in the case of single individuals; he has also given a specimen of it in the whole posterity of Abraham, to make it plain that the future condition of each nation was entirely at his disposal: . . .

John Calvin, *Institutes of the Christian Religion,* translated by Henry Beveridge (London: James Clarke & Co. Ltd., 1949), Vol. II, pp. 206–207, 210–211. Used by permission of the publisher.

We say, then, that Scripture clearly proves this much, that God by his eternal and immutable counsel determined once for all those whom it was his pleasure one day to admit to salvation, and those whom, on the other hand, it was his pleasure to doom to destruction. We maintain that this counsel, as regards the elect, is founded on his free mercy, without any respect to human worth, while those whom he dooms to destruction are excluded from access to life by a just and blameless, but at the same time incomprehensible judgment. In regard to the elect, we regard calling as the evidence of election, and justification as another symbol of its manifestation, until it is fully accomplished by the attainment of glory. But as the Lord seals his elect by calling and justification, so by excluding the reprobate either from the knowledge of his name or the sanctification of his Spirit, he by these marks in a manner discloses the judgment which awaits them.

4. CALVIN ATTEMPTS TO LEGISLATE MORALITY IN GENEVA

Between 1521 and his death in 1564, Calvin strove to make Geneva a model of Christian government. A group of elders or presbyters, "persons of upright life and good repute," were assigned to all parts of the city to keep watch over the life and conduct of each individual. The regulations the elders were enjoined to enforce were embodied in a long list of ordinances, excerpts from which follow.

CONCERNING THE TIME OF ASSEMBLING AT CHURCH. That the temples be closed for the rest of the time, in order that no one shall enter therein out of hours, impelled thereto by superstition; and if any one be found engaged in any special act of devotion therein or nearby he shall be admonished for it: if it be found to be of a superstitious nature for which simple correction is inadequate, then he shall be chastised.

BLASPHEMY. Whoever shall have blasphemed, swearing by the body or by the blood of our Lord, or in similar manner, he shall be made to kiss the earth for the first offence; for the second to pay 5 *sous,* and for the third 6 *sous,* and for the last offence be put in the pillory for one hour.

DRUNKENNESS. 1. That no one shall invite another to drink under penalty of 3 *sous.*

2. That taverns shall be closed during the sermon, under penalty that the tavern-keeper shall pay 3 *sous,* and whoever may be found therein shall pay the same amount.

3. If any one be found intoxicated he shall pay for the first offence

J. Calvin, *Opera,* X, 51 *et seq.*, in *Translations and Reprints from the Original Sources of European History* (Philadelphia: University of Pennsylvania, 1902), Series II, Vol. III, No. 3, pp. 10–11.

3 *sous* and shall be remanded to the consistory; for the second offence he shall be held to pay the sum of 6 *sous,* and for the third 10 *sous* and be put in prison.

SONGS AND DANCES. If any one sing immoral, dissolute or outrageous songs, or dance the *virollet* or other dance, he shall be put in prison for three days and then sent to the consistory.

USURY. That no one shall take upon interest or profit more than five per cent. upon penalty of confiscation of the principal and of being condemned to make restitution as the case may demand.

GAMES. That no one shall play at any dissolute game or at any game whatsoever it may be, neither for gold nor silver nor for any excessive stake, upon penalty of 5 *sous* and forfeiture of stake played for.

5. LUTHER AND CALVIN DIVERGE ON THE NATURE OF THE EUCHARIST

One of the theological points on which Luther and Calvin could not agree was the vital question of the nature of the Eucharist, the sacrament of the Lord's Supper. Both denounced the Catholic doctrine which held that by the hand of the priest the bread and wine were changed into the actual body and blood of Christ. Luther, however, arrived at a position much closer to the Catholic than to Calvin's, as can be seen from the selections below taken from the Lutheran Catechism of 1529 and the Genevan Catechism of 1541.

From Luther's Catechism, 1529

How the master of the house should explain it simply to his household.

What is the Sacrament of the Altar?

ANSWER. It is the very Body and Blood of our Lord Jesus Christ, under the Bread and Wine, for us Christians to eat and to drink, under the institution of Christ Himself.

Where is this written?

ANSWER. Thus say the holy Evangelists Matthew, Mark, Luke, and St. Paul:—

The Lord Jesus, in the same night in which He was betrayed, took bread, and when He had given thanks, He brake it, and gave it to His disciples, and said, Take; eat. This is My body, which is given for you; this do in remembrance of Me.

After the same manner also He took the cup when He had supped, and gave it to them, saying, Take this and drink ye all of it. This cup is the new

Henry Bettenson, ed., *Documents of the Christian Church* (Oxford: Oxford University Press, 1943), pp. 291–292. Used by permission of the publisher; *Translation and Reprints from the Original Sources of European History* (Philadelphia: University of Pennsylvania, 1902), Series II, Vol. III, No. 3, pp. 8–9.

testament in My blood, which is shed for you for the forgiveness of sins; this do ye, as oft as ye drink it, in remembrance of Me.

What avails it to eat and drink thus?

ANSWER. This is shown us by the words, *Given for you and shed for you for the remission of sins.* That is to say, that in the Sacrament forgiveness of sins, life, and salvation are bestowed on us by these words. For where forgiveness of sins is, there is also life and salvation.

How can bodily eating and drinking accomplish these great things?

ANSWER. Eating and drinking do not indeed accomplish this, but the words which stand there, *Given for you and shed for you for the remission of sins.* These words, together with the bodily eating and drinking, are the most important part of this Sacrament, and whoever believes these words, he has what they say, and as they speak, namely, remission of sins.

* * *

From Calvin's Catechism, 1541

THE MINISTER. Have we in the supper simply a signification of the things above mentioned, or are they given to us in reality?

THE CHILD. Since Jesus Christ is truth itself there can be no doubt that the promises he has made regarding the supper are accomplished, and that what is figured there is verified there also. Wherefore according as he promises and represents I have no doubt that he makes us partakers of his own substance, in order that he may unite us with him in one life.

THE MINISTER. But how may this be, when the body of Jesus Christ is in heaven, and we are on this earthly pilgrimage?

THE CHILD. It comes about through the incomprehensible power of his spirit, which may indeed unite things widely separated in space.

THE MINISTER. You do not understand then that the body is enclosed in the bread, or the blood in the cup?

THE CHILD. No. On the contrary, in order that the reality of the sacrament be achieved our hearts must be raised to heaven, where Jesus Christ dwells in the glory of the Father, whence we await him for our redemption; and we are not to seek him in these corruptible elements.

THE MINISTER. You understand then that there are two things in this sacrament: the natural bread and wine, which we see with the eye, touch with the hand and perceive with the taste; and Jesus Christ, through whom our souls are inwardly nourished?

THE CHILD. I do. In such a way moreover that we have there the very witness and so say a pledge of the resurrection of our bodies; since they are made partakers in the symbol of life.

20

THE PROTESTANT REVOLT IN ENGLAND

The Protestant Revolt in England took a form quite different from that of the Continent. Personal and national issues, rather than doctrinal, caused the break with the traditional authority of Rome. Henry VIII prided himself on his Catholic orthodoxy and persecuted with equal severity followers of the Continental Reformers and Catholics who refused to recognize the King as "Protector and Only Supreme Head of the Church and Clergy of England." But in the reigns of succeeding monarchs the demand for doctrinal changes became irresistible. Well before the end of the century, many characteristically Protestant beliefs and practices had been permanently incorporated into the Church of England.

1. CATHERINE OF ARAGON DEFENDS HERSELF BEFORE THE PAPAL LEGATE, 1529

When Henry VIII insisted on an annulment of his seventeen-year marriage with Catherine of Aragon, Pope Clement VII appointed Cardinals Campeggio and Wolsey to examine Henry's claims. It was before these prelates that Catherine made the following pitiful plea for justice. No decision was reached at this time, and the case was transferred to the Pope himself. The selection is from the Chronicle of Edward Hall (d. 1547).

The court being thus furnished and ordered, the judges commanded the crier to proclaim silence; then was the judges' commission, which they had of the pope, published and read openly before all the audience there assembled. That done, the crier called the king, by the name of "King

Hall, *Chronicle,* as found in Edward P. Cheyney, ed., *Readings in English History* (New York: Ginn and Company, 1908), pp. 337–39. Copyright 1908 by Edward P. Cheyney. Used by permission of the publisher.

Henry of England, come into the court," etc. With that the king answered and said, "Here, my lords!" Then he called also the queen, by the name of "Catherine Queen of England, come into the court," etc.; who made no answer to the same, but rose up incontinent out of her chair, where as she sat, and because she could not come directly to the king for the distance which severed them, she took pain to go about unto the king, kneeling down at his feet in the sight of all the court and assembly, to whom she said in effect, in broken English, as followeth:

"Sir," quoth she, "I beseech you for all the loves that hath been between us, and for the love of God, let me have justice and right; take of me some pity and compassion, for I am a poor woman and a stranger born out of your dominion; I have here no assured friend, and much less impartial counsel; I flee to you as to the head of justice within this realm. Alas! sir, wherein have I offended you, or what occasion of displeasure have I designed against your will and pleasure, intending, as I perceive, to put me from you? I take God and all the world to witness, that I have been to you a true, humble, and obedient wife. . . .

"This twenty years I have been your true wife or more, and by me ye have had divers children, although it hath pleased God to call them out of this world, which hath been no default in me. And when ye had me at the first, I take God to be my judge, I was a true maid, without touch of man; and whether this be true or no, I put it to your conscience. If there be any just cause by the law that ye can allege against me, either of dishonesty or any other impediment, to banish and put me from you, I am well content to depart to my great shame and dishonor; and if there be none, then here I most lowly beseech you let me remain in my former estate, and receive justice at your hands. . . .

". . . I most humbly require you, in the way of charity, and for the love of God, who is the just judge, to spare me the extremity of this new court, until I may be advertised what way and order my friends in Spain will advise me to take. And if ye will not extend to me so much indifferent favor, your pleasure then be fulfilled, and to God I commit my cause!"

And with that she rose up, making a low courtesy to the king, and so departed from thence. Many supposed that she would have resorted again to her former place; but she took her way straight out of the house, leaning (as she was wont always to do) upon the arm of her general receiver, called Master Griffith. And the king being advertised of her departure, commanded the crier to call her again, who called her by the name of "Catherine Queen of England, come into the court," etc. With that quoth Master Griffith, "Madam, ye be called again." "On, on," quoth she; "it maketh no matter, for it is no impartial court for me, therefore I will not tarry. Go on your ways." And thus she departed out of that court, without any farther answer at that time, or at any other, nor would ever appear at any other court after.

2. *PARLIAMENT DECLARES THE KING THE ONLY SUPREME HEAD OF THE CHURCH*

The crowning touch of the English religious revolt was furnished by Parliament's Act of Supremacy in November, 1534. It summed up briefly all that had been done during the preceding three years.

Albeit the king's majesty justly and rightfully is and ought to be the supreme head of the Church of England, and so is recognized by the clergy of this realm in their Convocations, yet nevertheless for corroboration and confirmation thereof, and for increase of virtue in Christ's religion within this realm of England, and to repress and extirp all errors, heresies, and other enormities and abuses heretofore used in the same; be it enacted by authority of this present Parliament, that the king our sovereign lord, his heirs and successors, kings of this realm, shall be taken, accepted, and reputed the only supreme head in earth of the Church of England, called *Anglicana Ecclesia*; . . . and that our said sovereign lord, his heirs and successors, kings of this realm, shall have full power and authority from time to time to visit, repress, redress, reform, order, correct, restrain, and amend all such errors, heresies, abuses, offences, contempts, and enormities, whatsoever they be, which by any manner spiritual authority or jurisdiction ought or may lawfully be reformed, repressed, ordered, redressed, corrected, restrained, or amended, most to the pleasure of Almighty God, the increase of virtue in Christ's religion, and for the conservation of the peace, unity, and tranquillity of this realm; . . .

Henry Bettenson, ed., *Documents of the Christian Church* (London: Oxford University Press, 1943), p. 319. Used by permission of the publisher.

3. *SIR THOMAS MORE IS BEHEADED FOR TREASON*

Among the Englishmen who refused to accept the foregoing Act of Supremacy was the brilliant ex-Chancellor of the King, Sir Thomas More. His last days are described in the closing pages of a notable biography written by his son-in-law, William Roper.

. . . early in the morning [of his day of execution] came to him Sir Thomas Pope, his singular friend, on message from the King and his Council, that

William Roper, *The Life of Sir Thomas More*, in *The Harvard Classics*, edited by Charles W. Eliot (New York: P.F. Collier & Son Corp., 1910), Vol. XXXVI, pp. 138–141. Copyright 1910 by P.F. Collier & Son Corp. Used by permission.

he should before nine of the clock in the same morning suffer death, and that therefore forthwith he should prepare himself thereto. "Mr. Pope," saith he, "for your good tidings I most heartily thank you. I have been always bounden much to the King's Highness for the benefits and honours which he hath still from time to time most bountifully heaped upon me, and yet more bounded I am to his Grace for putting me into this place, where I have had convenient time and space to have remembrance of my end, and so help me God most of all, Mr. Pope, am I bound to his Highness, that it pleased him so shortly to rid me of the miseries of this wretched world. And therefore will I not fail most earnestly to pray for his Grace both here, and also in another world." "The King's pleasure is further," quoth Mr. Pope, "that at your execution you shall not use many words." "Mr. Pope" (quoth he), "you do well that you give me warning of his Grace's pleasure. For otherwise had I purposed at that time somewhat to have spoken, but of no matter wherewith his Grace, or any other should have had cause to be offended. Nevertheless, whatsoever I intend I am ready obediently to conform myself to his Grace's commandment. . . ."

Wherewithal Mr. Pope taking his leave of him could not refrain from weeping, which Sir Thomas More perceiving, comforted him in this wise, "Quiet yourself, good Mr. Pope, and be not discomforted. For I trust that we shall once in heaven see each other full merrily, where we shall be sure to live and love together in joyful bliss eternally." Upon whose departure Sir Thomas More, as one that had been invited to a solemn feast, changed himself into his best apparel; which Mr. Lieutenant espying, advised him to put it off, saying, That he that should have it was but a worthless fellow. "What Mr. Lieutenant" (quoth he), "shall I account him a worthless fellow, that will do me this day so singular a benefit? Nay, I assure you, were it cloth of gold I would account it well bestowed on him, as St. Cyprian did, who gave his executioner thirty pieces of gold." And albeit at length, through Mr. Lieutenant's persuasions, he altered his apparel, yet, after the example of that holy martyr St. Cyprian, did he of that little money that was left him, send one angel of gold to his executioner. And so was he brought by Mr. Lieutenant out of the Tower, and from thence led towards the place of execution, where going up the scaffold, which was so weak that it was ready to fall, he said to Mr. Lieutenant, "I pray you, I pray you, Mr. Lieutenant, see me safe up, and for my coming down let me shift for myself." Then desired he all the people thereabouts to pray for him, and to bear witness with him, that he should then suffer death in and for the faith of the holy Catholic Church, which done he kneeled down, and after his prayers said, he turned to the executioner, and with a cheerful countenance spake unto him. "Pluck up thy spirits, man, and be not afraid to do thine office, my neck is very short. Take heed therefore thou shoot not awry for saving thine honesty." So passed Sir Thomas More out of this world to God upon the very same day in which himself had most desired.

Soon after whose death came intelligence thereof to the Emperor Charles, whereupon he sent for Sir Thomas Eliott, our English Ambassador, and said unto him, "My Lord Ambassador, we understand that the King your master hath put his faithful servant and grave wise councillor Sir Thomas More to death." Whereunto Sir Thomas Eliott answered, that he understood nothing thereof. "Well," said the Emperor, "it is very true, and this will we say, that if we had been master of such a servant, of whose doings ourselves have had these many years no small experience, we would rather have lost the best city of our dominions, than have lost such a worthy councillor." Which matter was by Sir Thomas Eliott to myself, to my wife, to Mr. Clement and his wife, to Mr. John Haywood and his wife, and divers others of his friends accordingly reported.

4. A MONASTERY IS SUPPRESSED AND ITS ABBOT EXECUTED

Glastonbury, in southwest England, was one of the oldest and most famous English monasteries. By a parliamentary act of 1539 it, and many other similar establishments, was given to the King. Its abbot, Richard Whiting, refused to surrender the monastery when Cromwell's agents appeared. He was charged with high treason and executed. His death caused a great sensation and was long remembered in the west of England.

Letter of the Visitors Sent to Examine the Abbot of Glastonbury to Thomas Cromwell, September 22, 1539

Please it your lordship to be advertised, that we came to Glastonbury on Friday last past, about ten of the clock in the forenoon: and [because] . . . the Abbot was then at Sharpham, a place of his, a mile and somewhat more from the abbey, we, without any delay, went unto the same place; and there . . . examined him upon certain articles. And [because] . . . his answer was not then to our purpose, we advised him to call to his remembrance that which he had as then forgotten, and so declare the truth, and then came with him the same day to the abbey; and there of new proceeded that night to search his study for letters and books: and found in his study . . . a written book of arguments against the divorce of his king's majesty and the lady dowager, as also divers pardons, copies of bulls, and the

T. Wright, ed., *Letters Relating to the Suppression of Monasteries* (London: Camden Society, 1843), pp. 255–256, 261–262.

counterfeit life of Thomas Becket in print; but we could not find any letter that was material. And so we proceeded again to his examination concerning the articles we received from your lordship, in the answers whereof, as we take it, shall appear his cankered and traitorous heart and mind against the king's majesty and his succession; as by the same answers, signed with his hand, and sent to your lordship by this bearer, more plainly shall appear. And so, with as fair words as we could, we have conveyed him from hence into the tower, being but a very weak man and sickly. . . . We have in money 300*l.* and above; but the certainty of plate and other stuff there as yet we know not, for we have not had opportunity for the same, but shortly we intend (God willing) to proceed to the same; whereof we shall ascertain your lordship so shortly as we may. This is also to advertise your lordship, that we have found a fair chalice of gold, and divers other parcels of plate, which the abbot had hid secretly from all such commissioners as have been there in times past; . . . It may please your lordship to advertise us of the king's pleasure by this bearer, to whom we shall deliver the custody and keeping of the house, with such stuff as we intend to leave there convenient to the king's use. We assure your lordship it is the goodliest house of that sort that ever we have seen. We would that your lordship did know it as we do; then we doubt not but your lordship would judge it a house meet for the king's majesty, and for no man else: which is to our great comfort; and we trust verily that there shall never come any double hood within that house again. Also this is to advertise your lordship, that there is never a one doctor within that house; but there be three bachelors of divinity, which be but meanly learned, as we can perceive. And thus our Lord preserve your good lordship.

Letter of One of the Visitors, Richard Pollard, to Cromwell, November 16, 1539

Pleaseth it your lordship to be advertised, that . . . [on November 15] the late abbot of Glastonbury went from Wells to Glastonbury, and there was drawn through the town upon a hurdle to the hill called the Torre, where he was put to execution; at which time he asked God mercy and the king for his great offences towards his highness. . . . Afore his execution, [he] was examined upon divers articles and interrogatories to him ministered by me, but he could accuse no man but himself of any offence against the king's highness, nor he would confess no more gold nor silver nor any other thing more than he did before your lordship in the Tower. . . . I suppose it will be near Christmas before I shall have surveyed the lands at Glastonbury, and taken the audit there. . . .

5. *HENRY VIII CLOSES THE DOOR ON DOCTRINAL INNOVATION: THE SIX ARTICLES*

In 1539, the very year in which Glastonbury and many other great monasteries were suppressed, Henry VIII issued the Six Articles. The pope himself could not have been more Catholic. Opposition in Parliament and among the ministers was widespread but unavailing. Cranmer, among others, put away his wife for the time being.

First, that in the most blessed Sacrament of the altar, by the strength and efficacy of Christ's mighty word (it being spoken by the priest), is present really, under the form of bread and wine, the natural body and blood of our Saviour Jesus Christ, conceived of the Virgin Mary; and that after the consecration there remaineth no substance of bread or wine, nor any other substance, but the substance of Christ, God and man.

Secondly, that communion in both kinds is not necessary *ad salutem*, by the law of God, to all persons; and that it is to be believed, and not doubted of, but that in the flesh, under the form of bread, is the very blood; and with the blood, under the form of wine, is the very flesh; as well apart, as though they were both together.

Thirdly, that priests after the order of priesthood received, as afore, may not marry, by the law of God.

Fourthly, that vows of chastity or widowhood, by man or woman made to God advisedly, ought to be observed by the law of God; and that it exempts them from other liberties of Christian people, which without that they might enjoy.

Fifthly, that it is meet and necessary that private masses be continued and admitted in this the king's English Church and congregation, as whereby good Christian people, ordering themselves accordingly, do receive both godly and goodly consolations and benefits; and it is agreeable also to God's law.

Sixthly, that auricular confession is expedient and necessary to be retained and continued, used and frequented in the Church of God.

Henry Bettenson, ed., *Documents of the Christian Church* (London: Oxford University Press, 1943), pp. 328–329. Used by permission of the publisher.

6. *THE "INVINCIBLE ARMADA" MEETS DISASTER*

On May 30, 1588, the Armada sailed from Lisbon. The plan called for a rendezvous with the duke of Parma and his 17,000-man army near Calais, from which point the invasion of England would be launched. English seamanship, the ele-

Victor von Klarwill, ed., *The Fugger News-Letters*, Second Series (New York: G.P. Putnam's Sons, 1926), pp. 133–185 *passim*.

ments, and Spanish bungling saved the island kingdom. The following account of the disaster is culled from the dispatches of the correspondents of the great German banking family, the Fuggers. Note the confusion in dating. The new calendar of Pope Gregory XIII, by which ten days had been dropped, had gone into effect in Catholic Europe in 1582.

MADRID, MAY 30, 1587. On the 24th inst. . . . Francis Drake, the English pirate, made a surprise landing [at Cadiz] with forty-eight ships great and small, not all warships. He pillaged and stripped about fourteen ships laden with all sorts of merchandise and lying in the roads, and stayed there for some days. Those ships which he could not take with him he afterwards burnt or sank. Thereupon the chief citizens with women and property fled to Seville and elsewhere. . . .

ANTWERP, NOVEMBER 5, 1587. As the King of Spain is arming so heavily at Lisbon and Biscay and assembling a powerful fleet, the Queen of England also is arming heavily, for it is considered certain that the King of Spain will send his Armada to Scotland since the King of that country seems to have risen against the Queen of England and to have promised the King of Spain a port for his vessels to take shelter in. . . .

COLOGNE, DECEMBER 24, 1587. The presumption in Brussels is that the vessels being pressed forward at Antwerp and other places are to sail next year against England. Four regiments of German mercenaries are to be put on board them. . . .

ANTWERP, JANUARY 23, 1588. Letters from Lisbon of December 16 have been received here this week reporting that the Armada there is ready and that twenty thousand men are awaiting embarkation. It is, however, not supposed that they will sail before the spring. The English with thirty-five warships are lying off Cape St. Vincent not far from Lisbon, awaiting vessels which move to and fro and carrying off what they can. . . .

ANTWERP, JANUARY 30, 1588. . . . The Queen of England is still arming vigorously and equipping a large number of warships. It is also reported that in addition to soldiers 4500 sailors have been recruited. Drake is to put them on fifty or sixty war-vessels and sail to Spain with them, though his precise destination is unknown. . . . Moreover, the Queen of England has called up and inscribed the whole male population, and all her harbours along the coast are garrisoned and warships in the ports near Scotland and Ireland are ready for sea, so that the Spanish Armada cannot get into England. Altogether she is handling maritime affairs with great boldness.

HAMBURG, JUNE 23, 1588 (O.S.). I simply must tell you that the skipper, Hans Limburger, has arrived here with his vessel from Cadiz. He broke through the embargo, and has a cargo of salt, wine, raisins, cinnamon, and a little sugar. He put out from there on the 20th ult., O.S., and passed Lisbon on the 24th. In the distance he saw the Spanish Armada and sailed abreast of it all day. The next day it was blowing rather hard and he could not see it. He is of opinion that the Armada put out on the 23rd of May Old Style or the 2nd of June New Style and was shaping a course for the Channel. The skipper met an English warship on his way and this brought him into Plymouth, to Drake's Armada. He was entertained by Drake for three days and the English were rejoicing that the Spanish Armada was at sea. Afterwards Captain Drake gave the Skipper a permit, so that he might be allowed to pass, and quickly formed in order and put to sea in spite of a contrary wind. If an action is fought, there will be terrible loss of life. On two consecutive days here the sun and moon have been quite bloody. What this signifies the merciful God alone knows. May he defend the Right!

ROME, JUNE 25, 1588. The Pope recently signified to one of the Cardinals that he was in alliance with the King of Spain. He intended to grant him a million crowns in aid, so soon as news reached him that the Spanish Armada had disembarked its men in England.

HAMBURG, AUGUST 3 AND 4, 1588. Hans Buttber has arrived off the town in a big ship. He comes through the Channel from San Lucar. He was with Captain Drake for four or five days and joined the Englishman on the 21st, O.S., of last month, just after the latter had had an engagement with the Spanish Armada. From the 21st to the 26th they had skirmished and fired heavily at each other, but they could not board, and the English with their little ships sailed so well and manoeuvred so skilfully, firing meanwhile, that the galleasses could not get at them. Drake captured Don Pedro de Valdez, Admiral of fourteen vessels, and had him and ten other nobles brought on to his own ship. He gave them a banquet and treated them very handsomely and entertained them besides with trumpets and music. On this ship he took sixty guns and made four hundred and fifty men prisoners. . . .

This noon there comes from Holland a vessel which was at Enkhuizen actually on the last day of July. It brings news that eighteen ships of the Spanish Armada were sunk by gunfire, and eight taken and brought to England. The rest of the Spanish Armada has fled to the French coast. If this is true it will somewhat abate Spanish insolence and give the English fresh courage, though they have no lack of insolence either.

MIDDELBURG, AUGUST 12, 1588. . . . The sea is driving ashore near Flushing much artillery and wreckage from the burnt ships as well as burnt corpses, so that it is a horrible sight. In Flushing there are heaps of captured Spaniards. They say the Prince of Parma has betrayed them, for the Spanish Armada went thus far up the country relying on his promises, and hoping to receive great assistance from him. Indeed, they were of opinion that he would accomplish more than the Armada, for he had always promised them to come out with 500 sail and be a match for the English alone. He was going to make the invasion with 70,000 men, but now he is bringing woe and misery on all the splendid Spanish ships. They curse him horribly, and it is to be feared he will fall into complete disfavour with the King and be recalled from the Netherlands. Altogether the wretched devils here do nothing but complain. Our sailors wanted to kill all the Spaniards because they would not surrender. Their ships are built as high as churches. But we took pity upon them. The seamen who brought in the ships above mentioned numbered 150 in all. They marched through the town at noon in procession two abreast with all the Spaniards' best clothes on. In costume one looked like a Portuguese, another like a Spaniard, a third like a Biscayan, a fourth like an Italian. People here thought they were prisoners from the Armada, because of the many expensive costumes. In the two ships there was plenty of booty, about 120 brass guns, many of iron and a quantity of provisions.

A vessel has also arrived at Flushing from Calais with the report that Duke Medina Sidonia and de San Lucar, in command of the Spanish Armada, has been brought in there. Half his head seems to have been shot off. They say he was the most powerful man in all Spain. The Spanish Armada has had a terrible time of it. A Scotchman has come in here also. He saw the Spanish Armada in the distance on the North Sea and says it is barely over 80 vessels strong and the English are after it with 250 and firing heavily with a favourable wind. The Spaniards have had no rest day or night for sixteen to eighteen days.

VENICE, AUGUST 19, 1588. . . . Although His Majesty of Spain was already suffering greatly from gout, his pains redoubled when he heard news how greatly the Spanish Armada had suffered in the storm and how it was somewhat hindered in its operations.

ANTWERP, OCTOBER 22, 1588. Several letters arrived here from London by Zeeland on the 17th inst., announcing that of the 80 ships of the Spanish Armada still remaining 34 of the biggest were driven ashore in Ireland by bad weather and a south-westerly gale. Where the rest have escaped to is not yet known. So when these vessels anchored on the Irish coast in a miserable state without masts and rudders, the gentlemen on board sent a boat to the Governor of Ireland to beg him to allow them on land to recover and to purchase necessities and also to repair their badly damaged vessels. This was granted, and the gentlemen with many of their men stayed ashore for some days and passed to and fro to their ships. They even presumed to throw up an entrenchment along the sea. But as soon as this was bruited abroad the people flew to arms and slaughtered all the

Spaniards they could catch on land. However the most important were kept prisoners, and fourteen grandees, among them the Duke of Medina Sidonia, were hourly expected in London as captives. They overpowered the vessels and took or threw into the sea all on board. It is said, though, that the Duke of Medina Sidonia is not among these, but has escaped to Spain.

ANTWERP, DECEMBER 24, 1588. Letters of the 18th inst. from England announce that during that week in all London churches great services of thanksgiving were held for delivery from the tyrannous projects of the Spaniards against England and against the Queen in particular. Like Pharaoh, the King of Spain has been punished. During these thanksgivings the Queen seemed very magnificent and devout.

21

THE CATHOLIC REFORMATION

By the time of Luther's death in 1546 Roman Catholicism gave the appearance of a dying institution. Northern and central Germany, England, and part of Switzerland were lost to the old faith. Protestants were making steady gains in the Lowlands, France, Poland, and Hungary. The Catholic Church was on the defensive nearly everywhere. But a generation later the situation had been reversed. The growth of the Protestant churches had been checked, and Catholicism was recouping many of its earlier losses. Thanks to a reformed Papacy, the Council of Trent, new religious orders like the Jesuits, and strong political support, the Roman Catholic Church was reinvigorated.

1. A PAPAL COMMISSION SPEAKS FRANKLY OF CHURCH ABUSES

In 1537 the reform-minded Pope Paul III selected a commission of nine cardinals to investigate the ills of the Church. A year later the commission rendered a remarkably candid report, a condensation of which is given below. Although intended to be secret, the report fell into the hands of the Lutherans. It was widely disseminated and regarded by Protestants as justification for their rebellion against Rome.

You [the Pope] have summoned us to yourself, unskilled as we are and unequal to such a great task . . . and with the most serious words you have enjoined that we collect all these abuses and report them to you. . . .

(1) The first abuse is that in the ordination of clerics and even of priests . . . no diligence is employed: the most ignorant men, those born

B.J. Kidd, ed., *Documents Illustrative of the Continental Reformation* (Oxford: The Clarendon Press, 1921), pp. 307–318. Used by permission of the publisher. An original translation by Peter Ford.

of the most worthless family, reprobates, and adolescents are admitted to Holy Orders and even to the priesthood. . . . In some places the divine worship has not only diminished, but is even already extinct. . . . Your Holiness should not allow anyone to be ordained except by his bishop, or with the permission of his bishop or of the deputies in the city: in addition, each bishop should have in his diocese a teacher to instruct clerics in minor orders in both letters and morals. . . .

(2) Another abuse of great seriousness is in the granting of ecclesiastical benefices, especially of parishes, and above all of bishoprics, in which it has become customary that the persons to whom benefices are granted are provided for, and not the flock of Christ and the Church. Therefore benefices, parishes, and especially bishoprics should be granted . . . to holy and learned men: . . . Nor should a benefice in Spain or Britain be granted to an Italian, or vice versa. . . .

(3) When benefices are conferred on or granted to others, another abuse has crept in by the fixing of payments on their fruits: . . . A great abuse which should be reformed is the granting of payments to rich clerics, who can live quite comfortably and honestly on the revenues they already have.

(4) Another such abuse is in the exchanging of benefices by simoniacal bargains with no consideration except for profit.

(5) . . . Although the law of the Church prohibits the bequeathing of benefices by will, because they belong not to the testator but to the Church . . . human . . . ingenuity finds many ways of evading this law. . . .

. . . there is an ancient law . . . that the sons of priests should not inherit the benefices of their parents . . . however (as we hear) dispensations are being given in regard to this venerable law. . . .

(6) Another abuse is in regard to expectations . . . of benefices whereby the occasion is presented that the death of another might be desired and eagerly listened for. . . .

. . . bishops . . . and curates should not absent themselves from their churches and parishes, except for some serious reason. . . . What more wretched sight is there visible to a Christian man traveling through the Christian world than this desertion of churches? Almost all pastors have left their flocks, almost all [parishes] have been entrusted to hirelings. . . .

(9) Another abuse is that so many . . . cardinals absent themselves from this Curia, and perform no part of their duties. . . .

(11) Another abuse which ought to be corrected is in the orders of religious, because so many are corrupt that they injure the seculars by great scandal and bad example. . . .

(13) Another abuse troubles the Christian people, namely in regard

to nuns who are under the care of conventual friars, for in many monasteries public sacrileges are committed, to the great scandal of all. . . .

(14) Another great and dangerous abuse is in the public schools, especially in Italy, in which professors of philosophy teach impiety. . . .

(15) . . . friars and religious . . . after a solemn vow leave their orders and obtain permission not to be obliged to wear their habits. . . .

(17) Another abuse is . . . a dispensation granted to a person in Holy Orders to marry. . . .

(18) An abuse is in regard to dispensation from marital impediments of consanguinity and affinity. Certainly a dispensation in the second degree should not be granted except for a serious public cause. . . .

(19) Another abuse is in the absolution of a simoniac. . . . This deadly disease reigns in the Church of God to such a degree that certain men are not afraid to commit simony, then immediately seek absolution from punishment . . . and in this way keep the benefice which they bought. . . .

(23) . . . many foreigners are scandalized who go into the Church of St. Peter where there are filthy, ignorant priests . . . celebrating Mass. . . .

(24) In this city public prostitutes walk or ride on mule as honorable women followed . . . by clerics and noble retinues of cardinals. . . .

These, Holy Father, are the abuses . . . which would seem to us ought to be corrected. . . . We have satisfied our consciences, not without a great hope that under your leadership we may see the Church of God purged, beautiful as a dove . . . with the eternal memory of your name. You have taken the name of Paul: we hope that you will imitate the love of Paul: chosen as he was as the vessel to carry the name of Christ to the Gentiles: we hope that you have been chosen, that you might restore the name of Christ which has been so forgotten by the people and us clergy.

2. *A GENERAL COUNCIL LEADS THE WAY TO CATHOLIC REVIVAL*

The Council of Trent met in twenty-five sessions from 1545 to 1563. Its work was two-fold: to restate and clarify the doctrines of the Church, particularly those tenets which had been repudiated by Luther, Calvin, and other Protestant leaders; and, secondly, to reform the discipline of the Church. The doctrinal work took two forms: definitions of doctrine (Part A below), and anathemas against specific heretical opinions (Part B).

[A] *Excerpts from the Formulation of Doctrine*

ON THE INSTITUTION OF THE SACRIFICE OF THE MASS. . . . He, therefore, our God and Lord, though He was about to offer Himself once on the altar

J. Waterworth, trans., *The Canons and Decrees of the Sacred and Oecumenical Council of Trent* (London: C. Dolman, 1848), *passim.*

of the cross unto God the Father by means of His death there to operate an eternal redemption; nevertheless, [so] that His priesthood [would] not be extinguished by His death, in the last supper, on the night in which He was betrayed . . . offered up to God the Father His own body and blood under the species of bread and wine; and, under the symbols of those same things, He delivered (His own body and blood) to be received by His apostles, whom He then constituted priests of the New Testament; and by those words, *Do this in commemoration of me,* He commanded them and their successors in the priesthood, to offer (them); even as the Catholic Church has always understood and taught. . . . [Twenty-second Session, 1562.]

ON THE INSTITUTION OF THE PRIESTHOOD. Sacrifice and priesthood are, by the ordinance of God, in such wise conjoined, as that both have existed in every law. Whereas, therefore, in the New Testament, the Catholic Church has received, from the institution of Christ, the holy visible sacrifice of the Eucharist; it must needs also be confessed, that there is, in that Church, a new, visible, and external priesthood, into which the old has been translated. And the sacred Scriptures show, and the tradition of the Catholic Church has always taught, that this priesthood was instituted by the same Lord our Saviour, and that to the apostles, and their successors in the priesthood, was the power delivered of consecrating, offering, and administering His Body and Blood, as also of forgiving and of retaining sins. [Twenty-third Session, 1563.]

ON TRANSUBSTANTIATION. And because that Christ, our Redeemer, declared that which He offered under the species of bread to be truly His own body, therefore has it ever been a firm belief in the Church of God, and this holy Synod doth now declare it anew, that, by the consecration of the bread and of the wine, a conversion is made of the whole substance of the bread into the substance of the body of Christ our Lord, and of the whole substance of the wine into the substance of His blood; which conversion is, by the holy Catholic Church, suitably and properly called Transubstantiation. [Thirteenth Session, 1551.]

DECREE CONCERNING THE USE OF THE SACRED BOOKS. The same sacred and holy Synod,—considering that no small utility may accrue to the Church of God, if it be made known which out of all the Latin editions, now in circulation, of the sacred books, is to be held as authentic,—ordains and declares, that the said old and vulgate edition, which, by the lengthened usage of so many ages, has been approved of in the Church, be, in public lectures, disputations, sermons and expositions, held as authentic; and that no one is to dare, or presume to reject it under any pretext whatever. Furthermore, in order to restrain petulant spirits, It decrees, that no one, relying on his own skill, shall,—in matters of faith, and of morals pertaining to the edification of Christian doctrine,—wresting the sacred Scripture to his own senses, presume to interpret the said sacred Scripture contrary to that sense which holy mother Church . . . hath held and doth hold; . . . [Fourth Session, 1546.]

ON THE INVOCATION AND RELICS OF SAINTS. The holy Synod enjoins on all bishops, and others who sustain the office and charge of teaching, that, agreeably to the usage of the Catholic and Apostolic Church, received from the primitive times of the Christian religion, and agreeably to the consent of the holy Fathers, and to the decrees of sacred Councils, they especially instruct the faithful diligently concerning the intercession and invocation of saints; the honour (paid) to relics; and the legitimate use of images: teaching them, that the saints, who reign together with Christ, offer up their own prayers to God for men; that it is good and useful suppliantly to invoke them, and to have recourse to their prayers, aid, (and) help for obtaining benefits from God, through His Son, Jesus Christ our Lord, who is our alone Redeemer and Saviour; . . . [Twenty-fifth Session, 1563.]

[B] *Excerpts from the Anathemas*

ON JUSTIFICATION. If any one saith, that man may be justified before God by his own works, whether done through the teaching of human nature, or that of the law, without the grace of God through Jesus Christ; let him be anathema. . . . [Sixth Session, 1547.]

ON THE SACRIFICE OF THE MASS. If any one saith, that in the mass a true and proper sacrifice is not offered to God; or, that to be offered is nothing else but that Christ is given us to eat; let him be anathema.

If any one saith, that by those words, *Do this for the commemoration of me* (Luke xxii. 19), Christ did not institute the apostles priests; or, did not ordain that they, and other priests should offer His own body and blood; let him be anathema. . . .

If any one saith, that the rite of the Roman Church, according to which a part of the canon and the words of consecration are pronounced in a low tone, is to be condemned; or, that the mass ought to be celebrated in the vulgar tongue only; . . . let him be anathema. . . . [Twenty-second Session, 1562.]

ON THE SACRAMENTS IN GENERAL. If any one saith, that the sacraments of the New Law were not all instituted by Jesus Christ, our Lord; or, that they are more, or less, than seven, to wit, Baptism, Confirmation, the Eucharist, Penance, Extreme Unction, Order, and Matrimony; or even that any one of these seven is not truly and properly a sacrament; let him be anathema. . . .

If any one saith, that the sacraments of the New Law are not necessary unto salvation, but superfluous; and that, without them, or without the desire thereof, men obtain of God, through faith alone, the grace of justification;—though all (the sacraments) are not indeed necessary for every individual; let him be anathema. . . .

If any one saith, that all Christians have power to administer the word, and all the sacraments; let him be anathema. . . .

If any one saith, that a minister, being in mortal sin,—if so be that he observe all the essentials which belong to the effecting, or conferring of, the sacrament,—neither effects, nor confers the sacrament; let him be anathema. . . . [Seventh Session, 1547.]

ON THE EUCHARIST. If any one saith, that Christ, given in the Eucharist, is eaten spiritually only, and not also sacramentally and really; let him be anathema. . . . [Thirteenth Session, 1551.]

ON THE SACRAMENT OF MATRIMONY. If any one saith, that the Church has erred, in that she hath taught, and doth teach, in accordance with the evangelical and apostolical doctrine, that the bond of matrimony cannot be dissolved on account of the adultery of one of the married parties; . . . let him be anathema. . . .

If any one saith, that the marriage state is to be placed above the state of virginity, or of celibacy, and that it is not better and more blessed to remain in virginity, or in celibacy, than to be united in matrimony; let him be anathema. . . . [Twenty-fourth Session, 1563.]

[C] *Excerpts from the Reformatory Decrees*

ON THE ESTABLISHMENT OF SEMINARIES FOR CLERICS. . . . the holy Synod ordains, that all cathedral, metropolitan, and other churches greater than these, shall be bound, each according to its means and the extent of the diocese, to maintain, to educate religiously, and to train in ecclesiastical discipline, a certain number of youths of their city and diocese. . . . [Twenty-third Session, 1563.]

ON THE NECESSITY FOR PREACHING. The holy Synod, desirous that the office of preaching . . . may be exercised as frequently as possible . . . ordains, that the bishops shall themselves in person, each in his own church, announce the sacred Scriptures and the divine law . . . and in the other churches the parish priests . . . and this at least on all Lord's Days and solemn festivals; but, during the season of the fasts, of Lent and of the Advent of the Lord, daily. . . . [Twenty-fourth Session, 1563.]

ON THE FURNITURE AND TABLE OF PRELATES. . . . [The Synod] not only orders that bishops be content with modest furniture, and a frugal table and diet, but that they also give heed that in the rest of their manner of living, and in their whole house, there be nothing seen that is alien from this holy institution, and which does not manifest simplicity, zeal towards God, and a contempt of vanities. Also, It wholly forbids them to strive to enrich their own kindred or domestics out of the revenues of the church: . . . [Twenty-fifth Session, 1563.]

ON THE USE OF THE POWER OF EXCOMMUNICATION. Although the sword of excommunication is the very sinews of ecclesiastical discipline, and very salutary for keeping the people in their duty, yet is it to be used with sobriety and great circumspection; seeing that experience teaches, that if it be rashly or for slight causes wielded, it is more despised than feared, and produces ruin rather than safety. . . . nor shall [the bishops] be induced to grant the said excommunications by the authority of any Secular person whatever, even though a magistrate; . . . [Twenty-fifth Session, 1563.]

ON INDULGENCES. Whereas the power of conferring Indulgences was granted by Christ to the Church; and she has, even in the most ancient times, used the said power, delivered unto her of God; the sacred holy Synod teaches, and enjoins, that the use of Indulgences . . . is to be retained in the Church; and It condemns with anathema those who either assert, that they are useless; or who deny that there is in the Church the power of granting them. In granting them, however, It desires that, in accordance with the ancient and approved custom in the Church, moderation be observed; . . . [Twenty-fifth Session, 1563.]

ON DUELLING. The detestable custom of duelling, introduced by the contrivance of the devil, that by the bloody death of the body, he may accomplish the ruin of the soul, shall be utterly exterminated from the Christian world. . . . [Twenty-fifth Session, 1563.]

3. *AUSTERITY BECOMES THE KEYNOTE AT ROME*

In the years after the Council of Trent, the popes set the example for all Catholic clerics. Characteristic of the new moral tone of the Papacy is the description sent in 1600 by the Fugger correspondent in that city.

The Pope is quite determined to lead a monastic life as an example to the whole world. On account of this he has already ordered all carpets and ornaments to be removed from his rooms and especially from his sleeping chamber, allowing nothing to remain therein except a bedstead, a table and several skulls, as he wishes only to lie between four walls. Near him sleep two Benedictine monks, who stand in very good repute. He has sum-

Victor von Karwill, ed., *The Fugger News-Letters* (New York: G.P. Putnam's Sons, 1924), p. 227.

moned them to his presence, in order to pass his time with them and only to think of spiritual matters.

Last Saturday the Pope sat in the chair of the Chief Penitentiary in the Church of St. Peter with a white rod in his hand, and heard confessions there for three hours, granting the people absolution. Among these were many pilgrims, such as the Viceroy of Naples and the Duke of Sessa, as well as the bandit chief and the former most intimate advisor of the Sciarra. . . .

4. LOYOLA WRITES AN EXERCISE TO BRING SOULS TO GOD

One of the world's great works on asceticism is the* Spiritual Exercises *of Ignatius Loyola, the founder of the Society of Jesus (Jesuits). It is not a book designed to be read in the conventional way but rather an outline for a four-week spiritual retreat under the guidance of a retreat-master. During this period the person, through the exercise of his mind and heart, is led step by step towards a spiritual union with God. As will be seen below, St. Ignatius makes a novel and somewhat disturbing appeal to the senses to achieve his aim.

Exercise on Death

Application of the *sight.* Consider—1. A few moments after your death. Your body laid on a funeral bed, wrapped in a shroud, a veil thrown over your face; beside you the crucifix, the holy water, friends, relatives, a priest kneeling by your sad remains . . . the public officer who writes in the register of the dead all the particulars of your decease,—such a death, such a year, such a day, such an hour,—the servants all occupied with the preparation for your funeral.

2. The day after your death. Your inanimate body enclosed in a coffin, covered with a pall, taken from your apartment, sadly carried to the foot of the altar. . . . Consider well the dismal field where the eye sees nothing but tombs; this open grave where they are laying your body. . . .

3. Some months after your death. Contemplate this stone already blackened by time, this inscription beginning to be effaced; and under that stone, in that coffin which is crumbling bit by bit, contemplate the sad state of your body; see how the worms devour the remains of putrid flesh; how all the limbs are separating; how the bones are eaten away by the corruption of the tomb! . . .

Application of the *hearing.* Go through again the different scenes

Adapted from *Manresa: or the Spiritual Exercises of St. Ignatius* (New York: The Catholic Publication Society, n.d.). The order of the "Third Exercise on Death" and the "Second Exercise on Hell" has been reversed.

where you are the spectacle. Listen—(1.) To the dismal sound of the bells which announce your death, and which beg the prayers of the faithful for your soul. (2.) The prayers which they recite at the foot of your bed: . . . (3.) The remarks of the servants who speak of you. (4.) Your friends and relatives, who communicate to each other their reflections on your death, and mutually console each other for your loss. (5.) The assistants called in to arrange your funeral, who speak of you with cold indifference. . . .

Application of the *smell* and the *touch*. Imagine yourself respiring the odour your body exhales when the soul is departed; the infection it would give out, if it were taken from the coffin a few months after your death. Imagine you touch this damp earth, where they have laid you; this shroud in which they have wrapped you, and which is now in rags; this bare skull, once the seat of thought; these dismembered limbs, which once obeyed all the orders of your will;—in fine, this mass of corruption, which the sepulchre has enclosed a few months, and the sight of which is horrible. In presence of this terrible scene, ask yourself what are health, fortune, friendship of the world, pleasures of the senses, life itself: "Vanity of vanities, all is vanity" (Eccles. i. 2).

End by a colloquy with our Saviour dying: "Into Thy hands I commend my spirit, O Lord."

* * *

Exercise on Hell

Application of the Senses

1. APPLICATION OF THE SIGHT. Consider in your mind the vast fire of hell; souls shut up in bodies of fire, as in an eternal prison; wicked spirits constantly employed in tormenting them.

2. APPLICATION OF THE HEARING. Listen to the groans, the howls, the cries of rage, the blasphemies against Christ and His saints, the mutual maledictions of the damned.

3. APPLICATION OF THE SMELL. Imagine you smell the fire, the brimstone, the infection which exhales from so many hideous corpses.

4. APPLICATION OF THE TASTE. Taste in spirit all the bitterness, the tears, the regrets, the remorse of the damned.

5. APPLICATION OF THE TOUCH. Touch in imagination those devouring flames which in hell consume not only the bodies of the reprobate, but the souls themselves. What do you think of them? Could you inhabit these eternal furnaces for a few hours? . . .

* * *

Exercise on the Blessed Life of Jesus Christ in Heaven

Preparatory Prayer

FIRST PRELUDE. Represent to yourself our Lord seated on His throne at the right hand of His Father; beside Him the Blessed Virgin; around the throne the angels and the elect.

SECOND PRELUDE. Beg for an ardent desire of heaven, and the courage to suffer on earth with Jesus Christ, that you may one day reign with Him in eternity.

FIRST POINT

Jesus Christ in heaven suffers no more.

In heaven the Christian, like his Divine Head, will be for ever freed from all bodily pains and from all afflictions of the soul.

1. IN HEAVEN THERE ARE NO MORE INFIRMITIES. . . . In this abode of perfect beatitude the blessed no longer know what it is to suffer and die: "And death shall be no more" (Apoc. xxi. 4).

2. IN HEAVEN THERE IS NO MORE GRIEF OR SORROW. "Nor mourning, nor crying, nor sorrow shall be any more" (Apoc. xxi. 4). Here below, what is life but one long unceasing affliction? In heaven all tears are dried: "God shall wipe away all tears from their eyes" (Apoc. vii. 17). . . .

3. IN HEAVEN THERE ARE NO MORE SEPARATIONS. Here below, to poison the sweets of friendship, this thought alone suffices: "How long will the society of these friends, of these relatives so tenderly loved, continue?" But once in the bosom of God, the elect meet to part no more. What joy for a Christian family to meet again, after the long and sad separation of the grave! What joy to be able to say with confidence, "We are again united, and it is for eternity!"

4. IN HEAVEN THERE ARE NO MORE TEMPTATIONS. Here on earth is for the Christian a struggle of every day and every moment; and in this struggle a continual danger of losing the grace of God, his soul, and eternity. . . .

5. IN HEAVEN, ABOVE ALL, THERE IS NO MORE SIN. Recall what you have meditated on the malice of sin. It is the supreme evil, the one only evil of time and eternity; the sole evil of the creature, the great evil done against God. Banished into hell, sin cannot penetrate into the kingdom of charity. Oh, the happiness of that day, when, entering into heaven, the elect shall say, My God is now mine, and I am His! . . .

5. FATHER RICCI DEBATES WITH A CHINESE MINISTER OF THE IDOLS

One of the ablest of the Jesuit missionaries was Father Matthew Ricci, who worked in China from 1583 until his death in 1610. He became renowned among Chinese intellectuals for his wisdom and wrote several works in flawless Chinese which are still regarded as classics of the language. The following incident in his life took place in Nanking and was recorded by one of Ricci's co-workers.

. . . Father Ricci wore the costume of the literary class, and of that particular branch of it known as the Expounders of the Law. It was a modest garb, and the hat that went with it was somewhat like our own biretta, designed in the form of a cross. Not only by his costume but by his preaching also he showed himself to be in truth an expounder of the law, but of the Christian law, and in both respects a confounder of the ministers of the idols. He did not find fault with the literary sect, on the contrary, he praised them and particularly their great philosopher, Confucius, who preferred to observe silence relative to the future life, rather than put forth erroneous ideas about it, and to explain the law by offering precepts for regulating the life of the individual, for the direction of the family, and for the proper government of the kingdom.

Father Matthew's custom of going about in his newly adopted raiment was something unusual for a foreigner, but it had the approval of the literary class. . . . This subject of Father Matthew's attire was a common topic of conversation among the most distinguished people, and he was always invited to the meetings of the literary leaders, as a man who adored one God, held to one religion which he believed to be true, and refused to associate with those who sacrificed to misleading deities. This same was true of many of the educated class of that period.

There was a venerable septuagenarian living in Nankin at that time; one of the City Judges, with a reputation for virtue as well as for learning. People came to him from all parts, as to an oracle for instruction, and he must have had a thousand followers. He had abandoned the teachings of the literati and gone over to the worshippers of idols, and to preaching their cult. . . . [One day Ricci received an invitation to go to this gentleman's house for dinner.] His host . . . had invited a celebrated minister of the temple idols, who was said to have had a great following of disciples and of the laity f both sexes, who called him Master. . . . He was an

China in the Sixteenth Century: The Journals of Matthew Ricci: 1583–1610, translated by L.J. Gallagher, S.J. (New York: Random House, Inc., 1953), pp. 337–343.

ardent scholar, a philosopher, an orator and a poet, and well versed in the doctrines of the other sects from which he differed. He was at the house when Father Matthew arrived, and surrounded by a coterie of his admirers, twenty or more in number, who had paid their respects to the host and were seated, waiting for the rest of the company. . . .

. . . The first place at table was assigned to Father Matthew, because he was a stranger, and during the dinner, they opened a discussion on a question frequently introduced at their gatherings, namely, What are we to think of human nature? Is it essentially good, or bad, or neither? If good, whence the evil it begets? If bad, whence the good it often produces? If neither, how does it happen that it produces both good and evil? Since these men lacked the rules of logic and knew of no distinction between natural and moral goodness, they confounded what is innate in human nature with what is acquired by it. Concerning the fall of human nature in original sin, and likewise concerning divine grace and its operation, of course, they knew absolutely nothing, because they had never even dreamed of such things. Up to this day their philosophers continue to argue about human nature, without ever being able to come to any definite conclusion concerning it. On this occasion they talked and argued about it for a whole hour, and as Father Matthew sat there quietly listening, some of them concluded that perhaps their arguments on the subject were too subtle for him to comprehend. Others, however, were eager to hear what he had to say in solution of so intricate a problem, and as he was about to speak, they all became quiet and settled back to listen with attention.

He began by making a detailed summary, from memory, of all that had been said on the question, which caused them all to open their eyes in wonder, after which he said, "There is no room for doubt that the God of heaven and earth must be considered as infinitely good. Now, if human nature is so weak that we doubt whether it is good or bad in itself, and if man as well as God is the creator of heaven and earth, as the master Sanhoi asserted he was, only a few minutes ago, then we must admit that it is open to doubt as to whether God also is good or bad." Sitting next to Father Ricci there was one of the literati of the class of Licentiates, who was so pleased with this argument, that fearing lest it might not be understood by the company, he stood up and gave a fuller and an excellent explanation of what it meant. At the end of his discourse he turned to the temple cenobite, with a smile, and said, "How will you answer that?" And the only answer to his question was a supercilious grin. At this, Father Matthew and several others insisted upon a verbal answer, rather than a nod or a gesture. To this the minister of the idols retorted with a narrative of peculiar hallucinations from the doctrine of his sect, which Father Matthew interrupted, saying: "Our arguments must be drawn from reason, not from authority. Since we disagree in doctrine and neither of us admits the validity of the books of the other, and since I could quote any number of examples from my books, our argument now is to be settled by reason which is common to us both." The minister of the idols, however, did not appear to be vanquished. Instead of taking up the argument, he rambled on slyly with a flow of nicely formed and sonorous sentences from the idiom of the Chinese language, pretending to prove that he who was good could also be bad. Then Father Matthew continued, just as cleverly as his opponent, saying that the sun was so bright that it could never be anything but bright, because of its natural, innate brightness. This was a new idea to them which had great force, for the simple reason that they knew of no distinction between substance and accident.

There were other subjects discussed at this dinner and when it was over, the temple minister was the only one who would not admit that he was vanquished, though all the others agreed that he was. They were so pleased with Father Matthew's presentation of his side of the question, that they carried on the discussion of the same subjects at their meetings for months afterwards. . . .

After the debate at the banquet, some of the disciples of the host became frequent callers on Father Ricci and soon put aside their pantheistic ideas. In order to help others to correct this fallacy, he wrote a treatise on that particular question, and inserted it as a separate chapter in his catechism. When this commentary was read by one of the disciples of the banquet host, he remarked that anyone denying its truth would deny that the sun was bright. The story of the debate at the banquet came to the President of the Magistrates and he congratulated the Father, as did others also, who had concluded that what they had formerly considered to be a barbarous law was not so barbarous as they had imagined. Father Ricci, himself, thanked God that the foundations of the Christian law were finally being laid in the kingdom of China.

22

THE THIRTY YEARS' WAR

No general European war has ever been more complex or confusing than the Thirty Years' War, the last of the wars of religion. It began as a German civil war between Catholics and Protestants, but from the start the constitutional question of the precise relation between the imperial power and the three hundred odd German states cut across the religious issue. The situation was further complicated by the intervention of a number of foreign powers, each more or less pursuing its own interest. To compound the confusion, some of the leading generals tended to behave like free agents rather than instruments of state or dynastic policy.

1. AN OLD RELIGIOUS SETTLEMENT CAUSES TROUBLE IN THE EMPIRE

The Peace of Augsburg (1555) had effected a truce between Lutherans and Catholics. Two aspects of the Peace, however, caused friction in later years and helped cause the Thirty Years' War: first, its failure to give legal recognition to the Calvinists; and, secondly, the "ecclesiastical reservation."

15. In order to bring peace into the holy Empire of the Germanic Nation between the Roman Imperial Majesty and the Electors, Princes, and Estates: let neither his Imperial Majesty nor the Electors, Princes, &c., do any violence or harm to any estate of the Empire on account of the Augsburg Confession [Lutheranism], but let them enjoy their religious belief, liturgy and ceremonies as well as their estates and other rights and privileges in peace; and complete religious peace shall be obtained only by Christian means of amity, or under threat of the punishment of the imperial ban.

B.J. Kidd, ed., *Documents Illustrative of the Continental Reformation* (Oxford: The Clarendon Press, 1921), No. 149, pp. 363–364. Used by permission of the publisher.

16. Likewise the Estates espousing the Augsburg Confession shall let all the Estates and Princes who cling to the old religion live in absolute peace and in the enjoyment of all their estates, rights and privileges.

17. However, all such as do not belong to the two above-named religions shall not be included in the present peace but be totally excluded from it.

18. And since it has proved to be matter of great dispute what was to happen with the bishoprics, priories, and other ecclesiastical benefices of such Catholic priests as would in course of time abandon the old religion, we have in virtue of the powers of Roman Emperors ordained as follows: Where an archbishop, bishop or prelate or any other priest of our old religion shall abandon the same, his archbishopric, bishopric, prelacy, and other benefices, together with all their income and revenues which he has so far possessed, shall be abandoned by him without any further objection or delay. The chapters and such as are entitled to it by common law or the custom of the place shall elect a person espousing the old religion, who may enter on the possession and enjoyment of all the rights and incomes of the place without any further hindrance and without prejudging any ultimate amicable settlement of religion.

23. No Estate shall try to persuade the subjects of other Estates to abandon their religion nor protect them against their own magistrates. . . .

24. In case our subjects, whether belonging to the old religion or to the Augsburg Confession, should intend leaving their homes, with their wives and children, in order to settle in another place, they shall neither be hindered in the sale of their estates after due payment of the local taxes nor injured in their honour. . . .

2. *GERMAN PROTESTANTS SUSPECT A JESUIT PLOT*

Uneasy German Protestants, watching the impressive resurgence of Catholic power after the Council of Trent, began to suspect a plot to restore the old faith throughout the Empire. The focal point of their suspicions was the Jesuits, as can be seen in the following letter written by the Lutheran elector of Saxony to his representative at the Diet in 1608.

How violently the restless Jesuits and their followers are exerting themselves to undo, by their absurd interpretations and preposterous attacks, the precious and solemnly ratified Religious Peace [of Augsburg] which was drawn up long years ago for many weighty reasons by his Roman Imperial Majesty and all the estates of the empire, is but too clear. Nay, they

J.H. Robinson, *Readings in European History* (New York: Ginn and Company, 1904), Vol. II, pp. 200–201.

would completely abolish it and then do away altogether with our true Christian religion, in which we were born and brought up and in which we would live and die. All this is sufficiently proved by the innumerable, violent, and poisonous books which they issue throughout the Roman Empire, directed against the said Religious Peace and its clear provisions, declaring it to be no more than *ad interim,*—a temporary concession of toleration, designed to last only until the conclusion of the Council of Trent; even going so far as to imply that his Imperial Majesty of happy memory had no authority to arrange the peace among the estates of the empire without the consent of the pope. Moreover they stir up harsh persecutions hitherto unheard of in the Holy Roman Empire, all with a view to accomplishing their end,—namely, to promote discord among the estates of the Holy Roman Empire, to rouse the several governments against their subjects and *vice versa,* and to check and suppress our true Christian religion and bring it back into the condition and contempt in which it was before the establishment of the religious and secular peace.

We know, however, that his Roman Imperial Majesty [Rudolf II] and the peace-loving Catholic estates, with their Christian and loyal German feelings, have no pleasure in the dangerous practices of the Jesuits and their adherents. . . . Moreover, since the nature and character of the Jesuits and their followers are as notorious among Catholics as among Protestants, and since what they have been up to in Sweden, Poland, France, the Netherlands, and, recently, in Italy, is well known, they should be estimated accordingly and precautions taken against their dangerous plots.

3. *A DEFENESTRATION AT PRAGUE TOUCHES OFF THE WAR*

On May 23, 1618, certain rabid Bohemian Protestants led by Count Matthias of Thurn showed their determination to maintain their religious and political independence by throwing two imperial governors out of a palace window. The scene is described by a modern historian, C.V. Wedgwood.

Thurn called a meeting of Protestant officials and deputies from all over Bohemia and appealed for the release of the prisoners. When this demonstration proved useless, he urged . . . a yet larger assembly of Protestants. This second meeting was fixed for May 1618; it was now March. In the intervening time both parties set themselves to work up the feelings of the people and of the townsfolk of Prague in particular. In spite of Catholic propaganda the Protestant meeting assembled on May 21st, a formidable gathering of noblemen, gentry and burghers from all over the province.

C.V. Wedgwood, *The Thirty Years' War* (New Haven, Conn.: Yale University Press, 1949), pp. 78–80. Used by permission of Jonathan Cape Limited, London, copyright holder.

The imperial governors in vain commanded them to dissolve. Only then did Slavata and Martinitz grasp the danger in which they stood, and on the evening of the 22nd a secretary of state escaped in disguise towards Vienna to implore immediate help.

It was too late. That very night Thurn called on the leading nobility to form a plan of action. . . . He demanded death for Slavata and Martinitz and the establishment of a Protestant emergency government. The city was already alive with excitement and when on the following morning the Protestant deputies were seen making their way towards the royal castle of the Hradschin an immense crowd followed in their wake. Through the portals surmounted by the outspread eagle of the Hapsburg they surged into the courtyard; up the staircase the deputies led the way, through the audience hall and into the small room where the governors sat. Trapped between the council table and the wall, the crowd before and the blank stones behind, Slavata and Martinitz stood at bay. Neither doubted that his last hour had come.

A hundred hands dragged them towards the high window, flung back the casement and hoisted them upwards. Martinitz went first. "Jesu Maria! Help!" he screamed and crashed over the sill. Slavata fought longer, calling on the Blessed Virgin and clawing at the window frame under a rain of blows until someone knocked him senseless and the bleeding hands relaxed. Their shivering secretary clung to Schlick for protection; out of sheer intoxication the crowd hoisted him up and sent him to join his masters.

One of the rebels leant over the ledge, jeering: "We will see if your Mary can help you!" A second later, between exasperation and amazement, "By God, his Mary has helped," he exclaimed, for Martinitz was already stirring. Suddenly a ladder protruded from a neighbouring window; Martinitz and the secretary made for it under a hail of misdirected missiles. Some of Slavata's servants, braving the mob, went down to his help and carried him after the others, unconscious but alive.

The extraordinary chance which had saved three lives was a holy miracle or a comic accident according to the religion of the beholder, but it had no political significance. Martinitz fled that night in disguise and Slavata continued, ill and a prisoner, in the house whither he had been carried. That evening his wife knelt before the Countess Thurn entreating some guarantee for her husband's life, a request which the lady granted with the pessimistic stipulation that the Countess Slavata should do her a like service after the next Bohemian revolution.

Murder or no murder, the *coup d'état* was complete, and since Thurn had overruled many of his supporters in demanding death it was as well for the conscience of his allies that a pile of mouldering filth in the courtyard of the Hradschin had made soft falling for the governors.

4. THE WAR SPREADS: THE EDICT OF RESTITUTION, 1629

By 1629 the Emperor had crushed the German Protestant resistance. He then overreached himself by issuing the Edict of Restitution. This action alienated many hitherto neutralist princes, who found foreign support in Gustavus Adolphus of Sweden.

We are determined for the realisation both of the religious and profane peace to despatch our imperial commissioners into the Empire; to reclaim all the archbishoprics, bishoprics, prelacies, monasteries, hospitals and endowments which the Catholics had possessed at the time of the treaty of Passau (1552) and of which they have been illegally deprived; and to put into all these Catholic foundations duly qualified persons so that each may get his proper due. We herewith declare that the religious peace (of 1555) refers only to the Augsburg Confession as it was submitted to our Ancestor Emperor Charles Vth twenty-fifth of June 1530; and that all other doctrines and sects, whatever names they may have, not included in the Peace are forbidden and cannot be tolerated. We therefore command to all and everybody under punishment of the religious and the land ban that they shall at once cease opposing our ordinance and carry it out in their lands and territories and also assist our commissioners. Such as hold the archbishoprics and bishoprics, prelacies, monasteries, hospitals &c., shall forthwith return them to our imperial commissioners with all their appurtenances. Should they not carry out this behest they will not only expose themselves to the imperial ban and to the immediate loss of all their privileges and rights without any further sentence on commendation, but to the inevitable real execution of that order.

Emil Reich, ed., *Select Documents Illustrating Mediaeval and Modern History* (London: Staples Press, 1915), pp. 234–235. Used by permission of the publisher.

5. A GREAT GERMAN CITY IS PUT TO THE SWORD

One of the worst acts of barbarism in a consistently savage war was the massacre of the inhabitants of Magdeburg by the imperialist troops under Tilly and Pappenheim in 1631. This event induced many Protestant princes to join Gustavus Adolphus. It is described by a writer of the period.

So then General Pappenheim collected a number of his people on the ramparts by the New Town, and brought them from there into the streets of the city. Von Falckenberg was shot, and fires were kindled in different quarters; then indeed it was all over with the city, and further resistance

J.H. Robinson, *Readings in European History* (New York: Ginn and Company, 1904), Vol. II, pp. 211–212. Copyright 1904 by James Harvey Robinson. Used by permission of the publisher.

was useless. Nevertheless some of the soldiers and citizens did try to make a stand here and there, but the imperial troops kept bringing on more and more forces—cavalry, too—to help them, and finally they got the Kröckenthor open and let in the whole imperial army and the forces of the Catholic League,—Hungarians, Croats, Poles, Walloons, Italians, Spaniards, French, North and South Germans.

Thus it came about that the city and all its inhabitants fell into the hands of the enemy, whose violence and cruelty were due in part to their common hatred of the adherents of the Augsburg Confession, and in part to their being imbittered by the chain shot which had been fired at them and by the derision and insults that the Magdeburgers had heaped upon them from the ramparts.

Then was there naught but beating and burning, plundering, torture, and murder. Most especially was every one of the enemy bent on securing much booty. When a marauding party entered a house, if its master had anything to give he might thereby purchase respite and protection for himself and his family till the next man, who also wanted something, should come along. It was only when everything had been brought forth and there was nothing left to give that the real trouble commenced. Then, what with blows and threats of shooting, stabbing, and hanging, the poor people were so terrified that if they had had anything left they would have brought it forth if it had been buried in the earth or hidden away in a thousand castles. In this frenzied rage, the great and splendid city that had stood like a fair princess in the land was now, in its hour of direst need and unutterable distress and woe, given over to the flames, and thousands of innocent men, women, and children, in the midst of a horrible din of heartrending shrieks and cries, were tortured and put to death in so cruel and shameful a manner that no words would suffice to describe, nor no tears to bewail it. . . .

Thus in a single day this noble and famous city, the pride of the whole country, went up in fire and smoke; and the remnant of its citizens, with their wives and children, were taken prisoners and driven away by the enemy with a noise of weeping and wailing that could be heard from afar, while the cinders and ashes from the town were carried by the wind to Wanzleben, Egeln, and still more distant places. . . .

In addition to all this, quantities of sumptuous and irreplaceable house furnishings and movable property of all kinds, such as books, manuscripts, paintings, memorials of all sorts . . . which money could not buy, were either burned or carried away by the soldiers as booty. The most magnificent garments, hangings, silk stuffs, gold and silver lace, linen of all sorts, and other household goods were bought by the army sutlers for a mere song and peddled about by the cart load all through the archbishopric of Magdeburg and in Anhalt and Brunswick. Gold chains and rings, jewels, and every kind of gold and silver utensils were to be bought from the common soldiers for a tenth of their real value. . . .

6. GUSTAVUS ADOLPHUS IS KILLED AT LÜTZEN

In November, 1632, the anti-imperialist forces lost their most capable general, Gustavus Adolphus, king of Sweden. The following account of the battle and the King's death is by a modern historian.

The morning of November 16th broke fair, but a thick mist gathered over the flat, sodden country at about ten o'clock and continued for the rest of the day. The ground was perfectly flat, the fields stretching away, almost without cover save for an occasional straggling hedge, on either side of the main road as far as eye could see. The road ran roughly east and west; north of it there was a ditch, and a little farther back three windmills. Between the ditch and the windmills, having Lützen on his right, Wallenstein drew up his forces, placing a line of musketeers in the ditch, whence they could shoot upwards at the bellies of the Swedish horses when they charged. He did not depart from the time-honoured formation, placing his cavalry on the wings, his infantry in the centre, his artillery in front of the infantry. Owing to Pappenheim's absence he had only between twelve and fifteen thousand men, very ill-armed he subsequently asserted, and to improve the appearance of his reduced forces he herded the camp followers out of the town, grouped them together loosely in squares, the men in front, provided them with a few standards and hoped that in the grey distance the Swedes would take them for a powerful reserve.

The King [Gustavus] drew up his troops on the south side of the road, having the town of Lützen a little in front of him and to the left. His right wing was against a small plantation of trees. He formed his troops once again in the manner which had been so successful at Breitenfeld, he himself commanding on the right wing and Bernard of Saxe-Weimar on the left; but the disposition of the battle, unlike Breitenfeld, was entirely in his hands, and both left and right wings were drawn up in the Swedish fashion. On the farther side of the road Holk faced the King, Wallenstein himself was opposite Saxe-Weimar.

As was his custom, the King prayed before the whole army, asking the blessing of God on the Protestant Cause. This was at about eight o'clock and the firing had already begun, but not for two hours did either army move. The Swedes once or twice attempted a feint attack to draw Wallen-

C.V. Wedgwood, *The Thirty Years' War* (New Haven, Conn.: Yale University Press, 1949), pp. 324–327. Used by permission of Jonathan Cape Limited, London, copyright holder.

stein out of his position, but in vain, and at last at ten o'clock, just as the mist was coming up, the King on the right wing charged Holk's cavalry. A sharp contest ensued at the ditch, from which the musketeers were eventually ousted, and in a desperate struggle the imperial horse were driven back on to the guns, while the terrified 'reserves' of camp-followers broke and fled, leaving the baggage unattended and the tracehorses unsecured. But on the farther side of the battle Wallenstein had set fire to Lützen, and the smoke blew across Bernard's lines. Under cover of this the Croatian cavalry on this wing charged against Bernard's half-blinded men. His troops were bolder than the Saxons had been at Breitenfeld, and stood their ground until the King came galloping across to encourage them.

From that moment the mist and smoke, which cut off one side of the conflict from the other and divided troop from troop, seemed to blow across the very memories of the observers. It may have been at noon, or not until evening, that Pappenheim appeared on Wallenstein's left wing and at once charged the flank of the victorious Swedes, forcing them back over the ditch which they had so hardly won. At some moment in this attack Pappenheim received that bullet in the lung which sent him, choking blood, to die in his coach on the Leipzig road. Towards midday the King of Sweden's horse, riderless and wild with pain from a neck-wound, was seen plunging across the field. The imperialists shouted that Gustavus was dead. Octavio Piccolomini swore he had seen him stretched on the ground. Holk spread the news. But on the Swedish side the officers denied it, desperate lest it might be true. It could not be denied for ever, for the King was no longer leading them, and to his army this had but one meaning.

Bernard of Saxe-Weimar took command. On the right wing his troops swept forward once again, driving Wallenstein's men back on to flaming Lützen; wheeling, they then charged the centre and seized the batteries at the windmills. On the right, frantic at their King's death, the soldiers cleared the long-contested ditch once again, and put Pappenheim's wild but unreliable cavalry to flight. Three horses were shot under Octavio Piccolomini as he tried to rally them; seven times he was grazed by bullets, but never by word or sign let it be known. At nightfall Wallenstein, crippled with gout, raging with pain and mortification, drew off under cover of darkness to Halle. Exhausted, his men fell and slept by the way, while all night long he sent scouts to find out who was left that could fight. An English captain, roused from the sleep of exhaustion in a ditch, his head propped against his horse's flank, indicated three officers of his company lying close by, but thought there were no other survivors. If there were, he had lost them. Tracehorses were gone, so that the baggage and artillery had to be left, and Holk appears to have been the only man in the imperial army who regarded the engagement as a victory.

In the dank November darkness the Swedes were seeking the body of their King. They found him at last; he had been shot between the ear and the right eye, the wound that killed him, but he had other wounds, a dagger thrust and a shot in the side, two balls in the arm and one—which caused great rumour of treachery—in the back. He lay on what had been the enemy's side of the contested ditch, naked, under a heap of dead. That night, over his whole camp, among Swedes and Germans, Scots, English, Irish, Poles, French and Dutch, among mercenaries as among his subjects, there hung the silence of unutterable sorrow.

7. *THE WAR AS SEEN BY A GERMAN PEASANT*

One of the best accounts of the devastation wrought by the Thirty Years' War is the semiautobiographical novel,* The Adventurous Simplicissimus, *by Grimmelshausen. The author was himself a soldier in the latter part of the war.

How Simplicissimus's Palace [i.e., Hut] Was Stormed, Plundered, and Ruinated, and in What Sorry Fashion the Soldiers Kept House There

Although it was not my intention to take the peace-loving reader with these troopers to my dad's house and farm, seeing that matters will go ill therein, yet the course of my history demands that I should leave to kind posterity an account of what manner of cruelties were now and again practised in this our German war. . . .

The first thing these troopers did was, that they stabled their horses: thereafter each fell to his appointed task: which task was neither more nor less than ruin and destruction. For though some began to slaughter and to boil and to roast so that it looked as if there should be a merry banquet forward, yet others there were who did but storm through the house above and below stairs. Others stowed together great parcels of cloth and apparel and all manner of household stuff, as if they would set up a frippery market. All that they had no mind to take with them they cut in pieces. Some thrust their swords through the hay and straw as if they had not enough sheep and swine to slaughter: and some shook the feathers out of the beds and in their stead stuffed in bacon and other dried meat and provisions as if such were better and softer to sleep upon. Others broke the stove and the windows as if they had a never-ending summer to promise. Houseware of copper and tin they beat flat, and packed such vessels, all bent and spoiled, in with the rest. Bedsteads, tables, chairs, and benches they burned, though there lay many cords of dry wood in the yard. Pots and pipkins must all

Hans J.C. von Grimmelshausen, *The Adventurous Simplicissimus,* translated by A.T.S. Goodrick (London: William Heinemann Ltd., 1912), pp. 28–31. Used by permission of the publisher.

go to pieces, either because they would eat none but roast flesh, or because their purpose was to make there but a single meal.

Our maid was so handled in the stable that she could not come out; which is a shame to tell of. Our man they laid bound upon the ground, thrust a gag into his mouth, and poured a pailful of filthy water into his body: and by this, which they called a Swedish draught, they forced him to lead a party of them to another place where they captured men and beasts, and brought them back to our farm, in which company were my dad, my mother, and our Ursula.

And now they began: first to take the flints out of their pistols and in place of them to jam the peasants' thumbs in and so to torture the poor rogues as if they had been about the burning of witches: for one of them they had taken they thrust into the baking oven and there lit a fire under him, although he had as yet confessed no crime: as for another, they put a cord round his head and so twisted it tight with a piece of wood that the blood gushed from his mouth and nose and ears. In a word, each had his own device to torture the peasants, and each peasant his several torture. But as it seemed to me then, my dad was the luckiest, for he with a laughing face confessed what others must out with in the midst of pains and miserable lamentations: and such honour without doubt fell to him because he was the householder. For they set him before a fire and bound him fast so that he could neither stir hand nor foot, and smeared the soles of his feet with wet salt, and this they made our old goat lick off, and so tickle him that he well nigh burst his sides with laughing. And this seemed to me so merry a thing that I must needs laugh with him for the sake of fellowship, or because I knew no better. In the midst of such laughter he must needs confess all that they would have of him, and indeed revealed to them a secret treasure, which proved far richer in pearls, gold, and trinkets than any would have looked for among peasants. Of the women, girls, and maidservants whom they took, I have not much to say in particular, for the soldiers would not have me see how they dealt with them. Yet this I know, that one heard some of them scream most piteously in divers corners of the house; and well I can judge it fared no better with my mother and our Ursel than with the rest. Yet in the midst of all this miserable ruin I helped to turn the spit, and in the afternoon to give the horses drink, in which employ I encountered our maid in the stable, who seemed to me wondrously tumbled, so that I knew her not, but with a weak voice she called to me, "O lad, run away, or the troopers will have thee away with them. Look to it well that thou get hence: thou seest in what plight. . . ." And more she could not say.

VI

POWER POLITICS AND "ENLIGHTENMENT"

23

THE AGE OF LOUIS XIV

Louis XIV's reign began at an auspicious moment in the history of France. For the first time in a century and a half, thanks largely to Richelieu, the monarchy could feel secure against both internal and foreign foes: feudal nobility, Huguenots, and Hapsburgs. Young Louis XIV recognized his opportunity. With Colbert, he launched an era of reform without equal in the history of the Old Regime. Unfortunately, the King's mounting devotion to military glory and conquest terminated his ambitious plans for internal reform. The latter part of the reign is a depressing chronicle of wars, religious fanaticism, and economic woes.

1. LOUIS XIV INSTRUCTS HIS SON IN THE FUNCTIONS OF A MONARCH

Early in his reign Louis XIV began to write memoirs for the future instruction of his son. The following was probably written in 1666. In describing himself as a hard-working, reform-minded monarch, he was telling no more than the truth, at least at this period of his reign. Note the obvious pleasure he derives from ruling.

Two things without doubt were absolutely necessary: very hard work on my part, and a wise choice of persons capable of seconding it.

As for work, it may be, my son, that you will begin to read these Memoirs at an age when one is far more in the habit of dreading than loving it, only too happy to have escaped subjection to tutors and to have your hours regulated no longer, nor lengthy and prescribed study laid down for you.

A King's Lessons in Statecraft: Louis XIV, translated by Herbert Wilson (New York: Albert and Charles Boni, 1925), pp. 48–50. Used by permission of Routledge & Kegan Paul Ltd., London.

. . . it is . . . toil *by which* one reigns, and *for which* one reigns. . . .

I laid a rule on myself to work regularly twice every day, and for two or three hours each time with different persons, without counting the hours which I passed privately and alone, nor the time which I was able to give on particular occasions to any special affairs that might arise. There was no moment when I did not permit people to talk to me about them, provided that they were urgent; with the exception of foreign ministers who sometimes find too favourable moments in the familiarity allowed to them, either to obtain or to discover something, and whom one should not hear without being previously prepared.

I cannot tell you what fruit I gathered immediately I had taken this resolution. I felt myself, as it were, uplifted in thought and courage; I found myself quite another man, and with joy reproached myself for having been too long unaware of it. This first timidity, which a little self-judgment always produces and which at the beginning gave me pain, especially on occasions when I had to speak in public, disappeared in less than no time. The only thing I felt then was that I was King, and born to be one. I experienced next a delicious feeling, hard to express, and which you will not know yourself except by tasting it as I have done. For you must not imagine, my son, that the affairs of State are like some obscure and thorny path of learning which may possibly have already wearied you, wherein the mind strives to raise itself with effort above its purview, more often to arrive at no conclusion, and whose utility or apparent utility is repugnant to us as much as its difficulty. The function of Kings consists principally in allowing good sense to act, which always acts naturally and without effort. What we apply ourselves to is sometimes less difficult than what we do only for our amusement. Its usefulness always follows. A King, however skilful and enlightened be his ministers, cannot put his own hand to the work without its effect being seen. Success, which is agreeable in everything, even in the smallest matters, gratifies us in these as well as in the greatest, and there is no satisfaction to equal that of noting every day some progress in glorious and lofty enterprises, and in the happiness of the people which has been planned and thought out by oneself. All that is most necessary to this work is at the same time agreeable; for, in a word, my son, it is to have one's eyes open to the whole earth; to learn each hour the news concerning every province and every nation, the secrets of every court, the mood and the weaknesses of each Prince and of every foreign minister; to be well-informed on an infinite number of matters about which we are supposed to know nothing; to elicit from our subjects what they hide from us with the greatest care; to discover the most remote opinions of our own courtiers and the most hidden interests of those who come to us with quite contrary professions. I do not know of any other pleasure we would not renounce for that, even if curiosity alone gave us the opportunity. . . .

2. SAINT-SIMON DESCRIBES THE DAILY ROUTINE OF THE SUN KING

One of the greatest writers of memoirs was the Duke of Saint-Simon. He tells the "inside story" of thirty years of the reigns of Louis XIV and Louis XV. In reading the following excerpt, note the importance Saint-Simon attaches to getting the King's ear. For a courtier nothing was more important.

At eight o'clock the chief *valet de chambre* on duty, who alone had slept in the royal chamber, and who had dressed himself, awoke the King. The chief physician, the chief surgeon, and the nurse (as long as she lived), entered at the same time. The latter kissed the King; the others rubbed and changed his shirt, because he was in the habit of sweating a great deal. At the quarter, the grand chamberlain was called (or, in his absence, the first gentleman of the chamber), and those who had what was called the *grandes entrées*. The chamberlain (or chief gentleman) drew back the curtains which had been closed again, and presented the holy water from the vase, at the head of the bed. These gentlemen stayed but a moment, and that was the time to speak to the King, if anyone had anything to ask of him; in which case the rest stood aside. . . . Then all passed into the cabinet of the council. A very short religious service being over, the King called, they re-entered. The same officer gave him his dressing gown; immediately after, other priviliged courtiers entered, and then everybody, in time to find the King putting on his shoes and stockings, for he did almost everything himself and with address and grace. Every other day we saw the King shave himself; and he had a little short wig in which he always appeared, even in bed, and on medicine days. He often spoke of the chase, and sometimes said a word to somebody. No toilet table was near him; he had simply a mirror held before him.

As soon as he was dressed, he prayed to God, at the side of his bed, where all the clergy present knelt, the cardinals without cushions, all the laity remaining standing; and the captain of the guards came to the balustrade during the prayer, after which the King passed into his cabinet.

He found there, or was followed by all who had the *entrée,* a very numerous company, for it included everybody in any office. He gave orders to each for the day; thus within a half a quarter of an hour it was known what he meant to do; and then all this crowd left directly. The bastards,

Saint-Simon, *Memoirs of Louis XIV and the Regency,* translated by Bayle St. John (New York: M. Walter Dunne, 1901), Vol. III, pp. 30–37.

a few favorites, and the valets alone were left. It was then a good opportunity for talking with the King; for example, about plans of gardens and buildings; and conversation lasted more or less according to the person engaged in it. . . .

The King went to mass, where his musicians always sang an anthem. . . . During the mass the ministers assembled in the King's chamber where distinguished people could go and speak or chat with them. The King amused himself a little upon returning from mass and asked almost immediately for the Council. Then the morning was finished. . . .

The dinner was always *au petit couvert,* that is, the King ate by himself in his chamber upon a square table in front of the middle window. It was more or less abundant, for he ordered in the morning whether it was to be "a little," or "very little" service. . . .

Upon leaving the table the King immediately entered his cabinet. That was the time for distinguished people to speak to him. He stopped at the door a moment to listen, then entered; very rarely did anyone follow him, never without asking him for permission to do so; and for this few had the courage. If followed he placed himself in the embrasure of the window nearest to the door of the cabinet, which immediately closed of itself, and which you were obliged to open yourself on quitting the King. This also was the time for the bastards and the valets.

The King amused himself by feeding his dogs, and remained with them more or less time, then asked for his wardrobe, changed before the very few distinguished people it pleased the first gentleman of the chamber to admit there, and immediately went out by the back stairs into the court of marble to get into his coach. . . .

The King was fond of air, and when deprived of it his health suffered; he had headaches and vapors caused by the undue use he had formerly made of perfumes, so that for many years he could not endure any, except the odor of orange flowers; therefore if you had to approach anywhere near him you did well not to carry them.

As he was but little sensitive to heat or cold, or even rain, the weather was seldom sufficiently bad to prevent his going abroad. He went out for three objects: stag hunting, once or more each week; shooting in his parks (and no man handled a gun with more grace and skill), once or twice each week; and walking in his gardens for exercise, and to see his workmen. Sometimes he made picnics with ladies, in the forest at Marly or at Fontainebleau, and in this last place, promenades with all the Court around the canal, which was a magnificent spectacle. . . .

Upon returning home from walks or drives, anybody, as I have said, might speak to the King from the moment he left his coach till he reached the foot of his staircase. He changed his dress again, and rested in his cabinet an hour or more, then went to Madame de Maintenon's and on the way anyone who wished might speak to him.

At ten o'clock his supper was served. . . . This supper was always on a grand scale. . . .

After supper the King stood some moments, his back to the balustrade of the foot of his bed, encircled by all his Court; then, with bows to the ladies, passed into his cabinet, where on arriving, he gave his orders. He passed a little less than an hour there, seated in an armchair, with his legitimate children and bastards, his grandchildren, legitimate and otherwise, and their husbands or wives. . . .

The King, wishing to retire, went and fed his dogs; then said good night, passed into his chamber to the ruelle of his bed, where he said his prayers, as in the morning, then undressed. He said good night with an inclination of the head, and while everybody was leaving the room stood at the corner of the mantlepiece, where he gave the order to the colonel of the guards alone. Then commenced what was called the *petit coucher*, at which only the specially privileged remained. That was short. They did not leave until he got into bed. It was a moment to speak to him. . . .

On medicine days, which occurred about once a month, the King remained in bed, then heard mass. The royal household came to see him for a moment, and Madame de Maintenon seated herself in the armchair at the head of his bed. The King dined in bed about three o'clock, everybody being allowed to enter the room, then rose, and the privileged alone remained. . . .

3. *MOLIÈRE SATIRIZES THE MEDICAL PROFESSION*

Prominent among the cluster of brilliant writers and artists who made the reign of Louis XIV the golden age of French culture was the dramatist Molière. One of his fortes was deflating pretentious individuals, particularly physicians. In the following scene from **The Physician in Spite of Himself,** ***Sganarelle is the bogus doctor, Géronte is the bourgeois father intent upon arranging an advantageous marriage for his daughter Lucinde. Jacqueline and Lucas are Géronte's servants.***

SGANARELLE. Is this the patient?

GÉRONTE. Yes I have but one daughter; and I would never get over it if she were to die.

SGANARELLE. Do not let her do anything of the kind. She must not die without a prescription of the physician. . . .

Molière, *The Physician in Spite of Himself,* Act II, Scene VI, in *The Dramatic Works of Molière* (Philadelphia: Gebbie and Barrie, 1878), pp. 276–280.

GÉRONTE. . . . She has become dumb, without our having been able till now to discover the cause. This accident has obliged us to postpone her marriage.

SGANARELLE. And why so?

GÉRONTE. He whom she is going to marry wishes to wait for her recovery to conclude the marriage.

SGANARELLE. And who is this fool that does not want his wife to be dumb? Would to Heaven that mine had that complaint! I should take particular care not to have her cured. . . .

SGANARELLE. (*Turning to the patient.*) Give me your hand. (*To Géronte.*) The pulse tells me that your daughter is dumb.

GÉRONTE. Sir, that is what is the matter with her; ah! yes, you have found it out at the first touch.

SGANARELLE. Of course!

JACQUELINE. See how he has guessed her complaint.

SGANARELLE. We great physicians, we know matters at once. An ignoramus would have been nonplussed, and would have told you: it is this, that or the other; but I hit the nail on the head from the very first, and I tell you that your daughter is dumb.

GÉRONTE. Yes; but I should like you to tell me whence it arises.

SGANARELLE. Nothing is easier; it arises from loss of speech.

GÉRONTE. Very good. But the reason of her having lost her speech, pray?

SGANARELLE. Our best authorities will tell you that it is because there is an impediment in the action of her tongue.

GÉRONTE. But, once more, your opinion upon this impediment in the action of her tongue.

SGANARELLE. Aristotle on this subject says . . . a great many clever things.

GÉRONTE. I dare say.

SGANARELLI. Ah! He was a great man!

GÉRONTE. No doubt.

SGANARELLE. Yes, a very great man. (*Holding out his arm, and putting a finger of the other hand in the bend.*) A man who was, by this, much greater than I. But to come back to our argument: I am of opinion that this impediment in the action of her tongue is caused by certain humours, which among us learned men, we call peccant humours; peccant—that is to say . . . peccant humours; inasmuch as the vapours formed by the exhallations of the influences which rise in the very region of diseases, coming . . . as we may say to. . . . Do you understand Latin?

GÉRONTE. Not in the least.

SGANARELLE. (*Suddenly rising.*) You do not understand Latin?

GÉRONTE. No.

STANARELLE. (*Assuming various comic attitudes.*) *Cabricias arci thuram, catalamus, singulariter, nominativo, haec musa,* the muse, *bonus, bona, bonum. Deus sanctus, estne oratio latinas? Etiam,* Yes. *Quare?* Why. *Quia substantivo et adjectivum, concordat in generi, numerum, et casus.*

GÉRONTE. Ah! Why did I not study?

JACQUELINE. What a clever man!

LUCAS. Yes, it is so beautiful that I do not understand a word of it.

SGANARELLE. Thus these vapours which I speak of, passing from the left side, where the liver is, to the right side, where we find the heart, it so happens that the lungs, which in Latin we call *armyan,* having communication with the brain, which in Greek we style *nasmus,* by means of the *vena cava,* which in Hebrew, is termed *cubile,* meet in their course the said vapours, which fill the ventricles of the omoplata; and because the said vapours . . . now understand well this argument, pray . . . and because these said vapours are endowed with a certain malignity . . . listen well to this, I beseech you.

GÉRONTE. Yes.

SGANARELLE. Are endowed with a certain malignity which is caused . . . pay attention here, if you please.

GÉRONTE. I do.

SGANARELLE. Which is caused by the acridity of these humours engendered in the concavity of the diaphragm, it happens that these vapours. . . . *Ossabandus, nequeis, nequer, potarinum, puipsa milus.* That is exactly the reason that your daughter is dumb.

JACQUELINE. Ah! How well this gentleman explains all this.

LUCAS. Why does not my tongue wag as well as his?

GÉRONTE. It is undoubtedly impossible to argue better. There is but one thing that I cannot exactly make out: that is the whereabouts of the liver and the heart. It appears to me that you place them differently from what they are; that the heart is on the left side, and the liver on the right.

SGANARELLE. Yes; this was so formerly; but we have changed all that, and we now-a-days practise the medical art on an entirely new system.

GÉRONTE. I did not know that, and I pray you pardon my ignorance.

SGANARELLE. There is no harm done; and you are not obliged to be so clever as we are.

GÉRONTE. Certainly not. But what think you, Sir, ought to be done for this complaint?

SGANARELLE. What do I think ought to be done?

GÉRONTE. Yes.

SGANARELLE. My advice is to put her to bed again, and make her, as a remedy, take plenty of bread soaked in wine.

GÉRONTE. Why so, sir?

SGANARELLE. Because there is in bread and wine mixed together a sympathetic virtue which produces speech. Do you not see that they give nothing else to parrots, and that, by eating it, they learn to speak?

GÉRONTE. That is true. Oh! the great man! Quick, plenty of bread and wine.

SGANARELLE. I shall come back to-night to see how the patient is getting on. . . .

4. COLBERT REGULATES FRENCH INDUSTRY

An essential feature of the mercantilism which Colbert symbolized was the minute regulation of private industry, the principal aim being to raise production standards and thereby increase the demand for French goods abroad. In 1669 a sort of master code was drawn up for the textile industry. Suspecting that manufacturers were not paying much attention to the code, Colbert in 1670 created inspectors to enforce the law, as we read in the following selection.

TO THE INTENDANTS: The King, desiring to remedy the abuses which are committed in the . . . manufactures of France . . . had the goodness to have drawn up general regulations and to have them registered in his presence in his parlement of Paris, August 13, 1669. His Majesty has resolved to send inspectors into all the provinces of his kingdom . . . to inform the judges, the merchants, and the workers of his wishes. . . . That is why, on the express order of His Majesty, we have prepared the following directive. . . . Signed, Colbert.

1. The said inspector shall report to Monsieur ——, [intendant] of His Majesty. . . .

2. The said inspector, having received his orders from the intendant, will betake himself immediately to the nearest manufacturing center and consult with the mayor and aldermen; . . . he will ascertain from them if the regulation for manufactures . . . has been registered and published. . . .

3. There will be established a community room in the City Hall . . . where the examiners can see, inspect, and mark the merchandise which will be taken there at set times by the cloth-workers, where they can settle on the spot disputes which might develop because of defects in the said manufactures and instil fear [of the laws] in the minds of the said cloth-workers. . . . And since the merchants have a particular knowledge of the good quality or defects of merchandise, and since it is in their interest that the

Lettres, Instructions, et Mémoires de Colbert, edited by Pierre Clément (Paris: Imprimerie Impériale, 1863), Vol. II, pp. 832–837. Our translation.

merchandise be perfect, it will also be necessary that the aldermen elect one of the more prominent merchants to be present at the said inspections and markings. . . .

11. The said inspector will assemble all the . . . [guild] masters in the community room, and will read the said regulation to them [the general regulation concerning textile manufacture of 1669], explaining to them article by article what they must do to carry it out properly, and informing them that if they contravene it that their ruin will surely follow, because their goods will be confiscated and the selvedges torn to bits [causing the cloth to unravel]. . . . Do not neglect to inform [the masters] that the goods of the same name, kind, and quality must be uniform throughout the kingdom in length, width, and strength. . . .

18. The said inspector will inform himself . . . of all the important fairs which will be held in his department and will betake himself there . . . to inspect the said merchandise, to see whether it has been marked at the place of manufacture and meets the quality called for by the regulation; if not, to seize and confiscate it and tear the selvedge publicly on the spot. . . . But as it is very important not to disturb the fairs . . . this must be carried out with much prudence . . . on the days and hours most convenient to the sellers and buyers. . . .

27. The said inspectors will give the greatest encouragement to all the masters and cloth-workers . . . to make [their cloth] the most perfect possible in order to strengthen the commerce and manufactures of France and to outstrip foreign competitors. . . .

5. LOUIS XIV REVOKES THE EDICT OF NANTES, 1685

The revocation of Henry IV's edict of toleration of 1598 was preceded by a long and often savage campaign to convert the Huguenots to orthodoxy. The pretext given for the revocation was that by 1685 the "greater part of the R.P.R. **[Religion prétendue réformée,** ***the 'so-called reformed religion'] have embraced the Catholic faith." Since there were no Huguenots, the Edict of Nantes had been rendered nugatory.***

1. Be it known that . . . we have, by this present perpetual and irrevocable edict, suppressed and revoked, and do suppress and revoke, the edict of our said grandfather, given at Nantes in April, 1598, in its whole extent. . . .

2. We forbid our subjects of the R.P.R. to meet any more for the exercise of the said religion in any place or private house, under any pretext whatever. . . .

J.H. Robinson, *Readings in European History* (New York: Ginn and Company, 1904), Vol. II, pp. 289–291.

3. We likewise forbid all noblemen, of what condition soever, to hold such religious exercises in their houses or fiefs, under penalty to be inflicted upon all our said subjects who shall engage in the said exercises, of imprisonment and confiscation.

4. We enjoin all ministers of the said R.P.R., who do not choose to become converts and to embrace the Catholic, apostolic, and Roman religion, to leave our kingdom and the territories subject to us within a fortnight of the publication of our present edict. . . .

7. We forbid private schools for the instruction of children of the said R.P.R., and in general all things whatever which can be regarded as a concession of any kind in favor of the said religion.

8. As for children who may be born of persons of the said R.P.R., we desire that from henceforth they be baptized by the parish priests. We enjoin parents to send them to the churches for that purpose, under penalty of five hundred livres fine, to be increased as circumstances may demand; and thereafter the children shall be brought up in the Catholic, apostolic, and Roman religion, which we expressly enjoin the local magistrates to see done.

10. We repeat our most express prohibition to all our subjects of the said R.P.R., together with their wives and children, against leaving our kingdom, lands, and territories subject to us, or transporting their goods and effects therefrom under penalty, as respects the men, of being sent to the galleys, and as respects the women, of imprisonment and confiscation.

12. As for the rest, liberty is granted to the said persons of the R.P.R., pending the time when it shall please God to enlighten them as well as others, to remain in the cities and places of our kingdom, lands, and territories subject to us, and there to continue their commerce, and to enjoy their possessions, without being subjected to molestation or hindrance on account of the said R.P.R., on condition of not engaging in the exercise of the said religion, or of meeting under pretext of prayers or religious services, of whatever nature these may be, under the penalties above mentioned of imprisonment and confiscation. This do we give in charge of our trusty and well-beloved counselors, etc.

6. LOUIS XIV ACCEPTS THE THRONE OF SPAIN FOR HIS GRANDSON

When Charles II, the last of the Spanish Hapsburgs, died in 1700, he left a will making the grandson of Louis XIV his successor. The French King knew full well that acceptance meant war with most of Europe. Nevertheless, he accepted, and

Saint-Simon, *Memoirs of Louis XIV and the Regency*, translated by Bayle St. John (New York: M. Walter Dunne, 1901), Vol. I, pp. 198–200.

the greatest war the world had known up to that time began. Saint-Simon describes this historic moment.

. . . The news arrived at Court (Fontainebleau) in the month of November. The King was going out shooting that day; but, upon learning what had taken place, at once countermanded the sport, announced the death of the King of Spain, and at three o'clock held a council of the ministers in the apartments of Madame de Maintenon. This council lasted until past seven o'clock in the evening. Monseigneur [the Dauphin], who had been out wolf hunting, returned in time to attend it. On the next morning, Wednesday, another council was held, and in the evening a third, in the apartments of Madame de Maintenon. . . .

At the first receipt of the news the King and his ministers had been overwhelmed with a surprise that they could not recover from for several days. When the news was spread abroad, the Court was equally surprised. The foreign ministers passed whole nights deliberating upon the course the King would adopt. Nothing else was spoken of but this matter. The King, one evening, to divert himself, asked the princesses their opinion. They replied that he should send M. le Duc d'Anjou (the second son of Monseigneur) into Spain, and that this was the general sentiment. "I am sure," replied the King, "that whatever course I adopt many people will condemn me."

At last, on Tuesday, the 16th of November, the King publicly declared himself. The Spanish ambassador had received intelligence which proved the eagerness of Spain to welcome the Duc d'Anjou as its King. There seemed to be no doubt of the matter. The King, immediately after getting up, called the ambassador into his cabinet, where M. le Duc d'Anjou had already arrived. Then, pointing to the Duke, he told the ambassador he might salute him as King of Spain. The ambassador threw himself upon his knees after the fashion of his country, and addressed to the Duke a tolerable long compliment in the Spanish language. Immediately afterward, the King, contrary to all custom, opened the two folding doors of his cabinet, and commanded everybody to enter. It was a very full Court that day. The King, majestically turning his eyes toward the numerous company, and showing them M. le Duc d'Anjou said: "Gentlemen, behold the King of Spain. His birth called him to that crown; the late King also has called him to it by his will; the whole nation wished for him, and has asked me for him eagerly; it is the will of heaven; I have obeyed it with pleasure." And then, turning toward his grandson, he said, "Be a good Spaniard, that is your first duty; but remember that you are a Frenchman born, in order that the union between the two nations may be preserved; it will be the means of rendering both happy, and of preserving the peace of Europe." . . .

7. A GREAT REIGN ENDS, AND FEW MOURN

The passing of Louis XIV, it is generally agreed, was not an occasion for sadness, least of all for the Duke of Saint-Simon. Like many French noblemen, Saint-Simon could not forgive Louis XIV for making fawning parasites out of the old nobility. His account of the termination of the reign follows.

The King was but little regretted. His valets and a few other people felt his loss, scarcely anybody else. . . .

Paris, tired of a dependence which had enslaved everything, breathed again in the hope of liberty, and with joy at seeing at an end the authority of so many people who abused it. The provinces in despair at their ruin and their annihilation breathed again and leaped for joy; and the Parliament and the [nobility of the] robe destroyed by edicts and by revolutions, flattered themselves the first that they should figure, the other that they should find themselves free. The people ruined, overwhelmed, desperate, gave thanks to God, with a scandalous *éclat*, for a deliverance, . . .

Foreigners delighted to be at last, after so many years, quit of a monarch who had so long imposed his law upon them, and who had escaped from them by a species of miracle at the very moment in which they counted upon having subjugated him, contained themselves with much more decency than the French. The marvels of the first three quarters of this reign of more than seventy years, and the personal magnanimity of this King until then so successful, and so abandoned afterward by fortune during the last quarter of his reign—had justly dazzled them. They made it a point of honor to render to him after his death what they had constantly refused him during life. No foreign Court exulted: all plumed themselves upon praising and honoring his memory. The Emperor wore mourning as for a father. . . .

To finish at once all that regards the King, let me here say, that his entrails were taken to Notre Dame, on the 4th of September, without any ceremony, by two almoners of the King, without accompaniment. On Friday, the 6th of September, the Cardinal de Rohan, carried the heart to the Grand Jesuits, with very little accompaniment or pomp. Except the persons necessary for the ceremony, not half a dozen courtiers were present. . . . On the 9th of September, the body of the late King, was buried at St. Denis. The Bishop of Aleth pronounced the oration. Very little expense was gone to; and nobody was found who cared sufficiently for the late King to murmur at the economy. On Friday, the 25th of October, his solemn obsequies took place at St. Denis in a confusion, as to rank and precedence, without example. On Thursday, the 28th of November, the solemn obsequies were again performed, this time at Notre Dame, and with the usual ceremonies.

Saint-Simon, *Memoirs of Louis XIV and the Regency*, translated by Bayle St. John (New York: M. Walter Dunne, 1901), Vol. III, pp. 38–42.

24

THE ENGLISH REVOLUTIONS OF THE SEVENTEENTH CENTURY

The political stability which we have come to associate with the English nation was definitely not characteristic of its seventeenth century history. To the Continental of that period, the English people must have seemed extremely fickle and excitable. Two revolutions, a royal execution, and a prolonged civil war, among other things, disturbed the tranquility of the English scene. But by the end of the century England had obtained the type of liberal, parliamentary, and Protestant monarchy that most of her citizens desired. So "advanced" did the English form of government become that many enlightened Europeans began to think of it as a model which all progressive states might well emulate.

1. THE DIFFICULTIES OF THE EARLY STUARTS: CONSTITUTIONAL, RELIGIOUS, FINANCIAL

The first two Stuart kings, James I (1603–1625) and Charles I (1625–1649), managed to estrange a large part of the English people for one reason or another. Their high-handed interpretation of monarchy as an institution responsible only to God (Selection A) brought them into conflict with powerful parliamentary interests. Their intense dislike of the Puritans led them to such deliberate affronts as the Declaration of Sports (Selection B). Finally, their financial embarrassments caused them to resort to extra-legal taxes, an example of which is ship money. The first writ for ship money (Selection C) was really intended for its declared purpose, but later issues were deviated to the King's own purposes.

[A] J.H. Robinson, *Readings in European History* (New York: Ginn and Company, 1904), Vol. II, pp. 219–221. Copyright 1904 by James Harvey Robinson. Used by permission of the publisher. [B] and [C] Edward P. Cheyney, ed., *Readings in English History* (New York: Ginn and Company, 1908), pp. 421–422 and pp. 465–466. Copyright 1908 by Edward P. Cheyney. Used by permission of the publisher.

[A] *James I's Speech in Parliament, 1609*

The state of monarchy is the supremest thing upon earth; for kings are not only God's lieutenants upon earth, and sit upon God's throne, but even by God himself they are called gods. . . .

Kings are justly called gods, for that they exercise a manner or resemblance of divine power upon earth; for if you will consider the attributes to God, you shall see how they agree in the person of a king. God hath power to create or destroy, make or unmake at his pleasure, to give life or send death, to judge all and to be judged nor accountable to none, to raise low things and to make high things low at his pleasure, and to God are both soul and body due. And the like power have kings: they make and unmake their subjects, they have power of raising and casting down, of life and of death, judges over all their subjects and in all causes and yet accountable to none but God only. . . .

I would wish you to be careful to avoid three things in the matter of grievances:

First, that you do not meddle with the main points of government; that is my craft: . . . I am now an old king; for six and thirty years have I governed in Scotland personally, and now have I accomplished my apprenticeship of seven years here; and seven years is a great time for a king's experience in government; therefore there should not be too many Phormios to teach Hannibal: I must not be taught my office.

Secondly, I would not have you meddle with such ancient rights of mine as I have received from my predecessors, possessing them, *more majorum*; such things I would be sorry should be accounted for grievances. All novelties are dangerous as well in a politic as in a natural body, and therefore I would be loath to be quarreled in my ancient rights and possessions; for that were to judge me unworthy of that which my predecessors had and left me.

And, lastly, I pray you beware to exhibit for grievance anything that is established by settled law, and whereunto (as you have already had a proof) you know I will never give a plausible answer; for it is an undutiful part in subjects to press their king, wherein they know beforehand he will refuse them.

[B] *James I's Declaration of Sports, 1617*

. . . no lawful recreation shall be barred to our good people which shall not tend to the breach of our aforesaid laws and canons of our church. . . . Our pleasure is, that after the end of divine service our good people be not disturbed, letted, or discouraged from any lawful recreation, such as dancing, either men or women, archery for men, leaping, vaulting, or any other such harmless recreation, nor from having of May games, Whitsun ales, and morris dances; and the setting of Maypoles and other sports therewith used; so as the same be had in due and convenient time, without impediment or neglect of divine service. And that women shall have leave to carry rushes to the church for the decorating of it, according to their old custom. But withal we do here account still as prohibited all unlawful games to be used upon Sundays only, as bear and bull baitings, interludes, and at all times in the meaner sort of people, by law prohibited, bowling.

And likewise we bar from this benefit and liberty all such known recusants, either men or women, as will abstain from coming to church or divine service, being therefore unworthy of lawful recreation after the said service, that will not first come to the church and serve God; prohibiting in like sort the said recreation to any that, though conformed in religion, are not present in the church at the service of God before their going to the said recreations. . . .

[*C*] *The First Writ of Ship Money, 1634*

To the mayor, commonalty, and citizens of our city of London, and to the sheriffs of the same city and good men in the said city and in the liberties and members of the same, greeting: Because we are given to understand that certain thieves, pirates, and robbers of the sea, as well Turks, enemies of the Christian name, as others, being gathered together, wickedly taking by force and spoiling the ships and goods and merchandises, not only of our subjects but also the subjects of our friends on the sea. . . .

We command, firmly enjoining you the aforesaid mayor, commonalty, and citizens, and sheriffs of the said city, and the good men in the same city and in the liberties and members of the same, in the faith and allegiance wherein you are bound unto us, and as you do love us and our honor, and under the forfeiture of all which you can forfeit to us, that you cause to be prepared and brought to the port of Portsmouth, before the first day of March now next ensuing, one ship of war of the burden of nine hundred tons, with three hundred and fifty men at the least, as well expert masters as very able and skillful mariners; one other ship of war of the burden of eight hundred tons, with two hundred and sixty men at the least, as well skillful masters as very able and expert mariners; four other ships of war, every of them of the burden of five hundred tons, and every of them with two hundred men at the least as well expert masters as very able and skillful mariners; and one other ship of war of the burden of three hundred tons, with a hundred and fifty men, as well expert masters as very able and skillful mariners. . . .

2. *CHARLES I SACRIFICES THE EARL OF STRAFFORD, 1641*

One of Charles I's ablest ministers was the Earl of Strafford. Accused of an assortment of despotic acts, he was the object of a bill of attainder passed by Parliament and approved by a frightened monarch in 1641. Conscience-stricken, Charles addressed the following half-hearted appeal for clemency to the House of Lords.

My Lords, I did yesterday satisfy the justice of the kingdom, by passing of the bill of attainder against the earl of Strafford; but mercy being as inherent and inseparable to a king as justice, I desire at this time in some measure, to show that likewise, by suffering that unfortunate man to fulfil the natural course of his life in a close imprisonment, yet so that, if ever he make the least offer to escape, or offer, directly or indirectly, to meddle with any sort of public business, especially with me, either by message or letter, it shall cost him his life, without further press.

This, if it may be done without the discontent of my people, will be an unspeakable comfort to me; to which end, as in the first place, I by this letter do earnestly desire your approbation; and to endear it the more, have chosen him to carry, that of all your house is most dear to me [the Prince of Wales]; so I do desire, that by a conference you will endeavour to give the House of Commons contentment; likewise assuring you, that the exercise is no more pleasing to me than to see both Houses of Parliament consent, for my sake, that I should moderate the severity of the law in so important a case. I will not say, that your complying with me in this my pretended mercy, shall make me more willing, but certainly it will make me more cheerful in granting your just grievances; but, if no less than his life can satisfy my people, I must say, *fiat justitia.*

Thus again earnestly recommending the consideration of my intentions to you, I rest,

Your unalterable and affectionate friend,

Charles R.

Whitehall, 11th May, 1641

If he *must* die, it were charity to reprieve him till Saturday.

Harleian Ms. 1769, Art. 12, as found in Elizabeth Kimball Kendall, ed., *Source-Book of English History* (New York: The Macmillan Company, 1900), pp. 236–237.

3. *CHARLES I INVADES PARLIAMENT TO ARREST FIVE "ROGUES"*

Relations between monarch and Parliament steadily worsened between 1640 and 1642. Matters came to a climax when Charles strode into Parliament at the head of an armed escort to arrest five troublesome members. The following account of this tumultuous scene (1642) is provided by John Rushworth, a member of the parliamentary faction.

. . . The said five accused Members this day *after dinner* came into the House. . . .

They were no sooner sate in their places, but the House was informed . . . that his Majesty was coming with a Guard of Military Men, Commanders and Souldiers, to the House of Commons. . . . Whereupon a certain Member of the House having also private Intimation . . . that endeavours would be used this day to apprehend the five Members, the House required the five Members to depart the House forthwith, to the end to avoid Combustion in the House, if the said Souldiers should use Violence to pull any of them out. To which Command of the House, four of the said Members yielded ready Obedience, but Mr. *Stroud* was obstinate, till Sir *Walter Earle* (his ancient acquaintance) pulled him out by force, the King being at that time entering into the *New Pallace-yard*, in *Westminster*: And as his Majesty came through *Westminster Hall*, the Commanders, Reformadoes, &c. that attended him, made a Lane on both sides the Hall (through which his Majesty passed and came up the Stairs to the House of Commons) and stood before the Guard of Pentioners, and Halberteers, (who also attended the Kings Person,) and the door of the House of Commons being thrown open, his Majesty entered the House, and as he passed up towards *the Chair* he cast his eye on the Right-hand near the Bar of the House, where Mr. *Pym* used to sit, but his Majesty not seeing him there (knowing him well) went up to the Chair, and said, "By your leave, (Mr. Speaker) I must borrow your Chair a little," whereupon the Speaker came out of the Chair, and his Majesty stept up into it, after he had stood in the Chair a while, casting his Eye upon the Members as they stood up *uncovered*, but could not discern any of the five Members to be there, nor indeed were they easie to be discerned (had they been there) among so many bare Faces all standing up together.

Then his Majesty made this Speech,

"Gentlemen,

"I Am sorry for this occasion of coming unto you: Yesterday I sent a

John Rushworth, *Historical Collections* (London: 1691), Vol. IV, pp. 477–478, as found in Elizabeth Kimball Kendall, ed., *Source-Book of English History* (New York: The Macmillan Company, 1900), pp. 237–240.

Serjeant at Arms upon a very Important occasion to apprehend some that by my command were accused of High Treason, whereunto I did expect Obedience and not a Message. And I must declare unto you here, that albeit, no King that ever was in *England*, shall be more careful of your Priviledges, to maintain them to the uttermost of his power then I shall be; yet you must know that in Cases of Treason, no person hath a priviledge. And therefore I am come to know if any of these persons that were accused are here: For I must tell you Gentlemen, that so long as these persons that I have accused (for no slight Crime but for Treason) are here, I cannot expect that this House will be in the Right way that I do heartily wish it; Therefore I am come to tell you that I must have them wheresoever I find them. Well since I see all the Birds are Flown, I do expect from you, that you shall send them unto me, as soon as they return hither. But I assure you, in the word of a King, I never did intend any Force, but shall proceed against them in a legal and fair way, for I never meant any other.

"And now since I see I cannot do what I came for, I think this no unfit occasion to repeat what I have said formerly, That whatsoever I have done in favour, and to the good of my Subjects, I do mean to maintain it.

"I will trouble you no more, but tell you I do expect as soon as they come to the House, you will send them to me; otherwise I must take my own Course to find them."

When the King was looking about the House, the Speaker standing below by the Chair, his Majesty ask'd him, whether any of these persons were in the House? Whether he saw any of them? and where they were? To which the Speaker falling on his Knee, thus Answered.

"*May it please your Majesty*, I Have neither Eyes to see, nor Tongue to speak in this place, but as the House is pleased to direct me, whose Servant I am here, and humbly beg your Majesties Pardon, that I cannot give any other Answer than this, to what your Majesty is pleased to demand of me."

The King having Concluded his Speech, went out of the House again which was in great disorder, and many Members cried out, aloud so as he might hear them, "Priviledge! Priviledge!" and forthwith Adjourned till the next Day at One of the Clock. . . .

4. CROMWELL PUTS THE "BARBAROUS" IRISH TO THE SWORD, 1650

After the execution of Charles I in 1649, Cromwell was faced with a rebellion in Ireland of Roman Catholics allied with Protestant royalists. His savage suppres-

sion of the rebellion has left a stain on his memory. In his view, he was doing God's work in exterminating the Catholic Irish. The following account of the storming of Drogheda is from one of Cromwell's letters to Parliament.

Upon Tuesday the 10th of this instant, about five o'clock in the evening, we began the storm, and after some hot dispute we entered about seven or eight hundred men, the enemy disputing it very stiffly with us. And indeed, through the advantages of the place, and the courage God was pleased to give the defenders, our men were forced to retreat quite out of the breach, not without some considerable loss; . . .

Although our men that stormed the breaches were forced to recoil . . . yet, being encouraged to recover their loss, they made a second attempt, wherein God was pleased [so] to animate them that they got ground of the enemy, and by the goodness of God, forced him to quit his entrenchments. And after a very hot dispute, the enemy having both horse and foot, and we only foot, within the wall, they gave ground, and our men became masters both of their retrenchments and the church; . . .

The enemy retreated, divers of them, into the Mill-Mount: a place very strong and of difficult access, being exceedingly high, having a good graft, and strongly palisadoed. The Governor, Sir Arthur Ashton, and divers considerable Officers being there, our men getting up to them, were ordered by me to put them all to the sword. And indeed, being in the heat of action, I forbade them to spare any that were in arms in the town, and, I think, that night they put to the sword about 2,000 men, divers of the officers and soldiers being fled over the Bridge into the other part of the Town, where about one hundred of them possessed St. Peter's church-steeple, some the west gate, and others a strong round tower next the gate called St. Sunday's. These being summoned to yield to mercy, refused, whereupon I ordered the steeple of St. Peter's Church to be fired, where one of them was heard to say in the midst of the flames: "God damn me, God confound me; I burn, I burn."

The next day, the other two towers were summoned, in one of which was about six or seven score; but they refused to yield themselves, and we knowing that hunger must compel them, set only good guards to secure them from running away until their stomachs were come down. From one of the said towers, notwithstanding their condition, they killed and wounded some of our men. When they submitted, their officers were knocked on the head, and every tenth man of the soldiers killed, and the rest shipped for the Barbadoes. The soldiers in the other tower were all spared, as to their lives only, and shipped likewise for the Barbadoes. . . .

And now give me leave to say how it comes to pass that this work is wrought. It was set upon some of our hearts, That a great thing should be done, not by power or might, but by the Spirit of God. And is it not so clear? That which caused your men to storm so courageously, it was the Spirit of God, who gave your men courage, and took it away again; and gave the enemy courage, and took it away again; and gave your men courage again, and therewith this happy success. And therefore it is good that God alone have all the glory. . . .

5. SAMUEL PEPYS DESCRIBES THE GREAT LONDON FIRE, 1666

Hard on the heels of the great plague of 1665, London experienced another disaster, the fire of 1666. Some 450 acres, 13,000 houses, and 89 churches were consumed. A fine description of the fire can be found in the inimitable diary of Samuel Pepys.

SEPTEMBER 2ND (LORD'S DAY). Some of our maids sitting up late last night . . . called us up about three in the morning, to tell us of a great fire they saw in the City. So I rose, and slipped on my night-gown, and went to her window; and thought it to be on the back-side of Marke-lane at the farthest, but being unused to such fires as followed, I thought it far enough off; and so went to bed again, and to sleep. About seven rose again to dress myself, and there looked out at the window, and saw the fire not so much as it was, and further off. . . . I made myself ready presently, and walked to the Tower, and there got up upon one of the high places, Sir J. Robinson's little son going up with me; and there I did see the houses at that end of the bridge all on fire, and an infinite great fire on this and the other side the end of the bridge; . . . So down with my heart full of trouble to the Lieutenant of the Tower, who tells me that it begun this morning in the King's baker's house in Pudding-lane. . . . I down to the water-side, and there got a boat, and through bridge, and there saw a lamentable fire. . . . Every body endeavouring to remove their goods, and flinging into the river, or bringing them into lighters that lay off; poor people staying in their houses as long as till the very fire touched them, and then running into boats, or clambering from one pair of stairs by the water-side to another. And among other things, the poor pigeons, I perceive, were loth to leave their houses, but hovered about the windows and balconys, till they burned their wings, and fell down. Having staid, and in an hour's time seen the fire rage every way, and nobody, to my sight endeavouring to quench it, but to remove their goods, and leave all to the fire, and having seen it get as far as the Steele-yard, and the wind mighty high, and driving it into the City: and every thing after so long a drought proving combustible, even

The Diary of Samuel Pepys (London: Library of Classics, n.d.), pp. 329–338.

the very stones of churches. . . . At last met my Lord Mayor in Canning-street, like a man spent, with a hankercher about his neck. . . . he cried, like a fainting woman, "Lord! what can I do? I am spent: people will not obey me. I have been pulling down houses; but the fire overtakes us faster than we can do it." . . .

3RD. About four o'clock in the morning, my Lady Batten sent me a cart to carry away all my money, and plate, and best things, to Sir W. Rider's at Bednallgreene. Which I did, riding myself in my night-gown, in the cart; and, Lord! to see how the streets and the highways are crowded with people running and riding, and getting of carts at any rate to fetch away things. . . . Then home, and with much ado to find a way, nor any sleep all this night to me nor my poor wife. But then all this day she and I, and all my people labouring to get away the rest of our things. . . . At night lay down a little upon a quilt of W. Hewer's, in the office, all my own things being packed up or gone; and after me my poor wife did the like, we having fed upon the remains of yesterday's dinner, having no fire nor dishes, nor any opportunity of dressing any thing.

4TH. Up by break of day, to get away the remainder of my things; which I did by a lighter at the Iron gate: and my hands so full, that it was the afternoon before we could get them all away. Sir W. Pen and I to the Tower-street, and there met the fire burning three or four doors beyond Mr. Howell's, whose goods, poor man, his trayes, and dishes, shovells, &c., were flung all along Tower-street in the kennels, and people working therewith from one end to the other; the fire coming on in that narrow street, on both sides, with infinite fury. Sir W. Batten not knowing how to remove his wine, did dig a pit in the garden, and laid it in there; and I took the opportunity of laying all the papers of my office that I could not otherwise dispose of. And in the evening Sir W. Pen and I did dig another, and put our wine in it; and I my parmazan cheese, as well as my wine and some other things. . . . Now begins the practice of blowing up of houses in Tower-street, those next the Tower, which at first did frighten people more than any thing; but it stopped the fire where it was done, it bringing down the houses to the ground in the same places they stood, and then it was easy to quench what little fire was in it, though it kindled nothing almost. . . .

5TH. I lay down in the office again upon W. Hewer's quilt, being mighty weary, and sore in my feet with going till I was hardly able to stand. About two in the morning my wife calls me up, and tells me of new cryes of fire, it being come to Barking Church, which is the bottom of our lane. I up; and finding it so, resolved presently to take her away, and did, and took my gold, which was about 2350£. . . . I up to the top of Barking steeple, and there saw the saddest sight of desolation that I ever saw; every where great fires, oyle-cellars, and brimstone, and other things burning. I became afraid to stay there long, and therefore down again as fast as I could, the fire being spread as far as I could see it; and to Sir W. Pen's, and there eat a piece of cold meat, having eaten nothing since Sunday, but the remains of Sunday's dinner. . . .

6TH. Up about five o'clock; and met Mr. Gauden at the gate of the office, (I intending to go out, as I used, every now and then to-day, to see how the fire is,) to call our men to Bishop's-gate, where no fire had yet been near, and there is now one broke out: which did give great grounds to people, and to me too, to think that there is some kind of plot in this, (on which many by this time have been taken, and it hath been dangerous for any stranger to walk in the streets,) but I went with the men, and we did put it out in a little time; so that that was well again. It was pretty to see how hard the women did work in the cannells, sweeping of water; but then they would scold for drink, and be as drunk as devils. I saw good butts of sugar broke open in the street, and people give and take handfulls out, and put into beer, and drink it. And now all being pretty well, I took boat, and over to Southwarke, and took boat on the other side the bridge, and so to Westminster, thinking to shift myself, being all in dirt from top to bottom; but could not there find any place to buy a shirt or a pair of gloves. . . . To Sir R. Ford's, and there dined in an earthen platter—a fried breast of mutton; a great many of us, but very merry, and indeed as good a meal, though as ugly a one, as ever I had in my life. Thence down to Deptford, and there with great satisfaction landed all my goods at Sir G. Carteret's safe, and nothing missed I could see or hear. This being done to my great content, I home, and to Sir W. Batten's, and there with Sir R. Ford, Mr. Knightly, and one Withers, a professed lying rogue, supped well, and mighty merry, and our fears over. . . .

6. A SCAPEGOAT IS FOUND FOR THE GREAT FIRE

The anti-Catholic hysteria of the latter part of Charles II's reign led to the erection of the following monument in London. It stood until 1831.

This Pillar was set up in Perpetuall Remembrance of that most dreadful burning of this Protestant city, begun and carryed on by ye treachery and malice of ye Popish faction, in ye beginning of Septem. in ye year of our

H. Wheatley, *London, Past and Present,* as found in Elizabeth Kimball Kendall, ed., *Source-Book of English History* (New York: The Macmillan Company, 1900), p. 283.

Lord 1666, in order to ye carrying on their horrid Plott for extirpating the Protestant Religion and old English Liberty, and the introducing Popery and Slavery.

7. *ENGLAND EXCHANGES A CATHOLIC KING FOR A PROTESTANT*

Although political and constitutional issues played a role, the main reason for the Glorious Revolution of 1688 was religious. James II's open espousal of Roman Catholicism was extremely distasteful to the great majority of Englishmen. John Evelyn's* Diary*, excerpts from which follow, reflects the state of public opinion in England.

29TH DECEMBER, 1686. I went to hear the music of the Italians in the new chapel, now first opened publicly at Whitehall for the Popish Service. . . . Here we saw the Bishop in his mitre and rich copes, with six or seven Jesuits and others in rich copes, sumptuously habited, often taking off and putting on the Bishop's mitre, who sat in a chair with arms pontifically, was adored and censed by three Jesuits in their copes; . . . I could not have believed I should ever have seen such things in the King of England's palace, after it had pleased God to enlighten this nation; . . .

20TH MARCH, 1687. . . . His Majesty again prorogued the Parliament, foreseeing it would not remit the laws against Papists. . . .

15TH JANUARY, 1688. There was a solemn and particular office used at our, and all the churches of London and ten miles round, for a thanksgiving to God, for her Majesty being with child. . . .

18TH MAY, 1688. The King enjoining the ministers to read his Declaration for giving liberty of conscience (as it was styled) in all churches of England, this evening, six Bishops . . . in the name of all the rest of the Bishops, came to his Majesty to petition him, that he would not impose the reading of it to the several congregations within their dioceses; . . .

8TH JUNE, 1688. This day, the Archbishop of Canterbury, with the Bishops of Ely, Chichester, St. Asaph, Bristol, Peterborough, and Bath and Wells, were sent from the Privy Council prisoners to the Tower. . . .

10TH JUNE, 1688. A YOUNG PRINCE born, which will cause disputes.

About two o'clock, we heard the Tower ordnance discharged, and the bells ring for the birth of a Prince of Wales. This was very surprising, it having been universally given out that her Majesty did not look till the next month. . . .

29TH JUNE, 1688. They [the bishops] appeared; the trial lasted from

The Diary of John Evelyn, in the Universal Classics Library (Washington and London: M. Walter Dunne, 1901), pp. 258–284.

nine in the morning to past six in the evening. . . . The jury were locked up till that time, eleven of them being for an acquittal; but one (Arnold, a brewer) would not consent. At length he agreed with the others. . . . When this was heard, there was great rejoicing; and there was a lane of people from the King's Bench to the water side, on their knees, as the Bishops passed and repassed, to beg their blessing. Bonfires were made that night, and bells rung, which was taken very ill at Court. . . .

10TH AUGUST, 1688. Dr. Tenison now told me there would suddenly be some great thing discovered. This was the Prince of Orange intending to come over. . . .

30TH SEPTEMBER, 1688. The Court in extraordinary a consternation, on assurance of the Prince of Orange's intention to land. . . .

28TH OCTOBER, 1688. A tumult in London on the rabble demolishing a Popish chapel, that had been set up in the city. . . .

5TH NOVEMBER, 1688. I went to London; heard the news of the Prince having landed at Torbay, coming with a fleet of near 700 sail, passing through the Channel with so favorable a wind, that our navy could not intercept, or molest them. This put the King and Court into great consternation. . . .

14TH NOVEMBER, 1688. The Prince increases every day in force. Several Lords go in to him. Lord Cornbury carries some regiments, and marches to Honiton, the Prince's headquarters. The city of London in disorder; the rabble pulled down the nunnery newly bought by the Papists of Lord Berkeley, at St. John's. . . .

2ND DECEMBER, 1688. . . . The great favorites at Court, Priests and Jesuits, fly or abscond. . . . The Papists in offices lay down their commissions, and fly. Universal consternation among them; it looks like a revolution. . . .

13TH DECEMBER, 1688. The King flies to sea, puts in at Faversham for ballast; is rudely treated by the people; comes back to Whitehall. . . .

18TH DECEMBER, 1688. I saw the King take barge to Gravesend at twelve o'clock—a sad sight! The Prince comes to St. James's, and fills Whitehall with Dutch guards. . . .

All the world go to see the Prince at St. James's, where there is a great Court. There I saw him, and several of my acquaintance who came over with him. He is very stately, serious and reserved. The English soldiers sent out of town to disband them; not well pleased.

24TH DECEMBER, 1688. The King passes into France, whither the Queen and child were gone a few days before. . . .

25

RISE OF RUSSIA AND PRUSSIA

During the eighteenth century the rise of two states, Russia and Prussia, transformed the politics of eastern and central Europe. At the same time, a much older state, Austria, whose dreams of converting the Holy Roman Empire into a modern state had been shattered by the Treaty of Westphalia, began to reach down the Danube Valley. All three grew steadily in size and strength, mastering their weaker neighbors (Poland, Sweden, the Ottoman Empire), and finally coming to adjoin one another. They shared central-eastern Europe until they were all three destroyed by the upheavals of World War I.

1. PETER THE GREAT VISITS ENGLAND

In 1697 and 1698, Czar Peter made a historic visit to western Europe. His trip was cut short by news of an uprising in Moscow, which he proceeded to suppress in a way which suggests that he had learned a good deal more about technical matters than about Western humanitarianism. The following account of his stay in London was written by the Anglican Bishop and historian Gilbert Burnet.

. . . [The Czar] came this Winter over to England, and stayed some Months among us; I waited often on him, and was ordered, both by the King and the Archbishop and Bishops, to attend upon him, and to offer him such Informations of our Religion and Constitution, as he was willing to receive: I had good Interpreters, so I had much free discourse with him. He is a man of a very hot temper, soon inflamed, and very brutal in his Passion; he raises his natural heat, by drinking much Brandy, which he rectifies himself with great application: He is subject to convulsive Motions all over his Body, and his Head seems to be affected with these; he wants not Capacity, and

Bishop Burnet, *History of His Own Time* (London: 1753), Vol. III, pp. 306–308.

has a larger measure of Knowledge than might be expected from his Education, which was very indifferent: A want of Judgment, with an instability of Temper, appear in him too often and too evidently; he is mechanically turned, and seems designed by Nature rather to be a Ship Carpenter, than a great Prince: this was his chief study and exercise while he stayed here: He wrought much with his own hands, and made all about him work at the Models of Ships: He told me, he designed a great Fleet at Azor, and with it to attack the Turkish Empire; but he did not seem capable of conducting so great a Design, though his conduct in his Wars since this, has discovered a greater Genius in him, than appeared at that time. He was disposed to understand our Doctrine, but he did not seem desirous to mend matters in Muscovy: He was indeed resolved to encourage Learning, and to polish his People, by sending some of them to travel in other Countries, and to draw Strangers to come and live among them. He seemed apprehensive still of his Sister's Intrigues. There was a mixture both of Passion and Severity in his temper. He is resolute, but understands little of War, and seemed not at all inquisitive that way. After I had seen him often, and had conversed much with him, I could not but adore the depth of the Providence of God, that had raised up such a furious man, to so absolute an Authority over so great a part of the World. . . .

. . . He went from hence to the Court of Vienna, where he purposed to have stayed some time, but he was called home sooner than he had intended, upon a discovery or a suspicion of Intrigues managed by his Sister: The Strangers to whom he trusted most, were so true to him, that those designs were crushed before he came back; but on this occasion, he let loose his fury on all whom he suspected; some hundred of them were hanged all round Moscow, and it was said, that he cut off many Heads with his own hand, and so far was he from relenting or showing any sort of tenderness, that he seemed delighted with it. How long he is to be the Scourge of that Nation, or of his Neighbours, God only knows: So extraordinary an incident will, I hope, justify such a digression. . . .

2. *AN ENGLISH ENGINEER DESCRIBES PETER THE GREAT'S RUSSIA*

During his visit to England, Peter the Great arranged to have a number of English technicians return with him to Russia to help modernize the country. One of these men was the hydraulic engineer John Perry, who spent fourteen frustrating

John Perry, *The State of Russia Under the Present Czar*, in *Seven Britons in Imperial Russia, 1698–1812*, edited by Peter Putnam (Princeton, N.J.: Princeton University Press, 1952), pp. 31–62.

and unrewarded years in Russia. Finally, in grave peril of his life, he managed to escape in 1712. His book on Russia was widely read and influential in western Europe in the eighteenth century.

[The Czar during his visit to London] was likewise shown both Houses of Parliament when they were sitting, and was prevail'd upon to go once or twice to the play, but that was what he did not like. He spent most of his time in what related to war and shipping, and upon the water. He often took the carpenter's tools in his hands, and often work'd himself in Deptford Yard, as he had done before in Holland. He would sometimes be at the smith's, and sometimes at the gun-founder's, and there was scarce any art or mechanick trade whatsoever, from the watch-maker to the coffin-maker, but he more or less inspected it, and even caused a model of an English coffin to be sent into Russia, as he did also of many other things. . . .

It was a very rare thing in Russia before this present Czar's time to have found any man, even among the highest and most learned of the clergy, to have understood any language but their own; and as they were themselves void of learning, so they were wary and cautious to keep out all means that might bring it in, lest their ignorance should be discovered . . . for which reason the learning of foreign languages and books were always formerly discouraged; even as they are to this day in the Turkish Empire. . . .

There came once a press and letters out of Poland to Mosco, where a printing-house was set up with the approbation of one of the former Czars; but not long after the house was fir'd in the night-time, and the press and letters were burnt, as was thought by the procurement of the priests, they looking upon all other books except the history of their own countrey, and the exploits and victories of their Czars, and the lives and miracles of their saints, to be as dangerous as witchcraft.

This ignorance was not so much to be wonder'd at when it is consider'd that they neither suffer'd their sons to travel, nor was there ever any university in the countrey, or considerable school of any learning, till this Czar's time. . . .

. . . notwithstanding their pretended purity in keeping their fasts, and abstaining from flesh, there is nothing more common than to have both the people and the priest, too, go to church on a holiday in the morning, and get drunk in the afternoon long before night; especially the greater the holiday, the more it is excusable, and the custom, to be drunk. It is very ordinary at such times, if you ride through Mosco in the evening on a great holiday, to see the priests, as well as other men, lie drunk about the streets . . . and so far from it being accounted a scandal to be drunk, that the very women, not only the meaner sort, but even women of distinction and fashion, will make no scruple to own, that they have been very drunk; and in publick company will thank them for the civility and kindness, as they call it, of making them drunk, when they have been entertained any place, the next time they meet them. And, indeed, when I first went into the countrey, and for some years after, it was the common way, not only at all great entertainments where the court was invited and present, but even among private friends, to make their visitants drunk before they parted, or it was not accounted that they had been made welcome; . . .

It had been the manner of the Russes, like the Patriarchs of old, to wear long beards hanging down upon their bosoms, which they comb'd out with pride, and kept smooth and fine, without one hair to be diminish'd. . . . The Czar, therefore, to reform this foolish custom, and to make them look like other Europeans, ordered a tax to be laid, on all gentlemen, merchants, and others of his subjects (excepting the priests and common peasants, or slaves) that they should each of them pay a hundred rubles per annum, for the wearing of their beards, and that even the common people should pay a copeck at the entrance of the gates of any of the towns or cities of Russia. . . .

. . . the Czar came down to Veronize, where I was then on service, and a great many of my men that had worn their beards all their lives, were now obliged to part with them, amongst which . . . was an old Russ carpenter that had been with me at Camishinka. . . . I jested a little with him on this occasion, telling him that he was become a young man, and asked him what he had done with his beard? Upon which he put his hand in his bosom and pull'd it out, and shed'd it to me: farther telling me, that when he came home, he would lay it up to have it put in his coffin and buried along with him, that he might be able to give an account of it to St. Nicholas, when he came to the other world; and that all his brothers (meaning his fellow-workmen, who had been shaved that day) had taken the same care. . . .

The Czar . . . gave orders that all his boyars and people whatsoever, that came near his court, and that were in his pay should . . . equip themselves with handsome cloathes made after the English fashion. . . . And next he commanded, that a pattern of cloathes of the English fashion should be hung up at all the gates of the city of Mosco, and that publication should be made, that all persons (excepting the common peasants who brought goods and provisions into the city) should make their cloathes according to the said patterns; and that whosoever should disobey the said orders, and should be found passing any of the gates of the city in their long habits, should either pay two grevens (which is 20 pence) or be obliged to kneel down at the gates of the city, and to have their coats cut off just even with the ground. . . .

It had been the custom of Russia, in case of marriages, that the match always be made up between the parents on each side, without any previous meeting, consent or liking of one another. . . . It [is] a thing common in Russia to beat wives in a most barbarous manner, very often so unhumanly that they die with the blows; the wives being thus many times made desperate, murther their husbands in revenge for the ill usage they receive; on which occasion there is a law made, that when they murther their husbands, they are set alive in the ground, standing upright, with the earth fill'd about them, and only their heads left just above the earth, and a watch set over them, that they shall not be relieved till they are starved to death; which is a common sight in that countrey, and I have known them live sometimes seven or eight days in that posture.

. . . among some other causes, one of the chief which makes the generality of the nobility at present uneasy, is, that the Czar obliges them against their will, to come and live at Petersburgh, with their wives and their families, where they are oblig'd to build new houses for themselves, and where all manner of provisions are usually three or four times as dear, and forage for their horses, etc. at least six or eight times as dear as it at Mosco; which happens from the small quantity which the countrey thereabouts produces, being more than two thirds woods and bogs; and not only the nobility, but merchants and tradesmen of all sorts, are oblig'd to go and live there. . . .

As for the Czar, he is a great lover of the water, and entirely delights in ships and boats, and in sailing. . . . But his lords have no relish nor pleasure in those things, and though they seemingly compliment the Czar whenever he talks to them of the beauties and delights of Petersburgh; yet when they get together by themselves, they complain and say that there are tears and water enough at Petersburgh, but they pray God to send them to live again at Mosco.

3. *CATHERINE THE GREAT TELLS HOW SHE ROSE TO POWER*

The following account of the palace revolution which overthrew Czar Peter III in 1762 and put his wife Catherine on the throne is taken from a letter written by Catherine to her lover Stanislaw Poniatowski, later king of Poland. Catherine's

Letter of Catherine to Stanislaw Poniatowski, August, 1762, as found in *Readings in Russian History,* edited by W.B. Walsh (Syracuse, N.Y.: Syracuse University Press, 1950), pp. 184–188. From the book *Peter III, Emperor of Russia* by R.N. Bain. Published by E.P. Dutton & Co., Inc. Copyright 1902 by E.P. Dutton & Co., Inc. Reprinted by permission of the copyright holders.

explanation of her husband's death can hardly be taken literally; there is little doubt that he was murdered.

. . . It is six months ago since my accession to the throne was first put in hand. Peter III. had lost the little wit he had. He ran his head against everything. He wanted to break up the Guards. . . . He wanted to change his religion, marry Elizabeth Vorontsov and shut me up.

The day of the celebration of the peace with [Prussia,] after having publicly insulted me at table, he ordered my arrest the same evening. My uncle, Prince George, got this order retracted, and from thenceforth I lent an ear to the propositions which had been made to me [ever] since the death of the Empress [Elizabeth].

The [original] design was to seize him in his apartments and shut him up as was done with the Princess Anne and her children. He went off [however] to Oranienbaum. We were sure of a great number of the captains of the Guards. The fate of the secret was in the hands of the three brothers Orlov. . . . They are extremely determined people and much beloved by the common soldiers, having served in the Guards. I am under great obligation to these people, all Petersburg is my witness. . . .

I was at Peterhof. Peter III. was making merry and dwelling at Oranienbaum. . . . I was sleeping calmly. . . . At 6 o'clock in the morning of the 28th . . . Alexius Orlov enters my room and says quite gently: "It is time to get up; all is ready for your proclamation." . . . I dressed myself quickly without making my toilet and got into the carriage which he had brought with him. . . .

Five versts from the town I met the elder Orlov with the younger Prince Bariatinsky. Orlov gave up his carriage to me, for my horses were done up, and we got out at the barracks of the Ismailovsky Regiment. [At the gates] were only twelve men, and a drummer, who began sounding an alarm, when the soldiers came running out, kissing me, embracing my hands and feet and clothes, and calling me their deliverer. Then they began swearing allegiance to me. When this had been done, they begged me to get into the carriage, and the priest, cross in hand, walked on in front. We went [first] to the [barracks of the] Semenovsky Regiment, but the regiment came marching out to meet us, crying, "Vivat!" Then we went to the church of Kazan, where I got out. Then the Preobrazhensky Regiment arrived, crying, "Vivat!" "We beg your pardon," they said to me, "for being the last. Our officers stopped us, but here are four of them whom we have arrested to show you our zeal. We want what our brothers want." Then the horse-guards arrived frantic with joy, I never saw anything like it, weeping and crying at the deliverance of their country. . . . I went to the new Winter Palace where the Synod and the Senate were assembled. A manifesto and a form of oath were hastily drawn up. Then I went down and received the troops on foot. There were more than 14,000 men, guards and country regiments. As soon as they saw me they uttered cries of joy which were taken up by an innumerable crowd. . . . it was resolved to go to Peterhof. . . . on leaving town, three soldiers of the Guards . . . came to me and said: "Here! take what Peter III. has entrusted us with [a manifesto], we give it to you. We are very glad of the opportunity of joining our brethren."

After the first letter came a second, the bearer whereof, General Michal Ismailov, threw himself at my feet and said: "Do you take me for an honest man?" On my replying, "Yes!" "Well," says he, "it is pleasant to have to do with sensible folk. The Emperor offers to resign. I will bring to you [a form of abdication] after a very few alterations. I will save my country from a civil war without any difficulty."

I charged him with this commission, and off he went to accomplish it. Peter III. abdicated, at Oranienbaum, in full liberty, surrounded by 5000 Holsteiners, and came with Elizabeth Vorontsov, Gudovich and Ismailov to Peterhof, where, to protect his person, I gave him five officers and some soldiers. . . . Thereupon I sent the deposed Emperor to a remote and very agreeable place called Ropsha, 25 versts from Peterhof, under the command of Alexius Orlov, with four officers and a detachment of picked, good-natured men, whilst decent and convenient rooms were being prepared for him at Schlusselburg. But God disposed otherwise. Fear had given him a diarrhoea which lasted three days and passed away on the fourth; in this [fourth] day he drank excessively, for he had all he wanted except liberty. Nevertheless, the only things he asked me for were his mistress, his dog, his Negro and his violin; but for fear of scandal and increasing the agitation of the persons who guarded him, I only sent him the last three things.

The hemorrhoidal colic which seized him affected his brain: two days he was delirious, and the delirium was followed by very great exhaustion, and despite all the assistance of the doctors, he expired whilst demanding a Lutheran priest. I feared that the officers might have poisoned him, so I had him opened, but it is an absolute fact that not the slightest trace of poison was found inside him. The stomach was quite sound, but inflammation of the bowels and a stroke of apoplexy had carried him off. His heart was extraordinarily small and quite decayed. . . .

At last, then God has brought everything to pass according to His predisposition. The whole thing is rather a miracle than a fact foreseen and arranged beforehand, for so many felicitous combinations could not have coincided unless God's hand had been over it all.

. . . Be assured, too, that hatred of foreigners was the leading principle of the whole affair, and that Peter III. himself passed for a foreigner.

Adieu, there are some very strange situations in this world.

4. *CATHERINE'S WILL, 1792*

If I should die in Tsarskoe Selo, I wish to be buried in the Sophien town cemetery.

If in the town of St. Peter—in the Nevsky monastery in the cathedral or funereal church.

If in Pella—to be brought by sea to the Nevsky monastery.

If in Moscow—in the Don monastery or the nearest town cemetery.

If in Peterhof—in the Troitza-Sergiev monastery.

If in any other place—in the nearest cemetery.

The coffin should be carried by Chevalier Guards and nobody else.

My body should be dressed in white and a golden crown bearing my name should be placed on my head.

The mourning to last six months, not more and even better if less.

After the first six weeks all public entertainments to be resumed.

Marriages and music to be allowed immediately after the burial. . . .

My desire is to bring Constantine to the throne of the Great Eastern Empire.

For the good of the Russian and Greek Empires I advise that the Princes of Wurtemberg should be banished from the affairs of these Empires and have as little to do with them as possible; I also advise avoiding consulting all Germans of both sexes.

The Memoirs of Catherine the Great, edited by Dominique Maroger and translated by Baroness Moura Budberg (New York: The Macmillan Company, n.d.), pp. 377–378. Used by permission of The Macmillan Company and Hamish Hamilton Ltd., London, publisher of the original edition.

5. *CROWN PRINCE FREDERICK IS TAUGHT PRUSSIAN DISCIPLINE*

Few princes have been brought up with greater rigor than was Frederick the Great by his father, Frederick William I. The first two selections below are an exchange of letters between the sixteen-year-old Frederick and his father. The third selection tells the unhappy consequences of an attempt by Frederick (eighteen at the time) to run away to England. He and his companion, Lieutenant Katte, were apprehended, tried by a court-martial acting under the King's thumb, and condemned to death.

[A] and [B] J.H. Robinson, *Readings in European History* (New York: Ginn and Company, 1904), Vol. II, pp. 321–322. Copyright 1904 by James Harvey Robinson. Used by permission of the publisher. [C] *Memoirs of Frederica Sophia Wilhemina,* edited by W.D. Howells (Boston: James R. Osgood, 1877), Vol. I, pp. 239–245.

[A] *Frederick to His Father, September 11, 1728*

I have not ventured for a long time to present myself before my dear papa, partly because I was advised against it, but chiefly because I anticipated an even worse reception than usual and feared to vex my dear papa still further by the favor I have now to ask; so I have preferred to put it in writing.

I beg my dear papa that he will be kindly disposed toward me. I do assure him that after long examination of my conscience I do not find the slightest thing with which to reproach myself; but if, against my wish and will, I have vexed my dear papa, I hereby beg most humbly for forgiveness, and hope that my dear papa will give over the fearful hate which has appeared so plainly in his whole behavior and to which I cannot accustom myself. I have always thought hitherto that I had a kind father, but now I see the contrary. However, I will take courage and hope that my dear papa will think this all over and take me again into his favor. Meantime I assure him that I will never, my life long, willingly fail him, and in spite of his disfavor I am still, with most dutiful and childlike respect, my dear papa's

Most obedient and faithful servant and son,

FREDERICK

[B] *Frederick William in Reply*

A bad, obstinate boy, who does not love his father; for when one does one's best, and especially when one loves one's father, one does what he wishes not only when he is standing by but when he is not there to see. Moreover you know very well that I cannot stand an effeminate fellow who has no manly tastes, who cannot ride or shoot (to his shame be it said!), is untidy about his person, and wears his hair curled like a fool instead of cutting it; and that I have condemned all these things a thousand times, and yet there is no sign of improvement. For the rest, haughty, offish as a country lout, conversing with none but a favored few instead of being affable and popular, grimacing like a fool, and never following my wishes out of love for me but only when forced into it, caring for nothing but to have his own way, and thinking nothing else is of any importance. This is my answer. . . .

[C] *Frederick's Sister Tells of Katte's Execution*

The king would have suffered the sentence to be executed had not all the foreign powers interceded for the prince [Frederick], and particularly the emperor and the states-general. Seckendorff exerted himself very much;

as he had caused the mischief, he wished to repair it. He told the king that though the prince royal was his son, he belonged to the empire, and that his Majesty had no right over him. It was with very great difficulty he obtained his pardon. His continual solicitations, however, gradually weakened the sanguinary intentions of the king. Grumkow, who became aware of this change, sought to take to himself the merit of it with my brother. He went to Cüstrin, and prevailed with the prince to write and make his submission to the king.

Seckendorff also attempted to save Katte; but the king remained inflexible. . . .

Major Schenk now came to inform him [Katte] that his execution was to take place at Cüstrin, and that the coach, which was to convey him thither, was waiting for him. He appeared somewhat surprised at this intelligence; but soon resuming his tranquillity, he with a smiling countenance followed M. de Schenk, who got into the coach with him, besides two other officers of the horse-guards. . . . He arrived at Cüstrin at nine o'clock in the morning, and was taken directly to the scaffold.

The day before, General Lepel, governor of the fortress, and President Munchow had conducted my brother to an apartment that had been purposely prepared for him on the floor above that where he had lodged. He there found a bed and some furniture. The window-curtains were let down, which at first prevented his seeing what was going on without. A plain brown coat was brought to him, in which he was obliged to dress himself. I forgot to state that a similar coat had been given to Katte. The general, having then drawn up the curtains, pointed out to the prince a scaffold covered with black, and as high as the window, which had been widened and the bars of which had been removed. After this, both the general and Munchow retired. This sight, and the downcast look of Munchow, induced my brother to think that sentence of death was going to be passed upon him, and that these preparations regarded himself, which caused him a violent agitation.

General Lepel and President Munchow entered the prince's room in the morning a little before Katte appeared, and endeavored to prepare the prince in the best manner they could for this horrible scene. It is said that he was in such a state of despair and grief as had never before been witnessed. In the meantime Schenk was rendering the like friendly office to Katte. On entering the fortress he said to him: "Continue firm, my dear Katte; you are going to undergo a severe trial; you are at Cüstrin, and you will see the prince royal." "Rather say," answered Katte, "that I am going to have the greatest consolation that could have been granted to me." With these words he ascended the scaffold. My unfortunate brother was then forced to stand at the window. He attempted to throw himself out of it, but was prevented. "I entreat you, for Heaven's sake," said the prince to those who were around him, "delay the execution; I shall inform the king that I am ready to renounce my right to the crown, if his Majesty will pardon Katte." M. de Munchow stopped the prince's mouth with a handkerchief. When the prince saw Katte, he exclaimed: "How wretched I am, my dear Katte! I am the cause of your death. Would to Heaven I were in your place!" "Ah!" replied Katte, "if I had a thousand lives, I would sacrifice them all for your royal highness." At the same time he dropped on his knees. One of his servants attempted to blindfold him, but he would not suffer it, and elevating his thoughts to Heaven, he ejaculated: "My God! I commit my soul into thy hands!" Scarcely had he pronounced these words, when his head, cut off at one blow, rolled at his feet. . . . [My brother] fainted away, and the gentlemen about him had laid him on his bed, where he remained senseless for some hours. . . . M. de Munchow, in spite of the orders of the king, let the curtains down, and sent for physicians, who found the prince in a very dangerous state. He would not take anything that was given him. His mind was so bewildered, and his agitation so great, that he would have destroyed himself had he not been prevented. Religious considerations, it was thought, would soften him; a clergyman was sent for to comfort him: but all in vain; the violent convulsions ceased only when his strength was exhausted. Tears succeeded to these dreadful agitations. It was with extreme difficulty that he was prevailed upon to take medicine. Nothing could induce him to do it, but the representation that he would also cause the queen's death and mine, if he persisted in his own destruction. A profound melancholy fastened upon him for a long time, and for three successive days his life was in imminent danger. The body of Katte remained exposed on the scaffold until sunset. It was buried in one of the bastions of the fortress. . . .

6. THE PARTITION OF POLAND DRIVES MARIA THERESA TO "BLACK MELANCHOLY"

It is to be doubted whether either Frederick the Great or Catherine the Great had any qualms of conscience about their part in that act of eighteenth century international gangsterism, the Partition of Poland. The same is not true of the third party in the scheme, Maria Theresa, as evidenced by the following letter written by her in September, 1772.

J.H. Robinson, *Readings in European History* (New York: Ginn and Company, 1904), Vol. II, p. 328. Copyright 1904 by James Harvey Robinson. Used by permission of the publisher.

. . . Firmian will receive a lengthy document with instructions in regard to our present situation, our engagements toward Russia, Prussia, and the Turks, but particularly in regard to this unfortunate partition of Poland, which is costing me ten years of my life. It will make plain the whole unhappy history of that affair. How many times have I refused to agree to it! But disaster after disaster heaped upon us by the Turks; misery, famine, and pestilence at home; no hope of assistance either from France or England, and the prospect of being isolated and threatened with a war both with Russia and Prussia,—it was all these considerations that finally forced me to accede to that unhappy proposal, which will remain a blot on my whole reign. God grant that I be not held responsible for it in the other world! I confess that I cannot keep from talking about this affair. I have taken it so to heart that it poisons and imbitters all my days, which even without that are sad enough. I must stop writing about it at once, or I shall worry myself into the blackest melancholy. . . .

26

THE SEVEN YEARS' WAR

The Seven Years' War was basically a continuation of the War of the Austrian Succession, but with partners reversed. Austria, sufficiently bent on revenge against Prussia to forget her long enmity towards France, obtained the aid of that state plus Russia in what bid fair to be a war to exterminate Prussia. Frederick the Great found himself opposed to a coalition whose combined populations were more than fifteen times that of Prussia. His only ally was England, whose interest in the conflict was mainly colonial and naval.

1. FREDERICK THE GREAT ADDRESSES HIS OFFICERS BEFORE BATTLE

Capitalizing on the failure of his opponents to coordinate their armies, Frederick the Great took the offensive at the war's start and launched a series of brilliant attacks on enemy forces. One of his greatest victories was against the Austrians at Leuthen, December 5, 1757. The following selection gives his address to his officers just prior to the start of the battle.

You are aware, gentlemen, that Prince Karl of Lorraine has succeeded in taking Schweidnitz, defeating the duke of Bevern and making himself master of Breslau, while I was engaged in checking the advance of the French and imperial forces. A part of Schleswig, my capital, and all the military stores it contained, are lost, and I should feel myself in dire straits indeed if it were not for my unbounded confidence in your courage, your constancy, and your love for the fatherland, which you have proved to me on so many occasions in the past. These services to me and to the fatherland have touched the deepest fibers of my heart. There is hardly one among

J.H. Robinson, *Readings in European History* (New York: Ginn and Company, 1904), Vol. II, pp. 323–324.

you who has not distinguished himself by some conspicuous deed of valor, wherefore I flatter myself that in the approaching opportunity also you will not fail in any sacrifice that your country may demand of you.

And this opportunity is close at hand. I should feel that I had accomplished nothing if Austria were left in possession of Schleswig. Let me tell you then that I propose, in defiance of all the rules of the art of war, to attack the army of Prince Karl, three times as large as ours, wherever I find it. It is here no question of the numbers of the enemy nor of the importance of the positions they have occupied; all this I hope to overcome by the devotion of my troops and the careful carrying out of my plans. I must take this step or all will be lost; we must defeat the enemy, else we shall all lie buried under his batteries. So I believe—so I shall act.

Communicate my decision to all the officers of the army; prepare the common soldier for the exertions that are to come, and tell him that I feel justified in expecting unquestioning obedience from him. Remember that you are Prussians and you cannot show yourselves unworthy of that distinction. But if there be one or other among you who fears to share with me any and all danger, he shall at once be given his discharge without reproach from me.

[Convinced that he had produced the effect he desired, Frederick smilingly continued:]

I was convinced that no one of you would wish to leave me; I count then, absolutely, on your faithful help and on certain victory. Should I not return to reward you for your devotion, the fatherland itself must do it. Return now to camp and repeat to your troops what you have heard from me. [Then, becoming once more the stern ruler, he announced the punishment that awaited the slightest hesitation in following orders.] The regiment of cavalry that does not immediately on the receipt of orders throw itself upon the enemy I will have unmounted immediately after the battle and make it a garrison regiment. The battalion of infantry that even begins to hesitate, no matter what the danger may be, shall lose its flags and its swords and have the gold lace stripped from its uniforms.

And now, gentlemen, farewell; erelong we shall either have defeated the enemy or we shall see each other no more.

2. *THE DEATH OF THE CZARINA (1762) SAVES FREDERICK II AND PRUSSIA*

After his spectacular victories in the opening years of the Seven Years' War, Frederick II was worn down by the weight of his enemies and forced to stage a

Oeuvres de Frédéric Le Grand (Berlin: Rodolphe Decker, 1855), Vol. XXVI, pp. 234–237. Our translation.

long and exhausting defensive war. By the beginning of 1762, as the following correspondence indicates, Frederick was in a despairing mood. He was saved in the nick of time by the death of the Czarina and the accession of the mad but friendly Peter III.

Frederick to Prince Henry, His Brother, January 9, 1762

. . . you want me to tell you what course should be followed in an extremity like this. I suggest that we gather all our forces and employ this mass to strike at our enemies by turn. That is the best thing to do. It is not enough, and I can already hear all the obstacles and objections you are going to present. But think it over; after all, to perish by bits or to perish *en masse,* is it not all the same?

Prince Henry to Frederick, January 16, 1762

You had the kindness to reply, on the subject of the next campaign, that you intend to assemble all your forces and strike against one after another of the enemy. . . . The solution you have decided upon seems to me very desperate. . . . I admit all the difficulties which result from dividing our forces; but since it is only a question of perishing, it is merely necessary to know what is the slowest way to die. If the end is prolonged there is some hope that some unforseen event will take place. . . . A skillful doctor tries to drag out the life of his patient, if he cannot cure him, so that, when he dies, he at least has the consolation that it is according to the rule of Galen and the precepts of Hippocrates, and I consequently think that regiments placed opposite the enemy would at least check them, and that is all that can be done and hoped for. . . .

Frederick to Prince Henry, January 19, 1762

I have just received your letter of the sixteenth of this month. You know that there are two doctors in Molière, Dr. So-Much-the-Worst and Dr. So-Much-the-Better, and it is impossible for them to agree. [The King is confusing Molière with La Fontaine's *Fables.*] I have a sick person to treat who has a violent fever. Despairing, I order an emetic for him, and you want to give him an anodyne. . . . I will say no more about the situation in which I find myself here, neither of all that I fear. I hope to keep going until the month of March. . . .

To Prince Henry, January 20, 1762

I did not want to leave you uninformed of the important news which I have just received of the death of the Empress of Russia, which took place the fifth of this month.

I would not as yet be able to tell you the consequences of this event, and we will have to be patient for a couple of weeks to see where this will lead . . . but what I fully expect is that it will not turn out at all badly for us.

To Prince Henry, January 31, 1762

I have to tell you the good news that Czernichew leaves for Poland with his Russians. We have nothing more to fear, for the moment, from those people. Here we are, thank heavens, with no one on our back. . . . I hope this news will cause you to cheer up.

3. THE ANNUAL REGISTER *PRAISES WILLIAM PITT*

The great organizer of victory in England's overseas duel with France was William Pitt, later made earl of Chatham. Unfortunately, because of a quarrel with the other members of the Cabinet, he resigned in 1761. The editors of* The Annual Register, *an influential review of world news, review Pitt's accomplishments.

. . . we may affirm with truth and impartiality, that no man was ever better fitted than Mr. Pitt to be the minister in a great and powerful nation, or better qualified to carry that power and greatness to their utmost limits. There was in all his designs a magnitude, and even a vastness, which was not easily comprehended by every mind, and which nothing but success could have made to appear reasonable. If he was sometimes incorrect, he was never vulgar.

His power, as it was not acquired, so neither was it exercised in an ordinary manner. With very little parliamentary, and with less court influence, he swayed both at court and in parliament with an authority unknown before to the best supported ministers. He was called to the ministry by the voice of the people; and what is more rare, he held it with that approbation; and under him for the first time, administration and popularity were seen united. Under him Great Britain carried on the most important war in which she ever was engaged, alone and unassisted, with greater splendour, and with more success than she had ever enjoyed at the head of the most powerful alliances. Alone this island seemed to balance the rest of Europe.

In the conduct of the war he never suffered the enemy to breathe, but overwhelmed them with reiterated blows, and kept up the alarm in every quarter. If one of his expeditions was not so well calculated or so successfully executed, amends were made by another, and by a third. The spirit of the nation once roused, was not suffered for a moment to subside; and

The Annual Register . . . of the Year 1761, p. 47.

the French, dazzled, as it were, by the multitude and celerity of his enterprizes, seemed to have lost all power of resistance. In short, he revived the military genius of our people; he supported our allies; he extended our trade; he raised our reputation; he augmented our dominions; and on his departure from administration, left the nation in no other danger than that which ever must attend exorbitant power, and the temptation which may be, to the invidious exertion of it. Happy it had been for him, for his sovereign, and his country, if a temper less austere, and a disposition more practicable, more compliant, and conciliating, had been joined to his other great virtues. The want of these qualities disabled him from acting any otherwise than alone: it prevented our enjoying the joint fruit of the wisdom of many able men, who might mutually have tempered, and mutually forwarded each other; and finally, which was not the meanest loss, it deprived us of his own immediate services. . . .

4. A SURVIVOR TELLS OF THE BLACK HOLE OF CALCUTTA

In 1756 the Nawab of the Bengal region captured British headquarters at Calcutta and placed 146 prisoners in the "Black Hole." What ensued in the course of one terrible night is described by one of the survivors, J.Z. Holwell.

Figure to yourself, my friend, if possible, the situation of a hundred and forty-six wretches, exhausted by continual fatigue and action, crammed togather in a cube of eighteen feet, in a close sultry night, in Bengal, shut up to the eastward and southward (the only quarters from whence air could reach us) by dead walls, and by a wall and door to the north, open only to the westward by two windows, strongly barred with iron, from which we could receive scarce any circulation of fresh air. . . .

We had been but a few minutes confined before every one fell into a perspiration so profuse, you can form no idea of it. This brought on a raging thirst, which increased in proportion as the body was drained of its moisture.

Various expedients were thought of to give more room and air. To obtain the former, it was moved to put off their cloaths; this was approved as a happy motion, and in a few minutes I believe every man was stripped (myself, Mr. Court, and the two young gentlemen by me excepted.) For a little time they flattered themselves with having gained a mighty advantage; every hat was put in motion to produce a circulation of air, and Mr.

Narrative of J.Z. Holwell in *The Annual Register . . . for the Year 1758*, pp. 279–285.

Baillie proposed that every man should sit down on his hams. This expedient was several times put in practice, and at each time many of the poor creatures, whose natural strength was less than that of others, or who had been more exhausted and could not immediately recover their legs, as others did when the word was given to rise, fell to rise no more; for they were instantly trod to death or suffocated. When the whole body sat down, they were so closely wedged together, that they were obliged to use many efforts before they could put themselves in motion to get up again. . . .

Now every body, excepting those situated in and near the windows, began to grow outrageous, and many delirious: *Water, water,* became the general cry. And the old Jemmautdaar before mentioned, taking pity on us, ordered the people to bring some skins of water. This was what I dreaded. I foresaw it would prove the ruin of the small chance left us, and essayed many times to speak to him privately to forbid its being brought; but the clamour was so loud, it became impossible. The water appeared. Words cannot paint to you the universal agitation and raving the sight of it threw us into. I flattered myself that some, by preserving an equal temper of mind, might out-live the night; but now the reflection, which gave me the greatest pain, was, that I saw no possibility of one escaping to tell the dismal tale.

Until the water came, I had myself not suffered much from thirst, which instantly grew excessive. We had no means of conveying it into the prison, but by hats forced through the bars; and thus myself and Messieurs Coles and Scott (notwithstanding the pains they suffered from their wounds) supplied them as fast as possible. But those who have experienced intense thirst, or are acquainted with the cause and nature of this appetite, will be sufficiently sensible it could receive no more than a momentary alleviation; the cause still subsisted. Though we brought full hats within the bars, there ensued such violent struggles, and frequent contests to get at it, that before it reached the lips of any one, there would be scarcely a small tea cup full left in them. These supplies, like sprinkling water on fire, only served to feed and raise the flame. . . .

By half an hour past eleven, the much greater number of those living were in an outrageous delirium, and the others quite ungovernable; few retaining any calmness, but the ranks next the windows. They all now found, that water, instead of relieving, rather heightened their uneasiness; and, *Air, air,* was the general cry. Every insult that could be devised against the guard, all the approbrious names and abuse that the suba, Monickchund, &c. could be loaded with, were repeated to provoke the guard to fire upon us, every man that could, rushing tumultuously towards the windows, with eager hopes of meeting the first shot. Then a general prayer to heaven to hasten the approach of the flames to the right and left of us, and put a period to our misery. But these failing, they whose strength and spirits were quite exhausted, laid themselves down and expired quietly upon their fellows: others who had yet some strength and vigour left, made a last effort for the windows, and several succeeded by leaping and scrambling over the backs and heads of those in the first ranks; and got hold of the bars, from which there was no removing them. Many to the right and left sunk with the violent pressure, and were soon suffocated; for now a steam arose from the living and the dead. . . .

I need not, my dear friend, ask your commiseration, when I tell you, that in this plight, from half an hour after eleven till near two in the morning, I sustained the weight of a heavy man, with his knees on my back, and the pressure of his whole body on my head; a Dutch serjeant, who had taken his seat upon my left shoulder, and a Topaz [a black Christian soldier] bearing on my right: all which, nothing could have enabled me long to support, but the props and pressure equally sustaining me all around. The two latter I frequently dislodged, by shifting my hold on the bars, and driving my knuckles into their ribs; but my friend above stuck fast, and, as he held by two bars, was immoveable. . . .

When the day broke, and the gentlemen found that no entreaties could prevail to get the door opened, it occurred to one of them (I think to Mr. Secretary Cooke) to make a search for me, in hopes I might have influence enough to gain a release from this scene of misery. Accordingly Messrs. Lushington and Walcot undertook the search, and by my shirt discovered me under the dead upon the platform. They took me from thence, and imagining I had some signs of life, brought me towards the window I had first possession of.

But as life was equally dear to every man (and the stench arising from the dead bodies was grown so intolerable) no one would give up his station in or near the window: so they were obliged to carry me back again. But soon after Captain Mills, (now captain of the company's yacht) who was in possession of a seat in the window, had the humanity to offer to resign it. I was again brought by the same gentlemen and placed in the window.

At this juncture the suba, who had received an account of the havoc death had made amongst us, sent one of his Jemmautdaars to enquire if the chief survived. They showed me to him; told I had appearance of life remaining; and believed I might recover if the door was opened very soon. This answer being returned to the suba, an order came immediately for our release, it being then near six in the morning.

As the door opened inwards, and as the dead were piled up against it, and covered all the rest of the floor, it was impossible to open it by any efforts from without; it was therefore necessary that the dead should be removed by the few that were within, who were become so feeble, that the task, though it was the condition of life, was not performed without the utmost difficulty, and it was 20 minutes after the order came, before the door could be opened.

About a quarter after six in the morning, the poor remains of 146 souls, being no more than three and twenty, came out of the Blackhole alive, but in a condition which made it very doubtful whether they would see the morning of the next day; among the living was Mrs. Carey, but poor Leech was among the dead. The bodies were dragged out of the hole by the soldiers, and thrown promiscuously into the ditch of an unfinished ravelin, which was afterwards filled with earth. . . .

5. THE FRENCH LOSE QUEBEC, 1759

The key to Canada was the city of Quebec. When Wolfe forced its surrender it was the beginning of the end of the French empire in North America. This episode in the Seven Years' War is told by Captain John Knox, who took part in the battle he describes.

Before daybreak this morning we made a descent upon the north shore, about half a quarter of a mile to the eastward of Sillery, and the light troops were fortunately, by the rapidity of the current, carried lower down, between us and Cape Diamond; we had, in this debarkation, thirty flat-bottomed boats, containing about sixteen hundred men. This was a great surprise on the enemy, who, from the natural strength of the place, did not suspect, and consequently were not prepared against, so bold an attempt. The chain of sentries, which they had posted along the summit of the heights, galled us a little, and picked off several men, and some officers, before our light infantry got up to dislodge them.

This grand enterprise was conducted and executed with great good order and discretion; as fast as we landed, the boats put off for reënforcements, and the troops formed with much regularity: the general, with Brigadiers Monckton and Murray, were ashore with the first division. We lost no time here, but clambered up one of the steepest precipices than can be conceived, being almost a perpendicular, and of an incredible height. As soon as we gained the summit all was quiet, and not a shot was heard, owing to the excellent conduct of the light infantry under Colonel Howe;

John Knox, *Historical Journal*, Vol. II, pp. 66–79, as found in Edward P. Cheyney, ed., *Readings in English History* (New York: Ginn and Company, 1908), pp. 598–600.

it was by this time clear daylight. Here we formed again, the river and the south country in our rear, our right extending to the town, our left to Sillery, and halted a few minutes. The general then detached the light troops to our left to rout the enemy from their battery and to disable their guns, except they could be rendered serviceable to the party who were to remain there; and this service was soon performed. We then faced to the right, and marched towards the town by files, till we came to the Plains of Abraham: an even piece of ground which Mr. Wolfe had made choice of, while we stood forming upon the hill. Weather showery; about six o'clock the enemy first made their appearance upon the heights, between us and the town; whereupon we halted, and wheeled to the right, thereby forming the line of battle.

About eight o'clock we had two pieces of short brass six-pounders playing on the enemy, which threw them into some confusion, and obliged them to alter their disposition, and Montcalm formed them into three large columns; about nine the two armies moved a little nearer each other. The light cavalry made a faint attempt upon our parties at the battery of Sillery, but were soon beat off, and Monsieur de Bougainville, with his troops from Cape Rouge, came down to attack the flank of our second line, hoping to penetrate there; but, by a masterly disposition of Brigadier Townshend, they were forced to desist, and the third battalion of Royal Americans was then detached to the first ground we had formed on after we gained the heights, to preserve the communication with the beach and our boats.

About ten o'clock the enemy began to advance briskly in three columns, with loud shouts and recovered arms, two of them inclining to the left of our army, and the third towards our right, firing obliquely at the two extremities of our line, from the distance of one hundred and thirty, until they came within forty, yards; which our troops withstood with the greatest intrepidity and firmness, still reserving their fire, and paying the strictest obedience to their officers. This uncommon steadiness, together with the havoc which the grapeshot from our fieldpieces made among them, threw them into some disorder, and was most critically maintained by a well-timed, regular, and heavy discharge of our small arms, such as they could no longer oppose. Hereupon they gave way, and fled with precipitation, so that, by the time the cloud of smoke was vanished, our men were again loaded, and, profiting by the advantage we had over them, pursued them almost to the gates of the town and the bridge over the little river, redoubling our fire with great eagerness, making many officers and men prisoners. . . .

Our joy at this success is inexpressibly damped by the loss we sustained of one of the greatest heroes which this or any other age can boast of,—General James Wolfe, who received his mortal wound as he was exerting himself at the head of the grenadiers of Louisbourg.

. . . The Sieur de Montcalm died late last night: when his wound was dressed, and he settled in bed, the surgeons who attended him were desired to acquaint him ingenuously with their sentiments of him, and being answered that his wound was mortal, he calmly replied that he was glad of it. His excellency then demanded whether he could survive it long, and how long. He was told, "about a dozen hours, perhaps more, peradventure less." "So much the better," rejoined this eminent warrior; "I am happy I shall not live to see the surrender of Quebec." . . .

After our late worthy general, of renowned memory, was carried off wounded to the rear of the front line, he desired those who were about him to lay him down; being asked if he would have a surgeon he replied, "It is needless; it is all over with me." One of them cried out, "They run, see how they run!" "Who runs?" demanded our hero with great earnestness, like a person aroused from sleep. The officer answered, "The enemy, sir; egad, they give way everywhere." Thereupon the general rejoined, "Go one of you, my lads, to Colonel Burton; tell him to march Webb's regiment with all speed down to Charles's river, to cut off the retreat of the fugitives from the bridge." Then, turning on his side, he added, "Now, God be praised, I will die in peace"; and thus expired. . . .

27

THE "ENLIGHTENMENT"

The great intellectual and moral revolution of modern Europe was the eighteenth century "Enlightenment," which attempted to replace the traditional God-centered, supernatural world with the rationalist heaven on earth. By the application of reason to all problems—political, religious, economic, social—man would lift himself from the alleged superstition and darkness of the past and create a perfect world. The principal practitioners of the new ideas were a class of writers and thinkers called *philosophes* (who were often anything but philosophical) and a group of rulers and ministers styled "enlightened despots" (who were more often despotic than enlightened).

1. MONTESQUIEU SATIRIZES THRONE AND ALTAR

The principal targets of the French philosophes *were irrational government and dogmatic religion, especially the Catholic Church. Typical is a masterpiece of satire entitled* The Persian Letters *(1721), often called the opening gun of the* philosophes. *Its author, Montesquieu, was a prominent member of the nobility of the robe. The book is in the form of letters written by two visiting Persians, Usbek and Rica, to their friends at home.*

Rica to Ibben, Paris, the 4th of the Second Moon of Rebiab, 1712

We have now been a month at Paris, and all the time constantly moving about. There is much to do before one can get settled, find out the people with whom one has business, and procure the many requisites which are all wanted at the same time.

Paris is quite as large as Ispahan. The houses are so high that you

Montesquieu, *The Persian Letters,* Letter XXIV (New York and London: M. Walter Dunne, 1901), pp. 65–68.

would swear they must be inhabited by astrologers. You can easily imagine that a city built in the air, with six or seven houses one above the other, is densely peopled; and that when everybody is abroad, there is a mighty bustle.

You will scarcely believe that during the month I have been here I have not yet seen any one walking. There is no people in the world who hold more by their vehicles than the French: they run; they fly: the slow carriages of Asia, the measured step of our camels, would put them into a state of coma. As for me, who am not made for such hurry, and who often go a-foot without changing my pace, I am sometimes as mad as a Christian; for, passing over splashing from head to foot, I cannot pardon the elbowings I meet with regularly and periodically. A man, coming up behind me, passes me, and turns me half round; then another, crossing me on the opposite side, spins me suddenly round to my first position. Before I have walked a hundred paces, I am more bruised than if I had gone ten leagues.

You must not expect from me an exhaustive account of the manners and customs of the Europeans: I have myself but a faint notion of them yet, and have hardly had time to recover from my astonishment.

The King of France [Louis XIV] is the most powerful of European potentates. He has no mines of gold like his neighbor, the King of Spain; but he is much wealthier than that prince, because his riches are drawn from a more inexhaustible source, the vanity of his subjects. He has undertaken and carried on great wars, without any other supplies than those derived from the sale of titles of honor; and it is by a prodigy of human pride that his troops are paid, his towns fortified, and his fleets equipped.

Then again, the king is a great magician, for his dominion extends to the minds of his subjects; he makes them think what he wishes. . . . If he has a costly war on hand, and is short of money, he simply suggests to his subjects that a piece of paper is coin of the realm, and they are straightway convinced of it. He has even succeeded in persuading them that his touch is a sovereign cure for all sorts of diseases, so great is the power and influence he has over their minds.

What I have told you of this prince need not astonish you: there is another magician more powerful still, who is master of the king's mind, as absolutely as the king is master of the minds of his subjects. This magician is called the Pope. Sometimes he makes the king believe that three are no more than one; that the bread which he eats is not bread; the wine which he drinks not wine; and a thousand things of a like nature.

I will continue to write you, and acquaint you with matters differing widely from the Persian character and genius. We tread, indeed, the same earth; but it seems incredible, remembering in the presence of the men of this country those of the country in which you are.

2. *ROUSSEAU TRIES TO RECONCILE LIBERTY AND GOVERNMENT*

One of Rousseau's principal ideas—and one which ran counter to the eighteenth century dogma of progress—was that civilization corrupted man; man was at his best in a state of nature. Government, in the opinion of Rousseau, was an evil, but, because of the obvious impossibility of returning to a state of nature, a necessary evil. The first selection below illustrates Rousseau's views of natural man, while the second shows how Rousseau would reconcile individual liberty and the need for government.

[A] *From "A Discourse on the Origin of Inequality," 1755*

O man, of whatever country you are, and whatever your opinions may be, behold your history, such as I have thought to read it, not in books written by your fellow-creatures, who are liars, but in nature, which never lies. All that comes from her will be true; nor will you meet with anything false, unless I have involuntarily put in something of my own. The times of which I am going to speak are very remote: how much are you changed from what you once were! It is, so to speak, the life of your species which I am going to write, after the qualities which you have received, which your education and habits may have depraved, but cannot have entirely destroyed. . . . Discontented with your present state, for reasons which threaten your unfortunate descendants with still greater discontent, you will perhaps wish it were in your power to go back; and this feeling should be a panegyric on your first ancestors, a criticism of your contemporaries, and a terror to the unfortunates who will come after you.

Important as it may be, in order to judge rightly of the natural state of man, to consider him from his origin, and to examine him, as it were, in the embryo of his species; I shall not follow his organisation through its successive developments, nor shall I stay to inquire what his animal system must have been at the beginning, in order to become at length what it actually is. . . . I shall suppose his conformation to have been at all times what it appears to us at this day; that he always walked on two legs, made

[A] Jean Jacques Rousseau, *The Social Contract and Other Essays* (New York: Carlton House, n.d.), pp. 165–170. [B] Jean Jacques Rousseau, *The Social Contract*, I, 6, translated by Gerard Hopkins, as found in *Social Contract*, published by the Oxford University Press in the World's Classics series (London and New York: 1945), pp. 254–257. Used by permission of the publisher.

use of his hands as we do, directed his looks over all nature, and measured with his eyes the vast expanse of Heaven.

Hobbes contends that man is naturally intrepid, and is intent only upon attacking and fighting. Another illustrious philosopher holds the opposite, and Cumberland and Puffendorf also affirm that nothing is more timid and fearful than man in the state of nature; that he is always in a tremble, and ready to fly at the least noise or the slightest movement. This may be true of things he does not know; and I do not doubt his being terrified by every novelty that presents itself, when he neither knows the physical good or evil he may expect from it, nor can make a comparison between his own strength and the dangers he is about to encounter. Such circumstances, however, rarely occur in a state of nature, in which all things proceed in a uniform manner, and the face of the earth is not subject to those sudden and continual changes which arise from the passions and caprices of bodies of men living together. But savage man, living dispersed among other animals, and finding himself betimes in a situation to measure his strength with theirs, soon comes to compare himself with them; and, perceiving that he surpasses them more in adroitness than they surpass him in strength, learns to be no longer afraid of them. . . .

With respect to sickness, I shall not repeat the vain and false declamations which most healthy people pronounce against medicine; but I shall ask if any solid observations have been made from which it may be justly concluded that, in the countries where the art of medicine is most neglected, the mean duration of man's life is less than in those where it is most cultivated. How indeed can this be the case, if we bring on ourselves more diseases than medicine can furnish remedies? The great inequality in manner of living, the extreme idleness of some, and the excessive labour of others, the easiness of exciting and gratifying our sensual appetites, the too exquisite foods of the wealthy which overheat and fill them with indigestion, and, on the other hand, the unwholesome food of the poor, often, bad as it is, insufficient for their needs, which induces them, when opportunity offers, to eat voraciously and overchange their stomachs; all these, together with sitting up late, and excesses of every kind, immoderate transports of every passion, fatigue, mental exhaustion, the innumerable pains and anxieties inseparable from every condition of life, by which the mind of man is incessantly tormented; these are too fatal proofs that the greater part of our ills are of our own making, and that we might have avoided them nearly all by adhering to that simple, uniform and solitary manner of life which nature prescribed. If she destined man to be healthy, I venture to declare that a state of reflection is a state contrary to nature, and that a thinking man is a depraved animal. . . .

[*B*] *From* The Social Contract

I assume, for the sake of argument, that a point was reached in the history of mankind when the obstacles to continuing in a state of Nature were stronger than the forces which each individual could employ to the end of continuing in it. The original state of Nature, therefore, could no longer endure, and the human race would have perished had it not changed its manner of existence.

Now, since men can by no means engender new powers, but can only unite and control those of which they are already possessed, there is no way in which they can maintain themselves save by coming together and pooling their strength in a way that will enable them to withstand any resistance exerted upon them from without. They must develop some sort of central direction and learn to act in concert.

Such a concentration of powers can be brought about only as the consequence of an agreement reached between individuals. But the self-preservation of each single man derives primarily from his own freedom. How, then, can he limit these without, at the same time, doing himself an injury and neglecting that care which it is his duty to devote to his own concerns? This difficulty, in so far as it is relevant to my subject, can be expressed as follows:

'Some form of association must be found as a result of which the whole strength of the community will be enlisted for the protection of the person and property of each constituent member, in such a way that each, when united to his fellows, renders obedience to his own will, and remains as free as he was before.' That is the basic problem of which the Social Contract provides the solution.

The clauses of this Contract are determined by the Act of Association in such a way that the least modification must render them null and void. Even though they may never have been formally enunciated, they must be everywhere the same, and everywhere tacitly admitted and recognized. So completely must this be the case that, should the social compact be violated, each associated individual would at once resume all the rights which once were his, and regain his natural liberty, by the mere fact of losing the agreed liberty for which he renounced it.

It must be clearly understood that the clauses in question can be reduced, in the last analysis, to one only, to wit, the complete alienation by each associate member to the community of *all his rights*. For, in the first place, since each has made surrender of himself without reservation, the resultant conditions are the same for all: and, because they are the same for all, it is in the interest of none to make them onerous to his fellows.

Furthermore, this alienation having been made unreservedly, the union of individuals is as perfect as it well can be, none of the associated members having any claim against the community. For should there be any rights left to individuals, and no common authority be empowered to pronounce as between them and the public, then each, being in some things his own judge, would soon claim to be so in all. Were that so, a state of Nature would still remain in being, the conditions of association becoming either despotic or ineffective.

In short, whoso gives himself to all gives himself to none. And, since there is no member of the social group over whom we do not acquire precisely the same rights as those over ourselves which we have surrendered to him, it follows that we gain the exact equivalent of what we lose, as well as an added power to conserve what we already have.

If, then, we take from the social pact everything which is not essential to it, we shall find it to be reduced to the following terms: 'each of us contributes to the group his person and the powers which he wields as a person, and we receive into the body politic each individual as forming an indivisible part of the whole.'

As soon as the act of association becomes a reality, it substitutes for the person of each of the contracting parties a moral and collective body made up of as many members as the constituting assembly has votes, which body receives from this very act of constitution its unity, its dispersed *self*, and its will. . . .

3. VOLTAIRE STRIKES AT SOME FAVORITE TARGETS

***Voltaire felt only contempt for Rousseau's doctrine that primitive man was "purer" than civilized man (see above). When Rousseau's "Discourse on the Origin of Inequality" appeared, Voltaire wrote him the letter in the first of the following selections. The other selections are extracts from* The Philosophical Dictionary.**

[A] *Voltaire to Rousseau, 1755*

I have received, sir, your new book against the human species, and I thank you for it. You will please people by your manner of telling them the truth about themselves, but you will not alter them. The horrors of that human society—from which in our feebleness and ignorance we expect so many consolations—have never been painted in more striking colours: no one has ever been so witty as you are in trying to turn us into brutes: to read

[A] E.R. Hall (S.G. Tallentyre, pseud.), *Voltaire in His Letters* (New York: G.P. Putnam's Sons, 1919), pp. 149–154. Copyright 1919 by G.P. Putnam's Sons. Used by permission. [B] and [C] *The Philosophical Dictionary* (London and New York: E.R. Dumont, 1901), Vol. III, pp. 49–54; Vol. VIII, 293–295.

your book makes one long to go on all fours. Since, however, it is now some sixty years since I gave up the practice, I feel that it is unfortunately impossible for me to resume it: I leave this natural habit to those more fit for it than are you and I. Nor can I set sail to discover the aborigines of Canada, in the first place because my ill-health ties me to the side of the greatest doctor in Europe, and I should not find the same professional assistance among the Missouris: and secondly because war is going on in that country, and the example of the civilised nations has made the barbarians almost as wicked as we are ourselves. I must confine myself to being a peaceful savage in the retreat I have chosen—close to your country, where you yourself should be.

I agree with you that science and literature have sometimes done a great deal of harm. Tasso's enemies made his life a long series of misfortunes: Galileo's enemies kept him languishing in prison, at seventy years of age. . . .

If I might venture to include myself among those whose works have brought them persecution as their sole recompense, I could tell you of men set on ruining me from the day I produced my tragedy *Œdipe*: of a perfect library of absurd calumnies which have been written against me: of an ex-Jesuit priest whom I saved from utter disgrace rewarding me by defamatory libels: of a man yet more contemptible printing my *Century of Louis XIV* with *Notes* in which crass ignorance gave birth to the most abominable falsehoods: . . .

Confess, sir, that all these things are, after all, but little personal pinpricks, which society scarcely notices. What matter to humankind that a few drones steal the honey of a few bees? Literary men make a great fuss of their petty quarrels: the rest of the world ignores them, or laughs at them.

They are, perhaps, the least serious of all the ills attendant on human life. The thorns inseparable from literature and a modest degree of fame are flowers in comparison with the other evils which from all time have flooded the world. Neither Cicero, Varron, Lucretius, Virgil, or Horace had any part in the proscriptions of Marius, Sulla, that profligate Antony, or that fool Lepidus; while as for that cowardly tyrant, Octavius Caesar—servilely entitled Augustus—he only became an assassin when he was deprived of the society of men of letters.

Confess that Italy owed none of her troubles to Petrarch or to Boccaccio: that Marot's jests were not responsible for the massacre of St. Bartholomew: or the tragedy of the *Cid* for the wars of the Fronde. Great crimes are always committed by great ignoramuses. What makes, and will always make, this world a vale of tears is the insatiable greediness and the indomitable pride of men, from Thomas Koulikan, who did not know how to read, to a customhouse officer who can just count. Letters support, refine, and comfort the soul: they are serving you, sir, at the very moment you decry them: . . .

If anyone has a right to complain of letters, I am that person, for in all times and in all places they have led to my being persecuted: still, we must needs love them in spite of the way they are abused—as we cling to society, though the wicked spoil its pleasantness: as we must love our country, though it treats us unjustly: and as we must love and serve the Supreme Being, despite the superstition and fanaticism which too often dishonour His service.

[*B*] *"On Certainty"*

I am certain: I have friends: my fortune is secure; my relations will never abandon me; I shall have justice done me; my work is good, it will be well received; what is owing to me will be paid; my friend will be faithful, he has sworn it; the minister will advance me—he has, by the way, promised it—all these are words which a man who has lived a short time in the world erases from his dictionary.

There is no certainty, except when it is physically or morally impossible that the thing can be otherwise. What! is a strict demonstration necessary to enable us to assert that the surface of a sphere is equal to four times the area of its great circle; and is not one required to warrant taking away the life of a citizen by a disgraceful punishment?

If such is the misfortune of humanity that judges must be contented with extreme probabilities, they should at least consult the age, the rank, the conduct of the accused—the interest which he could have in committing the crime, and the interest of his enemies to destroy him. Every judge should say to himself: Will not posterity, will not entire Europe condemn my sentence? Shall I sleep tranquilly with my hands tainted with innocent blood? . . .

If you had asked the whole earth before the time of Copernicus: has the sun risen? has it set to-day? all men would have answered: We are quite certain of it. They were certain and they were in error.

Witchcraft, divinations, and possessions were for a long time the most certain things in the world in the eyes of society. What an innumerable crowd of people who have seen all these fine things and who have been certain of them! At present this certainty is a little shaken.

A young man who is beginning to study geometry comes to me; he is only at the definition of triangles. Are you not certain, said I to him, that the three angles of a triangle are equal to two right angles? He answered that not only was he not certain of it, but that he had not the slightest idea of the proposition. I demonstrated it to him. He then became very certain of it, and will remain so all his life. This is a certainty very different from the others; they were only probabilities and these probabilities, when examined, have turned out errors, but mathematical certainty is immutable and eternal.

I exist, I think, I feel grief—is all that as certain as a geometrical truth? Yes, skeptical as I am, I avow it. Why? It is that these truths are proved by the same principle that it is impossible for a thing to exist and not exist at the same time. I cannot at the same time feel and not feel. A triangle cannot at the same time contain a hundred and eighty degrees, which are the sum of two right angles, and not contain them. The physical certainty of my existence, of my identity, is of the same value as mathematical certainty, although it is of a different kind.

It is not the same with the certainty founded on appearances, or on the unanimous testimony of mankind.

But how, you will say to me, are you not certain that Pekin exists? Have you not merchandise from Pekin? People of different countries and different opinions have vehemently written against one another while preaching the truth at Pekin; then are you not assured of the existence of this town? I answer that it is extremely probable that there may be a city of Pekin but I would not wager my life that such a town exists, and I would at any time wager my life that the three angles of a triangle are equal to two right angles.

[C] *"On the Presbyterians"*

The Anglican religion is predominant only in England and Ireland; Presbyterianism is the established religion of Scotland. This Presbyterianism is nothing more than pure Calvinism, such as once existed in France, and still exists at Geneva.

In comparison with a young and lively French bachelor in divinity, brawling during the morning in the schools of theology, and singing with the ladies in the evening, a Church-of-England divine is a Cato; but this Cato is himself a gallant in presence of the Scottish Presbyterians. The latter affect a solemn walk, a serious demeanor, a large hat, a long robe beneath a short one, and preach through the nose. All churches in which the ecclesiastics are so happy as to receive an annual income of fifty thousand livres, and to be addressed by the people as "my lord," "your grace," or "your eminence," they denominate the whore of Babylon. These gentlemen have also several churches in England, where they maintain the same manners and gravity as in Scotland. It is to them chiefly that the English are indebted for the strict sanctification of Sunday throughout the three kingdoms. They are forbidden either to labor or to amuse themselves. No opera, no concert, no comedy, in London on a Sunday. Even cards are expressly forbidden; and there are only certain people of quality, who are deemed open souls, who play on that day. The rest of the nation attend sermons, taverns, and their small affairs of love.

Although Episcopacy and Presbyterianism predominate in Great Britain, all other opinions are welcome and live tolerably well together, although the various preachers reciprocally detest one another with nearly the same cordiality as a Jansenist damns a Jesuit.

Enter into the Royal Exchange of London, a place more respectable than many courts, in which deputies from all nations assemble for the advantage of mankind. There the Jew, the Mahometan, and the Christian bargain with one another as if they were of the same religion, and bestow the name of infidel on bankrupts only. There the Presbyterian gives credit to the Anabaptist, and the votary of the establishment accepts the promise of the Quaker. On the separation of these free and pacific assemblies, some visit the synagogue, others repair to the tavern. Here one proceeds to baptize his son in a great tub, in the name of the Father, Son, and Holy Ghost; there another deprives his boy of a small portion of his foreskin, and mutters over the child some Hebrew words which he cannot understand; a third kind hasten to their chapels to wait for the inspiration of the Lord with their hats on; and all are content.

Was there in London but one religion, despotism might be apprehended; if two only, they would seek to cut each other's throats; but as there are at least thirty, they live together in peace and happiness.

4. DIDEROT TELLS WHAT MAKES A PHILOSOPHE

***While Diderot does not possess the stature of Montesquieu, Rousseau, or Voltaire, his importance in the "Enlightenment" is considerable. He was the principal editor of the great literary monument of the century, the* Encyclopédie, *and the author of several influential philosophical works. The excerpt below is from the* Encyclopédie.**

There is nothing which costs less to acquire nowadays than the name of *Philosopher;* an obscure and retired life, some outward signs of wisdom, with a little reading, suffice to attach this name to persons who enjoy the honor without meriting it.

Translations and Reprints from the Original Sources of European History (Philadelphia: University of Pennsylvania, 1900), Series I, Vol. VI, No. 1, pp. 20–22.

Others in whom freedom of thought takes the place of reasoning, regard themselves as the only true philosophers, because they have dared to overturn the consecrated limits placed by religion, and have broken the fetters which faith laid upon their reason. Proud of having gotten rid of the prejudices of education, in the matter of religion, they look upon others with scorn as feeble souls, servile and pusillanimous spirits, who allow themselves to be frightened by the consequences to which irreligion leads, and who, not daring to emerge for an instant from the circle of established verities, nor to proceed along unaccustomed paths, sink to sleep under the yoke of superstition. But one ought to have a more adequate idea of the philosopher, and here is the character which we give him:

Other men make up their minds to act without thinking, nor are they conscious of the causes which move them, not even knowing that such exist. The philosopher, on the contrary, distinguishes the causes to what extent he may, and often anticipates them, and knowingly surrenders himself to them. In this manner he avoids objects that may cause him sensations that are not conducive to his well being or his rational existence, and seeks those which may excite in him affections agreeable with the state in which he finds himself. Reason is in the estimation of the philosopher what grace is to the Christian. Grace determines the Christian's action; reason the philosopher's.

Other men are carried away by their passions, so that the acts which they produce do not proceed from reflection. These are the men who move in darkness; while the philosopher, even in his passions, moves only after reflection. He marches at night, but a torch goes on ahead.

The philosopher forms his principles upon an infinity of individual observations. The people adopt the principle without a thought of the observations which have produced it, believing that the maxim exists, so to speak, of itself; but the philosopher takes the maxim at its source, he examines its origin, he knows its real value, and only makes use of it, if it seems to him satisfactory.

Truth is not for the philosopher a mistress who vitiates his imagination, and whom he believes to find everywhere. He contents himself with being able to discover it wherever he may chance to find it. He does not confound it with its semblance; but takes for true that which is true, for false that which is false, for doubtful that which is doubtful, and for probable that which is only probable. He does more—and this is the great perfection of philosophy; that when he has no real grounds for passing judgment, he knows how to remain undetermined.

The philosopher is then an honest man, actuated in everything by reason. . . .

VII

LIBERAL AND NATIONALIST UPHEAVALS

28

THE FRENCH REVOLUTION

The French Revolution is an event of transcendent importance not only in French history but in world history as well. Many of the basic movements which have determined nineteenth and twentieth century history stem in whole or in part from the French Revolution: liberalism, radicalism, nationalism, among others. The men of 1789 and 1792 pointed the way to the type of liberal, democratic, and secular state which is today taken for granted in the Western World. Until the Bolshevik Revolution of 1917 evoked a whole new set of competing and contradictory values, no single event in European history could compare in world importance with the French Revolution.

1. THE ESTATES GENERAL IS TRANSFORMED INTO A NATIONAL ASSEMBLY

The Estates General of 1789 was originally designed by its aristocratic initiators to advance the interests of the privileged classes as against the monarchy. However, the deputies of the Third Estate transformed the medieval Estates into a modern assembly representing not classes but the nation. The three selections below help to show how this came about. Note in the first selection the reluctance of the bourgeois deputies to play the part of revolutionaries.

[A] Bailly, *Mémoires,* and [C] Letter of Jefferson to John Jay, both as found in E.L. Higgins, *The French Revolution as Told by Contemporaries* (Boston: Houghton Mifflin Company, 1939), p. 82 and pp. 88–89. Copyright 1938 by E.L. Higgins. The selections from E.L. Higgins, *The French Revolution as Told by Contemporaries,* are reprinted by permission of and arrangement with Houghton Mifflin Company, the authorized publishers. [B] J.H. Stewart, *A Documentary Survey of the French Revolution* (New York: The Macmillan Company, 1951), p. 88. Copyright 1951 by The Macmillan Company. Used by permission.

[*A*] *A Name Is Sought for the Assembly*

One debated the great question of deciding in what manner and under what form the assembly should constitute itself; some wished it to declare itself the *Nation;* M. de Mirabeau proposed the denomination of *Representatives of the French People.* M. Mounier proposed the constitution of a *Lawful Assembly of the Representatives of the Greater Part of the Nation Acting in the Absence of the Minor Part;* M. Pison du Garland, *The Active and Lawful Assembly of the Representatives of the French Nation;* M. Barère de Vieuzac, deputy of Bigorre, *The Representatives of the Much Greater Part of the French in the National Assembly.* Messieurs Target, Biauzat, and Rabaut Saint-Etienne likewise proposed plans of constitution more or less similar to the first; others, *The Representatives of Almost the Whole of the French People;* another, *The Representatives of Twenty-Four Million Men;* and finally M. de Grand, the denomination of *National Assembly.*

[*B*] *The Tennis Court Oath*

The National Assembly, considering that it has been summoned to establish the constitution of the kingdom, to effect the regeneration of public order, and to maintain the true principles of monarchy; that nothing can prevent it from continuing its deliberations in whatever place it may be forced to establish itself; and, finally, that wheresoever its members are assembled, *there* is the National Assembly;

Decrees that all members of this Assembly shall immediately take a solemn oath not to separate, and to reassemble wherever circumstances require, until the constitution of the kingdom is established and consolidated upon firm foundations; and that, the said oath taken, all members and each one of them individually shall ratify this steadfast resolution by signature.

[*C*] *Thomas Jefferson Tells How the King Yielded to the Third Estate*

I have before mentioned . . . the ferment into which the proceedings at the *séance royale* of [July] 23rd had thrown the people. The soldiery was also affected by it. It began in the French guards, extended to those of every other denomination (except the Swiss), and even to the bodyguards of the king. They began to quit their barracks, to assemble in squads, to declare they would defend the life of the king, but would not cut the throats of their fellow citizens. . . . Similar accounts came in from the troops in other parts of the kingdom, as well from those which had not heard of the *séance royale,* as those which had, and gave good reason to apprehend that the soldiery, in general, would side with their fathers and brothers, rather than with their officers. The operation of this medicine, at

Versailles, was as sudden as it was powerful. The alarm there was so complete that in the afternoon of the 27th the king wrote a letter to the president of the clergy, the Cardinal de La Rochefoucauld, in these words:

MY COUSIN: Wholly engaged in promoting the general good of the kingdom, and desirous, above all things, that the Assembly of the States-General should apply themselves to objects of general interest, after the voluntary acceptance by your order of my declaration of the 23rd of the present month, I pass my word that my faithful clergy will, without delay, unite themselves with the other two orders, to hasten the accomplishment of my paternal views. Those, whose powers are too limited, may decline voting until new powers are procured. This will be a new mark of attachment which my clergy will give me. I pray God, my Cousin, to have you in His holy keeping.

LOUIS

A like letter was written to the Duc de Luxembourg, president of the *noblesse.* The two chambers entered into debate on the question, whether they should obey the letter of the king. There was considerable opposition; when notes written by the Comte d'Artois to sundry members, and handed about among the rest, decided the matter, and they went in a body and took their seats with the *Tiers,* and thus rendered the union of the orders in one chamber complete. As soon as this was known to the people of Versailles, they assembled about the palace, demanded the king and queen, who came and showed themselves in a balcony. They rent the skies with cries of "*Vive le roi!*"—"*Vive la reine!*" They called for the dauphin, who was also produced, and was the subject of new acclamations. . . . Similar emotions of joy took place in Paris, and at this moment the triumph of the *Tiers* is considered as complete.

2. *THE NATIONAL (CONSTITUENT) ASSEMBLY RECONSTRUCTS FRANCE*

From July, 1789, until its dissolution in September, 1791, the Assembly worked to "regenerate" France. The principles of the Age of Reason began to be translated into reality. Time-sanctioned customs and institutions were given short shrift. Following are some of the more important acts of the Assembly.

[A] *Feudalism Abolished, August 4, 1789*

1. The National Assembly . . . decrees that feudal rights and dues deriving from real or personal *mainmorte* and personal servitude, and those

[A], [B], [C], and [D] J.H. Stewart, *A Documentary Survey of the French Revolution* (New York: The Macmillan Company, 1951), pp. 107–110, 113–115, 142–143, and 174–176. Copyright 1951 by The Macmillan Company. Used by permission. [E] E.L. Higgins, *The French Revolution as Told by Contemporaries* (Boston: Houghton Mifflin Company, 1939), pp. 153–155. Copyright 1938 by E.L. Higgins. The selection from E.L. Higgins, *The French Revolution as Told by Contemporaries,* is reprinted by permission of and arrangement with Houghton Mifflin Company, the authorized publishers.

representative thereof, are abolished without indemnity, and all others declared redeemable; . . .

2. . . . pigeons shall be confined at times determined by the communities; and during such periods they shall be regarded as game, and everyone shall have the right to kill them on his own land.

3. The exclusive right of hunting and open warrens is likewise abolished; and every proprietor has the right to destroy and to have destroyed, on his own property only, every kind of game. . . .

4. All seigneurial courts of justice are suppressed without any indemnity; . . .

5. Tithes of every kind and dues which take the place thereof . . . are abolished. . . .

7. Venality of judicial and municipal offices is suppressed henceforth. Justice shall be rendered gratuitously; . . .

9. Pecuniary privileges, personal or real, in matters of taxation are abolished forever. . . .

11. All citizens may be admitted, without distinction of birth, to all ecclesiastical, civil, and military employments and offices, and no useful profession shall entail forfeiture.

12. In the future no *deniers* for annates or for any other cause whatsoever shall be dispatched to the court of Rome. . . .

14. Plurality of benefices shall no longer exist when the revenues of the benefice or benefices of an incumbent exceed the sum of 3,000 *livres*. . . .

16. The National Assembly decrees that, in memory of the impressive and momentous deliberations just held for the welfare of France, a medal shall be struck, and that, as an expression of gratitude, a *Te Deum* shall be sung in all parishes and churches of the kingdom.

17. The National Assembly solemnly proclaims King Louis XVI *Restorer of French Liberty.*

18. The National Assembly shall repair *en masse* to the King to present to His Majesty the decree just pronounced, to bear him the homage of its most respectful gratitude, and to supplicate him to permit the *Te Deum* to be sung in his chapel, and to be present there himself. . . .

[*B*] *Declaration of the Rights of Man, August 27, 1789*

The National Assembly recognizes and proclaims in the presence and under the auspices of the Supreme Being, the following rights of man and citizen.

1. Men are born and remain free and equal in rights; social distinctions may be based only upon general usefulness.

2. The aim of every political association is the preservation of the natural and inalienable rights of man; these rights are liberty, property, security, and resistance to oppression.

3. The source of all sovereignty resides essentially in the nation; no group, no individual may exercise authority not emanating expressly therefrom.

4. Liberty consists of the power to do whatever is not injurious to others; thus the enjoyment of the natural rights of every man has for its limits only those that assure other members of society the enjoyment of those same rights; such limits may be determined only by law.

5. The law has the right to forbid only actions which are injurious to society. Whatever is not forbidden by law may not be prevented, and no one may be constrained to do what it does not prescribe.

6. Law is the expression of the general will; all citizens have the right to concur personally, or through their representatives, in its formation; it must be the same for all, whether it protects or punishes. All citizens, being equal before it, are equally admissible to all public offices, positions, and employments, according to their capacity, and without other distinction than that of virtues and talents.

7. No man may be accused, arrested, or detained except in the cases determined by law, and according to the forms prescribed thereby. . . .

8. The law is to establish only penalties that are absolutely and obviously necessary; and no one may be punished except by virtue of a law established and promulgated prior to the offence and legally applied.

9. Since every man is presumed innocent until declared guilty, if arrest be deemed indispensable, all unnecessary severity for securing the person of the accused must be severely repressed by law.

10. No one is to be disquieted because of his opinions, even religious, provided their manifestation does not disturb the public order established by law.

11. Free communication of ideas and opinions is one of the most precious of the rights of man. Consequently, every citizen may speak, write, and print freely, subject to responsibility for the abuse of such liberty in the cases determined by law. . . .

14. Citizens have the right to ascertain, by themselves or through their representatives, the necessity of the public tax, to consent to it freely, to supervise its use, and to determine its quota, assessment, payment, and duration. . . .

17. Since property is a sacred and inviolable right, no one may be deprived thereof unless a legally established public necessity obviously requires it, and upon condition of a just and previous indemnity.

[*C*] *Hereditary Nobility and Titles Abolished, June 19, 1790*

1. Hereditary nobility is abolished forever; accordingly, the titles of prince, duke, count, marquis, viscount, *vidame*, baron, knight, *messire*, squire, noble, and all other similar titles shall neither be accepted by nor bestowed upon anyone whomsoever.

2. A citizen may assume only his real family name; no one may wear liveries or have them worn, or have coats of arms; incense shall be burned in the churches only to honor the Divinity, and shall not be offered to any person whomsoever.

3. The titles of *monseigneur* and *messeigneurs* shall not be bestowed upon any group or individual; likewise, the titles of excellency, highness, eminence, grace, etc.; . . .

[*D*] *The Civil Constitution of the Clergy, July 12, 1790*

1. Dating from the day of publication of the present decree, appointments to bishoprics and cures are to be made by election only.

2. All elections shall be by ballot and absolute majority of votes.

3. The election of bishops shall take place according to the form prescribed by . . . the decree of 22 December, 1789, for the appointment of members of the departmental assembly. . . .

7. To be eligible for a bishopric, one must have performed for at least fifteen years the duties of ecclesiastical ministry in the diocese, in the capacity of *curé*, officiating minister or vicar, or as superior or directing vicar of the seminary. . . .

16. Not later than a month subsequent to his election, the bishop-elect shall present himself in person to his metropolitan bishop; and if elected to the metropolitan see, to the oldest bishop of the *arrondissement*, with the *procès-verbal* of the election and proclamation, and shall request him to grant canonical confirmation.

17. The metropolitan or the senior bishop shall have the right to examine the bishop-elect, in the presence of his council, concerning his doctrine and morals. If he considers him qualified, he shall give him canonical institution; if he believes it his duty to refuse, the reasons for such refusal shall be given in writing, signed by the metropolitan bishop and his council, reserving to the interested parties the right to appeal by writ of error as provided hereinafter. . . .

19. The new bishop may not apply to the Pope for confirmation, but shall write to him as the Visible Head of the Universal Church, in testimony of the unity of faith and communion which he is to maintain therewith. . . .

21. Before the ceremony of consecration begins, the bishop-elect shall

take a solemn oath, in the presence of the municipal officials, the people, and the clergy, to watch with care over the faithful of the diocese entrusted to him, to be faithful to the nation, to the law, and to the King, and to maintain with all his power the Constitution decreed by the National Assembly and accepted by the King. . . .

25. The election of *curés* shall be conducted according to the forms prescribed by, and by the electors designated in, the decree of 22 December, 1789, for the election of members of the district administrative assembly. . . .

[*E*] *The New National Spirit: the Festival of July 14, 1790*

More than three hundred thousand people of both sexes, from Paris and the environs, had been assembled since six in the morning at the Champ-de-Mars. Sitting on turf seats, which formed an immense circus, drenched, draggled, sheltering themselves with parasols from the torrents of rain which descended upon them, and at the least ray of sunshine adjusting their dresses, they waited, laughing and chatting, for the federates and the National Assembly. A spacious amphitheater had been erected for the king, the royal family, the ambassadors, and the deputies. The federates, who first arrived, began to dance *farandoles*; those who followed joined them, forming a round which soon embraced part of the Champ-de-Mars. A sight worthy of the philosophic observer was that exhibited by this host of men, who had come from the most opposite parts of France, hurried away by the impulse of the national character, banishing all remembrance of the past, all idea of the present, all fear of the future, and indulging in a delicious thoughtlessness. Three hundred thousand spectators, of all ages and of both sexes, followed their motions, beating time with their hands, forgetting the rain, hunger, and the weariness of long waiting. At length, the whole procession having entered the Champ-de-Mars, the dance ceased, each federate repaired to his banner. The Bishop of Autun prepared to perform mass at an altar in the antique style, erected in the center of the Champ-de-Mars. Three hundred priests in white surplices, girt with broad tri-colored scarfs, ranged themselves at the four corners of the altar. The Bishop of Autun blessed the oriflamme and the eighty-three banners: he struck up the *Te Deum.* Twelve hundred musicians played that hymn. . . .

. . . The federates, before they quitted the capital, went to pay homage to the king: all of them testified the most profound respect, the warmest attachment. The chief of the Bretons dropped on his knee, and presented his sword to Louis XVI. "Sire," said he, "I deliver to you, pure and sacred, the sword of the faithful Bretons: it shall never be stained but with the blood of your enemies." "That sword cannot be in better hands than those of my dear Bretons," replied Louis XVI, raising the chief of the Bretons, and returning him his sword. . . . A mutual emotion prolonged for some moments this touching scene. The chief of the Bretons was the first to speak. "Sire," said he, "all the French, if I may judge from our hearts, love and will love you, because you are a citizen king."

3. *THE CONSTITUTIONAL MONARCHY IS OVERTHROWN, AUGUST 10, 1792*

The constitutional monarchy created in September, 1791, lasted less than a year. For one thing, Louis XVI was widely, and rightly, suspected of treasonous activity. For another, despite the "free and equal" clause of the Declaration of the Rights of Man, the Constitution of 1791 denied full political rights to about half the adult males of France. On August 10, 1792, occurred the "Second French Revolution" which led to the deposition of the King and the proclamation of a democratic republic. The following accounts of the attack on the King's palace and the September Massacres are by eyewitnesses.

[A] *The Attack on the Tuileries*

Nobles and persons attached to the king had come in great numbers to the palace, armed with swords and pistols. Their intention can only be praised; it was excellent; but one must disapprove of their action and avow that armed as they were they could only embarrass the defense and inspire distrust in the national guard.

At eleven o'clock in the evening [August 9, 1792], the information was received that the tocsin would sound at midnight. A little later it was known at the palace that the Faubourg Saint-Antoine had passed a resolution of which the principal articles were "to attack the palace; exterminate everybody, with particular attention to the Swiss; force the king to abdicate; and conduct the king, queen, and royal family to Vincennes to serve as hostages in case the foreigners launched themselves upon Paris."

At midnight, the tocsin was heard to sound. . . .

. . . At two in the morning, four battalions from the faubourgs had already arrived on the Place du Carrousel. They were ready to execute their horrible projects and only awaited their comrades.

Between four and five o'clock, M. Mandat [in charge of the defense of

[A] Colonel Pfyffer d'Altishoffen, *Récit*, and [B] Ferrières, *Mémoires*, both as found in E.L. Higgins, *The French Revolution as Told by Contemporaries* (Boston: Houghton Mifflin Company, 1939), pp. 238–240 and pp. 249–250.

the Tuileries] received an order to go to the commune. They were waiting to cut his throat on the steps of the Hôtel de Ville. They knew that he had in his pocket an order signed by Pétion [mayor of Paris] authorizing him to repel force with force, and were willing to employ murder to keep this written document from becoming public. . . .

Between eight and nine o'clock, the king decided to repair to the midst of the National Assembly. He was accompanied by all the royal family and some of the nobles. . . .

The army of Santerre put itself into movement, preceded by cannon, and soon was seen advancing towards the gates of the palace. . . .

Here is the state of things at the moment the combat was about to begin. There were seven hundred and fifty Swiss distributed over more than twenty posts, two hundred noblemen without arms, and some national guards who had remained faithful. Without commander-in-chief, without munitions, and without cannon, they were attacked from all sides by nearly a hundred thousand furious people having with them fifty pieces of artillery. This mob felt that it was encouraged by the legislative body, and that it was in control of the municipality.

The troops of Santerre let loose a discharge that wounded several soldiers. The Filles-Saint-Thomas grenadiers replied, followed by the Swiss. . . .

The action became general. It was soon decided in favor of the Swiss; the fire from the windows and that of M. de Durler's reserve had been deadly. In a short time the court found itself evacuated, heaped with dead, dying, and wounded. . . .

But the Swiss saw with anxiety that the moment was approaching when lack of munitions would leave them exposed to the fire of the enemy, without means of responding to it.

At this critical moment, M. d'Hervilly (since dead for the royal cause at Quiberon) arrived without arms, hatless, through musket and cannon fire. [The officers] wished to show him the dispositions that had just been made on the side of the garden. "Never mind that," he said. "You have to betake yourselves to the Assembly." . . .

Finally they arrived in the corridors of the National Assembly. The Baron de Salis, becoming too ardent, entered the hall of the legislative body sword in hand, to the great fright of the Left of the Assembly. The deputies there cried out, "The Swiss, the Swiss!" and several sought to escape through the windows.

A deputy came to order the commander to lay down his arms; he refused to do so. M. de Durler was brought before His Majesty. He said to the king, "Sire, they want us to lay down our arms." The king replied, "Yield them to the national guard; I do not want brave men like you to perish." A moment afterwards, the king sent him a note in his own writing conceived in these terms: "The king orders the Swiss to lay down their arms and retire to the barracks." This order was a thunderbolt to these brave soldiers. They cried out that they could still defend themselves with the bayonet. Several cried with rage, but in this frightful extremity discipline and fidelity prevailed. All obeyed.

This order to abandon their weapons and deliver themselves over defenseless to tigers thirsting for their blood was the final sacrifice demanded of the Swiss. . . .

The palace being no longer defended, the army of Santerre entered it, and began a cowardly massacring of the wounded and those who had lost their way in the immensity of the palace. . . .

[*B*] *The September Massacres Begin*

While the commissaries of the commune inflame the populace by recitals of imaginary facts, and inspire all hearts with the fury which animates them, two or three hundred scoundrels repair to Les Carmes and to Saint-Germain to murder four hundred priests. They go next to the Abbaye, and soon the cries of the dying, mingled with the shrieks of the people as they call incessantly for new victims, bring terror to the souls of the prisoners. Each awaits in tortured anxiety the instant that is to mark his fate. . . .

The commune, seeking to give this horrible butchery the semblance of popular justice, hastily organizes a tribunal in each prison. He who presides [Maillard] has a long sword at his side; he sits before a table strewn with papers, pipes, and bottles. A dozen men compose the monstrous jury. Some, in workmen's blouses, remain standing. Others lie upon benches, dozing with fatigue and drunkenness. Three cutthroats bring in each prisoner. Their sabers cross his breast and he is warned that at the least movement he will be pierced. Two butchers with naked swords and their sleeves rolled up, their shirts spotted with blood, guard the door. The jailer has his hand on the bolts that secure it. A candle in the middle of the table adds shadowed somberness to the scene. Its wavering light is reflected on the sinister faces of the judges, and reveals their fierce and hideous features. "Your name and your profession," comes in harsh tones from the president. "Take care; a lie will be your ruin."

No plea can save the designated victim. A man of sixty is presented as the president consults his jail-book. Two national guards appear to speak for the accused in the name of the Croix-Rouge section. They insist that he has always been a good citizen. "Recommendations are useless in the case of traitors," says the president shortly. "But that is horrible," the man cries out. "Your trial is an assassination." "My hands have been washed of it," the president replies. "Please conduct the gentleman." He is hustled out into the court and slaughtered.

4. TERROR DECLARED THE ORDER OF THE DAY

The Reign of Terror extended from September, 1793, to the overthrow of Robespierre, July 27, 1794. It was motivated by many considerations: the intrigues of the* émigrés; *the imminent danger of invasion by the foreign coalition; civil war in several parts of France; a desperate economic situation which demanded scapegoats. At least 15,000 people were put to death during the Terror.

[A] *A Parisian Newspaper Justifies the Principle of Terror*

Yes, terror is the order of the day, and ought to be for the selfish, for the federalists, for the heartless rich, for dishonest opportunists, for shameless intriguers, for unpatriotic cowards, for all who do not feel the dignity of being free men and pure republicans. Rivers of blood have been shed for the gold of Peru and the diamonds of Golconda. Well! Does not liberty, that inestimable blessing which one would surely not tarnish by comparing it with the vile metals of the Indies, have the same right to sacrifice lives, fortunes, and even, for a time, individual liberties? In the thick of battle is there any foolish wailing over the soldiers fallen from the ranks? They are promptly replaced by others, and with the perfidious aggressor repulsed, one is free to weep over the unfortunate victims mowed down on the field of battle. Is not the French Revolution just such a deadly combat, a war to the death between those who want to be free and those content to be slaves? This is the situation, and the French people have gone too far to retreat with honor and safety. There is no middle ground; France must be entirely free or perish in the attempt, and any means are justifiable in fighting for so fine a cause. But our resources are being exhausted, say some. Well, when the Revolution is finished, they will be replenished by peace. A free people, as long as they have weapons and hands, can fight their enemies and plow their fields. . . .

[A] *Révolutions de Paris, No. 212,* as found in E.L. Higgins, *The French Revolution as Told by Contemporaries* (Boston: Houghton Mifflin Company, 1939), pp. 306–307. [B] and [C] J.H. Stewart, *A Documentary Survey of the French Revolution* (New York: The Macmillan Company, 1951), pp. 472–474 and pp. 477–478.

[*B*] ***Defense of the Republic: the Levy en masse, August 23, 1793***

1. Henceforth, until the enemies have been driven from the territory of the Republic, the French people are in permanent requisition for army service.

The young men shall go to battle; the married men shall forge arms and transport provisions; the women shall make tents and clothes, and shall serve in the hospitals; the children shall turn old linen into lint; the old men shall repair to the public places, to stimulate the courage of the warriors and preach the unity of the Republic and hatred of kings.

2. National buildings shall be converted into barracks; public places into armament workshops; the soil of cellars shall be washed in lye to extract saltpeter therefrom.

3. Arms of caliber shall be turned over exclusively to those who march against the enemy; the service of the interior shall be carried on with fowling pieces and sabers.

5. The Committee of Public Safety is charged with taking all measures necessary for establishing, without delay, a special manufacture of arms of all kinds, in harmony with the *élan* and the energy of the French people. . . .

11. The battalion organized in each district shall be united under a banner bearing the inscription: *The French people risen against tyrants*. . . .

[*C*] ***The Law of Suspects, September 17, 1793***

1. Immediately after the publication of the present decree, all suspected persons within the territory of the Republic and still at liberty shall be placed in custody.

2. The following are deemed suspected persons: 1st, those who, by their conduct, associations, talk, or writings have shown themselves partisans of tyranny or federalism and enemies of liberty; 2nd, those who are unable to justify, in the manner prescribed by the decree of 21 March last, their means of existence and the performance of their civic duties; 3rd, those to whom certificates of patriotism have been refused; 4th, public functionaries suspended or dismissed from their positions by the National Convention or by its commissioners, and not reinstated, especially those who have been or are to be dismissed by virtue of the decree of 14 August last; 5th, those former nobles, husbands, wives, fathers, mothers, sons or daughters, brothers or sisters, and agents of the *émigrés*, who have not steadily manifested their devotion to the Revolution; 6th, those who have emigrated during the interval between 1 July, 1789, and the publication of the decree of 30 March–8 April, 1792, even though they have returned to France within the period established by said decree or prior thereto. . . .

5. Individuals arrested as suspects shall be taken first to the jails of the place of their detention; in default of jails, they shall be kept under surveillance in their respective dwellings.

6. Within the following week, they shall be transferred to national buildings, which the departmental administrations shall be required to designate and to have prepared for such purpose immediately after the receipt of the present decree. . . .

5. *THE CONVENTION TURNS AGAINST ROBESPIERRE*

The virtual dictator of France in the latter months of the Reign of Terror was Robespierre. But as no member of the Convention could be certain when his turn on the guillotine would be next, the inevitable conspiracy formed against Robespierre. He was seized on July 27, 1794, and quickly guillotined. His death brought the Terror to an end. Following is a contemporary account of the famous session of 9 Thermidor.

. . . Robespierre, whose rage may easily be imagined, rushes to the rostrum, thinking to overawe them with the imperious tone that has always been successful. But the charm has been broken; all have been convinced, and from every side they cry at him, "Down with the tyrant!" Overwhelmed by this terrible word, he drops his head, and descends several steps. Still they discuss his crimes, and he begins to suffer torture. . . .

The orator, after comparing Robespierre to Catiline, and his followers to Verres, demands that there be no adjournment until the glaive of the law has safeguarded the Revolution by arresting Hanriot. These two propositions are decreed, and acclaimed by the Assembly and the people amidst cries of "Long live the Republic!" . . .

Robespierre attempts to speak; but a member rises and puts forward new grievances. . . .

Robespierre once more presents himself at the rostrum, but is met by a unanimous cry of indignation. He persists, acting in a furious fashion. "Down with the tyrant" re-echoes on all sides. He turns around for a moment towards Saint-Just, whose attitude shows his despair at being unmasked, and is little calculated to encourage him; he obstinately persists in his attempt to speak, but all members cry out at him anew, "Down with the tyrant!" . . .

Robespierre, tortured in conscience, becomes greatly agitated and cries

E.L. Higgins, *The French Revolution as Told by Contemporaries* (Boston: Houghton Mifflin Company, 1939), pp. 357–359.

out that they are bringing his death. "You deserve a thousand deaths," says a member. The younger Robespierre now joins his brother and asks to share his fate. With eyes that gleam with frenzy, and in despair of dominating by affected calm, they reveal the hidden depths of their souls. They abuse the National Convention; they insult; they menace. A general indignation arises in reply to the cries of these madmen; the turmoil steadily increases; the president covers himself. The elder Robespierre, profiting by the moment of silence which always follows this act, denounces the president and the members of the Assembly in the most abusive terms. There is a violent hub-bub of murmurs and the National Convention rises as one man. Members demand the arrest of this man who dares to attack the majesty of the people in the person of its representatives. Another cries out that Robespierre has incontestably been a tyrant, and for that alone should have his arrest decreed. All are demanding the arrest of the two brothers. . . .

. . . Robespierre threatens and struggles in vain; he tries various points of the chamber; in vain with furious looks he ascends and descends the steps of the rostrum where he has reigned so long as despot. A violent hatred of tyranny is exhaled from every soul, enveloping him in an atmosphere where he can no longer breathe. He falls gasping upon a seat, and there the indignation of republicans holds him as if enchained. His arrest, and that of his brother, are demanded on all sides. This is finally decreed amid numerous and violent bursts of applause.

"The National Convention decrees the immediate arrest of Maximilien Robespierre, one of its members. . . ."

29

NAPOLEON

The period from 1799 to 1814 is usually labeled the "Napoleonic Era." No man has come closer to mastering all of Europe than Napoleon. In France he instituted a government based on the new catchwords of order, stability, and moderation. The individual liberties guaranteed earlier by the Declaration of the Rights of Man were largely disregarded, but the social gains of the Revolution—notably equality before the law and the abolition of feudalism—were preserved. Making use of national patriotism and national armies created by the Revolution, he spread many of the ideas and institutions of revolutionary France throughout the Continent. Whatever they thought of Napoleon, the European peoples would never be quite the same thereafter.

1. NAPOLEON GIVES HIS VERSION OF THE COUP OF BRUMAIRE

The following account of the* coup d'état *of November 10, 1799, which put Napoleon in power as consul, is taken from Napoleon's* Memoirs *written at St. Helena. It is a somewhat colored version of the occurrence. Instead of remaining the calm master of the situation, as he claims, Napoleon lost his nerve completely and was carried half-fainting from the Council of Five Hundred, the lower house of the legislature. It was his brother Lucien, the president of the Council, who saved the day for Napoleon.

Napoleon . . . entered the Council of Ancients [the upper house of the legislature], and placed himself at the bar, opposite to the president:

"You stand," said he, "upon a volcano; the Republic no longer possesses

Memoirs of the History of France During the Reign of Napoleon, Dictated by the Emperor (London: Henry Colburn and Co., and Martin Bossange and Co., 1823), Vol. I, pp. 92–98.

a government; the Directory is dissolved; factions are at work; the hour of decision is come. You have called in my arm, and the arms of my comrades, to the support of your wisdom: but the moments are precious; . . . I desire nothing but the safety of the Republic. . . .

Upon this a member (Linglet) rose and said with a loud voice, "General, we applaud what you say; swear then, with us, obedience to the Constitution of the year III. which alone can preserve the Republic."

The astonishment caused by these words produced the most profound silence.

Napoleon recollected himself for a moment; and then went on again emphatically: "The Constitution of the year III.!—you have it no longer—you violated it on the eighteenth of Fructidor, when the Government infringed on the independence of the Legislative Body; you violated it on the thirtieth of Prairial, in the year VII., when the Legislative Body struck at the independence of the Government; you violated it on the twenty-second of Floréal, when, by a sacrilegious decree, the Government and the Legislative Body invaded the sovereignty of the people, by annulling the elections made by them. The Constitution being violated, there must be a new compact, new guarantees."

The force of this speech, and the energy of the General, brought over three-fourths of the members of Council, who rose to indicate their approbation. . . . At this moment Napoleon was informed that [the Council of Five Hundred was] endeavouring to force the president Lucien to put the outlawry of his brother to the vote. Napoleon immediately hastened to the Five Hundred, entered the chamber with his hat off, and ordered the officers and soldiers who accompanied him to remain at the doors: he was desirous to present himself at the bar, to rally his party, which was numerous, but which had lost all unity and resolution. But to get to the bar, it was necessary to cross half the chamber, because the President had his seat on one of the wings. When Napoleon had advanced alone across one-third of the orangery, two or three hundred members suddenly rose, crying, "Death to the tyrant! down with the dictator!"

Two grenadiers, who, by the order of the General, had remained at the door, and who had reluctantly obeyed, saying to him, "You do not know them, they are capable of any thing!" rushed in, sabre in hand, overthrowing all that opposed their passage, to join the General, and cover him with their bodies. All the other grenadiers followed this example, and forced Napoleon out of the chamber. . . .

The General descended into the court-yard, called the troops into a circle by beat of drum, got on horseback, and harangued them: "I was about," said he, "to point out to them the means of saving the Republic, and restoring our glory. They answered me with their daggers. It was thus they would have accomplished the wishes of the Allied Kings. What more could England have done? Soldiers, may I rely upon you?"

Unanimous acclamations formed the reply to this speech. Napoleon instantly ordered a captain to go with ten men into the chamber of the Five Hundred, and to liberate the President.

. . . The officer of grenadiers then presented himself at the door of the chamber, exclaiming, "*Vive la Republique!*" . . .

. . . No opposition was offered to the departure of the President, who left the chamber, rushed into the court-yard, mounted a horse, and cried out in his stentorian voice, "General—and you, soldiers—the President of the Council of Five Hundred proclaims to you that factious men, with drawn daggers, have interrupted the deliberations of that assembly. He calls upon you to employ force against these disturbers. The Council of Five Hundred is dissolved."

"President," replied the General, "it shall be done."

He then ordered Murat into the chamber, at the head of a detachment in close column. At this crisis General B—— ventured to ask him for fifty men, in order to place himself in ambuscade upon the way, and fire upon the fugitives. Napoleon replied to this request only by enjoining the grenadiers to commit no excesses. "It is my wish," said he, "that not one drop of blood may be shed."

Murat presented himself at the door, and summoned the Council to disperse. The shouts and vociferations continued. Colonel Moulins, Brune's aide-de-camp, who had just arrived from Holland, ordered the charge to be beaten. The drum put an end to the clamour. The soldiers entered the chamber charging bayonets. The deputies leaped out at the windows, and dispersed, leaving their gowns, caps, &c.: in one moment the chamber was empty.

2. *NAPOLEON PROCLAIMS THE END OF THE FRENCH REVOLUTION*

This is the first proclamation (December 15, 1799) of the new consular government to the French people. Note the emphasis on such words as "property," "strong," "stable," along with the old stand-bys "equality and liberty."

Frenchmen!

A Constitution is presented to you.

It terminates the uncertainties which the provisional government intro-

J.H. Stewart, *A Documentary Survey of the French Revolution* (New York: The Macmillan Company, 1951), p. 780.

duced into external relations, into the internal and military situation of the Republic.

It places in the institutions which it establishes first magistrates whose devotion has appeared necessary for its success.

The Constitution is founded on the true principles of representative government, on the sacred rights of property, equality, and liberty.

The powers which it institutes will be strong and stable, as they must be in order to guarantee the rights of citizens and the interests of the State.

Citizens, the Revolution is established upon the principles which began it: It is ended.

3. *NAPOLEON REGULATES PUBLIC OPINION*

Like all dictators, Napoleon felt it essential to manufacture public opinion favorable to his regime. The great majority of newspapers in Paris were suppressed within a few months of Napoleon's advent to power. Theatrical and literary censorship quickly followed. The importance Napoleon attached to these matters is shown in the ensuing letters.

To Citizen Ripault, Napoleon's Librarian, July 23, 1801

Citizen Ripault is to see that he is supplied every day with all the papers that come out, except the eleven political papers. He will read them carefully, make an abstract of everything they contain likely to influence public opinion, especially with regard to religion, philosophy, and political opinion. He will send me this abstract daily between five and six o'clock.

Once every ten days he will send me an analysis of all the books or pamphlets which have appeared during that period, calling attention to any passages on moral questions. . . .

He will take pains to procure copies of all the plays which are produced, and to analyse them for me, with observations of the same character as those mentioned above. This analysis must be made, at the latest, within forty-eight hours of the production of the plays.

He is to send me every first and sixth day, between five and six o'clock, a list of all the bills, advertisements, etc. which deserve attention, as well as anything that has come to his knowledge, and anything that has been done or said in the various institutes, or important trials, that might be of interest from a political and moral point of view.

The first four letters are from *Correspondance de Napoléon I* (Paris: 1854–1869), Vol. VII, p. 5647; Vol. X, p. 8821; Vol. XI, p. 9243; Vol. XII, p. 10209. The last letter is from L. Lecestre, *Lettres inédites de Napoléon I*er (Paris: 1897), Vol. I, p. 150. Our translation.

To Fouché, June 1, 1805

I would like newspaper editors [to have] enough sense not to publish news harmful to the nation. The attention of the papers ought to be directed toward attacking England—English fashions, English customs, English literature, the English constitution. . . . Voltaire did us great harm by his constant essays in Anglomania.

It seems to me that the success of the tragedy *The Templars* is turning attention to that incident in French history. That is good, but I don't think we ought to allow plays on subjects of too recent a date. I see in one of the papers that there is talk of putting on a tragedy about Henry IV [d. 1610]. That period is not distant enough to rouse no passions. The stage needs a touch of antiquity: and I think that, without interfering with the theater too much, you ought to veto this particular play: but don't make your intervention public. . . .

To Portalis, September 19, 1805

Inform M. Robert, a priest at Bourges, of my displeasure at the extremely bad sermon on August 15.

To Fouché, May 7, 1806

A fourth volume of Millot has just been published, containing all kinds of ridiculous nonsense and harmful to the glory of our arms. It is the height of indecency that such an ignoramus should write in the grand manner about contemporary events. Have the book suppressed. . . .

To Fouché, April 21, 1807

I want you to get up a great agitation . . . against the persecution which the Irish Catholics are suffering at the hands of the Anglican Church. . . . I will get M. Portalis to make private arrangements with some of the bishops, so that, when these newspaper articles have had time to produce their effect, prayers will be offered entreating an end to the persecution. But the administration must move very delicately and make use of the newspapers without their realizing what the government is driving at. . . . You must make people realize the cruelties and indignities committed by England against the Irish Catholics, whom they have been massacring in St. Bartholomew's Eve fashion for the last hundred years. Don't talk of "Protestants": say "the Anglican Church"; for there are Protestants in France, but there are no Anglicans.

4. *FOUCHÉ ORGANIZES THE IMPERIAL SECRET POLICE*

Joseph Fouché was the organizer of a system of secret police which in its ruthless efficiency surpassed anything Europe had previously known. Opportunistic to an incredible degree, devoid of any sense of virtue, he in the end betrayed Napoleon. He tells in this passage how he organized the secret police.

. . . [I reserved] to myself the duty of alone regulating the superior police; . . . It was to the central focus of my cabinet that all the great affairs of state, of which I grasped the strings, finally converged. It will not be doubted, that I had salaried spies in all ranks and all orders; I had them of both sexes, hired at the rate of a thousand or two thousand francs per month, according to their importance and their services. I received their reports directly in writing, having a conventional mark. Every three months, I communicated my list to the emperor, in order that there might be no double employment; and also in order that the nature of the service, occasionally permanent, often temporary, might be rewarded either by places or remunerations. As to the department of foreign police, it had two essential objects, namely, to watch friendly powers, and counteract hostile governments. In both cases, it was composed of individuals purchased or pensioned, and commissioned to reside near each government, or in each principal town, independent of numerous secret agents sent into all countries, either by the minister of foreign affairs, or by the emperor himself.

. . . It was in my department, also, that the foreign gazettes prohibited to the perusal of the French people, and transcripts of which were sent to me, were treasured up. By that means, I held in my hands the most important strings of foreign politics; and I discharged, in conjunction with the chief of the government, a task capable of controlling or balancing that of the minister charged with the function of foreign relations.

I was thus far from limiting my duties to *espionnage*. All the state prisons were under my control, as well as the *gendarmerie*. The delivery and the *visa* of passports belonged to me. To me was assigned the duty of overlooking amnestied individuals and foreigners. I established general commissariats in the principal towns of the kingdom, which extended the network of the police over the whole of France, and especially our frontiers.

My police acquired so high a renown, that the world went so far as to pretend that I had, among my secret agents, three nobles of the *ancien régime*, distinguished by princely titles, and who daily communicated to me the result of their observations.

The Memoirs of Joseph Fouché (Boston: Wells and Lilly, 1825), pp. 195–198.

I confess that such an establishment was expensive; it swallowed up several millions, the funds of which were secretly provided from taxes laid upon gambling and prostitution, and from the granting of passports. . . . I nominated as superintendent-general of the gambling-houses in France, Perrein the elder, who already farmed them, and who, after the coronation, extended his privilege over all the chief towns of the empire, upon condition of paying fourteen millions yearly, independent of three thousand francs daily to the minister of the police. All, however, did not remain in his hands. . . . I succeeded much more by the force of informations and of apprehension, than by restraint and the employment of coercive measures. I revived the ancient police maxim, namely, that three persons could not meet and speak indiscreetly upon public affairs, without its coming the next day to the ears of the minister of police. Certain it is, that I had the address to make it universally believed that where-ever four persons assembled, there, in my pay, were eyes to see and ears to hear. Such a belief, no doubt, tended to general corruption and debasement; but, on the other hand, what evils, what wretchedness, what tears has it prevented? Such then was this vast and terrific machine called the general police of the empire.

5. NAPOLEON WINS A CLASSIC VICTORY: AUSTERLITZ, 1805

The battle from which Napoleon professed to take the greatest satisfaction was one fought on December 2, 1805, near the small Austrian village of Austerlitz. Employing masterful tactics, Napoleon cut in half and routed an Austro-Russian force. The ensuing account is taken from Napoleon's battle orders, official bulletins, and proclamations on the battle.

General Dispositions for the Day of Battle, Issued from the Emperor's Bivouac, 8:30 P.M., December 1, 1805

Marshal Soult will give orders so that his three divisions shall be placed beyond the ravine (Bösenitz Brook) at seven o'clock in the morning, in such a manner as to be ready to commence the manoeuvre of the day, which is to be a march forward by echelons, the right wing leading. Marshal Soult will be personally at half-past seven in the morning near the emperor at his bivouac.

His Highness Prince Murat will give orders to the cavalry of General Kellermann, to that of Generals Walther, Beaumont, Nansouty and Hautpoul,

T.A. Dodge, *Napoleon* (Boston: Houghton Mifflin Company, 1904), Vol. II, pp. 275–307. Copyright 1904 by Theodore Ayrault Dodge. The selection from T.A. Dodge, *Napoleon,* is reprinted by permission of and arrangement with Houghton Mifflin Company, the authorized publishers.

so that the divisions may be placed at seven o'clock in the morning between the left of Marshal Soult and the right of Marshal Lannes, in a manner to occupy the least possible space, and so that at the moment when Marshal Soult shall begin his march, all the cavalry under the orders of Prince Murat shall pass the brook, and find itself placed in the centre of the army.

General Caffarelli is ordered to move at seven o'clock in the morning with his divisions so as to place himself on the right of Suchet's divisions, after having passed the brook. . . .

Marshal Bernadotte with his two infantry divisions will move at seven o'clock in the morning into the same position which is occupied to-day, the 10th, by Caffarelli's division, except that his left shall be close to and behind the Santon (hill), and will remain there in column by regiments.

Marshal Lannes will order a division of grenadiers to place itself in line in front of his present position, the left behind the right of General Caffarelli. . . .

Marshal Davout, with Friant's division and the division of dragoons of General Bourcier, will start at five o'clock in the morning from the Raigern Abbey, to reach the right of Marshal Soult. . . .

At half-past seven the marshals will be near the emperor in his bivouac, so that, according to the movements the enemy may have made during the night, he may give new orders. . . .

All the troops will remain in the dispositions indicated above until new orders. . . .

Each of the marshals will give the orders which apply to him in consequence of the present dispositions.

NAPOLEON

Proclamation Read to Each Battalion, December 1

Soldiers, a Russian army presents itself before you to avenge the Austrian army of Ulm. These are the same battalions which you beat at Hollabrünn, and which you have constantly pursued to this place. The positions we occupy are formidable, and while they are marching to turn my right, they will present me their flank.

Soldiers, I shall myself direct all your battalions. I shall hold myself distant from the fire, if with your accustomed bravery you carry disorder and confusion into the enemy's ranks; but should victory for a moment be uncertain, you would see your emperor expose himself to the first strokes; for victory ought not to hesitate, in this day especially where there is at stake the honor of the French infantry, which means so much to the honor of all the nation.

On pretext of carrying off the wounded, let not the ranks be disgarnished, and let each one be fully penetrated with this idea, that we must vanquish these stipendiaries of England, who are animated with so great a hatred against our nation.

This victory will finish our campaign, and we can retake our winter quarters, where we shall be joined by new armies which are forming in France; and then the peace I shall make will be worthy of my people, of you and of me.

NAPOLEON

Napoleon Visits His Troops

In the evening [December 1st] the emperor desired to visit on foot and *incognito* all the bivouacs, but he had scarcely taken a few steps when he was recognized. It would be impossible to paint the enthusiasm of the soldiers on seeing him. Torches of straw were put in an instant at the tops of thousands of poles, and eighty thousand men presented themselves before the emperor, and saluted him with exclamations, some to feast the anniversary of the crowning, others saying that the army would to-morrow give its bouquet to the emperor. One of the old grenadiers approached him and said: "Sire, thou hast no need to expose thyself. I promise thee in the name of the grenadiers of the army that thou shalt have to fight but with thine eyes, and that we will bring thee to-morrow the flags and the artillery of the Russian army to celebrate the anniversary of thy crowning." The emperor said in returning to his bivouac, which consisted of a poor cabin of straw without a roof, which the grenadiers had made him, "This is the finest evening of my life . . . but I regret to think that I shall lose a great number of these brave men. I feel, by the way it hurts me, that these are really my children, and in truth I sometimes reproach myself with the sentiment, for I fear that it may end by making me unable to carry on war."

Excerpts from the Thirtieth Bulletin of the Grand Army, December 3, 1805

Never battlefield was more horrible. From the middle of the immense ponds one yet hears the cries of thousands of men whom one cannot save. It will take three days to send all the enemy's wounded to Brünn. One's heart bleeds; may so much blood shed, may so many misfortunes, finally fall on the perfidious islanders who are its cause: may the oligarchs of London bear the load of so many evils. . . . The Russian troops are brave, but much less brave than the French troops. . . . The Russians in fighting have the habit of leaving behind their haversacks. As the whole Russian army was routed, our soldiers took all the haversacks. We also took a great part of the baggage, and the men found a great deal of money. The French soldiers picked up a large quantity of medals and decorations. . . . General Valhubert had his leg carried off by a cannonball. Four soldiers came to pick him up. Remembering the order of the day, he cried in a voice of thunder, "Join your ranks. If you come back victors, you can take me up after the battle. If you are vanquished, I attach no price to my life."

Napoleon's Proclamation to the Army, December 3

Soldiers, I am satisfied with you. You have in the day of Austerlitz justified all that I expected of your intrepidity. You have decorated your eagles with an immemorial glory. An army of one hundred thousand men, commanded by the Emperors of Austria and Russia, has been, in less than four hours, either cut off or dispersed. Those who escaped your steel were drowned in the ponds; forty flags, the standards of the Imperial Guard of Russia, one hundred and twenty pieces of cannon, twenty generals, more than thirty thousand prisoners, are the result of this day forever celebrated. This so much vaunted infantry in superior numbers was unable to resist your shock, and from now on you have no rivals to fear. Thus in two months this Third Coalition has been vanquished and dissolved. Peace cannot be distant. . . . Soldiers, when all that is necessary to assure the happiness and the prosperity of our country shall be accomplished, I will lead you back to France. There you will be the object of my most tender solicitude. My people will see you back with joy, and it will suffice you to say, "I was at the battle of Austerlitz," for people to answer, "There stands a brave man."

NAPOLEON

Napoleon's Decree of December 7

1. We adopt all the children of the French generals, officers and soldiers killed at the battle of Austerlitz. 2. They shall be kept and educated at our expense, the boys in our Imperial Palace of Rambouillet, and the girls in our Imperial Palace of St. Germain. The boys shall be placed in situations and the girls married by us. 3. Independently of their names of baptism and family, they shall have the right to join thereto the name of Napoleon.

Napoleon's Proclamation of December 27

Soldiers! Peace between me and the Emperor of Austria is signed. You have in this late season made two campaigns. You have performed everything that I expected of you. I am leaving to go to my capital. I have given promotion and rewards to those who most distinguished themselves.

I will do all that I have promised you. You have seen your emperor partake your perils and fatigues. I also wish you to come and see me surrounded by the grandeur and the splendor which belong to the sovereign of the first people of the universe. I will give a great Fete in the first days of May in Paris. You shall all be there, and after that we shall see where the happiness of our country and the interests of our glory will call us.

NAPOLEON

Bestowal of Awards to the Marshals, April 26, 1806, to Be Paid by the Italian Provinces Designated

To	Ney	from	Dalmatia	100,000	francs
"	Lannes	"	Istria	100,000	"
"	Soult	"	Friuli	60,000	"
"	Bessieres	"	Cadore	60,000	"
"	Serurier	"	Belluno	60,000	"
"	Perignon	"	Conegliano	60,000	"
"	Moncey	"	Treviso	60,000	"
"	Mortier	"	Feltre	60,000	"
"	Dejean	"	Bassano	60,000	"
"	Champagny	"	Vicenza	60,000	"
"	Davout	"	Padua	60,000	"
"	Fouché	"	Rovigo	60,000	"

6. METTERNICH DRAWS THE PORTRAIT OF NAPOLEON

One of the men best qualified to judge Napoleon was the Austrian statesman and diplomat Prince Metternich. He was Austrian ambassador at Paris between 1806 and 1809 and was influential in securing Marie Louise as Napoleon's second wife. He came to know Napoleon as few other foreigners knew him.

I had never seen Napoleon till the audience which he gave me at St. Cloud, when I delivered my credentials. I found him standing in the middle of one of the rooms, with the Minister for Foreign Affairs and six other members of the Court. He wore the Guards uniform, and had his hat on his head. This latter circumstance, improper in any case, for the audience was not a public one, struck me as misplaced pretension, showing the *parvenu;* I even hesitated for a moment, whether I too should not cover. . . .

His attitude seemed to me to show constraint and even embarrassment. His short, broad figure, negligent dress, and marked endeavour to make an imposing effect, combined to weaken in me the feeling of grandeur nat-

Memoirs of Prince Metternich, translated by Mrs. Alexander Napier (New York: Charles Scribner's Sons, 1880), Vol. I, pp. 270–286.

urally attached to the idea of a man before whom the world trembled. This impression has never been entirely effaced from my mind; it was present with me in the most important interviews which I have had with Napoleon, at different epochs in his career. Possibly it helped to show me the man as he was, behind the masks with which he knew how to cover himself. In his freaks, in his fits of passion, in his brusque interpellations, I saw prepared scenes, studied and calculated to produce a certain effect on the person to whom he was speaking.

. . . The turn of his mind always led him towards the positive; he disliked vague ideas, and hated equally the dreams of visionaries and the abstraction of idealists, and treated as mere nonsense everything that was not clearly and practically presented to him. He valued only those sciences which can be controlled and verified by the senses or which rest on observation and experience. He had the greatest contempt for the false philosophy and the false philanthropy of the eighteenth century. Among the chief teachers of these doctrines, Voltaire was the special object of his aversion, and he even went so far as to attack, whenever he had the opportunity, the general opinion as to his literary power. . . .

In private life, without being amiable, he was good-natured, and even carried indulgence to the point of weakness. . . . His sisters, in particular, got from him everything that they wanted.

Neither of his wives had ever anything to complain of from Napoleon's personal manners. Although the fact is well known already, a saying of the Archduchesse Marie Louise will put it in a new light. "I am sure," she said to me some time after her marriage, "that they think a great deal about me in Vienna, and that the general opinion is that I live a life of daily suffering. So true is it that truth is often not probable. I have no fear of Napoleon, but I begin to think that he is afraid of me."

Simple and even easy as he was in private life, he showed himself to little advantage in the great world. It is difficult to imagine anything more awkward than Napoleon's manner in a drawing-room. The pains which he took to correct the faults of his nature and education only served to make his deficiencies more evident. I am satisfied that he would have made great sacrifices to add to his height and give dignity to his appearance, which became more common in proportion as his *embonpoint* increased. He walked by preference on tiptoe. His costumes were studied to form a contrast by comparison with the circle which surrounded him, either by their extreme simplicity or by their extreme magnificence. . . . Out of his mouth there never came one graceful or even a well-turned speech to a woman, although the effort to make one was often expressed on his face and in the sound of his voice. He spoke to ladies only of their dress, of which he declared himself a severe judge, or perhaps of the number of their children, and one of his usual questions was if they had nursed their children themselves, a question which he commonly made in terms seldom used in good society. . . .

The opinion of the world is still divided, and perhaps will always be, on the question, Whether Napoleon did in fact deserve to be called a great man? It would be impossible to dispute the great qualities of one who, rising from obscurity, has become in a few years the strongest and most powerful of his contemporaries. But strength, power, and superiority are more or less relative terms. To appreciate properly the degree of genius which has been required for a man to dominate his age, it is necessary to have the measure of that age. This is the point from which opinions with regard to Napoleon diverge so essentially. If the era of the Revolution was, as its admirers think, the most brilliant, the most glorious epoch of modern history, Napoleon, who has been able to take the first place in it, and to keep it for fifteen years, was, certainly, one of the greatest men who have ever appeared. If, on the contrary, he has only had to move like a meteor above the mists of a general dissolution; if he has found nothing around him but the *débris* of a social condition ruined by the excess of false civilisation; if he has only had to combat a resistance weakened by universal lassitude, feeble rivalries, ignoble passions, in fact, adversaries everywhere disunited and paralysed by their disagreements, the splendour of his success diminishes with the facility with which he obtained it. . . .

30

REACTION AND REFORM, 1815–1832

With the exile of Napoleon to Elba in 1814, the rulers of Europe faced a rare opportunity to negotiate a lasting peace. Meeting at Vienna in 1814 and 1815, the monarchs and their advisors applied the principles of "legitimacy" and "compensation" in restoring former dynasties and settling territorial disputes. Metternich, Austrian chief minister, created the Concert of Europe, an arrangement for periodic consultation among the conservative powers belonging to the Quadruple Alliance for the purpose of suppressing any future liberal or national revolution. Metternich's conservative order was challenged by spotty local revolts in 1820 and 1821, shaken by the revolutions of 1830, and destroyed by the European-wide revolutions of 1848. In England, Tory reaction was overcome by Liberals and Whigs who carried through the Reform Bill of 1832.

1. TALLEYRAND GAINS INFLUENCE AT THE CONGRESS OF VIENNA

Behind the brilliant pageantry of the Congress of Vienna, the actual work was undertaken by representatives of the "Big Four" powers. A fifth power, defeated France, was represented by Talleyrand. He had been a bishop before the French Revolution and had served successively the governments of the Revolution, Napoleon, and Louis XVIII. Talleyrand possessed the rare talent of being able to anticipate political changes, and he capped his career by serving after 1830 as Louis Philippe's ambassador to England.

. . . at the opening of the negotiations, all the cabinets regarded themselves as being, notwithstanding the peace, in an attitude which, if not hostile, was at least very equivocal, with France! They all thought, more or less,

Memoires of the Prince de Talleyrand, edited by the Duc de Broglie and translated by R.L. de Beaufort (New York and London: G.P. Putnam's Sons, 1891), Vol. II, pp. 200–205.

that it would have been to their interest that she should have been more enfeebled still. Unable to do anything in that direction, they endeavoured to diminish, at least, her influence. I saw that they all agreed on those various points.

It remained for me to hope that there would be among the powers some divergence of opinion, when they came to distribute the numerous territories that the war had put at their disposal, each one desiring, either to obtain for himself, or to give to the states dependent upon her, a considerable portion of the conquered territories. It was specially desired, at the same time, to exclude from the division those countries which it was feared would prove too independent. That variety of contest, however, offered me but scant opportunity to interfere with matters; for previous arrangements, by which the disposal of the most important territories had been regulated, existed between the powers. To succeed in modifying those arrangements, or to have them completely renounced, according to the dictates of justice, there were more than prejudices to remove, more than pretensions to check, more than ambition to defeat. It was necessary to annul all that had been done without France. For if they consented to admit us to take a share in the acts of the congress, it was for the sake of form only, and in order to deprive us of the means of contesting their validity; but it was pretended that France should have nothing to see in the resolutions already settled, and that were looked upon as accomplished facts. . . .

The opening of congress had been fixed for the 1st of October. I had been at Vienna since September 23, but I had been preceded there by several days, by the ministers who, having directed the war, and repented of peace, wished to take up their advantages again at the congress. It was not long before I was informed that they had already formed a committee, and were holding conferences among themselves, of which a protocol had been prepared. Their object was to decide alone, what ought to be submitted to the deliberations of the congress, and that too, without the assistance of either France, Spain, or any power of the second order; to these however they would afterwards communicate, in the form of a proposition what would in reality be a resolution, viz., the different articles they should have determined upon. I made no remonstrances. I continued to see them, without speaking of business. I limited myself to communicating to the ministers of the secondary powers, who had a common interest with me, the dissatisfaction I felt. Discovering also, in the past policy of their countries, traces of confidence in France, they very soon looked upon me as their support, and once assured of their assent in all that I was about to do, I officially pressed the opening of the congress. In my first requests I acted as though I had no knowledge of the conferences that had been held. The opening of the congress was fixed for a certain day. That day passed; I entreated that another should be fixed in the near future. I gave it to be understood that it was necessary that I should not remain too long absent from France. A few replies, evasive at first, caused me to repeat my entreaties. I even went so far as to complain a little, but was finally obliged to make use of the personal influence that I had fortunately acquired in the previous negotiations, over the principal personages of the congress. Prince Metternich, and the Count Nesselrode, not wishing to be disobliging to me, both had me invited to a conference which was to have been held at the office of the minister of foreign affairs. Count de Labrador, minister of Spain, with whom I had the honour to support a common cause in the deliberations of the congress, received the same invitation.

I went to the office of the minister of state at the hour indicated, and found there, Lord Castlereagh, Prince von Hardenberg, Herr von Humboldt, and Herr von Gentz, a man of distinguished talents, who fulfilled the functions of secretary. The protocol of the preceding sittings was on the table. I mention all the details of that first sitting, because it decided the position of France at the congress. Prince Metternich opened it by a few sentences on the duty of the congress to give solidity to the peace which had just been restored to Europe. The Prince von Hardenberg added, that in order to consolidate the peace it was indispensable that the engagements that followed perforce from the war should be religiously kept, and that such was the intention of the allied powers.

Placed by the side of Prince von Hardenberg, I was naturally forced to speak after him, and after having said a few words on the good fortune of France in finding herself in relations of confidence and friendship with all the cabinets of Europe, I remarked that the Prince von Hardenberg had let fall an expression that appeared to me to belong to other times, for that they had both of them spoken of the intentions of the *allied powers*. I declared that *allied powers,* and a *congress* in which powers that were not allied were to be found, were in my eyes very little able to arrange affairs loyally together. I repeated with some astonishment and even warmth, the word *allied powers* . . . "*allied,*" I said, "and against whom? It is no longer against Napoleon—he is on the isle of Elba . . . it is no longer against France; for peace has been made . . . it is surely not against the King of France; he is a guarantee of the duration of that peace. Gentlemen, let us speak frankly; if there are still *allied powers*, I am one too many here." —I perceived that I had produced some impression, and especially on Herr von Gentz. I continued: "And nevertheless if I were not here, I should decidedly be missed. Gentlemen, I am perhaps the only one who asks nothing. Great esteem is all I would have for France. She is sufficiently powerful by her resources, her extent of territory, by the number and intelligence of her inhabitants, by the contiguity of her provinces, by the unity of her administration, by the defences with which nature and art have guaranteed her frontiers. I want nothing, I repeat it, but I bring you a great deal. The presence of a minister of Louis XVIII. consecrates here the principle upon which all social order rests. The first need of Europe is to banish for ever the opinion that right can be acquired by conquest alone, and to cause the revival of that sacred principle of legitimacy from which all order and stability spring. . . ."

After a few moments' silence, Count Labrador [of Spain] made, in his proud and piquant language, a declaration almost identical with my own. Embarrassment was depicted on every face. They denied and explained in the same breath all that had taken place before this meeting. I profited by this moment in order to make a few concessions to the pride that I saw thus hurt. I said that in an assembly as numerous as the congress, where one was obliged to occupy oneself with so many different matters, to regulate questions of the first importance, and to decide a host of secondary interests, it was very difficult, nay even impossible, to reach any result by treating of all these subjects in general assemblies, but that some means of distributing and classifying all the business could be found without wounding either the interest or the dignity of any of the powers.

This language, though vague, yet pointed out the possibility of a particular direction being given to general business, and thus permitted the assembled ministers to reconsider what they had done, and to regard it all as null; while Herr von Gentz drew up the protocols of the previous sittings, and arranged one for that day. That protocol constituted the reports of the first sitting, and, in order to officially date our arrival at the congress, I signed it. From that time there was no conference among the great powers in which France did not take a part. . . .

Thus, at the end of the month of October, 1814, I was able to write to Paris, that the house of Bourbon, which had only returned to France five months ago, and France herself, who had been conquered five months previously, found themselves already replaced to their proper place in Europe, and had again regained that influence that belonged to them, in the most important deliberations of the congress. . . .

2. CZAR ALEXANDER PROPOSES A HOLY ALLIANCE

Czar Alexander I, the creator of the Holy Alliance, was probably the only ruler who took the document seriously. Yet, the Holy Alliance was so well publicized

Translations and Reprints from the Original Sources of European History (Philadelphia: University of Pennsylvania, 1894), Series I, Vol. I, No. 3, pp. 9–10.

that to many liberals it seemed to symbolize reactionary repression. Actually, the basis for the Concert of Europe was the more effective bond of the Quadruple Alliance.

In the Name of the Very Holy and Indivisible Trinity.

Their majesties, the Emperor of Austria, the King of Prussia and the Emperor of Russia, in view of the great events which the last three years have brought to pass in Europe and in view especially of the benefits which it has pleased Divine Providence to confer upon those states whose governments have placed their confidence and their hope in Him alone, having reached the profound conviction that the policy of the powers, in their mutual relations, ought to be guided by the sublime truths taught by the eternal religion of God our Saviour, solemnly declare that the present act has no other aim than to manifest to the world their unchangeable determination to adopt no other rule of conduct, either in the government of their respective countries or in their political relations with other governments, than the precepts of that holy religion, the precepts of justice, charity and peace. These, far from being applicable exclusively to private life, ought on the contrary directly to control the resolutions of princes and to guide their steps as the sole means of establishing human institutions and of remedying their imperfections. Hence their majesties have agreed upon the following articles:

ARTICLE I. Conformably to the words of Holy Scripture which command all men to look upon each other as brothers, the three contracting monarchs will continue united by the bonds of a true and indissoluble fraternity and, regarding themselves as compatriots, they shall lend aid and assistance to each other on all occasions and in all places, viewing themselves, in their relations to their subjects and to their armies, as fathers of families, they shall direct them in the same spirit of fraternity by which they are animated for the protection of religion, peace and justice.

ARTICLE II. Hence the sole principle of conduct, be it between the said government or their subjects, shall be that of rendering mutual service, and testifying by unceasing good-will, the mutual affection with which they should be animated. Considering themselves all as members of one great Christian nation, the three allied princes look upon themselves as delegates of Providence called upon to govern three branches of the same family, viz: Austria, Russia and Prussia. They thus confess that the Christian nation, of which they and their people form a part, has in reality no other sovereign than He alone to whom belongs by right the power, for in Him alone are to be found all the treasures of love, of knowledge and of infinite wisdom, that is to say God, our Divine Saviour Jesus Christ, the word of the Most

High, the word of life. Their majesties recommend, therefore, to their peoples, as the sole means of enjoying that peace which springs from a good conscience and is alone enduring, to fortify themselves each day in the principles and practice of those duties which the Divine Saviour has taught to men.

ARTICLE III. All those powers who wish solemnly to make avowal of the sacred principles which have dictated the present act, and who would recognize how important it is to the happiness of nations, too long agitated, that these truths should hereafter exercise upon human destiny all the influence belonging to them, shall be received into this Holy Alliance with as much cordiality as affection.

Engrossed in three copies and signed at Paris, year of grace, 1815, September 14/26.

Signed { FRANCIS
FREDERICK WILLIAM
ALEXANDER

3. *METTERNICH EXPLAINS HIS POLITICAL FAITH*

Prince Clemens von Metternich (1773–1859), Austrian chief minister for nearly forty years, established within the vast Austrian Empire a model conservative state. In Germany, Metternich used the mechanism of the Germanic Confederation to enforce a program of reaction. The same policy was imposed on most of Italy by the presence of Austrian troops and Hapsburg princes. The selection below forms part of a secret memorandum of 1820 from Metternich to Czar Alexander.

Kings have to calculate the chances of their very existence in the immediate future; passions are let loose, and league together to overthrow everything which society respects as the basis of its existence; religion, public morality, laws, customs, rights, and duties, all are attacked, confounded, overthrown, or called in question. The great mass of the people are tranquil spectators of these attacks and revolutions, and of the absolute want of all means of defence. A few are carried off by the torrent, but the wishes of the immense majority are to maintain a repose which exists no longer, and of which even the first elements seem to be lost. . . .

The scenes of horror which accompanied the first phases of the French Revolution prevented the rapid propagation of its subversive principles beyond the frontiers of France, and the wars of conquest which succeeded them gave to the public mind a direction little favourable to revolutionary

Memoires of Prince Metternich, edited by Prince Richard Metternich and translated by Mrs. Alexander Napier (New York: Charles Scribner's Sons, 1881), Vol. III, pp. 455, 462–463, 465–467, 469–471, 475.

principles. Thus the Jacobin propaganda failed entirely to realise criminal hopes.

Nevertheless the revolutionary seed had penertated into every country and spread more or less. It was greatly developed under the *régime* of the military despotism of Bonaparte. His conquests displaced a number of laws, institutions, and customs; broke through bonds sacred among all nations, strong enough to resist time itself; which is more than can be said of certain benefits conferred by these innovators. From these perturbations it followed that the revolutionary spirit could in Germany, Italy, and later on in Spain, easily hide itself under the veil of patriotism. . . .

The evil exists and it is enormous. We do not think we can better define it and its cause at all times and in all places than we have already done by the word 'presumption,' that inseparable companion of the half-educated, that spring of an unmeasured ambition, and yet easy to satisfy in times of trouble and confusion.

It is principally the middle classes of society which this moral gangrene has affected, and it is only among them that the real heads of the party are found.

For the great mass of the people it has no attraction and can have none. The labours to which this class—the real people—are obliged to devote themselves, are too continuous and too positive to allow them to throw themselves into vague abstractions and ambitions. The people know what is the happiest thing for them: namely, to be able to count on the morrow, for it is the morrow which will repay them for the cares and sorrows of to-day. The laws which afford a just protection to individuals, to families, and to property, are quite simple in their essence. The people dread any movement which injures industry and brings new burdens in its train. . . .

There is besides scarcely any epoch which does not offer a rallying cry to some particular faction. This cry, since 1815, has been *Constitution.* But do not let us deceive ourselves: this word, susceptible of great latitude of interpretation, would be but imperfectly understood if we supposed that the factions attached quite the same meaning to it under the different *régimes.* Such is certainly not the case. In pure monarchies it is qualified by the name of 'national representation.' In countries which have lately been brought under the representative *régime* it is called 'development,' and promises charters and fundamental laws. In the only State which possesses an ancient national representation it takes 'reform' as its object. Everywhere it means change and trouble. . . .

We are convinced that society can no longer be saved without strong and vigorous resolutions on the part of the Governments still free in their opinions and actions.

We are also convinced that this may yet be, if the Governments face the truth, if they free themselves from all illusion, if they join their ranks and take their stand on a line of correct, unambiguous, and frankly announced principles.

By this course the monarchs will fulfil the duties imposed upon them by Him who, by entrusting them with power, has charged them to watch over the maintenance of justice, and the rights of all, to avoid the paths of error, and tread firmly in the way of truth. . . .

Union between the monarchs is the basis of the policy which must now be followed to save society from total ruin. . . .

In short, let the great monarchs strengthen their union, and prove to the world that if it exists, it is beneficent, and ensures the political peace of Europe: that it is powerful only for the maintenance of tranquillity at a time when so many attacks are directed against it; that the principles which they profess are paternal and protective, menacing only the disturbers of public tranquillity.

4. THE CARLSBAD DECREES MARK THE CONSERVATIVE TRIUMPH IN GERMANY

August von Kotzebue, a German dramatist and propagandist in the pay of the Russian Czar, was murdered in 1819 by a liberal university student. Metternich, thoroughly alarmed by the spread of liberalism among German professors, students, and journalists, called other German conservative statesmen to an emergency conference at Carlsbad, where the following resolutions were agreed upon. They were subsequently approved by the Diet of the Germanic Confederation.

Provisional Decree Relating to the Universities, Unanimously Adopted September 20, 1819

1. A special representative of the ruler of each state shall be appointed for each university with appropriate instructions and extended powers, and who shall reside in the place where the university is situated. This office may devolve upon the existing Curator or upon any other individual whom the government may deem qualified.

The function of this agent shall be to see to the strictest enforcement of existing laws and disciplinary regulations; to observe carefully the spirit which is shown by the instructors in the university in their public lectures and regular courses, and, without directly interfering in scientific matters or in the methods of teaching, to give a salutary direction to the instruction,

Translations and Reprints from the Original Sources of European History (Philadelphia: University of Pennsylvania, 1894), Series I, Vol. I, No. 3, pp. 16–20.

having in view the future attitude of the students. Lastly, they shall devote unceasing attention to everything that may promote morality, good order and outward propriety among the students.

The relation of these special agents to the Senate of the university, as well as all details relating to the extent of their duties and to their manner of action, shall be included in the instructions furnished by the superior government officials. These instructions shall be as precise as the circumstances which have dictated the appointment of the agents in question shall permit.

2. The confederated governments mutually pledge themselves to remove from the universities or other public educational institutions all teachers who, by obvious deviation from their duty or by exceeding the limits of their functions, or by the abuse of their legitimate influence over the youthful minds, or by propagating harmful doctrines hostile to the public order or subversive of existing governmental institutions, shall have unmistakably proved their unfitness for the important office intrusted to them. No obstacle whatever shall prevent the execution of this provision so long as it shall remain in force and until such time as this matter shall be definitely regulated. Removals of this character shall, however, never be made except upon the recommendation, accompanied with full reasons, of the aforesaid special agent of the government at the university or in view of a report previously required from him.

No teacher who shall have been removed in this manner shall be again appointed to a position in any public institution of learning in another state of the Union.

3. Those laws which have for a long period been directed against secret and unauthorized societies in the universities, shall be strictly enforced. These laws apply especially to that association established some years since under the name Universal Students' Union (*Allgemeine Burschenschaft*), since the very conception of the society implies the utterly unallowable plan of permanent fellowship and constant communication between the various universities. The duty of especial watchfulness in this matter should be impressed upon the special agents of the government.

The governments mutually agree that such persons as shall, after the publication of the present decree, be shown to have remained in secret or unauthorized associations or shall have entered such associations, shall not be admitted to any public office.

4. No student, who shall be expelled from a university by a decision of the University Senate, which was ratified or prompted by the agent of the government, or who shall have left the institution in order to escape expulsion, shall be received in any other university. Nor, in general, shall any

student be admitted to another university without a satisfactory certificate of his good conduct at the university he has left.

Press Laws for Five Years

1. So long as this decree shall remain in force no publication which appears in the form of daily issues or as a serial not exceeding twenty sheets of printed matter shall go to press in any state of the Union without the previous knowledge and approval of the state officials. . . .

Establishment of an Investigating Committee at Mainz

ARTICLE I. Within a fortnight, reckoned from the passage of this decree, there shall convene, under the auspices of the Confederation, in the city and federal fortress of Mainz, an Extraordinary Commission of Investigation to consist of seven members including the chairman.

ARTICLE II. The object of the Commission shall be a joint investigation, as thorough and extensive as possible, of the facts relating to the origin and manifold ramifications of the revolutionary plots and demagogical associations directed against the existing Constitution and internal peace both of the Union and of the individual states: of the existence of which plots more or less clear evidence is to be had already, or may be produced in the course of the investigation.

5. *LORD JOHN RUSSELL PRESENTS THE REFORM BILL*

While Metternich's system of rigid reaction prevailed in most of Europe, Liberals and Radicals in England successfully overthrew the repressive Tory regime by concentrating their attacks on the inequality of voting districts. The Great Reform Act of 1832 eliminated rotten boroughs, gave representation to the new industrial cities, and enfranchised a few additional voters.

. . . parliament met . . . on the 3rd of February. Ministers had hitherto veiled in profound secrecy the plan of Reform which they intended to introduce. . . . it was not till the 1st of March, that it was introduced into the House of Commons. It was introduced by lord John Russell, to whom, although not a cabinet minister, this duty had been intrusted, in consideration of his lordship having made, on many occasions, many motions for many partial changes in the existing state of the representation.

His lordship declared in the outset that the measure which he was about to propose had been formed in the mind of earl Grey himself: the

"History," *The Annual Register, 1831* (London: 1832), pp. 5–7.

world believed that the greater portion of the premier's mind, had been found, on this occasion, to reside within the body of his son-in-law, lord Durham. His lordship farther declared, that the object of ministers had been . . . to frame a measure with which every reasonable man in the country would be satisfied: that they wished to take their stand between two hostile parties, neither agreeing with the bigotted on one hand, that no Reform was necessary, nor agreeing with the fanaticism of others, that only one particular reform could be wholesome or satisfactory, but taking a firm and steadfast ground between abuses which were to be amended, and convulsions which were to be averted. These were all most excellent general expressions.

His lordship next laid it down as one principle on which he and his colleagues agreed, that the question of *right* was in favour of the reformers; for the ancient constitution of the country declared, that no man should be taxed for the support of the state who had not consented, by himself or his representative to the imposition of the taxes. The statute *de Tallagio non concedendo* spoke the same language; and, although some historical doubts had been thrown upon it, its legal meaning had never been questioned. It included "all the freemen of the land;" and it provided that each county should send to the Commons two knights, each city two burgesses, and each borough two members. About an 100 places sent representatives, and thirty or forty others occasionally enjoyed the privilege; but it was discontinued or revived as they rose or fell in the scale of wealth, and importance. No doubt, at that early period, the House of Commons did represent the people of England; but, added his lordship, there is likewise no doubt, that the House of Commons, as it presently subsists, does not represent the people of England.

The right being thus in favour of reform, the house would find that the result would be the same, when they looked to what was reasonable; for it would be impossible to keep the constitution of the House as it at present existed. Who had not heard of the fame of this country, that in wealth it was unparalleled, in civilization unrivalled, and in freedom unequalled, in the history of the empires of the world? Now suppose that a foreigner, well acquainted with these facts, were told, that in this most wealthy, most civilized, and most free country, the representatives of the people, the guardians of her liberties, were chosen only every six years, would he not be very curious and very anxious to hear in what way that operation was performed, by which this great and wise nation selected the members who were to represent them, and upon whom depended their fortunes and their rights? Would not such a foreigner be much astonished if he were taken to a green mound and informed that it sent two members to the British parliament?—

if he were shown a stone wall, and told that it also sent two members to the British parliament? . . . He would, be still more astonished were he to go into the northern part of the country, and were to see flourishing towns, containing immense manufactories and depositories of every sort of merchandize, and be informed that these places sent no representatives to parliament. He would be still more astonished, were he taken to a great and opulent town—Liverpool for instance—and were to observe the manner in which general elections were there conducted. He would see bribery prevail to the greatest extent; he would see men openly paid for their votes; and he would be astonished that a nation, whose representatives were so chosen, should be at all competent to perform the functions of legislation. The people called loudly for reform, saying that whatever good existed in the constitution of this House—whatever confidence was placed in it by the people, was completely gone. Whatever might be thought of particular acts, the confidence of the country in the constitution of the House had long ceased; and so long as towns like Leeds and Manchester elected no representatives, while such places as Gatton and Old Sarum did, it was impossible to say that the representation was fairly and properly carried on. From these premises his lordship arrived at this conclusion—if the case be one of right, it is in favour of reform—if it be a question of reason it is in favour of reform—if it be a question of expediency, expedience calls loudly for it.

His lordship then stated the plan by which ministers proposed to meet and satisfy the demand for reform which they averred themselves to believe could no longer be resisted. That plan had been so framed as to remove the reasonable complaints of the people, and these complaints again were principally directed, first, against nomination by individuals; secondly, elections by close corporations; thirdly, the expenses of elections. In so far as concerned the first two grounds of complaint, the plan of ministers consisted first of disfranchisement, in order to get rid of places which had hitherto sent members to parliament: secondly, of enfranchisement, in order to enable places which had hitherto been unrepresented, to elect members: thirdly, of an extension of the franchise, in order to increase the number of electors in those places which were to be allowed to retain in whole, or in part, their existing privilege of sending members to the House of Commons.

31

ROMANTICISM AND SCIENCE

Classicism, which had dominated European culture since the Renaissance, gave way in the late eighteenth and early nineteenth centuries to the Romantic movement. Romantic writers and artists stressed emotion and sentiment rather than pure reason, studied the individual instead of society, and sought originality and diversity rather than conformity to fixed standards. In religion, Methodists and Baptists increased their numbers, while a group of English intellectuals followed John Henry Newman as converts to Catholicism. Romanticism harmonized well with the growing surge of nationalism, and such a writer as Mazzini was both a Romanticist and a liberal nationalist. Quite apart from the world of Romanticism, individual scientists produced valuable new theories based on personal observation, experiment, and reason.

1. CLASSICISM IS OVERTHROWN BY THE ROMANTIC REVOLUTION

The Romantic movement is difficult to define and has been frequently misunderstood and misinterpreted by its critics. Jacques Barzun, the perceptive author of the following selection, sees Romanticism as a form of realism and finds that Romantic writers were not only creative and imaginative, but were vigorously realistic as well.

Before we come to particulars, the general setting may be put in a few words: classicism perished from an excess of abstraction and generality. This was most visibly true in the several arts, and nothing shows more clearly the romanticists' realistic purpose than their refusal to go on imitat-

Jacques Barzun, *Romanticism and the Modern Ego* (Boston: Little, Brown & Company, 1943), pp. 82–84. Copyright 1943 by Jacques Barzun. Reprinted by permission of Little, Brown & Co.

ing forms whose contents had evaporated. Seeing this refusal, we believe too readily in the miscalled "romantic revolt." We imagine a sudden and irresponsible rebellion of brash young men against the wisdom and experience of their elders. It was nothing of the kind. The breaking away was reluctant, painful, and deliberate. A whole generation of geniuses came to see that to continue writing in the manner of Paley and Pye, Gottsched, Lebrun, and Delille, was intellectually impossible.

I use literary instances, but the other arts would furnish exact parallels. There was no choice but to begin afresh. The romanticist was in the position of a primitive with the seven arts to create out of nothing. At the same time, he labored under the handicap of having "inimitable" classical masterpieces held up to him to imitate, even though the substance of these great works had already been spread thin over fifty years of copying. This was like asking someone to produce the finest champagne by further diluting the weakest grape juice; the romantic revolt consisted solely in refusing to do the undoable.

Having perforce given up conventional abstractions, clichés, diction, and rules, what did the romanticists turn to? The answer can be generalized: for substance they turned to the world about them; they tried to meet the claims of every existing reality, both internal and external. For form, they relied on earlier romantic periods and on their own inventive genius.

The characteristics of romanticism which the textbooks list as if they were whimsical and isolated preferences are merely the embodiment of what I have just said. As against poetic diction and "noble" words, the romanticists admitted all words, especially the neglected host of common words; as against the exclusive use of a selected Graeco-Roman mythology, they took in the Celtic and Germanic; as against the uniform setting and tone of classical tragedy, they studied and reproduced the real diversities known as "local color." As against the antique subjects and the set scale of pictorial merits prescribed by the Academy, they took in the whole world, seen and unseen, and the whole range of colors. As against the academic rules prohibiting the use of certain chords, tonalities, and modulations, they sought to use and give shape to all manageable combinations of sound. As against the assumption that no civilization had existed since the fall of Rome, they rediscovered the Middle Ages and the sixteenth century, and made history their dominant avocation. As against the provincial belief that Paris and London were the sole centers of civilized life, they traveled to remote places such as America and the Near East, and earned the name of "exotic" for their pains. As against the snobbish idea that the products of sophistication and refined living are the only topics worth treating, they began to treasure folk literature and folk music, and to draw the subject matter of their art from every class and condition of men. As against the materialistic view that whatever is must be tangible, they made room in their notion of reality for the world of dreams, the mysterious in man and nature, and the supernatural.

All this they did knowingly, deliberately, with the patience and tenacity of pioneers and explorers. So that to those who speak sneeringly of the "romantic revolt" one may offer the answer of Liancourt to Louis XVI, "No Sire, it is a revolution." . . .

2. *BYRON CONDEMNS NAPOLEONIC TYRANNY AND EXTOLLS GREEK LIBERTY*

Enthusiastically Romantic in both his poetry and his private life, George Gordon, Lord Byron (1788–1824), was also a fervent advocate of freedom. Two aspects of Byron's Romantic liberalism are revealed here: In the first selection his hero, Harold, muses at the battlefield of Waterloo on the passing of Napoleonic tyranny; in the second, Harold encourages the Greeks to cast off Turkish domination.

XVII

Stop! for thy tread is on an Empire's dust!
An Earthquake's spoil is sepulchred below!
Is the spot marked with no colossal bust?
Nor column trophied for triumphal show?
None; but the moral's truth tells simpler so,
As the ground was before, thus let it be;–
How that red rain hath made the harvest grow!
And is this all the world has gained by thee,
Thou first and last of fields! king-making Victory?

XVIII

And Harold stands upon this place of skulls,
The grave of France, the deadly Waterloo!
How in an hour the power which gave annuls
Its gifts, transferring fame as fleeting too!
In "pride of place" here last the eagle flew,
Then tore with bloody talon the rent plain,
Pierced by the shaft of banded nations through;
Ambition's life and labours all were vain;
He wears the shattered links of the world's broken chain.

George Gordon, Lord Byron, *Childe Harold's Pilgrimage*, Canto II, Stanzas LXXIII–LXXVI; Canto III, Stanzas XVII–XX.

XIX

Fit retribution! Gaul may champ the bit
And foam in fetters;—but is Earth more free?
Did nations combat to make *One* submit;
Or league to teach all kings true sovereignty?
What! shall reviving thraldom again be
The patched-up idol of enlightened days?
Shall we, who struck the Lion down, shall we
Pay the Wolf homage? proffering lowly gaze
And servile knees to thrones? No; prove before ye praise!

XX

If not, o'er one fallen despot boast no more!
In vain fair cheeks were furrowed with hot tears
For Europe's flowers long rooted up before
The trampler of her vineyards; in vain years
Of death, depopulation, bondage, fears,
Have all been borne, and broken by the accord
Of roused-up millions: all that most endears
Glory, is when the myrtle wreathes a sword
Such as Harmodius drew on Athens' tyrant lord.

* * *

LXXIII

Fair Greece! sad relic of departed worth!
Immortal, though no more; though fallen, great;
Who now shall lead they scattered children forth,
And long accustomed bondage uncreate?
Not such thy sons who whilome did await,
The hopeless warriors of a willing doom,
In bleak Thermopylae's sepulchral strait—
Oh! who that gallant spirit shall resume,
Leap from Eurotas' banks, and call thee from the tomb?

LXXIV

Spirit of Freedom! when on Phyle's brow
Thou sat'st with Trasybulus and his train,
Couldst thou forebode the dismal hour which now
Dims the green beauties of thine Attic plain?

Not thirty tyrants now enforce the chain,
But every carle can lord it o'er thy land;
Nor rise thy sons, but idly rail in vain,
Trembling beneath the scourge of Turkish hand,
From birth till death enslaved; in word, in deed, unmanned.

LXXV

In all save form alone, how changed! and who
That marks the fire still sparkling in each eye,
Who but would deem their bosoms burned anew
With thy unquenchèd beam, lost Liberty!
And many dream withal the hour is nigh
That gives them back their father's heritage:
For foreign arms and aid they fondly sigh,
Nor solely dare encounter hostile rage,
Or tear their name defiled from Slavery's mournful page.

LXXVI

Hereditary bondsmen! know ye not
Who would be free themselves must strike the blow?
By their right arms the conquest must be wrought?
Will Gaul or Muscovite redress ye? no!
True, they may lay your proud despoilers low,
But not for you will Freedom's altars flame.
Shades of the Helots! triumph o'er your foe:
Greece! change thy lords, they state is still the same;
Thy glorious day is o'er, but not thine years of shame.

3. *DON CARLOS VISITS THE TOMB OF CHARLEMAGNE*

Victor Hugo (1802–1885), the greatest of the French Romantic writers, was equally at home in the fields of drama, poetry, essay, satire, novel, or literary criticism.* Hernani, *his most famous play, is intensely emotional and thoroughly Romantic. At its opening performance in Paris in 1830, angry Classicists staged a riot. In this scene from* Hernani *Don Carlos (Emperor Charles V) visits the tomb of Charlemagne, while awaiting his election as Holy Roman Emperor.

SCENE. *The monumental caverns of Aix-la-Chapelle. Spacious vaults of Lombard architecture, low and massy pillars, with ornamental capitals. On the right the tomb of Charlemagne, with a small low door of brass,*

Victor Hugo, *Hernani,* Act IV, in *Dramas* (Boston and New York: University Press Co., n.d.), Vol. I, pp. 60–63.

the inscription "Karolo Magno" rendered conspicuous by the light of a lamp, which is suspended singly from the centre of the vaults. The eye is lost in the undefined depths of the Arcades.

Enter CARLOS *and* RICARDO, *the latter leading the way with a lantern.*

DON RICARDO. We have now, my liege, wound through the murky labyrinth. Here, no doubt, the traitors will assemble; and here is your chosen concealment.

DON CARLOS. We'll use it anon. Thanks to our diligence and the speed of our horses, we are far in advance of their appointed hour. And this, then, is to be the council hall of conspiracy? They'll sharpen their daggers on the tomb of Charlemagne, as if Carlos of Castile were unworthy to succeed him. Your list of these formidable conspirators.

DON RICARDO. 'T is here, my liege, with the exception of two who have lately reinforced them, and who appear to be father and son; but their names I know not.

DON CARLOS. We may soon engrave them on their monument for public information. But in thus disposing of our pigmy foes, what is our dependence on our friends? The empire, Count, the empire! The crisis of its fate is near at hand.

DON RICARDO. The council, sire, is at this moment deliberating. You will succeed.

DON CARLOS. Three voices, as I think, would secure me. Three suffrages! Could I but purchase them for as many cities,—Ghent, Toledo, Salamanca. In Spain or Flanders let them make their choice, and they shall have the richest and the proudest.

DON RICARDO. 'T were a tempting bribe, sire.

DON CARLOS. 'T is nothing, Count,—a trifle. (*Tapping him familiarly.*) Cities, my sagacious friend, may be recovered; the empire once lost becomes a forlorn hope. (RICARDO *puts on his hat.*) Your hat, sir!

DON RICARDO. My liege, you have touched and familiarly accosted me. I am a grandee of Spain, *ipso facto*.

DON CARLOS. Ha, ha, ha! You are learned in the law, Count, and prompt at illustration. We venture not to litigate your claim, and therefore, grandee, we must admit you. Our Donna Zanthe, how has she sustained her journey?

DON RICARDO. Marvellously well, sire, since the worthy duchess you gave her in charge to, and her own experience, have assured her of your Highness's chivalrous forbearance.

DON CARLOS. Therein she flatters not *my* love, my lord.
But she is woman still, and should I triumph—
Have you considered our impatience, Count?
How shall we quickliest know the council's choice?

DON RICARDO. From the cannon's mouth, my liege. The discharge of one only will announce the election of the Duke of Saxony; two will report for Francis; and three will thunder for your Highness.

DON CARLOS. 'T is well devised. They'll boldly speak the worst, unminced with flattery. And now to prepare for our conspirators,—these self-elected guardians of the state and empire! Forget not my instructions.

DON RICARDO. I do not, my liege.

DON CARLOS. The key of the monument.

DON RICARDO. 'T is here! (*Gives it.*)

DON CARLOS. Now leave us, and obey our orders strictly.

(*Exit* RICARDO, *R.*)

DON CARLOS (*remains for a time in profound abstraction, then turns toward the tomb of Charlemagne*).

Charlemagne! mighty spirit! now enthroned
Above this coil and buzz of mortal passions,
Oh, let me commune with thee! Say, is all
Thy power, the wisdom and the mastery
Of soul, that with thy mortal nature came
On earth, gone with it,—perished, marbled up
With that poor dust, which balanced with the vilest,
Nor weighs, nor values more? Let them be dumb
Who deem so, while a heart is swelling here,
That unrebuked, even in this awful presence,
Dares hope to track thee in thy giant path,
And do thy mighty deeds. Oh, empire! empire!
Winning thee fairly shall I not desire thee?
And having won thee, when I spot thy purple
With sloth or slavish passion, to my bosom
Take other counsellors than truth and justice,
Then strip it from me, Heaven, and degrade
The mightiest monarch to the meanest man.
And thou, immortal spirit! by my strength;
Sustain me; poise me on my height, and yield me
Awhile thy sanctuary. Dare I enter?
Should I in shadowy majesty behold him,
How would he palsy my presumption? Hark!
What step, save mine, profanes thy sacred rest?
(*Smiling.*) I had forgot. I wait for my assassins.
They come.

(*He enters the tomb and closes it. Several Men enter with cautious step, enveloped in their mantles, finally meet each other, and speak in a low voice.*)

4. NEWMAN DESCRIBES HIS EARLY RELIGIOUS BELIEFS

John Henry Newman as an Oxford scholar was greatly disturbed by the intellectual dominance of liberalism and its effect on religion in England. Newman was ordained in the Church of England in 1824, but his study of the theological bases of his church led him to Catholicism by 1845. Several other members of the "Oxford Movement" were also converted to Catholicism, and Newman himself was created a cardinal in 1879.

I have spoken of my firm confidence in my position; and now let me state more definitely what the position was which I took up, and the propositions about which I was so confident. These were three:—

1. First was the principle of dogma: my battle was with liberalism; by liberalism I meant the anti-dogmatic principle and its developments. This was the first point on which I was certain. Here I make a remark: persistence in a given belief is no sufficient test of its truth; but departure from it is at least a slur upon the man who has felt so certain about it. In proportion then as I had in 1832 a strong persuasion in beliefs which I have since given up, so far a sort of guilt attaches to me, not only for that vain confidence, but for my multiform conduct in consequence of it. But here I have the satisfaction of feeling that I have nothing to retract, and nothing to repent of. The main principle of the [Oxford] Movement is as dear to me now as it ever was. I have changed in many things: in this I have not. From the age of fifteen, dogma has been the fundamental principle of my religion: I know no other religion; I cannot enter into the idea of any other sort of religion; religion, as a mere sentiment, is to me a dream and a mockery. As well can there be filial love without the fact of a father, as devotion without the fact of a Supreme Being. What I held in 1816, I held in 1833, and I hold in 1864. Please God, I shall hold it to the end. . . .

2. Secondly, I was confident in the truth of a certain definite religious teaching, based upon this foundation of dogma; viz., that there was a visible Church with sacraments and rites which are the channels of invisible grace. I thought that this was the doctrine of Scripture, of the early Church, and of the Anglican Church. Here again, I have not changed in opinion; I am as certain now on this point as I was in 1833, and have never ceased to be certain. In 1834 and the following years I put this ecclesiastical doctrine on a broader basis, after reading Laud, Bramhall, and Stillingfleet and other Anglican divines on the one hand, and after prosecuting the study of the Fathers on the other; but the doctrine of 1833 was strengthened in me, not changed. . . .

John Henry Newman, *Apologia Pro Vita Sua,* Third Edition (New York: D. Appleton and Company, 1865), pp. 95–99.

And further, as to the Episcopal system, I founded it upon the Epistles of St. Ignatius, which inculcated it in various ways. One passage especially impressed itself upon me: speaking of cases of disobedience to ecclesiastical authority, he says, "A man does not deceive that Bishop whom he sees, but he practises rather upon the Bishop Invisible, and so the question is not with flesh, but with God, who knows the secret heart." I wished to act on this principle to the letter, and I may say with confidence that I never consciously transgressed it. I loved to act in the sight of my Bishop, as if I was, as it were, in the sight of God. It was one of my special safeguards against myself and of my supports; I could not go very wrong while I had reason to believe that I was in no respect displeasing him. It was not a mere formal obedience to rule that I put before me, but I desired to please him personally, as I considered him set over me by the Divine Hand. I was strict in observing my clerical engagements, not only because they *were* engagements, but because I considered myself simply as the servant and instrument of my bishop. I did not care much for the Bench of Bishops, except as they might be the voice of my Church: nor should I have cared much for a Provincial Council; nor for a Diocesan Synod, presided over by my Bishop; all these matters seemed to me to be *jure ecclesiastico*, but what to me was *jure divino* was the voice of my Bishop in his own person. My own Bishop was my Pope; I knew no other; the successor of the Apostles, the Vicar of Christ. This was but a practical exhibition of the Anglican theory of Church Government, as I had already drawn it out myself. This continued all through my course; when at length in 1845 I wrote to Bishop Wiseman, in whose Vicariate I found myself, to announce my conversion [to Catholicism], I could find nothing better to say to him, than that I would obey the Pope as I had obeyed my own Bishop in the Anglican Church. My duty to him was my point of honour; his disapprobation was the one thing which I could not bear. . . .

And now in concluding my remarks on the second point on which my confidence rested, I observe that here again I have no retractation to announce as to its main outline. While I am now as clear in my acceptance of the principle of dogma, as I was in 1833 and 1816, so again I am now as firm in my belief of a visible Church, of the authority of Bishops, of the grace of the sacraments, of the religious worth of works of penance, as I was in 1833. I have added Articles to my Creed; but the old ones, which I then held with a divine faith, remain.

3. But now, as to the third point on which I stood in 1833, and which I have utterly renounced and trampled upon since, my then view of the Church of Rome;—I will speak about it as exactly as I can. When I was young, as I have said already, and after I was grown up, I thought the

Pope to be Antichrist. At Christmas, 1824–'5, I preached a Sermon to that effect. . . . From my boyhood and in 1824 I considered, after Protestant authorities, that St. Gregory I. about A.D. 600 was the first Pope that was Antichrist, and again that he was also a great and holy man; in 1832–'3 I thought the Church of Rome was bound up with the cause of Antichrist by the Council of Trent. When it was that in my deliberate judgment I gave up the notion altogether in any shape, that some special reproach was attached to her name, I cannot tell; but I had a shrinking from renouncing it, even when my reason so ordered me, from a sort of conscience or prejudice, I think up to 1843. Moreover, at least during the Tract Movement, I thought the essence of her offence to consist in the honours which she paid to the Blessed Virgin and the Saints; and the more I grew in devotion, both to the Saints and to Our Lady, the more impatient was I at the Roman practices, as if those glorified creations of God must be gravely shocked, if pain could be theirs, at the undue veneration of which they were the objects.

5. *MAZZINI FOUNDS THE YOUNG ITALY MOVEMENT*

Joseph (or Giuseppe) Mazzini (1805–1872), an unsuccessful revolutionary but a gifted writer, lifted the Italian movement for political unity to a high spiritual plane. He lived most of his life as an exile from his homeland and founded Young Italy in 1831 to inspire his fellow Italians to work for a united democratic republic.

It was during these months of imprisonment in Savona that I conceived the plan of the association of Young Italy (*La Giovina Italia*). I meditated deeply upon the principles upon which to base the organisation of the party, the aim and purpose of its labours—which I intended should be publicly declared—the method of its formation, the individuals to be selected to aid me in its creation, and the possibility of linking its operations with those of the existing revolutionary elements of Europe.

We were few in number, young in years, and of limited means and influence; but I believed the whole problem to consist in appealing to the true instincts and tendencies of the Italian heart, mute at that time, but revealed to us both by history and our own previsions of the future. Our strength must lie in our right appreciation of what those instincts and tendencies really were.

All great national enterprises have ever been originated by men of the

The Living Thoughts of Mazzini, presented by Ignazio Silone (New York: Longmans, Green and Company, 1939), pp. 47–50. Used by permission of the publisher and David McKay Company, Inc., New York.

people, whose sole strength lay in that power of *faith* and of *will*, which neither counts obstacles nor measures time. Men of means and influence follow after, either to support and carry on the movement created by the first, or, as too often happens, to divert it from its original aim.

I was not influenced by any mere political conception, nor idea of elevating the condition of the single people whom I saw thus dismembered, degraded, and oppressed; the parent thought of my every design was a presentiment that regenerated Italy was destined to arise the *initiatrix* of a new life, and a new and powerful Unity to all the nations of Europe.

Even at that time, in spite of the fascination exercised over my mind by the fervid words in which France at that day asserted her right of leadership amid the general silence, the idea was dimly stirring within me to which I gave expression six years later—the sense of a void, a want in Europe.

I felt that authority—true righteous and holy authority—the search after which, whether conscious or not, is in fact the secret of our human life, and which is only irrationally denied by those who confound it with its false semblance or shadow, and imagine they have abolished God himself, when they have but abolished an idol;—I felt that authority had vanished, and become extinct in Europe; and that for this reason no power of *initiative* existed in any of the peoples of Europe.

The labours, studies, and sorrows of my life have not only justified and confirmed this idea, but have transformed it into a *faith*. And if ever—though I may not think it—I should live to see Italy One, and to pass one year of solitude in some corner of my own land, or of this land where I now write, and which affection has rendered a second country to me, I shall endeavour to develop and reduce the consequences which flow from this idea, and are of far greater importance than most men believe.

At that time even the immature conception inspired me with a mighty hope that flashed before my spirit like a star. I saw regenerate Italy becoming at one bound the missionary of a religion of progress and fraternity, far grander and vaster than that she gave to humanity in the past.

The worship of Rome was a part of my being. The great Unity, the One Life of the world, had twice been elaborated within her walls. Other peoples—their brief mission fulfilled—disappeared for ever. To none save to her had it been given twice to guide and direct the world. There, life was eternal, death unknown. There, upon the vestiges of an epoch of civilisation anterior to the Grecian, which had had its seat in Italy, and which the historical science of the future will show to have had a far wider external influence than the learned of our own day imagine—the Rome of the Republic, concluded by the Caesars, had arisen to consign the former world to oblivion, and borne her eagles over the known world, carrying with them the idea of right, the source of liberty.

In later days, while men were mourning over her as the sepulchre of the living, she had again arisen, greater than before, and at once constituted herself, through her Popes—as venerable once as abject now—the accepted centre of a new Unity, elevating the law from earth to heaven, and substituting to the idea of right an idea of duty—a duty common to all men, and therefore source of their equality.

Why should not a new Rome, the Rome of the Italian people—portents of whose coming I deemed I saw—arise to create a third and still vaster unity; to link together and harmonize earth and heaven, right and duty; and utter, not to individuals but to peoples, the great word Association—to make known to free men and equals their mission here below?

The immediate result of these ideas was to convince me that the labour to be undertaken was not merely a political, but above all a moral work; not negative, but religious; not founded upon any theory of self-interest, or well-being, but upon principles and upon duty.

During the first months of my university life my mind had been somewhat tainted by the doctrines of the foreign materialist school; but the study of history and the intuition of conscience—the only tests of truth—soon led me back to the spiritualism of our Italian fathers.

6. MICHAEL FARADAY DISCOVERS ELECTRO-MAGNETISM

Michael Faraday (1791–1867) was a brilliant, self-educated scientist, who had served early in his career as assistant to the great Sir Humphrey Davy. The assistant soon surpassed the master in originality and versatility. Faraday's discovery of electro-magnetic induction in 1831 and his subsequent invention of the dynamo provided the bases for most later developments of electrical machinery. He also discovered the anaesthetic properties of ether, developed the electroplating industrial process, and proposed a theory of electrons which was ignored for decades.

His mode of attacking any problem was intuitive rather than logical, though when on the track of a solution his reasoning, proceeding by process of elimination, of trial and error, was sound and logical enough. . . . Helmholtz, in his Faraday Lecture of 1881, said: "It is in the highest degree astonishing to see what a large number of general theorems, the methodical deduction of which requires the highest powers of mathematical analysis,

Wilfred L. Randell, *Michael Faraday* (London: Leonard Parsons, 1924), pp. 14, 15–16, 105–110.

he found by a kind of intuition, with the security of instinct, without the help of a single mathematical formula." He repeats this, evidently impressed by such a gift: "With a quite wonderful sagacity and intellectual precision, Faraday performed in his brain the work of a great mathematician without using a single mathematical formula. . . . The fundamental conceptions by which Faraday was led to these much admired discoveries have not received an equal amount of consideration. They were very divergent from the trodden path of scientific theory, and appeared rather startling to his contemporaries. His principal aim was to express in his new conceptions only facts, with the least possible use of hypothetical substances and forces. This was really an advance in general scientific method, destined to purify science from the last remnants of metaphysics. Faraday was not the first, and not the only man, who had worked in this direction, but perhaps nobody else at his time did it so radically." . . .

Since 1824 he had held the belief that as a current of electricity can cause a piece of soft iron to become a magnet, so, somehow, a magnet *ought* to be able to cause a current of electricity, or in some way, at any rate, to affect an existing current. But, try as he would—and he tried several times during the intervening years—the expected, the logical event, would not happen. In 1831 he succeeded. Ampère had caused electricity to produce magnetic effects and magnets; Faraday now, by means of magnets, elicited electrical action. This foreshadowed another crowning feat, the exposition of the inductive effects of electrical currents—that is, more simply worded, the fact that a current flowing through one wire causes or "induces" another current to flow through another wire near it, but not in any way directly connected with it. In December, 1824, he tried to obtain an electric current by means of a magnet closely approached to a wire, and on three occasions had made elaborate but unsuccessful attempts to produce a current in one wire either by means of a current in another wire or by a magnet.

He persevered in spite of his disappointments, and on August 29, 1831, he obtained the first evidence that an electric current can induce another current in a different and unconnected circuit. Writing to a friend, on September 23, he says: "I am busy just now again on electro-magnetism, and think I have got hold of a good thing, but can't say. It may be a weed instead of a fish that, after all my labours, I may at last pull up." Had he been able to foresee how these comparatively few weeks of work would revolutionize the world of electrical science and of industry in general, even his unfailing modesty might have been pardoned for yielding, for once, to a sense of pride and elation. In nine more days he arrived at definite results, and he described the whole series of epoch-making experiments in his first "Experimental Researches," read before the Royal Society on November 24 of the same year. . . .

. . . I give here, for their historical interest, a few sentences from two paragraphs in which he describes electrical induction and the experiment with a magnet:

1. When an electric current is passed through one of two parallel wires, it causes at first a current in the same direction through the other, but this induced current does not last a moment, notwithstanding the inducing current (from the voltaic battery) is continued; all seems unchanged, except that the principal current continues its course. But when the current is stopped, then a return current occurs in the wire under induction, of about the same intensity and momentary duration, but in the opposite direction to that first formed. . . .

2. Then I found that magnets would induce just like voltaic currents, and by bringing helices and wires up to the poles of magnets, electrical currents were produced in them; these currents being able to deflect the galvonometer, or to make, by means of the helix, magnetic needles, or in one case even to give a spark. Hence the evolution of *electricity from magnetism.* The currents were not permanent. They ceased the moment the wires ceased to approach the magnet, because the new and apparently quiescent state was assumed, just as in the case of the induction of currents. But when the magnet was removed, and its induction therefore ceased, the return currents appeared as before.

32

THE REVOLUTIONS OF 1848

The revolutions of 1848 owed much to the liberal and nationalist heritage of the French Revolution. Revolutionary outbursts, beginning in Sicily and France in January and February, swept over central Europe in March and April, overthrowing Metternich's conservative order. In France, King Louis Philippe and his prime minister, Guizot, were replaced by a republican government. Elsewhere the revolutionists preserved monarchy but insisted upon written constitutions. In Italy and Germany liberals and nationalists sought unsuccessfully to achieve national unity. By mid-summer conservative forces (army, clergy, nobility, and peasantry) rallied so effectively that by the end of 1848 the revolts were largely crushed.

1. THE FEBRUARY REVOLUTION SWEEPS AWAY THE JULY MONARCHY

Opposition within France to the July Monarchy of Louis Philippe included such discontented groups as Legitimists, Catholics, Bonapartists, Liberal Reformers, Republicans, and Socialists. As these parties were prevented from airing their grievances in the press, they staged a series of political banquets. When the government forbade a banquet scheduled for February 22, 1848, the revolution began. In this selection Alexis de Tocqueville recalls the first few hours of the revolution.

The next morning was the 24th of February. On leaving my bedroom, I met the cook, who had been out; the good woman was quite beside herself, and poured out a sorrowing rigmarole, of which I failed to understand a

The Recollections of Alexis de Tocqueville, translated by Alexander Teixeira de Mattos and edited by J.P. Mayer (London: Harvill Press, Ltd., 1948), pp. 37–38, 58–59, 67. Used by permission of the publisher.

word, except that the Government was massacring the poor people. I went downstairs at once, and had no sooner set foot in the street than I breathed for the first time the atmosphere of revolutions. The roadway was empty; the shops were not open; there were no carriages nor pedestrians to be seen; none of the ordinary hawkers' cries were heard; neighbours stood talking in little groups at their doors, with subdued voices, with a frightened air; every face seemed distorted with fear or anger. I met a National Guard hurrying along, gun in hand, with a tragic gait; I accosted him, but could learn nothing from him, save that the Government was massacring the people (to which he added that the National Guard would know how to put that right). It was the same old refrain: it is easily understood that this explanation explained nothing. I was too well acquainted with the vices of the Government of July not to know that cruelty was not one of them. I considered it one of the most corrupt, but also one of the least bloodthirsty, that had ever existed, and I only repeat this observation in order to show the sort of rumour that assists the progress of revolutions. . .

. . . M. de Corcelles, whom I met in the street, gave me his account of what was happening, but in a very confused manner; for, in a city in state of revolution, as on a battle-field, each one readily regards the incidents of which himself is a witness as the events of the day. He told me of the firing on the Boulevard des Capucines, and of the rapid development of the insurrection of which this act of unnecessary violence was the cause or the pretext; . . .

I returned to the House and resumed my seat. Almost all the members had left; the benches were occupied by men of the populace. Lamartine was still in the tribune between the two banners, continuing to address the crowd, or rather conversing with them; for there seemed to be almost as many orators as listeners. The confusion was at its height. In a moment of semi-silence, Lamartine began to read out a list containing the names of the different people proposed by I don't know whom to take share in the Provisional Government that had just been decreed, nobody knows how. Most of these names were accepted with acclamations, some rejected with groans, others received with jest, for in scenes in which the people take part, as in the plays of Shakespeare, burlesque often rubs shoulders with tragedy, and wretched jokes sometimes come to the relief of the ardour of revolution. . . .

M. de Lamartine, I think, was beginning to grow greatly embarrassed at his position; for in a rebellion, as in a novel, the most difficult part to invent is the end. When, therefore, someone took it into his head to cry, "To the Hôtel de Ville!" Lamartine echoed, "Yes, to the Hôtel de Ville," and went out forthwith taking half the crowd with him; the others remained with Ledru-Rollin, who, in order, I suppose, to retain a leading part for himself, felt called upon in his turn to go through the same mock election, after which he too set out for the Hôtel de Ville. There the same electoral display was gone through once more; . . .

And so the Monarchy of July was fallen, fallen without a struggle, and before rather than beneath the blows of the victors, who were as astonished at their triumph as were the vanquished at their defeat. . . .

2. *KING FREDERICK WILLIAM IV ADDRESSES HIS BELOVED BERLINERS*

Frederick William IV, king of Prussia from 1840 to 1861, was a vaguely liberal dreamer, irresolute even in the calmest of circumstances. In the confusion of March 18, 1848, when barricades appeared in Berlin, he lost his courage entirely and made this ill-timed effort to win the affection of his subjects.

To My Beloved Berliners, . . . By my patent of convocation this day, you have received the pledge of the faithful sentiments of your King towards you and towards the whole of the German nation. The shout of joy which greeted me from unnumbered faithful hearts still resounded in my ears, when a crowd of peace-breakers mingled with the loyal throng, making seditious and bold demands, and augmenting in numbers as the well-disposed withdrew.

As their impetuous intrusion extended to the very portals of the Palace with apprehended sinister views, and insults were offered to my valiant and faithful soldiers, the court-yard was cleared by the cavalry, *at walking pace and with their weapons sheathed*; and two guns of the infantry went off of themselves, without, thanks be to God! causing any injury. A band of wicked men, chiefly consisting of foreigners, who, although searched for, have succeeded in concealing themselves for more than a week, have converted this circumstance into a palpable untruth, and have filled the excited minds of my faithful and beloved Berliners with thoughts of vengeance for supposed bloodshed; and thus have they become the fearful authors of bloodshed themselves. My troops, your brothers and fellow country-men, did not make use of their weapons till forced to do so by several shots fired at them from the Königs Strasse. The victorious advance of the troops was the necessary consequence.

It is now yours, inhabitants of my beloved native city, to avert a fearful evil. Acknowledge your fatal error; your King, your trusting friend, enjoins you, by all that is most sacred, to acknowledge your fatal error. Return to peace; remove the barricades which are still standing; and send to me men

"History," *The Annual Register, 1848* (London: 1849), pp. 378–379.

filled with the genuine ancient spirit of Berlin, speaking words which are seemly to your King; and I pledge you my royal truth that all the streets and squares shall be instantaneously cleared of the troops, and the military garrisons shall be confined solely to the most important buildings—to the Castle, the Arsenal, and a few others—and even here only for a brief space of time. Listen to the paternal voice of your King, ye inhabitants of my true and beautiful Berlin; and forget the past, as I shall forget it, for the sake of that great future which, under the peace-giving blessing of God, is dawning upon Prussia, and through Prussia upon all Germany.

Your loving Queen, and truly your genuine mother and friend, who is lying on a sick bed, joins her heartfelt and tearful supplications to mine.

Written during the night of the 18th and 19th March, 1848.

FREDERICK WILLIAM

3. *VIENNESE RIOTERS FORCE METTERNICH'S DISMISSAL*

In early March, 1848, when news of the February Revolution in Paris reached Austria, a wave of excitement swept over Viennese students. Middle-class businessmen, who were disturbed by the economic depression, and factory workers, who were close to starvation, joined a crowd of students on the morning of March 13 outside the* Landhaus *where the Estates of Lower Austria were meeting.

Just then a young man came plunging through the mob, joy beaming from his face, waving a paper and crying "Kossuth's speech. Kossuth's speech." The moment was electric. For ten days rumors had been going about town concerning a speech which the great Hungarian had given to his countrymen at the moment when he was inspired by the news of the Paris revolution. Everyone had heard of this speech, but very few had actually read the copies which were smuggled in and translated and passed from hand to hand. Now the mob hushed so that people as far away as possible could hear the magic words. For Kossuth was not afraid to use the word liberty. Hungary was a free country, he said, with an age-old constitution, and he demanded that the Hapsburgs should give her back her ancient rights. But Hungary could never count on her freedom, he insisted, under a king who was at the same time an absolute emperor to the rest of his dominions. Austria must have a constitution, too. (Hungary persisted in this demand right through 1867, when the system of the dual monarchy was set up and Austria then received a constitution at the hands of her sister nation.)

Priscilla Robertson, *Revolutions of 1848: A Social History* (Princeton, N.J.: Princeton University Press, 1952), pp. 210–212, 215–216.

When they heard this part of the speech, the people began yelling in spite of themselves. A constitution—hardly anyone in Vienna had dared to think of such a thing, not even the students. Here was courage, here was progress, pushing them beyond their dreams. As the young reader drew toward the end of his paper, a voice from a window in the *Landhaus* cried "From the Estates," and a hundred arms passed a piece of paper toward the young man who was standing on a fountain. But the mob would not let him read the news from the Estates until he had finished every last word from Kossuth. Then he opened the new paper and read a somewhat humble request to the Emperor to call a united diet (like Prussia's) to consider reform.

"That's nothing. Tear it up," people yelled, and the Estates' document was torn into a hundred pieces and scattered down on the heads of the crowd. "We want deeds, not words. No wishes, no prayers. We *demand.* We have the right to do it." A young man with dark face and flaming eyes climbed arrogantly on the fountain. "Dismiss the minister everyone hates," he cried. "What's his name? Tell us his name," roared the people below. "Metternich." This sally was met with bravos. . . .

All this time the press outside was getting thicker, if that were possible, and the good citizens who hoped for peaceful reforms were considerably surprised to find themselves mingling with a number of those workers from the suburbs whom the students had engaged to come and help them. With sudden shrinking, many burghers felt they would rather keep on with tyranny from above than be caught fighting on the same side as the rabble from the factories.

Ordinarily, the two classes never mixed, for the inner city of Vienna was still surrounded by its ancient walls and moat, and outside was a broad grass-covered glacis which separated it from the suburbs where the workers lived.

During the morning of March 13, the city gates were ordered shut, so that all but a few hundred workmen were successfully kept out of the city. Some students who happened to be shut out too were almost frantic at missing the excitement. One bribed a mail coach to let him hang on an axle and rode inside that way. But even the few workers who got in heartened the radicals and students and terrified the milder citizens to the point where they began shrieking for arms, a national guard to protect property. Up to this point, the national guard had seemed a very radical demand, stemming straight from Paris, but now it became one the government was almost eager to gratify. For the government was losing self-confidence rapidly and hoped the burghers would forget their other wishes in their excitement of being under arms. . . .

Just at the time when the students were winning their arms, their arch enemy, Prince Metternich, quit his office. He had known for a long time that the country suffered from incurable ailments—"I am too old a physician to be deceived"—and the news of Guizot's fall in Paris struck him like the death knell.

Not for a minute, though, did he lose his perfect composure. During the morning of March 13, he had telegraphed Pressburg that by evening all would be quiet. Later on in the day, he appeared at a state conference fastidiously dressed in a green morning coat and brightly colored trousers. Glancing out of the window, he made a comment about the rabble outdoors, and when someone observed that there were many well-dressed people in the street, he said, "If my son were among those people, I would still call them rabble." Towards evening his enemies proposed to his face that he resign. Metternich only bowed courteously, saying that he did not want his term of office to outlast his usefulness to the state, but that he had promised the Emperor's father never to abandon Ferdinand. That remark only sent people scurrying, with the natural bad manners of the court, to get poor Ferdinand to give an official kick to his old servant; it was not hard to do, and with perfect *sang-froid* Prince Metternich withdrew. Let no one think, he gently reminded protesting friends, that the fate of Austria depended on any one man. The country could be lost only if it gave itself up.

Outside the palace the crowds were yelling so fiercely against Metternich that Archduke Louis said he could not be responsible for his life—a fine admission from the very Hapsburg who had served with the great minister as a regent of the Empire for thirteen years. And the state treasury would not even advance him cash for a trip to England. The Prince finally got a loan from his friends, the Rothschilds, and made his way out of Vienna in a common cab. After various adventures, he succeeded in settling in England, from whence he watched the Empire he had held together so long, fall swiftly, though temporarily, to pieces.

4. *THE MILANESE RISE AGAINST AUSTRIA*

Five days after the student outburst in Vienna, revolutionaries seized Milan, the prosperous industrial and commercial center of the rich Lombard plain. The struggle of the Milanese against the Austrians included a mixture of comedy and tragedy. Before the end of 1848, however, Marshal Radetzky's Austrian forces reoccupied all of Lombardy and Venice.

Priscilla Robertson, *Revolutions of 1848: A Social History* (Princeton, N.J.: Princeton University Press, 1952), pp. 338–341.

. . . a professor at the university told the Milanese the story of the Boston tea party, and he urged that his fellow citizens copy American tactics. He thought they might stop using tobacco or playing the imperial lottery, for the tobacco monopoly brought in millions of lire to the imperial treasury, and the lottery was even more profitable. In answer the Milanese agreed to give up these pleasures beginning on New Year's Day, 1848.

For the first two days of the year things stayed fairly quiet, and Radetzky's impatience grew when he perceived that the citizens' boycott was a success. To provoke trouble, on January 3, every Austrian soldier was issued six cigars and a ration of brandy. Until this moment their manners had been impeccably correct, but now they swaggered around in groups of twenty or more, blowing smoke in civilians' faces and sometimes flaunting two cigars at once. Finally a civilian snatched a cigar from a soldier, and the fight for which both sides were spoiling was on. The results were tragic. Infantry cut down civilians, cavalry trampled them. At the end of the day there were 61 dead, including six children under eight and five old people over sixty. A man in a café who tried to shield his little girl with his own body was cut down along with the child. Soldiers fell on a group of workingmen coming out of a factory and tried to force them to smoke; the workmen refused and some of them were killed. Hospitals, which incidentally had been warned to get beds ready, were crowded with wounded.

Radetzky may have been pleased with this result. At any rate he refused for a whole week the civilian governor's request to hold his soldiers in their barracks. All the time he told the Milanese proletariat that the nobility started all the trouble—it was the work of a small party only.

Even though you call us twice a party, said the Marquis Massimo d' Azeglio in his report to the civilized world on the massacre, we will answer three times, "We are a nation, a nation, a nation." . . . To prove to the common people that they were not a separate party, Milanese nobles raised a subscription for the wounded and for the families of the dead. Fifty-two gentlemen took the unusual step of soliciting from door to door to give the lie to the Austrian assertions and show that Italians of all classes were united.

From that time until March the Milanese led their Austrian masters a dizzy dance. One day all patriots appeared with their hat bands buckled in front. When the bureaucracy caught on to this and passed an ordinance forbidding it, the same gentlemen came out the next day with the beaver fur of their hats brushed against the nap, and next another unusual fashion, and then another. Ladies too seemed under the sway of some powerful organization which told them what to do. Often La Scala was empty, except for the rows of white-coated Austrian officers, but on the night when Milan heard that the King of Naples had granted a constitution to his people, every great lady attended the performance in a gala gown. On the same day the poorer classes of people celebrated by eating Neapolitan spaghetti. "Here is a police far stronger than our own," complained a harassed Austrian who could not keep up with such tactics.

Some explosion would have come soon to any city so tense with feeling. As it happened, the news of the Vienna revolution reached Milanese patriots just as they were wondering what sort of a demonstration to make; as soon as they heard it Milan's date was moved up to March 18.

The night before, many Milanese youths took the sacrament. Afterwards, with glowing faces, they pulled out their strange and rusty assortment of hidden arms, even though their first orders were only to form a procession.

. . . 15,000 men answered the call to march to the Austrian government house. . . .

The highest Austrian official whom these patriots could find at his office was terrified, and he signed at once the order they asked for, an order to establish a civic guard for all citizens not living by their daily work. . . .

The barricades of Milan were the most fantastic of all the impromptu structures of 1848. Not only viceregal coaches and omnibusses, but sofas and pianos went into them. Rich merchants opened their warehouses and the people carried out bales of silk or coops of hens. Schools were emptied of their benches, churches of their confessionals. Rich citizens and factory workers helped each other in this work while children carried stones and tiles and boiling water to the roofs to hurl on any unlucky Austrian uniform below. Young girls pulled up the two white rows of flagstones which ran down the middle of each street for carriage wheels to pass over. Though a dozen chemists worked night and day to make powder, this item was so scarce that it was rationed out as if it were tobacco. Only men who knew how to shoot were allowed to use it, and they were happy whenever they got enough to charge their guns once or twice. They all felt that they could not afford two shots to kill a single Croat, so the young men shot in turn instead of simultaneously. Astronomers on a tower scanned the countryside with their telescopes and passed news down a wire on a little ring. University students, who were in charge of prisoners and of attacking the gates of the city, were the happiest of all. They hurried along the streets or over the roofs or through windows, intent on their business until they lost all idea of time. When they were hungry they begged a bit of bread at any doorway; if they were wounded all homes were open to them.

Radetzky's highly trained army was not prepared to deal with this sort of an insurrection, where cavalry and artillery were useless and his infantry patrols were all too easily picked off. So he decided to retire his foodless, sleepless troops from the interior of the city and make an iron ring outside from which he might starve the town and bombard it if it refused to come to terms.

5. *THE TIDE TURNS AGAINST THE REVOLUTIONISTS*

The first real defeat for the revolutionists of 1848 occurred in Prague, where a pan-Slavic congress had gathered to discuss Slavic autonomy within the Hapsburg empire. Prince Windischgrätz' capture of Prague, described below, heralded the end of the liberal movement in central Europe.

In the mean time national antipathies between the German and Slavonic races had broken out into open hostilities in Bohemia. Early in March a meeting had been held at Prague, for the purpose of petitioning the Austrian Government to grant certain demands upon which both the Czechs and Germans were agreed. They were principally these:—political equality of the two races (Czech or Slavonic and German); obligation on all public functionaries to speak both languages; union of Bohemia, Moravia, and Silesia, guaranteed by a Diet which was to meet alternately at Prague and Brunn; representative and municipal reform; liberty of the press; publicity of proceedings in courts of justice; arming of the people; suppression of feudal seignories and jurisdictions; security for personal liberty; impartiality in the demands of military service; and equality of all religious sects.

After considerable delay, the whole of these demands were, on the 8th of April, granted by a royal rescript of the Emperor, and the young Archduke Francis Joseph, the nephew of Ferdinand and heir presumptive of the throne, was nominated Viceroy of the kingdom of Bohemia.

The effect of this concession, however, was very different from what had been anticipated. Hitherto the German element of the population, though numerically inferior in the proportion of 1,830,000 to 2,558,000, had been the dominant body; but now, in consequence of the new constitution granted at their own request, they found themselves in a position of disadvantage. They had despised the Slavonic race too much to take the trouble to acquire a knowledge of their language, and owing to the provision which required all public officers to speak both tongues, they were suddenly incapacitated for state employments, and the Czechs became at

"History," *The Annual Register, 1848* (London: 1849), pp. 408–410.

once the powerful and dominant party. Count Leo Thun was elected by the latter as Burgrave of Prague, and it was resolved to convoke a great Panslavonic Congress, to meet at Prague on the 31st of May, in order to determine upon the measures necessary to protect Slavonic independence against the aggressive attempts of Teutonic supremacy.

Two days before this Assembly met, Count Leo Thun and the other leaders of the Czechs at Prague determined to established a Provisional Government there, which should be independent of the Government at Vienna. Accordingly, eight of the most conspicuous members of that party were chosen and invested with the direction of affairs, and two of the number left Prague for Innspruck, in order to obtain the formal sanction of the Emperor to their proceedings. . . .

In obedience to the summons issued by the Czechs of Prague, three hundred deputies from the different Slavonic States met there on the 2nd of June, when the Congress was formally opened. Their first act was to frame and publish a manifesto to the whole of Europe, in which they declared that their object was to claim and assert full justice for the whole Slavonic family; and to effect this they demanded that a great European Congress should meet, and settle the various conflicting interests of the States in which Slavs formed part of the population. But a sterner arbitrament was at hand. The Viennese ministry refused to recognize the Provisional Government at Prague, and declared that its constitution was illegal, and its acts void. At this time the Austrian Governor of Prague was Prince Windischgrätz (a lineal descendant of the great Wallenstein), and he took active measures to prepare for the struggle which he saw approaching. On the 12th of June a public meeting of the Czechs was held, to protest against the removal of artillery to points where it could be directed against the city. A tumult ensued, and the crowd rushed to the house of Prince Windischgrätz, where they gave vent to their feelings of hatred by abusive cries. The rioters were ordered to disperse, but they refused to quit the place, and some shots were fired by the mob, one of which, from a rifle, by a melancholy fatality, killed the Princess Windischgrätz, who was in an apartment of the house. The bereaved husband immediately came forward, and expostulated with the crowd in mild and dignified language, but in vain; at last an attempt was made to seize him, but the soldiers promptly interfered, and a general fight between them and the populace commenced. The contest raged with fury until the evening of the 14th, when Count Mensdorff arrived from Vienna, and assumed the command of the troops. This produced no cessation of the struggle, and on the following day the military quitted the town, and, taking up a position in the heights, began to bombard it with cannon. Even then the infuriated Czechs refused to yield; and it was not until the evening of the 17th, when a great part of the city had been destroyed, that the troops gained possession of Prague, and the insurrection was put down. The Slavonic Congress was of course at once dissolved, and the revolutionary Government overthrown.

6. LOUIS NAPOLEON BONAPARTE INTRODUCES HIMSELF TO FRENCH VOTERS

Louis Napoleon Bonaparte (1808–1873), nephew of Napoleon I, was living in England when the February Revolution occurred. Although he was elected to the National Assembly in the summer of 1848, most Frenchmen knew little about him. Hence, Louis Napoleon issued the following manifesto during the presidential campaign in the fall of 1848. The second selection is from a speech delivered at Bordeaux in October, 1852, by President Louis Napoleon Bonaparte shortly before the Second French Republic became the Second Empire.

LOUIS NAPOLEON TO HIS FELLOW-CITIZENS: In order to recall me from exile, you have elected me a representative of the people; on the eve of choosing a chief magistrate for the republic my name presents itself to you as a symbol of order and security.

Those proofs of so honorable a confidence are, I am well aware, addressed to my name rather than to myself, who, as yet, have done nothing for my country; but the more the memory of the Emperor protects me and inspires your suffrages, the more I feel compelled to acquaint you with my sentiments and principles. There must be no equivocation between us.

I am moved by no ambition which dreams one day of empire and war, the next of the application of subversive theories. Brought up in free countries, disciplined in the school of misfortune, I shall ever remain faithful to the duties which your suffrages and the will of the Assembly impose upon me.

If elected president, I shall shrink from no danger, from no sacrifice, in the defense of society, which has been so outrageously assailed. I shall devote myself wholly and without reservation to the consolidation of the republic, so that it may be wise in its laws, honest in its aims, great and strong in its deeds. My greatest honor wuold be to hand on to my successor, after four years of office, the public power consolidated, its liberties intact, and a genuine progress assured. . . .

LOUIS NAPOLEON BONAPARTE

J.H. Robinson, *Readings in European History* (New York: Ginn and Company, 1904), Vol. II, p. 562. Copyright 1904 by James Harvey Robinson. Used by permission of the publisher.

7. LOUIS NAPOLEON SUGGESTS THAT THE FRENCH REPUBLIC BECOME AN EMPIRE

The purpose of this journey, as you know, was to see for myself our beautiful provinces of the south and familiarize myself with their needs. It has, however, given rise to a much more important result. Indeed,—and I say it with a candor as far removed from arrogance as from false modesty,—never has a people testified in a manner more direct, spontaneous, and unanimous, the longing to be freed from anxiety as to the future by concentrating in a single person an authority which shall accord with their desires. They realize now both the false hopes with which they have been deluded and the dangers which threaten them. . . .

France to-day encompasses me with her sympathies because I do not belong to the group of dreamers. In order to benefit the country it is not necessary to resort to new systems, but, above all, to establish confidence in the present and security for the future. This is why France seems to wish to revert to the empire.

There is, nevertheless, one apprehension, and that I shall set at rest. A spirit of distrust leads certain persons to say that the empire means war. I say, the empire means peace. France longs for peace, and if France is satisfied the world is tranquil. Glory is rightly handed down hereditarily, but not war. . . .

I concede, nevertheless, that, like the Emperor, I have many conquests to make. I would, like him, conquer, for the sake of harmony, the warring parties and bring into the great popular current the wasteful and conflicting eddies. I would conquer, for the sake of religion, morality, and material ease, that portion of the population, still very numerous, which, in the midst of a country of faith and belief, hardly knows the precepts of Christ; which, in the midst of the most fertile country of the world, is hardly able to enjoy the primary necessities of life. We have immense uncultivated districts to bring under cultivation, roads to open, harbors to construct, rivers to render navigable, canals to finish, and our network of railroads to bring to completion. . . .

This is what I understand by the emipre, if the empire is to be reëstablished. These are the conquests which I contemplate, and all of you who surround me, who, like myself, wish the good of our common country, you are my soldiers.

J.H. Robinson, *Readings in European History* (New York: Ginn and Company, 1904), Vol. II, pp. 563–564. Copyright 1904 by James Harvey Robinson. Used by permission of the publisher.

VIII

MATERIAL PROGRESS AND DEMOCRATIC POLITICS

33

THE INDUSTRIAL REVOLUTION

The term "Industrial Revolution" refers to the economic and social changes that transformed an agricultural and commercial world into a modern industrial society. Beginning in England in the middle of the eighteenth century, the Industrial Revolution had spread by 1840 to France and Belgium. Germany remained relatively backward until economic unity was achieved by the *Zollverein* and the railroads. Watt's steam engine furnished power to heavy, expensive machinery installed in factories. With the factory system arose the industrial city, unattractive and unsanitary. Despite unhealthy working and living conditions, the population of Europe increased greatly as industrialization spread. In the course of time the Industrial Revolution brought to millions of workers a higher standard of living than nobles of earlier ages had known.

1. INVENTORS PLAY A LEADING ROLE IN THE INDUSTRIAL REVOLUTION

In eighteenth century England, wealth gained from overseas trade led to an increasing demand for goods, particularly cotton cloth, which exceeded the productive capacity of the cotton industry. Production was increased despite a labor shortage by means of a series of remarkable inventions in cotton spinning, weaving, bleaching, and printing. In the iron industry a shortage of wood led to use of coke as a smelting fuel, while the quality of wrought iron was improved by a series of inventions.

Some accounts of the technological revolution begin with the story of a dreamy boy watching the steam raise the lid of the kettle on the domestic hearth, or with that of a poor weaver gazing with stupefaction at his wife's

Thomas S. Ashton, *The Industrial Revolution, 1760–1830* (London: Oxford University Press, 1948), pp. 13–15. Used by permission of the publisher.

spinning wheel, overturned on the floor but still revolving. These, needless to say, are nothing but romantic fiction. Other accounts leave the impression that the inventions were the work of obscure millwrights, carpenters, or clock-makers, untutored in principles, who stumbled by chance on some device that was destined to bring others to fame and fortune and themselves to penury. It is true that there were inventors—men like Brindley and Murdoch—who were endowed with little learning, but with much native wit. It is true that there were others, such as Crompton and Cort, whose discoveries transformed whole industries, but left them to end their days in relative poverty. It is true that a few new products came into being as the result of accident. But such accounts have done harm by obscuring the fact that systematic thought lay behind most of the innovations in industrial practice, by making it appear that the distribution of rewards and penalties in the economic system was wholly irrational, and above all, by overstressing the part played by chance in technical progress. 'Chance', as Pasteur said, 'favours only the mind which is prepared': most discoveries are achieved only after repeated trial and error. Many involve two or more previously independent ideas or processes, which, brought together in the mind of the inventor, issue in a more or less complex and efficient mechanism. In this way, for example, the principle of the jenny was united by Crompton with that of spinning by rollers to produce the mule; and the iron rail, which had long been in use in the coal mine, was joined to the locomotive to create the railway. In such cases of what has been called cross-mutation the part played by chance must have been very small indeed.

Yet other accounts of the industrial revolution are misleading because they present discovery as the achievement of individual genius, and not as a social process. 'Invention', as a distinguished modern scientist, Michael Polanyi, has remarked, 'is a drama enacted on a crowded stage.' The applause tends to be given to those who happen to be on the boards in the final act, but the success of the performance depends on the close cooperation of many players, and of those behind the scenes. . . .

2. *JAMES WATT TAKES A SUNDAY AFTERNOON STROLL*

James Watt (1736–1819) possessed both inventive talents and considerable scientific knowledge. As an instrument maker at the University of Glasgow, Watt was repairing a model of the Newcomen steam engine, when he began thinking of

Conversation of James Watt with Robert Hart of Glasgow in 1813 or 1814, in H.W. Dickinson and Rhys Jenkins, *James Watt and the Steam Engine* (Oxford: The Clarendon Press, 1927), p. 23.

improvements. Newcomen's engine had only one cylinder, in which steam was alternately induced and condensed. Watt describes below his great fuel-saving invention of 1764. His separate condenser was the greatest single improvement ever made in a steam engine.

It was in the Green of Glasgow. I had gone to take a walk on a fine Sabbath afternoon. I had entered the Green by the gate at the foot of Charlotte Street—had passed the old washing-house. I was thinking upon the engine . . . and gone as far as the Herd's House, when the idea came into my mind that as steam was an elastic body it would rush into a vacuum, and if a communication was made between the cylinder and an exhausted vessel, it would rush into it and might be there condensed without cooling the cylinder. I then saw that I must get quit of the condensed steam and injection water, if I used a jet as in Newcomen's engine. Two ways of doing this occurred to me. First the water might be run off by a descending pipe, if an offlet could be got at the depth of 35 or 36 feet, and any air might be extracted by a small pump; the second was to make the pump large enough to extract both water and air. . . . I had not walked further than the Golf-house when the whole thing was arranged in my mind.

3. *A SURGEON DESCRIBES SANITARY CONDITIONS IN MANCHESTER*

As factories tended to concentrate in certain favorable locations with advantages of water power, coal, mineral deposits, or transportation, a new type of urban community emerged—the industrial city. Manchester, center of the cotton spinning industry, was England's fastest growing factory town in the early nineteenth century.

Until twelve years ago there was no paving and sewering Act in any of the townships; even in the township of Manchester, containing in the year 1831 upwards of 142,000 inhabitants, this was the case; and the disgraceful condition of the streets and sewers on the invasion of the cholera you have no doubt learned from Dr. Kay's able and valuable pamphlet. At the present time the paving of the streets proceeds rapidly in every direction, and great attention is given to the drains. Upon the whole, it is gratifying to bear testimony to the zeal of the authorities in carrying on the salutary improvements, especially when it is known that no street can be paved and

"Description of the Condition of Manchester by John Robertson, Surgeon," from *Report of Committee on Health of Towns* (1840), Vol. XI, pp. 221–222, App. II, as found in A.E. Bland, P.A. Brown, and R.H. Tawney, eds., *English Economic History: Select Documents* (London: G. Bell & Sons, Ltd., 1925), pp. 519–521. Used by permission of the publisher.

sewered without the consent of the owners of property, unless a certain large proportion of the land on either side is built upon. Owing to this cause several important streets remain to this hour disgraceful nuisances.

Manchester has no Building Act, and hence, with the exception of certain central streets, over which the Police Act gives the Commissioners power, each proprietor builds as he pleases. New cottages, with or without cellars, huddled together row behind row, may be seen springing up in many parts, but especially in the township of Manchester, where the land is higher in price than the land for cottage sites in other townships is. With such proceedings as these the authorities cannot interfere. A cottage row may be badly drained, the streets may be full of pits, brimful of stagnant water, the receptacle of dead cats and dogs, yet no one may find fault. The number of cellar residences, you have probably learned from the papers published by the Manchester Statistical Society, is very great in all quarters of the town; and even in Hulme, a large portion of which consists of cottages recently erected, the same practice is continued. That it is an evil must be obvious on the slightest consideration, for how can a hole underground of from 12 to 15 feet square admit of ventilation so as to fit it for a human habitation?

We have no authorized inspector of dwellings and streets. If an epidemic disease were to invade, as happened in 1832, the authorities would probably order inspection, as they did on that occasion, but it would be merely by general permission, not of right.

So long as this and other great manufacturing towns were multiplying and extending their branches of manufacture and were prosperous, every fresh addition of operatives found employment, good wages, and plenty of food; and so long as the families of working people are well fed, it is certain they maintain their health in a surprising manner, even in cellars and other close dwellings. Now, however, the case is different. Food is dear, labour scarce, and wages in many branches very low; consequently, as might be expected, disease and death are making unusual havoc. In the years 1833, 1834, 1835, and 1836 (years of prosperity), the number of fever cases admitted into the Manchester House of Recovery amounted only to 1,685, or 421 per annum; while in the two pinching years, 1838 and 1839, the number admitted was 2,414, or 1,207 per annum. It is in such a depressed state of the manufacturing districts as at present exists that unpaved and badly sewered streets, narrow alleys, close, unventilated courts and cellars, exhibit their malign influence in augmenting the sufferings which that greatest of all physical evils, want of sufficient food, inflicts on young and old in large towns, but especially on the young.

Manchester has no public park or other grounds where the population can walk and breathe the fresh air. New streets are rapidly extending in every direction, and so great already is the expanse of the town, that those who live in the more populous quarters can seldom hope to see the green face of nature. . . . In this respect Manchester is disgracefully defective; more so, perhaps, than any other town in the empire. Every advantage of this nature has been sacrificed to the getting of money in the shape of ground-rents.

4. ROBERT OWEN AND SIR ROBERT PEEL REPORT ON CHILDREN IN FACTORIES

Robert Owen (1771–1858) rose from humble origins to become a factory owner, humanitarian, and social reformer. Owen's factory community was a model of the best working and living conditions possible at that time. Sir Robert Peel (1788–1850), a parliamentary leader of the Conservative Party, came from a newly rich family of cotton manufacturers. Both Owen and Peel were familiar with child labor in factories, one of the most depressing aspects of the early Industrial Revolution.

Mr. Robert Owen, Again Called in, and Examined

Have you anything to add to your evidence of yesterday?—Some questions were put to me yesterday respecting the early age at which children are employed at Stockport; I knew I had made a memorandum at the time, but I could not then put my hand upon it; I have since found it; and I can now reply to the questions regarding those cases. Mr. George Oughton, secretary to the Sunday school in Stockport, informed me about a fortnight ago, in the presence of an individual, who will probably be here in the course of the morning, that he knows a little girl of the name of Hannah Downham, who was employed in a mill at Stockport at the age of four. Mr. Turner, treasurer to the Sunday school, knows a boy that was employed in a mill at Stockport when he was only three years old. . . .

They were mentioned to you as a rare instance?—They were mentioned to me in the midst of a very numerous assembly of very respectable people; I inquired of them whether they knew, as they were surrounded with, I believe, two or three thousand children at the time, what was the age at which children were generally admitted into cotton mills; their answer was, Some at five, many at six, and a greater number at seven. I have also received very important information from a very respectable individual at Manchester, relative to the age at which children are employed, the hours

Report of Committee on Children in Manufactories (1816), Vol. III, pp. 89, 132–133, as found in A.E. Bland, P.A. Brown, and R.H. Tawney, eds., *English Economic History: Select Documents* (London: G. Bell & Sons, Ltd., 1925), pp. 502–504. Used by permission of the publisher.

they are kept to work, and a variety of other particulars from very authentic sources. . . .

Does the information you propose to give come from the manufactory to which it relates?—No manufacturer would give information against himself.

State what you know relative to the number of hours which children and others are employed in their attendance on mills and manufactories?—About a fortnight ago I was in Leeds; and in conversation with Mr. Gott, whose name is well-known to many gentlemen in this room, he stated to me that it was a common practice, when the woollen trade was going on well, to work sixteen hours in the day: I was also informed by Mr. Marshall, who is another principal, and considered a highly respectable manufacturer in Leeds, that it was a common practice to work at flax-mills there sixteen hours a day whenever the trade went well: I was also informed by Mr. Gott, that when the Bill, generally known by the name of Sir Robert Peel's Bill, was brought in last session of Parliament, the night-work at Leeds was put an end to. In Stockport, on Sunday fortnight, I saw a number of small children going to the church; they appeared to me to be going from a Sunday school; the master was with them; I stopped the master, and asked him what he knew of the circumstances of the manufacturers in Stockport; he said he knew a great deal, because he himself had formerly, for many years, been a spinner in those mills; his name is Robert Mayor, of the National School in Stockport; he stated that he was willing to make oath that mills in Stockport, within the last twelve months, had been worked from three and four o'clock in the morning until nine at night, that he himself has frequently worked those hours.

Sir Robert Peel, Bart.

The house in which I have a concern gave employment at one time to near one thousand children of this description. Having other pursuits, it was not often in my power to visit the factories, but whenever such visits were made, I was struck with the uniform appearance of bad health, and, in many cases, stinted growth of the children; the hours of labour were regulated by the interest of the overseer, whose remuneration depending on the quantity of the work done, he was often induced to make the poor children work excessive hours, and to stop their complaints by trifling bribes. Finding our own factories under such management, and learning that the like practices prevailed in other parts of the kingdom where similar machinery was in use, the children being much over-worked, and often little or no regard paid to cleanliness and ventilation in the buildings; having the assistance of Dr. Percival and other eminent medical gentlemen of Manchester, together with some distinguished characters both in and out of Parliament, I brought in a Bill . . . for the regulation of factories containing such parish apprentices. The hours of work allowed by that Bill being fewer in number than those formerly practised, a visible improvement in the health and general appearance of the children soon became evident, and since the complete operation of the Act contagious disorders have rarely occurred.

5. MALTHUS VIEWS WITH ALARM THE RISE OF POPULATION

Thomas Robert Malthus (1766–1834) published his first* Essay on Population *in 1798, when the Industrial Revolution was gaining momentum, and when the population of England was rapidly increasing. His pessimistic view that population tends to increase faster than available food supplies led many to the conclusion that charity or higher wages served only to increase the population and bring renewed poverty and distress.

I have read some of the speculations on the perfectibility of man and of society with great pleasure. I have been warmed and delighted with the enchanting picture which they hold forth. I ardently wish for such happy improvements. But I see great, and, to my understanding, unconquerable difficulties in the way to them. . . .

I think I may fairly make two postulata.

First, That food is necessary to the existence of man.

Secondly, That the passion between the sexes is necessary, and will remain nearly in its present state.

These two laws ever since we have had any knowledge of mankind, appear to have been fixed laws of our nature; and, as we have not hitherto seen any alteration in them, we have no right to conclude that they will ever cease to be what they are now, without an immediate act of power in that Being who first arranged the system of the universe; and for the advantage of his creatures, still executes, according to fixed laws, all its various operations. . . .

Assuming, then, my postulata as granted, I say, that the power of population is indefinitely greater than the power in the earth to produce subsistence for man.

Population, when unchecked, increases in a geometrical ratio. Subsistence only increases in an arithmetical ratio. A slight acquaintance with

T.R. Malthus, *Parallel Chapters from the First and Second Editions of an Essay on the Principle of Population* (New York: The Macmillan Company, 1906), pp. 4, 6–8.

numbers will show the immensity of the first power in comparison of the second.

By that law of our nature which makes food necessary to the life of man, the effects of these two unequal powers must be kept equal.

This implies a strong and constantly operating check on population from the difficulty of subsistence. This difficulty must fall some where; and must necessarily be severely felt by a large portion of mankind.

Through the animal and vegetable kingdoms, nature has scattered the seeds of life abroad with the most profuse and liberal hand. She has been comparatively sparing in the room, and the nourishment necessary to rear them. The germs of existence contained in this spot of earth, with ample food, and ample room to expand it, would fill millions of worlds in the course of a few thousand years. Necessity, that imperious, all-pervading law of nature, restrains them within the prescribed bounds. The race of plants, and the race of animals shrink under this great restrictive law. And the race of man cannot, by any efforts of reason, escape from it. Among plants and animals its effects are waste of seed, sickness, and premature death. Among mankind, misery and vice. The former, misery, is an absolutely necessary consequence of it. Vice is a highly probable consequence, and we therefore see it abundantly prevail; but it ought not, perhaps, to be called an absolutely necessary consequence. The ordeal of virtue is to resist all temptation to evil.

This natural inequality of the two powers of population, and of production in the earth, and that great law of our nature which must constantly keep their effects equal, form the great difficulty that to me appears insurmountable in the way to perfectibility of society. . . .

6. *THE INDUSTRIAL REVOLUTION IS ACCOMPANIED BY AN UNPRECEDENTED POPULATION GROWTH*

Malthus' fears that increasing poverty would result from population growth failed to materialize. However, Europe would have experienced a lowering of the standard of living, had it not been for the technological advances, increased agricultural production, and improvements in transportation.

The outstanding feature of the social history of the period—the thing that above all others distinguishes the age from its predecessors—is the rapid growth of population. Careful estimates, based on figures of burials and christenings, put the number of people in England and Wales at about five and a half millions in 1700, and six and a half millions in 1750: when the

Thomas S. Ashton, *The Industrial Revolution, 1760–1830* (London: Oxford University Press, 1948), 2–5. Used by permission of the publisher.

first census was taken in 1801 it was a round nine millions, and by 1831 had reached fourteen millions. In the second half of the eighteenth century population had thus increased by 40 per cent., and in the first three decades of the nineteenth century by more than 50 per cent. For Great Britain the figures are approximately eleven millions in 1801, and sixteen and a half millions in 1831.

The growth of population was not the result of any marked change in the birth rate. During the first four decades of the eighteenth century, it is true, the number of births per thousand people seems to have risen a little. Farm labourers tended to set up households of their own instead of boarding with their employers, and a decline of the system of apprenticeship in industry also led to earlier marriage and larger families. But from 1740 to 1830 the birth rate appears to have fluctuated only very slightly: for no decade does the estimate rise above 37.7, or fall below 36.6. Throughout the industrial revolution fertility was high but steady.

Nor can the increase of people be attributed to an influx from other countries. In every decade men and women took ship from Ireland to England and Scotland, and at times of dearth the trickle became a stream. But there was no such torrent of Irish immigration as was to come in the last five years of the eighteen-forties. On the other hand, during the eighteenth century perhaps a million people left Britain to seek a living overseas, mainly in the colonies. Among them were some 50,000 criminals transported to Maryland or Botany Bay, and a number of artisans who defied the law by carrying their technical knowledge and skill to Europe—not in the long run, it may be guessed, to the disadvantage of their native land. On balance, Britain was not a receiving centre but a breeding-ground for new communities across the seas.

It was a fall of mortality that led to the increase of numbers. In the first four decades of the eighteenth century excessive indulgence in cheap gin and intermittent periods of famine took a heavy toll of lives; but between 1740 and 1820 the death rate fell almost continuously—from an estimated 35.8 for the ten years ending in 1740 to one of 21.1 for those ending in 1821. Many influences were operating to reduce the incidence of death. The introduction of root crops made it possible to feed more cattle in the winter months, and so to supply fresh meat throughout the year. The substitution of wheat for inferior cereals, and an increased consumption of vegetables, strengthened resistance to disease. Higher standards of personal cleanliness, associated with more soap and cheaper cotton underwear, lessened the dangers of infection. The use of brick in place of timber in the walls, and of slate or stone instead of thatch in the roofs, of cottages reduced the number of pests; and the removal of many noxious processes of manufacture from the homes of the workers brought greater domestic comfort. The larger towns were paved, drained, and supplied with running water; knowledge of medicine and surgery developed; hospitals and dispensaries increased; and more attention was paid to such things as the disposal of refuse and the proper burial of the dead.

Since there are no reliable statistics it is not possible to say which age groups of the population benefited most from these improvements. In a well-known passage of his *Autobiography* Edward Gibbon says:

> The death of a new-born child before that of its parents may seem an unnatural, but it is strictly a probable event; since of any given number, the greater part are extinguished before their ninth year, before they possess the faculties of mind or body. Without accusing the profuse waste or imperfect workmanship of Nature, I shall only observe that this unfavourable chance was multiplied against my infant existence. So feeble was my constitution, so precarious my life, that in the baptism of each of my brothers, my father's prudence repeated my Christian name of Edward, that in case of the departure of the eldest son, this patronymic appellation might be still perpetuated in the family.

This was written in 1792–3. By that time it is probable that the profuse waste of infant life was a little less than at the date of Gibbon's birth, and, if so, there would be a higher percentage of children and young people in the population. It is a matter to be borne in mind in considering the constitution of the labour force of the early factories.

7. *THE* ZOLLVEREIN *CONTRIBUTES TO GERMANY'S INDUSTRIAL REVOLUTION*

British industrial superiority, unrivaled in the first three-fourths of the nineteenth century, was challenged by Germany after 1870 with surprising success. The creation of the customs union* (Zollverein) *in 1833 was one of the major contributing factors. Other major elements in the German Industrial Revolution were: the excellent coal deposits in the Ruhr and Silesia, improved east-west communications by railway building, and Bismarck's political unification of 1870.

Communications were very poor in Germany in the early years of the nineteenth century. The character of one of Jean Paul's novels who took some splints with him when setting out on a journey was only taking a necessary precaution. In winter, travelling was particularly difficult. One traveller wrote that in Thuringia in 1814 his coach was stuck in a hole filled with snow and he had to be rescued by a detachment of Russian soldiers. Two years later another traveller took no less than five hours to go by coach from Weimar to Erfurt, a distance of about twelve miles. In

W.O. Henderson, *The Zollverein* (Cambridge: University Press, 1939), pp. 19–20, 21–23, 337–339. Used by permission of the publisher.

the early 'twenties the post-coach from Berlin to Breslau carried only three passengers and took forty hours for the journey. The fare was 12 thalers. Only those who could afford to secure frequent changes of horses moved with any speed. Some good roads, such as the one from Metz to Mainz and Bremen, were built in those parts of Germany that were under the control of the French but they were exceptional. On the whole, river and canal communications were also inadequate. Poor communications hampered trade and at times of bad harvest some towns suffered considerably owing to the difficulty of bringing food from any distance. It was not easy to bring coal and iron together for purposes of manufacture. As late as 1830 Harkort complained that the Westphalian iron industry could not develop as the coal and iron lay 46 miles apart.

Few could have foreseen in 1815 that Germany with her cumbersome federal constitution, her internal tariff barriers and her comparatively poor natural resources would one day become the leading industrial State on the Continent.

. . . It is estimated that in 1790 there were some eighteen hundred customs frontiers in Germany. "The Germans trade like prisoners behind prison bars", declared a Frenchman. In 1722 Bavaria had over four hundred customs houses. The shipper who took goods on the Rhine from Strassburg to the Dutch frontier, on the Main from Bamberg to Mainz, or on the Weser from Minden to Elsfleth (below Bremen) had to pay over thirty tolls on each of these journeys. Fourteen dues were charged on the Elbe between Magdeburg and Hamburg. The traveller who went from Dresden to Magdeburg had to pass sixteen customs houses. Tariffs were complicated. Prussia, for example, imposed over sixty different rates of customs and excise. . . .

Four of the most serious disadvantages of this state of affairs deserve notice. First, legitimate internal trade was seriously hampered. An influential Union of Merchants complained in a petition drawn up by Friedrich List in 1819, that numerous customs barriers "cripple trade and produce the same effect as ligatures which prevent the free circulation of the blood. The merchants trading between Hamburg and Austria, or Berlin and Switzerland must traverse ten States, must learn ten customs tariffs, must pay ten successive transit dues. Anyone who is so unfortunate as to live on the boundary line between three or four States spends his days among hostile tax-gatherers and customs house officials. He is a man without a country".

Secondly, the multiplicity of customs encouraged contraband traffic and "caused the country to swarm with petty smugglers." Thirdly, "the customs house administration was costly and generally inefficient, from the extent of frontier to be guarded". Fourthly, there were many complaints that owing to low duties imposed by ports like Hamburg and Bremen and by great markets like Frankfurt-am-Main, no adequate protection was afforded to German industry at a time when cheap British goods were flooding continental markets. "All States favour home industries by tariffs: Germany alone fails to protect her children", wrote seventy Rhineland manufacturers in a petition to the King of Prussia in April, 1818. . . .

. . . Germany's industrial successes after 1871 were based upon the firm foundations of earlier progress. Between 1815 and 1850 the first steps towards industrial expansion were taken by the founding and extending of the Zollverein and by the improvement of communications. The years 1850 to 1870 saw the rise of German industries—particularly coal, iron, steel and textiles—and the development of a capitalist organisation capable of great expansion in the future.

The development of the Zollverein had thus both an economic and a political significance. It contributed to that expansion of manufactures and commerce in the 'fifties and 'sixties which prepared the way for Germany's rapid rise after 1871 to the position of the chief industrial State on the Continent. It is impossible to estimate the extent to which the Zollverein was responsible for these changes, since many other factors favourable to industrial development have also to be considered. It is necessary to guard against the temptation to lay too much weight upon the part that treaties, laws and administrative decisions play in the economic life of a people.

The Zollverein was established in 1834. Germany's economic position improved somewhat in the next twenty years. It is easy to see a connection between the two. But it is a dangerous half-truth—an over-simplification of a highly complicated situation—to say that one caused the other. In its early days the Zollverein was far from complete and its influence was limited in many ways. The economic progress of the 'forties and 'fifties was satisfactory but by no means extraordinary. The construction of railways, the enterprise of capitalists, the activity of the great industrialists were probably as important as the customs union in promoting economic welfare. Thus the linking of the agricultural regions east of the Elbe with the manufacturing districts of the Rhineland and Saxony was due at least as much to railway developments as to establishment of the customs union. On the other hand, it is clear that if there had been no Zollverein Germany's economic progress would have been hindered, however strong might have been the other economic forces working in favour of expansion. Prussia—despite the gap between her eastern and western provinces—was probably large enough in area and population and sufficiently rich in natural resources and manufactures to make very considerable economic progress even if trade with other German States were hampered by tariff barriers. But smaller

States—except a few with special natural advantages—would probably have found themselves in serious difficulties if they had persisted in retaining their economic independence.

Germany's economic advance in the period 1815–71 may be considered from three angles—first, the gradual economic unification through the Zollverein and other agencies; secondly, the improvement in communications, particularly railways; and, thirdly, advances in manufactures, finance, agriculture and so forth. But such a division is one which should be adopted merely for convenience of discussion. It is essentially an artificial one since there is so much overlapping between the suggested factors. It would be fruitless to enquire which was the most important or which "caused" the others. Actually they are all of great importance and they sprang from similar fundamental causes. The period 1815–71 saw the genesis of the Industrial Revolution in Germany. The great capitalists and financiers and the commercial middle classes who stood to gain most from the industrialisation of the country supported such changes as would promote the progress of manufactures. The growth of the Zollverein and the construction of a railway system were changes of this nature. In this way the German environment was rendered more suitable for industrial advance. The difficulties in the way were due less to economic circumstances than to peculiar political conditions.

The Zollverein contributed to the attainment of German unity. The figure of Bismarck dominates Germany in the 'sixties, and students who investigate the history of the founding of the German Empire are tempted to confine their attention to his diplomacy and to the wars by which unity was attained. But, so far as her economic life was concerned, Germany had achieved a considerable measure of unification under Prussian leadership some time before Bismarck became Minister President in 1862. . . .

34

THE UNIFICATION OF ITALY AND GERMANY

The failure of idealistic liberals in both Italy and Germany to unify their lands in 1848 led to the more violent methods adopted by Cavour and Bismarck. Cavour, realizing the inability of Sardinia to overthrow Austrian domination of Italy unaided, pursued an elaborate plan to gain the support of Napoleon III and his French forces. Bismarck created a unified German Empire by utilizing Prussian military power and his own adroit diplomacy to achieve successive victories over Denmark, Austria, and France. In both Italy and Germany unification brought new problems of adjustment, including the relations of church and state.

1. CAVOUR AND NAPOLEON III CONSPIRE AGAINST AUSTRIA

Count Camillo Cavour (1810–1861), of a noble Piedmontese family, became prime minister of Sardinia in 1852 and worked tirelessly thereafter for Italian unity. By entering Sardinia in the Crimean War, Cavour was able to present the case for Italian unity at the Paris peace conference. In 1858, Napoleon III decided to work with Cavour to bring about a war with Austria. The details of the forthcoming conflict were cold-bloodedly arranged at a secret meeting at Plombières, France, in July, 1858, as described below.

The first interview began at 11 A.M. and lasted until 3 P.M. Napoleon commenced by saying that he had decided to support Sardinia with all his forces in a war against Austria, provided that a nonrevolutionary cause, which would justify the war in the eyes of diplomacy, and especially of public opinion in France and Europe, could be found. Cavour then sug-

A.J. Whyte, *The Political Life and Letters of Cavour, 1848–1861* (London: Oxford University Press, 1930), pp. 255–257. Used by permission of The Clarendon Press, Oxford.

gested, first, the trouble arising from the Treaty of Commerce with Austria, and then Austria's illegal expansion of power in Italy. Neither of these reasons satisfied Napoleon. They then examined together the map of Italy and finally found in Massa-Carrara a promising centre in which to foment the necessary rebellion. Sardinia was to provoke an appeal from the inhabitants, demanding annexation to Piedmont. The King would thereupon address a threatening note to the Duke of Modena who, relying on Austria, would probably reply in a similar tone. Victor Emmanuel would then occupy the Duchy and war would commence. After deciding that Naples should be left strictly alone, and that the Pope should be left in peaceful possession of Rome and the country round it, they passed on to the object of the war and the final settlement of Italy. Austria was to be completely driven out of the Peninsula and the country divided into a confederation of four powers. The Kingdom of Upper Italy, embracing North Italy from the Alps to the Adriatic with Romagna and the Duchies added, under the House of Savoy; a Kingdom of Central Italy composed of Tuscany and the greater part of the States of the Church; Rome and the Patriarchate, and the Kingdom of Naples. The Duchess of Parma was to be offered the throne of Central Italy, and the Pope was to be the President of the Confederation, which was to have a constitution based on that of Germany.

Having settled the future of Italy there came the question of the price to be paid. Napoleon demanded the cession of Savoy and Nice. Cavour, after stressing the severity of sacrificing the cradle of the race, agreed to surrender Savoy, but pointed out that to cede Nice was to infringe the principle of nationality, the people being Italian. At this the Emperor, after thoughtfully caressing his moustache several times, remarked that this was, after all, a secondary question which they could deal with later. The military aspect was next dealt with. France would provide 200,000 men and Italy half that number. To carry out their programme the complete defeat of Austria would be necessary and peace might have to be signed at Vienna before Austria would yield her Italian provinces. As to finance the Emperor agreed to furnish Piedmont with material, and facilitate the raising of a loan in France.

2. *GARIBALDI APPEALS TO THE SICILIANS*

Giuseppe Garibaldi (1807–1882), an early disciple of Mazzini, had followed an adventurous revolutionary career in Italy and South America. In Genoa in May, 1860, Garibaldi, with Sardinian approval, organized a volunteer force, the thousand "red shirts," for the conquest of Sicily and southern Italy. The following proclamation, issued by Garibaldi before reaching Sicily, evoked such sympa-

"Public Documents," *The Annual Register, 1860* (London: 1861), pp. 281–282.

thetic support in the south that all of the Kingdom of the Two Sicilies was rapidly overrun.

ITALIANS!—The Sicilians are fighting against the enemies of Italy, and for Italy. It is the duty of every Italian to succour them with words, money, and arms, and, above all, in person.

The misfortunes of Italy arise from the indifference of one province to the fate of the others.

The redemption of Italy began from the moment that men of the same land ran to help their distressed brothers.

Left to themselves, the brave Sicilians will have to fight, not only the mercenaries of the Bourbon, but also those of Austria and the Priest of Rome.

Let the inhabitants of the free provinces lift their voices in behalf of their struggling brethren, and impel their brave youth to the conflict.

Let the Marches, Umbria, Sabina, Rome, the Neapolitan, rise to divide the forces of our enemies.

Where the cities suffice not for the insurrection, let them send bands of their bravest into the country.

The brave man finds an arm everywhere. Listen not to the voice of cowards, but arm, and let us fight for our brethren, who will fight for us to-morrow.

A band of those who fought with me the country's battles marches with me to the fight. Good and generous, they will fight for their country to the last drop of their blood, nor ask for other reward than a clear conscience.

"Italy and Victor Emmanuel!" they cried, on passing the Ticino. "Italy and Victor Emmanuel!" shall re-echo in the blazing caves of Mongibello.

At this cry, thundering from the great rock of Italy to the Tarpeian, the rotten Throne of tyranny shall crumble, and, as one man, the brave descendants of Vespro shall rise.

To arms! Let me put an end, once for all, to the miseries of so many centuries. Prove to the world that it is no lie that Roman generations inhabited this land.

(Signed) G. GARIBALDI

3. *BISMARCK CALLS FOR BLOOD AND IRON*

William I, on his accession to the Prussian throne in 1861, desired to expand and reform the army. When his military budget was rejected by the liberals in

"Bismarck's Speech to the Budget Commission, 30 September, 1862," in G.A. Craig, trans. and ed., *The Development of National Feeling in Germany to 1871* (New Haven, Conn.: Yale University Press, 1940), p. 39.

the Prussian legislature, William named Otto von Bismarck (1815–1898) as chief minister. Bismarck, in the selection below, indicates his future program and methods.

Our blood is too hot; we prefer to wear armor which is too heavy for our slender body; but we should use it nonetheless. The eyes of Germany are fixed not upon Prussia's liberalism, but upon her armed might. Bavaria, Württemberg and Baden may indulge in liberal experiments; therefore, no one will assign to them Prussia's role. Prussia must harbor and maintain her strength for the favorable moment—a moment which has already, on one occasion, slipped by; Prussia's boundaries, as drawn by the Vienna treaties, are not suitable for a healthy State-life. The great questions of the day will not be decided by speeches or by majority decisions—that was the mistake of 1848 and 1849—but by blood and iron!

4. BISMARCK DISAGREES WITH THE KING ON PEACE TERMS FOR AUSTRIA

Ignoring the legislature, Bismarck proceeded to increase the Prussian army and to use it for the creation of a united Germany based on a more powerful Prussia. In 1866, Bismarck's well-planned war against Austria resulted in a quick victory for the Prussians at Sadowa on July 3, 1866.

On July 23, [1866], under the presidency of the King, a council of war was held, in which the question to be decided was whether we should make peace under the conditions offered or continue the war. A painful illness from which I was suffering made it necessary that the council should be held in my room. On this occasion I was the only civilian in uniform. I declared it to be my conviction that peace must be concluded on the Austrian terms, but remained alone in my opinion; the King supported the military majority. My nerves could not stand the strain which had been put upon them day and night; I got up in silence, walked into my adjoining bedchamber and was there overcome by a violent paroxysm of tears. Meanwhile, I heard the council dispersing in the next room. I thereupon set to work to commit to paper the reasons which in my opinion spoke for the conclusion of peace; and begged the King, in the event of his not accepting the advice for which I was responsible, to relieve me of my functions as minister if the war were continued. With this document I set out on the following day to explain it by word of mouth. In the antechamber I found two colonels with a report on the spread of cholera among their troops,

Bismarck, the Man and the Statesman, Being the Reflections and Reminiscences of Otto Prince von Bismarck, translated under the supervision of A.J. Butler (Leipzig: Bernhard Tauchnitz, 1899), Vol. II, pp. 228–233.

barely half of whom were fit for service. . . . Besides my political anxieties, I feared that by transferring the operations to Hungary, the nature of that country, which was well known to me, would soon make the disease overwhelming. The climate, especially in August, is dangerous. . . . Armed with my document I unfolded to the King the political and military reasons which opposed the continuation of the war.

We had to avoid wounding Austria too severely; we had to avoid leaving behind in her any unnecessary bitterness of feeling or desire for revenge; we ought rather to reserve the possibility of becoming friends again with our adversary of the moment, and in any case to regard the Austrian state as a piece on the European chessboard and the renewal of friendly relations with her as a move open to us. If Austria were severely injured, she would become the ally of France and of every other opponent of ours; she would even sacrifice her anti-Russian interests for the sake of revenge on Prussia.

On the other hand, I could see no future acceptable to us for the countries constituting the Austrian monarchy, in case the latter were split up by risings of the Hungarians and Slavs or made permanently dependent on those peoples. What would be put in that portion of Europe which the Austrian state from Tyrol to the Bukowina had hitherto occupied? Fresh formations on this surface could only be of a permanently revolutionary nature. German Austria we could neither wholly nor partly make use of. The acquisition of provinces like Austrian Silesia and portions of Bohemia could not strengthen the Prussian state; it would not lead to an amalgamation of German Austria with Prussia, and Vienna could not be governed from Berlin as a mere dependency. . . .

. . . We must finish off rapidly; before France won time to bring further diplomatic action to bear upon Austria.

To all this the King raised no objection, but declared the actual terms inadequate, without, however, definitely formulating his own demands. Only so much was clear, that his claims had grown considerably since July 4. He said that the chief culprit could not be allowed to escape unpunished, and that justice once satisfied, we could let the misguided partners off more easily, and he insisted on the cessions of territory from Austria which I have already mentioned. I replied that we were not there to sit in judgment, but to pursue the German policy. Austria's conflict in rivalry with us was no more culpable than ours with her; *our task was the establishment or initiation of German national unity under the leadership of the King of Prussia.*

Passing on to the German states, he spoke of various acquisitions by cutting down the territories of all our opponents. I repeated that we were there not to administer retributive justice, but to pursue a policy; that I wished to avoid, in the German federation of the future, the sight of mutilated territories, whose princes and peoples might very easily (such is human weakness) retain a lively wish to recover their former possessions by means of foreign help; such allies would be very unreliable. . . . What seemed to me to be paramount with his Majesty was the aversion of the military party to interrupt the victorious course of the army. The resistance which I was obliged, in accordance with my convictions, to offer to the King's views with regard to following up the military successes, and to his inclination to continue the victorious advance, excited him to such a degree that a prolongation of the discussion became impossible; and, under the impression that my opinion was rejected, I left the room with the idea of begging the King to allow me, in my capacity of officer, to join my regiment. On returning to my room I was in the mood that the thought occurred to me whether it would not be better to fall out of the open window, which was four storeys high; and I did not look round when I heard the door open, although I suspected that the person entering was the Crown Prince, whose room in the same corridor I had just passed. I felt his hand on my shoulder, while he said: "You know that I was against this war. You considered it necessary, and the responsibility for it lies on you. If you are now persuaded that our end is attained, and peace must now be concluded, I am ready to support you and defend your opinion with my father." He then repaired to the King, and came back after a short half-hour, in the same calm, friendly mood, but with the words: "It has been a very difficult business, but my father has consented." This consent found expression in a note written with lead pencil on the margin of one of my last memoranda, something to this effect: "Inasmuch as my Minister-President has left me in the lurch in the face of the enemy, and here I am not in a position to supply his place, I have discussed the question with my son; and as he has associated himself with the Minister-President's opinion, I find myself reluctantly compelled, after such brilliant victories on the part of the army, to bite this sour apple and accept so disgraceful a peace." . . .

5. *BISMARCK "EDITS" THE EMS TELEGRAM*

After the creation of the North German Confederation in 1867, and the exclusion of Austria from German affairs, Bismarck arranged a series of secret treaties with the independent states of South Germany, who feared French aggression. To complete German unification, Bismarck now needed only a war with France, in

Bismarck, the Man and the Statesman, Being the Reflections and Reminiscences of Otto Prince von Bismarck, translated under the supervision of A.J. Butler (Leipzig: Bernhard Tauchnitz, 1899), Vol. II, pp. 272–273, 275–276, 287–280, 282–283.

which the French would appear to be the aggressors. The Spanish succession problem fortuitously provided him with the opportunity for fulfilling his grand design.

The first demands of France respecting the candidature for the Spanish throne, and they were unjustifiable, had been presented on July 4, and answered by our Foreign Office evasively, though in accordance with truth, that the *ministry* knew nothing about the matter. This was correct so far, that the question of Prince Leopold's acceptance of his election had been treated by his Majesty simply as a family matter, which in no way concerned either Prussia or the North German Confederation, and which affected solely the personal relations between the Commander-in-Chief and a German officer, and those between the head of the family and, not the royal family of Prussia but, the entire family of Hohenzollern, or all the bearers of that name.

In France, however, a *casus belli* [an event which is a cause of war] was being sought against Prussia which should be as free as possible from German national colouring; and it was thought one had been discovered in the dynastic sphere by the accession to the Spanish throne of a candidate bearing the name of Hohenzollern. In this the overrating of the military superiority of France and the underrating of the national feeling in Germany was clearly the chief reason why the tenability of this pretext was not examined either with honesty or judgment. The German national outburst which followed the French declaration, and resembled a stream bursting its sluices, was a surprise to French politicians. . . .

On July 12 I decided to hurry off from Varzin to Ems to discuss with his Majesty about summoning the *Reichstag* for the purpose of the mobilisation. . . . As I entered the courtyard of my house at Berlin, and before leaving the carriage, I received telegrams from which it appeared that the King was continuing to treat with Benedetti [the French Ambassador], even after the French threats and outrages in parliament and in the press, and not referring him with calm reserve to his ministers. During dinner, at which Moltke and Roon were present, the announcement arrived from the embassy in Paris that the Prince of Hohenzollern had renounced his candidature in order to prevent the war with which France threatened us. My first idea was to retire from the service, because, after all the insolent challenges which had gone before, I perceived in this extorted submission a humiliation of Germany for which I did not desire to be responsible. This impression of a wound to our sense of national honour by the compulsory withdrawal so dominated me that I had already decided to announce my retirement at Ems. . . . I was very much depressed, for I saw no means of repairing the corroding injury I dreaded to our national position from a timorous policy, unless by picking quarrels clumsily and seeking them artificially. I saw by that time that war was a necessity, which we could no longer avoid with honour. . . .

Having decided to resign, in spite of the remonstrances which Roon made against it, I invited him and Moltke to dine with me alone on the 13th, and communicated to them at table my views and projects for doing so. Both were greatly depressed, and reproached me indirectly with selfishly availing myself of my greater facility for withdrawing from service. I maintained the position that I could not offer up my sense of honour to politics, that both of them, being professional soldiers and consequently without freedom of choice, need not take the same point of view as a responsible Foreign Minister. During our conversation I was informed that a telegram from Ems . . . was being deciphered. When the copy was handed to me it showed that Abeken had drawn up and signed the telegram at his Majesty's command, and I read it out to my guests, whose dejection was so great that they turned away from food and drink. [The telegram, handed in at Ems on July 13, 1870, at 3:50 P.M. and received in Berlin at 6:09, ran as deciphered:

His Majesty writes to me: "Count Benedetti spoke to me on the promenade, in order to demand from me, finally in a very importunate manner, that I should authorise him to telegraph at once that I bound myself for all future time never again to give my consent if the Hohenzollerns should renew their candidature. I refused at last somewhat sternly, as it is neither right nor possible to undertake engagements of this kind *à tout jamais*. Naturally I told him that I had as yet received no news, and as he was earlier informed about Paris and Madrid than myself, he could clearly see that my government once more had no hand in the matter." His Majesty has since received a letter from the Prince. His Majesty having told Count Benedetti that he was awaiting news from the Prince, has decided, with reference to the above demand, upon the representation of Count Eulenburg and myself, not to receive Count Benedetti again, but only to let him be informed through an aide-de-camp: That his Majesty had now received from the Prince confirmation of the news which Benedetti had already received from Paris, and had nothing further to say to the ambassador. His Majesty leaves it to your Excellency whether Benedetti's fresh demand and its rejection should not be at once communicated with to our ambassadors and to the press.]

On a repeated examination of the document I lingered upon the authorisation of his Majesty, which included a command, immediately to communicate Benedetti's fresh demand and its rejection both to our ambassadors and to the press. I put a few questions to Moltke as to the extent of his confidence in the state of our preparations, especially as to the time they would still require in order to meet this sudden risk of war. He answered that if there was to be war he expected no advantage to us by deferring its outbreak; and even if we should not be strong enough at first to protect all the territories on the left bank of the Rhine against French invasion, our preparations would nevertheless soon overtake those of the French, while at a later period this advantage would be diminished; he regarded a rapid outbreak as, on the whole, more favourable to us than delay.

In view of the attitude of France, our national sense of honour compelled us, in my opinion, to go to war; and if we did not act according to the demands of this feeling, we should lose, when on the way to its completion, the entire impetus towards our national development won in 1866, while the German national feeling south of the Main, aroused by our military successes in 1866, and shown by the readiness of the southern states to enter the alliances, would have to grow cold again. . . .

. . . Under this conviction I made use of the royal authorisation communicated to me through Abeken, to publish the contents of the telegram; and in the presence of my two guests I reduced the telegram by striking out words, but without adding or altering, to the following form: "After the news of the renunciation of the hereditary Prince of Hohenzollern had been officially communicated to the imperial government of France by the royal government of Spain, the French ambassador at Ems further demanded of his Majesty the King that he would authorise him to telegraph to Paris that his Majesty the King bound himself for all future time never again to give his consent if the Hohenzollerns should renew their candidature. His Majesty the King thereupon decided not to receive the French ambassador again, and sent to tell him through the aide-de-camp on duty that his Majesty had nothing further to communicate to the ambassador." The difference in the effect of the abbreviated text of the Ems telegram as compared with that produced by the original was not the result of stronger words but of the form, which made this announcement appear decisive, while Abeken's version would only have been regarded as a fragment of a negotiation still pending, and to be continued at Berlin.

After I had read out the concentrated edition to my two guests, Moltke remarked: "Now it has a different ring; it sounded before like a parley; now it is like a flourish in answer to a challenge." I went on to explain: "If in execution of his Majesty's order I at once communicate this text, which contains no alteration in or addition to the telegram, not only to the newspapers, but also by telegraph to all our embassies, it will be known in Paris before midnight, and not only on account of its contents, but also on account of the manner of its distribution, will have the effect of a red rag upon the Gallic bull." . . .

This explanation brought about in the two generals a revulsion to a more joyous mood, the liveliness of which surprised me. They had suddenly recovered their pleasure in eating and drinking and spoke in a more cheerful vein. Roon said: "Our God of old lives still and will not let us perish in disgrace." . . .

6. A GERMAN EMPIRE IS PROCLAIMED AT VERSAILLES

As Bismarck had anticipated, the enthusiasm of a common war effort by North and South Germans greatly facilitated the final step in unification. A series of treaties negotiated in the early stages of the Franco-Prussian War tied the southern states to the North German Confederation. All that remained was the formal proclamation of the German Empire. The following selection is the official account of that event.

In the palace of Louis XIV, in that ancient center of a hostile power which for centuries has striven to divide and humiliate Germany, the solemn proclamation of the German empire was made on January 18, exactly one hundred and seventy years after the assumption of the royal dignity by the Prussian sovereigns at Königsberg. Though the German people, owing to the necessities of the times, were represented at the ceremony only by the German army, the eyes of the entire nation were gratefully turned to the place where, surrounded by sovereigns, generals, and soldiers, King William announced to the world the assumption by himself and his heirs of a title for the reëstablishment of which we have been yearning during the sixty long years it has been in abeyance.

As yet the infatuation of the enemy does not permit us to throw aside the weapons we have taken up in self-defense; and as our unity arose out of the first part of the campaign, so will our empire be strengthened by the remaining feats of arms. By the self-sacrificing devotion of all classes of society, the nation has proved that it still possesses that warlike prowess which distinguished our ancestors. It has recovered its ancient position in Europe; and, neither fearing an adversary nor envying any neighbor, discreet and temperate in its acts and aims, it accepts the destiny prophesied for it in the proclamation of its new emperor. This destiny is to add to its power not by conquest but by promoting culture, liberty, and civilization. As far as the German people are concerned, there will be no more wars in Europe after the determination of the present campaign. . . .

Owing to the unfavorable weather the festive procession which was to conduct his Majesty from the prefecture to the palace did not take place. The crown prince, with Lieutenant-General Blumenthal, his chief of staff,

J.H. Robinson, *Readings in European History* (New York: Ginn and Company, 1904), Vol. II, pp. 594–596.

and an escort of Prussians, Würtembergers, Badeners, and Bavarians, drove to the palace to receive his royal father at the eastern portal in front of the Princes' Stairway. In the courtyard of the palace a company of the king's own troops was drawn up as a guard of honor. . . .

At a quarter past twelve his Majesty entered the hall, when a choir consisting of men of the Seventh, Forty-Seventh, and Fifty-Eighth regiments intoned the choral, "Let all the world rejoice in the Lord." . . . When the choir ceased, the congregation sang one verse of the choral, "Praise and honor unto the Lord." The ordinary military liturgy was then read by the clergymen. . . . The *Te Deum Laudamus* closed the service.

The king then walked up to where the colors were displayed, and, standing before them, read the document proclaiming the reëstablishment of the German empire. Count Bismarck having read the king's proclamation to the German nation, the grand duke of Baden stepped forth and exclaimed, "Long live his Majesty the emperor!" The cheers of the assembly were taken up by the bands playing the national anthem.

7. *BISMARCK STRUGGLES AGAINST THE CATHOLIC CHURCH*

In the German Empire of 1871, Catholics constituted a sizable minority which included Rhineland industrial workers and Bavarian farmers, subject Poles in the east, and conquered Alsatians in the west. Bismarck viewed Catholicism as a serious threat to the unity of the Empire and failed to understand how Catholics could be loyal both to Germany and to the pope. This struggle against the Church is known as the Kulturkampf (battle for civilization).

Before Bismarck's Empire was a year old his Kulturkampf was under way. On July 8, 1871, the Catholic section of the Prussian Ministry of Worship, which dated from 1841, was abolished and the destiny of the Church was entirely in Protestant hands. This was followed by a series of legislative acts, the first of which, on December 10 of the same year, was the "Pulpit law." . . . Accordingly penalties were laid upon any criticism of the Reich and its constitution. . . .

A crucial move was the appointment of Adalbert Falk as Minister of Worship. During eight years of persecution until his dismissal in 1879, as Bismarck's mouthpiece or his evil genius, he enjoyed an unenviable popularity and power. The "May laws," or "Falk laws" were his work. . . .

"The Kulturkampf began in frivolity, was carried through with brutal-

Raymond Corrigan, S.J., *The Church and the Nineteenth Century* (Milwaukee, Wis., The Bruce Publishing Company, 1938), pp. 209–215.

ity and ended ingloriously." So concludes a recent German historian of the Church. About the reasons, the motives behind the Kulturkampf, there is some obscurity. The main lines are clear enough. Bismarck had crushed internal and external opposition to found his mighty Empire. He would brush aside any obstacle to its unity and strength. The National-Liberal party, which should have withstood the absolute State, forgot its principles, as it conveniently could do on occasion, to fight the Catholic Church. But it is not so clear how much is to be attributed to incidental factors, to Protestant convictions, to Freemasonry, to Papal Infallibility and the "Old Catholics," to Polish activities, or to the political program of the Center Party.

Bismarck was a religious-minded man, in his own way, and he regarded the *Kleindeutsch* victory over Austria and the North German victory over France as a triumph of Protestantism. Falk was a Freemason, and so also was the Emperor. The Vatican Council and its definition of Infallibility aroused much resentment in the Fatherland. The religion of the Catholic Poles made it more difficult to make good Prussians of them. The Center Party stood for States' rights in an Empire that Bismarck was determined to centralize. In the pope, the Poles, and the Center Party Bismarck saw potential, if not actual obstruction to his dreams of absolutism. One looks in vain for light in the writings of the Iron Chancellor. His memoires and his recorded statements in formal speeches or in private conversation present a variety of contradictory views which effectually conceal his real mind. He wrote and he talked for effect. . . .

"God" was the God of Bismarck's Prussian State, and the enemies of Prussia or of Bismarck were the enemies of God. In politico-religious matters he was ruthlessly intolerant. . . .

When Leo XIII succeeded Pius IX in 1878 the Kulturkampf was seven years old. . . .

Less than twenty-four hours after his elevation to the papal throne Leo had written a kindly letter to the Emperor. Shortly after this Bismarck had an informal conversation with the Nuncio Massella. The obnoxious Minister Falk was dismissed and his work gradually undone. A sort of diplomatic hide-and-seek game went on until the last remnants of the mass of Kulturkampf legislation were swept away with the exception of the anti-Jesuit laws, the supervision of Catholic schools, and the government approval of appointments to parishes. The process was a slow one, but it was virtually complete in 1887. . . .

35

LIBERALISM AND DEMOCRACY IN WESTERN EUROPE, AND BACKWARDNESS IN EASTERN EUROPE

While Germany and Italy were emerging with some violence as unified nations, England and France, after centuries of national unity, appeared in the late nineteenth century as strongholds of liberalism, in which a considerable degree of political democracy had been attained. England's internal problems were ably handled in her Parliament, led by two outstanding party leaders, William E. Gladstone and Benjamin Disraeli. France, after a painful transition from the Second Empire to the Third Republic, was predominantly liberal and increasingly democratic. The multinational empires of eastern Europe, however, presented a marked contrast to the western democracies. Russia remained thoroughly autocratic, although serfdom was abolished in 1861, while in Turkey governmental corruption and incompetence were symptoms of impending collapse.

1. GLADSTONE REVIEWS THE PROGRESS OF THE WORKING CLASS

William Ewart Gladstone (1809–1898), leader of the British Liberal Party, served as prime minister on four occasions between 1868 and 1894. The speech below was delivered in Parliament in 1866 to support his own proposal to widen the suffrage sufficiently to include the urban working class. Gladstone's proposal served as a basis for the Reform Act of 1867, sponsored by Disraeli's Conservative cabinet.

Parliamentary Debates, Third Series, CLXXXII, 1132 f., as found in Carl Stephenson and Frederick George Marcham, eds. and trans., *Sources of English Constitutional History* (New York: Harper & Brothers, 1937), pp. 775–776. Copyright 1937 by Harper & Brothers. Used by permission.

. . . Since 1832 every kind of beneficial change has been in operation in favour of the working classes. There never was a period in which religious influences were more active than in the period I now name. It is hardly an exaggeration to say that within that time the civilizing and training powers of education have for all practical purposes been not so much improved as, I might almost say, brought into existence, as far as the mass of the people is concerned. As regards the press, an emancipation and extension have taken place to which it would be difficult to find a parallel. I will not believe that the mass of gentlemen opposite are really insensible to the enormous benefit that has been effected by that emancipation of the press—when, for the humble sum of a penny or for even less, newspapers are circulated from day to day by the million rather than by the thousand, in numbers almost defying the powers of statistics to follow, and carrying home to all classes of our fellow-countrymen accounts of public affairs; enabling them to feel a new interest in the transaction of those affairs and containing articles which, I must say, are written in a spirit, with an ability, with a sound moral sense, and with a refinement that have made the penny press of England the worthy companion—indeed say the worthy rival—of those dearer and older papers which have long secured for British journalism a renown perhaps without parallel in the world. By external and material as well as by higher means, by measures relating to labour, to police, and to sanitary arrangements, parliament has been labouring, has been striving with admitted success. And there is not a call which has been made upon the self-improving powers of the working community which has not been fully answered. Take, for instance, the working men's free libraries and institutes throughout the country. Take, as an example of the class, Liverpool. Who are the frequenters of that institution? I believe that the majority of the careful, honest, painstaking students who crowd that library are men belonging to the working classes, a large number of whom cannot attend without making some considerable sacrifice. Then again, sir, we called upon them to be provident; we instituted for them post-office savings banks, which may now be said to have been in full operation for four years. And what has been the result? During these four years we have received these names at the rate of thousands by the week, and there are now 650,000 depositors in those savings banks. This, then, is the way in which parliament has been acting towards the working classes. But what is the meaning of all this? Parliament has been striving to make the working classes progressively fitter and fitter for the franchise. And can anything be more unwise, not to say more senseless, than to persevere from year to year in this plan, and then blindly to refuse to recognize its legitimate upshot—namely, the increased fitness of the working classes for the exercise of political power? . . .

2. *PARNELL URGES HOME RULE FOR IRELAND*

Charles Stewart Parnell (1846–1891), an Irish Protestant landowner, was elected in 1875 to Parliament, where he organized the Irish Nationalist Party, advocating "home rule" for Ireland. Following the 1885 elections, during which Parnell delivered the speech below at Cork, the Irish Nationalists held the balance of power in Parliament. Gladstone gained the support of the Irish by accepting Parnell's home rule program, but the bill failed to pass in 1886.

. . . At the election in 1880 I laid certain principles before you, and you accepted them (applause, and cries of 'we do'). I said and I pledged myself, that I should form one of an independent Irish party to act in opposition to every English government which refused to concede the just rights of Ireland (applause). And the longer time which is gone by since then, the more I am convinced that that is the true policy to pursue so far as parliamentary policy is concerned, and that it will be impossible for either or both of the English parties to contend for any long time against a determined band of Irishmen acting honestly upon these principles, and backed by the Irish people (cheers). But we have not alone had that object in view—we have always been very careful not to fetter or control the people at home in any way, not to prevent them from doing any thing by their own strength which it is possible for them to do. Sometimes, perhaps, in our anxiety in this direction we have asked them to do what is beyond their strength, but I hold that it is better even to encourage you to do what is beyond your strength even should you fail sometimes in the attempt than to teach you to be subservient and unreliant (applause). You have been encouraged to organize yourselves, to depend upon the rectitude of your cause for your justification, and to depend upon the determination which has helped Irishmen through many centuries to retain the name of Ireland and to retain her nationhood. Nobody could point to any single action of ours in the house of commons or out of it which was not based upon the knowledge that behind us existed a strong and brave people, that without the help of the people our exertions would be as nothing, and that with their help and with their confidence we should be, as I believe we shall prove to be in the near future, invincible and unconquerable (great applause). . . . We shall struggle, as we have been struggling, for the great

The Freeman's Journal (January 22, 1885), as found in Edmund Curtis and R.B. McDowell, eds., *Irish Historical Documents, 1172–1922* (London: Methuen & Co., Ltd., 1943), pp. 282–284. Used by permission of the publisher.

and important interests of the Irish tenant farmer. We shall ask that his industry shall not be fettered by rent. We shall ask also from the farmer in return that he shall do what in him lies to encourage the struggling manufactures of Ireland, and that he shall not think it too great a sacrifice to be called upon when he wants anything, when he has to purchase anything, to consider how he may get it of Irish material and manufacture (hear, hear), even supposing he has to pay a little more for it (cheers). . . . Well, but gentlemen, I go back from the consideration of these questions to the land question, in which the labourers' question is also involved and the manufacturers' question. I come back, and every Irish politician must be forcibly driven back, to the consideration of the great question of national self-government for Ireland (cheers). I do not know how this great question will be eventually settled. I do not know whether England will be wise in time and concede to constitutional arguments and methods the restitution of that which was stolen from us towards the close of the last century (cheers). It is given to none of us to forecast the future, and just as it is impossible for us to say in what way or by what means the national question may be settled, in what way full justice may be done to Ireland, so it is impossible for us to say to what extent that justice should be done. . . . But, gentlemen, while we leave those things to time, circumstances and the future, we must each one of us resolve in our own hearts that we shall at all times do everything that within us lies to obtain for Ireland the fullest measure of her rights (applause). In this way we shall avoid difficulties and contentions amongst each other. In this way we shall not give up anything which the future may put in favour of our country; and while we struggle to-day for that which may seem possible for us with our combination, we must struggle for it with the proud consciousness that we shall not do anything to hinder or prevent better men who may come after us from gaining better things than those for which we now contend (prolonged applause).

3. *THE PARIS COMMUNE BECOMES DISTORTED BY MARXIST HISTORIANS*

Few historical episodes have been so misinterpreted and misunderstood as the Paris Commune of 1871. Following the humiliating defeat of France by Bismarck's Prussian Army, a new provisional government at Versailles seemed ready to accept an equally humiliating peace treaty. In March, 1871, the communal government of Paris revolted against the Versailles group. Although the Commune contained a number of radicals and a few socialists, it had no inten-

Edward S. Mason, *The Paris Commune* (New York: The Macmillan Company, 1930), pp. vii–viii, x–xi.

tion of setting up a communist regime. The siege of Paris by the Versailles army was marked by extreme ferocity, with the final assault on the city culminating in a gigantic massacre.

The close of the Franco-Prussian war, foreshadowed by the capitulation of Paris on January 28th, 1871, after four months of heroic resistance, was quickly followed by an uprising which has long ago taken its place beside the revolutions of 1830 and 1848. The radical republicans of Paris, among whom were mingled socialists of all shades of opinion, established a government which for two months ruled the capital and gave battle to established authority in France. This government collapsed during the last week of May in the bloodiest bit of street fighting of the century.

The Commune is often lost sight of in the larger panorama of the Franco-Prussian War. Despite the profound impression which it made upon contemporaries with its bombardment of Paris, its summary executions, the massacres in the streets, and the eccentricities of its revolutionary government, it quickly lost its separate identity. For a while conservatives in France and in Europe saw in the revolution of March 18th the hand of socialism. The Commune made the reputation of Karl Marx in France and generated in Europe a remarkable fear of the First International. But soon, as the real weakness of this organization became evident, opinion turned the other way and students of the Commune were inclined to regard it as a regrettable but inevitable by-product of the war. Its socialist origins were vague and its socialist intentions, dubious. Fifteen thousand men were dead, another fifteen thousand imprisoned, and a considerable part of the most beautiful city in Europe destroyed for apparently indefinable reasons and with inappreciable results. The Commune disappeared, leaving scarcely a trace on the institutional life or development of France.

It has been rescued, however, from its somewhat insignificant position as an incident in the history of France, by the activity of the socialists and the communists. In their hands it has become an event of world-shaking importance, a proletarian and socialist revolution par excellence, and the first real government of the working class. The Commune of Paris is, in the opinion of the communists, the immediate forbear of the Russian Soviet. . . .

In the light of this fact the history of the revolution of 1871 must be reconsidered. Was it proletarian and was it socialist? Was it a revolutionary class struggle or something quite other than this? The Marxian version has it that the Commune was socialist because proletarian, "for the proletariat can fight for no other cause than socialism." But this is a complete *non sequitur* to any other than a believer in the Marxian theory of an economically determined class struggle in which the participants are a class-conscious proletariat and a class-conscious bourgeoisie.

The Commune of Paris, as a matter of fact, sprang from an exceedingly complicated historical situation. Irritation and disgust at the loss of the war, the misery of the four-month siege of Paris, the struggle of republicanism against monarchy, socialist desires and aspirations clothed in the ideas of Proudhon and Blanqui, all mingled inextricably in the causes of the revolution. No simple explanation such as that implied in the socialist theory of the class struggle can be accepted.

4. *THE FRENCH REPUBLIC EXPERIENCES MINISTERIAL INSTABILITY*

With the collapse of Napoleon III's Empire in 1870, a hastily assembled group of political leaders formed a provisional government, vaguely termed a "republic." However, the National Assembly of 1871 contained a large majority of monarchists, who regarded the "republic" as a temporary device. Unable to agree upon details for restoring a king, the royalists acquiesced in 1875 to a republican constitution. Designed as a temporary, stog-gap measure, this constitution became the foundation of the Third Republic.

The Third Republic's constitution was monarchist by birth, republican only only by adoption. Its drafters in 1875 had been inspired both by French royalist tradition and by the example of the British parliamentary monarchy; they had designed their makeshift constitution to serve as the framework for a restored monarchy in France. The structure proved flexible enough, however, to adapt itself to republican needs; and so France unintentionally furnished the world with history's first example of the parliamentary republic.

The essence of the parliamentary system lay in the dominant role of the Chamber of Deputies, which could overthrow and replace the executive organ (the cabinet) at will. In contrast to the so-called presidential form of government, there was no attempt at a clear-cut separation of powers, with the executive and legislative branches both stemming directly from the people and kept in equilibrium by a series of checks and balances. At most, there was a separation of functions between the executive and legislative organs. The seat of national sovereignty, the source of executive authority lay in the Chamber of Deputies alone.

Between 1875 and 1940, practice altered certain aspects of the government's operation. The most significant change was a relative weakening of the executive organs in favor of the legislature. Above all, the executive's chief weapon against the legislature—the right to dissolve the Chamber and to order new elections—fell into complete disuse. The dissolution mechanism

Gordon Wright, *The Reshaping of French Democracy* (New York: Reynal and Hitchcock, 1948), pp. 8–10.

rusted for two reasons: because it was once utilized for partisan ends by the monarchist President MacMahon in 1877 (so that thereafter it bore an anti-republican odor), and because dissolution required the Senate's consent, which became more and more unlikely as the Senate fell under the control of the same parties which dominated the Chamber.

The decay of dissolution did much to produce that famous French phenomenon, cabinet instability. During the sixty-five-year life of the Third Republic, France had a sequence of 102 cabinets, which scarcely made for executive strength or authority. The changes became increasingly kaleidoscopic as time passed; calculators have figured that from 1875 to 1920, governments lasted an average of less than ten months each; but that from 1920 to 1940, the speed of rotation just about doubled. If the deputies had been faced by the prospect of dissolution and a subsequent campaign for re-election, they might have been much more cautious before putting the skids under a set of ministers.

A second factor which contributed heavily to cabinet instability was the multi-party system. Once the Republic got well under way, no party ever approached a clear majority in the Chamber; a coalition of from two to a half-dozen groups was always necessary in order to form a cabinet, and the life of such a coalition was at the mercy of each component group. Furthermore, the parties themselves were fluid and ill-disciplined, which added to the structural instability of cabinets. The largest single group, the Radical Socialist, was once described as "not a party but only a state of mind"; and the same was true of all groups except the Socialists and Communists, who arrived late on the scene. The average politician, it was sometimes said, felt that an ideal party would be one which included only himself plus enough voters to elect him to office.

A final aspect of executive decline was the creeping paralysis which afflicted the formal head of the state, the president of the republic. A series of presidents beginning with Jules Grévy consciously limited the scope of their office, and parliament helped this process along by usually electing men of distinctly second-rate qualities. Clemenceau was thinking of the presidency when he coined the caustic epigram, "I vote for the most stupid." It was not long before the president became the butt of French witticisms rather than the symbol of governmental authority. His role was sometimes important as a behind-the-scenes adviser, but in general he spent his time receiving ambassadors and presiding at cattle shows. He emerged into the limelight briefly when cabinets fell, for it was his important duty to name a new premier. Critics sometimes compared the president to the pin boy in a bowling alley, whose only function it was to pick up fallen cabinets as the Chamber knocked them down.

5. *THE RUSSIAN SERF LOOKS TOWARD LIBERATION*

Although the peasants of western Europe had progressed since the thirteenth century from serfdom to freedom, the rural population of Russia from the reign of Peter the Great at the end of the seventeenth century had been forced into a miserable, degrading serfdom. Nowhere else in Europe was the social gulf between noble and peasant so great.

It is difficult to-day to realise even approximately the nature of Russian serfdom. Those familiar with the history of the institution are apt to confine their attention to its legal and economic aspects. It is necessary to grasp the moral and social implications of serfdom as it affected concrete life. We have to understand that the peasant was in actual fact another's property, soul and body; that the lord could sell his serfs; that down to the year 1833 he could at will break up the serf's family as irrevocably as death breaks it up, by selling an individual member apart from the family—for the serf, bound to the soil, could not follow the one who was sold, as the wives of aristocrats were able at their own charges to follow husbands exiled to Siberia. The serf was money, was part of the natural economy. The landowner could gamble away his "souls" at the card-table, or could make his mistresses a present of them. The slaves were at the absolute disposal of the lord, who was free to settle whether a gifted child should become cook, musician, or surgeon. The lord disposed likewise of his slaves' wives and daughters, deciding what couples might marry and what couples might not; . . . Terrible is the picture of serfdom given by the best authors in their reminiscences. An attentive reader of the older Russian literature will discern everywhere this peculiar moral and social background. Those who have observed and described Russian village and rural life make express references to the matter. " 'Gryzlov,' said D.S., 'Marija Thedorova is making ready to go to Moscow. We need money. When I was driving through the villages I saw a number of children; our chattels have been increasing in number; take measures accordingly!' This signified that Gryzlov was commissioned to visit the villages of D.S., to seize some of the superfluous boys and girls, sell them, and hand the proceeds to the landowner." . . .

The liberation of the peasantry, as actually carried out, was the result of a compromise between the opponents and the supporters of serfdom and between the conflicting plans of the various parties. Whereas the peasants naturally desired their liberation to be accompanied by the assignment to them of the soil they tilled, no more than an infinitesimal minority of land-

Thomas G. Masaryk, *The Spirit of Russia,* translated by Eden and Cedar Paul (London: George Allen & Unwin Ltd., 1919), Vol. I, pp. 134–135, 141–142. Used by permission of the publisher.

owners favoured this idea. The best of the landowners proposed that liberation, if it was to be effected, should be accompanied by the granting of land to the peasants in return for compensation payable to the landowner by the peasant, by the state, or by both. In the Baltic provinces, liberation was effected without any grant of land, and the peasants had to rent whatever land they needed. Many landowners in other parts would doubtless have agreed to an arrangement of the kind, but even upon this matter there were conflicting currents. Some desired that the enfranchised peasant should have no land of his own at all; others were willing that he should be granted a small allotment; others proposed a partial enfranchisement with a definite legal formulation of peasant right. The manifesto of 1861 aimed at meeting the landowners' wishes as far as possible.

Serfdom was abolished, and agrarian difficulties, which still persist, were the sequel of enfranchisement.

6. CZAR ALEXANDER II EMANCIPATES THE SERFS

At the accession of Alexander II in 1855, nine-tenths of the Russian land was owned by the imperial family and 100,000 noble families. Except for a few small areas of free peasantry, serfs tilled the soil and served in the nobles' households. Alexander began a series of reforms by freeing the serfs on the imperial estates. This action was followed by the emancipation decree of March, 1861.

By the grace of God, we, Alexander II., Emperor and Autocrat of all the Russias, King of Poland, Grand Duke of Finland, &c., to all our faithful subjects make known: . . .

In considering the various classes and conditions of which the State is composed we came to the conviction that the legislation of the empire having wisely provided for the organization of the upper and middle classes and having defined with precision their obligations, their rights, and their privileges, has not attained the same degree of efficiency as regards the peasants attached to the soil, thus designated because either from ancient laws or from custom they have been hereditarily subjected to the authority of the proprietors, on whom it was incumbent at the same time to provide for their welfare. . . .

Having invoked the Divine assistance, we have resolved to carry this work into execution. . . .

. . . the peasants attached to the soil will be invested within a term fixed by the law with all the rights of free cultivators.

"History," *The Annual Register, 1861* (London: 1862), pp. 207–212.

The proprietors retaining their rights of property on all the land belonging to them, grant to the peasants for a fixed regulated rental the full enjoyment of their close; and, moreover, to assure their livelihood and to guarantee the fulfilment of their obligations towards the Government, the quantity of arable land is fixed by the said dispositions, as well as other rural appurtenances.

But, in the enjoyment of these territorial allotments, the peasants are obliged, in return, to acquit the rentals fixed by the same dispositions to the profit of the proprietors. In this state, which must be a transitory one, the peasants shall be designated as 'temporarily bound.'

At the same time, they are granted the right of purchasing their close, and, with the consent of the proprietors, they may acquire in full property the arable lands and other appurtenances which are allotted to them as a permanent holding. By the acquisition in full property of the quantity of land fixed, the peasants are free from their obligations towards the proprietors for land thus purchased, and they enter definitively into the condition of free peasants—landholders.

By a special disposition concerning the domestics, a transitory state is fixed for them, adapted to their occupations and the exigencies of their position. On the expiration of a term of two years, dating from the day of the promulgation of these dispositions, they shall receive their full enfranchisement and some temporary immunities. . . .

For which end, we have deemed it advisable to ordain—

1. To establish in each district a special Court for the question of the peasants; it will have to investigate the affairs of the rural communes established on the land of the lords of the soil.

2. To appoint in each district justices of the peace to investigate on the spot all misunderstandings and disputes which may arise on the occasion of the introduction of the new regulation, and to form district assemblies with these justices of the peace. . . .

6. Up to the expiration of this term, the peasants and domestics are to remain in the same obedience towards their proprietors, and to fulfil their former obligations without scruple. . . .

To render the transactions between the proprietors and the peasants more easy, in virtue of which the latter may acquire in full property their close (homestead) and the land they occupy, the Government will advance assistance, according to a special regulation, by means of loans or a transfer of debts encumbering an estate. . . .

Given at St. Petersburg, the 19th day of February (March 3), of the year of Grace 1861, and the seventh of our reign.

ALEXANDER

7. AN ENGLISHMAN DESCRIBES THE SULTAN OF TURKEY

The Turkish Empire in the late nineteenth century was looked upon by westerners as a decadent and decrepit survivor of the past. With its finances controlled by foreigners, its army often defeated, its administration corrupt, and its subject peoples in chronic revolt, Turkey maintained a precarious existence. Sir Edwin Pears, author of the selection below, was an English lawyer and newspaper correspondent, who lived for over forty years in the Turkish capital.

. . . When I arrived in the country Abdul Aziz was on the throne. He was a harmless sort of Eastern sovereign, who was not generally disliked by his subjects, and who probably thought of his own pleasures more than anything else. His hobby was building. The beautiful palace of Dolma Bagsche, about two miles from Seraglio Point and one of the most conspicuous objects on the Bosporus, was completed in his reign. It was rumoured that the Sultan was unwilling to occupy it on account of some superstitious fear. . . .

Public opinion in Turkey could hardly be said at any time to have existed outside Constantinople. But in that city there was a strong party opposed to the Sultan on account of his extravagance, and the show of palaces was the ever-present evidence of his failing. There was also a small group of men who wished to transform the absolutism of the Government into a limited monarchy, and to establish a Constitution. Amongst them Midhat Pasha was the leader. They succeeded in bringing about the revolution which placed Murad on the throne, which deposed him and appointed Abdul Hamid as his successor. It was not a military revolution, and though both soldiers and sailors took part in it, the movement was as spontaneous as such a change could be. After the short attempt at parliamentary government and the packing off of the members from the capital, Sultan Abdul Hamid soon showed himself bitterly hostile to all projects of parliamentary government, or to anything which should tend to diminish his absolute power. He is a man of a certain amount of cunning, but also of a meanness of character which is not Turkish. . . .

The moderate party amongst the Turks, reasonable men, even those, who wished the government to be conducted on the old lines and to be reformed quietly upon such lines, never had a hearing from him. They soon learned to distrust him, and he on his part became surrounded either by sycophants, working to fill their own pockets, or by unscrupulous adventurers. He had begun by believing that he was surrounded by enemies, and he ended by a general distrust of everybody with whom he came in contact,

Sir Edwin Pears, *Forty Years in Constantinople* (London: Herbert Jenkins Ltd., 1916), pp. 102–106. Used by permission of the publisher.

and with the conviction that he alone knew how to govern the country. Gradually we learned that the chief weapon for his own defence was a system of espionage which, limited at first to men in office, was gradually extended to comprise almost everybody of note in the country.

His surroundings had never been favourable to manliness or to the development of the talents required by a successful ruler. In this he was subject to the same disabilities that for upwards of three centuries have always weighed upon heirs to the Turkish throne. They are largely the results of the Turkish law of succession. Instead of following the European rule, the Crown Prince as already mentioned is the eldest surviving male member belonging to the Imperial family. . . .

The occupant of the throne in Turkey, and especially perhaps the mother of such occupant, desires that her son shall succeed. But in front of him there will probably stand half a dozen members of the family who are his seniors. Fourteen such members ranked before the present Sultan Mahomet V. and the eldest son of the deposed Murad. A century and a half ago children of the Royal family who were likely to stand in the way of a succession were often murdered, and some of the most pathetic passages in Turkish history relate to the intrigues which took place either to kill the heir to the throne, or to prevent an infant attaining to that position. The reigning sovereign has usually regarded the Crown Prince with suspicion, and has prevented him becoming acquainted with the Ministers or having any but strictly formal communication with the representatives of foreign states.

It was under this system that Abdul Hamid had been brought up. He was never allowed to see foreign Ambassadors or to take any part in discussing the affairs of the empire. His youthful want of training and his limited environment give the key to his subsequent characteristics, unconsidered action, and above all, suspicion. When on the deposition of Murad, Abdul Hamid was girded with the sword of Osman, he was the nominee of the party which had brought about two revolutions. That party had great hopes in him and his pliability. They were soon undeceived. . . .

From that time the Sultan turned his attention to removing from the capital all who had aided in placing him on the throne, with one exception. The exception was the Minister of Marine, who lived on and retained his office until his death in 1902. It was only towards the end of his life that I met with him, but he had the reputation of being a brave, bluff sailor who feared neither the Sultan nor anybody else. When he was reproached by Abdul for having pocketed £200,000 in one operation, he corrected his imperial master by saying that it was £300,000. None of us could understand why amidst the dismissal of so many Ministers, and of everybody connected with the deposition of his predecessors, Abdul Hamid did not get rid of the Minister of Marine. It was in vain that, in the long interval between 1876 and 1902, everyone knew that the fleet had been allowed to rot and rust, and that with one insignificant exception none of the really magnificent ironclads which the Sultan had found on his accession ever went out of the harbour of the Golden Horn.

Everyone saw that the naval school languished; though torpedo boats and new ironclads had been bought. They knew that the Minister was currently reported to do nothing unless he were heavily bribed, but throughout these long years Abdul Hamid retained him at his post. . .

36

DIPLOMACY AND IMPERIALISM

From 1870 to 1914 there were no wars among the major powers. Peace was preserved by a system of long-term military alliances, inaugurated by Bismarck and continued by his successors. With relative stability in Europe, with economic pressures from the increased industrialization, and with an upsurge of intense nationalism, a new imperialism emerged. In the 1880's, following Stanley's well-publicized explorations, a mad scramble for African colonies began. British imperialist expansion in South Africa, stimulated by discoveries of gold and diamonds, encountered stiff resistance from the Boers. Simultaneously, in the Far East another scramble for colonies, concessions, and special privileges led to imperialistic wars, such as the Russo-Japanese War, and to attempts like the "open door" notes to regulate and equalize the opportunities for imperialism.

1. BISMARCK'S DUAL ALLIANCE BECOMES A TRIPLE ALLIANCE

For twenty years after the Franco-Prussian War of 1870, Bismarck worked hard to keep the peace of Europe. In 1879 he concluded a secret defensive treaty with Austria-Hungary. Two years later France, with Bismarck's blessings, seized Tunis, a land which the Italians had looked on as their future colony. Feeling isolated in a hostile world, Italy sought an alliance with Germany. Bismarck agreed, on condition that Italy join in a three-way treaty which would include her traditional foe, Austria.

Their Majesties the Emperor of Austria, King of Bohemia, etc., and Apostolic King of Hungary, the Emperor of Germany, King of Prussia, and the

F. Pribram, *The Secret Treaties of Austria-Hungary*, translated by Denys P. Myers and J.G. D'Arcy Paul (Cambridge, Mass.: Harvard University Press, 1920), Vol. I, pp. 65–71.

King of Italy, animated by the desire to increase the guaranties of the general peace, to fortify the monarchical principle and thereby to assure the unimpaired maintenance of the social and political order in Their respective States, have agreed to conclude a Treaty which, by its essentially conservative and defensive nature pursues only the aim of forestalling the dangers which might threaten the security of Their States and the peace of Europe. . . .

ARTICLE 1. The High Contracting Parties mutually promise peace and friendship, and will enter into no alliance or engagement directed against any one of their States.

They engage to proceed to an exchange of ideas on political and economic questions of a general nature which may arise, and they further promise one another mutual support within the limits of their own interests.

ARTICLE 2. In case Italy, without direct provocation on her part, should be attacked by France for any reason whatsoever, the two other Contracting Parties shall be bound to lend help and assistance with all their forces to the Party attacked.

This same obligation shall devolve upon Italy in case of any aggression without direct provocation by France against Germany.

ARTICLE 3. If one, or two, of the High Contracting Parties, without direct provocation on their part, should chance to be attacked and to be engaged in a war with two or more Great Powers nonsignatory to the present Treaty, the *casus foederis* will arise simultaneously [1] for all the High Contracting Parties.

ARTICLE 4. In case a Great Power nonsignatory to the present Treaty should threaten the security of the states of one of the High Contracting Parties, and the threatened Party should find itself forced on that account to make war against it, the two others bind themselves to observe towards their Ally a benevolent neutrality. Each of them reserves to itself, in this case, the right to take part in the war, if it should see fit, to make common cause with its Ally.

ARTICLE 5. If the peace of any of the High Contracting Parties should chance to be threatened under the circumstances foreseen by the preceding Articles, the High Contracting Parties shall take counsel together in ample time as to the military measures to be taken with a view to eventual cooperation.

They engage henceforward, in all cases of common participation in a war, to conclude neither armistice, nor peace, nor treaty, except by common agreement among themselves.

[1] That is, the other parties in this alliance would come to the aid of one attacked.

ARTICLE 6. The High Contracting Parties mutually promise secrecy as to the contents and existence of the present Treaty.

ARTICLE 7. The present Treaty shall remain in force during the space of five years, dating from the day of the exchange of ratifications.

ARTICLE 8. . . . Done at Vienna, the twentieth day of the month of May of the year one thousand eight hundred and eighty-two.

Additional Declaration of Italy

The Royal Italian Government declares that the provisions of the secret Treaty concluded May 20, 1882, between Italy, Austria-Hungary, and Germany, cannot, as has been previously agreed, in any case be regarded as being directed against England. . . .

Rome, May 22, 1882

2. *FRANCE AND RUSSIA AGREE ON A MILITARY CONVENTION*

Bismarck's great success in keeping France isolated barely outlasted his term in office, as both France and Russia felt isolated and threatened by the Triple Alliance. Despite the extreme differences between Russian absolutism and French republicanism, the two powers drew together. Both parties were anxious to form an alliance; but to ensure complete secrecy, it took the form of a military convention rather than a formal treaty.

France and Russia, animated by a common desire to preserve the peace, and having no other aim than to prepare for the necessities of a defensive war, provoked against either of them by an attack by the forces of the Triple Alliance, have agreed upon the following provisions:

1. If France is attacked by Germany, or by Italy supported by Germany, Russia shall employ all her available forces to fight Germany.

If Russia is attacked by Germany, or by Austria supported by Germany, France shall employ all her available forces to fight Germany.

2. In case the forces of the Triple Alliance or of one of the Powers which compose it should be mobilized, France and Russia, at the first indication of the event, and without a previous agreement being necessary, shall mobilize all their forces immediately and simultaneously, and shall transport them as near to the frontiers as possible.

3. The forces available which must be employed against Germany shall be for France, 1,300,000 men; for Russia, from 700,000 to 800,000 men. These forces shall begin complete action with all speed, so that Germany will have to fight at the same time in the east and in the west.

Sidney B. Fay, *The Origins of the World War,* Second Edition, Revised (New York: The Macmillan Company, 1943), Vol. I, pp. 118–119.

4. The Staffs of the armies of the two countries shall constantly plan in concert in order to prepare for and facilitate the execution of the above measures. They shall communicate to each other in time of peace all the information regarding the armies of the Triple Alliance which is in or shall come into their possession. The ways and means of corresponding in time of war shall be studied and arranged in advance.

5. France and Russia shall not conclude peace separately.

6. The present Convention shall have the same duration as the Triple Alliance.

7. All the clauses enumerated above shall be kept absolutely secret.

3. *STANLEY FINDS LIVINGSTONE*

Henry Morton Stanley (1841–1904), born in Wales as John Rowlands, emigrated to America and fought on both sides in the Civil War. His war reporting won him such fame as a journalist that in 1871 he was sent by the New York* Herald *to find David Livingstone in Africa. Livingstone, a Scottish missionary and explorer, was found by Stanley at Ujiji, on the shores of Lake Tanganyika. Stanley's stories from "Darkest Africa" stirred the imaginations of millions, while Livingstone became a national hero of Britain and was buried in the shrine of heroes, Westminster Abbey.

. . . the news had been conveyed to the Doctor that it was surely a white man that was coming, whose guns were firing and whose flag could be seen; and the great Arab magnates of Ujiji . . . had gathered together before the Doctor's house, and the Doctor had come out from his veranda to discuss the matter and await my arrival.

In the meantime, the head of the Expedition had halted . . . and Selim said to me, "I see the Doctor, sir. Oh, what an old man! He has got a white beard." And I—what would I not have given for a bit of friendly wilderness, where, unseen, I might vent my joy in some mad freak, such as idiotically biting my hand, turning a somersault, or slashing at trees, in order to allay those exciting feelings that were well-nigh uncontrollable. My heart beats fast, but I must not let my face betray my emotions, lest it shall detract from the dignity of a white man appearing under such extraordinary circumstances.

So I did that which I thought was most dignified. I pushed back the crowds, and, passing from the rear, walked down a living avenue of people, until I came in front of the semicricle of Arabs, in the front of which stood

Henry M. Stanley, *How I Found Livingstone* (New York: Scribner, Armstrong and Company, 1872), pp. 410–413.

the white man with the grey beard. As I advanced slowly towards him I noticed he was pale, looked wearied, had a grey beard, wore a bluish cap with a faded gold band round it, had on a red-sleeved waistcoat, and a pair of grey tweed trousers. I would have run to him, only I was a coward in the presence of such a mob—would have embraced him, only, he being an Englishman, I did not know how he would receive me; so I did what cowardice and false pride suggested was the best thing—walked deliberately to him, took off my hat, and said:

"Dr. Livingstone, I presume?"

"YES," said he, with a kind smile, lifting his cap slightly.

I replace my hat on my head, and he puts on his cap, and we both grasp hands, and I then say aloud:

"I thank God, Doctor, I have been permitted to see you."

He answered, "I feel thankful that I am here to welcome you."

I turn to the Arabs, take off my hat to them in response to the saluting chorus of "Yambos" I receive, and the Doctor introduces them to me by name. Then, oblivious of the crowds, oblivious of the men who shared with me my dangers, we—Livingstone and I—turn our faces towards his tembe. He points to the veranda, or, rather, mud platform, under the broad overhanging eaves; he points to his own particular seat, which I see his age and experience in Africa has suggested, namely, a straw mat, with a goatskin over it, and another skin nailed against the wall to protect his back from contact with the cold mud. I protest against taking this seat, which so much more befits him than me, but the Doctor will not yield: I must take it.

We are seated—the Doctor and I—with our backs to the wall. The Arabs take seats on our left. More than a thousand natives are in our front, filling the whole square densely, indulging their curiosity, and discussing the fact of two white men meeting at Ujiji—one just come from Manyuema, in the west, the other from Unyanyembe, in the east.

Conversation began. What about? I declare I have forgotten. Oh! we mutually asked questions of one another, such as:

"How did you come here?" and "Where have you been all this long time?—the world has believed you to be dead." Yes, that was the way it began; but whatever the Doctor informed me, and that which I communicated to him, I cannot correctly report, for I found myself gazing at him, conning the wonderful man at whose side I now sat in Central Africa. Every hair of his head and beard, every wrinkle of his face, the wanness of his features, and the slightly wearied look he wore, were all imparting intelligence to me—the knowledge I craved for so much ever since I heard the words, "Take what you want, but find Livingstone."

4. SIR HARRY JOHNSTON ASCENDS THE CROSS RIVER

Sir Harry Johnston, a highly successful agent of the Royal Niger Company, became an empire builder by following a standard pattern of flag raising and treaty making. Using identical tactics, Carl Peters, an enthusiastic German adventurer, secured for Germany a vast territory in East Africa.

In a long native canoe Johnston and his forty Kruboys (negro porters) and Callabars paddled up the Cross River, through lonely glades, startling an occasional chimpanzee or elephant herd, but seeing no human beings, until they neared a large negro village. Savages rushed out into the water, dragged Johnston from his canoe, and carried him off to a native hut. There, with a hundred human skulls grinning at him from the walls, he had to sit, while a crowd of savages stared at his strange complexion and clothes. At length his captors question him, through his native interpreter. He came, he said, on a friendly mission from "a great white Queen who was the ruler of the White People." He wished to "make a book" with the ruler of the village —that is, a treaty—to "take home to the Woman Chief" who had sent him out. The natives, fortunately, were agreeable. A burly individual carried him back to the canoe, and there Johnston took a treaty form (he had a stock ready for such contingencies) from his dispatch box, while three or four negroes, apparently persons of authority, crowded into the canoe to make crosses on the treaty. The natives, it seemed, had consumed enough palm-wine to be genial, even boisterous. Seeing their condition, Johnston "was longing to get away." Accordingly "after the crosses had been splodged on the treaty-form" and he had given them a present of beads and cloth, he made his adieux, but not before the villagers had generously compelled him to accept a hundred yams and two sheep—and "a necklace of human knuckle bones." Then, fearing that the natives might kill and eat his servants, Johnston made "a judicious retreat."

Such, in a general way, was the process of treaty-making by which the negro tribes accepted Great Britain's protectorate. A courageous but nervous explorer, bravely concealing his fears; a half-explained treaty of "friendship"; presents of beads and cloth (and of liquor in the case of less high-minded explorers)—these were the typical elements in the situation.

Parker T. Moon, *Imperialism and World Politics* (New York: The Macmillan Company, 1926), pp. 101–102. Copyright 1926 by The Macmillan Company. Used by permission.

5. *KITCHENER MEETS MARCHAND AT FASHODA*

In the scramble for land in Africa, one of the few territories unclaimed by Europeans in 1898 was the Sudan, the upper valley of the Nile. A small French expedition under Captain J.B. Marchand journeyed by river and portage from French Congo to Fashoda on the upper Nile. There he claimed the town and the region for France. Learning of this, the British sent General Kitchener with 25,000 men up the Nile from Cairo to Fashoda. Kitchener claimed the Sudan for Britain, and both men wrote home for instructions. A European diplomatic crisis followed, in which France backed down in the face of an uncompromising British attitude. Marchand was recalled.

I have received the following telegram this morning from Sir Herbert Kitchener:—

"I have just returned here from Fashoda where I found Captain Marchand, accompanied by eight officers and 120 men, located in the old Government buildings, over which they had hoisted the French flag; I sent a letter announcing my approach the day before my arrival at Fashoda. A small rowboat carrying the French flag brought me a reply from Captain Marchand on the following morning, the 19th September, stating that he had reached Fashoda on the 10th July, his Government having given him instructions to occupy the Bahr-el-Ghazal as far as the confluence of the Bahr-el-Jebel, as well as the Shilluk country on the left bank of the White Nile as far as Fashoda. He stated that he had concluded a Treaty with the Chief of the Shilluk tribe, whereby the latter placed his country under the protection of France, and that he had sent this Treaty to his Government for ratification by way of Abyssinia, as well as by the Bahr-el-Ghazal, Captain Marchand described the fight which he had had with the Dervishes on the 25th August, and said that, in anticipation of a second and more severe attack, he had sent his steamer south for reinforcements, but our arrival had averted this danger.

"When we arrived at Fashoda, Captain Marchand and M. Germain came on board, and I at once stated that the presence of a French force at Fashoda and in the Valley of the Nile was regarded as a direct infringement of the rights of the Egyptian Government and of that of Great Britain, and I protested in the strongest terms against their occupation of Fashoda and their hoisting the French flag in the dominions of His Highness the Khedive. In reply, Captain Marchand stated that he had precise orders to occupy the

Letter of Rennell Rodd, British representative in Cairo, to the Marquess of Salisbury, British prime minister, September 25, 1898, in British Foreign Office, Turkey (Egypt), 4960, as found in W. Henry Cooke and Edith P. Stickney, *Readings in European International Relations Since 1879* (New York: Harper & Brothers, 1931), pp. 61–63.

country and to hoist the French flag over the Government buildings at Fashoda, and that it was impossible for him to retire without receiving orders from his Government to that effect, but he did not expect that these orders would be delayed. On my pressing him to say whether, seeing that I had a preponderating force, he was prepared to resist the hoisting of the Egyptian flag at Fashoda, he hesitated and replied that resistance was impossible. I then caused the flag to be hoisted on a ruined bastion of the old Egyptian fortifications about 500 yards south of the French flag, and on the only road which leads to the interior from the French position, which is surrounded by impassable marshes on all sides. Before leaving for the south, I handed to Captain Marchand a formal protest in writing, on behalf of the British and Egyptian Governments, against any occupation by France of any part of the Nile Valley, such occupation being an infringement of the rights of these Governments which I could not recognise.

"I appointed Major Jackson to be Commandant of the Fashoda district, where I left a garrison consisting of one Soudanese battalion, four guns, and a gun-boat, after which I proceeded to the Sobat, where, on the 20th September, a post was established and the flag hoisted. . . . On my way north, as I passed Fashoda, I sent a letter to Captain Marchand, stating that all transport of war material on the Nile was absolutely prohibited, as the country was under military law. The Shilluk Chief, with a large following, has come into Major Jackson's camp; the whole tribe are delighted to return to their allegiance to us, and the Chief absolutely denies having made any Treaty with the French.

"The position in which Captain Marchand finds himself at Fashoda is as impossible as it is absurd. He is cut off from the interior, and his water transport is quite inadequate; he is, moreover, short of ammunition and supplies, which must take months to reach him; he has no following in the country, and nothing could have saved him and his expedition from being annihilated by the Dervishes had we been a fortnight later in crushing the Khalifa.

"The futility of all their efforts is fully realised by Captain Marchand himself, and he seems quite as anxious to return as we are to facilitate his departure. In his present position he is powerless, but I hope that Her Majesty's Government will take the necessary steps for his removal as soon as possible, as the presence of a French force and flag on the Nile is manifestly extremely undesirable.

"Captain Marchand only lost four natives on the journey, and his expedition is all well.

"I am sending a complete despatch by Lord Edward Cecil, who is leaving with it for Cairo at once."

6. CECIL RHODES PRESENTS PLANS FOR SOUTH AFRICAN DEVELOPMENT

Cecil Rhodes (1853–1902) acquired an enormous fortune from South African gold and diamonds. Using his financial power to pursue political goals, Rhodes created the British South African Company in 1889 for developing an interior region, now known as Rhodesia. His distant goal was an Africa dominated by Britain, with a Cape-to-Cairo railway linking South Africa with Egypt. Alfred Milner, high commissioner for South Africa after 1897, found it very difficult to restrain the imperialistic Rhodes.

What I am in a hurry to write about to-day is *Rhodes*, especially with regard to the position in the North, which is perhaps going to be of more immediate urgency than the Transvaal. . . . He looks to making the territory of the B.S.A.C. [British South Africa Company] into a separate Colony ultimately self-governed (the Company keeping its mineral and other valuable rights, but giving up administration). The Colony (which I may remark in passing, though nominally self-governed, will be virtually an absolute monarchy with Rhodes as monarch) he means to unite with the Cape Colony and Natal, and then the three combined will bring *peaceful* pressure upon the Republics to drive them into a S. African federation. For the execution of this big scheme he wants the new northern colony (the virtual Rhodes Settlement) to be as big as possible. Therefore he wishes to incorporate the Protectorate, and not to run the risk of something like a Crown Colony springing up between the Northern boundary of the Cape Colony and the territory already in the hands of the Company. In my opinion the policy, in the main, is good. Everything depends upon the execution. And here we are in this peculiar position. Rhodes is the only man big enough to carry out such a work, but, on the other hand, Rhodes uncontrolled, in the same position in which he was before the [Jameson] Raid . . . will probably fail in carrying it out, because he is too self-willed, too violent, too sanguine, and in too great a hurry. He is just the same man as he always was, undaunted and unbroken by his former failure, but also untaught by it. He is much too strong a man to be merely *used.* He will work for his own ends in his own way—we must accept that—but, on the other hand we must, to a great extent, guide and restrain him. And, unless he is to make shipwreck both of his own ambitions and our permanent interests, it is necessary that we should do so. The great question is, how, without unduly interfering with or worrying

Letter of Sir Alfred Milner to Lord Selborne, June 2, 1897, in *The Milner Papers: South Africa 1897–1899*, edited by Cecil Headlam (London: Cassell & Company Ltd., 1931), Vol. I, pp. 105–107. Used by permission of the publisher and A.P. Watt & Son, owners of the copyright.

Rhodes, can we yet keep the necessary amount of control over him? . . . Men are ruled by their foibles, and Rhodes's foible is *size*. He really will be little or no better off for having the Protectorate. It does not materially affect the game. But he looks at that big map. He sees on the one side the Cape Colony, of which he once was master and hopes to be again, on the other side Rhodesia, of which he is master. Between the two he sees that huge patch, which he all but got once and is still without. It makes his mouth water and he will do all he can to get it. . . . Rhodes is a great developer, but he is not a good administrator, and it is most necessary that in his administrative arrangements *and in his choice of men*, he should listen to good advice, as he will readily if he sees something to gain by it. . . .

7. *BRITONS AND BOERS FACE A CRISIS IN SOUTH AFRICA*

The Boers, a farming people of Dutch descent in the republics of Transvaal and the Orange Free State, developed a strong anti-British feeling in the 1890's as Uitlanders (foreigners, mainly British) swarmed into gold and diamond mining camps. The British supported the mining companies against the Boers, resented Boer laws excluding Uitlanders from voting, and believed a struggle for control of South Africa was inevitable. Neither Paul Kruger, president of the Transvaal, nor Alfred Milner, high commissioner for South Africa, tried seriously to avert war in 1899.

The case for intervention is overwhelming. The only attempted answer is that things will right themselves if left alone. But, in fact, the policy of leaving things alone has been tried for years, and it has led to their going from bad to worse. . . .

The spectacle of thousands of British subjects kept permanently in the position of helots, constantly chafing under undoubted grievances, and calling vainly to Her Majesty's Government for redress, does steadily undermine the influence and reputation of Great Britain and the respect for the British Government within its own dominions. A certain section of the press, and not in the Transvaal only, preaches openly and constantly the doctrine of a Republic embracing all South Africa, and supports it by menacing references to the armaments of the Transvaal, its alliance with the Orange Free State, and the active sympathy which in case of war it would receive from a section of Her Majesty's subjects. I regret to say that this doctrine, supported as it is by a ceaseless stream of malignant lies about the inten-

Telegram from Sir Alfred Milner to Mr. Joseph Chamberlain, May 4, 1899, in *The Milner Papers: South Africa 1897–1899*, edited by Cecil Headlam (London: Cassell & Company Ltd., 1931), Vol. I, pp. 352–353. Used by permission of the publisher and A.P. Watt & Son, owners of the copyright.

tions of the British Government, is producing a great effect upon a large number of our Dutch fellow-colonists. Language is frequently used which seems to imply that the Dutch have some superior right even in this colony to their fellow-citizens of British birth. Thousands of men peaceably disposed, and, if left alone, perfectly satisfied with their position as British subjects, are being drawn into disaffection, and there is a corresponding exasperation on the side of the British.

I can see nothing which will put a stop to this mischievous propaganda but some striking proof of the intention, if it is the intention, of Her Majesty's Government not to be ousted from its position in South Africa. And the best proof alike of its power and its justice would be to obtain for the Uitlanders in the Transvaal a fair share in the Government of the country which owes everything to their exertions. It could be made perfectly clear that our action was not directed against the existence of the Republic. We should only be demanding the re-establishment of rights which now exist in the Orange Free State, and which existed in the Transvaal itself at the time of and long after the withdrawal of British sovereignty. It would be no selfish demand, as other Uitlanders besides those of British birth would benefit by it. It is asking for nothing from others which we do not give ourselves. And it would certainly go to the root of the political unrest in South Africa, and, though temporarily it might aggravate, it would ultimately extinguish the race feud which is the great bane of the country.

37

SCIENCE, SOCIALISM, AND RELIGION IN THE LATE NINETEENTH CENTURY

Science in the last half of the nineteenth century made enormous strides in many fields. The most startling and controversial discoveries were those of Charles Darwin, who proposed the theory of evolution by "natural selection." Darwinian ideas profoundly influenced literature in the direction of realism and turned philosophy toward materialism. Increasing industrialization and the social evils of the factory system led to the growth of various types of anarchism, syndicalism, and socialism, particularly the "scientific socialism" of Karl Marx. In this welter of confusion the Christian churches, Protestant and Catholic, were assailed from many sides by anti-clerical liberalism, Marxian Socialism, Darwinism, and an increasing amount of indifference to religion.

1. DARWIN EXPLAINS EVOLUTION BY NATURAL SELECTION

Early in the nineteenth century there had been considerable speculation by scientists on the evolution of complex species of life from simpler forms. Charles Darwin (1809–1882), in his famous work* Origin of Species, *carried the concept further than any of his predecessors by proposing a plausible theory of the evolutionary process, by supporting the theory with an impressive accumulation of facts, and by suggesting in the idea of natural selection an easy and universal explanation. Darwin's* Descent of Man *extended the theory from the world of plants and animals to man himself.

When on board H.M.S. 'Beagle,' as naturalist, I was much struck with certain facts in the distribution of the organic beings inhabiting South

Charles Darwin, *On the Origin of Species* (New York: D. Appleton and Company, 1873), pp. 1, 3, 61, 103.

America, and in the geological relations of the present to the past inhabitants of that continent. These facts, as will be seen in the latter chapters of this volume, seemed to throw some light on the origin of species—that mystery of mysteries, as it has been called by one of our greatest philosophers. On my return home, it occurred to me, in 1837, that something might perhaps be made out of this question by patiently accumulating and reflecting on all sorts of facts which could possibly have any bearing on it. After five years' work I allowed myself to speculate on the subject, and drew up some short notes; these I enlarged in 1844 into a sketch of the conclusions, which then seemed to me probable: from that period to the present day I have steadily pursued the same object. I hope that I may be excused for entering on these personal details, as I give them to show that I have not been hasty in coming to a decision. . . .

. . . I shall devote the first chapter of this Abstract to Variation under Domestication. We shall thus see that a large amount of hereditary modification is at least possible; and, what is equally or more important, we shall see how great is the power of man in accumulating by his Selection successive slight variations. I will then pass on to the variability of species in a state of nature; but I shall, unfortunately, be compelled to treat this subject far too briefly, as it can be treated properly only by giving long catalogues of facts. We shall, however, be enabled to discuss what circumstances are most favourable to variation. In the next chapter the Struggle for Existence amongst all organic beings throughout the world, which inevitably follows from the high geometrical ratio of their increase, will be considered. This is the doctrine of Malthus, applied to the whole animal and vegetable kingdoms. As many more individuals of each species are born than can possibly survive; and as, consequently, there is a frequently recurring struggle for existence, it follows that any being, if it vary however slightly in any manner profitable to itself, under the complex and sometimes varying conditions of life, will have a better chance of surviving, and thus be *naturally selected.* From the strong principle of inheritance, any selected variety will tend to propagate its new and modified form. . . .

. . . All that we can do, is to keep steadily in mind that each organic being is striving to increase in a geometrical ratio; that each at some period of its life, during some season of the year, during each generation or at intervals, has to struggle for life and to suffer great destruction. When we reflect on this struggle, we may console ourselves with the full belief, that the war of nature is not incessant, that no fear is felt, that death is generally prompt, and that the vigorous, the healthy, and the happy survive and multiply. . . .

We have seen that it is the common, the widely-diffused, and widely-ranging species, belonging to the larger genera within each class, which vary most; and these tend to transmit to their modified offspring that superiority which now makes them dominant in their own countries. Natural selection, as has been marked, leads to divergence of character and to much extinction of the less improved and intermediate forms of life. . . .

2. *DARWIN LINKS MAN TO LOWER ANIMALS*

The main conclusion here arrived at, and now held by many naturalists who are well competent to form a sound judgment, is that man is descended from some less highly organised form. The grounds upon which this conclusion rests will never be shaken, for the close similarity between man and the lower animals in embryonic development, as well as in innumerable points of structure and constitution, both of high and of the most trifling importance,—the rudiments which he retains, and the abnormal reversions to which he is occasionally liable,—are facts which cannot be disputed. They have long been known, but until recently they told us nothing with respect to the origin of man. Now when viewed by the light of our knowledge of the whole organic world, their meaning is unmistakable. The great principle of evolution stands up clear and firm, when these groups of facts are considered in connection with others, such as the mutual affinities of the members of the same group, their geographical distribution in past and present times, and their geological succession. . . .

The main conclusion arrived at in this work, namely that man is descended from some lowly organised form, will, I regret to think, be highly distasteful to many. But there can hardly be a doubt that we are descended from barbarians. . . . For my own part I would as soon be descended from that heroic little monkey, who braved his dreaded enemy in order to save the life of his keeper, or from that old baboon, who descending from the mountains, carried away in triumph his young comrade from a crowd of astonished dogs—as from a savage who delights to torture his enemies, offers up bloody sacrifices, practises infanticide without remorse, treats his wives like slaves, knows no decency, and is haunted by the grossest superstitions. . . .

. . . We must, however, acknowledge, as it seems to me, that man with all his noble qualities, with sympathy which feels for the most debased, with benevolence which extends not only to other men but to the humblest living creature, with his god-like intellect which has penetrated into the movements and constitution of the solar system—with all these exalted

Charles Darwin, *The Descent of Man* (New York: D. Appleton and Company, 1896), pp. 606–607, 618–619.

powers—Man still bears in his bodily frame the indelible stamp of his lowly origin.

3. *NIETZSCHE INVOKES THE SUPERMAN*

Friedrich Nietzsche (1844–1900) developed a brutal, pessimistic type of realism with his violent attacks on traditional morality. Nietzsche, greatly influenced by Darwin's concept of the struggle for existence, called on the will of man to create a race of supermen. Nietzsche despised Christianity and the Golden Rule and sought a victory of strength and will over humility and charity.

. . . And Zarathustra spake thus unto the people:

I teach you the Superman. Man is something that is to be surpassed. What have ye done to surpass man?

All beings hitherto have created something beyond themselves: and ye want to be the ebb of that great tide, and would rather go back to the beast than surpass man?

What is the ape to man? A laughing-stock, a thing of shame. And just the same shall man be to the Superman: a laughing-stock, a thing of shame.

Ye have made your way from the worm to man, and much within you is still worm. Once were ye apes, and even yet man is more of an ape than any of the apes.

Even the wisest among you is only a disharmony and hybrid of plant and phantom. But do I bid you become phantoms or plants?

Lo, I teach you the Superman!

The Superman is the meaning of the earth. Let your will say: The Superman *shall be* the meaning of the earth!

* * *

For to-day have the petty people become master: they all preach submission and humility and policy and diligence and consideration and the long *et cetera* of petty virtues.

Whatever is of the effeminate type, whatever originateth from the servile type, and especially the populace-mish-mash:—*that* wisheth now to be master of all human destiny—O disgust! Disgust! Disgust! . . .

These masters of to-day—surpass them, O my brethren—these petty people: *they* are the Superman's greatest danger! . . .

Friedrich Nietzsche, *Thus Spake Zarathustra,* translated by Thomas Common (New York: The Modern Library, n.d.), pp. 27–28, 286–287. Used by permission of George Allen & Unwin Ltd., London.

4. KARL MARX CALLS FOR A COMMUNIST REVOLUTION

Karl Marx (1818–1883), in collaboration with Friedrich Engels, issued the inflammatory pamphlet* The Communist Manifesto *early in 1848. This publication exerted almost no influence on the wave of revolutions of 1848, however. The* Manifesto *contains nearly all the basic doctrines of Marxian Socialism, and was widely circulated and read in the last half of the nineteenth century.

A spectre is haunting Europe—the spectre of Communism. All the Powers of old Europe have entered into a holy alliance to exorcise this spectre; Pope and Czar, Metternich and Guizot, French Radicals and German police-spies.

Where is the party in opposition that has not been decried as communistic by its opponents in power? Where the Opposition that has not hurled back the branding reproach of Communism against the more advanced opposition parties, as well as against its reactionary adversaries?

Two things result from this fact.

I. Communism is already acknowledged by all European Powers to be itself a Power.

II. It is high time that Communists should openly, in the face of the whole world, publish their views, their aims, their tendencies, and meet this nursery tale of the spectre of Communism with a Manifesto of the party itself. . . .

The history of all hitherto existing society is the history of class struggles.

Freeman and slave, patrician and plebeian, lord and serf, guild-master and journeyman, in a word, oppressor and oppressed, stood in constant opposition to one another, carried on uninterrupted, now hidden, now open fight, a fight that each time ended, either in a revolutionary re-constitution of society at large, or in the common ruin of the contending classes.

In the earlier epochs of history we find almost everywhere a complicated arrangement of society into various orders, a manifold gradation of social rank. In ancient Rome we have patricians, knights, plebeians, slaves; in the middle ages, feudal lords, vassals, guild-masters, journeymen, apprentices, serfs; in almost all of these classes, again, subordinate gradations.

The modern bourgeois society that has sprouted from the ruins of feudal society, has not done away with class antagonisms. It has but estab-

Karl Marx, "The Communist Manifesto," in *Capital, the Communist Manifesto, and Other Writings* (New York: The Modern Library, 1932), pp. 320–324, 326, 327–329, 330, 332, 333, 335, 343, 355.

lished new classes, new conditions of oppression, new forms of struggle in place of the old ones.

Our epoch, the epoch of the bourgeoisie, possesses, however, this distinctive feature; it has simplified the class antagonisms. Society as a whole is more and more splitting up into two great hostile camps, into two great classes directly facing each other: Bourgeoisie and Proletariat. . . .

. . . the bourgeoisie has at last, since the establishment of Modern Industry and of the world-market, conquered for itself, in the modern representative State, exclusive political sway. The executive of the modern State is but a committee for managing the common affairs of the whole bourgeoisie. . . .

The bourgeoisie has stripped of its halo every occupation hitherto honored and looked up to with reverent awe. It has converted the physician, the lawyer, the priest, the poet, the man of science, into its paid wage laborers.

The bourgeoisie has torn away from the family its sentimental veil, and has reduced the family relation to a mere money relation. . . .

The need of a constantly expanding market for its products chases the bourgeoisie over the whole surface of the globe. It must nestle everywhere, settle everywhere, establish connections everywhere. . . .

The bourgeoisie, during its rule of scarce one hundred years, has created more massive and more colossal productive forces than have all preceding generations together. . . .

The weapons with which the bourgeoisie felled feudalism to the ground are now turned against the bourgeoisie itself.

But not only has the bourgeoisie forged the weapons that bring death to itself; it has also called into existence the men who are to wield those weapons—the modern working-class—the proletarians.

In proportion as the bourgeoisie, *i.e.*, capital, is developed, in the same proportion is the proletariat, the modern working-class, developed, a class of laborers who live only so long as they find work, and who find work only so long as their labor increases capital. These laborers, who must sell themselves piecemeal, are a commodity, like every other article of commerce, and are consequently exposed to all the vicissitudes of competition, to all the fluctuations of the market. . . .

The lower strata of the middle class—the small trades-people, shopkeepers and retired tradesmen generally, the handicraftsmen and peasants —all these sink gradually into the proletariat, partly because their diminutive capital does not suffice for the scale on which Modern Industry is carried on, and is swamped in the competition with the large capitalists, partly because their specialized skill is rendered worthless by new methods of production. Thus the proletariat is recruited from all classes of the population. . . .

But with the development of industry the proletariat not only increases in number; it becomes concentrated in greater masses, its strength grows and it feels that strength more. The various interests and conditions of life within the ranks of the proletariat are more and more equalized, in proportion as machinery obliterates all distinctions of labor, and nearly everywhere reduces wages to the same low level. . . .

. . . The proletarian is without property; his relation to his wife and children has no longer anything in common with the bourgeois family relations; modern industrial labor, modern subjection to capital, the same in England as in France, in America as in Germany, has stripped him of every trace of national character. Law, morality, religion, are to him so many bourgeois prejudices, behind which lurk in ambush just as many bourgeois interests. . . .

. . . The modern laborer, on the contrary, instead of rising with the progress of industry, sinks deeper and deeper below the conditions of existence of his own class. He becomes a pauper, and pauperism develops more rapidly than population and wealth. And here it becomes evident that the bourgeoisie is unfit any longer to be the ruling class in society, and to impose its conditions of existence upon society as an over-riding law. It is unfit to rule, because it is incompetent to assure an existence to its slave within his slavery, because it cannot help letting him sink into such a state that it has to feed him, instead of being fed by him. Society can no longer live under this bourgeoisie; in other words, its existence is no longer compatible with society. . . .

. . . the theory of the Communists may be summed up in the single sentence: Abolition of private property. . . .

. . . If the proletariat during its contest with the bourgeoisie is compelled, by the force of circumstances, to organize itself as a class, if, by means of a revolution, it makes itself the ruling class, and, as such, sweeps away by force the old conditions of production, then it will, along with these conditions, have swept away the conditions for the existence of class antagonism, and of classes generally, and will thereby have abolished its own supremacy as a class.

In place of the old bourgeois society, with its classes and class antagonisms, we shall have an association in which the free development of each is the condition for the free development of all. . . .

In short, the Communists everywhere support every revolutionary movement against the existing social and political order of things.

In all these movements they bring to the front, as the leading question in each, the property question, no matter what its degree of development at the time.

Finally, they labor everywhere for the union and agreement of the democratic parties of all countries.

The Communists disdain to conceal their views and aims. They openly declare that their ends can be attained only by the forcible overthrow of all existing social conditions. Let the ruling classes tremble at a Communistic revolution. The proletarians have nothing to lose but their chains. They have a world to win.

Working men of all countries, unite!

5. *POPE PIUS IX CONDEMNS LIBERALISM IN THE* SYLLABUS OF ERRORS

At the end of the encyclical* Quanta Cura*, issued by Pius IX in 1864, appeared a list of eighty erroneous propositions, the* Syllabus of Errors*. Therein the Pope reaffirmed earlier condemnations of liberalism, rationalism, and indifferentism. The* Syllabus *was generally misunderstood by its critics. Anti-clerical liberals pointed with glee at the last proposition, in which the Pope seemed to be condemning all modern civilization.

1. There exists no supreme, all wise, most provident divine Being, distinct from the universe; God and nature are one, and God is therefore subject to change; actually, God is produced in man and in the world; God and the world are identical, as are spirit and matter, true and false, good and evil, just and unjust. . . .

4. All truths of religion derive from the natural force of human reason; hence reason is the principal rule by which man can and should attain the knowledge of all truths of whatever kind. . . .

7. Prophecies and miracles, set forth and narrated in Holy Scripture, are poetical fictions; the mysteries of Christian faith are the results of philosophic investigations; in the books of both Testaments are contained mythical inventions; and Jesus Christ Himself is a mythical fiction. . . .

9. Without exception, all the dogmas of the Christian religion are the object of natural science or philosophy; and human reason, developed solely by history, can by its own natural strength and principles arrive at the true knowledge of even the more abstruse dogmas, provided these dogmas be proposed as the object of reason. . . .

15. Every man is free to embrace and profess that religion which, guided by the light of reason, he shall believe true. . . .

The Syllabus of Errors, in Raymond Corrigan, S.J., *The Church and the Nineteenth Century* (Milwaukee, Wis., The Bruce Publishing Company, 1938), pp. 289–295.

20. The Ecclesiastical power must not exercise its authority without the permission and assent of civil government. . . .

26. The Church has no natural and legitimate right to acquire and possess property.

27. The ministers of the Church and the Roman Pontiff ought to be absolutely excluded from all care and dominion over temporal things. . . .

55. The Church should be separated from the State, and the State from the Church.

56. Moral laws do not require a divine sanction, nor is there any need for human laws to be conformable to the law of nature or to receive their binding force from God.

57. The science of philosophy and morals, and likewise of civil laws may and should be withdrawn from divine and ecclesiastical authority. . . .

67. The marriage bond is not indissoluble according to the natural law, and in certain cases divorce, properly so called, may be sanctioned by civil authority. . . .

77. In our times it is no longer necessary that the Catholic religion should be the only religion of the State to the exclusion of all others whatsoever. . . .

80. The Roman Pontiff can and should reconcile and align himself with progress, liberalism, and modern civilization.

6. THE VATICAN COUNCIL DEFINES PAPAL INFALLIBILITY

Pius IX convoked a general council of the Catholic Church, which met at the Vatican in December, 1869. This council, the first since that of Trent three hundred years earlier, adjourned in the summer of 1870 with its work unfinished, and was never reconvened. Its most spectacular achievement was the proclamation of the dogma of papal infallibility.

Wherefore, faithfully adhering to the tradition handed down from the beginning, for the glory of God our Savior, for the exaltation of the Catholic Religion, and the salvation of Christian peoples, with the approbation of the Sacred Council, we teach and we define the divinely revealed dogma that: when the Roman Pontiff speaks *ex cathedra*, that is, when in the discharge of his office as Doctor and Pastor of all Christians, in virtue of his supreme Apostolic authority, he defines a doctrine concerning faith or morals to be held by the whole Church, he enjoys, by the divine assistance promised him in Blessed Peter, that infallibility with which the divine Redeemer willed

"The Dogma of Papal Infallibility," in Raymond Corrigan, S.J., *The Church and the Nineteenth Century* (Milwaukee, Wis., The Bruce Publishing Company, 1938), p. 199.

that His Church should be endowed for the purpose of defining doctrines concerning faith or morals.

7. *LEO XIII IN* RERUM NOVARUM *ENCOURAGES A CATHOLIC SOCIAL MOVEMENT*

Leo XIII, greatest of the modern popes, issued his famous encyclical* On the Condition of the Workers (Rerum Novarum) *in 1891. The encyclical denied the Marxian concept of class warfare, defended the rights of private property, and called for a "living family wage" for the working man. In the years following, a number of Catholic political parties and Catholic labor unions arose to pursue a social program based on Christian principles, in opposition to Marxian Socialism and economic liberalism.

1. Once the passion for revolutionary change was aroused—a passion long disturbing governments—it was bound to follow sooner or later that eagerness for change would pass from the political sphere over into the related field of economics. In fact, new developments in industry, new techniques striking out on new paths, changed relations of employer and employee, abounding wealth among a very small number and destitution among the masses, increased self-reliance on the part of workers as well as a closer bond of union with one another, and, in addition to all this, a decline in morals have caused conflict to break forth.

2. The momentous nature of the questions involved in this conflict is evident from the fact that it keeps men's minds in anxious expectation, occupying the talents of the learned, the discussions of the wise and experienced, the assemblies of the people, the judgment of lawmakers, and the deliberations of rulers, so that now no topic more strongly holds men's interests.

3. Therefore, Venerable Brethren, with the cause of the Church and the common welfare before Us, We have thought it advisable, following Our custom on other occasions when We issued to you the Encyclicals *On Political Power, On Human Liberty, On the Christian Constitution of States,* and others of similar nature, which seemed opportune to refute erroneous opinions, that We ought to do the same now, and for the same reasons, *On the Condition of Workers.* We have on occasion touched more than once upon this subject. In this Encyclical, however, consciousness of Our Apostolic office admonishes Us to treat the entire question thoroughly, in order that the principles may stand out in clear light, and the conflict may thereby be brought to an end as required by truth and equity.

Two Basic Social Encyclicals: On the Condition of Workers, Leo XIII and Forty Years After, On Reconstructing Social Order, Pius XI. Latin text with English translation approved by the Holy See, pp. 3–81, *passim.*

4. The problem is difficult to resolve and is not free from dangers. It is hard indeed to fix the boundaries of the rights and duties within which the rich and the proletariat—those who furnish material things and those who furnish work—ought to be restricted in relation to each other. The controversy is truly dangerous, for in various places it is being twisted by turbulent and crafty men to pervert judgment as to truth and seditiously to incite the masses.

5. In any event, We see clearly, and all are agreed that the poor must be speedily and fittingly cared for, since the great majority of them live undeservedly in miserable and wretched conditions.

6. After the old trade guilds had been destroyed in the last century, and no protection was substituted in their place, and when public institutions and legislation had cast off traditional religious teaching, it gradually came about that the present age handed over the workers, each alone and defenseless, to the inhumanity of employers and the unbridled greed of competitors. A devouring usury, although often condemned by the Church, but practiced nevertheless under another form by avaricious and grasping men, has increased the evil; and in addition the whole process of production as well as trade in every kind of goods has been brought almost entirely under the power of a few, so that a very few rich and exceedingly rich men have laid a yoke almost of slavery on the unnumbered masses of non-owning workers.

7. To cure this evil, the Socialists, exciting the envy of the poor toward the rich, contend that it is necessary to do away with private possession of goods and in its place to make the goods of individuals common to all, and that the men who preside over a municipality or who direct the entire State should act as administrators of these goods. They hold that, by such a transfer of private goods from private individuals to the community, they can cure the present evil through dividing wealth and benefits equally among the citizens.

8. But their program is so unsuited for terminating the conflict that it actually injures the workers themselves. Moreover, it is highly unjust, because it violates the rights of lawful owners, perverts the functions of the State, and throws governments into utter confusion. . . .

. . . inasmuch as the Socialists seek to transfer the goods of private persons to the community at large, they make the lot of all wage earners worse, because in abolishing the freedom to dispose of wages they take away from them by this very act the hope and the opportunity of increasing their property and of securing advantages for themselves.

10. But, what is of more vital concern, they propose a remedy openly

in conflict with justice, inasmuch as nature confers on man the right to possess things privately as his own. . . .

21. To desire . . . that the civil power should enter arbitrarily into the privacy of homes is a great and pernicious error. If a family perchance is in such extreme difficulty and is so completely without plans that it is entirely unable to help itself, it is right that the distress be remedied by public aid, for each individual family is a part of the community. . . . for the very reason that children "are by nature part of their father . . . before they have the use of free will, they are kept under the care of their parents." Inasmuch as the Socialists, therefore, disregard care by parents and in its place introduce care by the State, they act *against natural justice* and dissolve the structure of the home. . . .

28. It is a capital evil with respect to the question We are discussing to take for granted that the one class of society is of itself hostile to the other, as if nature had set rich and poor against each other to fight fiercely in implacable war. This is so abhorrent to reason and truth that the exact opposite is true; for just as in the human body the different members harmonize with one another, whence arises that disposition of parts and proportion in the human figure rightly called symmetry, so likewise nature has commanded in the case of the State that the two classes mentioned should agree harmoniously and should properly form equally balanced counterparts to each other. Each needs the other completely: neither capital can do without labor, nor labor without capital. Concord begets beauty and order in things. Conversely, from perpetual strife there must arise disorder accompanied by bestial cruelty. But for putting an end to conflict and for cutting away its very roots, there is wondrous and multiple power in Christian institutions.

29. And first and foremost, the entire body of religious teaching and practice, of which the Church is the interpreter and guardian, can pre-eminently bring together and unite the rich and the poor by recalling the two classes of society to their mutual duties, and in particular to those duties which derive from justice.

30. Among these duties the following concern the poor and the workers: To perform entirely and conscientiously whatever work has been voluntarily and equitably agreed upon; not in any way to injure the property or to harm the person of employers; in protecting their own interests, to refrain from violence and never to engage in rioting; . . .

31. The following duties, on the other hand, concern rich men and employers: Workers are not to be treated as slaves; justice demands that the dignity of human personality be respected in them, ennobled as it has

been through what we call the Christian character. If we hearken to natural reason and to Christian philosophy, gainful occupations are not a mark of shame to man, but rather of respect, as they provide him with an honorable means of supporting life. It is shameful and inhuman, however, to use men as things for gain and to put no more value on them than what they are worth in muscle and energy. . . .

37. Those who lack fortune's goods are taught by the Church that, before God as Judge, poverty is no disgrace, and that no one should be ashamed because he makes his living by toil. . . .

49. . . . the State has one basic purpose for existence, which embraces in common the highest and the lowest of its members. Non-owning workers are unquestionably citizens by nature in virtue of the same right as the rich, that is, true and vital parts whence, through the medium of families, the body of the State is constituted; and it hardly need be added that they are by far the greatest number in every urban area. Since it would be quite absurd to look out for one portion of the citizens and to neglect another, it follows that public authority ought to exercise due care in safe-guarding the well-being and the interests of non-owning workers. . . .

59. Now as concerns the protection of corporeal and physical goods, the oppressed workers, above all, ought to be liberated from the savagery of greedy men, who inordinately use human beings as things for gain. Assuredly, neither justice nor humanity can countenance the exaction of so much work that the spirit is dulled from excessive toil and that along with it the body sinks crushed from exhaustion. . . .

69. . . . In our present age of greater culture, with its new customs and ways of living, and with the increased number of things required by daily life, it is most clearly necessary that workers' associations be adapted to meet the present need. It is gratifying that societies of this kind composed either of workers alone or of workers and employers together are being formed everywhere, and it is truly to be desired that they grow in number and in active vigor. . . .

81. The condition of workers is a subject of bitter controversy at the present time; and whether this controversy is resolved in accordance with reason or otherwise, is in either event of utmost importance to the State. But Christian workers will readily resolve it in accordance with reason, if, united in associations and under wise leaders, they enter upon the path which their fathers and their ancestors followed to their own best welfare as well as to that of the State. . . .

IX

EUROPE IN THE TWENTIETH CENTURY

38

WORLD WAR I AND VERSAILLES

In the decade from 1905 to 1914 a succession of crises increased tension between the Triple Entente and the Triple Alliance. Compromise became impossible as each of the great powers felt that its national interests were at stake. When war came, Germany found herself fighting a two-front war against Russia in the east and against England and France, later joined by Italy and America, in the west. The entry of America on the Allied side in 1917 compensated for the collapse of Russia and the near-exhaustion of England and France. Defeated, but not completely crushed, Germany sought an armistice in 1918. The victorious Allies, meeting at Paris and Versailles, drew up peace terms and established a League of Nations.

1. A RUSSIAN DIPLOMAT REVIEWS THE BOSNIAN CRISIS OF 1908

Austria-Hungary in 1908 took the dangerous step of annexing Bosnia and Herzogovina, Serb-speaking provinces nominally a part of the Turkish Empire but administered by Austria-Hungary since 1878. Serbia, enraged by this crushing blow to her expansion plans, appealed to Russia. The Russians, however, were too exhausted by their recent war with Japan to furnish aid. Germany, on the other hand, offered full military support to Austria. Serge Sazonov, author of this selection, was an able diplomat, serving as Russia's foreign minister from 1910 to 1916.

From this political rivalry in the Balkans sprang a perpetual enmity between Vienna and St. Petersburg, fated to lead sooner or later to open war—the

Serge Sazonov, *Fateful Years, 1909–1916* (London: Jonathan Cape Ltd., 1928; and New York: Frederick A. Stokes Company, 1928), pp. 14–20, as found in W. Henry Cooke and Edith P. Stickney, *Readings in European International Relations Since 1879* (New York: Harper & Brothers, 1931), pp. 135–136, 139.

inevitable outcome of the irreconcilable antipathy. It was always improbable, on account of the general European character which Balkan questions had long since assumed, that Russia and Austria-Hungary would be able to settle accounts with regard to the Balkans without drawing the other Powers into the struggle; but when Bismarck concluded an alliance with Austria in 1879 there was no longer any hope of confining the matter to a mere duel between the two rivals. This was recognized by all the European Cabinets. Nevertheless, up to 1909 Germany refrained from openly avowing her full solidarity with Austria-Hungary's Balkan policy; . . . The Bosnia and Herzegovina crisis in 1908–09 revealed the true state of affairs to the whole of Europe. Aehrenthal's unscrupulous conduct in converting the actual control of Bosnia and Herzegovina, which entailed no danger for the Austro-Hungarian Monarchy, into a juridical possession by means of a gross infringement of all law, was a challenge to the whole Serbian people and also to Russia; not only did it fail to evoke any expression of disapproval from the German Government—it actually received the support and protection of Germany's Imperial power. Europe was confronted with a *fait accompli*, and was forced either to accept it as such, or to engage in an armed struggle with Austria-Hungary, and possibly with the whole of the Triple Alliance.

The public opinion of Europe condemned the methods of Austrian diplomacy, recognizing in them a threat to the legal stability of international State life; but no one was eager to oppose them by force of arms. The direct interests of Western Europe were not affected by the Austrian *coup*, and the danger of provoking a European war, with its disastrous consequences, was apparent to all. Consequently neither France nor England could be expected to concern themselves with this question, beyond according their diplomatic support to the wronged party.

In Serbia and Russia, however, the Bosnia-Herzegovina crisis called forth very different feelings. For Serbia the absorption by Austria-Hungary of a considerable portion of the Serbian race was not only a heavy blow to her national pride, it was also an ominous forecast of the ulterior designs of the Viennese policy. Russia, although her interests were not directly affected, nevertheless felt insulted by the methods adopted by Count Aehrenthal in dealing with the Russian Minister for Foreign Affairs. By means of a palpable concealment he allowed himself to interpret certain general conversations between himself and Isvolsky [Russian minister for Foreign Affairs] as a consent on the part of the Russian Government to the immediate annexation of the occupied Turkish provinces. . . .

. . . Serbia obeyed the friendly advice of Russia and the Western Powers, and prudently refrained from kindling a European conflagration under political circumstances unfavourable to her own future. The diplomatic incident was closed; but the bad seed sown by Aehrenthal bore poisonous fruit in the injured sense of national dignity of which the Serbs remained conscious.

2. *DEATH COMES TO ARCHDUKE FRANCIS FERDINAND AT SARAJEVO*

Archduke Francis Ferdinand of Austria was the nephew and heir to the throne of the aged Hapsburg Emperor Francis Joseph. The announcement of the Archduke's intention of visiting Sarajevo, the Bosnian capital, led to a plot by a group of Bosnian youths to assassinate him. Trained and armed in Serbia by the "Black Hand" organization, three assassins returned to Sarajevo to await their victim.

Sarajevo, for some five hundred years, had been the capital of Bosnia and is still its principal city. It is crowded into a narrow valley at the foot of high hills. Through its center runs a little river, the Miljachka, half dry in summer. In the older parts of the city toward the cathedral the streets are crooked and narrow. But the Appel Quay, now known as the Stepanovitch Quay, is a fairly wide straight avenue lined with houses on one side, and with a low wall on the other, where the Quay follows the Miljachka. . . . Along the Appel Quay, which was the route the Archduke and his wife were to follow, Ilitch had placed the various murderers to whom he had distributed the bombs and revolvers a few hours before the assassination. . . .

On Vidov-Dan, Sunday, June 28, 1914, the day opened with glorious summer weather. The streets, at the request of the Mayor, had been beflagged in the Archduke's honor. His portrait stood in many windows. Considerable crowds were abroad in the streets to see him pass. No effort was made to keep them back, by forming a line of soldiers, as had been done in 1910 when Francis Joseph visited the city. Several of the loyal newspapers welcomed the Archduke's presence, but the leading Serb newspaper, *Narod*, contented itself with the bare announcement of his visit, and devoted the rest of its issue to a patriotic account of the significance of Vidov-Dan, an account of the Battle of Kossovo, and a picture of King Peter of Serbia framed in the national Serbian colors.

Franz Ferdinand and his party reached Sarajevo . . . about 10 A.M. After reviewing local troops, they started in autos toward the Town Hall for the formal reception in accordance with the announced program. The

Sidney B. Fay, *The Origins of the World War*, Second Edition, Revised (New York: The Macmillan Company, 1943), Vol. II, pp. 121–126.

Heir to the Throne was in full uniform, wearing all his decorations. His wife, in a white gown and large hat, sat beside him. On the seat facing them was General Potiorek, the military Governor of Bosnia, who pointed out the objects of interest as they drove along. In front of them, in another car, the Mayor and Chief of Police led the way. Then followed two other autos bearing various persons belonging to the Archduke's suite or General Potiorek's staff.

Just as they were approaching the Cumurja Bridge and Potiorek was calling the Archduke's attention to some new barracks, Chabrinovitch knocked off the cap of his bomb against a post, stepped forward, and hurled it at the Archduke's car. The chauffeur, observing him, put on speed, so that the missile fell onto the folded hood of the uncovered car and bounced off; or, according to another account, Franz Ferdinand, with extraordinary coolness, seized it and threw it back of him into the road. There it exploded with a heavy detonation, partly wrecking the following auto and seriously wounding Lieut.-Col. Merizzi and several bystanders. Chabrinovitch sprang over the wall into the river-bed, which was nearly dry at this season of the year, and tried to escape; but police agents quickly seized him and marched him off for examination. Meanwhile the fourth auto, uninjured except for a broken windshield, passed the wrecked car and closed up quickly to that of the Archduke, none of whose occupants had been hurt, except for a scratch on the Archduke's face, probably caused by the flying cap of the bomb. The Archduke ordered all the cars to stop, in order to learn what damage had been done. Having seen that the wounded men were dispatched to a hospital, he remarked with characteristic coolness and courage: "Come on. The fellow is insane. Gentlemen, let us proceed with our program."

So the party drove on to the Town Hall, at first rapidly, and then, at the Archduke's order, more slowly so that the people could see him better. The Archduke's wife met a deputation of Mohammedan women, while the Archduke was to receive the city officials. The Mayor, who had written out his speech of welcome, started to read it, as if nothing had happened. But it hardly suited the occasion. It dilated upon the loyalty of the Bosnian people and the overwhelming joy with which they welcomed the Heir to the Throne. Franz Ferdinand, by nature quick-tempered and outspoken, roughly interrupted the Mayor, saying: "Enough of that. What! I make you a visit, and you receive me with bombs." Nevertheless, he allowed the Mayor to finish his address. This terminated the formalities at the Town Hall.

The question then arose whether the party should still follow the prearranged program which provided for a drive through the narrow Franz

Josef Street in the crowded part of the city and a visit to the Museum; or whether, in view of another possible attack, they should drive straight to the Governor's residence on the other side of the river for luncheon. The Archduke insisited that he wanted to visit the hospital to inquire after the officer who had been wounded by Chabrinovitch's bomb. General Potiorek and the Chief of Police thought it very unlikely that any second attempt at murder would be made on the same day. But as a punishment for the first, and for the sake of safety, it was decided that the autos should not follow the prearranged route through the narrow Franz Josef Street, but should reach the hospital and Museum by driving rapidly straight along the Appel Quay. Therefore the Archduke and his wife and the others entered the cars in the same order as before, except that Count Harrach stood on the left running-board of the Archduke's car, as a protection from any attack from the Miljachka side of the Quay. On reaching the Franz Josef Street the Mayor's car in the lead turned to the right into it, according to the original program. The Archduke's chauffeur started to follow it, but Potiorek called out. "That's the wrong way! Drive straight down the Appel Quay!" The chauffeur put on the brakes in order to back up. It happened that it was precisely at this corner, where the car paused for a fatal moment, that Princip was now standing, having crossed over from his original position on the river side of the Quay. These chance occurrences gave him the best possible opportunity. He stepped forward and fired two shots point blank. One pierced the Archduke's neck so that blood spurted from his mouth. The other shot, aimed perhaps at Potiorek, entered the abdomen of Sophie Chotek [wife of the Archduke].

The car turned and sped over the Latin Bridge to the Konak. The Archduke's last words to his wife were: "Sophie, Sophie, do not die. Live for our children." But death overtook them both within a few minutes. It was about 11:30 A.M., St. Vitus's Day, Sunday, June 28, 1914.

3. *THE GERMANS LAUNCH A NIGHT ATTACK ON THE WESTERN FRONT*

By September, 1914, the initial German drive in the west had stalled along the Marne River, and both sides dug in. For the next four years a static trench warfare prevailed on the western front, punctuated by mass-attack offensives such as the German assault on Verdun in 1916, the longest and bloodiest action of the war. The selection below describes typical combat conditions of the battle of Verdun.

Jules Romains, *Verdun* (Vol. VIII of *Men of Good Will*), translated by Gerard Hopkins (New York: Alfred A. Knopf, Inc., 1939), pp. 307–309.

Along the line of these nocturnal woods were thus strung out hundreds of tiny independent battles and night-blanketed struggles, the participants in each one of which scarce knew of the existence of the others. Advances and retirements were measured in yards. The darkness was full of forms stumbling over stones and mounds of earth and steel plates. Feet were caught in wire. Men found themselves treading on yielding surfaces which could be nothing but corpses, or flung themselves head-foremost into something long and dark which turned out to be all that remained of a trench, to rest their rifles for a moment on the parapet and fire a few cartridges without aiming at a few shadows which they had reason to suppose were "on the opposite side," were "enemies." Everyone was hungry, since, needless to say, no rations had come up, and most of the men had finished what they carried on them, or refrained from touching the little that remained, for fear of having nothing with which to keep up their strength when dawn should come. Their insides were hollow, as though they had, indeed, been ghosts. . . .

Darkness covered everything. The various movements were carried out in comparative silence and almost furtively. Now and then might be heard a burst of rifle-fire, explosions of grenades, the tac-tac-tac of machine-guns. Scarcely a cry was audible. Many a manoeuvre was carried out in complete silence. A dozen or so men would creep forward through the trees, making use of the cover provided by heaps of rubbish or what remained of parapets, whispering among themselves. They would succeed in just edging round to the left of some field-work in which the enemy had managed to get a footing, and as though to mark the successful accomplishment of the movement, the two or three men forming the spear-head of the tiny thrust would start firing at the objective without aiming, almost without seeing. The occupants of the point attacked would run out, bent double, from the shell-holes where they had been crouching, and withdraw through the darkness and the trees, firing as they went. A little farther on, to right or left, a similar operation would develop in the opposite sense. Now and then a man would fall. The official reports would speak of "bitter fighting." That it was obstinate there could be no doubt. Not a blunder, not a sign of weakening on the part of either adversary, but was noted at once and exploited as far as the darkness would permit. But there was no fury of hand-to-hand fighting. Those who had not been there would reconstruct the scene in imagination as a struggle to the death of man with man, a madness of frenzied warriors, feeling for one another in the darkness and battling with fists and knives. In reality, this confused scramble which no one could see as a whole, know anything about, or, in any actual sense, control, was like some muddled sort of game. It was as though, vaguely visible in the darkness, confused teams, drawn from two opposing sides, were attempting to bring off a series of strokes against each other, scoring "points," for the time being at least, in accordance with a system of unspoken conventions. "Strictly speaking, you've worked round my flank. I'm in danger of being surrounded. All right, I shan't contest it. Let's go back and start again twenty yards to the rear." The mortal blows, beneath which from moment to moment some man would fall, were evidence that this was no bloodless sport. But their real value was that they served as "marks." In spite of them, and quite apart from what those engaged intended, the fight managed to retain a certain purely theoretical character. Its various phases were determined less by the actual clash of contending forces, by the effective destruction of one by the other, than by a balancing of possibilities and chances between the two. . . .

Suddenly, a hail of shells from the 75's. The French gunners had at last understood that something was going on out there in front which might be considered to have a personal interest for them.

The men's hearts rose, not so much because the assistance was effective, but because it was, at least, support. But their joy was shortlived. It is not wholly beneficial to take part in an action at quite so late a stage, to start doing something at eight o'clock which ought to have been done at four. The shells were falling not in front of the lines but on the wood itself. The gunners, who had set themselves to find out quite a lot of things, had discovered, among others, that the enemy had got a footing in the woods and could best be hit there. The trouble was that he was no longer the only person there, that the action now in full swing had become so confused that God Himself, had He been in charge of the artillery, could not have distinguished between French and German.

"That's enough! Tell 'em to stop! Send up flares! Send back runners. . . ."

Those who had survived the German bombardment were now to be blown to pieces by their own guns!

4. THE SOVIET OF WORKERS' DEPUTIES APPEALS TO THE RUSSIAN PEOPLE

Conditions in Russia by 1917 were becoming intolerable. Food shortages in the cities, munitions shortages at the front, the breakdown of rail transport, and the incompetence of the Czar's government led to a revolution in Petrograd, the

Izvestiia, No. 1, March 13, 1917, Soviet of Workers' Deputies, as found in Frank Alfred Golder, *Documents of Russian History, 1914–1917,* translated by Emanuel Aronsberg, pp. 287–288.

capital, in which soldiers and workers formed "soviets" or councils. The soviets joined with the Duma, the Russian parliament, to form a provisional government. The next day Czar Nicholas II abdicated.

The old régime has brought the country to ruin and the population to famine. It was impossible to bear this longer, and the inhabitants of Petrograd came out on the street to express their dissatisfaction. They were greeted by a volley of bullets. In place of bread, the Tsar's Ministers gave them lead.

But the soldiers would not act against the people and turned against the Government. Together with the people they seized guns, arsenals, and important governmental institutions.

The fight is still on and must go on to the end. The old power must be completely crushed to make way for popular government. In that lies the salvation of Russia.

In order to succeed in this struggle for democracy, the people must create their own governmental organ. Yesterday, March 12, there was formed at the capital a Soviet of Workers' Deputies, made up of representatives of factories, mills, revolted troops, and democratic and socialistic parties and groups. The Soviet, sitting in the Duma, has set for itself as its main task to organize the popular forces, and to fight for the consolidation of political freedom and popular government.

The Soviet has appointed commissars to establish the people's authority in the wards of Petrograd. We invite the entire population of the capital to rally at once to the Soviet, to organize local committees in their wards and take into their hands the management of local affairs.

All together, with our forces united, we will fight to wipe out completely the old Government and to call a constituent assembly on the basis of universal, equal, direct, and secret suffrage.

5. *LENIN AND THE BOLSHEVIKS OVERTHROW THE KERENSKY RÉGIME*

The provisional government which emerged from the first Russian Revolution of March, 1917, attempted, under Alexander Kerensky, to continue the unpopular war against Germany. As Kerensky failed to provide determined, effective leadership, a small group of Bolsheviks (Communists) won the support of soldiers, sailors, and workers in Petrograd. The Bolsheviks, ably led by Nicolai Lenin, who had returned from exile with German assistance, seized control from the Kerensky Régime on November 7, 1917.

Izvestiia, No. 207, November 8, 1917, as found in Frank Alfred Golder, *Documents of Russian History, 1914–1917*, translated by Emanuel Aronsberg, pp. 617–619.

Meeting of the Petrograd Soviet

The meeting opened at 2:35 P.M. with Trotsky in the chair. He said: "In the name of the War-Revolutionary Committee, I announce that the Provisional Government no longer exists. (Applause.) Some of the Ministers are already under arrest. (Bravo.) Others soon will be. (Applause.) The revolutionary garrison, under the control of the War-Revolutionary Committee, has dismissed the Assembly of the Pre-Parliament [Council of the Republic]. (Loud applause. "Long live the War-Revolutionary Committee.") . . . The railway stations, post and telegraph offices, the Petrograd Telegraph Agency, and State Banks are occupied." . . .

Trotsky continued by saying: "In our midst is Vladimir Ilich Lenin, who, by force of circumstances, had not been able to be with us all this time. . . . Hail the return of Lenin!" The audience gave him a noisy ovation. . . .

Lenin's Speech

Comrades, the workmen's and peasants' revolution, the need of which the Bolsheviks have emphasized many times, has come to pass.

What is the significance of this revolution? Its significance is, in the first place, that we shall have a soviet government, without the participation of bourgeoisie of any kind. The oppressed masses will of themselves form a government. The old state machinery will be smashed into bits and in its place will be created a new machinery of government by the soviet organizations. From now on there is a new page in the history of Russia, and the present, third Russian revolution shall in its final result lead to the victory of Socialism.

One of our immediate tasks is to put an end to the war at once. But in order to end the war, which is closely bound up with the present capitalistic system, it is necessary to overthrow capitalism itself. In this work we shall have the aid of the world labor movement, which has already begun to develop in Italy, England, and Germany.

A just and immediate offer of peace by us to the international democracy will find everywhere a warm response among the international proletariat masses. In order to secure the confidence of the proletariat, it is necessary to publish at once all secret treaties.

In the interior of Russia a very large part of the peasantry has said: Enough playing with the capitalists; we will go with the workers. We shall secure the confidence of the peasants by one decree, which will wipe out the private property of the landowners. The peasants will understand that their only salvation is in union with the workers.

We will establish a real labor control on production.

We have now learned to work together in a friendly manner, as is evident from this revolution. We have the force of mass organization which has conquered all and which will lead the proletariat to world revolution.

We should now occupy ourselves in Russia in building up a proletarian socialist state.

Long live the world-wide socialistic revolution.

6. THE TREATY OF VERSAILLES IS REVEALED TO THE GERMANS

The major decisions at the Paris Peace Conference of 1919 were made by the leaders of the three major Allied governments: Clemenceau of France, Wilson of the United States, and Lloyd George of Great Britain. The treaty with Germany contained a "war guilt" clause, declaring the Germans responsible for starting the war, and, hence, liable for "reparations" to the Allies. In addition, Germany lost territories and population. Only after the treaty was completed were German delegates summoned to Paris.

The Treaty of Versailles was formally presented to the German representatives on May 7, 1919, by coincidence the fourth anniversary of the sinking of the *Lusitania.*

The scene was the Trianon Palace at Versailles. The day was one of surpassing loveliness, and brilliant spring sunlight flooded the room. Dr. Walter Simons, Commissioner-General of the German delegation, noted that "outside of the big window at my right there was a wonderful cherry tree in bloom, and it seemed to me the only reality when compared with the performance in the hall. This cherry tree and its kind will still be blooming when the states whose representatives gathered here exist no longer."

The crowd was small, for the room was small—merely the delegates of both sides, with their assistants, and a few carefully selected press representatives. The grim-visaged Clemenceau sat at the center of the main table: Wilson at his right, Lloyd George at his left.

The air was surcharged with electricity: German and Allied diplomats had not met face to face since the fateful summer of 1914. Would the Germans do something to offend the proprieties?

When all were seated, the doors swung open. At the cry, "*Messieurs les plénipotentiares allemands!*" the whole assembly rose and stood in silence

Thomas A. Bailey, *Woodrow Wilson and the Lost Peace,* in *Wilson and the Peacemakers* (New York: The Macmillan Company, 1947), pp. 288–290.

while the German delegates filed in before their conquerors and sat at a table facing Clemenceau.

The Tiger rose to his feet, and, his voice vibrant with the venom of 1871, almost spat out his speech with staccato precision: "It is neither the time nor the place for superfluous words. . . . The time has come when we must settle our accounts. You have asked for peace. We are ready to give you peace."

Already a secretary had quietly walked over to the table at which the Germans sat, and laid before them the thick, two-hundred-odd-page treaty—"the book."

With Clemenceau still standing, the pale, black-clad Count Brockdorff-Rantzau, head of the German delegation, began reading his reply—*seated.*

An almost perceptible gasp swept the room, for the failure of the German to rise was taken as a studied discourtesy. Some felt that he was too nervous and shaken to stand. Others felt that he wanted to snub his "conquerors." The truth is that he planned to sit, not wishing to stand like a culprit before a judge to receive sentence.

Nothing could better reflect the spirit of the Germans. They felt that the war had been more or less a stalemate; they had laid down their arms expecting to negotiate with a chivalrous foe. As equals, why should they rise like criminals before the Allied bar?

If Brockdorff-Rantzau's posture was unfortunate, his words and the intonation of his words were doubly so.

The Germans had not yet read the Treaty, but they had every reason to believe that it would be severe. They had not been allowed to participate in its negotiation; they would not be allowed to discuss its provisions *orally* with their conquerors. Brockdorff-Rantzau decided to make the most of this his only opportunity to meet his adversaries face to face and comment on the unread Treaty. Both his manner and his words were sullen, arrogant, unrepentant.

Speaking with great deliberation and without the usual courteous salutation to the presiding officer, he began by saying that the Germans were under "no illusions" as to the extent of their defeat and the degree of their "powerlessness." This was not true, for both he and his people were under great illusions.

Then he referred defiantly but inaccurately to the demand that the Germans acknowledge that "we alone are guilty of having caused the war. Such a confession in my mouth would be a lie." And the word "lie" fairly hissed from between his teeth.

Bitterly he mentioned the "hundreds of thousands" of German non-combatants who had perished since Armistice Day as a result of Allied insistence on continuing the blockade during the peace negotiations. This shaft struck home, especially to the heart of Lloyd George.

When the echo of Brockdorff-Rantzau's last tactless word had died away, Clemenceau spoke. His face had gone red during the harangue, but he had held himself in check with remarkable self-restraint. Harshly and peremptorily he steam-rolled the proceedings to an end: "Has anybody any more observations to offer? Does no one wish to speak? If not, the meeting is closed."

The German delegates marched out, facing a battery of clicking moving picture cameras. Brockdorf-Rantzau lighted a cigarette with trembling fingers.

Lloyd George, who had snapped an ivory paper knife in his hands, remarked angrily: "It is hard to have won the war and to have to listen to that."

Thus, within a half-hour, was compressed one of the greatest dramas of all time.

39

THE RISE OF TOTALITARIANISM

America had entered World War I to "make the world safe for democracy," in the words of Woodrow Wilson. Yet, within a few years democracy was in full retreat as new types of authoritarian rule emerged. The first of these totalitarian dictatorships appeared in Russia in November, 1917, when Lenin overthrew the shaky liberal, democratic government. In Italy, Mussolini replaced a weak parliamentary government with a Fascist dictatorship. Similarly, in Germany economic distress and political confusion were skillfully exploited by Adolf Hitler to establish a Nazi dictatorship. Other types of dictatorial or authoritarian rule emerged in Hungary under Horthy, in Turkey under Kemal Ataturk, in Poland under Pilsudski, in Portugal under Salazar, and in Spain under Franco.

1. MUSSOLINI EXPLAINS FASCISM

Italy, although victorious in World War I, had experienced serious losses and deep humiliation in the war and had failed to gain the expected fruits of victory. Riots and strikes, and the inability of an unstable parliamentary government to cope with the violence, left the way open for the rise of a nationalist movement, Fascism, led by a former Socialist, Benito Mussolini (1883–1945). Before Mussolini's seizure of power in 1922, Fascism contained little coherent political theory. Its political philosophy was added in the following years.

First of all, as regards the future development of mankind,—and quite apart from all present political considerations—Fascism does not, generally speaking, believe in the possibility or utility of perpetual peace. It therefore discards pacifism as a cloak for cowardly supine renunciation in contra-distinc-

Benito Mussolini, *Fascism: Doctrine and Institutions* (Rome: Ardita Publishers, 1935), pp. 18–27, *passim*. Copyright 1935 by "Ardita," Rome.

tion to self-sacrifice. War alone keys up all human energies to their maximum tension and sets the seal of nobility on those peoples who have the courage to face it. . . .

Such a conception of life makes Fascism the resolute negation of the doctrine underlying so-called scientific and Marxian socialism, the doctrine of historic materialism which would explain the history of mankind in terms of the class-struggle and by changes in the processes and instruments of production, to the exclusion of all else. . . .

After socialism, Fascism trains its guns on the whole block of democratic ideologies, and rejects both their premises and their practical applications and implements. Fascism denies that numbers, as such, can be the determining factor in human society; it denies the right of numbers to govern by means of periodical consultations; it asserts the irremediable and fertile and beneficent inequality of men who cannot be levelled by any such mechanical and extrinsic device as universal suffrage. . . .

Fascism is definitely and absolutely opposed to the doctrines of liberalism, both in the political and the economic sphere. The importance of liberalism in the XIXth century should not be exaggerated for present-day polemical purposes, nor should we make of one of the many doctrines which flourished in that century a religion for mankind for the present and for all time to come. . . .

A party governing a nation "totalitarianly" is a new departure in history. There are no points of reference nor of comparison. From beneath the ruins of liberal, socialist, and democratic doctrines, Fascism extracts those elements which are still vital. . . . We are free to believe that this is the century of authority, a century tending to the "right", a Fascist century. If the XIXth century was the century of the individual (liberalism implies individualism) we are free to believe that this is the "collective" century, and therefore the century of the State. . . .

The key-stone of the Fascist doctrine is its conception of the State, of its essence, its functions, and its aims. For Fascism the State is absolute, individuals and groups relative. Individuals and groups are admissable in so far as they come within the State. . . .

2. *STALIN REVEALS THE PURPOSE OF THE FIRST FIVE-YEAR PLAN*

Joseph Stalin (1879–1953), Lenin's successor as dictator of Communist Russia, sought to create a socialist economy by means of a "Five-Year Plan" (1928–1932). As he explains below, one of the goals was the elimination of capitalism which

Joseph Stalin, *Selected Writings* (New York: International Publishers, 1942), p. 242.

Lenin had permitted in the form of the NEP (New Economic Policy) in small businesses and in agriculture.

What was the fundamental task of the Five-Year Plan? . . .

The fundamental task of the Five-Year Plan was, in converting the U.S.S.R. into an industrial country, fully to eliminate the capitalist elements, to widen the front of socialist forms of economy, and to create the economic base for the abolition of classes in the U.S.S.R., for the construction of socialist society.

The fundamental task of the Five-Year Plan was to create such an industry in our country as would be able to re-equip and reorganize, not only the whole of industry, but also transport and agriculture—on the basis of socialism.

The fundamental task of the Five-Year Plan was to transfer small and scattered agriculture to the lines of large-scale collective farming, so as to ensure the economic base for socialism in the rural districts and thus to eliminate the possibility of the restoration of capitalism in the U.S.S.R.

Finally, the task of the Five-Year Plan was to create in the country all the necessary technical and economic prerequisites for increasing to the utmost the defensive capacity of the country, to enable it to organize determined resistance to any and every attempt at military intervention from outside, to any and every attempt at military attack from without.

3. STALIN BUILDS A COMMUNIST DICTATORSHIP

Lenin, the creator of the Communist state in Russia, held dictatorial powers from 1917 to 1924. In the last two years of this period, with Lenin incapacitated by illness, a struggle for succession broke out between Trotsky, organizer of the Red Army, and Stalin, secretary of the Central Committee of the Communist Party. Control of the party proved to be the decisive factor, giving Stalin a complete victory over Trotsky and a firm grip on the Soviet government.

The Bolshevik regime had to maneuver in order to survive until proper conditions—namely, its own strength and the weakness of the other powers—would permit a new advance. . . .

The whole period of 1921–1927 can be characterized as a period in which the Soviet regime tried to gain strength for such a new advance. This period opened with Lenin's introduction of the New Economic Policy (NEP), designed to make concessions to the tired and exhausted masses. A limited free market and private trade were admitted in the interest of the

Waldemar Gurian, *Bolshevism: An Introduction to Soviet Communism* (Notre Dame, Ind.: University of Notre Dame Press, 1952), pp. 46–48, 51, 55–57.

peasants. Lenin even offered "concessions" to foreign capitalists in order to make investments in Soviet Russia attractive to them—a policy which did not have the success expected. Principles of calculation and the stringencies of legalistic rules were emphasized and introduced, replacing the former policies of confiscation without regulations, which had aided in winning the civil war. But the "commanding positions" remained in the hands of the party. The nationalized economy controlled the sector into which private initiative was admitted. Banks, big enterprises, and foreign trade remained under the control of the Soviet state. No other parties were permitted alongside the Bolshevik party. A committee which was organized in the hunger-catastrophe of 1922 was dissolved when its non-Bolshevik members tried to gain independent influence. The Che-Ka [secret police] was rechristened G-P-U; but even under formal legal supervision, it retained its basically unlimited powers. The consolidation of the regime advanced.

The loose confederation of Soviet Republics—of which the Russian and Ukrainian were the most important ones—was held together by the solidarity and unity of the Communists; it was replaced in 1922 by the Soviet Union. The USSR was nominally a federation, but in reality, despite the explicit statement of its constitution about the right of secession, it continued to concentrate power in Moscow. . . .

During Lenin's illness (he was incapacitated in 1922 and died in 1924), an internal struggle about who was to succeed him developed within the party leadership. Upon Zinoviev's suggestion Stalin had been made secretary general of the party in 1922. He used this office to bring the party machine, step by step, under his control. Together with Kamenev and Zinoviev, two typical Bolshevik intellectuals, he prevented Trotsky from becoming Lenin's heir and helped reduce his influence in the party. Then Stalin turned against his allies of the first hour and in their turn deprived them of power. Now they joined with Trotsky, opposing Stalin in a bloc. But it was too late. Stalin could use the party machine against the opposition; the party voted always in Stalin's favor and did not listen to the arguments of the opposition. Of course, all competitors in the fight for power cited Lenin as the highest infallible authority. . . . In 1927 the opposition was expelled from the party; its leaders submitted more or less eagerly to the official line; and Trotsky was exiled (1929) from the Soviet Union. . . .

The Bolsheviks under Stalin organized and consolidated their complete control of the Soviet Union according to a definite totalitarian pattern. The Five Year plans for the organization of production and the acceleration of industrialization were put into operation. After 1929, Stalin carried out the collectivization of agriculture from above, using every form of compulsion. For millions of people, this policy resulted in death through hunger, or in deportation to labor camps. For Stalin was determined to destroy the independence of the peasants who had threatened the process of industrialization by their refusal to supply cities with foodstuffs. The peasants were forced into kolhozes controlled by party officials and had to fulfill production quotas imposed from above. They were forced to adopt agricultural machinery in order to form a market for the products of the industrial plants; the government organized and controlled the centers (stations) for the machines.

The millions deported as forced labor brought a change in the activities of the GPU. Its concentration camps had served to isolate active or potential enemies of the regime; now these camps became enterprises for economic and colonizing purposes. The Volga-White Sea canal had served as preparatory experiment for the exploitation of forced labor; now deportees, political and criminal prisoners, could be used on a much larger scale in the almost unpopulated regions of Northern Europe as well as of Asiatic Russia. In other words, terror was now combined with economic planning. . . .

The great purge from 1936 to 1938 definitely established Stalin's absolute control over the Party. . . .

The great purge stabilized definitely a totalitarian rule by an omnipotent Soviet leadership. Perpetuating itself by controlling everything with the help of a subservient bureaucracy, it pretended (and still pretends) to fulfill and interpret authoritatively an absolutely true doctrine. But, as we have seen, this development was not a break with Lenin's principles; Stalin's extension of terroristic methods to the party was only an application of these principles. Stalin had instruments for establishing the regime which Lenin, fighting for a conquest of power, obviously did not yet have. . . .

The Bolshevik regime construes itself to have started as a dictatorship founded upon an alliance between the proletariat and the poor peasants. . . . Today the official doctrine explains that socialism is realized in the Soviet Union: the economy is entirely socialized; private ownership of the means of production (and therefore the division of society into classes) has been abolished; all-out planning, extending to agriculture, has been introduced. True, a Communism in which everybody will be rewarded according to his needs, has not yet been achieved. In the present phase the principle prevails that rewards are differentiated according to the individual's contribution to society. . . .

Contrary to Lenin's original expectations and announcements, formulated particularly in his *State and Revolution* (1917), the alleged realization of socialism was not accompanied by a corresponding withering away of the state (the instrument of coercion in the interest of one class). Lenin had hoped that with the advance of the dictatorship of the proletariat, the organs of the state separated from the people, like the army and the bureaucracy, would disappear. All these announcements, expectations and hopes have not come true. . . . Stalin emphasizes the necessity for the state's continuing existence even after the realization of socialism in the Soviet Union. This acceptance of the state as official doctrine has increased tremendously the employment of power and violence. Pressure is applied in order to accomplish the transformation of society and the education of the masses; the doctrine of the necessary development of society towards the aims of socialism and communism justifies this systematic, ruthlessly cool pressure. Terrorism is unavoidable in order to force the masses in the right direction. Here Bolshevist policies rejoin typical traditions of Russian Muscovite history where brutal power is applied from above to shape society (Ivan the Terrible, Peter the Great). Industrial backwardness must be overcome by promoting an artificial acceleration of economic developments through constant compulsion from above, disregarding, as the forced collectivization of agriculture and the large masses in the labor camps show, the will and welfare of the people and society.

4. *HITLER EXPLAINS NATIONAL SOCIALISM*

Adolf Hitler (1889–1945) joined the newly formed National Socialist Party (Nazis) in 1919 and soon became its leader. **Mein Kampf** ***was written by Hitler in prison, following his arrest in 1923 in an attempt to overthrow the government of Bavaria. The book is crudely written and repetitious and features racism and anti-Semitism as the main themes.***

. . . One blood demands one Reich. Never will the German nation possess the moral right to engage in colonial politics until, at least, it embraces its own sons within a single state. Only when the Reich borders include the very last German, but can no longer guarantee his daily bread, will the moral right to acquire foreign soil arise from the distress of our own people. Their sword will become our plow, and from the tears of war the daily bread of future generations will grow. . . .

Blood mixture and the resultant drop in the racial level is the sole cause of the dying out of old cultures; for men do not perish as a result of lost wars, but by the loss of that force of resistance which is contained only in pure blood.

Adolf Hitler, *Mein Kampf*, translated by Ralph Manheim (Boston: Houghton Mifflin Company, 1943), pp. 3, 296, 302, 339, 389, 427, 611, 624–625, 654.

All who are not of good race in this world are chaff.

And all occurrences in world history are only the expression of the races' instinct of self-preservation, in the good or bad sense. . . .

If the Jews were alone in this world, they would stifle in filth and offal; they would try to get ahead of one another in hate-filled struggle and exterminate one another, in so far as the absolute absence of all sense of self-sacrifice, expressing itself in their cowardice, did not turn battle into comedy here too.

So it is absolutely wrong to infer any ideal sense of sacrifice in the Jews from the fact that they stand together in struggle, or, better expressed, in the plundering of their fellow men. . . .

Without the clearest knowledge of the racial problem and hence of the Jewish problem there will never be a resurrection of the German nation.

The racial question gives the key not only to world history, but to all human culture. . . .

Since nationality or rather race does not happen to lie in language but in the blood, we would only be justified in speaking of a Germanization if by such a process we succeeded in transforming the blood of the subjected people. But this is impossible. Unless a blood mixture brings about a change, which, however, means the lowering of the level of the higher race. The final result of such a process would consequently be the destruction of precisely those qualities which had formerly made the conquering people capable of victory. Especially the cultural force would vanish through a mating with the lesser race, even if the resulting mongrels spoke the language of the earlier, higher race a thousand times over. . . .

The crown of the folkish state's entire work of education and training must be to burn the racial sense and racial feeling into the instinct and the intellect, the heart and brain of the youth entrusted to it. No boy and no girl must leave school without having been led to an ultimate realization of the necessity and essence of blood purity. . . .

. . . the presupposition for the gaining of lost territories is the intensive promotion and strengthening of the remaining remnant state and the unshakable decision slumbering in the heart to dedicate the new force thus arising to the freedom and unification of the entire nationality in the proper hour: therefore, *subordination* of the interests of the separated territories to the single interest of winning for the remaining remnant that measure of political power and strength which is the precondition for a correction of the will of hostile victors. *For oppressed territories are led back to the bosom of a common Reich, not by flaming protests, but by a mighty sword.*

To forge this sword is the task of a country's internal political leader-

ship; to safeguard the work of forging and seek comrades in arms is the function of diplomatic leadership. . . .

What France, spurred on by her own thirst for vengeance and systematically led by the Jew, is doing in Europe today is a sin against the existence of white humanity and some day will incite against this people all the avenging spirits of a race which has recognized racial pollution as the original sin of humanity.

For Germany, however, the French menace constitutes an obligation to subordinate all considerations of sentiment and hold out a hand to those who, threatened as much as we are, will neither suffer nor tolerate France's desires for domination.

In the predictable future there can be only two allies for Germany in Europe: England and Italy. . . .

And so we National Socialists consciously draw a line beneath the foreign policy tendency of our pre-War period. We take up where we broke off six hundred years ago. We stop the endless German movement to the south and west, and turn our gaze toward the land in the east. At long last we break off the colonial and commercial policy of the pre-War period and shift to the soil policy of the future.

If we speak of soil in Europe today, we can primarily have in mind only *Russia* and her vassal border states.

5. THE GERMAN PEOPLE ACCEPT HITLER'S POLICE STATE

By 1932, German democracy as practiced under the Weimar Constitution had virtually ceased to exist. Although the chancellors of that year ruled by decree, they were unable to achieve a stable government. In January, 1933, Hitler became chancellor in a constitutional manner, even though his Nazi Party did not command a parliamentary majority. Once in office Hitler began the creation of an authoritarian state.

Throughout the decade before Hitler came to power, the National Socialist German Workers Party (NSDAP) appealed to both the nationalists on the right and the workers on the left. It also gathered in elements of the population that lacked sufficient interest to vote or had no definite party affiliations—many youths as they came of voting age, and disillusioned veterans of the First World War. Hitler also profited from the world-wide depression which set in after 1929. But in the elections of November, 1932, the Nazi

Allen Welsh Dulles, *Germany's Underground* (New York: The Macmillan Company, 1947), pp. 12–22, *passim*. Copyright 1947 by Allen W. Dulles. Used by permission of the author.

party's voting strength, for the first time, declined. Many Germans who had viewed its uninterrupted progress with growing alarm felt that at last the tide was receding, the danger was over. But in those same elections the Communist party gained as much as the Nazis lost. Old and decrepit President Hindenburg, influenced by reactionary advisers—especially his son Oskar and his favorite Papen—was persuaded that the choice lay between Communism and Fascism, that with one more election the Communists would be in power. In a panic, he made Hitler Chancellor. This was done in such a constitutional and, to the Germans, orderly manner, that the majority in Germany failed to realize the significance of what was happening.

Many German industrialists, equally fearful of Communism, shared the view of the conservatives who helped Hitler into power and gave the Nazi party financial backing. . . .

Hitler then proceeded to destroy his opponents, playing them off against one another, and to wreck the institutions on which liberty and democratic government are based. At the outset he pleased the nationalists by his unconstitutional exclusion of the Communists from the Reichstag and his suppression of the Socialist party. Then he turned on the junkers—Hugenberg, Papen, and associates. He lured them into acquiescence by letting them keep their freedom, their property, and sometimes even their official positions, but saw to it that they were mere figureheads. He pleased the industrialists by destroying the labor unions, and then harnessed industry to the Nazi military machine. But he left the industrialists at least ostensible control of their properties. Then followed the destruction of *all* political parties, the suppression of the freedom of the press, the cruel extermination of the Jews and the creation of one of the most ruthlessly efficient police states in history. He even attacked the churches to prevent them from becoming an instrument for the preservation of political or personal liberty.

Finally Hitler turned his attention to the High Command of the German army and to those generals who had leadership potentialities. The army tried to remain immune from Nazi influence, but its independence was slowly undermined. Some generals were won over when Hitler repudiated the provision of the Versailles Treaty that restricted the size of the German army; others, who remained hostile, were ousted—simply or deviously. . . .

Hitler could not have accomplished all these things without the support of the German people, including, at the end, some eight million party members. Unfortunately he also found far too many supporters in England, France, the United States, and elsewhere throughout the world. The appeal of the "strong leader" was not limited to Germany. . . .

As for the Germans themselves, it was a commonplace, just after Hitler came to power, to hear even intelligent people say: "Let him have a taste of power. Six months of it will show up his inability to run a state—the responsibilities of government will ruin the Nazis and then we Germans will be rid of them forever." Intellectuals particularly succumbed to the illusion that Hitler and his crowd were too uncouth and too ignorant to direct the complicated mechanism of government. The experiences of the last few decades should teach all future intellectuals that it does not take "culture" to rule a state.

Even today we tend to fall into the smug and dangerous habit of dismissing Hitler as a mountebank and fool, a crazy fanatic. The truth is he was one of the smartest tyrants who ever hypnotized a people. He understood his Germans thoroughly. He bemused the common man and gave hope and confidence to millions who, under the Weimar government, had seen no way to escape from their frustrations. Hitler's firsthand knowledge of these frustrations and illusions of the masses equipped him well for the task of deceiving and leading the declassed, the uprooted and the unhappy of Germany. He had learned the secret of the demagogue, which is to proffer some explanation, no matter how specious, for mass discontent, and then to promise to ameliorate it. Hitler asserted, over and over until the least literate understood him, that the plight of the German nation and the unhappiness of the individual German were the result of the Versailles Treaty, the Jews, and the Weimar Republic, i.e., democracy. To the unemployed he promised jobs, to the veterans he promised a revival of militarism (though at first it was only the pseudo militarism of the S.A.), and to the hopeless he promised a renaissance of German glory.

Under Hitler there was a feeling of resurgence, and the average middle- and working-class German, the "little man," felt he had a better chance in the world and a new self-respect. Compared to these advantages, what, after all, were the liberties he had sacrificed? So thought the average German. . . .

National Socialism was in reality a revolt against the principles of civil rights and responsibilities, against enlightenment and human progress, against the achievements of the French and American revolutions. . . .

The German intelligentsia, with its cultural tradition, should have done far more than it did. Its misfortune was that it did not have political experience and had lost contact with the people. The intellectuals failed to realize that democracy must never be taken for granted. They did not see the vital need for coming to its defense. To the staid and aloof professors in the German universities Hitler's movement, exemplified in an incoherent book like *Mein Kampf*, was so ridiculous that they did not take it seriously. Before they knew it, many were removed, imprisoned, or, at best, forced into silence or exile.

It was under the guise of national and moral rebirth that Hitler built up his dictatorship. There is an almost unbelievable paradox here. Many Germans, and not a few foreigners, years after Hitler came to power, still believed that a system built on the vilest intrigue and unprecedented sadism was highly moral and virtuous. What impressed them was not that the Reichstag was burned, but that Nazi decrees legislated a new kind of morality—outlawed the use of lipstick, closed shady night clubs—and that the statistics showed that criminality had declined in the Third Reich. The height of hypocrisy was reached when the Nazi writers' association . . . decreed that no more than two murders were to occur in any mystery novel, so that "the low instincts are not incited."

By the time the German people realized what their "national rebirth" and "moral awakening" actually meant, one of the most ruthless police states the world has seen was firmly established. The Nazi leaders had studied the prototype of totalitarianism in Russia. . . .

Modern technology—the radio, telephotography, the concealed dictaphone—and the most efficient methods of detection and of torture were devoted to suppressing freedom and ferreting out any who dared to oppose the Nazi dictatorship. In a police state equipped with machine guns, tear gas, tanks and aircraft, revolutions are not made by aroused masses with their bare hands. . . .

. . . As Hitler gained one political and diplomatic victory after another, his popularity and power increased to the point where only a very small band of Germans dared to carry on a clandestine resistance. Those who opposed openly or whose secret opposition was discovered were relegated to concentration camps, of which some seventy to eighty existed even before the war. . . .

. . . A people that accepts regimentation is not likely to develop the virtue of individual initiative which a popular underground movement requires. The great majority of the German people, by 1939, either supported the Nazi regime, acquiesced in it because their livelihood depended upon it, or were terrified into silence and inaction by the political police.

6. THE ENABLING ACT CONSOLIDATES HITLER'S DICTATORSHIP

The Enabling Act of March, 1933, was pushed through a reluctant German parliament after a threat by Hitler that he would assume dictatorial powers in any case. The effect of this law was to provide a legal basis for Hitler's dictatorship. Parliamentary government henceforth ceased to exist in Germany.

"The Enabling Act of March 24, 1933," in William E. Rappard, Walter B. Sharp, Herbert W. Schneider, James K. Pollock, and Samuel N. Harper, eds., *Source Book on European Governments* (New York: D. Van Nostrand Co., Inc., 1937), pp. IV: 14–15.

The Reichstag has enacted the following law which, with the consent of the Reichsrat and after determination that the requirements for laws changing the constitution have been complied with, is hereby promulgated:

ARTICLE 1. National laws can be enacted by the national cabinet as well as in accordance with the procedure established in the constitution. This applies also to the laws referred to in article 85, paragraph 2, and in article 87 of the constitution.

ARTICLE 2. The national laws enacted by the national cabinet may deviate from the constitution insofar as they do not affect the position of the Reichstag and the Reichsrat. The powers of the president remain undisturbed.

ARTICLE 3. The national laws enacted by the national cabinet are prepared by the chancellor and published in the *Reichsgesetzblatt.* They come into effect, unless otherwise specified, upon the day following their publication. Articles 68 to 77 of the constitution do not apply to the laws enacted by the national cabinet.

ARTICLE 4. Treaties of the Reich with foreign states which concern matters of national legislation do not require the consent of the bodies participating in legislation. The national cabinet is empowered to issue the necessary provisions for the execution of these treaties.

ARTICLE 5. This law becomes effective on the day of its publication. It becomes invalid on April 1st, 1937; it further becomes invalid when the present national cabinet is replaced by another.

Berlin, March 24th, 1933

40

TOTALITARIAN AGGRESSION

The decade of the 1930's brought to the European world the double disasters of depression and aggression. The promising economic recovery of the late 1920's ended in the deepest depression the modern world has known. While America remained aloof from international controversies, a wave of aggressive acts by the totalitarian powers culminated in World War II. The Mukden Incident of 1931 presaged Japanese expansion in the Far East. Mussolini's conquests of Ethiopia and Albania were more than matched in audacity by Hitler's annexations in central Europe. France and Britain followed a policy of appeasement, dramatically demonstrated at Munich in 1938. In the next year Hitler's non-aggression pact with Russia and his subsequent attack on Poland brought on World War II.

1. THE GREAT DEPRESSION PARALYZES EUROPE AND AMERICA

The Wall Street crash in the autumn of 1929 led to a world-wide depression. In panic each nation looked to itself: tariffs were raised, imperial preferences arranged, and currencies manipulated to gain momentary advantages. In Germany depression and unemployment aided the rise of the Nazis. In America domestic economic troubles intensified the isolationist trend. In England and France prolonged internal distress paralyzed any potential resistance to totalitarian aggression.

. . . it is clear that the wave of prosperity which followed the depression of 1920–1921 was being broken down by recessionary movements before the year 1929 arrived. Yet 1929 is an important date, for it marks the crash of

Shepard Bancroft Clough and Charles Woolsey Cole, *Economic History of Europe*, Revised Edition (Boston: D.C. Heath and Company, 1946), pp. 803–808.

the stock-market boom in the United States. Speculative enthusiasm got under way in this country because people had come to believe that an increase in production and a steadiness of prices meant a long-continued period of prosperity. They therefore began to buy common stocks and to force security prices upward. As quotations of stocks rose, more people put their money in the market in order to get a profit from this rise. Before long money was being borrowed at 10 per cent in order to buy stocks which, if dividends on the basis of earnings were paid, could produce only 2 per cent on the purchase price. The Federal Reserve authorities contemplated raising the discount rate (1927) to stop this "race toward a fall," but did not do so until it was too late to be effective. From 1926 to September, 1929, the index of 421 common stocks in New York rose from 100 to 225, and in the twenty months ending in September, 1929, the value of stocks on the New York Exchange increased by over $51,000,000,000. In October, 1929, however, speculators discovered that the prices of stocks failed to go up; and they began to sell. Between September 3 and November 13, shares on the New York Stock Exchange fell by $30,000,000,000 and in June, 1932, reached an index of 34 (1926 = 100).

This speculative crash . . . had far-reaching effects. Immediately stocks on the European exchanges followed those in New York in their downward plunge. People began to withdraw their money from banks in order to pay their usual obligations and their stock-market debts. Capital in America was no longer available for export, and consequently Europeans, who had become accustomed to borrowing from the United States, were hard put to it to meet interest payments. This stringency in the money market brought such pressure on banks that those whose assets were not liquid began to go under. The Austrian Creditanstalt, founded by the Rothschilds in 1855, became insolvent in the early part of 1931; the great German Danatbank closed its doors in July of the same year; . . . Wholesale prices fell, production declined, unemployment increased, foreign trade went to pieces, and the investment of new capital was extremely low.

The depression also led many countries to abandon the so recently acquired gold standard. The credit crisis in Austria and Germany . . . tended to freeze many of the foreign loans to these states and caused nations, insofar as they could, to withdraw their holdings from abroad. This burden fell on the shoulders of the British, for they were heavy lenders in the areas mentioned and they held large amounts of foreign capital on deposit. Then when the drain on London got under way, it was obvious that other factors were involved. Great Britain had been importing more than usual . . . at the same time, it was exporting less because of its high domestic prices. . . .

. . . the English decided to abandon the gold standard September 20, 1931, and the pound was permitted to rest not on gold but on what businessmen would pay for it in gold or other currencies. By the end of 1931, it was about 30 per cent below its former level.

England's monetary depreciation was followed by similar moves on the part of other states. . . . By the end of 1932, thirty-five countries had left the gold standard. Those remaining on it—the United States, France, Switzerland, Holland, and Belgium—formed for a time a "gold bloc."

Problems arising from this upset of currencies were numerous and complex. There was, for instance, a great amount of "hot money"—capital which took flight from a country that was on the verge of depreciation and which sought refuge in a country that appeared to have a stable currency. These flights of capital worked mischief in the money markets, for they drained gold from the country whence they came and forced interest rates down in the nation to which they went. For these reasons, capital exports were limited by laws, which also had the effect of preventing persons from buying what they wanted or from settling their foreign debts. Furthermore, prices for various goods fluctuated widely from country to country. . . . Nor could these differences be easily ironed out, because quotas or other controls restricted foreign trade.

With cheap money in the countries which had devalued, with controlled currencies in many other places, and with embargoes of various kinds on trade, the "gold bloc" nations found that their currencies were so high that foreigners would not buy their goods. Hence agitation for devaluation got under way among them. . . . This agitation soon led to action. The United States abandoned the gold standard in April, 1933, and devalued the dollar by 40.94 per cent by act of 1934. . . . Those countries which did not devalue, and even some of those which did, increased their control of currencies and of prices (thirty-six countries in 1939).

The effect of these devaluations on international trade was again to give the country which had devalued an advantage in selling goods, but this advantage was usually temporary because some other state would soon devalue below the point fixed by the first nation. In international payments, the consequence was to make it easier for debtor states to pay off their obligations. In domestic economic relationships, the cheap money was similarly advantageous to debtors, for, if a rise in prices occurred, as it usually did, they could pay their creditors with less effort. In general, such conditions mean good times. Thus devaluation had its *raisons d'être*, but to work itself out to logical ends, time, peace, and relatively free economic exchanges were required. And these conditions were not present.

2. THE LEAGUE OF NATIONS INVESTIGATES THE MUKDEN INCIDENT

Violence, the prevailing spirit of the 1930's, was ushered in by the Mukden Incident of 1931, which led to the Japanese occupation of all Manchuria. For many decades Japan had coveted the rich agricultural lands and the mineral resources of Manchuria, a province nominally under Chinese sovereignty. In 1931 a large Japanese force was already on the scene, ostensibly to protect the South Manchuria Railway. The outbreak of hostilities brought the League of Nations Commission of Inquiry to Mukden. The following excerpt is taken from the Commission's report.

According to the Japanese versions, Lieutenant Kawamoto, with six men under his command, was on patrol duty on the night of September 18th, practising defence exercises along the track of the South Manchuria Railway to the north of Mukden. They were proceeding southwards in the direction of Mukden. The night was dark but clear and the field of vision was not wide. When they reached a point at which a small road crosses the line, they heard the noise of a loud explosion a little way behind them. They turned and ran back, and after going about 200 yards they discovered that a portion of one of the rails on the down track had been blown out. The explosion took place at the point of junction of two rails; the end of each rail had been cleanly severed, creating a gap in the line of 31 inches. On arrival at the site of the explosion, the patrol was fired upon from the fields on the east side of the line. Lieutenant Kawamoto immediately ordered his men to deploy and return the fire. The attacking body, estimated at five or six, then stopped firing and retreated northwards. The Japanese patrol at once started in pursuit and, having gone about 200 yards, they were again fired upon by a larger body, estimated at between three and four hundred. Finding himself in danger of being surrounded by this large force, Lieutenant Kawamoto then ordered one of his men to report to the Commander of the No. 3 Company, who was also engaged in night manoeuvres some 1500 yards to the north; at the same time, he ordered another of his men to telephone (by means of a box telephone near the spot) to Battalion Headquarters at Mukden for reinforcements.

At this moment the south-bound train from Changchun was heard approaching. Fearing that the train might be wrecked when it reached the damaged line, the Japanese patrol interrupted their engagement and placed detonators on the line in the hope of warning the train in time. The train, however, proceeded at full speed. When it reached the site of the explosion

"Report of the League of Nations Commission of Inquiry on Manchuria" (The Lytton Report), pp. 67–71, in Sara R. Smith, *The Manchurian Crisis, 1931–1932* (New York: Columbia University Press, 1948), pp. 19–21.

it was seen to sway and heel over to the side, but it recovered and passed on without stopping. As the train was due at Mukden at 10:30 P.M., where it arrived punctually, it must have been about 10 o'clock P.M., according to Lieutenant Kawamoto, when he first heard the explosion.

Fighting was then resumed. . . .

Lieutenant Kawamoto's patrol, reinforced by Captain Kawashima's Company, was still sustaining the fire of the Chinese troops concealed in the tall kaoliang grass, when the two Companies arrived from Mukden. Although his force was then only 500, and he believed the Chinese army in the North Barracks numbered 10,000, Lieutenant-Colonel Shinamoto at once ordered an attack on the Barracks. . . . When the Japanese reached the North Barracks, which were described as glittering with electric light, an attack was made by the 3rd Company, which succeeded in occupying a corner of the left wing. The attack was vigorously contested by the Chinese troops within, and there was fierce fighting for some hours. . . . by 6 o'clock A.M. the entire barracks were captured at the cost of two Japanese privates killed and twenty-two wounded. . . .

According to the Chinese version, the Japanese attack on the Barracks . . . was entirely unprovoked and came as a complete surprise. On the night of September 18th, all the soldiers of the 7th Brigade, numbering about 10,000 were in the North Barracks. As instructions had been received from Marshal Chang Hsueh-liang on September 6th that special care was to be taken to avoid any clash with Japanese troops in the tense state of feeling existing at the time, the sentries at the walls of the Barracks were armed only with dummy rifles. For the same reason the west gate in the mud wall surrounding the camp which gave access to the railway had been closed. The Japanese had been carrying out night manoeuvres around the barracks on the nights of September 14th, 15th, 16th and 17th. . . . At 10 P.M. (of the 18th) the sound of a loud explosion was heard, immediately followed by rifle fire. This was reported over the telephone by the Chief of Staff to the Commanding Officer, General Wang I-Cheh. . . . While the Chief of Staff was still at the telephone, news was brought to him that the Japanese were attacking the barracks. . . . As soon as the attack began, the Chief of Staff . . . again reported to General Wang I-Cheh by telephone. The latter replied that no resistance was to be offered. . . .

. . . the Commission has come to the following conclusions:

Tense feeling undoubtedly existed between the Japanese and Chinese military forces. The Japanese, as was explained to the Commission in evidence, had a carefully prepared plan to meet the case of possible hostilities between themselves and the Chinese. On the night of September 18th–19th, this plan was put into operation with swiftness and precision. The Chinese . . . had no plan of attacking the Japanese troops, or of endangering the lives or property of Japanese nationals at this particular time or place. They made no concerted or authorised attack on the Japanese forces and were surprised by the Japanese attack and subsequent operations. An explosion undoubtedly occurred on or near the railroad between 10 and 10:30 P.M. on September 18th, but the damage, if any to the railroad did not in fact prevent the punctual arrival of the south-bound train from Changchun, and was not in itself sufficient to justify military action. The military operations of the Japanese troops during this night, which have been described above cannot be regarded as measures of legitimate self-defence. . . .

3. *A DEFENDER OF THE REPUBLIC REVIEWS THE SPANISH CIVIL WAR*

In July, 1936, in response to chaotic conditions in Spain, General Franco led a military uprising against the leftist popular-front government. The civil war dragged on for nearly three years amid conditions of shocking barbarity. France and England maintained neutrality, while Germany and Italy intervened directly on behalf of Franco's insurgents, or Nationalists. The Republican forces, or Loyalists, received considerable aid from Soviet Russia.

The rebels counted on a short war. The confusion and disorder prevailing in the democratic camp, the mutual suspicion between the parties, the hostility between the leaders, the indiscipline of the masses, the weakness of the Government—all led them to believe that the rebellion would not encounter any serious obstacle. . . .

The lack of weapons of war from which [Republican] Spain suffered, due to the backwardness of the nation, led naturally to a display of great virtues by the people. Individual man, natural man, still counted in Spain. Six months afterwards, he was to count less, because the war would be waged on modern methods, when, with foreign aid, mechanized warfare superseded the period of street barricades. But in the meantime, the proletariat of Madrid and Barcelona did memorable things and saved the Republic. . . .

. . . In a matter of a few days, Spain split up into rebal territory and loyal territory. Two Spains, each hating the other, were locked in combat. . . . The two Spains which were tearing each other to pieces were the Spain that was sick, where the structure of property and the character of economic life were concerned, and the Spain that was healthy. . . . The industrial and commercial regions, the regions of the middle class and modern proletariat, rose then, spontaneously, for the Republic.

A. Ramos Oliveira, *Politics, Economics and Men of Modern Spain, 1808–1946,* translated by Teener Hall (London: Victor Gollancz, Ltd., 1946), pp. 567, 568, 579–580, 582, 594, 598–599.

On the other side, the insurgents made themselves master with hardly any opposition (which makes the opposition they did encounter all the more honourable and heroic), of the whole of the Spain which was socially sick. . . .

This peculiar division of the country into rebel and loyal, absolutist and Liberal, even were it not so nicely adjusted to social conditions, certainly affords, in my opinion, the most profound historical lesson to be learned from the civil war. It uncovers the root of the national problem of our days and confirms the fact that a Republic or a parliamentary democracy can only flourish where the middle classes predominate, preferably in regions where industry and commerce are fairly well developed. . . .

. . . the insurgents were in a desperate situation. They were rising against the State—an always risky enterprise—they had the people against them, and, to complete their discomfiture, the country's important industry, an indispensable factor in war, was located in regions which remained under the legitimate Government. . . . The confidence or faith of the rebels could only be explained by the negotiations they had concluded with foreign Powers.

The military rising had been mastered; that it finally triumphed was due entirely to the favour, expressed in aid of every shape and form, of the great Fascist and parliamentary Powers. . . .

Towards the end of 1936, when German, Italian and Portuguese intervention had already lasted three months, the first Russian aeroplanes and war material appeared in Spain. But the Republic never succeeded in solving the problem of war material and this spelt its doom. Franco had armaments and to spare, but he was always short of men; the Republic, on the other hand, had plenty of soldiers, but no arms. But the rebels could import Italian troops and German technicians without let or hindrance, and the Republican Government encountered insuperable obstacles in obtaining war material. . . .

The Communist Party, which had only a few thousand members in 1931, the year of the Republic, had been adding to its numbers in proportion as the proletariat veered towards radicalism as a result of the opposition of the oligarchy to all reform. . . . For the rest, internal unanimity, enthusiasm, and a facility for expounding without prolixity constructive formulas of action, made the Communist Party a group which was more important for its methods of combat than for its numbers. . . .

That meant that, at the outbreak of the military rising, no party of the Republic was better placed for the struggle than the Communist Party. None was so coherent, so disciplined or so sure of itself. And when the parliamentary democracies—the inspiration of all the other parties of the régime—abandoned the Spanish people, and the U.S.S.R. fulfilled its obligations under international law, the Communist Party inevitably came to the fore in the moral leadership of the régime. The people, contrasting the war material and supplies of all kinds arriving from Russia, with the blockade maintained by France and England, ascribed their salvation to the Soviet State. The Republican middle class, surprised by the moderate tone of Communist propaganda and impressed by the unity and realism which prevailed in this party, flocked in great numbers to join its ranks. Nothing succeeds like success; and the Communists, at home and abroad, were a force to be reckoned with. . . .

4. HITLER AND GOERING SEIZE AUSTRIA BY TELEPHONE

In 1934, Hitler's attempt to annex German-speaking Austria had failed because Austrian Nazis were poorly prepared, and because Mussolini firmly backed Austria. Four years later in more favorable circumstances Hitler applied pressure to Austrian Chancellor Schuschnigg to surrender his nation to the Nazis. Schuschnigg defiantly called for a plebiscite by which Austrians might present their views on annexation to the world. The plebiscite was never held, for Hitler, Goering, and the Austrian Nazis acted quickly to seize control, as revealed in these transcriptions of telephone conversations.

Keppler [Goering's Agent in Vienna] to Goering, March 11, 1938, 8:48 P.M.

KEPPLER: I would like to report what has happened: President Miklas [of Austria] has refused to do anything whatsoever. The cabinet, however, has ceased to function all the same. I talked to Schuschnigg and he told me that they had laid down their posts. . . . Seyss [-Inquart, leader of Austrian Nazis] spoke on the radio and announced that in his capacity as Minister of the Interior he would carry on the business of government. The old cabinet has given orders to the army not to resist in any way or form. So there won't be any shooting.

GOERING: Ah, well, that doesn't make any difference anyway. Now listen here: The main thing is that Seyss-Inquart takes charge of all functions of the government now, that he secures the broadcasting facilities, et cetera. And listen—Seyss is to send the following telegram to us. Take it down: "The provisional Austrian government, which after the resignation of the Schuschnigg cabinet sees its duty in the re-establishment of law and order

Transcriptions of telephone conversations, March 11, 1938, found by Allied authorities in the Reichkanzlei in Berlin in 1945, from Kurt von Schuschnigg, *Austrian Requiem,* translated by Franz von Hildebrand (New York: G.P. Putnam's Sons, 1946), pp. 308–310.

in Austria, urgently asks the German government to assist them in this task and to help them to avoid bloodshed. It therefore asks the German government to send German troops into Austria as quickly as possible."

K: Well, SA and SS [armed units of the Nazi party] are on the streets here but everything is quiet and orderly.

G: Oh, yes, another thing: Seyss is to occupy the borders at once so that they won't smuggle the money out of the country.

K: Yes, sir.

G: And above all he is to take over Foreign Affairs now.

K: Yes, of course, we have not got anyone yet for that post.

G: That makes no difference. Seyss will take over, and he will call in a couple of men to assist him. He is to take those whom we have suggested. He is to form a provisional government. It is quite unimportant now how the President feels about it.

K: Yes, sir.

G: Form a provisional government as he had planned and inform the other countries.

K: Yes, sir.

G: He is the only one who has any power in Austria now. Well, our troops will be across the border tonight.

K: Yes, sir.

G: All right. And he is to send the telegram as soon as possible. And tell him also that we would like. . . . He does not really have to send the telegram. He only has to say that he did. You get me? All right then. You will call me about this either at the Fuehrer's or at my place. Now get going. Heil Hitler!

Prince Phillip of Hesse, German Ambassador in Rome, to Hitler, March 11, 1938, 10:25 P.M.

HESSE: I have just returned from the Palazzo Venezia. The Duce [Mussolini] took the news very well indeed. He sends his very best regards to you. He said that he had heard the story about the plebiscite directly from Austria. Schuschnigg told him last Monday. Upon which Mussolini replied that such a plebiscite would be outright nonsense, an impossibility, a bluff—and that one could not do things like that. And Schuschnigg replied that he could not change anything now, everything had been arranged and settled already. So Mussolini said if that was so the Austrian question no longer interested him.

HITLER: Then please tell Mussolini that I shall never forget this.

HESSE: Yes, *mein Fuehrer.*

HITLER: Never, never, never. Come what may. I am also ready to sign quite another agreement with him.

HESSE: Yes, I have told him that already.

HITLER: Once the Austrian thing is out of the way I am ready to go with Mussolini through thick and thin, it's all the same to me now. . . .

HESSE: Yes, *mein Fuehrer.*

HITLER: And listen—sign any agreement he would like. I feel no longer in that terrible position which we faced only a short while ago, militarily, I mean, in case I might have got into a conflict. You can tell him again: I thank him most heartily. I will never forget him for that! I will never forget him!

HESSE: Yes, *mein Fuehrer.*

HITLER: I will never forget that. Come what may—oh, I will never forget him. Whenever he should be in need, or in danger, he can be sure that I will stick with him, rain or shine . . . come what may . . . and if the whole world would rise against him. I will, I shall. . . .

HESSE: Yes, *mein Fuehrer.*

5. *CHAMBERLAIN AT MUNICH SEEKS TO APPEASE HITLER*

In the summer of 1938, Hitler launched a violent propaganda attack against the Czechoslovak Republic, claiming that Sudeten Germans living in Czechoslovakia were being brutally persecuted. By September, as Hitler was clearly preparing for war, British Prime Minister Chamberlain made three dramatic flights to Germany. At the last of these, at Munich, Chamberlain and Daladier of France, meeting with Hitler and Mussolini, agreed to German occupation of Sudetenland. This was the tragic culmination of Chamberlain's appeasement policy.

. . . September 28, "Black Wednesday", dawned bright and clear over Paris and over London. Men and women woke with an eerie feeling that this was "the last day", and that by to-morrow night Paris and London might be in flaming ruins. In each capital there were some who remembered that, if this were so, Prague might have disappeared even earlier. In Paris they were fighting for seats on trains, and the roads out of the city were choked with traffic; in London they were digging trenches.

It was known that the Prime Minister would meet Parliament that afternoon to report on his negotiations with Hitler and the subsequent situation. It was impossible not to recall a parallel event on August 4, 1914, when Sir Edward Grey had addressed the House on a terribly similar occasion. Would Mr. Chamberlain close his speech with an ultimatum to Germany? The gloom deepened as the day drew on. . . .

John W. Wheeler-Bennett, *Munich: Prologue to Tragedy* (New York: Duell, Sloan & Pearce, Inc., 1948), pp. 167–171, 173, 177, *passim.*

Despite the tenseness the House of Commons adhered strictly to its established ritual. . . . Everything was done decently and in order. When the Prime Minister entered the Chamber, there was subdued applause, for the moment was too poignant for lively demonstration, and he was applauded again by his supporters when he rose to speak. . . .

It was 4.15 P.M. and Mr. Chamberlain had been speaking for some eighty minutes when the now historic scene took place. . . .

At this point Sir John Simon, after two unsuccessful efforts, succeeded in distracting the Prime Minister from his text. Mr. Chamberlain paused to read the paper handed to him, then he whispered to Sir John: "Shall I tell them now?" and the Chancellor nodded assent. When the Prime Minister again faced the House he was smiling:

> That is not all [he said]. I have something further to say to the House yet. I have now been informed by Herr Hitler that he invites me to meet him at Munich to-morrow morning. He has also invited Signor Mussolini and M. Daladier. Signor Mussolini has accepted and I have no doubt M. Daladier will accept. I need not say what my answer will be. (Interruption.) We are all patriots and there can be no hon. member of this House who did not feel his heart leap that the crisis has been once more postponed to give us once more an opportunity to try what reason and good-will and discussion will do to settle a problem which is already within sight of settlement. Mr. Speaker, I cannot say any more. I am sure that the House will be ready to release me now to go and see what I can make of this last effort. Perhaps they may think it will be well, in view of this new development, that the Debate shall stand adjourned for a few days, when perhaps we may meet in happier circumstances.

"Thank God for the Prime Minister!" cried an unidentified member, and with that cry touched off a demonstration of mass-hysteria which the Mother of Parliaments had never before witnessed. So great was the relief—so great, hon. members suddenly realized, had been their fear—that tears mingled with the cheering, as the whole House stood throwing its Order Papers in the air. . . .

To Jan Masaryk [Czech ambassador] the scene appeared fantastic, amazing, and he could scarcely believe his ears as to what he had just heard the Prime Minister announce. Was it possible that at this eleventh hour Britain and France had completely abandoned Czechoslovakia? that the Four Powers were about to settle the fate of his country without her voice even being heard? For a moment he stood alone in the Diplomatic Gallery, looking down at the weeping, cheering throng beneath. Then he left the House of Commons, not to enter it again for four years.

From Mr. Chamberlain and Lord Halifax Jan Masaryk sought explanation in the latter's room at the Foreign Office. He was told that Hitler had only consented to a conference on condition that Czechoslovakia and Russia were excluded. Public opinion in Britain and France, it was said later, would not support their national leaders if they now refused to go to Munich because the Czechs and the Russians were not to be represented.

Jan Masaryk stood silently mastering his emotions. Then he faced the two gaunt Englishmen across the table: "If you have sacrificed my nation to preserve the peace of the world, I will be the first to applaud you," he said. "But if not, gentlemen, God help your souls."

In reality the Munich Conference was but a ceremony. . . .

At half-past two on the morning of September 30, 1938, the Munich Agreement was signed by the representatives of the Four Powers, amid the flashlights of press photographers and the whirring of movie cameras. The only untoward event which marred the ceremony was the sudden discovery that the ink-well was empty. . . .

In effect, however, Hitler had gained everything. He had said that his troops would enter the Sudetenland by October 1, and they would do so—the only difference being that now they would not have to fight their way in, and would complete the occupation in ten days without resistance. He had inflicted a defeat of the first magnitude on France and on Britain without firing a shot. They had been forced to participate in the dismemberment of a small State for which the only historical parallels were the partitions of Poland in the eighteenth century.

In addition, Hitler had paved the way for his next step, already premeditated: the total destruction of the Czechoslovak State. He had shattered the French system of security, driven Russia out of the European alignment, and isolated Poland. Such were the fruits of Munich.

6. NEVILE HENDERSON MAKES A LAST ATTEMPT TO PREVENT WAR

Hitler had announced at Munich that he had no more territorial claims in Europe. Early in 1939, however, the Nazis seized the remnant of Czechoslovakia and took Memel from Lithuania. Then followed a bitter propaganda assault on Poland, obviously the next victim. Sir Nevile Henderson, British ambassador to Germany, faced the impossible task of trying to restrain Hitler. Secret negotiations in Moscow led to the signing of the Russo-German Non-Aggression Pact in August, 1939. On September 1, Hitler invaded Poland.

At the moment when Herr von Ribbentrop was preparing to fly to Moscow, I received shortly before 9 P.M. on August 22nd instructions to convey without delay a personal letter from the Prime Minister to Herr Hitler. . . . In the course of that night, after several telephonic communications, an inter-

Sir Nevile Henderson, *Failure of a Mission: Berlin 1937–1939* (New York: G.P. Putnam's Sons, 1940), pp. 268–270. Copyright 1940 by Sir Nevile Henderson. Used by permission of the publisher and Raymond Savage Limited, London, literary executor for Sir Nevile Henderson.

view was arranged for me with Hitler for the following day at Berchtesgaden; . . .

I reached Salzburg about midday and I had my first audience with Hitler at Berchtesgaden at 1 P.M. . . .

The three main points of the Prime Minister's letter were (1) insistence on the determination of His Majesty's Government to fulfill their obligations to Poland; (2) their readiness, if a peace atmosphere could be created, to discuss all the problems at issue between our two countries; and (3) their anxiety, during a period of truce, to see immediate direct discussion initiated between Germany and Poland in regard to the reciprocal treatment of minorities. Hitler's reply, which was no less uncompromising than I had anticipated, was to the effect that Great Britain's determination to support Poland could not modify his policy as expressed in the German verbal note to the Polish Government of August 9th; that he was prepared to accept even a long war rather than sacrifice German national interests and honor; and that, if Great Britain persisted in her own measures of mobilization, he would at once order the mobilization of the whole of the German forces.

At my first interview with him on that day Hitler was in a mood of extreme excitability. His language as regards the Poles and British responsibility for the Polish attitude was violent, recriminatory, and exaggerated. He referred, for instance, to 100,000 German refugees from Poland, a figure which was at least five times greater than the reality. Again I cannot say whether he was persuaded or persuaded himself of the reality of these figures. At my second interview, when he handed me his reply, he had recovered his calm but was not less obdurate. Everything was England's fault. She had encouraged the Czechs last year, and she was now giving a blank check to Poland. No longer, he told me, did he trust Mr. Chamberlain. He preferred war, he said, when he was fifty to when he was fifty-five or sixty. He had himself always sought and believed in the possibility of friendship with England. He now realized, he said, that those who had argued to the contrary had been right and nothing short of a complete change in British policy toward Germany could ever convince him of any sincere British desire for good relations. My last remark to him was that I could only deduce from his language that my mission to Germany had failed and that I bitterly regretted it.

I flew back from Berchtesgaden to Berlin the same evening. I had, in fact, little hope that either the Prime Minister's letter or my own language to Hitler, however direct and straightforward, would give him pause. The Russian Pact had, I felt, created in his opinion a situation which was favorable to his designs; and I believed his mind to be definitely made up. . . .

41

THE SECOND WORLD WAR

In the first two years of World War II, Hitler's mighty war machine overran Poland and western Europe, except for the British Isles, rescued Italy from an impending defeat by the Greeks, and finally launched an attack on Russia. Japan's early successes in the Pacific area were equally startling, as she followed the Pearl Harbor attack with conquest of Southeast Asia. However, Allied victories in North Africa, the South Pacific, and Stalingrad turned the tide by early 1943. In the final two years, Allied landings in France, a massive air attack on Germany, and the Russian advance from the east brought victory over Nazi Germany; while in the Pacific an island-hopping campaign, combined with naval and air assaults and the dropping of an atomic bomb on Hiroshima, defeated Japan.

1. THE MAGINOT LINE FAILS TO PROTECT FRANCE

France's Maginot Line, built in the 1930's to defend the northeast frontier facing Germany, was the world's most elaborate fortification system. It reflected the defensive strategy of French military leaders after World War I, and lulled the French people into a false sense of security. Hitler's blitzkrieg attack on the West on May 10, 1940, was directed against the Low Countries, so that the Maginot Line was outflanked as the Nazis poured into France from the north.

How can one explain the immovable calm of the generalissimo, the confidence with which he looked forward to a future of flame, steel, and blood? The answer is that General Gamelin had settled down into the certainties

Pertinax, *The Gravediggers of France* (Garden City, N. Y.: Doubleday & Company, Inc., 1942), pp. 11–15.

of what may be called the *Credo* of the Maginot Line. Here are the central articles of this faith:

1. Men defending fieldworks can hold out against an offensive, even if they are outnumbered three to one, or if the attack is carried out with bombers and tanks in massive quantities. This is even more true of the defense of concrete and steel fortifications. In order to do this successfully, they need only know how to handle their automatic rifles, machine guns, mortars, grenades, trench cannon, anti-tank and anti-aircraft cannon, avail themselves of the various types of artillery, and, in counter-attacks, combine planes and tanks with all other arms.

The French Command was well aware that tanks would be launched against our lines in a density of one hundred units to the kilometer. . . . But this avalanche of steel did not worry the High Command. Besides, they ignored that there was such a thing as air artillery which was to work in conjunction with fortresses on wheels. . . .

2. The ground gained by an enemy attack will always be limited, since it will be easier for the defense to organize resistance than for the attack to assemble the fresh troops required to widen the breach it has made. . . .

3. Besides, the Maginot Line has replaced the fieldworks of twenty-five years ago. These works were continuous; the Maginot Line is not only continuous, it has a strength far above anything we have ever seen. True enough, it lacks depth and elasticity. The lack of these is the price we paid for building strength into continuity and permanence. All in all, nevertheless, this combination probably excludes the possibility even of a minor break-through. . . .

The Maginot Line ends at Montmédy; from the Meuse to the Pas-de-Calais the terrain is open or slightly protected. How were we to ward against the dangers which arose from this solution of continuity, supposing that we did not get the hoped-for chance to attack along the Belgian-German frontier? Various answers were given. They amounted to this: fieldworks will be constructed. The natural obstacle which consists of the Ardennes Forest and the Meuse River rules out a break-through in that area. And the French-British-Belgian armies will be able to get to the relatively narrow stretch of territory between Givet and Antwerp quickly enough to prevent an enemy outflanking action. In the defensive credo here was the point which remained ill defined and vague. But this must be emphasized: Under the military philosophy which goes by the name of Maginot an appendix was set apart for strategy in open space. The "Maginot" credo was not a closed one—and that was the worst of it. In May–June 1940 the fortifications were not actually stormed by the enemy. They were turned.

2. CHURCHILL'S SPEECHES STIFFEN BRITISH MORALE

On May 10, 1940, the day Hitler attacked the Low Countries, Winston S. Churchill succeeded Neville Chamberlain as British prime minister. Churchill, a master of the English language, in a series of resounding speeches found the words to inspire his people. Excerpt A below is from a speech of May, 1940, on his accession as prime minister; B, after the Dunkirk evacuation; C, two weeks later at the beginning of the Battle of Britain; D, an address to the Italian people on December 23, 1940.

[A] On Monday, May 13, I asked the House of Commons . . . for a vote of confidence in the new Administration. After reporting the progress which had been made in filling the various offices, I said, "I have nothing to offer but blood, toil, tears and sweat." In all our long history no Prime Minister had ever been able to present to Parliament and the nation a programme at once so short and so popular. I ended:

You ask, what is our policy? I will say: It is to wage war, by sea, land, and air, with all our might and with all the strength that God can give us: to wage war against a monstrous tyranny, never surpassed in the dark, lamentable catalogue of human crime. That is our policy. You ask, What is our aim? I can answer in one word: Victory—victory at all costs, victory in spite of all terror; victory, however long and hard the road may be; for without victory, there is no survival. Let that be realised; no survival for the British Empire; no survival for all that the British Empire has stood for, no survival for the urge and impulse of the ages, that mankind will move forward towards its goal. But I take up my task with buoyancy and hope. I feel sure that our cause will not be suffered to fail among men. At this time I feel entitled to claim the aid of all, and I say, "Come, then, let us go forward together with our united strength."

[B] Even though large tracts of Europe and many old and famous States have fallen or may fall into the grip of the Gestapo and all the odious apparatus of Nazi rule, we shall not flag or fail. We shall go on to the end, we shall fight in France, we shall fight in the seas and oceans, we shall fight with growing confidence and growing strength in the air, we shall defend our island, whatever the cost may be, we shall fight on the beaches, we shall fight on the landing-grounds, we shall fight in the fields and in the streets, we shall fight in the hills; we shall never surrender, and even if, which I do not for a moment believe, this island or a large part of it were

Winston S. Churchill, *Their Finest Hour*, in *The Second World War* (Boston: Houghton Mifflin Company, 1949), Vol. II, pp. 25–26, 118, 225–226, 620–621.

subjugated and starving, then our Empire beyond the seas, armed and guarded by the British Fleet, would carry on the struggle, until, in God's good time, the New World, with all its power and might, steps forth to the rescue and the liberation of the Old.

[C] During the first four years of the last war the Allies experienced nothing but disaster and disappointments. . . . We repeatedly asked ourselves the question "How are we going to win?" and no one was ever able to answer it with much precision, until at the end, quite suddenly, quite unexpectedly, our terrible foe collapsed before us, and we were so glutted with victory that in our folly we threw it away.

However matters may go in France or with the French Government or other French Governments, we in this island and in the British Empire will never lose our sense of comradeship with the French people. . . . If final victory rewards our toils they shall share the gains—aye, and freedom shall be restored to all. We abate nothing of our just demands; not one jot or tittle do we recede. . . . Czechs, Poles, Norwegians, Dutch, Belgians, have joined their causes to our own. All these shall be restored.

What General Weygand called the Battle of France is over. I expect that the Battle of Britain is about to begin. Upon this battle depends the survival of Christian civilisation. Upon it depends our own British life, and the long continuity of our institutions and our Empire. The whole fury and might of the enemy must very soon be turned on us. Hitler knows that he will have to break us in this island or lose the war. If we can stand up to him, all Europe may be free and the life of the world may move forward into broad, sunlit uplands. But if we fail, then the whole world, including the United States, including all that we have known and cared for, will sink into the abyss of a new Dark Age, made more sinister, and perhaps more protracted, by the lights of perverted science. Let us therefore brace ourselves to our duties, and so bear ourselves that, if the British Empire and its Commonwealth last for a thousand years, men will say,"This was their finest hour."

[D] Where is it that the Duce has led his trusting people after eighteen years of dictatorial power? What hard choice is open to them now? It is to stand up to the battery of the whole British Empire on sea, in the air, and in Africa, and the vigorous counter-attack of the Greek nation; or, on the other hand, to call in Attila over the Brenner Pass with his hordes of ravenous soldiery and his gangs of Gestapo policemen to occupy, hold down, and protect the Italian people, for whom he and his Nazi followers cherish the most bitter and outspoken contempt that is on record between races.

There is where one man and one man only has led you; and there I leave this unfolding story until the day comes—as come it will—when the Italian nation will once more take a hand in shaping its own fortunes.

3. ROOSEVELT ADDRESSES CONGRESS ON THE DAY AFTER PEARL HARBOR

The Japanese air attack on Pearl Harbor was a carefully planned operation which completely surprised the American defenders early on Sunday morning, December 7, 1941. Through a series of blunders the American commanders failed to receive adequate warning. The American Pacific fleet and air force were put out of action, leaving American possessions in the Pacific defenseless and isolated.

Address Delivered by President Roosevelt to the Congress, December 8, 1941

Yesterday, December 7, 1941—a date which will live in infamy—the United States of America was suddenly and deliberately attacked by naval and air forces of the Empire of Japan.

The United States was at peace with that Nation and, at the solicitation of Japan, was still in conversation with its Government and its Emperor looking toward the maintenance of peace in the Pacific. Indeed, one hour after Japanese air squadrons had commenced bombing in Oahu, the Japanese Ambassador to the United States and his colleague delivered to the Secretary of State a formal reply to a recent American message. While this reply stated that it seemed useless to continue the existing diplomatic negotiations, it contained no threat or hint of war or armed attack.

It will be recorded that the distance of Hawaii from Japan makes it obvious that the attack was deliberately planned many days or even weeks ago. During the intervening time the Japanese Government has deliberately sought to deceive the United States by false statements and expressions of hope for continued peace.

The attack yesterday on the Hawaiian Islands has caused severe damage to American naval and military forces. Very many American lives have been lost. In addition American ships have been reported torpedoed on the high seas between San Francisco and Honolulu.

Yesterday the Japanese Government also launched an attack against Malaya.

Last night Japanese forces attacked Hong Kong.

Last night Japanese forces attacked Guam.

Last night Japanese forces attacked the Philippine Islands.

Department of State Bulletin, Vol. V, p. 474, in United States Department of State, *Peace and War: United States Foreign Policy, 1931–1941* (Washington, D.C., 1943), Document No. 267, pp. 839–840.

Last night the Japanese attacked Wake Island.

This morning the Japanese attacked Midway Island.

Japan has, therefore, undertaken a surprise offensive extending throughout the Pacific area. The facts of yesterday speak for themselves. The people of the United States have already formed their opinions and well understand the implications to the very life and safety of our Nation.

As Commander in Chief of the Army and Navy I have directed that all measures be taken for our defense.

Always will we remember the character of the onslaught against us.

No matter how long it may take us to overcome this premeditated invasion, the American people in their righteous might will win through to absolute victory.

I believe I interpret the will of the Congress and of the people when I assert that we will not only defend ourselves to the uttermost but will make very certain that this form of treachery shall never endanger us again.

Hostilities exist. There is no blinking at the fact that our people, our territory, and our interests are in grave danger.

With confidence in our armed forces—with the unbounded determination of our people—we will gain the inevitable triumph—so help us God.

I ask that the Congress declare that since the unprovoked and dastardly attack by Japan on Sunday, December 7, a state of war has existed between the United States and the Japanese Empire.

4. EISENHOWER SETS THE DATE FOR THE NORMANDY INVASION

In November, 1942, British, American, and Allied forces, under General Dwight D. Eisenhower, undertook their first major offensive action, the landing in North Africa. Although slowed by a setback in Tunisia, Eisenhower's forces by May, 1943, had taken all of North Africa, and by the end of the year Sicily and southern Italy were in Allied hands. In 1943 and 1944 men and materials of the free world were gathered in England for a great cross-Channel invasion of Hitler's Europe. General Eisenhower was transferred to England and installed as supreme allied commander.

Two considerations, one of them decisive in character, combined to postpone the target date from May to June. The first and important one was our insistence that the attack be on a larger scale than that originally planned by the staff assembled in London under Lieutenant General Frederick Morgan. . . . he had no recourse except to work out an attack along a

Dwight D. Eisenhower, *Crusade in Europe* (Garden City, N.Y.: Doubleday & Company, Inc., 1948), pp. 230–231, 239, 250.

three-division front, whereas I insisted upon five and informed the Combined Chiefs of Staff that we had to have the additional landing craft and other gear essential to the larger operation, even if this meant delaying the assault by a month. To this the Combined Chiefs of Staff agreed.

Another factor that made the later date a desirable one was the degree of dependence we were placing upon the preparatory effort of the air force. An early attack would provide the air force with only a minimum opportunity for pinpoint bombing of critical transportation centers in France, whereas the improved weather anticipated for the month of May would give them much more time and better opportunity to impede the movement of German reserves and demolish German defenses along the coast line. . . . Nevertheless, acceptance of the later date was disappointing. We wanted all the summer weather we could get for the European campaign.

Along with the general plan of operations we thoroughly considered means of deceiving the enemy as to the point and timing of attack. Our purpose was to convince him that we intended to strike directly across the Channel at its narrowest point, against the stronghold of Calais. In many ways great advantages would have accrued to us could we have successfully attacked in this region. Not only were the beaches the best along the coast, they were closest to the British ports and to the German border. The enemy, fully appreciating these facts, kept strong forces in the area and fortified that particular section of coast line more strongly than any other. The defenses were so strong that none of us believed that a successful assault from the sea could be made except at such terrific cost that the whole expedition might find itself helpless to accomplish anything of a positive character, after it got ashore. But we counted upon the enemy believing that we would be tempted into this operation, and the wide variety of measures we took for convincing him were given extraordinary credence by his Intelligence division. . . .

After the abandonment of the May target date, the next combination of moon, tide, and time of sunrise that we considered practicable for the attack occurred on June 5, 6, and 7. We wanted to cross the Channel with our convoys at night so that darkness would conceal the strength and direction of our several attacks. We wanted a moon for our airborne assaults. We needed approximately forty minutes of daylight preceding the ground assault to complete our bombing and preparatory bombardment. We had to attack on a relatively low tide because of beach obstacles which had to be removed while uncovered. These principal factors dictated the general period; but the selection of the actual day would depend upon weather forecasts. . . .

The conference on the evening of June 4 presented little, if any, added brightness to the picture of the morning, and tension mounted even higher because the inescapable consequences of postponement were almost too bitter to contemplate.

At three-thirty the next morning our little camp was shaking and shuddering under a wind of almost hurricane proportions and the accompanying rain seemed to be traveling in horizontal streaks. The mile-long trip through muddy roads to the naval headquarters was anything but a cheerful one, since it seemed impossible that in such conditions there was any reason for even discussing the situation.

When the conference started the first report given us by Group Captain Stagg and the Meteorologic Staff was that the bad conditions predicted the day before for the coast of France were actually prevailing there and that if we had persisted in the attempt to land on June 5 a major disaster would almost surely have resulted. This they probably told us to inspire more confidence in their next astonishing declaration, which was that by the following morning a period of relatively good weather, heretofore completely unexpected, would ensue, lasting probably thirty-six hours. The long-term prediction was not good but they did give us assurance that this short period of calm weather would intervene between the exhaustion of the storm we were then experiencing and the beginning of the next spell of really bad weather.

The prospect was not bright because of the possibility that we might land the first several waves successfully and then find later build-up impracticable, and so have to leave the isolated original attacking forces easy prey to German counteraction. However, the consequences of the delay justified great risk and I quickly announced the decision to go ahead with the attack on June 6. The time was then 4:15 A.M., June 5. No one present disagreed and there was a definite brightening of faces as, without a further word, each went off to his respective post of duty to flash out to his command the messages that would set the whole host in motion.

5. ALLIED AIR POWER DESTROYS GERMAN INDUSTRY AND TRANSPORTATION

At the start of World War II Germany possessed a superior air force which not only effectively supported the blitzkrieg tactics of ground forces, but also devastated such cities as Warsaw, Rotterdam, and London. By 1944, however, air supremacy passed to the British and Americans, who carried out a systematic bombardment of German industrial cities and communications centers. In early

The United States Strategic Bombing Survey, *The Effects of Strategic Bombing on the German War Economy* (Overall Economic Effects Division, October, 1945), pp. 6–14.

1945, Allied armies entering Germany found the cities in ruins and transportation paralyzed.

The outstanding feature of the German war effort is the surprisingly low output of armaments in the first three years of the war—surprisingly low as measured not only by Germany's later achievement, but also by the general expectations of the time and by the level of production of her enemy, Britain. In aircraft, trucks, tanks, self-propelled guns, and several other types of armaments, British production was greater than Germany's in 1940, 1941, and 1942.

For these early years the conclusion is inescapable that Germany's war production was not limited by her war potential—by the resources at her disposal—but by demand; in other words, by the notions of the German war leaders as to what was required for achieving their aim. The Germans did not plan for a long war, nor were they prepared for it. Hitler's strategy contemplated a series of separate thrusts and quick victories over enemies that were even less prepared than Germany; he did not expect to fight a prolonged war against a combination of major world powers. The Polish campaign, while it brought an unexpected declaration of war from France and England, went according to plan. The Norwegian and later the French campaign further justified the German faith in "Blitzkrieg." Both ended in complete victory within a very short time and with an unexpectedly small expenditure of military resources. After the occupation of France, England, though not invaded or brought to heel through aerial bombardment, was no longer considered an immediate threat. Eventual intervention by the United States was not taken seriously. The attack on Russia was started in the confident expectation that the experience of the earlier campaigns was to be repeated; Russia was to be completely subjugated in three to four months.

The underestimation of Russia's strength was the major miscalculation in this strategy. The Polish and French campaigns had shown that Germany's military preparedness, large or small, was fully adequate for achieving her strategic objectives. But in the case of Russia the same strategy would have required preparations on a far greater scale; and in the critical nine months that separated the decision to invade Russia from the actual beginning of the campaign, such reparations were not made, even though there were no serious obstacles to an all-around expansion of armaments production. The first three months of the Russian campaign did, in fact, go entirely "according to plan"; and at the end of September Hitler, believing the war about won, ordered a large scale reduction in armaments production. This order, even though only partially carried out caused important reductions in stocks, particularly of ammuntion, the effects of which were not overcome for a considerable time.

The defeat before Moscow, and the entry of the United States into the war in December 1941, brought the German leaders for the first time face to face with the prospect of a prolonged war with the three greatest powers ranged against them. From that time onward limitations of demand no longer played a role in restricting armaments production; Germany's leaders called for an all-out effort. Yet, measured by the standards of other belligerents, there was no "total mobilization" and no long-term planning to bring the war effort to its attainable maximum. The production of civilian goods was restricted only to a moderate extent; there was no further mobilization of women and no large scale transfer of labor from nonessential to essential industries.

In February 1942, Albert Speer, Hitler's personal architect, was appointed Minister of Armament Production with wide powers; and the production history of the following two and a half years bears the stamp of the "Speer Period." Speer set about replacing the existing machinery of control with a new organization (the "Rings" and "Committees"), manned by people selected from among the production managers and technicians of industry. They were charged with the task of increasing production by rationalizing German war industry; that is, by simplifying designs, standardizing components, concentrating production in the most suitable plants, reducing the number of different armaments orders given to a single firm, exchanging patents and secret processes, and generally adopting, throughout industry, the most efficient processes of production. The result of this policy was a more than threefold increase in Germany's munition production. . . .

There can be no doubt that Germany started the conversion of her economy to a wartime footing far too late. Had Germany's leaders decided to make an all-out war effort in 1939 instead of 1942, they would have had time to arm in "depth"; that is, to lay the foundations of a war economy by expanding their basic industries and building up equipment for the mass production of munitions. Starting their armament program as late as 1942, they could only arm in "width"; that is, accept their equipment and material base as given and expand munitions production on the basis of available capacity. . . .

. . . Production capacity, except in a few special cases, of which oil was the most notable, was never really short; machinery capacity was never fully utilized. Manpower—particularly woman power—was never fully mobilized. Raw material stocks of the most important categories, such as steel, were rising up to mid-1944. The output of civilian consumption goods, after the restriction of the first two years of the war (which still left the civilian standard of living at a fairly comfortable level and above that of the depression years in the early thirties), was maintained virtually stable until the second quarter of 1944. . . .

. . . apart from the aero-engine industry and a few other exceptions, the German armament industries worked only a single shift throughout the war, and the great capacity reserve that would have been available from double or triple shift operations was largely unutilized. Furthermore, the German machine tool industry hardly expanded during the war, worked on a single shift basis throughout, and converted almost 30 percent of its capacity to direct munitions production.

Germany's easy machine tool position is in striking contrast with the experience of the United States and Great Britain, where machine tools were kept working 24 hours a day seven days a week, and the machine tool industry was very much expanded and strained to the utmost to supply requirements. . . .

Germany's experience was fundamentally different from that of the Anglo-American Allies also as far as the manpower problem is concerned. While England and America both entered the war with substantial unemployment, Germany's labor force was fully employed already in 1939. Total employment increased by 8 million, or 30 percent, between 1933 and 1939. Industrial employment nearly doubled, with most of the increase concentrated on the heavy goods industries.

The absence of unemployment does not mean, however, that Germany was fully mobilized for war in 1939. The percentage of workers in her non-agricultural population of working age was hardly greater than it was in Great Britain at the time; and what manpower she utilized was not concentrated unduly on war production. According to German statistics, civilian consumption in 1939 was above the 1929 level and had only fallen slightly by 1941. This shows that Germany entered the war with a "guns *and* butter" philosophy which was continued well after the initial defeats in Russia. . . .

Prior to the summer of 1943, air raids had no appreciable effect either on German munitions production or on the national output in general. . . .

The effects of air raids became more noticeable from the summer of 1943 onward. This was partly due to the heavier weight of the RAF attacks and partly to the appearance of the AAF in major strength. Area raids on the Ruhr caused an estimated 8 percent loss of steel output, but adequate stocks in the hands of industrial users prevented the loss from affecting armament outputs. . . .

For the first four months of 1944 the AAF, capable for the first time of carrying out repeated attacks deep into Germany, concentrated its strength on aircraft and ball bearing targets. During the attacks beginning in February, about 90 percent of German fighter production capacity was attacked and 70 percent destroyed. . . .

The attack on transportation beginning in September 1944 was the most important single cause of Germany's ultimate economic collapse. Between August and December freight car loadings fell by approximately 50 percent. The progressive traffic tie-up was found to have first affected commodities normally shipped in less than full trainload lots—finished and semifinished manufactured goods, components and perishables. The effects of the attack are best seen, however, in the figures of coal transport, which normally constituted 40 percent of rail traffic. Shipments by rail and water fell from 7.4 million tons in August to 2.7 million tons in December. By March coal shipments were scarcely adequate even for the needs of the railroads. The operation of Germany's raw material industries, her manufacturing industries, and her power supply were all dependent on coal. By January their stocks were becoming exhausted and collapse was inevitable. . . .

From December 1944 onwards, all sectors of the German economy were in rapid decline. This collapse was due to the results of air raids working in combination with other causes. The armament index fell from 322 in July to 263 in December and to 145 in March. . . .

. . . "The German economy," Speer wrote in his report of March 15 [1945], "is heading for an inevitable collapse within 4–8 weeks." Even if the final military victories that carried the Allied armies across the Rhine and the Oder had not taken place, armament production would have come to a virtual standstill by May; the German armies, completely bereft of ammunition and motive power, would almost certainly have had to cease fighting by June or July.

6. THE UNESCO PREAMBLE EXPRESSES THE HOPES OF THE WORLD FOR PEACE

The tremendous suffering and destruction of World War II led to the firm conviction, shared by the leaders and peoples of the anti-Axis nations, that a world organization stronger than the League of Nations should be established to preserve the peace. The charter of the United Nations, as drawn up at San Francisco in the spring of 1945, provided for a number of important secondary agencies, including the United Nations Scientific and Cultural Organization (UNESCO), which was to promote the exchange of cultural, technological, and scientific information.

"Preamble to the Constitution of the United Nations Educational, Scientific, and Cultural Organization (UNESCO)," in United States Department of State, *Bulletin XIII*, p. 802.

The Governments of the States parties to this Constitution on behalf of their peoples declare that since wars begin in the minds of men it is in the minds of men that the defenses of peace must be constructed; that ignorance of each other's ways and lives has been a common cause throughout the history of mankind of that suspicion and mistrust between the peoples of the world through which their differences have all too often broken into war; that the great and terrible war which has now ended was a war made possible by the denial of the democratic principles of the dignity, equality and mutual respect of men and by the propagation in their place through ignorance and prejudice of the doctrine of the inequality of men and races; that the wide diffusion of culture and the education of humanity for justice and liberty and peace are indispensable to the dignity of man and constitute a sacred duty which all the nations must fulfill in a spirit of mutual assistance and concern; that a peace based exclusively upon the political and economic arrangements of Governments would not be a peace which could secure the unanimous, lasting and sincere support of the peoples of the world and that the peace must, therefore, be founded, if it is not to fail, upon the intellectual and moral solidarity of mankind. *For these reasons* the States parties to this Constitution, believing in full and equal opportunities for education for all in the unrestricted pursuit of objective truth and in the free exchange of ideas and knowledge, are agreed and determined to develop and to increase the means of communication between their peoples and to employ these means for the purposes of mutual understanding and a truer and more perfect knowledge of each other's lives; *In consequence whereof* they do hereby create the United Nations Educational, Scientific and Cultural Organization for the purpose of advancing through the educational and scientific and cultural relations of the peoples of the world the objectives of international peace and of the common welfare of mankind for which the United Nations Organization was established and which its Charter proclaims.